WILLIAM SHAKESPEARE was born in Stratford-upon-Avon in April, 1564, and his birth is traditionally celebrated on April 23. The facts of his life, known from surviving documents, are sparse. He was one of eight children born to John Shakespeare, a merchant of some standing in his community. William probably went to the King's New School in Stratford, but he had no university education. In November 1582, at the age of eighteen, he married Anne Hathaway, eight years his senior, who was pregnant with their first child, Susanna. She was born on May 26, 1583. Twins, a boy, Hamnet (who would die at age eleven), and a girl, Judith, were born in 1585. By 1592 Shakespeare had gone to London, working as an actor and already known as a playwright. A rival dramatist, Robert Greene, referred to him as "an upstart crow, beautified with our feathers." Shakespeare became a principal shareholder and playwright of the successful acting troupe the Lord Chamberlain's men (later, under James I, called the King's men). In 1599 the Lord Chamberlain's men built and occupied the Globe Theatre in Southwark near the Thames River. Here many of Shakespeare's plays were performed by the most famous actors of his time, including Richard Burbage, Will Kempe, and Robert Armin. In addition to his 37 plays, Shakespeare had a hand in others, including *Sir Thomas More* and *The Two Noble Kinsmen*, and he wrote poems, including *Venus and Adonis* and *The Rape of Lucrece*. His 154 sonnets were published, probably without his authorization, in 1609. In 1611 or 1612 he gave up his lodgings in London and devoted more and more of his time to retirement in Stratford, though he continued writing such plays as *The Tempest* and *Henry VIII* until about 1613. He died on April 23, 1616, and was buried in Holy Trinity Church, Stratford. No collected edition of his plays was published during his lifetime, but in 1623 two members of his acting company, John Heminges and Henry Condell, published the great collection now called the First Folio.

Bantam Shakespeare
The Complete Works—29 Volumes
Edited by David Bevington
With forewords by Joseph Papp on the plays

The Poems: Venus and Adonis, The Rape of Lucrece, The
        Phoenix and Turtle, A Lover's Complaint,
        the Sonnets

Antony and Cleopatra	*The Merchant of Venice*
As You Like It	*A Midsummer Night's Dream*
The Comedy of Errors	*Much Ado about Nothing*
Hamlet	*Othello*
Henry IV, Part One	*Richard II*
Henry IV, Part Two	*Richard III*
Henry V	*Romeo and Juliet*
Julius Caesar	*The Taming of the Shrew*
King Lear	*The Tempest*
Macbeth	*Twelfth Night*

Together in one volume:

Henry VI, Parts One, Two, and Three
King John and Henry VIII
*Measure for Measure, All's Well that Ends Well, and
        Troilus and Cressida*
Three Early Comedies: Love's Labor's Lost, The Two
                        Gentlemen of Verona, The Merry
                        Wives of Windsor
Three Classical Tragedies: Titus Andronicus, Timon
                            of Athens, Coriolanus
The Late Romances: Pericles, Cymbeline, The Winter's
        Tale, The Tempest

Two collections:

Four Comedies: The Taming of the Shrew, A Midsummer
                Night's Dream, The Merchant of Venice,
                Twelfth Night
Four Tragedies: Hamlet, Othello, King Lear, Macbeth

William Shakespeare

FOUR TRAGEDIES

Hamlet
Othello
King Lear
Macbeth

Edited by
David Bevington

David Scott Kastan,
James Hammersmith,
and Robert Kean Turner,
Associate Editors

With a Foreword by
Joseph Papp

BANTAM BOOKS
NEW YORK · TORONTO · LONDON · SYDNEY · AUCKLAND

FOUR TRAGEDIES

*A Bantam Book / published by arrangement
with Scott, Foresman and Company*

PUBLISHING HISTORY

*Scott, Foresman edition published / January 1980
Bantam edition, with newly edited text and substantially revised, edited, and
amplified notes, introductions, and other materials,
published / February 1988
Valuable advice on staging matters has been provided by Richard Hosley.
Collations checked by Eric Rasmussen.
Additional editorial assistance by Claire McEachern.*

ISBN 0-553-21283-4

Published simultaneously in the United States and Canada

*Bantam Books are published by Bantam Books, a division of Bantam Double-
day Dell Publishing Group, Inc. Its trademark, consisting of the words
"Bantam Books" and the portrayal of a rooster, is Registered in U.S. Patent
and Trademark Office and in other countries. Marca Registrada. Bantam
Books, 1540 Broadway, New York, New York 10036.*

PRINTED IN THE UNITED STATES OF AMERICA

O   0 9 8

Contents

Foreword

It's hard to imagine, but Shakespeare wrote all of his plays with a quill pen, a goose feather whose hard end had to be sharpened frequently. How many times did he scrape the dull end to a point with his knife, dip it into the inkwell, and bring up, dripping wet, those wonderful words and ideas that are known all over the world?

In the age of word processors, typewriters, and ballpoint pens, we have almost forgotten the meaning of the word "blot." Yet when I went to school, in the 1930s, my classmates and I knew all too well what an inkblot from the metal-tipped pens we used would do to a nice clean page of a test paper, and we groaned whenever a splotch fell across the sheet. Most of us finished the school day with ink-stained fingers; those who were less careful also went home with ink-stained shirts, which were almost impossible to get clean.

When I think about how long it took me to write the simplest composition with a metal-tipped pen and ink, I can only marvel at how many plays Shakespeare scratched out with his goose-feather quill pen, year after year. Imagine him walking down one of the narrow cobblestoned streets of London, or perhaps drinking a pint of beer in his local alehouse. Suddenly his mind catches fire with an idea, or a sentence, or a previously elusive phrase. He is burning with impatience to write it down—but because he doesn't have a ballpoint pen or even a pencil in his pocket, he has to keep the idea in his head until he can get to his quill and parchment.

He rushes back to his lodgings on Silver Street, ignoring the vendors hawking brooms, the coaches clattering by, the piteous wails of beggars and prisoners. Bounding up the stairs, he snatches his quill and starts to write furiously, not even bothering to light a candle against the dusk. "To be, or not to be," he scrawls, "that is the—." But the quill point has gone dull, the letters have fattened out illegibly, and in the middle of writing one of the most famous passages in the history of dramatic literature, Shakespeare has to stop to sharpen his pen.

Taking a deep breath, he lights a candle now that it's dark, sits down, and begins again. By the time the candle has burned out and the noisy apprentices of his French Huguenot landlord have quieted down, Shakespeare has finished Act 3 of *Hamlet* with scarcely a blot.

Early the next morning, he hurries through the fog of a London summer morning to the rooms of his colleague Richard Burbage, the actor for whom the role of Hamlet is being written. He finds Burbage asleep and snoring loudly, sprawled across his straw mattress. Not only had the actor performed in *Henry V* the previous afternoon, but he had then gone out carousing all night with some friends who had come to the performance.

Shakespeare shakes his friend awake, until, bleary-eyed, Burbage sits up in his bed. "Dammit, Will," he grumbles, "can't you let an honest man sleep?" But the playwright, his eyes shining and the words tumbling out of his mouth, says, "Shut up and listen—tell me what you think of *this*!"

He begins to read to the still half-asleep Burbage, pacing around the room as he speaks. ". . . Whether 'tis nobler in the mind to suffer the slings and arrows of outrageous fortune—"

Burbage interrupts, suddenly wide awake, "That's excellent, very good, 'the slings and arrows of outrageous fortune,' yes, I think it will work quite well. . . ." He takes the parchment from Shakespeare and murmurs the lines to himself, slowly at first but with growing excitement.

The sun is just coming up, and the words of one of Shakespeare's most famous soliloquies are being uttered for the first time by the first actor ever to bring Hamlet to life. It must have been an exhilarating moment.

Shakespeare wrote most of his plays to be performed live by the actor Richard Burbage and the rest of the Lord Chamberlain's men (later the King's men). Today, however, our first encounter with the plays is usually in the form of the printed word. And there is no question that reading Shakespeare for the first time isn't easy. His plays aren't comic books or magazines or the dime-store detective novels I read when I was young. A lot of his sentences are complex. Many of his words are no longer used in our everyday speech. His profound thoughts are often condensed into poetry, which is not as straightforward as prose.

Yet when you hear the words spoken aloud, a lot of the language may strike you as unexpectedly modern. For Shakespeare's plays, like any dramatic work, weren't really meant to be read; they were meant to be spoken, seen, and performed. It's amazing how lines that are so troublesome in print can flow so naturally and easily when spoken.

I think it was precisely this music that first fascinated me. When I was growing up, Shakespeare was a stranger to me. I had no particular interest in him, for I was from a different cultural tradition. It never occurred to me that his plays might be more than just something to "get through" in school, like science or math or the physical education requirement we had to fulfill. My passions then were movies, radio, and vaudeville—certainly not Elizabethan drama.

I was, however, fascinated by words and language. Because I grew up in a home where Yiddish was spoken, and English was only a second language, I was acutely sensitive to the musical sounds of different languages and had an ear for lilt and cadence and rhythm in the spoken word. And so I loved reciting poems and speeches even as a very young child. In first grade I learned lots of short nature verses— "Who has seen the wind?," one of them began. My first foray into drama was playing the role of Scrooge in Charles Dickens's *A Christmas Carol* when I was eight years old. I liked summoning all the scorn and coldness I possessed and putting them into the words, "Bah, humbug!"

From there I moved on to longer and more famous poems and other works by writers of the 1930s. Then, in junior high school, I made my first acquaintance with Shakespeare through his play *Julius Caesar*. Our teacher, Miss McKay, assigned the class a passage to memorize from the opening scene of the play, the one that begins "Wherefore rejoice? What conquest brings he home?" The passage seemed so wonderfully theatrical and alive to me, and the experience of memorizing and reciting it was so much fun, that I went on to memorize another speech from the play on my own.

I chose Mark Antony's address to the crowd in Act 3,

scene 2, which struck me then as incredibly high drama. Even today, when I speak the words, I feel the same thrill I did that first time. There is the strong and athletic Antony descending from the raised pulpit where he has been speaking, right into the midst of a crowded Roman square. Holding the torn and bloody cloak of the murdered Julius Caesar in his hand, he begins to speak to the people of Rome:

> If you have tears, prepare to shed them now.
> You all do know this mantle. I remember
> The first time ever Caesar put it on;
> 'Twas on a summer's evening in his tent,
> That day he overcame the Nervii.
> Look, in this place ran Cassius' dagger through.
> See what a rent the envious Casca made.
> Through this the well-belovèd Brutus stabbed,
> And as he plucked his cursèd steel away,
> Mark how the blood of Caesar followed it,
> As rushing out of doors to be resolved
> If Brutus so unkindly knocked or no;
> For Brutus, as you know, was Caesar's angel.
> Judge, O you gods, how dearly Caesar loved him!
> This was the most unkindest cut of all . . .

I'm not sure now that I even knew Shakespeare had written a lot of other plays, or that he was considered "timeless," "universal," or "classic"—but I knew a good speech when I heard one, and I found the splendid rhythms of Antony's rhetoric as exciting as anything I'd ever come across.

Fifty years later, I still feel that way. Hearing good actors speak Shakespeare gracefully and naturally is a wonderful experience, unlike any other I know. There's a satisfying fullness to the spoken word that the printed page just can't convey. This is why seeing the plays of Shakespeare performed live in a theater is the best way to appreciate them. If you can't do that, listening to sound recordings or watching film versions of the plays is the next best thing.

But if you do start with the printed word, use the play as a script. Be an actor yourself and say the lines out loud. Don't worry too much at first about words you don't immediately understand. Look them up in the footnotes or a dictionary, but don't spend too much time on this. It is more profitable (and fun) to get the sense of a passage and sing it out. Speak naturally, almost as if you were talking to a friend, but be sure to enunciate the words properly. You'll be surprised at how much you understand simply by speaking the speech "trippingly on the tongue," as Hamlet advises the Players.

You might start, as I once did, with a speech from *Julius Caesar*, in which the tribune (city official) Marullus scolds the commoners for transferring their loyalties so quickly from the defeated and murdered general Pompey to the newly victorious Julius Caesar:

> Wherefore rejoice? What conquest brings he home?
> What tributaries follow him to Rome
> To grace in captive bonds his chariot wheels?
> You blocks, you stones, you worse than senseless
>   things!
> O you hard hearts, you cruel men of Rome,
> Knew you not Pompey? Many a time and oft
> Have you climbed up to walls and battlements,
> To towers and windows, yea, to chimney tops,
> Your infants in your arms, and there have sat
> The livelong day, with patient expectation,
> To see great Pompey pass the streets of Rome.

With the exception of one or two words like "wherefore" (which means "why," not "where"), "tributaries" (which means "captives"), and "patient expectation" (which means patient waiting), the meaning and emotions of this speech can be easily understood.

From here you can go on to dialogues or other more challenging scenes. Although you may stumble over unaccustomed phrases or unfamiliar words at first, and even fall flat when you're crossing some particularly rocky passages, pick yourself up and stay with it. Remember that it takes time to feel at home with anything new. Soon you'll come to recognize Shakespeare's unique sense of humor and way of saying things as easily as you recognize a friend's laughter.

And then it will just be a matter of choosing which one of Shakespeare's plays you want to tackle next. As a true fan of his, you'll find that you're constantly learning from his plays. It's a journey of discovery that you can continue for the rest of your life. For no matter how many times you read or see a particular play, there will always be something new there that you won't have noticed before.

Why do so many thousands of people get hooked on Shakespeare and develop a habit that lasts a lifetime? What can he really say to us today, in a world filled with inventions and problems he never could have imagined? And how do you get past his special language and difficult sentence structure to understand him?

The best way to answer these questions is to go see a live production. You might not know much about Shakespeare, or much about the theater, but when you watch actors performing one of his plays on the stage, it will soon become clear to you why people get so excited about a playwright who lived hundreds of years ago.

For the story—what's happening in the play—is the most accessible part of Shakespeare. In *A Midsummer Night's Dream*, for example, you can immediately understand the situation: a girl is chasing a guy who's chasing a girl who's chasing another guy. No wonder *A Midsummer Night's Dream* is one of the most popular of Shakespeare's plays: it's about one of the world's most popular pastimes—falling in love.

But the course of true love never did run smooth, as the young suitor Lysander says. Often in Shakespeare's comedies the girl whom the guy loves doesn't love him back, or she loves him but he loves someone else. In *The Two Gentlemen of Verona*, Julia loves Proteus, Proteus loves Sylvia, and Sylvia loves Valentine, who is Proteus's best friend. In the end, of course, true love prevails, but not without lots of complications along the way.

For in all of his plays—comedies, histories, and tragedies—Shakespeare is showing you human nature. His characters act and react in the most extraordinary ways—and sometimes in the most incomprehensible ways. People are always trying to find motivations for what a character does. They ask, "Why does Iago want to destroy Othello?"

The answer, to me, is very simple—because that's the way Iago is. That's just his nature. Shakespeare doesn't explain his characters; he sets them in motion—and away they go. He doesn't worry about whether they're likable or not. He's interested in interesting people, and his most fascinating characters are those who are unpredictable. If you lean back in your chair early on in one of his plays, thinking you've figured out what Iago or Shylock (in *The Merchant of Venice*) is up to, don't be too sure—because that great judge of human nature, Shakespeare, will surprise you every time.

He is just as wily in the way he structures a play. In *Macbeth*, a comic scene is suddenly introduced just after the bloodiest and most treacherous slaughter imaginable, of a guest and king by his host and subject, when in comes a drunk porter who has to go to the bathroom. Shakespeare is tickling your emotions by bringing a stand-up comic on-stage right on the heels of a savage murder.

It has taken me thirty years to understand even some of these things, and so I'm not suggesting that Shakespeare is immediately understandable. I've gotten to know him not through theory but through practice, the practice of the *living* Shakespeare—the playwright of the theater.

Of course the plays are a great achievement of dramatic literature, and they should be studied and analyzed in schools and universities. But you must always remember, when reading all the words *about* the playwright and his plays, that *Shakespeare's* words came first and that in the end there is nothing greater than a single actor on the stage speaking the lines of Shakespeare.

Everything important that I know about Shakespeare comes from the practical business of producing and directing his plays in the theater. The task of classifying, criticizing, and editing Shakespeare's printed works I happily leave to others. For me, his plays really do live on the stage, not on the page. That is what he wrote them for and that is how they are best appreciated.

Although Shakespeare lived and wrote hundreds of years ago, his name rolls off my tongue as if he were my brother. As a producer and director, I feel that there is a professional relationship between us that spans the centuries. As a human being, I feel that Shakespeare has enriched my understanding of life immeasurably. I hope you'll let him do the same for you.

❖

Hamlet has got just about all the ingredients of exciting, interesting theater—grand soliloquies, complex philosophizing, love relationships, family conflicts, ghosts, murder, revenge, swordplay, and a great death scene where bodies pile up on the stage. Young actors want to cut their teeth on the title role, and indeed, there is no more complex and challenging role for them, partly because of the weight of all the Hamlets who have gone before—among them Edwin Booth, the nineteenth-century American player, and Laurence Olivier, the great British actor of this century.

As I've been thinking about the play recently, it has struck me that *Hamlet* is a study of death and dying. Shakespeare's preoccupation is with life and death, and in his *Hamlet* he takes the popular form of the revenge tragedy and reduces it to its most basic elements. Death is the most recurrent theme in the play. From his first appearance onstage wearing the "inky cloak" of mourning and "customary suits of solemn black" that are "but the trappings and the suits of woe," Hamlet is fundamentally contemplating death. He sustains this preoccupation throughout the play, in his soliloquies—"To die, to sleep; / To sleep, perchance to dream. Ay, there's the rub, / For in that sleep of death what dreams may come, / When we have shuffled off this mortal coil, / Must give us pause."

In the end, death is the victor. Eight people die in the course of the play, the stage is littered with bodies in the last scene, and two entire families are wiped out, two bloodlines cut off forever. Yet this bloodbath at the end doesn't really solve anything, or answer the questions that plague Hamlet and perhaps plague us. To Hamlet, who has spent the entire play thinking about it and maybe even preparing for it, death comes too soon—as it always does:

> You that look pale and tremble at this chance,
> That are but mutes or audience to this act,
> Had I but time—as this fell sergeant, Death,
> Is strict in his arrest—O, I could tell you—

Yet in the midst of death, the wonder of the theater and the wonder of life persist. In his instructions to the Players, (3.2), Hamlet gives the greatest lesson in acting ever, better than anything modern theories or teachers can offer. He counsels restraint—"Nor do not saw the air too much with your hand, thus, but use all gently"—and decorum—"Suit the action to the word, the word to the action"—and reminds the Players that the purpose of acting, "both at the first and now, was and is to hold as 'twere the mirror up to nature."

Hamlet is a play *about* the theater, about the techniques of acting. In the entire middle section, beginning with the arrival of the traveling players in Act 2, scene 2, Shakespeare is reflecting on the uses and purposes of the theater by putting them inside the play itself. And Hamlet's method, like Shakespeare's, is to use theater to further his plot—"The play's the thing / Wherein I'll catch the conscience of the King"—to answer unanswerable questions, and ultimately, perhaps, to put off the death that haunts him.

❖

Othello is filled with extraordinary characters and speeches. There's Othello himself, with his blind and fatal trust in the wrong people. There's the remarkably strong Desdemona, whose defiance of her father to marry Othello would have been exceptional for that time. Lieutenant Cassio plays a vital role as the instrument employed by Iago to feed Othello's jealousy by winning Desdemona's sympathy.

And of course, Iago is Shakespeare's ultimate villain, that fiendishly smooth serpent of a man. I see him as a graceful, slender, elegant type, sophisticated, and, like Richard III, totally devoid of any moral sense. Possessed of that fine-tuned awareness of other people's weaknesses that psychopathic people often have, Iago knows precisely where to prick Othello. Slowly and surely, he moves in for the kill; we marvel at his finesse and subtlety as we watch.

How he does it—and not *why*—is what makes the play interesting. Iago himself gives several reasons for his hatred of the Moor—Iago wasn't promoted, he suspects Othello of sleeping with his wife, he loves Othello's wife Desdemona—but in the end none of these really account for what he does. He has the capacity to create the right circumstances, and then he makes them work for his purposes.

To all of these characters Shakespeare brings his amazing powers of perception as he examines a variety of human natures. We recognize Othello, or Desdemona, or Cassio, because we've seen them recreated countless times in ourselves and in other people—people who are jealous, or unfairly accused, or unwitting victims of someone else's cruelty. There's nothing in Shakespeare that isn't within the realm of human possibility. His characters aren't false, soap opera versions of real people; they *are* real people.

As in all of his plays, Shakespeare wrote some extraordinary speeches for *Othello*. Cassio's heartbroken outcry in Act 2, scene 3, about his reputation—in contrast to Falstaff's disdaining of "honor" as a mere word—is one example. Othello's explanation to the Venetian senators of how he and Desdemona fell in love, as he told her the story of his life, is gorgeously eloquent:

> She thanked me,
> And bade me, if I had a friend that loved her,
> I should but teach him how to tell my story
> And that would woo her. Upon this hint I spake.
> She loved me for the dangers I had passed,
> And I loved her that she did pity them.

The frank, surprisingly contemporary discussion Desdemona and Emilia have about marriage and infidelity, in Act 4, scene 3, has always been a favorite of mine.

DESDEMONA
    Dost thou in conscience think—tell me, Emilia—
    That there be women do abuse their husbands
    In such gross kind?
EMILIA   There be some such, no question.
DESDEMONA
    Wouldst thou do such a deed for all the world?
EMILIA
    Why, would not you?
DESDEMONA   No, by this heavenly light!
EMILIA
    Nor I neither by this heavenly light;
    I might do 't as well i' the dark.

DESDEMONA
   Wouldst thou do such a deed for all the world?
EMILIA
   The world's a huge thing. It is a great price
   For a small vice.
DESDEMONA
   Good troth, I think thou wouldst not.

Throughout this scene, Emilia's worldliness is contrasted to Desdemona's utter innocence and faith, which Shakespeare deliberately emphasizes shortly before Othello comes in to murder her. It's an ingenious dramatic prelude to the crime.

Othello's murder of Desdemona is one of Shakespeare's great scenes, though it can cause a slight problem for the director, who has to figure out how Desdemona can speak after she's been throttled. If not handled gingerly, this can easily lead to laughter, which will obviously destroy the delicate pathos of the scene. Nineteenth-century producers often solved the problem by having Othello stab Desdemona with a dagger instead of smothering her, but I consider that a coward's way out.

In a moving conclusion to the tragedy, before he takes his own life, Othello utters the poignant speech that begins, "Soft you; a word or two before you go":

               I pray you, in your letters,
   When you shall these unlucky deeds relate,
   Speak of me as I am; nothing extenuate,
   Nor set down aught in malice. Then must you speak
   Of one that loved not wisely but too well.

Othello is such a rich play, with its characters drawn straight from life and its array of gorgeous speeches, that it deserves to be read and performed over and over—as does all of Shakespeare.

❖

Once it gets past the hurdle of the opening scene, *King Lear* moves quickly and inexorably to "the promised end." But the first scene poses a real problem, because every-

thing in it seems so arbitrary. Why has Lear decided to divide his kingdom? Why are his daughters Goneril and
Regan playing up to him? Why is the youngest, Cordelia, so
stiff-necked? We watch perplexed as this super-egotist of a
king disowns his youngest daughter, banishes his most
loyal supporter, Kent, and stomps around the stage in a
childish rage that no one can appease. We feel a sense of
imminent doom as we see Lear so consumed with the sense
of his own power that he fails to realize the terrible consequences of giving it away.

Blinded by his anger, he can't see properly and so proceeds headlong on his disastrous course. Aside from his inability to judge his daughters accurately, Lear is also not
wise enough to know that once he's abdicated his power, he
can never get it back. For him to imagine that he can hold
on to the trappings of power—his one hundred knights, for
example—after he has given away its substance is terribly
naive and unworldly. Shakespeare gives Lear the Fool to remind him constantly of the terrible mistake he made in giving everything away. "Dost thou call me fool, boy?" Lear
asks; "All thy other titles thou hast given away; that thou
wast born with," the Fool replies. Indeed, as the Fool observes, Lear is the real fool of the play.

King Lear is a play about the problem of getting older but
not wiser. Lear is obviously a poor judge of character. He
has had a life of luxury, protected from poverty and unaware of the injustice in the world. The play charts his journey from the heights of wealth and power to the point where
he has neither and is set naked against nature, an old man
stripped of everything but his shaky wits and his aging
body.

An important part of Lear's fantastic journey is his learning firsthand about the world he has never known, the
world of hunger and corruption. I am reminded of an improvisation I created at Florida State University around a
concept of Lear that introduced the King as a jovial fat
man. As this improvisation progressed, it became clear to
me that *Lear* is essentially a play about hunger, old age,
madness, and dying. In the scene where Lear meets the
blinded Gloucester on the heath (4.6), the unseeing lord
begs to kiss Lear's hand. Lear replies, "Let me wipe it first;

it smells of mortality." In fact, the entire play smells of mortality; it is the quintessential play about old age and death.

❧

People always say that *Macbeth* is a play about ambition. But ambition is too vague a word to describe what goes on in the minds of Macbeth and Lady Macbeth. Their ambition is a dark driving force that will never be satisfied by what it achieves. It's an ambition that relies purely on getting other people out of the way, an ambition that requires one murder after another until Macbeth is "in blood / Stepped in so far that, should I wade no more, / Returning were as tedious as go o'er." The kind of ambition that Macbeth and his wife have feeds on itself, growing steadily and inevitably until it finally comes to rest with their deaths.

Though it is a tragedy, *Macbeth* is preoccupied with the perpetuation of the royal bloodline, as are many of Shakespeare's history plays. This concern seems to be at the core of Macbeth's ambition. His own quest, strangely resembling Richard III's, focuses on eliminating whoever is in the way of his becoming king.

And so he starts with the murder of King Duncan, the hereditary monarch. But it's clear to the murdered king's sons, Malcolm and Donalbain, that they are the next targets, and so they immediately flee Macbeth's castle. Then, in order to thwart the prophecy that Banquo will be father to a line of kings, Macbeth arranges to have him and his heir, Fleance, killed. When he learns to his horror that Fleance, like Malcolm and Donalbain, has escaped, he grows frantic at the failure of his efforts to achieve his bloody goal.

With an unquenchable appetite for murder, he orders the slaughter of Macduff's wife, children, and servants. The scene where Macduff learns of this butchery by Macbeth's henchmen is tremendously moving. Is there any greater expression of human grief than these lines spoken by the stricken Macduff?

He has no children. All my pretty ones?
Did you say all? O hell-kite! All?

What, all my pretty chickens and their dam
At one fell swoop?

The adolescent Malcolm, who has little experience in human affairs, appeals to his maleness, saying, "Dispute it like a man." Macduff's quiet reply, which always moves me deeply, is: "I shall do so; / But I must also feel it as a man." This is beautiful writing.

Gray, misty, and dark, *Macbeth* is a play in charcoal, with splotches of red providing the only color. Shakespeare, always attentive to his audience, gives them the revenge they want—everyone is eager to see Macbeth get it at the end, and he does. But Shakespeare doesn't satisfy the crowd's bloodlust right away. Macbeth is given his day in court, too, as he invites all comers into the fray: "Blow wind, come wrack, / At least we'll die with harness on our back."

Obviously Shakespeare doesn't resort to simplistic stereotypes. He lets good and bad mingle within Macbeth's heart—and within the hearts of all his bloody villains, for that matter. Richard III, that villain-king par excellence, fights to the bitter end, uttering those immortal lines. "A horse! A horse! My kingdom for a horse!" And Iago, the consummate evildoer, retains a shred of self-possession—even self-respect—at the end of *Othello* when he says, "Demand me nothing. What you know, you know. / From this time forth I never will speak word." With Iago, as with Richard and Macbeth, Shakespeare reminds us that people are never as simple as they seem.

JOSEPH PAPP

JOSEPH PAPP GRATEFULLY ACKNOWLEDGES THE HELP OF ELIZABETH KIRKLAND IN PREPARING THIS FOREWORD.

FOUR TRAGEDIES

Four Tragedies

Hamlet, Othello, King Lear, and *Macbeth* form a cohesive group in Shakespeare's dramatic production. They rank among the greatest tragedies he wrote—indeed, that anyone ever wrote. Shakespeare produced them all in one period of his life, in a steady outpouring of tragic eloquence: *Hamlet* (by 1601), *Othello* (c. 1603–1604), *King Lear* (c. 1605), and *Macbeth* (1606–1607). He also wrote several dark comedies and problematic plays—*All's Well That Ends Well, Measure for Measure,* and *Troilus and Cressida*—during the early years of this tragic period; they too are touched by a dark view of humanity's carnality and penchant for self-destruction. We encounter quite a separate tragic world of political struggle and social disillusionment in *Titus Andronicus* (c. 1589–1591), *Julius Caesar* (1599), *Timon of Athens* (c. 1605–1608), *Antony and Cleopatra* (1606–1607), and *Coriolanus* (c. 1608), plays where Shakespeare, in other periods, turned to the ancient classical world for tragic material.

The four tragedies in this volume are linked in a number of thematic ways. They all confront the nature of evil, as Shakespeare's classical tragedies generally do not. Human failure is often measured in terms of good and evil. Claudius, in *Hamlet,* confesses in soliloquy to being guilty of "the primal eldest curse" (3.3.37) of having killed his own brother, thus reenacting the crime of Cain against Abel (see Genesis 4) that began the history of human violence on earth. Othello, realizing too late what he has done in killing his innocent wife, begs divine punishment: "Whip me, ye devils, / From the possession of this heavenly sight! / Blow me about in winds! Roast me in sulfur! / Wash me in steep-down gulfs of liquid fire!" (5.2.286–289). The appalling evil manifested in *King Lear* by Goneril, Regan, Edmund, and others obliges Albany to question what will become of the human race if some restraint is not found: "If that the heavens do not their visible spirits / Send quickly down to tame these vile offenses, / It will come, / Humanity must perforce prey on itself, / Like monsters of the deep" (4.2.47–51). Macbeth is painfully aware that every decent consideration argues against the murder he is contemplating: "this Duncan / Hath borne his faculties so meek, hath been / So clear in his great office, that his virtues / Will plead like angels, trumpet-tongued, against / The deep damnation of his taking-off" (1.7.16–20). These four plays center on crimes that strike at everything civilization holds most dear: murder of a brother, usurpation of a crown through murder, murder to obtain one's brother's wife, murder of a wife, abandonment of a parent to life-threatening circumstances, adultery, conspiracy against a brother and a father, murder of one's king and one's guest.

Notably, these crimes are all contained within the family, which is one reason, perhaps, that we find Shakespeare's great tragedies so moving; they embody with such fearful clarity the struggles and rivalries within the family group. Hamlet must avenge his father's murder by killing his own uncle, and in doing so he must also confront the contrast between these two parental figures, his father and his stepfather. "Look here upon this picture, and on this," he urges his mother, as he shows her likenesses of the two. "Could you on this fair mountain leave to feed / And batten on this moor?" (3.4.54–68). It is as though Hamlet's father and Claudius personify what is best and worst in humanity, "Hyperion to a satyr" (1.2.140). Iago's rivalry with Cassio for Othello's favor, and his own hostility toward Othello, suggest a kind of family in which destructive anger has gone amok. *King Lear* structures its two parallel plots on two family groupings, in both of which the innocent child is betrayed by siblings and rejected by credulous and willfully unknowing parents. *Macbeth*'s crime is domestic, not only in that it is shared with such terrible intimacy by husband and wife, but in that the victim is a parental figure. "Had he not resembled / My father as he slept, I had done 't," says Lady Macbeth to her husband (2.2.12–13). Part of what is so frightening about Shakespeare's tragic vision is that it locates hatred so centrally in the struggle to survive within the family.

Evil is frightening in these plays also because it operates so insidiously, makes such canny use of false appearances, knows how to tempt human weakness at just the right time, and triumphs with such lamentable ease and frequency. Hamlet is obsessed with the human and especially femi-

nine susceptibility demonstrated by his mother and by
Ophelia. "Frailty, thy name is woman!" he exclaims in soliloquy (1.2.146). Yet men are no better, as Hamlet knows from
the example of Claudius or even of himself. "We are arrant
knaves all; believe none of us," he urges Ophelia (3.1.130).
"Use every man after his desert, and who shall scape whipping?" he observes to Polonius (2.2.529–530). Custom is a
"monster" (3.4.168) in Hamlet's view, something that too
readily produces the heavy drinking and lechery of his
uncle or the sliding into complicity of his mother, though
habit can also be enlisted more laboriously in the slow
work of reform. Othello quickly surrenders to the evil innu-
endos of Iago—despite the happiness of Othello in his marriage and his awareness of what losing Desdemona will cost
him—because Othello is all too ready to believe what Iago
proposes: that women are corruptible, and that it would be
"unnatural" for an attractive young white woman to continue loving an older black man once the novelty has worn
off. Edmund's practicing of evil against his brother and
father in *King Lear* succeeds so well because Edmund, like
Iago, is diabolically skillful at deception, and because villains who readily dispense with moral compunctions enjoy
an inherent competitive advantage over those who obey an
ethical code. The witches in *Macbeth* offer temptations that
are explicitly diabolical: they entice Macbeth into giving his
"eternal jewel," his soul, to "the common enemy of man,"
the devil, and they win because Macbeth consents knowingly to evil. The perpetrators of evil in these tragedies bear
responsibility for their own crimes, and yet their inability
to resist evil seems so profoundly human that their failure
touches us all. The bleak prospect of a world in which there
may be no gods and hence no restraints on human conduct
is equally dismaying; the villains prosper, for a while at
least, guided by this unsettling credo.

Shakespeare's great tragedies do nonetheless offer a
countervailing vision of goodness in which his virtuous
characters believe, no matter what the cost to themselves.
Hamlet knows that he is capable of evil like most people,
that he can be vindictive and ruthless—indeed, he is commanded to avenge his father's murder through some violent
action. Yet he yearns to think well of the human race, so
"noble in reason," so "infinite in faculties," the "beauty of

the world" and the "paragon of animals" (2.2.305–308), and the resolution of his dilemma comes paradoxically when he has laid aside scheming and is ready to affirm that "There's a divinity that shapes our ends, / Rough-hew them how we will" (5.2.10–11). Othello destroys Desdemona but cannot destroy her innocence. She must suffer, but her reputation is at last vindicated, while Iago's evil is disclosed. Iago had wished to poison Othello's mind forever against Desdemona, and to that extent he has failed. *King Lear*, though nominally pagan in setting, is filled with images of grace and charity offsetting those of depravity and hatred. Cordelia is, in the words of her husband-to-be (and of the Beatitudes, Matthew 5:1–12), "most rich being poor, / Most choice, forsaken, and most loved, despised" (1.1.254–255). She too must be sacrificed wantonly and unnecessarily, but the unselfish love she offers is a gift that no evil can undo. Erotic love and marriage are presented in negative terms in *King Lear*, as are many filial and parental relationships as well, but the devastating selfishness in such instances is at least partly countered by other generous and unselfish attachments between parent and child, master and follower. *King Lear* leaves us in no doubt that we should prefer to be a Cordelia rather than a Goneril, an Edgar rather than an Edmund—however much innocent "fools" may suffer in the world. Macbeth's crime unnerves us because it is so representatively human, and yet this play shows that humanity can also produce a Duncan, a Macduff, and an English king able to cure by the touch of his hand (4.3). The tragic world of these plays is a spiritual battleground in which failure is nearly universal, but in which our tragic response is tempered by the realization that one must understand evil if one is to resist it.

The Playhouse

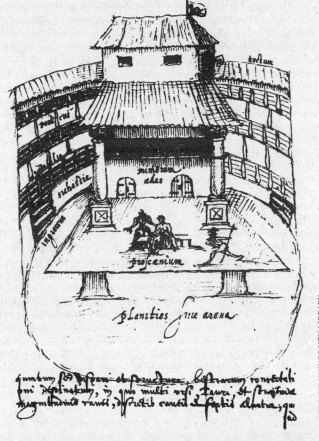

This early copy of a drawing by Johannes de Witt of the
Swan Theatre in London (c. 1596), made by his friend Arend
van Buchell, is the only surviving contemporary sketch of
the interior of a public theater in the 1590s.

From other contemporary evidence, including the stage directions and dialogue of Elizabethan plays, we can surmise that the various public theaters where Shakespeare's plays were produced (the Theatre, the Curtain, the Globe) resembled the Swan in many important particulars, though there must have been some variations as well. The public playhouses were essentially round, or polygonal, and open to the sky, forming an acting arena approximately 70 feet in diameter; they did not have a large curtain with which to open and close a scene, such as we see today in opera and some traditional theater. A platform measuring approximately 43 feet across and 27 feet deep, referred to in the de Witt drawing as the *proscaenium*, projected into the yard, *planities sive arena*. The roof, *tectum*, above the stage and supported by two pillars, could contain machinery for ascents and descents, as were required in several of Shakespeare's late plays. Above this roof was a hut, shown in the drawing with a flag flying atop it and a trumpeter at its door announcing the performance of a play. The underside of the stage roof, called the heavens, was usually richly decorated with symbolic figures of the sun, the moon, and the constellations. The platform stage stood at a height of 5½ feet or so above the yard, providing room under the stage for underworldly effects. A trapdoor, which is not visible in this drawing, gave access to the space below.

The structure at the back of the platform (labeled *mimorum aedes*), known as the tiring-house because it was the actors' attiring (dressing) space, featured at least two doors, as shown here. Some theaters seem to have also had a discovery space, or curtained recessed alcove, perhaps between the two doors—in which Falstaff could have hidden from the sheriff (*1 Henry IV*, 2.4) or Polonius could have eavesdropped on Hamlet and his mother (*Hamlet*, 3.4). This discovery space probably gave the actors a means of access to and from the tiring-house. Curtains may also have been hung in front of the stage doors on occasion. The de Witt drawing shows a gallery above the doors that extends across the back and evidently contains spectators. On occasions when action "above" demanded the use of this space, as when Juliet appears at her "window" (*Romeo and Juliet*, 2.2 and 3.5), the gallery seems to have been used by the actors, but large scenes there were impractical.

The three-tiered auditorium is perhaps best described by Thomas Platter, a visitor to London in 1599 who saw on that occasion Shakespeare's *Julius Caesar* performed at the Globe:

> The playhouses are so constructed that they play on a raised platform, so that everyone has a good view. There are different galleries and places [*orchestra, sedilia, porticus*], however, where the seating is better and more comfortable and therefore more expensive. For whoever cares to stand below only pays one English penny, but if he wishes to sit, he enters by another door [*ingressus*] and pays another penny, while if he desires to sit in the most comfortable seats, which are cushioned, where he not only sees everything well but can also be seen, then he pays yet another English penny at another door. And during the performance food and drink are carried round the audience, so that for what one cares to pay one may also have refreshment.

Scenery was not used, though the theater building itself was handsome enough to invoke a feeling of order and hierarchy that lent itself to the splendor and pageantry onstage. Portable properties, such as thrones, stools, tables, and beds, could be carried or thrust on as needed. In the scene pictured here by de Witt, a lady on a bench, attended perhaps by her waiting-gentlewoman, receives the address of a male figure. If Shakespeare had written *Twelfth Night* by 1596 for performance at the Swan, we could imagine Malvolio appearing like this as he bows before the Countess Olivia and her gentlewoman, Maria.

HAMLET

Introduction

A recurring motif in *Hamlet* is of a seemingly healthy exterior concealing an interior sickness. Mere pretense of virtue, as Hamlet warns his mother, "will but skin and film the ulcerous place, / Whiles rank corruption, mining all within, / Infects unseen" (3.4.154–156). Polonius confesses, when he is about to use his daughter as a decoy for Hamlet, that "with devotion's visage / And pious action we do sugar o'er / The devil himself"; and his observation elicits a more anguished mea culpa from Claudius in an aside: "How smart a lash that speech doth give my conscience! / The harlot's cheek, beautied with plastering art, / Is not more ugly to the thing that helps it / Than is my deed to my most painted word" (3.1.47–54).

This motif of concealed evil and disease continually reminds us that, in both a specific and a broader sense, "Something is rotten in the state of Denmark" (1.4.90). The specific source of contamination is a poison: the poison with which Claudius has killed Hamlet's father, the poison in the players' version of this same murder, and the two poisons (envenomed sword and poisoned drink) with which Claudius and Laertes plot to rid themselves of young Hamlet. More generally, the poison is an evil nature seeking to destroy humanity's better nature, as in the archetypal murder of Abel by Cain. "O, my offense is rank, it smells to heaven," laments Claudius, "It hath the primal eldest curse upon 't, / A brother's murder" (3.3.36–38). Hamlet's father and Claudius typify what is best and worst in humanity; one is the sun-god Hyperion, the other a satyr. Claudius is a "serpent" and a "mildewed ear, / Blasting his wholesome brother" (1.5.40; 3.4.65–66). Many a person, in Hamlet's view, is tragically destined to behold his or her better qualities corrupted by "some vicious mole of nature" over which the individual seems to have no control. "His virtues else, be they as pure as grace, / As infinite as man may undergo, / Shall in the general censure take corruption / From that particular fault." The "dram of evil" pollutes "all the noble substance" (1.4.24–37). Thus poison spreads outward to infect individual persons, just as bad individuals can infect an entire court or nation.

Hamlet, his mind attuned to philosophical matters, is keenly and poetically aware of humanity's fallen condition. He is, moreover, a shrewd observer of the Danish court, one familiar with its ways and at the same time newly returned from abroad, looking at Denmark with a stranger's eyes. What particularly darkens his view of humanity, however, is not the general fact of corrupted human nature but rather Hamlet's knowledge of a dreadful secret. Even before he learns of his father's murder, Hamlet senses that there is something more deeply amiss than his mother's overhasty marriage to her deceased husband's brother. This is serious enough, to be sure, for it violates a taboo (parallel to the marriage of a widower to his deceased wife's sister, long regarded as incestuous by the English) and is thus understandably referred to as "incest" by Hamlet and his father's ghost. The appalling spectacle of Gertrude's "wicked speed, to post / With such dexterity to incestuous sheets" (1.2.156–157) overwhelms Hamlet with revulsion at carnal appetite and intensifies the emotional crisis any son would go through when forced to contemplate his father's death and his mother's remarriage. Still, the Ghost's revelation is of something far worse, something Hamlet has subconsciously feared and suspected. "O my prophetic soul! My uncle!" (1.5.42). Now Hamlet has confirming evidence for his intuition that the world itself is "an unweeded garden / That grows to seed. Things rank and gross in nature / Possess it merely" (1.2.135–137).

Something is indeed rotten in the state of Denmark. The monarch on whom the health and safety of the kingdom depend is a murderer. Yet few persons know his secret: Hamlet, Horatio only belatedly, Claudius himself, and ourselves as audience. Many ironies and misunderstandings of the play cannot be understood without a proper awareness of this gap between Hamlet's knowledge and most others' ignorance of the murder. For, according to their own lights, Polonius and the rest behave as courtiers normally behave, obeying and flattering a king whom they acknowledge as their legitimate ruler. Hamlet, for his part, is so obsessed with the secret murder that he overreacts to those around him, rejecting overtures of friendship and becoming embittered, callous, brutal, and even violent. His antisocial behavior gives the others good reason to fear him as a menace to the state. Nevertheless, we share with Hamlet a knowledge of the truth and know that he is right, whereas the others are at best unhappily deceived by their own blind complicity in evil.

Rosencrantz and Guildenstern, for instance, are boyhood friends of Hamlet but are now dependent on the favor of King Claudius. Despite their seeming concern for their one-time comrade, and Hamlet's initial pleasure in receiving them, they are faceless courtiers whose very names, like their personalities, are virtually interchangeable. "Thanks, Rosencrantz and gentle Guildenstern," says the King, and "Thanks, Guildenstern and gentle Rosencrantz," echoes the Queen (2.2.33–34). They cannot understand why Hamlet increasingly mocks their overtures of friendship, whereas Hamlet cannot stomach their subservience to the King. The secret murder divides Hamlet from them, since only he knows of it. As the confrontation between Hamlet and Claudius grows more deadly, Rosencrantz and Guildenstern, not knowing the true cause, can only interpret Hamlet's behavior as dangerous madness. The wild display he puts on during the performance of "The Murder of Gonzago" and the killing of Polonius are evidence of a treasonous threat to the crown, eliciting from them staunch assertions of the divine right of kings. "Most holy and religious fear it is / To keep those many many bodies safe / That live and feed upon Your Majesty," professes Guildenstern, and Rosencrantz reiterates the theme: "The cess of majesty / Dies not alone, but like a gulf doth draw / What's near it with it" (3.3.8–17). These sentiments of Elizabethan orthodoxy, similar to ones frequently heard in Shakespeare's history plays, are here undercut by a devastating irony, since they are spoken unwittingly in defense of a murderer. This irony pursues Rosencrantz and Guildenstern to their graves, for they are killed performing what they see as their duty to convey Hamlet safely to England. They are as ignorant of Claudius's secret orders for the murder of Hamlet in England as they are of Claudius's real reason for wishing to be rid of his stepson. That Hamlet should ingeniously remove the secret commission from Rosencrantz and Guildenstern's packet and substitute an order for their execution is ironically fitting, even though they are guiltless of having plotted Hamlet's death. "Why, man, they did make love to this employment," says Hamlet to Horatio. "They are not near my conscience. Their defeat / Does by their own insinuation grow" (5.2.57–59). They have condemned themselves, in Hamlet's eyes, by interceding officiously in deadly affairs of which they had no comprehension. Hamlet's judgment of them is harsh, and he himself appears hardened and pitiless in his role as agent in their deaths, but he is right that they have courted their own destiny.

Polonius, too, dies for meddling. It seems an unfair fate, since he wishes no physical harm to Hamlet, and is only trying to ingratiate himself with Claudius. Yet Polonius's complicity in jaded court politics is deeper than his fatuous parental sententiousness might lead one to suppose. His famous advice to his son, often quoted out of context as though it were wise counsel, is in fact a worldly gospel of self-interest and concern for appearances. Like his son, Laertes, he cynically presumes that Hamlet's affection for Ophelia cannot be serious, since princes are not free to marry ladies of the court; accordingly, Polonius obliges his daughter to return the love letters she so cherishes. Polonius's spies are everywhere, seeking to entrap Polonius's own son in fleshly sin or to discover symptoms of Hamlet's presumed lovesickness. Polonius may cut a ridiculous figure as a prattling busybody, but he is wily and even menacing in his intent. He has actually helped Claudius to the throne and is an essential instrument of royal policy. His ineffectuality and ignorance of the murder do not really excuse his guilty involvement.

Ophelia is more innocent than her father and brother, and more truly affectionate toward Hamlet. She earns our sympathy because she is caught between the conflicting wills of the men who are supremely important to her—her lover, her father, her brother. Obedient by instinct and training to patriarchal instruction, she is unprepared to cope with divided authority and so takes refuge in passivity. Nevertheless her pitiable story suggests that weak-willed acquiescence is poisoned by the evil to which it surrenders. However passively, Ophelia becomes an instrument through which Claudius attempts to spy on Hamlet. She is much like Gertrude, for the Queen has yielded to Claudius's importunity without ever knowing fully what awful price Claudius has paid for her and for the throne. The resemblance between Ophelia and Gertrude confirms Hamlet's tendency to generalize about feminine weakness—"frailty, thy name is woman" (1.2.146)—and prompts his misogynistic outburst against Ophelia when he concludes she, too, is spying on him. His rejection of love and friendship (except for Horatio's) seems paranoid in character and yet is at least partially justified by the fact that so many of the court are in fact conspiring to learn what he is up to.

Their oversimplification of his dilemma and their facile analyses vex Hamlet as much as their meddling. When they presume to diagnose his malady, the courtiers actually reveal more about themselves than about Hamlet—something we as readers and viewers might well bear in mind. Rosencrantz and Guildenstern think in political terms, reflecting their own ambitious natures, and Hamlet takes mordant delight in leading them on. "Sir, I lack advancement," he mockingly answers Rosencrantz's questioning as to the cause of his distemper. Rosencrantz is immediately taken in: "How can that be, when you have the voice of the King himself for your succession in Denmark?" (3.2.338–341). Actually Hamlet does hold a grudge against Claudius for having "Popped in between th' election and my hopes" (5.2.65) by using the Danish custom of "election" by the chief lords of the realm to deprive young Hamlet of the succession that would normally have been his. Nevertheless, it is a gross oversimplification to suppose that political frustration is the key to Hamlet's sorrow, and to speculate thus is presumptuous. "Why, look you now, how unworthy a thing you make of me!" Hamlet protests to Rosencrantz and Guildenstern. "You would play upon me, you would seem to know my stops, you would pluck out the heart of my mystery" (3.2.362–365). Yet the worst offender in these distortions of complex truth is Polonius, whose diagnosis of lovesickness appears to have been inspired by recollections of Polonius's own far-off youth. ("Truly in my

youth I suffered much extremity for love, very near this,"
2.2.189–191.) Polonius's fatuous complacency in his own
powers of analysis—"If circumstances lead me, I will find /
Where truth is hid, though it were hid indeed / Within the
center" (2.2.157–159)—reads like a parody of Hamlet's
struggle to discover what is true and what is not.

Thus, although Hamlet may seem to react with excessive
bitterness toward those who are set to watch over him, the
corruption he decries in Denmark is both real and universal. "The time is out of joint," he laments. "O cursèd spite /
That ever I was born to set it right!" (1.5.197–198). How is
he to proceed in setting things right? Ever since the nineteenth century it has been fashionable to discover reasons
for Hamlet's delaying his revenge. The basic Romantic approach is to find a defect, or tragic flaw, in Hamlet himself.
In Coleridge's words, Hamlet suffers from "an overbalance
in the contemplative faculty" and is "one who vacillates
from sensibility and procrastinates from thought, and loses
the power of action in the energy of resolve." More recent
psychological critics, such as Freud's disciple Ernest Jones,
still seek answers to the Romantics' question by explaining
Hamlet's failure of will. In Jones's interpretation, Hamlet
is the victim of an Oedipal trauma; he has longed uncon-
sciously to possess his mother and for that very reason cannot bring himself to punish the hated uncle who has
supplanted him in his incestuous and forbidden desire.
Such interpretations suggest, among other things, that
Hamlet continues to serve as a mirror in which analysts
who would pluck out the heart of his mystery see an image
of their own concerns—just as Rosencrantz and Guildenstern read politics, and Polonius lovesickness, into Hamlet's distress.

We can ask, however, not only whether the explanations
for Hamlet's supposed delay are valid but whether the
question they seek to answer is itself valid. Is the delay unnecessary or excessive? The question did not even arise until the nineteenth century. Earlier audiences were evidently
satisfied that Hamlet must test the Ghost's credibility,
since apparitions can tell half-truths to deceive men, and
that once Hamlet has confirmed the Ghost's word, he proceeds as resolutely as his canny adversary allows. More re-

cent criticism, perhaps reflecting a modern absorption in existentialist philosophy, has proposed that Hamlet's dilemma is a matter not of personal failure but of the absurdity of action itself in a corrupt world. Does what Hamlet is asked to do make any sense, given the bestial nature of man and the impossibility of knowing what is right? In part it is a matter of style: Claudius's Denmark is crassly vulgar, and to combat this vulgarity on its own terms seems to require the sort of bad histrionics Hamlet derides in actors who mouth their lines or tear a passion to tatters. Hamlet's dilemma of action can best be studied in the play by comparing him with various characters who are obliged to act in situations similar to his own and who respond in meaningfully different ways.

Three young men—Hamlet, Laertes, and Fortinbras—are called upon to avenge their fathers' violent deaths. Ophelia, too, has lost a father by violent means, and her madness and death are another kind of reaction to such a loss. The responses of Laertes and Fortinbras offer implicit lessons to Hamlet, and in both cases the lesson seems to be of the futility of positive and forceful action. Laertes thinks he has received an unambiguous mandate to revenge, since Hamlet has undoubtedly slain Polonius and helped to deprive Ophelia of her sanity. Accordingly Laertes comes back to Denmark in a fury, stirring the rabble with his demagoguery and spouting Senecan rant about dismissing conscience "to the profoundest pit" in his quest for vengeance (4.5.135). When Claudius asks what Laertes would do to Hamlet "To show yourself in deed your father's son / More than in words," Laertes fires back: "To cut his throat i' the church" (4.7.126–127). This resolution is understandable. The pity is, however, that Laertes has only superficially identified the murderer in the case. He is too easily deceived by Claudius because he has accepted easy and fallacious conclusions, and so is doomed to become a pawn in Claudius's sly maneuverings. Too late he sees his error and must die for it, begging and receiving Hamlet's forgiveness. Before we accuse Hamlet of thinking too deliberately before acting, we must consider that Laertes does not think enough.

Fortinbras of Norway, as his name implies ("strong in

arms"), is one who believes in decisive action. At the beginning of the play we learn that his father has been slain in battle by old Hamlet, and that Fortinbras has collected an army to win back by force the territory fairly won by the Danes in that encounter. Like Hamlet, young Fortinbras does not succeed his father to the throne, but must now contend with an uncle-king. When this uncle, at Claudius's instigation, forbids Fortinbras to march against the Danes, and rewards him for his restraint with a huge annual income and a commission to fight the Poles instead, Fortinbras sagaciously welcomes the new opportunity. He pockets the money, marches against Poland, and waits for occasion to deliver Denmark as well into his hands. Clearly this is more of a success story than that of Laertes, and Hamlet does after all give his blessing to the "election" of Fortinbras to the Danish throne. Fortinbras is the man of the hour, the representative of a restored political stability. Yet Hamlet's admiration for this man on horseback is qualified by a profound reservation. The spectacle of Fortinbras marching against Poland "to gain a little patch of ground / That hath in it no profit but the name" prompts Hamlet to berate himself for inaction, but he cannot ignore the absurdity of the effort. "Two thousand souls and twenty thousand ducats / Will not debate the question of this straw." The soldiers will risk their very lives "Even for an eggshell" (4.4.19–54). It is only one step from this view of the vanity of ambitious striving to the speculation that great Caesar or Alexander, dead and turned to dust, may one day produce the loam or clay with which to stop the bunghole of a beer barrel. Fortinbras epitomizes the ongoing political order after Hamlet's death, but is that order of any consequence to us after we have imagined with Hamlet the futility of most human endeavor?

To ask such a question is to seek passive or self-abnegating answers to the riddle of life, and Hamlet is attuned to such inquiries. Even before he learns of his father's murder, he contemplates suicide, wishing "that the Everlasting had not fixed / His canon 'gainst self-slaughter" (1.2.131–132). As with the alternative of action, other characters serve as foils to Hamlet, revealing both the attractions and perils of withdrawal. Ophelia is destroyed by meekly acquiescing in others' desires. Whether she commits suicide is uncertain, but the very possibility reminds us that Hamlet has considered and reluctantly rejected this despairing path as forbidden by Christian teaching. He has also playacted at the madness to which Ophelia succumbs. Gertrude identifies herself with Ophelia and, like her, has surrendered her will to male aggressiveness. We suspect she knows little of the actual murder but dares not think how deeply she may be implicated. Her death may possibly be a suicide also, one of atonement. A more attractive alternative to decisive action for Hamlet is acting in the theater, and he is full of advice to the visiting players. The play they perform before Claudius at Hamlet's request and with some lines added by him, a play consciously archaic in style, offers to the Danish court a kind of heightened reflection of itself, a homiletic artifact rendering in conventional terms the taut anxieties and terrors of murder for the sake of ignoble passion. We are not surprised when, in his conversations with the players, Hamlet openly professes his admiration for the way in which art holds "the mirror up to nature, to show virtue her feature, scorn her own image, and the very age and body of the time his form and pressure" (3.2.22–24). Hamlet admires the dramatist's ability to transmute raw human feeling into tragic art, depicting and ordering reality as Shakespeare's play of *Hamlet* does for us. Yet playacting is also, Hamlet recognizes, a self-indulgent escape for him, a way of unpacking his heart with words, of verbalizing his situation without doing something to remedy it. Acting and talking remind him too much of Polonius, who was an actor in his youth and who continues to be, like Hamlet, an inveterate punster.

Of the passive responses in the play, the stoicism of Horatio is by far the most attractive to Hamlet. "More an antique Roman than a Dane" (5.2.343), Horatio is, as Hamlet praises him, immune to flattering or to opportunities for cheap self-advancement. He is "As one, in suffering all, that suffers nothing, / A man that Fortune's buffets and rewards / Hast ta'en with equal thanks" (3.2.65–67). Such a person has a sure defense against the worst that life can offer. Hamlet can trust and love Horatio as he can no one else. Yet even here there are limits, for Horatio's skeptical and Ro-

man philosophy cuts him off from a Christian and metaphysical overview. "There are more things in heaven and
earth, Horatio, / Than are dreamt of in your philosophy"
(1.5.175–176). After they have beheld together the skulls of
Yorick's graveyard, Horatio seemingly does not share with
Hamlet the exulting Christian perception that, although
human life is indeed vain, providence will reveal a pattern
transcending human sorrow.

Hamlet's path must lie somewhere between the rash sud-
denness of Laertes or the canny resoluteness of Fortinbras
on the one hand, and the passivity of Ophelia or Gertrude
and the stoic resignation of Horatio on the other, but he al-
ternates between action and inaction, finding neither satis-
factory. The Ghost has commanded Hamlet to revenge, but
has not explained how this is to be done; indeed, Gertrude
is to be left passively to heaven and her conscience. If this
method will suffice for her (and Christian wisdom taught
that such a purgation was as thorough as it was sure), why
not for Claudius? If Claudius must be killed, should it be
while he is at his sin rather than at his prayers? The play is
full of questions, stemming chiefly from the enigmatic commands of the Ghost. "Say, why is this? Wherefore? What
should we do?" (1.4.57). Hamlet is not incapable of action.
He shows unusual strength and cunning on the pirate ship,
or in his duel with Laertes ("I shall win at the odds";
5.2.209–210), or especially in his slaying of Polonius—an
action hardly characterized by "thinking too precisely on
th' event" (4.4.42). Here is forthright action of the sort
Laertes espouses. Yet when the corpse behind his mother's
arras turns out to be Polonius rather than Claudius, Hamlet
knows he has offended heaven. Even if Polonius deserves
what he got, Hamlet has made himself into a cruel
"scourge" of providence who must himself suffer retribution as well as deal it out. Swift action has not accomplished what the Ghost commanded.

The Ghost in fact does not appear to speak for providence. His message is of revenge, a pagan concept basic to
all primitive societies but at odds with Christian teaching.
His wish that Claudius be sent to hell and that Gertrude be
more gently treated is not the judgment of an impartial deity but the emotional reaction of a murdered man's restless

spirit. This is not to say that Hamlet is being tempted to perform a damnable act, as he fears is possible, but that the Ghost's command cannot readily be reconciled with a complex and balanced view of justice. If Hamlet were to spring on Claudius in the fullness of his vice and cut his throat, we would pronounce Hamlet a murderer. What Hamlet believes he has learned instead is that he must become the instrument of providence according to *its* plans, not his own. After his return from England, he senses triumphantly that all will be for the best if he allows an unseen power to decide the time and place for his final act. Under these conditions, rash action will be right. "Rashly, / And praised be rashness for it—let us know / Our indiscretion sometimes serves us well / When our deep plots do pall, and that should learn us / There's a divinity that shapes our ends, / Rough-hew them how we will" (5.2.6–11). Passivity, too, is now a proper course, for Hamlet puts himself wholly at the disposal of providence. What had seemed so impossible when Hamlet tried to formulate his own design now proves elementary once he trusts to heaven's justice. Rashness and passivity are perfectly fused. Hamlet is revenged without having to commit premeditated murder and is relieved of his painful existence without having to commit suicide.

The circumstances of *Hamlet*'s catastrophe do indeed accomplish all that Hamlet desires, by a route so circuitous that no man could ever have foreseen or devised it. Polonius's death, as it turns out, was instrumental after all, for it led to Laertes's angry return to Denmark and the challenge to a duel. Every seemingly unrelated event has its place; "There is special providence in the fall of a sparrow" (5.2.217–218). Repeatedly the characters stress the role of seeming accident leading to just retribution. Horatio sums up a pattern "Of accidental judgments, casual slaughters . . . And, in this upshot, purposes mistook / Fall'n on th' inventors' heads" (5.2.384–387). Laertes confesses himself "a woodcock to mine own springe" (l. 309). As Hamlet had said earlier, of Rosencrantz and Guildenstern, " 'tis the sport to have the enginer / Hoist with his own petard" (3.4.213–214). Thus, too, Claudius's poisoned cup, intended for Hamlet, kills the Queen for whom Claudius had done such evil in order to acquire.

In its final resolution, *Hamlet* incorporates a broader conception of justice than its revenge formula seemed at first to make possible. Yet in its origins *Hamlet* is a revenge story, and these traditions have left some residual savagery in the play. In the *Historia Danica* of Saxo Grammaticus, 1180–1208, and in the rather free translation of Saxo into French by François de Belleforest, *Histoires Tragiques* (1576), Hamlet is cunning and bloodily resolute throughout. He kills an eavesdropper without a qualm during the interview with his mother and exchanges letters on his way to England with characteristic shrewdness. Ultimately he returns to Denmark, sets fire to his uncle's hall, slays its courtly inhabitants, and claims his rightful throne from a grateful people. The Ghost, absent in this account, may well have been supplied by Thomas Kyd, author of *The Spanish Tragedy* (c. 1587) and seemingly of a lost *Hamlet* play in existence by 1589. *The Spanish Tragedy* bears many resemblances to our *Hamlet* and suggests what the lost *Hamlet* may well have contained: a sensational murder, a Senecan Ghost demanding revenge, the avenger hampered by court intrigue, his resort to a feigned madness, his difficulty in authenticating the ghostly vision. A German version of *Hamlet*, called *Der bestrafte Brudermord* (1710), based seemingly on the older *Hamlet*, includes such details as the play within the play, the sparing of the King at his prayers in order to damn his soul, Ophelia's madness, the fencing match with poisoned swords and poisoned drink, and the final catastrophe of vengeance and death. Similarly, the early pirated first quarto of *Hamlet* (1603) offers some passages seemingly based on the older play by Kyd.

Although this evidence suggests that Shakespeare received most of the material for the plot intact, his transformation of that material was nonetheless immeasurable. To be sure, Kyd's *The Spanish Tragedy* contains many rhetorical passages on the inadequacy of human justice, but the overall effect is still sensational and the outcome is a triumph for the pagan spirit of revenge. So, too, with the many revenge plays of the 1590s and 1600s that Kyd's dramatic genius had inspired, including Shakespeare's own *Titus Andronicus* (c. 1589–1591). *Hamlet*, written in about 1599–1601 (it is not mentioned by Francis Meres in his *Palladis Tamia: Wit's Treasury*, in 1598, and was entered in the Stationers'

Register, the official record book of the London Company of Stationers [booksellers and printers], in 1602), is unparalleled in its philosophical richness. Its ending is truly cathartic, for Hamlet dies not as a bloodied avenger but as one who has affirmed the tragic dignity of man. His courage and faith, maintained in the face of great odds, atone for the dismal corruption in which Denmark has festered. His resolutely honest inquiries have taken him beyond the revulsion and doubt that express so eloquently, among other matters, the fearful response of Shakespeare's own generation to a seeming breakdown of established political, theological, and cosmological beliefs. Hamlet finally perceives that "if it be not now, yet it will come," and that "The readiness is all" (5.2.219–220). This discovery, this revelation of necessity and meaning in Hamlet's great reversal of fortune, enables him to confront the tragic circumstance of his life with understanding and heroism, and to demonstrate the triumph of the human spirit even in the moment of his catastrophe.

Such an assertion of the individual will does not lessen the tragic waste with which *Hamlet* ends. Hamlet is dead, the great promise of his life forever lost. Few others have survived. Justice has seemingly been fulfilled in the deaths of Claudius, Gertrude, Rosencrantz and Guildenstern, Polonius, Laertes, and perhaps even Ophelia, but in a wild and extravagant way, as though Justice herself, more vengeful than providential, were unceasingly hungry for victims. Hamlet, the minister of that justice, has likewise grown indifferent to the spilling of blood, even if he submits himself at last to the will of a force he recognizes as providential. Denmark faces the kind of political uncertainty with which the play began. However much Hamlet may admire Fortinbras's resolution, the prince of Norway seems an alien choice for Denmark, even an ironic one. Horatio sees so little point in outliving the catastrophe of this play that he would choose death were it not that he must draw his breath in pain to ensure that Hamlet's story is truly told. Still, that truth has been rescued from oblivion. Amid the ruin of the final scene we share the artist's vision, through which we struggle to interpret and give order to the tragedy of human existence.

Hamlet
in Performance

Most people who know their Shakespeare are surprised and disconcerted by the cutting of so much material when they see the otherwise admirable film of *Hamlet* by Laurence Olivier (1948): all of Fortinbras's role and the negotiations with Norway, all of Rosencrantz and Guildenstern, a good deal of Act 4, and still more. The supposed reason, that a film must cut heavily to make room for visual material and to be of an acceptable length, is of course true in the main, but it overlooks the long history of the play in production. Many of the same cuts prevailed from the Restoration until the later nineteenth century as a way not only of shortening a long play but of highlighting the role of Hamlet for the lead actor.

Even in its own day, *Hamlet* (with Richard Burbage in the title role) must have been heavily cut at times, especially in the fourth act; the so-called "bad" quarto of 1603, though garbled presumably by the actors who helped to prepare a stolen copy, appears to be the report of a shortened acting text. During the Restoration, the published edition of the version that diarist Samuel Pepys saw and enjoyed five times during the 1660s was offered to its readers with a warning: "This play being too long to be conveniently acted, such places as might be least prejudicial to the plot or sense are left out upon the stage." This *Hamlet*, prepared by William Davenant and acted by Thomas Betterton at intervals from 1661 until 1709, took out some 841 lines, including most of Fortinbras's part, Polonius's advice to Laertes and instructions to Reynaldo, much of Rosencrantz and Guildenstern, the scene between Hamlet and Fortinbras's captain (4.4), and other matters, though the appearance of Fortinbras at the end was retained. Betterton's successor, Robert Wilks (active in the part until 1732), went further by removing Fortinbras from Act 5 entirely, concluding the play instead with Horatio's farewell and eulogy to his sweet prince. This ending was the only one to be seen onstage from 1732 until 1897. An operatic version of *Ham-*

let in 1712 bore even less resemblance to Shakespeare's play, taking its inspiration chiefly from Saxo Grammaticus's *Historia Danica*, the twelfth-century narrative from which the history of Hamlet derives.

David Garrick used for a time a version of the Wilks text from which he also cut Hamlet's soliloquy in Act 3, scene 3 ("Now might I do it pat"), and all mention of Hamlet's voyage to England. Then, in 1772, Garrick ventured to remove nearly all of the fifth act. In Garrick's *Hamlet* the protagonist never embarks for England at all, having been prevented from doing so by the arrival of Fortinbras. Laertes, hindered by a shipwreck, never gets to France. Laertes is a more estimable person than in Shakespeare's play, since he is entirely freed of the taint of plotting to kill Hamlet with a poisoned sword. Hamlet and Laertes fight, but without the poisoned sword; Claudius tries to intervene in the duel of the two young men and is slain by Hamlet, who then runs on Laertes's sword and falls, exchanging forgiveness with Laertes as he dies. Horatio, after attempting to kill Laertes in revenge, is persuaded by the dying Hamlet to accept the will of Heaven and to rule jointly with Laertes. The gravediggers are not needed since Ophelia's burial is omitted. Gertrude is not poisoned but, we are told, is in a trance and on the verge of madness from remorse. We do not hear of the execution of Rosencrantz and Guildenstern. Garrick's intention in all this novelty seems to have been to ennoble Hamlet by pairing him in the last scene with a worthy opponent, by reducing the bloodthirstiness of his killing of Claudius, and by omitting all mention of his part in the deaths of Rosencrantz and Guildenstern. Classical decorum was served by excising long gaps of time and travels into other lands, and by refusing to countenance the comedy of the gravediggers in a tragic play. Garrick restored the soliloquy, "How all occasions do inform against me" (4.4), again enhancing the role of the protagonist, along with some of Polonius's advice to his son.

Garrick called his alterations of *Hamlet* "the most imprudent thing" he had ever done. Although he was "sanguine" about the results, modern audiences are more likely to feel that the Romantic era was not an auspicious time for the play. In addition to Garrick's adaptations, German actors in England at the end of the century provided the play a happy ending, with the Queen's illness warning Hamlet in time. John Philip Kemble, acting the part at various times from 1783 to 1817, cut the play back to a series of well-known theatrical vignettes, prompting critic William Hazlitt, while admiring Kemble's acting, to complain that *Hamlet* is better not acted at all.

As if to confirm Hazlitt's worry about the often empty theatricality of the nineteenth-century stage, a chief preoccupation of the time was to add pictorial splendor to stage production. Actor-manager William Charles Macready, at the Theatre Royal, Covent Garden, in 1838, won praise for "a series of glorious pictures." Charles Kean, who in 1838 had a great success acting Hamlet at the Theatre Royal, Drury Lane, lavished money and attention on the fortress of Elsinore in his own production of the play at the Princess's Theatre in 1850. With his customary passion for scenic elaboration, he showed, among other scenes, a guard platform of the castle and then another part of the platform, the royal court of Denmark and its handsome theater, the Queen's "closet" or chamber, and the ancient burying ground in the vicinity of the palace to which Ophelia was borne with impressive if maimed rites. Nineteenth-century illustrations of Shakespeare's plays testify to the age's interest in pictorially detailed reproductions of the play within the play, Ophelia's mad scenes, and other emotionally powerful moments in *Hamlet*. Ophelia became a favorite subject for the visual arts, in the theater and out of it, perhaps because she was so well suited, like the Lady of Shalott, for pre-Raphaelite interpretation. Pictorialism in the theater thus accentuated the trend, already seen among earlier actor-managers, toward highlighting the play's great iconic moments at the expense of the rest of the text. Ophelia became a leading role for actresses such as Julia Bennett, Ellen and Kate Terry, and Helena Modjeska, especially in the latter part of the century.

Charles Fechter appears to have been the first, at the Princess's Theatre in 1861 and then at the Lyceum Theatre in 1864, to garb Hamlet, not in the velvet and lace of an English aristocrat, but in Viking attire appropriate to the play's Danish setting, which was matched with surrounding sets in primitive and medieval decor. His Hamlet was flaxen-haired; Rosencrantz and Guildenstern were bearded Scandinavian warriors in coarse cross-gartered leggings. Much of the action took place in the large main hall of Elsinore. Edwin Booth in America and Henry Irving in England were the leading Hamlets of the late century. Booth appeared first in the role in 1853, in San Francisco, winning instant renown both in America and abroad. In 1861, in Manchester, England, he played Hamlet to Irving's Laertes. Three years later, Irving himself first played Hamlet, and he continued in the role until 1885. Irving chose a decor of the fifth or sixth century, though not rigorously so, and his costumes retained the attractiveness of Elizabethan dress. Hamlet's first encounter with his father's ghost was impressively set in a remote part of the battlements of the castle, amid massive rocks, with the soft light of the moon filtering onto the Ghost while hints of dawn appeared over the expanse of water to be seen in the background. The scenes on the battlements showed the illuminated windows of the palace in the distance. The funeral of Ophelia took place on a hill near the palace. Irving portrayed Hamlet as deeply affected by his love for Ophelia in a sentimental interpretation that gave prominence to Ellen Terry's Ophelia. Irving made little of Hamlet's voyage to England or his encounter with Fortinbras's captain, devoting most of Act 4 instead to Ophelia's mad scenes and ending the play with "The rest is silence." These descriptions suggest the extent to which the actor-managers of that age turned to favorite scenes for their theatrical effects, cutting much else to accommodate the ponderous scenery.

Beginning with Johnston Forbes-Robertson's restoration of the Fortinbras ending in 1897, as he was encouraged to do by George Bernard Shaw, twentieth-century directors have generally shown more respect for the play's text than did their predecessors. In 1881 at St. George's Hall, William Poel had already directed a group of amateur actors in a reading of the play based on the 1603 quarto, and in 1899 Frank Benson staged an uncut composite Folio-quarto text (something never acted in Shakespeare's day) at the Shakespeare Memorial Theatre in Stratford-upon-Avon. These were experimental performances and not rigorously fol-

lowed since, though Harcourt Williams directed John
Gielgud, in his first Hamlet, at the Old Vic in 1930 in a production without significant cuts. Tyrone Guthrie successfully produced the play in an uncut version, which starred
Laurence Olivier, at the Old Vic in 1937, and Olivier himself
directed an uncut *Hamlet* at London's National Theatre
starring Peter O'Toole in 1963. At the same time, directors
have turned away from the nineteenth-century sentimental
focus on Hamlet's delay and love melancholy to explore ironies and conflict. *Hamlet* in modern dress, beginning with
H. K. Ayliff at the Birmingham Repertory Theatre in 1925,
and followed by, among others, Tyrone Guthrie in 1938, in
another production at the Old Vic, explored the existential
challenges of the play in the context of Europe between two
world wars. Freudian interpretation played a major part in
Laurence Olivier's film version of 1948, as evidenced by the
camera's preoccupation with Gertrude's bedroom and by
the intimate scenes between mother and son. Olivier's cutting and rearranging of scenes owed much to eighteenth-
and nineteenth-century traditions, as we have seen, even
while his camera work found new ways to explore the mysterious and labyrinthine corridors of Elsinore Castle. Joseph Papp's *Hamlet* (Public Theater, New York, 1968) went
beyond Olivier in an iconoclastic and deliberately overstated psychological shocker, featuring a manacled Hamlet (Martin Sheen) in a coffinlike cradle at the feet of
Claudius's and Gertrude's bed. Grigori Kozintsev's Russian film version of 1964, using a cut text by Boris Pas-
ternak, found eloquent visual metaphors for Hamlet's
story in the recurring images of stone, iron, fire, sea, and
earth. Among the best Hamlets have been those of Richard
Burton (in 1964 at New York's Lunt-Fontanne Theater, directed by John Gielgud), Nicol Williamson (in 1969 at the
Roundhouse Theatre in London, directed by Tony Richardson), and Derek Jacobi (in 1979 at the Old Vic, directed by
Toby Robertson) portraying the protagonist as tough and serious, capable of great tenderness in friendship and love,
but faced with hard necessities and pursuing them with
fierce energy. Jacobi's *Hamlet* can be seen today in the generally excellent BBC Shakespeare television version, with a
strong supporting cast.

The melancholic, pale, introspective Hamlet of Kemble and the lovestruck prince of Irving have thus seldom been seen on the modern stage, though Olivier recalls the tradition of melancholy with his voice-over soliloquies, and John Gielgud's sonorously spectral voice excels in the meditations on suicide. Today the play is more apt to be satirical, even funny at times, presenting a mordant and disillusioned view of life at court, as in Peter Hall's 1965 production at Stratford-upon-Avon, or in Jonathan Miller's more austere *Hamlet* at London's Warehouse Theatre in 1982, both of which disturbingly portray a world in which, as Hall wrote, "politics are a game and a lie." Polonius, long regarded in the theater as little more than a "tedious old fool," as Hamlet calls him, can reveal in the performance of Felix Alymer or Hume Cronyn or Del Close a canniness in political survival that fits well with his matter-of-fact and philistine outlook. The scenes at court lend themselves to contemporary political analogies: Claudius can become the Great Communicator, adept at public relations gimmicks, the darling of television, while the creatures who bustle about him do their part to "sell" Claudius to a complacent court and a thoroughly skeptical Hamlet. As the outsider, Hamlet today is likely to be the rebel, a misfit, and justly so in view of what he sees in Denmark. Stacy Keach, in Gerald Freedman's *Hamlet* at New York's Delacorte Theater in 1972, was neither melancholy nor vulnerable; rather he was bitter, shrewd, and, as the drama critic of *The New York Times* wrote, "hell-bent for revenge."

As originally staged, *Hamlet* must have made good use of the handsome Globe Theatre, where it first appeared. Without scenery, the Globe offered its spectators an impressive evocation of an idea of order, with the heavens above, hell below the trapdoor, and on the main stage the ceremonial magnificence of the court of Denmark. Claudius's appearances are generally marked by ritual, by the presence of throne and crown, by an entourage of obsequious courtiers. Yet Claudius has vitiated all this seeming order by his secret murder, and Hamlet's presence is a continual reminder that all is not well in Denmark. Hamlet attires himself in black, acts strangely, insults the courtiers, makes fun of their ceremoniousness, and prefers to be alone or on the battlements with Horatio and the guard. The Ghost's appearances, too, betoken inversions of order; he reminds us of a greatness now lost to Denmark as he stalks on, usually through the stage doors, in armor and in the full light of day during an afternoon performance at the Globe. He also speaks from beneath the stage. The performance of Hamlet's "Mousetrap" play is a scene of rich panoply that is once again undercut by the secret act of murder now represented in a mimetic drama for the King who is also a murderer. The final scene of *Hamlet* is Claudius's most splendid moment of presiding over the court, until it is suddenly his last moment. The play's reflexive interest in the art of theater is everywhere evident, in Hamlet's instructions to the players and in his appraisal of himself as an actor, as he explores all that it might mean to "act." Shakespeare wrote *Hamlet* with his own theater very much in mind, and, paradoxically, precisely this has allowed it to remain so vibrantly alive in the modern theater.

HAMLET

1.1 *Enter Bernardo and Francisco, two sentinels,*
       [meeting].

BERNARDO   Who's there?

FRANCISCO
  Nay, answer me. Stand and unfold yourself.   2

BERNARDO   Long live the King!

FRANCISCO   Bernardo?

BERNARDO   He.

FRANCISCO
  You come most carefully upon your hour.

BERNARDO
  'Tis now struck twelve. Get thee to bed, Francisco.

FRANCISCO
  For this relief much thanks. 'Tis bitter cold,
  And I am sick at heart.

BERNARDO   Have you had quiet guard?

FRANCISCO   Not a mouse stirring.

BERNARDO   Well, good night.
  If you do meet Horatio and Marcellus,
  The rivals of my watch, bid them make haste.   14

       Enter Horatio and Marcellus.

FRANCISCO
  I think I hear them.—Stand, ho! Who is there?

HORATIO   Friends to this ground.   16

MARCELLUS   And liegemen to the Dane.   17

FRANCISCO   Give you good night.   18

MARCELLUS
  O, farewell, honest soldier. Who hath relieved you?

FRANCISCO
  Bernardo hath my place. Give you good night.
                                      Exit Francisco.

MARCELLUS   Holla! Bernardo!

BERNARDO   Say, what, is Horatio there?

HORATIO   A piece of him.

1.1. Location: Elsinore castle. A guard platform.
2 me (Francisco emphasizes that *he* is the sentry currently on watch.)
unfold yourself reveal your identity   **14 rivals** partners   **16 ground**
country, land   **17 liegemen to the Dane** men sworn to serve the Danish
king   **18 Give** i.e., may God give

BERNARDO
Welcome, Horatio. Welcome, good Marcellus.
HORATIO
What, has this thing appeared again tonight?
BERNARDO   I have seen nothing.
MARCELLUS
Horatio says 'tis but our fantasy,   27
And will not let belief take hold of him
Touching this dreaded sight twice seen of us.
Therefore I have entreated him along   30
With us to watch the minutes of this night,   31
That if again this apparition come
He may approve our eyes and speak to it.   33
HORATIO
Tush, tush, 'twill not appear.
BERNARDO   Sit down awhile,
And let us once again assail your ears,
That are so fortified against our story,
What we have two nights seen.
HORATIO   Well, sit we down,   37
And let us hear Bernardo speak of this.
BERNARDO   Last night of all,   39
When yond same star that's westward from the pole   40
Had made his course t' illume that part of heaven   41
Where now it burns, Marcellus and myself,
The bell then beating one—

Enter Ghost.

MARCELLUS
Peace, break thee off! Look where it comes again!
BERNARDO
In the same figure like the King that's dead.
MARCELLUS
Thou art a scholar. Speak to it, Horatio.   46
BERNARDO
Looks 'a not like the King? Mark it, Horatio.   47

---

27 fantasy imagination   **30 along** i.e., to come along   **31 watch** i.e.,
keep watch during   **33 approve** corroborate   **37 What** i.e., with what
39 Last . . . all i.e., this *very* last night. (Emphatic.)   **40 pole** polestar,
north star   **41 his** its.   **illume** illuminate   **46 scholar** one learned
enough to know how to question a ghost properly   **47 'a** he

HORATIO
    Most like. It harrows me with fear and wonder.
BERNARDO
    It would be spoke to.
MARCELLUS　　　　　　Speak to it, Horatio.　　　　　　49
HORATIO
    What art thou that usurp'st this time of night,　　50
    Together with that fair and warlike form
    In which the majesty of buried Denmark　　　52
    Did sometime march? By heaven, I charge thee speak!　53
MARCELLUS
    It is offended.
BERNARDO　　　　　See, it stalks away.
HORATIO
    Stay! Speak, speak! I charge thee, speak!　*Exit Ghost.*
MARCELLUS　'Tis gone and will not answer.
BERNARDO
    How now, Horatio? You tremble and look pale.
    Is not this something more than fantasy?
    What think you on 't?　　　　　　　　　　59
HORATIO
    Before my God, I might not this believe
    Without the sensible and true avouch　　　　61
    Of mine own eyes.
MARCELLUS　　　　　Is it not like the King?
HORATIO　As thou art to thyself.
    Such was the very armor he had on
    When he the ambitious Norway combated.　　　65
    So frowned he once when, in an angry parle,　　66
    He smote the sledded Polacks on the ice.　　　67
    'Tis strange.
MARCELLUS
    Thus twice before, and jump at this dead hour,　69
    With martial stalk hath he gone by our watch.
HORATIO
    In what particular thought to work I know not,　71

49 It . . . to (It was commonly believed that a ghost could not speak until spoken to.)　**50 usurp'st** wrongfully takes over　**52 buried Denmark** the buried King of Denmark　**53 sometime** formerly　**59 on 't** of it　**61 sensible** confirmed by the senses.　**avouch** warrant, evidence　**65 Norway** King of Norway　**66 parle** parley　**67 sledded** traveling on sleds.　**Polacks** Poles　**69 jump** exactly　**71 to work** i.e., to collect my thoughts and try to understand this

But in the gross and scope of mine opinion   72
This bodes some strange eruption to our state.

MARCELLUS

Good now, sit down, and tell me, he that knows,   74
Why this same strict and most observant watch
So nightly toils the subject of the land,   76
And why such daily cast of brazen cannon   77
And foreign mart for implements of war,   78
Why such impress of shipwrights, whose sore task   79
Does not divide the Sunday from the week.
What might be toward, that this sweaty haste   81
Doth make the night joint-laborer with the day?
Who is 't that can inform me?

HORATIO   That can I;
At least, the whisper goes so. Our last king,
Whose image even but now appeared to us,
Was, as you know, by Fortinbras of Norway,
Thereto pricked on by a most emulate pride,   87
Dared to the combat; in which our valiant Hamlet—
For so this side of our known world esteemed him—   89
Did slay this Fortinbras; who by a sealed compact   90
Well ratified by law and heraldry
Did forfeit, with his life, all those his lands
Which he stood seized of to the conqueror;   93
Against the which a moiety competent   94
Was gagèd by our king, which had returned   95
To the inheritance of Fortinbras
Had he been vanquisher, as, by the same covenant   97
And carriage of the article designed,   98
His fell to Hamlet. Now, sir, young Fortinbras,
Of unimprovèd mettle hot and full,   100

---

72 gross and scope general drift   **74 Good now** (An expression denoting
entreaty or expostulation.)   **76 toils** causes to toil.   **subject** subjects
77 cast casting   **78 mart** buying and selling   **79 impress** impressment,
conscription   **81 toward** in preparation   **87 Thereto . . . pride** (Refers
to old Fortinbras, not the Danish King.)   **pricked on** incited.
emulate emulous, ambitious   **89 this . . . world** i.e., all Europe, the
Western world   **90 sealed** certified, confirmed   **93 seized** possessed
94 Against the in return for.   **moiety competent** sufficient portion
95 gagèd engaged, pledged   **97 covenant** i.e., the *sealed compact* of
l. 90   **98 carriage** import, bearing.   **article designed** article or clause
drawn up or prearranged   **100 unimprovèd** unrestrained, undisciplined

Hath in the skirts of Norway here and there   101
Sharked up a list of lawless resolutes   102
For food and diet to some enterprise   103
That hath a stomach in 't, which is no other—   104
As it doth well appear unto our state—
But to recover of us, by strong hand
And terms compulsatory, those foresaid lands
So by his father lost. And this, I take it,
Is the main motive of our preparations,
The source of this our watch, and the chief head   110
Of this posthaste and rummage in the land.   111

BERNARDO
I think it be no other but e'en so.
Well may it sort that this portentous figure   113
Comes armèd through our watch so like the King
That was and is the question of these wars.   115

HORATIO
A mote it is to trouble the mind's eye.   116
In the most high and palmy state of Rome,   117
A little ere the mightiest Julius fell,
The graves stood tenantless and the sheeted dead   119
Did squeak and gibber in the Roman streets;
As stars with trains of fire and dews of blood,   121
Disasters in the sun; and the moist star   122
Upon whose influence Neptune's empire stands   123
Was sick almost to doomsday with eclipse.   124
And even the like precurse of feared events,   125
As harbingers preceding still the fates   126
And prologue to the omen coming on,   127
Have heaven and earth together demonstrated
Unto our climatures and countrymen.   129

101 skirts outlying regions, outskirts   **102 Sharked up** got together in irregular fashion. **list** i.e., troop. **resolutes** desperadoes   **103 For food and diet** i.e., they are to serve as *food*, or means, *to some enterprise* **104 stomach** (1) a spirit of daring (2) an appetite that is fed by the *lawless resolutes*   **110 head** source   **111 rummage** bustle, commotion   **113 sort** suit **115 question** focus of contention   **116 mote** speck of dust **117 palmy** flourishing   **119 sheeted** shrouded   **121 As** (This abrupt transition suggests that matter is possibly omitted between ll. 120 and 121.)   **122 Disasters** unfavorable signs or aspects. **moist star** i.e., moon, governing tides   **123 Neptune** god of the sea. **stands** depends **124 sick . . . doomsday** (See Matthew 24:29 and Revelation 6:12.) **125 precurse** heralding, foreshadowing   **126 harbingers** forerunners. **still** continually   **127 omen** calamitous event   **129 climatures** regions

Enter Ghost.

But soft, behold! Lo, where it comes again!   130
I'll cross it, though it blast me. *(It spreads his arms.)*
     Stay, illusion!   131
If thou hast any sound or use of voice,
Speak to me!
If there be any good thing to be done
That may to thee do ease and grace to me,
Speak to me!
If thou art privy to thy country's fate,
Which, happily, foreknowing may avoid,   138
O, speak!
Or if thou hast uphoarded in thy life
Extorted treasure in the womb of earth,
For which, they say, you spirits oft walk in death,
Speak of it! *(The cock crows.)* Stay and speak!—
     Stop it, Marcellus.

MARCELLUS
Shall I strike at it with my partisan?   144

HORATIO   Do, if it will not stand.   [*They strike at it.*]
BERNARDO   'Tis here!
HORATIO   'Tis here!   [*Exit Ghost.*]
MARCELLUS   'Tis gone.
We do it wrong, being so majestical,
To offer it the show of violence,
For it is as the air invulnerable,
And our vain blows malicious mockery.

BERNARDO
It was about to speak when the cock crew.

HORATIO
And then it started like a guilty thing
Upon a fearful summons. I have heard
The cock, that is the trumpet to the morn,   156
Doth with his lofty and shrill-sounding throat
Awake the god of day, and at his warning,
Whether in sea or fire, in earth or air,
Th' extravagant and erring spirit hies   160

130 **soft** i.e., enough, break off   131 **cross** stand in its path, confront.
blast wither, strike with a curse   **s.d. his** its   138 **happily** haply, perchance   144 **partisan** long-handled spear   156 **trumpet** trumpeter
160 **extravagant and erring** wandering beyond bounds. (The words have
similar meaning.)

To his confine; and of the truth herein
This present object made probation.   162

MARCELLUS
  It faded on the crowing of the cock.
  Some say that ever 'gainst that season comes   164
  Wherein our Savior's birth is celebrated,
  This bird of dawning singeth all night long,
  And then, they say, no spirit dare stir abroad;
  The nights are wholesome, then no planets strike,   168
  No fairy takes, nor witch hath power to charm,   169
  So hallowed and so gracious is that time.   170

HORATIO
  So have I heard and do in part believe it.
  But, look, the morn in russet mantle clad
  Walks o'er the dew of yon high eastward hill.
  Break we our watch up, and by my advice
  Let us impart what we have seen tonight
  Unto young Hamlet; for upon my life,
  This spirit, dumb to us, will speak to him.
  Do you consent we shall acquaint him with it,
  As needful in our loves, fitting our duty?

MARCELLUS
  Let's do 't, I pray, and I this morning know
  Where we shall find him most conveniently.

                                        Exeunt.

                          ❖

1.2   *Flourish. Enter Claudius, King of Denmark,
          Gertrude the Queen, [the] Council, as Polonius
          and his son Laertes, Hamlet, cum aliis
          [including Voltimand and Cornelius].*

KING
  Though yet of Hamlet our dear brother's death   1
  The memory be green, and that it us befitted
  To bear our hearts in grief and our whole kingdom

---

162 probation proof   **164 'gainst** just before   **168 strike** destroy by evil
influence   **169 takes** bewitches   **170 gracious** full of grace

1.2. Location: The castle.
s.d. as i.e., such as, including.   **cum aliis** with others   **1 our** my. (The
royal "we"; also in the following lines.)

To be contracted in one brow of woe,
Yet so far hath discretion fought with nature
That we with wisest sorrow think on him
Together with remembrance of ourselves.
Therefore our sometime sister, now our queen,   8
Th' imperial jointress to this warlike state,   9
Have we, as 'twere with a defeated joy—
With an auspicious and a dropping eye,   11
With mirth in funeral and with dirge in marriage,
In equal scale weighing delight and dole—   13
Taken to wife. Nor have we herein barred
Your better wisdoms, which have freely gone
With this affair along. For all, our thanks.
Now follows that you know young Fortinbras,   17
Holding a weak supposal of our worth,   18
Or thinking by our late dear brother's death
Our state to be disjoint and out of frame,
Colleaguèd with this dream of his advantage,   21
He hath not failed to pester us with message
Importing the surrender of those lands   23
Lost by his father, with all bonds of law,   24
To our most valiant brother. So much for him.
Now for ourself and for this time of meeting.
Thus much the business is: we have here writ
To Norway, uncle of young Fortinbras—
Who, impotent and bedrid, scarcely hears   29
Of this his nephew's purpose—to suppress
His further gait herein, in that the levies,   31
The lists, and full proportions are all made   32
Out of his subject; and we here dispatch   33
You, good Cornelius, and you, Voltimand,
For bearers of this greeting to old Norway,
Giving to you no further personal power
To business with the King more than the scope

---

8 sometime former **9 jointress** woman possessing property with her
husband **11 With . . . eye** with one eye smiling and the other weeping
13 dole grief **17 know** be informed (that) **18 weak supposal** low
estimate **21 Colleaguèd with** joined to, allied with. **dream . . . advantage** illusory hope of success. (His only ally is this hope.) **23 Importing**
pertaining to **24 bonds** contracts **29 impotent** helpless **31 His** i.e.,
Fortinbras's. **gait** proceeding **31–33 in that . . . subject** since the
levying of troops and supplies is drawn entirely from the King of Norway's own subjects

Of these dilated articles allow.   [*He gives a paper.*] 38
Farewell, and let your haste commend your duty.   39
CORNELIUS, VOLTIMAND
  In that, and all things, will we show our duty.
KING
  We doubt it nothing. Heartily farewell.   41
              [*Exeunt Voltimand and Cornelius.*]
  And now, Laertes, what's the news with you?
  You told us of some suit; what is 't, Laertes?
  You cannot speak of reason to the Dane   44
  And lose your voice. What wouldst thou beg, Laertes,   45
  That shall not be my offer, not thy asking?
  The head is not more native to the heart,   47
  The hand more instrumental to the mouth,   48
  Than is the throne of Denmark to thy father.
  What wouldst thou have, Laertes?
LAERTES   My dread lord,
  Your leave and favor to return to France,   51
  From whence though willingly I came to Denmark
  To show my duty in your coronation,
  Yet now I must confess, that duty done,
  My thoughts and wishes bend again toward France
  And bow them to your gracious leave and pardon.   56
KING
  Have you your father's leave? What says Polonius?
POLONIUS
  H'ath, my lord, wrung from me my slow leave   58
  By laborsome petition, and at last
  Upon his will I sealed my hard consent.   60
  I do beseech you, give him leave to go.
KING
  Take thy fair hour, Laertes. Time be thine,   62
  And thy best graces spend it at thy will!   63

---

38 dilated set out at length   **39 commend** recommend to friendly
remembrance. (Their haste will impress the King with their attention to
duty.)   **41 nothing** not at all   **44 the Dane** the Danish king   **45 lose
your voice** waste your speech   **47 native** closely connected, related
48 instrumental serviceable   **51 leave and favor** kind permission
56 leave and pardon permission to depart   **58 H'ath** he has   **60 sealed**
(as if sealing a legal document).   **hard** reluctant   **62 Take thy fair hour**
enjoy your time of youth   **63 And . . . will** and may your finest qualities
guide the way you choose to spend your time

But now, my cousin Hamlet, and my son—   64
HAMLET
A little more than kin, and less than kind.   65
KING
How is it that the clouds still hang on you?
HAMLET
Not so, my lord. I am too much in the sun.   67
QUEEN
Good Hamlet, cast thy nighted color off,   68
And let thine eye look like a friend on Denmark.   69
Do not forever with thy vailèd lids   70
Seek for thy noble father in the dust.
Thou know'st 'tis common, all that lives must die,   72
Passing through nature to eternity.
HAMLET
Ay, madam, it is common.
QUEEN   If it be,
Why seems it so particular with thee?   75
HAMLET
Seems, madam? Nay, it is. I know not "seems."
'Tis not alone my inky cloak, good Mother,
Nor customary suits of solemn black,   78
Nor windy suspiration of forced breath,   79
No, nor the fruitful river in the eye,   80
Nor the dejected havior of the visage,   81
Together with all forms, moods, shapes of grief,   82
That can denote me truly. These indeed seem,
For they are actions that a man might play.
But I have that within which passes show;
These but the trappings and the suits of woe.

---

64 cousin any kin not of the immediate family   **65 A little . . . kind** i.e.,
closer than an ordinary nephew (since I am stepson), and yet more
separated in natural feeling (with pun on *kind* meaning "affectionate"
and "natural," "lawful." This line is often read as an aside, but it need
not be. The King chooses perhaps not to respond to Hamlet's cryptic
and bitter remark.)   **67 the sun** i.e., the sunshine of the King's
royal favor (with pun on *son*)   **68 nighted color** (1) mourning garments of
black (2) dark melancholy   **69 Denmark** the King of Denmark
70 vailèd lids lowered eyes   **72 common** of universal occurrence. (But
Hamlet plays on the sense of "vulgar" in l. 74.)   **75 particular** personal   **78 customary** (1) socially conventional (2) habitual with me
79 suspiration sighing   **80 fruitful** abundant   **81 havior** expression
82 moods outward expressions of feeling

KING

   'Tis sweet and commendable in your nature, Hamlet,
   To give these mourning duties to your father.
   But you must know your father lost a father,
   That father lost, lost his, and the survivor bound
   In filial obligation for some term
   To do obsequious sorrow. But to persever   92
   In obstinate condolement is a course   93
   Of impious stubbornness. 'Tis unmanly grief.
   It shows a will most incorrect to heaven,
   A heart unfortified, a mind impatient,   96
   An understanding simple and unschooled.   97
   For what we know must be and is as common
   As any the most vulgar thing to sense,   99
   Why should we in our peevish opposition
   Take it to heart? Fie, 'tis a fault to heaven,
   A fault against the dead, a fault to nature,
   To reason most absurd, whose common theme
   Is death of fathers, and who still hath cried,   104
   From the first corpse till he that died today,   105
   "This must be so." We pray you, throw to earth
   This unprevailing woe and think of us   107
   As of a father; for let the world take note,
   You are the most immediate to our throne,   109
   And with no less nobility of love
   Than that which dearest father bears his son
   Do I impart toward you. For your intent   112
   In going back to school in Wittenberg,   113
   It is most retrograde to our desire,   114
   And we beseech you bend you to remain   115
   Here in the cheer and comfort of our eye,
   Our chiefest courtier, cousin, and our son.

QUEEN

   Let not thy mother lose her prayers, Hamlet.
   I pray thee, stay with us, go not to Wittenberg.

---

92 obsequious suited to obsequies or funerals.   **persever** persevere
93 condolement sorrowing   **96 unfortified** i.e., against adversity
97 simple ignorant   **99 As . . . sense** as the most ordinary experience
104 still always   **105 the first corpse** (Abel's)   **107 unprevailing** unavailing   **109 most immediate** next in succession   **112 impart toward** i.e.,
bestow my affection on.   **For** as for   **113 to school** i.e., to your studies.   **Wittenberg** famous German university founded in 1502
114 retrograde contrary   **115 bend you** incline yourself

HAMLET

I shall in all my best obey you, madam.   120

KING

Why, 'tis a loving and a fair reply.
Be as ourself in Denmark. Madam, come.
This gentle and unforced accord of Hamlet
Sits smiling to my heart, in grace whereof   124
No jocund health that Denmark drinks today   125
But the great cannon to the clouds shall tell,
And the King's rouse the heaven shall bruit again,   127
Respeaking earthly thunder. Come away.   128

Flourish. Exeunt all but Hamlet.

HAMLET

O, that this too too sullied flesh would melt,   129
Thaw, and resolve itself into a dew!
Or that the Everlasting had not fixed
His canon 'gainst self-slaughter! O God, God,   132
How weary, stale, flat, and unprofitable
Seem to me all the uses of this world!   134
Fie on 't, ah fie! 'Tis an unweeded garden
That grows to seed. Things rank and gross in nature
Possess it merely. That it should come to this!   137
But two months dead—nay, not so much, not two.
So excellent a king, that was to this   139
Hyperion to a satyr, so loving to my mother   140
That he might not beteem the winds of heaven   141
Visit her face too roughly. Heaven and earth,
Must I remember? Why, she would hang on him
As if increase of appetite had grown
By what it fed on, and yet within a month—
Let me not think on 't; frailty, thy name is woman!—
A little month, or ere those shoes were old   147
With which she followed my poor father's body,

120 in all my best to the best of my ability **124 to** i.e., at. **grace** thanksgiving **125 jocund** merry **127 rouse** drinking of a draft of liquor. **bruit again** loudly echo **128 thunder** i.e., of trumpet and kettledrum, sounded when the King drinks; see 1.4.8–12 **129 sullied** defiled. (The early quartos read *sallied,* the Folio *solid.*) **132 canon** law **134 all the uses** the whole routine **137 merely** completely **139 to** in comparison to **140 Hyperion** Titan sun-god, father of Helios. **satyr** a lecherous creature of classical mythology, half-human but with a goat's legs, tail, ears, and horns **141 beteem** allow **147 or ere** even before

Like Niobe, all tears, why she, even she—   149
O God, a beast, that wants discourse of reason,   150
Would have mourned longer—married with my uncle,
My father's brother, but no more like my father
Than I to Hercules. Within a month,
Ere yet the salt of most unrighteous tears
Had left the flushing in her gallèd eyes,   155
She married. O, most wicked speed, to post
With such dexterity to incestuous sheets!   157
It is not, nor it cannot come to good.
But break, my heart, for I must hold my tongue.

Enter Horatio, Marcellus, and Bernardo.

HORATIO
　Hail to your lordship!
HAMLET　　　　　　　　　　I am glad to see you well.
　Horatio!—or I do forget myself.
HORATIO
　The same, my lord, and your poor servant ever.
HAMLET
　Sir, my good friend; I'll change that name with you.   163
　And what make you from Wittenberg, Horatio?—   164
　Marcellus.
MARCELLUS　My good lord.
HAMLET
　I am very glad to see you. [*To Bernardo.*] Good even, sir.—
　But what in faith make you from Wittenberg?
HORATIO
　A truant disposition, good my lord.
HAMLET
　I would not hear your enemy say so,
　Nor shall you do my ear that violence
　To make it truster of your own report
　Against yourself. I know you are no truant.

---

149 Niobe Tantalus' daughter, Queen of Thebes, who boasted that she
had more sons and daughters than Leto; for this, Apollo and Artemis,
children of Leto, slew her fourteen children. She was turned by Zeus
into a stone that continually dropped tears.　**150 wants . . . reason** lacks
the faculty of reason　**155 gallèd** irritated, inflamed　**157 incestuous** (In
Shakespeare's day, the marriage of a man like Claudius to his deceased
brother's wife was considered incestuous.)　**163 change** exchange (i.e.,
the name of friend)　**164 make** do

But what is your affair in Elsinore?
We'll teach you to drink deep ere you depart.

HORATIO
My lord, I came to see your father's funeral.

HAMLET
I prithee, do not mock me, fellow student;
I think it was to see my mother's wedding.

HORATIO
Indeed, my lord, it followed hard upon.   179

HAMLET
Thrift, thrift, Horatio! The funeral baked meats   180
Did coldly furnish forth the marriage tables.   181
Would I had met my dearest foe in heaven   182
Or ever I had seen that day, Horatio!   183
My father!—Methinks I see my father.

HORATIO
Where, my lord?

HAMLET   In my mind's eye, Horatio.

HORATIO
I saw him once. 'A was a goodly king.   186

HAMLET
'A was a man. Take him for all in all,
I shall not look upon his like again.

HORATIO
My lord, I think I saw him yesternight.

HAMLET   Saw? Who?

HORATIO   My lord, the King your father.

HAMLET   The King my father?

HORATIO
Season your admiration for a while   193
With an attent ear till I may deliver,   194
Upon the witness of these gentlemen,
This marvel to you.

HAMLET   For God's love, let me hear!

HORATIO
Two nights together had these gentlemen,
Marcellus and Bernardo, on their watch,
In the dead waste and middle of the night,

179 hard close   180 baked meats meat pies   181 coldly i.e., as cold
leftovers   182 dearest closest (and therefore deadliest)   183 Or ever
before   186 'A he   193 Season your admiration restrain your astonishment   194 attent attentive

Been thus encountered. A figure like your father,
Armèd at point exactly, cap-à-pie,   201
Appears before them, and with solemn march
Goes slow and stately by them. Thrice he walked
By their oppressed and fear-surprisèd eyes
Within his truncheon's length, whilst they, distilled   205
Almost to jelly with the act of fear,   206
Stand dumb and speak not to him. This to me
In dreadful secrecy impart they did,
And I with them the third night kept the watch,
Where, as they had delivered, both in time,
Form of the thing, each word made true and good,
The apparition comes. I knew your father;
These hands are not more like.

HAMLET   But where was this?

MARCELLUS
My lord, upon the platform where we watch.

HAMLET
Did you not speak to it?

HORATIO   My lord, I did,
But answer made it none. Yet once methought
It lifted up its head and did address   217
Itself to motion, like as it would speak;   218
But even then the morning cock crew loud,   219
And at the sound it shrunk in haste away
And vanished from our sight.

HAMLET   'Tis very strange.

HORATIO
As I do live, my honored lord, 'tis true,
And we did think it writ down in our duty
To let you know of it.

HAMLET
Indeed, indeed, sirs. But this troubles me.
Hold you the watch tonight?

ALL   We do, my lord.

HAMLET Armed, say you?

ALL Armed, my lord.

HAMLET From top to toe?

201 at point correctly in every detail.   **cap-à-pie** from head to foot
205 truncheon officer's staff.   **distilled** dissolved   **206 act** action,
operation   **217–218 did . . . speak** began to move as though it were
about to speak   **219 even then** at that very instant

ALL   My lord, from head to foot.

HAMLET   Then saw you not his face?

HORATIO

O, yes, my lord, he wore his beaver up.   232

HAMLET   What looked he, frowningly?   233

HORATIO

A countenance more in sorrow than in anger.

HAMLET   Pale or red?

HORATIO   Nay, very pale.

HAMLET   And fixed his eyes upon you?

HORATIO   Most constantly.

HAMLET   I would I had been there.

HORATIO   It would have much amazed you.

HAMLET   Very like, very like. Stayed it long?

HORATIO

While one with moderate haste might tell a hundred.   242

MARCELLUS, BERNARDO   Longer, longer.

HORATIO   Not when I saw 't.

HAMLET   His beard was grizzled—no?   245

HORATIO

It was, as I have seen it in his life,

A sable silvered.

HAMLET   I will watch tonight.   247

Perchance 'twill walk again.

HORATIO   I warrant it will.

HAMLET

If it assume my noble father's person,

I'll speak to it though hell itself should gape

And bid me hold my peace. I pray you all,

If you have hitherto concealed this sight,

Let it be tenable in your silence still,   253

And whatsoever else shall hap tonight,

Give it an understanding but no tongue.

I will requite your loves. So, fare you well.

Upon the platform twixt eleven and twelve

I'll visit you.

ALL   Our duty to your honor.

---

232 beaver visor on the helmet   **233 What** how   **242 tell** count
245 grizzled gray   **247 sable silvered** black mixed with white
253 tenable held tightly

HAMLET
Your loves, as mine to you. Farewell.
> *Exeunt [all but Hamlet].*
My father's spirit in arms! All is not well.
I doubt some foul play. Would the night were come!   261
Till then sit still, my soul. Foul deeds will rise,
Though all the earth o'erwhelm them, to men's eyes.
> *Exit.*

❖

1.3   *Enter Laertes and Ophelia, his sister.*

LAERTES
My necessaries are embarked. Farewell.
And, sister, as the winds give benefit
And convoy is assistant, do not sleep   3
But let me hear from you.
OPHELIA   Do you doubt that?
LAERTES
For Hamlet, and the trifling of his favor,
Hold it a fashion and a toy in blood,   6
A violet in the youth of primy nature,   7
Forward, not permanent, sweet, not lasting,   8
The perfume and suppliance of a minute—   9
No more.
OPHELIA   No more but so?
LAERTES   Think it no more.
For nature crescent does not grow alone   11
In thews and bulk, but as this temple waxes   12
The inward service of the mind and soul
Grows wide withal. Perhaps he loves you now,   14
And now no soil nor cautel doth besmirch   15
The virtue of his will; but you must fear,   16

261 doubt suspect

1.3 Location: Polonius's chambers.
3 convoy is assistant means of conveyance are available   **6 toy in blood**
passing amorous fancy   **7 primy** in its prime, springtime   **8 Forward**
precocious   **9 suppliance** supply, filler   **11 crescent** growing, waxing
12 thews bodily strength. **temple** i.e., body   **14 Grows wide withal**
grows along with it   **15 soil** blemish. **cautel** deceit   **16 will** desire

His greatness weighed, his will is not his own.   17
For he himself is subject to his birth.
He may not, as unvalued persons do,
Carve for himself, for on his choice depends   20
The safety and health of this whole state,
And therefore must his choice be circumscribed
Unto the voice and yielding of that body   23
Whereof he is the head. Then if he says he loves you,
It fits your wisdom so far to believe it
As he in his particular act and place   26
May give his saying deed, which is no further   27
Than the main voice of Denmark goes withal.   28
Then weigh what loss your honor may sustain
If with too credent ear you list his songs,   30
Or lose your heart, or your chaste treasure open
To his unmastered importunity.
Fear it, Ophelia, fear it, my dear sister,
And keep you in the rear of your affection,   34
Out of the shot and danger of desire.   35
The chariest maid is prodigal enough   36
If she unmask her beauty to the moon.   37
Virtue itself scapes not calumnious strokes.
The canker galls the infants of the spring   39
Too oft before their buttons be disclosed,   40
And in the morn and liquid dew of youth   41
Contagious blastments are most imminent.   42
Be wary then; best safety lies in fear.
Youth to itself rebels, though none else near.   44

OPHELIA
I shall the effect of this good lesson keep
As watchman to my heart. But, good my brother,
Do not, as some ungracious pastors do,   47

17 His greatness weighed considering his high position   **20 Carve** i.e.,
choose   **23 voice and yielding** assent, approval   **26 in . . . place** in his
particular restricted circumstances   **27 deed** effect   **28 main voice**
general assent.   **withal** along with   **30 credent** credulous.   **list** listen
to   **34 keep . . . affection** don't advance as far as your affection might
lead you. (A military metaphor.)   **35 shot** range   **36 chariest** most
scrupulously modest   **37 If she unmask** if she does no more than show
her beauty.   **moon** (Symbol of chastity.)   **39 canker galls** cankerworm
destroys   **40 buttons** buds.   **disclosed** opened   **41 liquid dew** i.e., time
when dew is fresh and bright   **42 blastments** blights   **44 Youth . . .
rebels** youth is inherently rebellious   **47 ungracious** ungodly

Show me the steep and thorny way to heaven,
Whiles like a puffed and reckless libertine   49
Himself the primrose path of dalliance treads,
And recks not his own rede.

    Enter Polonius.

LAERTES   O, fear me not.   51
I stay too long. But here my father comes.
A double blessing is a double grace;   53
Occasion smiles upon a second leave.   54

POLONIUS
Yet here, Laertes? Aboard, aboard, for shame!
The wind sits in the shoulder of your sail,
And you are stayed for. There—my blessing with thee!
And these few precepts in thy memory
Look thou character. Give thy thoughts no tongue,   59
Nor any unproportioned thought his act.   60
Be thou familiar, but by no means vulgar.   61
Those friends thou hast, and their adoption tried,   62
Grapple them unto thy soul with hoops of steel,
But do not dull thy palm with entertainment   64
Of each new-hatched, unfledged courage. Beware   65
Of entrance to a quarrel, but being in,
Bear 't that th' opposèd may beware of thee.   67
Give every man thy ear, but few thy voice;
Take each man's censure, but reserve thy judgment.   69
Costly thy habit as thy purse can buy,   70
But not expressed in fancy; rich, not gaudy,   71
For the apparel oft proclaims the man,
And they in France of the best rank and station
Are of a most select and generous chief in that.   74
Neither a borrower nor a lender be,

---

49 puffed bloated, or swollen with pride   **51 recks** heeds.   **rede** counsel   **53 double** (Laertes has already bidden his father good-bye.)
54 Occasion . . . leave-happy is the circumstance that provides a second leave-taking. (The goddess Occasion, or Opportunity, smiles.)   **59 Look** be sure that.   **character** inscribe   **60 unproportioned** badly calculated, intemperate.   **his** its   **61 familiar** sociable.   **vulgar** common   **62 tried** tested   **64 dull thy palm** i.e., shake hands so often as to make the gesture meaningless   **65 courage** young man of spirit   **67 Bear 't that** manage it so that   **69 censure** opinion, judgment   **70 habit** clothing   **71 fancy** excessive ornament, decadent fashion   **74 Are . . . that** i.e., are of a most refined and well-bred preeminence in choosing what to wear

For loan oft loses both itself and friend,
And borrowing dulls the edge of husbandry.   77
This above all: to thine own self be true,
And it must follow, as the night the day,
Thou canst not then be false to any man.
Farewell. My blessing season this in thee!   81

LAERTES
Most humbly do I take my leave, my lord.

POLONIUS
The time invests you. Go, your servants tend.   83

LAERTES
Farewell, Ophelia, and remember well
What I have said to you.

OPHELIA   'Tis in my memory locked,
And you yourself shall keep the key of it.

LAERTES   Farewell.   *Exit Laertes.*

POLONIUS
What is 't, Ophelia, he hath said to you?

OPHELIA
So please you, something touching the Lord Hamlet.

POLONIUS   Marry, well bethought.   91
'Tis told me he hath very oft of late
Given private time to you, and you yourself
Have of your audience been most free and bounteous.
If it be so—as so 'tis put on me,   95
And that in way of caution—I must tell you
You do not understand yourself so clearly
As it behooves my daughter and your honor.   98
What is between you? Give me up the truth.

OPHELIA
He hath, my lord, of late made many tenders   100
Of his affection to me.

POLONIUS
Affection? Pooh! You speak like a green girl,
Unsifted in such perilous circumstance.   103
Do you believe his tenders, as you call them?

---

77 husbandry thrift **81 season** mature **83 invests** besieges, presses
upon. **tend** attend, wait **91 Marry** i.e., by the Virgin Mary. (A mild
oath.) **95 put on** impressed on, told to **98 behooves** befits
100 tenders offers **103 Unsifted** i.e., untried

OPHELIA
I do not know, my lord, what I should think.

POLONIUS
Marry, I will teach you. Think yourself a baby
That you have ta'en these tenders for true pay   107
Which are not sterling. Tender yourself more dearly, 108
Or—not to crack the wind of the poor phrase,   109
Running it thus—you'll tender me a fool.   110

OPHELIA
My lord, he hath importuned me with love
In honorable fashion.

POLONIUS
Ay, fashion you may call it. Go to, go to.   113

OPHELIA
And hath given countenance to his speech, my lord, 114
With almost all the holy vows of heaven.

POLONIUS
Ay, springes to catch woodcocks. I do know,   116
When the blood burns, how prodigal the soul   117
Lends the tongue vows. These blazes, daughter,
Giving more light than heat, extinct in both
Even in their promise as it is a-making,   120
You must not take for fire. From this time
Be something scanter of your maiden presence.   122
Set your entreatments at a higher rate   123
Than a command to parle. For Lord Hamlet,   124
Believe so much in him that he is young,   125
And with a larger tether may he walk
Than may be given you. In few, Ophelia,   127

---

107 tenders (with added meaning here of "promises to pay")
108 sterling legal currency. **Tender** hold, look after, offer **109 crack the wind** i.e., run it until it is broken-winded **110 tender me a fool** (1) show yourself to me as a fool (2) show me up as a fool (3) present me with a grandchild. (*Fool* was a term of endearment for a child.)
113 fashion mere form, pretense. **Go to** (An expression of impatience.) **114 countenance** credit, confirmation **116 springes** snares. **woodcocks** birds easily caught; here used to connote gullibility
117 prodigal i.e., prodigally **120 it** i.e., the promise **122 something** somewhat **123 entreatments** negotiations for surrender. (A military term.) **124 parle** discuss terms with the enemy. (Polonius urges his daughter, in the metaphor of military language, not to meet with Hamlet and consider giving in to him merely because he requests an interview.) **125 so . . . him** this much concerning him **127 In few** briefly

Do not believe his vows, for they are brokers,   128
Not of that dye which their investments show,   129
But mere implorators of unholy suits,   130
Breathing like sanctified and pious bawds   131
The better to beguile. This is for all: 132
I would not, in plain terms, from this time forth
Have you so slander any moment leisure   134
As to give words or talk with the Lord Hamlet.
Look to 't, I charge you. Come your ways.   136
OPHELIA   I shall obey, my lord.   *Exeunt.*

❖

1.4   *Enter Hamlet, Horatio, and Marcellus.*

HAMLET
The air bites shrewdly; it is very cold.   1
HORATIO
It is a nipping and an eager air.   2
HAMLET
What hour now?
HORATIO   I think it lacks of twelve.   3
MARCELLUS
No, it is struck.
HORATIO   Indeed? I heard it not.
It then draws near the season   5
Wherein the spirit held his wont to walk.   6
                    A flourish of trumpets, and two pieces go off
                    [*within*].
What does this mean, my lord?
HAMLET
The King doth wake tonight and takes his rouse,   8

128 brokers go-betweens, procurers   **129 dye** color or sort.   **investments** clothes. (The vows are not what they seem.)   **130 mere implorators** out and out solicitors   **131 Breathing** speaking   **132 for all**
once for all, in sum   **134 slander** abuse, misuse.   **moment** moment's
136 Come your ways come along

1.4. Location: The guard platform.
1 shrewdly keenly, sharply   **2 eager** biting   **3 lacks of** is just short of
5 season time   **6 held his wont** was accustomed   **s.d. pieces** i.e.,
of ordnance, cannon   **8 wake** stay awake and hold revel.   **rouse** carouse, drinking bout

Keeps wassail, and the swaggering upspring reels;　9
And as he drains his drafts of Rhenish down,　10
The kettledrum and trumpet thus bray out
The triumph of his pledge.
HORATIO　　　　　　　　　　Is it a custom?　12
HAMLET　Ay, marry, is 't,
But to my mind, though I am native here
And to the manner born, it is a custom　15
More honored in the breach than the observance.　16
This heavy-headed revel east and west　17
Makes us traduced and taxed of other nations.　18
They clepe us drunkards, and with swinish phrase　19
Soil our addition; and indeed it takes　20
From our achievements, though performed at height,　21
The pith and marrow of our attribute.　22
So, oft it chances in particular men,
That for some vicious mole of nature in them,　24
As in their birth—wherein they are not guilty,
Since nature cannot choose his origin—　26
By their o'ergrowth of some complexion,　27
Oft breaking down the pales and forts of reason,　28
Or by some habit that too much o'erleavens　29
The form of plausive manners, that these men,　30
Carrying, I say, the stamp of one defect,
Being nature's livery or fortune's star,　32
His virtues else, be they as pure as grace,　33
As infinite as man may undergo,　34
Shall in the general censure take corruption　35

9 **wassail** carousal. **upspring** wild German dance. **reels** dances
10 **Rhenish** Rhine wine　12 **the triumph . . . pledge** i.e., his feat in
draining the wine in a single draft　15 **manner** custom (of drinking)
16 **More . . . observance** better neglected than followed　17 **east and
west** i.e., everywhere　18 **taxed of** censured by　19 **clepe** call.　**with
swinish phrase** i.e., by calling us swine　20 **addition** reputation　21 **at
height** outstandingly　22 **The pith . . . attribute** the essence of the
reputation that others attribute to us　24 **for** on account of.　**mole of
nature** natural blemish in one's constitution　26 **his** its　27 **their
o'ergrowth . . . complexion** the excessive growth in individuals of
some natural trait　28 **pales** palings, fences (as of a fortification)
29 **o'erleavens** induces a change throughout (as yeast works in dough)
30 **plausive** pleasing　32 **nature's livery** sign of one's servitude to
nature.　**fortune's star** the destiny that chance brings　33 **His virtues
else** i.e., the other qualities of *these men* (l. 30)　34 **may undergo** can
sustain　35 **general censure** general opinion that people have of him

From that particular fault. The dram of evil   36
Doth all the noble substance often dout   37
To his own scandal.

    Enter Ghost.

HORATIO   Look, my lord, it comes!   38
HAMLET
Angels and ministers of grace defend us!
Be thou a spirit of health or goblin damned,   40
Bring with thee airs from heaven or blasts from hell,   41
Be thy intents wicked or charitable,   42
Thou com'st in such a questionable shape   43
That I will speak to thee. I'll call thee Hamlet,
King, Father, royal Dane. O, answer me!
Let me not burst in ignorance, but tell
Why thy canonized bones, hearsèd in death,   47
Have burst their cerements; why the sepulcher   48
Wherein we saw thee quietly inurned   49
Hath oped his ponderous and marble jaws
To cast thee up again. What may this mean,
That thou, dead corpse, again in complete steel,   52
Revisits thus the glimpses of the moon,   53
Making night hideous, and we fools of nature   54
So horridly to shake our disposition   55
With thoughts beyond the reaches of our souls?
Say, why is this? Wherefore? What should we do?
        [The Ghost] beckons [Hamlet].

HORATIO
It beckons you to go away with it,
As if it some impartment did desire   59
To you alone.

36–38 **The dram . . . scandal** i.e., the small drop of evil blots out or
works against the noble substance of the whole and brings it into
disrepute. To *dout* is to blot out. (A famous crux.) **38 To . . . scandal**
i.e., with consequent ruin or disgrace to that man **40 Be thou** i.e.,
whether you are. **spirit of health** good angel **41 Bring** i.e., whether
you bring **42 Be thy intents** i.e., whether your intents are **43 questionable** inviting question **47 canonized** buried according to the canons
of the church. **hearsèd** coffined **48 cerements** grave-clothes
49 inurned entombed **52 complete steel** full armor **53 glimpses of the
moon** pale and uncertain moonlight **54 fools of nature** mere men,
limited to natural knowledge and subject to the caprices of nature
55 So . . . disposition to distress our mental composure so violently
59 impartment communication

MARCELLUS   Look with what courteous action
It wafts you to a more removèd ground.
But do not go with it.

HORATIO   No, by no means.

HAMLET
It will not speak. Then I will follow it.

HORATIO
Do not, my lord!

HAMLET   Why, what should be the fear?
I do not set my life at a pin's fee,   65
And for my soul, what can it do to that,
Being a thing immortal as itself?
It waves me forth again. I'll follow it.

HORATIO
What if it tempt you toward the flood, my lord,   69
Or to the dreadful summit of the cliff
That beetles o'er his base into the sea,   71
And there assume some other horrible form
Which might deprive your sovereignty of reason   73
And draw you into madness? Think of it.
The very place puts toys of desperation,   75
Without more motive, into every brain
That looks so many fathoms to the sea
And hears it roar beneath.

HAMLET
It wafts me still.—Go on, I'll follow thee.

MARCELLUS
You shall not go, my lord.   [*They try to stop him.*]

HAMLET   Hold off your hands!

HORATIO
Be ruled. You shall not go.

HAMLET   My fate cries out,   81
And makes each petty artery in this body   82
As hardy as the Nemean lion's nerve.   83
Still am I called. Unhand me, gentlemen.

---

65 fee value   **69 flood** sea   **71 beetles o'er** overhangs threateningly (like bushy eyebrows).   **his** its   **73 deprive . . . reason** take away the rule of reason over your mind   **75 toys of desperation** fancies of desperate acts, i.e., suicide   **81 My fate cries out** my destiny summons me   **82 petty** weak.   **artery** (through which the vital spirits were thought to have been conveyed)   **83 Nemean lion** one of the monsters slain by Hercules in his twelve labors.   **nerve** sinew

By heaven, I'll make a ghost of him that lets me!   85
I say, away!—Go on, I'll follow thee.
                              Exeunt Ghost and Hamlet.

HORATIO
  He waxes desperate with imagination.
MARCELLUS
  Let's follow. 'Tis not fit thus to obey him.
HORATIO
  Have after. To what issue will this come?   89
MARCELLUS
  Something is rotten in the state of Denmark.
HORATIO
  Heaven will direct it.
MARCELLUS   Nay, let's follow him.   *Exeunt.* 91

❖

1.5   *Enter Ghost and Hamlet.*

HAMLET
  Whither wilt thou lead me? Speak. I'll go no further.
GHOST
  Mark me.
HAMLET   I will.
GHOST   My hour is almost come,
  When I to sulfurous and tormenting flames
  Must render up myself.
HAMLET   Alas, poor ghost!
GHOST
  Pity me not, but lend thy serious hearing
  To what I shall unfold.
HAMLET   Speak. I am bound to hear.   7
GHOST
  So art thou to revenge, when thou shalt hear.
HAMLET   What?
GHOST   I am thy father's spirit,
  Doomed for a certain term to walk the night,

85 lets hinder   **89 Have after** let's go after him.   **issue** outcome
91 it i.e., the outcome

1.5. Location: The battlements of the castle.
7 bound (1) ready (2) obligated by duty and fate. (The Ghost, in l. 8,
answers in the second sense.)

And for the day confined to fast in fires,   12
Till the foul crimes done in my days of nature   13
Are burnt and purged away. But that I am forbid   14
To tell the secrets of my prison house,
I could a tale unfold whose lightest word
Would harrow up thy soul, freeze thy young blood,   17
Make thy two eyes like stars start from their spheres, 18
Thy knotted and combinèd locks to part,   19
And each particular hair to stand on end
Like quills upon the fretful porpentine.   21
But this eternal blazon must not be   22
To ears of flesh and blood. List, list, O, list!
If thou didst ever thy dear father love—

HAMLET   O God!

GHOST
Revenge his foul and most unnatural murder.

HAMLET   Murder?

GHOST
Murder most foul, as in the best it is,   28
But this most foul, strange, and unnatural.

HAMLET
Haste me to know 't, that I, with wings as swift
As meditation or the thoughts of love
May sweep to my revenge.

GHOST   I find thee apt;
And duller shouldst thou be than the fat weed   33
That roots itself in ease on Lethe wharf,   34
Wouldst thou not stir in this. Now, Hamlet, hear.
'Tis given out that, sleeping in my orchard,   36
A serpent stung me. So the whole ear of Denmark
Is by a forgèd process of my death   38
Rankly abused. But know, thou noble youth,   39
The serpent that did sting thy father's life
Now wears his crown.

---

12 fast do penance   **13 crimes** sins   **14 But that** were it not that   **17 harrow up** lacerate, tear   **18 spheres** i.e., eye-sockets, here compared to the orbits or transparent revolving spheres in which, according to Ptolemaic astronomy, the heavenly bodies were fixed   **19 knotted . . . locks** i.e., hair neatly arranged and confined   **21 porpentine** porcupine   **22 eternal blazon** revelation of the secrets of eternity   **28 in the best** even at best   **33 shouldst thou be** you would have to be.   **fat** torpid, lethargic   **34 Lethe** the river of forgetfulness in Hades.   **wharf** bank   **36 orchard** garden   **38 forgèd process** falsified account   **39 abused** deceived

HAMLET   O, my prophetic soul! My uncle!

GHOST

Ay, that incestuous, that adulterate beast,   43

With witchcraft of his wit, with traitorous gifts—   44

O wicked wit and gifts, that have the power

So to seduce!—won to his shameful lust

The will of my most seeming-virtuous queen.

O Hamlet, what a falling off was there!

From me, whose love was of that dignity

That it went hand in hand even with the vow   50

I made to her in marriage, and to decline

Upon a wretch whose natural gifts were poor

To those of mine!   53

But virtue, as it never will be moved,   54

Though lewdness court it in a shape of heaven,   55

So lust, though to a radiant angel linked,

Will sate itself in a celestial bed   57

And prey on garbage.

But soft, methinks I scent the morning air.

Brief let me be. Sleeping within my orchard,

My custom always of the afternoon,

Upon my secure hour thy uncle stole,   62

With juice of cursèd hebona in a vial,   63

And in the porches of my ears did pour   64

The leprous distillment, whose effect   65

Holds such an enmity with blood of man

That swift as quicksilver it courses through

The natural gates and alleys of the body,

And with a sudden vigor it doth posset   69

And curd, like eager droppings into milk,   70

The thin and wholesome blood. So did it mine,

And a most instant tetter barked about,   72

---

43 adulterate adulterous   **44 gifts** (1) talents (2) presents   **50 even with the vow** with the very vow   **53 To** compared to   **54 virtue, as it** as virtue   **55 shape of heaven** heavenly form   **57 sate . . . bed** i.e., cease to find sexual pleasure in a virtuously lawful marriage   **62 secure** confident, unsuspicious   **63 hebona** a poison. (The word seems to be a form of *ebony*, though it is thought perhaps to be related to *henbane*, a poison, or to *ebenus*, yew.)   **64 porches of my ears** ears as a porch or entrance of the body   **65 leprous distillment** distillation causing leprosy-like disfigurement   **69 posset** coagulate, curdle   **70 eager** sour, acid   **72 tetter** eruption of scabs.   **barked** covered with a rough covering, like bark on a tree

Most lazar-like, with vile and loathsome crust,   73
All my smooth body.
Thus was I, sleeping, by a brother's hand
Of life, of crown, of queen at once dispatched,   76
Cut off even in the blossoms of my sin,
Unhouseled, disappointed, unaneled,   78
No reckoning made, but sent to my account   79
With all my imperfections on my head.
O, horrible! O, horrible, most horrible!
If thou hast nature in thee, bear it not.   82
Let not the royal bed of Denmark be
A couch for luxury and damnèd incest.   84
But, howsoever thou pursues this act,
Taint not thy mind nor let thy soul contrive
Against thy mother aught. Leave her to heaven
And to those thorns that in her bosom lodge,
To prick and sting her. Fare thee well at once.
The glowworm shows the matin to be near,   90
And 'gins to pale his uneffectual fire.   91
Adieu, adieu, adieu! Remember me.   [*Exit.*]

HAMLET
O all you host of heaven! O earth! What else?
And shall I couple hell? O, fie! Hold, hold, my heart,   94
And you, my sinews, grow not instant old,   95
But bear me stiffly up. Remember thee?
Ay, thou poor ghost, whiles memory holds a seat
In this distracted globe. Remember thee?   98
Yea, from the table of my memory   99
I'll wipe away all trivial fond records,   100
All saws of books, all forms, all pressures past   101
That youth and observation copied there,
And thy commandment all alone shall live
Within the book and volume of my brain,

---

73 lazar-like leper-like   **76 dispatched** suddenly deprived   **78 Unhouseled** without having received the Sacrament.   **disappointed** unready (spiritually) for the last journey.   **unaneled** without having received extreme unction   **79 reckoning** settling of accounts   **82 nature** i.e., the promptings of a son   **84 luxury** lechery   **90 matin** i.e., morning   **91 uneffectual fire** light rendered ineffectual by the approach of bright day   **94 couple** add.   **Hold** hold together   **95 instant** instantly   **98 globe** (1) head (2) world   **99 table** tablet, slate   **100 fond** foolish   **101 saws** wise sayings.   **forms** shapes or images copied onto the slate; general ideas.   **pressures** impressions stamped

Unmixed with baser matter. Yes, by heaven!
O most pernicious woman!
O villain, villain, smiling, damnèd villain!
My tables—meet it is I set it down   108
That one may smile, and smile, and be a villain.
At least I am sure it may be so in Denmark.

                                        [*Writing.*]

So, uncle, there you are. Now to my word: 111
It is "Adieu, adieu! Remember me."
I have sworn 't.

    Enter Horatio and Marcellus.

HORATIO   My lord, my lord!
MARCELLUS   Lord Hamlet!
HORATIO   Heavens secure him!   116
HAMLET   So be it.
MARCELLUS   Hillo, ho, ho, my lord!
HAMLET   Hillo, ho, ho, boy! Come, bird, come.   119
MARCELLUS   How is 't, my noble lord?
HORATIO   What news, my lord?
HAMLET   O, wonderful!
HORATIO   Good my lord, tell it.
HAMLET   No, you will reveal it.
HORATIO   Not I, my lord, by heaven.
MARCELLUS   Nor I, my lord.
HAMLET
  How say you, then, would heart of man once think it? 127
  But you'll be secret?
HORATIO, MARCELLUS   Ay, by heaven, my lord.
HAMLET
  There's never a villain dwelling in all Denmark
  But he's an arrant knave.   130
HORATIO
  There needs no ghost, my lord, come from the grave
  To tell us this.
HAMLET   Why, right, you are in the right.

---

108 tables writing tablets.   **meet it is** it is fitting   **111 there you are** i.e.,
there, I've written that down against you   **116 secure him** keep him
safe   **119 Hillo . . . come** (A falconer's call to a hawk in air. Hamlet
mocks the hallooing as though it were a part of hawking.)   **127 once**
ever   **130 arrant** thoroughgoing

And so, without more circumstance at all,   133
I hold it fit that we shake hands and part,
You as your business and desire shall point you—
For every man hath business and desire,
Such as it is—and for my own poor part,
Look you, I'll go pray.

HORATIO
These are but wild and whirling words, my lord.

HAMLET
I am sorry they offend you, heartily;
Yes, faith, heartily.

HORATIO   There's no offense, my lord.

HAMLET
Yes, by Saint Patrick, but there is, Horatio,   142
And much offense too. Touching this vision here,   143
It is an honest ghost, that let me tell you.   144
For your desire to know what is between us,
O'ermaster 't as you may. And now, good friends,
As you are friends, scholars, and soldiers,
Give me one poor request.

HORATIO   What is 't, my lord? We will.

HAMLET
Never make known what you have seen tonight.

HORATIO, MARCELLUS   My lord, we will not.

HAMLET   Nay, but swear 't.

HORATIO   In faith, my lord, not I.   153

MARCELLUS   Nor I, my lord, in faith.

HAMLET   Upon my sword.   [*He holds out his sword.*]   155

MARCELLUS   We have sworn, my lord, already.   156

HAMLET   Indeed, upon my sword, indeed.

GHOST (*Cries under the stage*)   Swear.

HAMLET
Ha, ha, boy, sayst thou so? Art thou there, truepenny?   159

---

133 circumstance ceremony, elaboration   **142 Saint Patrick** (The
keeper of Purgatory and patron saint of all blunders and confusion.)
143 offense (Hamlet deliberately changes Horatio's "no offense taken"
to "an offense against all decency.")   **144 an honest ghost** i.e., a real
ghost and not an evil spirit   **153 In faith . . . I** i.e., I swear not to tell
what I have seen. (Horatio is not refusing to swear.)   **155 sword** i.e., the
hilt in the form of a cross   **156 We . . . already** i.e., we swore *in faith*
159 truepenny honest old fellow

Come on, you hear this fellow in the cellarage.
Consent to swear.

HORATIO   Propose the oath, my lord.

HAMLET
Never to speak of this that you have seen,
Swear by my sword.

GHOST [*Beneath*]   Swear.   [*They swear.*] 164

HAMLET
Hic et ubique? Then we'll shift our ground.   165
                    [*He moves to another spot.*]
Come hither, gentlemen,
And lay your hands again upon my sword.
Swear by my sword
Never to speak of this that you have heard.

GHOST [*Beneath*]   Swear by his sword.   [*They swear.*]

HAMLET
Well said, old mole. Canst work i' th' earth so fast?
A worthy pioner! Once more remove, good friends.   172
                    [*He moves again.*]

HORATIO
O day and night, but this is wondrous strange!

HAMLET
And therefore as a stranger give it welcome.   174
There are more things in heaven and earth, Horatio,
Than are dreamt of in your philosophy.   176
But come;
Here, as before, never, so help you mercy,   178
How strange or odd soe'er I bear myself—
As I perchance hereafter shall think meet
To put an antic disposition on—   181
That you, at such times seeing me, never shall,
With arms encumbered thus, or this headshake,   183

164 s.d. They swear (Seemingly they swear here, and at ll. 170 and 190,
as they lay their hands on Hamlet's sword. Triple oaths would have
particular force; these three oaths deal with what they have seen, what
they have heard, and what they promise about Hamlet's *antic disposition*.)   **165 Hic et ubique** here and everywhere. (Latin.)   **172 pioner** foot
soldier assigned to dig tunnels and excavations   **174 as a stranger** i.e.,
since it is a stranger and hence needing your hospitality   **176 your
philosophy** i.e., this subject called "natural philosophy" or "science"
that people talk about   **178 so help you mercy** i.e., as you hope for
God's mercy when you are judged   **181 antic** fantastic   **183 encumbered** folded or entwined

Or by pronouncing of some doubtful phrase
As "Well, we know," or "We could, an if we would,"   185
Or "If we list to speak," or "There be, an if they might,"   186
Or such ambiguous giving out, to note   187
That you know aught of me—this do swear,   188
So grace and mercy at your most need help you.

GHOST [*Beneath*]   Swear.   [*They swear.*]

HAMLET

Rest, rest, perturbèd spirit! So, gentlemen,
With all my love I do commend me to you;   192
And what so poor a man as Hamlet is
May do t' express his love and friending to you,   194
God willing, shall not lack. Let us go in together,   195
And still your fingers on your lips, I pray.   196
The time is out of joint. O cursèd spite   197
That ever I was born to set it right!
         [*They wait for him to leave first.*]
Nay, come, let's go together.   *Exeunt.* 199

❖

185 **an if** if   186 **list** wished.   **There . . . might** i.e., there are people here (we, in fact) who could tell news if we were at liberty to do so   187 **giving out** intimidation, promulgating.   **note** draw attention to the fact 188 **aught** i.e., something secret   192 **do . . . you** entrust myself to you 194 **friending** friendliness   195 **lack** be lacking   196 **still** always 197 **The time** i.e., the state of affairs.   **spite** i.e., the spite of Fortune 199 **let's go together** (Probably they wait for him to leave first, but he refuses this ceremoniousness.)

2.1

Enter old Polonius with his man [Reynaldo].

POLONIUS
Give him this money and these notes, Reynaldo.
> [*He gives money and papers.*]

REYNALDO   I will, my lord.

POLONIUS
You shall do marvelous wisely, good Reynaldo,   3
Before you visit him, to make inquire   4
Of his behavior.

REYNALDO   My lord, I did intend it.

POLONIUS
Marry, well said, very well said. Look you, sir,
Inquire me first what Danskers are in Paris,   7
And how, and who, what means, and where they keep,   8
What company, at what expense; and finding
By this encompassment and drift of question   10
That they do know my son, come you more nearer   11
Than your particular demands will touch it.   12
Take you, as 'twere, some distant knowledge of him, 13
As thus, "I know his father and his friends,
And in part him." Do you mark this, Reynaldo?

REYNALDO   Ay, very well, my lord.

POLONIUS
"And in part him, but," you may say, "not well.
But if 't be he I mean, he's very wild,
Addicted so and so," and there put on him   19
What forgeries you please—marry, none so rank   20
As may dishonor him, take heed of that,
But, sir, such wanton, wild, and usual slips   22
As are companions noted and most known
To youth and liberty.

REYNALDO   As gaming, my lord.

2.1. Location: Polonius' chambers.
3 **marvelous** marvelously   4 **inquire** inquiry   7 **Danskers** Danes
8 **what means** what wealth (they have).   **keep** dwell   10 **encompassment** roundabout talking.   **drift** gradual approach or course
11–12 **come . . . it** i.e., you will find out more this way than by asking pointed questions (*particular demands*)   13 **Take you** assume, pretend
19 **put on** impute to   20 **forgeries** invented tales.   **rank** gross
22 **wanton** sportive, unrestrained

POLONIUS   Ay, or drinking, fencing, swearing,
  Quarreling, drabbing—you may go so far.   27
REYNALDO   My lord, that would dishonor him.
POLONIUS
  Faith, no, as you may season it in the charge.   29
  You must not put another scandal on him
  That he is open to incontinency;   31
  That's not my meaning. But breathe his faults so
    quaintly   32
  That they may seem the taints of liberty,   33
  The flash and outbreak of a fiery mind,
  A savageness in unreclaimèd blood,   35
  Of general assault.   36
REYNALDO   But, my good lord—
POLONIUS
  Wherefore should you do this?
REYNALDO   Ay, my lord, I would know that.
POLONIUS   Marry, sir, here's my drift,
  And I believe it is a fetch of warrant.   41
  You laying these slight sullies on my son,
  As 'twere a thing a little soiled wi' the working,   43
  Mark you,
  Your party in converse, him you would sound,   45
  Having ever seen in the prenominate crimes   46
  The youth you breathe of guilty, be assured   47
  He closes with you in this consequence: 48
  "Good sir," or so, or "friend," or "gentleman,"
  According to the phrase or the addition   50
  Of man and country.
REYNALDO   Very good, my lord.
POLONIUS   And then, sir, does 'a this—'a does—what was I
  about to say? By the Mass, I was about to say something.
  Where did I leave?

27 drabbing keeping company with loose women   **29 season** temper, soften
31 incontinency habitual sexual excess   **32 quaintly** artfully, subtly
33 taints of liberty faults resulting from free living   **35–36 A savageness
. . . assault** a wildness in untamed youth that assails all indiscriminately
41 fetch of warrant legitimate trick   **43 soiled wi' the working** soiled by
handling while it is being made   **45 converse** conversation.   **sound** i.e.,
sound out   **46 Having ever** if he has ever.   **prenominate crimes** before-
mentioned offenses   **47 breathe** speak   **48 closes . . . consequence**
follows your lead in some fashion as follows   **50 addition** title

REYNALDO   At "closes in the consequence."

POLONIUS

At "closes in the consequence," ay, marry.
He closes thus: "I know the gentleman,
I saw him yesterday," or "th' other day,"
Or then, or then, with such or such, "and as you say,
There was 'a gaming,'" "there o'ertook in 's rouse,"   60
"There falling out at tennis," or perchance   61
"I saw him enter such a house of sale,"
Videlicet a brothel, or so forth. See you now,   63
Your bait of falsehood takes this carp of truth;   64
And thus do we of wisdom and of reach,   65
With windlasses and with assays of bias,   66
By indirections find directions out.   67
So by my former lecture and advice
Shall you my son. You have me, have you not?   69

REYNALDO

My lord, I have.

POLONIUS   God b' wi' ye; fare ye well.   70

REYNALDO   Good my lord.

POLONIUS

Observe his inclination in yourself.   72

REYNALDO   I shall, my lord.

POLONIUS   And let him ply his music.   74

REYNALDO   Well, my lord.

POLONIUS

Farewell.   *Exit Reynaldo.*

    Enter Ophelia.

            How now, Ophelia, what's the matter?

OPHELIA

O my lord, my lord, I have been so affrighted!

POLONIUS   With what, i' the name of God?

---

60 o'ertook in 's rouse overcome by drink   **61 falling out** quarreling
63 Videlicet namely   **64 carp** a fish   **65 reach** capacity, ability
66 windlasses i.e., circuitous paths. (Literally, circuits made to head off
the game in hunting.)   **assays of bias** attempts through indirection (like
the curving path of the bowling ball which is biased or weighted to one
side)   **67 directions** i.e., the way things really are   **69 have** understand   **70 b' wi'** be with   **72 in yourself** in your own person (as well as
by asking questions)   **74 let him ply** see that he continues to study

OPHELIA

My lord, as I was sewing in my closet,   79
Lord Hamlet, with his doublet all unbraced,   80
No hat upon his head, his stockings fouled,
Ungartered, and down-gyvèd to his ankle,   82
Pale as his shirt, his knees knocking each other,
And with a look so piteous in purport   84
As if he had been loosèd out of hell
To speak of horrors—he comes before me.

POLONIUS

Mad for thy love?

OPHELIA   My lord, I do not know,
But truly I do fear it.

POLONIUS   What said he?

OPHELIA

He took me by the wrist and held me hard.
Then goes he to the length of all his arm,
And with his other hand thus o'er his brow
He falls to such perusal of my face
As 'a would draw it. Long stayed he so.   93
At last, a little shaking of mine arm
And thrice his head thus waving up and down,
He raised a sigh so piteous and profound
As it did seem to shatter all his bulk   97
And end his being. That done, he lets me go,
And with his head over his shoulder turned
He seemed to find his way without his eyes,
For out o' doors he went without their helps,
And to the last bended their light on me.

POLONIUS

Come, go with me. I will go seek the King.
This is the very ecstasy of love,   104
Whose violent property fordoes itself   105
And leads the will to desperate undertakings
As oft as any passion under heaven
That does afflict our natures. I am sorry.
What, have you given him any hard words of late?

---

79 closet private chamber   **80 doublet** close-fitting jacket.   **unbraced**
unfastened   **82 down-gyvèd** fallen to the ankles (like gyves or fetters)
84 in purport in what it expressed   **93 As** as if (also in l. 97)   **97 bulk**
body   **104 ecstasy** madness   **105 property** nature.   **fordoes** destroys

OPHELIA
No, my good lord, but as you did command
I did repel his letters and denied
His access to me.
POLONIUS   That hath made him mad.
I am sorry that with better heed and judgment
I had not quoted him. I feared he did but trifle   114
And meant to wrack thee. But beshrew my jealousy!   115
By heaven, it is as proper to our age   116
To cast beyond ourselves in our opinions   117
As it is common for the younger sort
To lack discretion. Come, go we to the King.
This must be known, which, being kept close, might
     move   120
More grief to hide than hate to utter love.   121
Come.   *Exeunt.*

❖

2.2 *Flourish. Enter King and Queen, Rosencrantz,*
     and Guildenstern [with others].

KING
Welcome, dear Rosencrantz and Guildenstern.
Moreover that we much did long to see you,   2
The need we have to use you did provoke
Our hasty sending. Something have you heard
Of Hamlet's transformation—so call it,
Sith nor th' exterior nor the inward man   6
Resembles that it was. What it should be,   7
More than his father's death, that thus hath put him
So much from th' understanding of himself,
I cannot dream of. I entreat you both

114 quoted observed **115 wrack** i.e., ruin, seduce. **beshrew my jealousy** a plague upon my suspicious nature **116 proper . . . age** characteristic of us (old) men **117 cast beyond** overshoot, miscalculate
120 close secret **120–121 might . . . love** i.e., might cause more grief
(because of what Hamlet might do) by hiding the knowledge of Hamlet's strange behavior to Ophelia than unpleasantness by telling it

2.2. Location: The castle.
2 Moreover that besides the fact that **6 Sith** since. **nor . . . nor** neither
. . . nor **7 that** what

That, being of so young days brought up with him,   11
And sith so neighbored to his youth and havior,   12
That you vouchsafe your rest here in our court   13
Some little time, so by your companies
To draw him on to pleasures, and to gather
So much as from occasion you may glean,   16
Whether aught to us unknown afflicts him thus
That, opened, lies within our remedy.   18

QUEEN
Good gentlemen, he hath much talked of you,
And sure I am two men there is not living
To whom he more adheres. If it will please you
To show us so much gentry and good will   22
As to expend your time with us awhile
For the supply and profit of our hope,   24
Your visitation shall receive such thanks
As fits a king's remembrance.

ROSENCRANTZ   Both Your Majesties   26
Might, by the sovereign power you have of us,   27
Put your dread pleasures more into command   28
Than to entreaty.

GUILDENSTERN   But we both obey,
And here give up ourselves in the full bent   30
To lay our service freely at your feet,
To be commanded.

KING
Thanks, Rosencrantz and gentle Guildenstern.

QUEEN
Thanks, Guildenstern and gentle Rosencrantz.
And I beseech you instantly to visit
My too much changèd son. Go, some of you,
And bring these gentlemen where Hamlet is.

GUILDENSTERN
Heavens make our presence and our practices   38
Pleasant and helpful to him!

11 of . . . days from such early youth   12 And sith so neighbored to i.e.,
and since you are (or, and since that time you are) intimately acquainted
with.   havior demeanor   13 vouchsafe your rest please to stay
16 occasion opportunity   18 opened being revealed   22 gentry courtesy   24 supply . . . hope aid and furtherance of what we hope for
26 As fits . . . remembrance i.e., as would be a fitting gift of a king who
rewards true service   27 of over   28 dread inspiring awe   30 in . . .
bent to the utmost degree of our capacity   38 practices doings

QUEEN   Ay, amen!
Exeunt Rosencrantz and Guildenstern [with
some attendants].

   Enter Polonius.

POLONIUS
  Th' ambassadors from Norway, my good lord,
  Are joyfully returned.
KING
  Thou still hast been the father of good news.   42
POLONIUS
  Have I, my lord? I assure my good liege
  I hold my duty, as I hold my soul,   44
  Both to my God and to my gracious king;
  And I do think, or else this brain of mine
  Hunts not the trail of policy so sure   47
  As it hath used to do, that I have found
  The very cause of Hamlet's lunacy.
KING
  O, speak of that! That do I long to hear.
POLONIUS
  Give first admittance to th' ambassadors.
  My news shall be the fruit to that great feast.   52
KING
  Thyself do grace to them and bring them in.
                        [Exit Polonius.]
  He tells me, my dear Gertrude, he hath found
  The head and source of all your son's distemper.
QUEEN
  I doubt it is no other but the main,   56
  His father's death and our o'erhasty marriage.

   Enter Ambassadors [Voltimand and Cornelius,
   with Polonius].

KING
  Well, we shall sift him.—Welcome, my good friends!   58
  Say, Voltimand, what from our brother Norway?   59

---

42 still always **44 hold** maintain. **as** as firmly as **47 policy** state-
craft **52 fruit** dessert **56 doubt** fear, suspect. **main** chief point,
principal concern **58 sift him** i.e., question Polonius closely
59 brother i.e., fellow king

VOLTIMAND
Most fair return of greetings and desires.   60
Upon our first, he sent out to suppress   61
His nephew's levies, which to him appeared
To be a preparation 'gainst the Polack,
But, better looked into, he truly found
It was against Your Highness. Whereat grieved
That so his sickness, age, and impotence   66
Was falsely borne in hand, sends out arrests   67
On Fortinbras, which he, in brief, obeys,
Receives rebuke from Norway, and in fine   69
Makes vow before his uncle never more
To give th' assay of arms against Your Majesty.   71
Whereon old Norway, overcome with joy,
Gives him three thousand crowns in annual fee
And his commission to employ those soldiers,
So levied as before, against the Polack,
With an entreaty, herein further shown,
                          [*Giving a paper*]
That it might please you to give quiet pass
Through your dominions for this enterprise
On such regards of safety and allowance   79
As therein are set down.
KING   It likes us well,   80
And at our more considered time we'll read,   81
Answer, and think upon this business.
Meantime we thank you for your well-took labor.
Go to your rest; at night we'll feast together.
Most welcome home!   *Exeunt Ambassadors.*
POLONIUS   This business is well ended.
My liege, and madam, to expostulate   86
What majesty should be, what duty is,
Why day is day, night night, and time is time,
Were nothing but to waste night, day, and time.

---

60 desires good wishes   **61 Upon our first** at our first words on the business   **66 impotence** helplessness   **67 borne in hand** deluded, taken advantage of.   **arrests** orders to desist   **69 in fine** in conclusion   **71 give th' assay** make trial of strength, challenge   **79 On . . . allowance** i.e., with such considerations or conditions for the safety of Denmark and terms of permission for Fortinbras   **80 likes** pleases   **81 considered** suitable for deliberation   **86 expostulate** expound, inquire into

Therefore, since brevity is the soul of wit,   90
And tediousness the limbs and outward flourishes,
I will be brief. Your noble son is mad.
Mad call I it, for, to define true madness,
What is 't but to be nothing else but mad?
But let that go.

QUEEN   More matter, with less art.

POLONIUS
Madam, I swear I use no art at all.
That he's mad, 'tis true; 'tis true 'tis pity,
And pity 'tis 'tis true—a foolish figure,
But farewell it, for I will use no art.   98
Mad let us grant him, then, and now remains
That we find out the cause of this effect,
Or rather say, the cause of this defect,
For this effect defective comes by cause.   103
Thus it remains, and the remainder thus.
Perpend.   105
I have a daughter—have while she is mine—
Who, in her duty and obedience, mark,
Hath given me this. Now gather and surmise.   108
[*He reads the letter.*] "To the celestial and my soul's idol,
the most beautified Ophelia"—
That's an ill phrase, a vile phrase; "beautified" is a vile
phrase. But you shall hear. Thus: [*He reads.*]
"In her excellent white bosom, these, etc."   113

QUEEN   Came this from Hamlet to her?

POLONIUS
Good madam, stay awhile. I will be faithful.   115

        [*He reads.*]

        "Doubt thou the stars are fire,
            Doubt that the sun doth move,
        Doubt truth to be a liar,   118
            But never doubt I love.
O dear Ophelia, I am ill at these numbers. I have not   120

---

90 wit sound sense or judgment, intellectual keenness   **98 figure** figure
of speech   **103 For . . . cause** i.e., for this defective behavior, this madness, has a cause   **105 Perpend** consider   **108 gather and surmise** draw
your own conclusions   **113 In . . . bosom** (The letter is poetically ad-
dressed to her heart.)   **these** i.e., the letter   **115 stay** wait.   **faithful** i.e.,
in reading the letter accurately   **118 Doubt** suspect   **120 ill . . . numbers** unskilled at writing verses

art to reckon my groans. But that I love thee best, O   121
most best, believe it. Adieu.

         Thine evermore, most dear lady, whilst this
                machine is to him, Hamlet."   124
This in obedience hath my daughter shown me,
And, more above, hath his solicitings,   126
As they fell out by time, by means, and place,   127
All given to mine ear.

KING   But how hath she   128
Received his love?

POLONIUS   What do you think of me?

KING
As of a man faithful and honorable.

POLONIUS
I would fain prove so. But what might you think,   131
When I had seen this hot love on the wing—
As I perceived it, I must tell you that,
Before my daughter told me—what might you,
Or my dear Majesty your queen here, think,
If I had played the desk or table book,   136
Or given my heart a winking, mute and dumb,   137
Or looked upon this love with idle sight?   138
What might you think? No, I went round to work,   139
And my young mistress thus I did bespeak: 140
"Lord Hamlet is a prince out of thy star;   141
This must not be." And then I prescripts gave her   142
That she should lock herself from his resort,   143
Admit no messengers, receive no tokens.
Which done, she took the fruits of my advice;
And he, repellèd—a short tale to make—
Fell into a sadness, then into a fast,
Thence to a watch, thence into a weakness,   148
Thence to a lightness, and by this declension   149

---

121 reckon (1) count (2) number metrically, scan   **124 machine** i.e.,
body   **126 more above** moreover   **127 fell out** occurred. **by** according
to   **128 given . . . ear** i.e., told me about   **131 fain** gladly   **136 played
. . . table book** i.e., remained shut up, concealing the information; or,
acted as a go-between, provided communication   **137 given . . . winking**
closed the eyes of my heart to this   **138 with idle sight** complacently or
incomprehendingly   **139 round** roundly, plainly   **140 bespeak** address   **141 out of thy star** above your sphere, position   **142 prescripts**
orders   **143 his resort** his visits   **148 watch** state of sleeplessness
149 lightness lightheadedness. **declension** decline, deterioration

Into the madness wherein now he raves
And all we mourn for.

KING [*To Queen*]   Do you think 'tis this?   151

QUEEN   It may be, very like.

POLONIUS
Hath there been such a time—I would fain know that—
That I have positively said " 'Tis so,"
When it proved otherwise?

KING   Not that I know.

POLONIUS
Take this from this, if this be otherwise.   156
If circumstances lead me, I will find
Where truth is hid, though it were hid indeed
Within the center.

KING   How may we try it further?   159

POLONIUS
You know sometimes he walks four hours together
Here in the lobby.

QUEEN   So he does indeed.

POLONIUS
At such a time I'll loose my daughter to him.   162
Be you and I behind an arras then.   163
Mark the encounter. If he love her not
And be not from his reason fallen thereon,   165
Let me be no assistant for a state,
But keep a farm and carters.

KING   We will try it.

Enter Hamlet [reading on a book].

QUEEN
But look where sadly the poor wretch comes reading.   168

POLONIUS
Away, I do beseech you both, away.

---

151 all i.e., into everything that   **156 Take this from this** (The actor
gestures, indicating that he means his head from his shoulders, or his
staff of office or chain from his hands or neck, or something similar.)
159 center middle point of the earth (which is also the center of the
Ptolemaic universe).   **try** test, judge   **162 loose** (as one might release an
animal that is being mated)   **163 arras** hanging, tapestry   **165 thereon**
on that account   **168 sadly** seriously

I'll board him presently. O, give me leave.   170
   Exeunt King and Queen [with attendants].
How does my good Lord Hamlet?

HAMLET   Well, God-a-mercy.   172

POLONIUS   Do you know me, my lord?

HAMLET   Excellent well. You are a fishmonger.   174

POLONIUS   Not I, my lord.

HAMLET   Then I would you were so honest a man.

POLONIUS   Honest, my lord?

HAMLET   Ay, sir. To be honest, as this world goes, is to
be one man picked out of ten thousand.

POLONIUS   That's very true, my lord.

HAMLET   For if the sun breed maggots in a dead dog,
being a good kissing carrion—Have you a daughter?   182

POLONIUS   I have, my lord.

HAMLET   Let her not walk i' the sun. Conception is a   184
blessing, but as your daughter may conceive, friend,
look to 't.

POLONIUS   [*Aside*]   How say you by that? Still harping
on my daughter. Yet he knew me not at first; 'a said I   188
was a fishmonger. 'A is far gone. And truly in my
youth I suffered much extremity for love, very near
this. I'll speak to him again.—What do you read, my
lord?

HAMLET   Words, words, words.

POLONIUS   What is the matter, my lord?   194

HAMLET   Between who?

POLONIUS   I mean, the matter that you read, my lord.

HAMLET   Slanders, sir; for the satirical rogue says here
that old men have gray beards, that their faces are wrin-
kled, their eyes purging thick amber and plum-tree   199
gum, and that they have a plentiful lack of wit, to-   200

170 board accost.   **presently** at once.   **give me leave** i.e., excuse me.
(Said to those he hurries offstage, including the King and Queen.)
172 God-a-mercy i.e., thank you   **174 fishmonger** fish merchant   **182 a
good kissing carrion** i.e., a good piece of flesh for kissing, or for the sun
to kiss   **184 i' the sun** (with additional implication of the sunshine of
princely favors).   **Conception** (1) understanding (2) pregnancy   **188 'a**
he   **194 matter** substance. (But Hamlet plays on the sense of "basis for
a dispute.")   **199 purging** discharging.   **amber** i.e., resin, like the
resinous *plum-tree gum*   **200 wit** understanding

gether with most weak hams. All which, sir, though I
most powerfully and potently believe, yet I hold it not
honesty to have it thus set down, for yourself, sir, shall   203
grow old as I am, if like a crab you could go backward.   204
POLONIUS [*Aside*] Though this be madness, yet there is
method in 't.—Will you walk out of the air, my lord?   206
HAMLET Into my grave.
POLONIUS Indeed, that's out of the air. [*Aside.*] How
pregnant sometimes his replies are! A happiness that   209
often madness hits on, which reason and sanity could
not so prosperously be delivered of. I will leave him   211
and suddenly contrive the means of meeting between   212
him and my daughter.—My honorable lord, I will
most humbly take my leave of you.
HAMLET You cannot, sir, take from me anything that I
will more willingly part withal—except my life, except   216
my life, except my life.

Enter Guildenstern and Rosencrantz.

POLONIUS Fare you well, my lord.
HAMLET These tedious old fools!   219
POLONIUS You go to seek the Lord Hamlet. There he is.
ROSENCRANTZ [*To Polonius*] God save you, sir!
                                        [*Exit Polonius.*]
GUILDENSTERN My honored lord!
ROSENCRANTZ My most dear lord!
HAMLET My excellent good friends! How dost thou,
Guildenstern? Ah, Rosencrantz! Good lads, how do
you both?
ROSENCRANTZ
As the indifferent children of the earth.   227
GUILDENSTERN
Happy in that we are not overhappy.
On Fortune's cap we are not the very button.

---

203 honesty decency, decorum **204 old** as old **206 out of the air** (The
open air was considered dangerous for sick people.) **209 pregnant**
quick-witted, full of meaning. **happiness** felicity of expression
211 prosperously successfully **212 suddenly** immediately **216 withal**
with **219 old fools** i.e., old men like Polonius **227 indifferent** ordinary,
at neither extreme of fortune or misfortune

HAMLET   Nor the soles of her shoe?

ROSENCRANTZ   Neither, my lord.

HAMLET   Then you live about her waist, or in the middle of her favors? 233

GUILDENSTERN   Faith, her privates we. 234

HAMLET   In the secret parts of Fortune? O, most true, she is a strumpet. What news? 236

ROSENCRANTZ   None, my lord, but the world's grown honest.

HAMLET   Then is doomsday near. But your news is not true. Let me question more in particular. What have you, my good friends, deserved at the hands of Fortune that she sends you to prison hither?

GUILDENSTERN   Prison, my lord?

HAMLET   Denmark's a prison.

ROSENCRANTZ   Then is the world one.

HAMLET   A goodly one, in which there are many confines, wards, and dungeons, Denmark being one o' the worst. 246 247

ROSENCRANTZ   We think not so, my lord.

HAMLET   Why then 'tis none to you, for there is nothing either good or bad but thinking makes it so. To me it is a prison.

ROSENCRANTZ   Why then, your ambition makes it one. 'Tis too narrow for your mind.

HAMLET   O God, I could be bounded in a nutshell and count myself a king of infinite space, were it not that I have bad dreams.

GUILDENSTERN   Which dreams indeed are ambition, for the very substance of the ambitious is merely the shadow of a dream. 259

HAMLET   A dream itself is but a shadow.

ROSENCRANTZ   Truly, and I hold ambition of so airy and light a quality that it is but a shadow's shadow.

---

233 favors i.e., sexual favors   **234 her privates we** i.e., (1) we are sexually intimate with Fortune, the fickle goddess who bestows her favors indiscriminately (2) we are her ordinary citizens   **236 strumpet** prostitute. (A common epithet for indiscriminate Fortune; see l. 493 below.) **246–247 confines** places of confinement   **247 wards** cells   **259 the very . . . ambitious** that seemingly very substantial thing that the ambitious pursue

HAMLET   Then are our beggars bodies, and our mon- 264
archs and outstretched heroes the beggars' shadows. 265
Shall we to the court? For, by my fay, I cannot reason. 266
ROSENCRANTZ, GUILDENSTERN   We'll wait upon you.   267
HAMLET   No such matter. I will not sort you with the 268
rest of my servants, for, to speak to you like an honest
man, I am most dreadfully attended. But, in the 270
beaten way of friendship, what make you at Elsinore? 271
ROSENCRANTZ   To visit you, my lord, no other occasion.
HAMLET   Beggar that I am, I am even poor in thanks;
but I thank you, and sure, dear friends, my thanks are
too dear a halfpenny. Were you not sent for? Is it your 275
own inclining? Is it a free visitation? Come, come, deal 276
justly with me. Come, come; nay, speak.
GUILDENSTERN   What should we say, my lord?
HAMLET   Anything but to the purpose. You were sent 279
for, and there is a kind of confession in your looks which
your modesties have not craft enough to color. I know 281
the good King and Queen have sent for you.
ROSENCRANTZ   To what end, my lord?
HAMLET   That you must teach me. But let me conjure 284
you, by the rights of our fellowship, by the conso- 285
nancy of our youth, by the obligation of our ever-pre- 286
served love, and by what more dear a better proposer 287
could charge you withal, be even and direct with me 288
whether you were sent for or no.
ROSENCRANTZ [*Aside to Guildenstern*]   What say you?
HAMLET [*Aside*]   Nay, then, I have an eye of you.—If 291
you love me, hold not off.   292

264 bodies i.e., solid substances rather than shadows (since beggars are
not ambitious)   **265 outstretched** (1) far-reaching in their ambition (2) elon-
gated as shadows   **266 fay** faith   **267 wait upon** accompany, attend. (But
Hamlet uses the phrase in the sense of providing menial service.)
268 sort class, categorize   **270 dreadfully attended** waited upon in
slovenly fashion   **271 beaten way** familiar path, tried-and-true course.
make do   **275 dear a halfpenny** expensive at the price of a halfpenny,
i.e., of little worth   **276 free** voluntary   **279 Anything but to the purpose** anything except a straightforward answer. (Said ironically.)
281 modesties sense of shame.   **color** disguise   **284 conjure** adjure,
entreat   **285–286 the consonancy of our youth** our closeness in
our younger days   **287 better proposer** more skillful propounder
288 charge urge.   **even** straight, honest   **291 of** on   **292 hold not
off** don't hold back

GUILDENSTERN My lord, we were sent for.

HAMLET I will tell you why; so shall my anticipation 294
prevent your discovery, and your secrecy to the King 295
and Queen molt no feather. I have of late—but 296
wherefore I know not—lost all my mirth, forgone all
custom of exercises; and indeed it goes so heavily with
my disposition that this goodly frame, the earth,
seems to me a sterile promontory; this most excellent
canopy, the air, look you, this brave o'erhanging fir- 301
mament, this majestical roof fretted with golden fire, 302
why, it appeareth nothing to me but a foul and pestilent congregation of vapors. What a piece of work is a 304
man! How noble in reason, how infinite in faculties,
in form and moving how express and admirable, in 306
action how like an angel, in apprehension how like a 307
god! The beauty of the world, the paragon of animals!
And yet, to me, what is this quintessence of dust? 309
Man delights not me—no, nor woman neither,
though by your smiling you seem to say so.

ROSENCRANTZ My lord, there was no such stuff in my
thoughts.

HAMLET Why did you laugh then, when I said man
delights not me?

ROSENCRANTZ To think, my lord, if you delight not in
man, what Lenten entertainment the players shall re- 317
ceive from you. We coted them on the way, and hither 318
are they coming to offer you service.

HAMLET He that plays the king shall be welcome; His
Majesty shall have tribute of me. The adventurous 321
knight shall use his foil and target, the lover shall not 322

294–295 so . . . discovery in that way my saying it first will spare you
from revealing the truth **296 molt no feather** i.e., not diminish in the
least **301 brave** splendid **302 fretted** adorned (with fretwork, as in a
vaulted ceiling) **304 congregation** mass. **piece of work** masterpiece
306 express well-framed, exact, expressive (?) **307 apprehension** power
of comprehending **309 quintessence** the fifth essence of ancient philosophy, beyond earth, water, air, and fire, supposed to be the substance of
the heavenly bodies and to be latent in all things **317 Lenten entertainment** meager reception (appropriate to Lent) **318 coted** overtook and
passed by **321 shall . . . of me** will receive my tribute of praise
322 foil and target sword and shield

sigh gratis, the humorous man shall end his part in 323
peace, the clown shall make those laugh whose lungs 324
are tickle o' the sear, and the lady shall say her mind 325
freely, or the blank verse shall halt for 't. What players 326
are they?

ROSENCRANTZ   Even those you were wont to take such
delight in, the tragedians of the city.

HAMLET   How chances it they travel? Their residence, 330
both in reputation and profit, was better both ways.

ROSENCRANTZ   I think their inhibition comes by the 332
means of the late innovation. 333

HAMLET   Do they hold the same estimation they did
when I was in the city? Are they so followed?

ROSENCRANTZ   No, indeed are they not.

HAMLET   How comes it? Do they grow rusty? 337

ROSENCRANTZ   Nay, their endeavor keeps in the wonted 338
pace. But there is, sir, an aerie of children, little eyases, 339
that cry out on the top of question and are most tyran- 340
nically clapped for 't. These are now the fashion, and 341
so berattle the common stages—so they call them— 342
that many wearing rapiers are afraid of goose quills 343
and dare scarce come thither.

HAMLET   What, are they children? Who maintains 'em?
How are they escoted? Will they pursue the quality no 346
longer than they can sing? Will they not say after- 347

323 gratis for nothing.   **humorous man** eccentric character, dominated
by one trait or "humor"   **323–324 in peace** i.e., with full license
325 tickle o' the sear easy on the trigger, ready to laugh easily. (A *sear* is
part of a gunlock.)   **326 halt** limp   **330 residence** remaining in one
place, i.e., in the city   **332 inhibition** formal prohibition (from acting
plays in the city)   **333 late** recent.   **innovation** i.e., the new fashion in
satirical plays performed by boy actors in the "private" theaters; or
possibly a political uprising; or the strict limitations set on the theaters
in London in 1600   **337–362 How . . . load too** (The passage, omitted
from the early quartos, alludes to the so-called War of the Theaters,
1599–1602, the rivalry between the children's companies and the adult
actors.)   **338 keeps** continues.   **wonted** usual   **339 aerie** nest.   **eyases**
young hawks   **340 cry . . . question** speak shrilly, dominating the controversy (in decrying the public theaters)   **340–341 tyrannically** outra-
geously   **342 berattle** berate, clamor against.   **common stages** public
theaters   **343 many wearing rapiers** i.e., many men of fashion, afraid to
patronize the common players for fear of being satirized by the poets
writing for the boy actors.   **goose quills** i.e., pens of satirists
346 escoted maintained.   **quality** (acting) profession   **346–347 no
longer . . . sing** i.e., only until their voices change

wards, if they should grow themselves to common 348
players—as it is most like, if their means are no bet- 349
ter—their writers do them wrong to make them ex- 350
claim against their own succession? 351

ROSENCRANTZ Faith, there has been much to-do on 352
both sides, and the nation holds it no sin to tar them 353
to controversy. There was for a while no money bid
for argument unless the poet and the player went to 355
cuffs in the question. 356

HAMLET Is 't possible?

GUILDENSTERN O, there has been much throwing about
of brains.

HAMLET Do the boys carry it away? 360

ROSENCRANTZ Ay, that they do, my lord—Hercules 361
and his load too. 362

HAMLET It is not very strange; for my uncle is King of
Denmark, and those that would make mouths at him 364
while my father lived give twenty, forty, fifty, a
hundred ducats apiece for his picture in little. 'Sblood, 366
there is something in this more than natural, if philos- 367
ophy could find it out. 368

A flourish [*of trumpets within*].

GUILDENSTERN There are the players.

HAMLET Gentlemen, you are welcome to Elsinore. Your
hands, come then. Th' appurtenance of welcome is 371
fashion and ceremony. Let me comply with you in this 372
garb, lest my extent to the players, which, I tell you, 373
must show fairly outwards, should more appear like 374
entertainment than yours. You are welcome. But my 375
uncle-father and aunt-mother are deceived.

---

348 common regular, adult **349 like** likely **349–350 if . . . better** if
they find no better way to support themselves **351 succession** i.e.,
future careers **352 to-do** ado **353 tar** set on (as dogs) **355 argument**
plot for a play **355–356 went . . . question** came to blows in the play
itself **360 carry it away** i.e., win the day **361–362 Hercules . . . load**
(Thought to be an allusion to the sign of the Globe Theatre, which was
Hercules bearing the world on his shoulder.) **364 mouths** faces
366 ducats gold coins. **in little** in miniature. **'Sblood** by God's
(Christ's) blood **367–368 philosophy** i.e., scientific inquiry
371 appurtenance proper accompaniment **372 comply** observe the
formalities of courtesy **373 garb** i.e., manner. **my extent** that which I
extend, i.e., my polite behavior **374 show fairly outwards** show every
evidence of cordiality **375 entertainment** a (warm) reception

GUILDENSTERN   In what, my dear lord?

HAMLET   I am but mad north-north-west. When the 378
wind is southerly I know a hawk from a handsaw. 379

Enter Polonius.

POLONIUS   Well be with you, gentlemen!

HAMLET   Hark you, Guildenstern, and you too; at each
ear a hearer. That great baby you see there is not yet
out of his swaddling clouts. 383

ROSENCRANTZ   Haply he is the second time come to 384
them, for they say an old man is twice a child.

HAMLET   I will prophesy he comes to tell me of the players; mark it.—You say right, sir, o' Monday morning,
'twas then indeed.

POLONIUS   My lord, I have news to tell you.

HAMLET   My lord, I have news to tell you. When Ros- 390
cius was an actor in Rome— 391

POLONIUS   The actors are come hither, my lord.

HAMLET   Buzz, buzz! 393

POLONIUS   Upon my honor—

HAMLET   Then came each actor on his ass.

POLONIUS   The best actors in the world, either for
tragedy, comedy, history, pastoral, pastoral-comical,
historical-pastoral, tragical-historical, tragical-comical-
historical-pastoral, scene individable, or poem unlim- 399
ited. Seneca cannot be too heavy, nor Plautus too light. 400
For the law of writ and the liberty, these are the only 401
men.

HAMLET   O Jephthah, judge of Israel, what a treasure 403
hadst thou!

378 north-north-west i.e., only partly, at times   **379 hawk, handsaw** i.e.,
two very different things, though also perhaps meaning a mattock (or
hack) and a carpenter's cutting tool respectively; also birds, with a play
on *hernshaw* or heron   **383 swaddling clouts** cloths in which to wrap a
newborn baby   **384 Haply** perhaps   **390–391 Roscius** a famous Roman
actor who died in 62 B.C.   **393 Buzz** (An interjection used to denote
stale news.)   **399 scene individable** a play observing the unity of place;
or perhaps one that is unclassifiable   **399–400 poem unlimited** a play
disregarding the unities of time and place; one that is all-inclusive
400 Seneca writer of Latin tragedies.   **Plautus** writer of Latin comedy
401 law . . . liberty dramatic composition both according to rules and
without rules, i.e., "classical" and "romantic" dramas.   **these** i.e., the
actors   **403 Jephthah . . . Israel** (Jephthah had to sacrifice his daughter;
see Judges 11. Hamlet goes on to quote from a ballad on the theme.)

POLONIUS What a treasure had he, my lord?
HAMLET Why,
    "One fair daughter, and no more,
    The which he lovèd passing well."   408
POLONIUS [*Aside*] Still on my daughter.
HAMLET Am I not i' the right, old Jephthah?
POLONIUS If you call me Jephthah, my lord, I have a
    daughter that I love passing well.
HAMLET Nay, that follows not.
POLONIUS What follows then, my lord?
HAMLET Why,
    "As by lot, God wot,"   416
and then, you know,
    "It came to pass, as most like it was"—   418
the first row of the pious chanson will show you more,   419
for look where my abridgment comes.   420

    Enter the Players.

You are welcome, masters; welcome, all. I am glad to
see thee well. Welcome, good friends. O, old friend!
Why, thy face is valanced since I saw thee last. Com'st 423
thou to beard me in Denmark? What, my young lady   424
and mistress! By 'r Lady, your ladyship is nearer to   425
heaven than when I saw you last, by the altitude of a
chopine. Pray God your voice, like a piece of uncur-   427
rent gold, be not cracked within the ring. Masters, you 428
are all welcome. We'll e'en to 't like French falconers, 429
fly at anything we see. We'll have a speech straight.   430
Come, give us a taste of your quality. Come, a passion- 431
ate speech.
FIRST PLAYER What speech, my good lord?

408 passing surpassingly **416 lot** chance. **wot** knows **418 like** likely,
probable **419 row** stanza. **chanson** ballad, song **420 my abridgment**
something that cuts short my conversation; also, a diversion **423 valanced** fringed (with a beard) **424 beard** confront, challenge (with
obvious pun). **young lady** i.e., boy playing women's parts **425 By 'r
Lady** by Our Lady **427 chopine** thick-soled shoe of Italian fashion
427–428 uncurrent not passable as lawful coinage **428 cracked . . . ring**
i.e., changed from adolescent to male voice, no longer suitable for women's
roles. (Coins featured rings enclosing the sovereign's head; if the coin
was cracked within this ring, it was unfit for currency.) **429 e'en to 't**
go at it **430 straight** at once **431 quality** professional skill

HAMLET I heard thee speak me a speech once, but it
was never acted, or if it was, not above once, for the
play, I remember, pleased not the million; 'twas cav- 436
iar to the general. But it was—as I received it, and 437
others, whose judgments in such matters cried in the 438
top of mine—an excellent play, well digested in the 439
scenes, set down with as much modesty as cunning. I 440
remember one said there were no sallets in the lines to 441
make the matter savory, nor no matter in the phrase
that might indict the author of affectation, but called it 443
an honest method, as wholesome as sweet, and by
very much more handsome than fine. One speech in 't 445
I chiefly loved: 'twas Aeneas' tale to Dido, and there-
about of it especially when he speaks of Priam's 447
slaughter. If it live in your memory, begin at this line: 448
let me see, let me see—
     "The rugged Pyrrhus, like th' Hyrcanian beast"— 450
'Tis not so. It begins with Pyrrhus:
     "The rugged Pyrrhus, he whose sable arms, 452
     Black as his purpose, did the night resemble
     When he lay couchèd in the ominous horse, 454
     Hath now this dread and black complexion smeared
     With heraldry more dismal. Head to foot 456
     Now is he total gules, horridly tricked 457
     With blood of fathers, mothers, daughters, sons,
     Baked and impasted with the parching streets, 459

436–437 caviar to the general caviar to the multitude, i.e., a choice dish
too elegant for coarse tastes **438–439 cried in the top of** i.e., spoke
with greater authority than **439 digested** arranged, ordered
440 modesty moderation, restraint. **cunning** skill **441 sallets** i.e.,
something savory, spicy improprieties **443 indict** convict **445 fine**
elaborately ornamented, showy **447–448 Priam's slaughter** the slaying
of the ruler of Troy, when the Greeks finally took the city **450 Pyrrhus**
a Greek hero in the Trojan War, also known as Neoptolemus, son of
Achilles—another avenging son. **Hyrcanian beast** i.e., tiger. (On the
death of Priam, see Virgil, *Aeneid*, 2.506–558; compare the whole speech
with Marlowe's *Dido Queen of Carthage*, 2.1.214 ff. On the *Hyrcanian*
tiger, see *Aeneid*, 4.366–367. Hyrcania is on the Caspian Sea.) **452 sable**
black (for reasons of camouflage during the episode of the Trojan
horse) **454 couchèd** concealed. **ominous horse** Trojan horse, by which
the Greeks gained access to Troy **456 dismal** ill-omened **457 gules**
red. (A heraldic term.) **tricked** adorned, decorated **459 impasted**
crusted, like a thick paste. **with . . . streets** by the parching heat of the
streets (because of the fires everywhere)

That lend a tyrannous and a damnèd light
To their lord's murder. Roasted in wrath and fire, 461
And thus o'ersizèd with coagulate gore, 462
With eyes like carbuncles, the hellish Pyrrhus 463
Old grandsire Priam seeks."
So proceed you.
POLONIUS 'Fore God, my lord, well spoken, with good
accent and good discretion.
FIRST PLAYER "Anon he finds him
Striking too short at Greeks. His antique sword,
Rebellious to his arm, lies where it falls,
Repugnant to command. Unequal matched, 471
Pyrrhus at Priam drives, in rage strikes wide,
But with the whiff and wind of his fell sword 473
Th' unnervèd father falls. Then senseless Ilium, 474
Seeming to feel this blow, with flaming top
Stoops to his base, and with a hideous crash 476
Takes prisoner Pyrrhus' ear. For, lo! His sword,
Which was declining on the milky head 478
Of reverend Priam, seemed i' th' air to stick.
So as a painted tyrant Pyrrhus stood, 480
And, like a neutral to his will and matter, 481
Did nothing.
But as we often see against some storm 483
A silence in the heavens, the rack stand still, 484
The bold winds speechless, and the orb below 485
As hush as death, anon the dreadful thunder
Doth rend the region, so, after Pyrrhus' pause, 487
Arousèd vengeance sets him new a-work,
And never did the Cyclops' hammers fall 489
On Mars's armor forged for proof eterne 490
With less remorse than Pyrrhus' bleeding sword 491
Now falls on Priam.

461 their lord's i.e., Priam's   **462 o'ersizèd** covered as with size or glue
463 carbuncles large fiery-red precious stones thought to emit their own
light   **471 Repugnant** disobedient, resistant   **473 fell** cruel   **474 unnervèd**
strengthless.   **senseless Ilium** inanimate citadel of Troy   **476 his** its
478 declining descending.   **milky** white-haired   **480 painted** i.e., painted in
a picture   **481 like . . . matter** i.e., as though suspended between his
intention and its fulfillment   **483 against** just before   **484 rack** mass of
clouds   **485 orb** globe, earth   **487 region** sky   **489 Cyclops** giant armor-
makers in the smithy of Vulcan   **490 proof eterne** eternal resistance to
assault   **491 remorse** pity

Out, out, thou strumpet Fortune! All you gods
In general synod take away her power!　　　　494
Break all the spokes and fellies from her wheel,　　　495
And bowl the round nave down the hill of heaven　　496
As low as to the fiends!"

POLONIUS　This is too long.

HAMLET　It shall to the barber's with your beard.—Prithee, say on. He's for a jig or a tale of bawdry, or he　500
sleeps. Say on; come to Hecuba.　　　　501

FIRST PLAYER
"But who, ah woe! had seen the moblèd queen"—　　502

HAMLET　"The moblèd queen"?

POLONIUS　That's good. "Moblèd queen" is good.

FIRST PLAYER
"Run barefoot up and down, threat'ning the flames
With bisson rheum, a clout upon that head　　　506
Where late the diadem stood, and, for a robe,　　507
About her lank and all o'erteemèd loins　　　508
A blanket, in the alarm of fear caught up—
Who this had seen, with tongue in venom steeped,
'Gainst Fortune's state would treason have
　pronounced.
　　　　　　　　　　　　　　　　　　　　511
But if the gods themselves did see her then
When she saw Pyrrhus make malicious sport
In mincing with his sword her husband's limbs,
The instant burst of clamor that she made,
Unless things mortal move them not at all,
Would have made milch the burning eyes of heaven,　517
And passion in the gods."　　　　518

POLONIUS　Look whe'er he has not turned his color and　519
has tears in 's eyes. Prithee, no more.

HAMLET　'Tis well. I'll have thee speak out the rest of
this soon.—Good my lord, will you see the players well

---

494 synod assembly　**495 fellies** pieces of wood forming the rim of a
wheel　**496 nave** hub　**500 jig** comic song and dance often given at the
end of a play　**501 Hecuba** wife of Priam　**502 who . . . had** anyone who
had (also in l. 510).　**moblèd** muffled　**506 bisson rheum** blinding
tears.　**clout** cloth　**507 late** lately　**508 o'erteemèd** worn out with
bearing children　**511 state** rule, managing.　**pronounced** proclaimed
517 milch milky, moist with tears　**518 passion** overpowering emotion
519 whe'er whether

bestowed? Do you hear, let them be well used, for they 523
are the abstract and brief chronicles of the time. After 524
your death you were better have a bad epitaph than
their ill report while you live.

POLONIUS My lord, I will use them according to their
desert.

HAMLET God's bodikin, man, much better. Use every 529
man after his desert, and who shall scape whipping?
Use them after your own honor and dignity. The less
they deserve, the more merit is in your bounty. Take
them in.

POLONIUS Come, sirs.

HAMLET Follow him, friends. We'll hear a play tomor-
row. [*As they start to leave, Hamlet detains the First
Player.*] Dost thou hear me, old friend? Can you play
The Murder of Gonzago?

FIRST PLAYER Ay, my lord.

HAMLET We'll ha 't tomorrow night. You could, for 540
a need, study a speech of some dozen or sixteen lines 541
which I would set down and insert in 't, could you
not?

FIRST PLAYER Ay, my lord.

HAMLET Very well. Follow that lord, and look you mock 545
him not. (*Exeunt Polonius and Players.*) My good friends,
I'll leave you till night. You are welcome to Elsinore.

ROSENCRANTZ Good my lord!
            Exeunt [*Rosencrantz and Guildenstern*].

HAMLET
Ay, so, goodbye to you.—Now I am alone.
O, what a rogue and peasant slave am I!
Is it not monstrous that this player here,
But in a fiction, in a dream of passion,   552
Could force his soul so to his own conceit   553
That from her working all his visage wanned,   554
Tears in his eyes, distraction in his aspect,

---

523 bestowed lodged   **524 abstract** summary account   **529 God's
bodikin** by God's (Christ's) little body, *bodykin*. (Not to be confused with
bodkin, dagger.)   **540 ha 't** have it   **541 study** memorize   **545 mock**
mimic derisively   **552 But** merely   **553 to** in accord with.   **conceit**
conception   **554 from her working** as a result of, or in response to, his
soul's activity.   **wanned** grew pale

A broken voice, and his whole function suiting   556
With forms to his conceit? And all for nothing!   557
For Hecuba!
What's Hecuba to him, or he to Hecuba,
That he should weep for her? What would he do
Had he the motive and the cue for passion
That I have? He would drown the stage with tears
And cleave the general ear with horrid speech,   563
Make mad the guilty and appall the free,   564
Confound the ignorant, and amaze indeed
The very faculties of eyes and ears. Yet I,
A dull and muddy-mettled rascal, peak   567
Like John-a-dreams, unpregnant of my cause,   568
And can say nothing—no, not for a king
Upon whose property and most dear life   570
A damned defeat was made. Am I a coward?   571
Who calls me villain? Breaks my pate across?
Plucks off my beard and blows it in my face?
Tweaks me by the nose? Gives me the lie i' the throat   574
As deep as to the lungs? Who does me this?
Ha, 'swounds, I should take it; for it cannot be   576
But I am pigeon-livered and lack gall   577
To make oppression bitter, or ere this   578
I should ha' fatted all the region kites   579
With this slave's offal. Bloody, bawdy villain!
Remorseless, treacherous, lecherous, kindless villain!   581
O, vengeance!
Why, what an ass am I! This is most brave,   583
That I, the son of a dear father murdered,
Prompted to my revenge by heaven and hell,
Must like a whore unpack my heart with words

556-557 **his whole . . . conceit** all his bodily powers responding with
actions to suit his thought   **563 the general ear** everyone's ear.   **horrid**
horrible   **564 appall** (Literally, make pale.)   **free** innocent   **567 muddy-
mettled** dull-spirited.   **peak** mope, pine   **568 John-a-dreams** a sleepy,
dreaming idler.   **unpregnant of** not quickened by   **570 property** i.e., the
crown; perhaps also character, quality   **571 defeat** destruction
574 Gives me the lie calls me a liar   **576 'swounds** by his (Christ's)
wounds   **577 pigeon-livered** (The pigeon or dove was popularly supposed to be mild because it secreted no gall.)   **578 To . . . bitter** to make
tyranny bitter to itself   **579 region kites** kites (birds of prey) of the air
581 Remorseless pitiless.   **kindless** unnatural   **583 brave** fine, admirable. (Said ironically.)

And fall a-cursing, like a very drab,   587
A scullion! Fie upon 't, foh! About, my brain!   588
Hum, I have heard
That guilty creatures sitting at a play
Have by the very cunning of the scene   591
Been struck so to the soul that presently   592
They have proclaimed their malefactions;
For murder, though it have no tongue, will speak
With most miraculous organ. I'll have these players
Play something like the murder of my father
Before mine uncle. I'll observe his looks;
I'll tent him to the quick. If 'a do blench,   598
I know my course. The spirit that I have seen
May be the devil, and the devil hath power
T' assume a pleasing shape; yea, and perhaps,
Out of my weakness and my melancholy,
As he is very potent with such spirits,   603
Abuses me to damn me. I'll have grounds   604
More relative than this. The play's the thing   605
Wherein I'll catch the conscience of the King.   *Exit.*

❖

---

587 drab prostitute   **588 scullion** menial kitchen servant (apt to be foulmouthed).   **About** about it, to work   **591 cunning** art, skill.   **scene** dramatic presentation   **592 presently** at once   **598 tent** probe.   **blench** quail, flinch   **603 spirits** humors (of melancholy)   **604 Abuses** deludes   **605 relative** cogent, pertinent

3.1 *Enter King, Queen, Polonius, Ophelia, Rosencrantz, Guildenstern, lords.*

KING
   And can you by no drift of conference   1
   Get from him why he puts on this confusion,
   Grating so harshly all his days of quiet
   With turbulent and dangerous lunacy?

ROSENCRANTZ
   He does confess he feels himself distracted,
   But from what cause 'a will by no means speak.

GUILDENSTERN
   Nor do we find him forward to be sounded,   7
   But with a crafty madness keeps aloof
   When we would bring him on to some confession
   Of his true state.

QUEEN   Did he receive you well?
ROSENCRANTZ   Most like a gentleman.

GUILDENSTERN
   But with much forcing of his disposition.   12

ROSENCRANTZ
   Niggard of question, but of our demands   13
   Most free in his reply.

QUEEN   Did you assay him   14
   To any pastime?

ROSENCRANTZ
   Madam, it so fell out that certain players
   We o'erraught on the way. Of these we told him,   17
   And there did seem in him a kind of joy
   To hear of it. They are here about the court,
   And, as I think, they have already order
   This night to play before him.

POLONIUS   'Tis most true,
   And he beseeched me to entreat Your Majesties
   To hear and see the matter.

KING
   With all my heart, and it doth much content me
   To hear him so inclined.

3.1. Location: The castle.
1 drift of conference directing of conversation   **7 forward** willing.
sounded questioned   **12 disposition** inclination   **13 question** conversation   **14 assay** try to win   **17 o'erraught** overtook and passed

Good gentlemen, give him a further edge   26
And drive his purpose into these delights.

ROSENCRANTZ
We shall, my lord.
                    Exeunt Rosencrantz and Guildenstern.

KING   Sweet Gertrude, leave us too,
For we have closely sent for Hamlet hither,   29
That he, as 'twere by accident, may here
Affront Ophelia.   31
Her father and myself, lawful espials,   32
Will so bestow ourselves that seeing, unseen,
We may of their encounter frankly judge,
And gather by him, as he is behaved,
If 't be th' affliction of his love or no
That thus he suffers for.

QUEEN   I shall obey you.
And for your part, Ophelia, I do wish
That your good beauties be the happy cause
Of Hamlet's wildness. So shall I hope your virtues
Will bring him to his wonted way again,
To both your honors.

OPHELIA   Madam, I wish it may.
                                        [*Exit Queen.*]

POLONIUS
Ophelia, walk you here.—Gracious, so please you,   43
We will bestow ourselves. [*To Ophelia.*] Read on this
     book,   [*Giving her a book*]   44
That show of such an exercise may color   45
Your loneliness. We are oft to blame in this—   46
'Tis too much proved—that with devotion's visage   47
And pious action we do sugar o'er
The devil himself.

KING [*Aside*]   O, 'tis too true!
How smart a lash that speech doth give my conscience!
The harlot's cheek, beautied with plastering art,
Is not more ugly to the thing that helps it   53

---

26 edge incitement   **29 closely** privately   **31 Affront** confront, meet
32 espials spies   **43 Gracious** Your Grace (i.e., the King)   **44 bestow**
conceal   **45 exercise** act of devotion. (The book she reads is one of
devotion.)   **color** give a plausible appearance to   **46 loneliness** being
alone   **47 too much proved** too often shown to be true, too often practiced   **53 to** compared to.   **the thing** i.e., the cosmetic

Than is my deed to my most painted word.
O heavy burden!

POLONIUS
I hear him coming. Let's withdraw, my lord.   56
                    [*The King and Polonius withdraw.*]

          Enter Hamlet. [*Ophelia pretends to read a book.*]

HAMLET
To be, or not to be, that is the question:
Whether 'tis nobler in the mind to suffer
The slings and arrows of outrageous fortune,   59
Or to take arms against a sea of troubles
And by opposing end them. To die, to sleep—
No more—and by a sleep to say we end
The heartache and the thousand natural shocks
That flesh is heir to. 'Tis a consummation
Devoutly to be wished. To die, to sleep;
To sleep, perchance to dream. Ay, there's the rub,   66
For in that sleep of death what dreams may come,
When we have shuffled off this mortal coil,   68
Must give us pause. There's the respect   69
That makes calamity of so long life.   70
For who would bear the whips and scorns of time,   71
Th' oppressor's wrong, the proud man's contumely,   72
The pangs of disprized love, the law's delay,   73
The insolence of office, and the spurns   74
That patient merit of th' unworthy takes,   75
When he himself might his quietus make   76
With a bare bodkin? Who would fardels bear,   77
To grunt and sweat under a weary life,
But that the dread of something after death,
The undiscovered country from whose bourn   80
No traveler returns, puzzles the will,

---

56 s.d. withdraw (The King and Polonius may retire behind an arras.
The stage directions specify that they "enter" again near the end of the
scene.)   **59 slings** missiles   **66 rub** (Literally, an obstacle in the game of
bowls.)   **68 shuffled** sloughed, cast.   **coil** turmoil   **69 respect** consideration   **70 of . . . life** so long-lived (also suggesting that long life is itself
a calamity)   **71 time** the world we live in   **72 contumely** insolent
abuse   **73 disprized** unvalued   **74 office** officialdom.   **spurns** insults
75 of . . . takes receives from unworthy persons   **76 quietus** acquittance; here, death   **77 a bare** merely a.   **bodkin** dagger.   **fardels** bur-
dens   **80 bourn** boundary

And makes us rather bear those ills we have
Than fly to others that we know not of?
Thus conscience does make cowards of us all;
And thus the native hue of resolution   85
Is sicklied o'er with the pale cast of thought,   86
And enterprises of great pitch and moment   87
With this regard their currents turn awry   88
And lose the name of action.—Soft you now,   89
The fair Ophelia. Nymph, in thy orisons   90
Be all my sins remembered.

OPHELIA   Good my lord.
How does your honor for this many a day?

HAMLET
I humbly thank you; well, well, well.

OPHELIA
My lord, I have remembrances of yours,
That I have longèd long to redeliver.
I pray you, now receive them.   [*She offers tokens.*]

HAMLET
No, not I. I never gave you aught.

OPHELIA
My honored lord, you know right well you did,
And with them words of so sweet breath composed
As made the things more rich. Their perfume lost,
Take these again, for to the noble mind
Rich gifts wax poor when givers prove unkind.
There, my lord.   [*She gives tokens.*]

HAMLET   Ha, ha! Are you honest?   104

OPHELIA   My lord?

HAMLET   Are you fair?   106

OPHELIA   What means your lordship?

HAMLET   That if you be honest and fair, your honesty   108
should admit no discourse to your beauty.   109

OPHELIA   Could beauty, my lord, have better commerce   110
than with honesty?

---

85 native hue natural color, complexion   **86 cast** tinge, shade of color
87 pitch height (as of a falcon's flight).   **moment** importance   **88 regard**
respect, consideration.   **currents** courses   **89 Soft you** i.e., wait a minute,
gently   **90 orisons** prayers   **104 honest** (1) truthful (2) chaste   **106 fair**
(1) beautiful (2) just, honorable   **108 your honesty** your chastity
109 discourse to familiar dealings with   **110 commerce** dealings,
intercourse

HAMLET   Ay, truly, for the power of beauty will sooner
transform honesty from what it is to a bawd than the
force of honesty can translate beauty into his likeness. 114
This was sometime a paradox, but now the time gives 115
it proof. I did love you once.

OPHELIA   Indeed, my lord, you made me believe so.

HAMLET   You should not have believed me, for virtue
cannot so inoculate our old stock but we shall relish of 119
it. I loved you not. 120

OPHELIA   I was the more deceived.

HAMLET   Get thee to a nunnery. Why wouldst thou be a 122
breeder of sinners? I am myself indifferent honest, but 123
yet I could accuse me of such things that it were better
my mother had not borne me: I am very proud, re-
vengeful, ambitious, with more offenses at my beck 126
than I have thoughts to put them in, imagination to
give them shape, or time to act them in. What should
such fellows as I do crawling between earth and
heaven? We are arrant knaves all; believe none of us.
Go thy ways to a nunnery. Where's your father?

OPHELIA   At home, my lord.

HAMLET   Let the doors be shut upon him, that he may
play the fool nowhere but in 's own house. Farewell.

OPHELIA   O, help him, you sweet heavens!

HAMLET   If thou dost marry, I'll give thee this plague for
thy dowry: be thou as chaste as ice, as pure as snow,
thou shalt not escape calumny. Get thee to a nunnery,
farewell. Or, if thou wilt needs marry, marry a fool,
for wise men know well enough what monsters you 140
make of them. To a nunnery, go, and quickly too. Farewell.

OPHELIA   Heavenly powers, restore him!

HAMLET   I have heard of your paintings too, well
enough. God hath given you one face, and you make

---

114 his its   **115 sometime** formerly.   **a paradox** a view opposite to
commonly held opinion.   **the time** the present age   **119 inoculate** graft,
be engrafted to   **119–120 but . . . it** i.e., that we do not still have about
us a taste of the old stock, i.e., retain our sinfulness   **122 nunnery**
convent (with possibly an awareness that the word was also used derisively to denote a brothel)   **123 indifferent honest** reasonably virtuous   **126 beck** command   **140 monsters** (An allusion to the horns of a
cuckold.)   **you** i.e., you women

yourselves another. You jig, you amble, and you 146
lisp, you nickname God's creatures, and make your 147
wantonness your ignorance. Go to, I'll no more on 't; 148
it hath made me mad. I say we will have no more
marriage. Those that are married already—all but
one—shall live. The rest shall keep as they are. To a
nunnery, go.　　　　　　　　　　　　　　　　*Exit.*

OPHELIA
O, what a noble mind is here o'erthrown!
The courtier's, soldier's, scholar's, eye, tongue, sword,
Th' expectancy and rose of the fair state, 155
The glass of fashion and the mold of form, 156
Th' observed of all observers, quite, quite down! 157
And I, of ladies most deject and wretched,
That sucked the honey of his music vows,
Now see that noble and most sovereign reason
Like sweet bells jangled out of tune and harsh,
That unmatched form and feature of blown youth 162
Blasted with ecstasy. O, woe is me, 163
T' have seen what I have seen, see what I see!

Enter King and Polonius.

KING
Love? His affections do not that way tend; 165
Nor what he spake, though it lacked form a little,
Was not like madness. There's something in his soul
O'er which his melancholy sits on brood, 168
And I do doubt the hatch and the disclose 169
Will be some danger; which for to prevent,
I have in quick determination
Thus set it down: he shall with speed to England 172

---

146 jig i.e., dance and sing affectedly and wantonly.　**amble** dance,
move coquettishly　**147 lisp** (A wanton affectation.)　**nickname** find a
new name for, transform (as in using cosmetics)　**147–148 make . . .
ignorance** i.e., excuse your affectation on the grounds of your ignorance　**148 on 't** of it　**155 Th' expectancy . . . state** the hope and
ornament of the kingdom made fair (by him)　**156 The glass . . . form**
the mirror of true self-fashioning and the pattern of courtly behavior
157 Th' observed . . . observers i.e., the center of attention and honor in
the court　**162 blown** blooming　**163 Blasted** withered.　**ecstasy** madness　**165 affections** emotions, feelings　**168 sits on brood** sits like a
bird on a nest, about to *hatch* mischief (l. 169)　**169 doubt** fear.
disclose disclosure, hatching　**172 set it down** resolved

For the demand of our neglected tribute.   173
Haply the seas and countries different
With variable objects shall expel   175
This something settled matter in his heart,   176
Whereon his brains still beating puts him thus   177
From fashion of himself. What think you on 't?   178

POLONIUS
It shall do well. But yet do I believe
The origin and commencement of his grief
Sprung from neglected love.—How now, Ophelia?
You need not tell us what Lord Hamlet said;
We heard it all.—My lord, do as you please,
But, if you hold it fit, after the play
Let his queen-mother all alone entreat him   185
To show his grief. Let her be round with him;   186
And I'll be placed, so please you, in the ear
Of all their conference. If she find him not,   188
To England send him, or confine him where
Your wisdom best shall think.

KING   It shall be so.
Madness in great ones must not unwatched go.
                                                    Exeunt.

❖

3.2   *Enter Hamlet and three of the Players.*

HAMLET   Speak the speech, I pray you, as I pronounced
it to you, trippingly on the tongue. But if you mouth
it, as many of our players do, I had as lief the town   3
crier spoke my lines. Nor do not saw the air too much
with your hand, thus, but use all gently; for in the very
torrent, tempest, and, as I may say, whirlwind of your

---

173 For . . . of to demand   175 variable objects various sights and
surroundings to divert him   176 This something . . . heart the strange
unidentified matter settled in his heart   177 still continually
178 From . . . himself out of his natural manner   185 queen-mother
queen and mother, not widowed dowager   186 round blunt   188 find
him not fails to discover what is troubling him

3.2. Location: The castle.
3 our players (Indefinite use; i.e., players nowadays.)   I had as lief I
would just as soon

passion, you must acquire and beget a temperance
that may give it smoothness. O, it offends me to the
soul to hear a robustious periwig-pated fellow tear a 9
passion to tatters, to very rags, to split the ears of the
groundlings, who for the most part are capable of 11
nothing but inexplicable dumb shows and noise. I
would have such a fellow whipped for o'erdoing Ter- 13
magant. It out-Herods Herod. Pray you, avoid it. 14

FIRST PLAYER I warrant your honor.

HAMLET Be not too tame neither, but let your own discretion be your tutor. Suit the action to the word, the
word to the action, with this special observance, that
you o'erstep not the modesty of nature. For anything 19
so o'erdone is from the purpose of playing, whose 20
end, both at the first and now, was and is to hold as
'twere the mirror up to nature, to show virtue her
feature, scorn her own image, and the very age and 23
body of the time his form and pressure. Now this 24
overdone or come tardy off, though it makes the un- 25
skillful laugh, cannot but make the judicious grieve, 26
the censure of the which one must in your allowance 27
o'erweigh a whole theater of others. O, there be players that I have seen play, and heard others praise, and
that highly, not to speak it profanely, that, neither 30
having th' accent of Christians nor the gait of Chris- 31
tian, pagan, nor man, have so strutted and bellowed 32
that I have thought some of nature's journeymen had 33

---

9 robustious violent, boisterous. **periwig-pated** wearing a wig
11 groundlings spectators who paid least and stood in the yard of the
theater. **capable of** able to understand **13–14 Termagant** a supposed
deity of the Mohammedans, not found in any English medieval play but
elsewhere portrayed as violent and blustering **14 Herod** Herod of
Jewry. (A character in *The Slaughter of the Innocents* and other cycle
plays. The part was played with great noise and fury.) **19 modesty**
restraint, moderation **20 from** contrary to **23 scorn** i.e., something
foolish and deserving of scorn **23–24 the very ... time** i.e., the present
state of affairs **24 his** its. **pressure** stamp, impressed character
25 come tardy off inadequately done **25–26 the unskillful** those lacking in judgment **27 the censure ... one** the judgment of even one of
whom. **your allowance** your scale of values **30 not ... profanely**
(Hamlet anticipates his idea in ll. 33–34 that some men were not made
by God at all.) **31 Christians** i.e., ordinary decent folk **32 nor man** i.e.,
nor any human being at all **33 journeymen** laborers not yet masters in
their trade

made men and not made them well, they imitated humanity so abominably.   35
FIRST PLAYER   I hope we have reformed that indifferently   36
with us, sir.
HAMLET   O, reform it altogether. And let those that play
your clowns speak no more than is set down for them;
for there be of them that will themselves laugh, to set   40
on some quantity of barren spectators to laugh too,   41
though in the meantime some necessary question of
the play be then to be considered. That's villainous,
and shows a most pitiful ambition in the fool that uses
it. Go make you ready.   [*Exeunt Players.*]

Enter Polonius, Guildenstern, and Rosencrantz.

How now, my lord, will the King hear this piece of
work?
POLONIUS   And the Queen too, and that presently.   48
HAMLET   Bid the players make haste.   [*Exit Polonius.*]
Will you two help to hasten them?
ROSENCRANTZ
Ay, my lord.   *Exeunt they two.*
HAMLET   What ho, Horatio!

Enter Horatio.

HORATIO   Here, sweet lord, at your service.
HAMLET
Horatio, thou art e'en as just a man
As e'er my conversation coped withal.   54
HORATIO
O, my dear lord—
HAMLET   Nay, do not think I flatter,
For what advancement may I hope from thee
That no revenue hast but thy good spirits
To feed and clothe thee? Why should the poor be
flattered?

---

35 abominably (Shakespeare's usual spelling, *abhominably*, suggests a
literal though etymologically incorrect meaning, "removed from human
nature.")   **36 indifferently** tolerably   **40 of them** i.e., some among
them   **41 barren** i.e., of wit   **48 presently** at once   **54 my . . . withal** my
contact with people provided opportunity for encounter with

No, let the candied tongue lick absurd pomp, 59
And crook the pregnant hinges of the knee 60
Where thrift may follow fawning. Dost thou hear? 61
Since my dear soul was mistress of her choice
And could of men distinguish her election, 63
Sh' hath sealed thee for herself, for thou hast been 64
As one, in suffering all, that suffers nothing,
A man that Fortune's buffets and rewards
Hast ta'en with equal thanks; and blest are those
Whose blood and judgment are so well commeddled 68
That they are not a pipe for Fortune's finger
To sound what stop she please. Give me that man 70
That is not passion's slave, and I will wear him
In my heart's core, ay, in my heart of heart,
As I do thee.—Something too much of this.—
There is a play tonight before the King.
One scene of it comes near the circumstance
Which I have told thee of my father's death.
I prithee, when thou seest that act afoot,
Even with the very comment of thy soul 78
Observe my uncle. If his occulted guilt 79
Do not itself unkennel in one speech, 80
It is a damnèd ghost that we have seen, 81
And my imaginations are as foul
As Vulcan's stithy. Give him heedful note, 83
For I mine eyes will rivet to his face,
And after we will both our judgments join
In censure of his seeming.
HORATIO   Well, my lord. 86
If 'a steal aught the whilst this play is playing 87
And scape detecting, I will pay the theft.

---

59 candied sugared, flattering **60 pregnant** compliant **61 thrift**
profit **63 could . . . election** could make distinguishing choices among
men **64 sealed thee** (Literally, as one would seal a legal document to
mark possession.) **68 blood** passion. **68 commeddled** commingled
70 stop hole in a wind instrument for controlling the sound **78 very**
. . . soul i.e., your most penetrating observation and consideration
79 occulted hidden **80 unkennel** (As one would say of a fox driven from
its lair.) **81 damnèd** in league with Satan **83 stithy** smithy, place of
stiths (anvils) **86 censure of his seeming** judgment of his appearance or
behavior **87 If 'a steal aught** i.e., if he hides anything

[*Flourish.*] *Enter trumpets and kettledrums,*
King, Queen, Polonius, Ophelia, [Rosencrantz,
Guildenstern, and other lords, with guards
carrying torches].

HAMLET   They are coming to the play. I must be idle. 89
Get you a place. [*The King, Queen, and courtiers sit.*]

KING   How fares our cousin Hamlet? 91

HAMLET   Excellent, i' faith, of the chameleon's dish: I eat 92
the air, promise-crammed. You cannot feed capons so. 93

KING   I have nothing with this answer, Hamlet. These 94
words are not mine. 95

HAMLET   No, nor mine now. [*To Polonius.*] My lord, 96
you played once i' th' university, you say?

POLONIUS   That did I, my lord, and was accounted a
good actor.

HAMLET   What did you enact?

POLONIUS   I did enact Julius Caesar. I was killed i' the
Capitol; Brutus killed me.

HAMLET   It was a brute part of him to kill so capital a 103
calf there.—Be the players ready? 104

ROSENCRANTZ   Ay, my lord. They stay upon your patience.

QUEEN   Come hither, my dear Hamlet, sit by me.

HAMLET   No, good Mother, here's metal more attractive. 108

POLONIUS [*To the King*]   Oho, do you mark that?

HAMLET   Lady, shall I lie in your lap?
[*Lying down at Ophelia's feet.*]

OPHELIA   No, my lord.

HAMLET   I mean, my head upon your lap?

OPHELIA   Ay, my lord.

---

89 idle (1) unoccupied (2) mad   **91 cousin** i.e., close relative
92 chameleon's dish (Chameleons were supposed to feed on air. Hamlet
deliberately misinterprets the King's *fares* as "feeds." By his phrase *eat*
the air he also plays on the idea of feeding himself with the promise of
succession, of being the *heir*.)   **93 capons** roosters castrated and
crammed with feed to make them succulent   **94 have . . . with** make
nothing of, or gain nothing from   **95 are not mine** do not respond to
what I asked   **96 nor mine now** (Once spoken, words are proverbially
no longer the speaker's own—and hence should be uttered warily.)
103 brute (The Latin meaning of *brutus*, "stupid," was often used
punningly with the name Brutus.)   **part** (1) deed (2) role   **104 calf**
fool   **108 metal** substance that is *attractive*, i.e., magnetic, but with
suggestion also of *mettle*, disposition

HAMLET   Do you think I meant country matters?   114

OPHELIA   I think nothing, my lord.

HAMLET   That's a fair thought to lie between maids' legs.

OPHELIA   What is, my lord?

HAMLET   Nothing.   119

OPHELIA   You are merry, my lord.

HAMLET   Who, I?

OPHELIA   Ay, my lord.

HAMLET   O God, your only jig maker. What should a   123
man do but be merry? For look you how cheerfully my
mother looks, and my father died within 's two hours.   125

OPHELIA   Nay, 'tis twice two months, my lord.

HAMLET   So long? Nay then, let the devil wear black, for
I'll have a suit of sables. O heavens! Die two months   128
ago, and not forgotten yet? Then there's hope a great
man's memory may outlive his life half a year. But,
by 'r Lady, 'a must build churches, then, or else shall
'a suffer not thinking on, with the hobbyhorse, whose   132
epitaph is "For O, for O, the hobbyhorse is forgot."   133

The trumpets sound. Dumb show follows.

*Enter a King and a Queen [very lovingly]; the
Queen embracing him, and he her. [She kneels,
and makes show of protestation unto him.] He
takes her up, and declines his head upon her neck.
He lies him down upon a bank of flowers. She,
seeing him asleep, leaves him. Anon comes in*

114 country matters the coarse and bawdy things that country folk do
(with a pun on the first syllable of *country*)   **119 Nothing** the figure
zero or naught, suggesting the female anatomy. (*Thing* not infrequently
has a bawdy connotation of male or female anatomy, and the reference
here could be male.)   **123 only jig maker** very best composer of jigs
(song and dance). (Hamlet replies sardonically to Ophelia's observation
that he is merry by saying, "If you're looking for someone who is really
merry, you've come to the right person.")   **125 within 's** within this
128 suit of sables garments trimmed with the fur of the sable, and
hence suited for a wealthy person, not a mourner (but with a pun on
sable, black, ironically suggesting mourning once again)   **132 suffer . . .
on** undergo oblivion   **133 For . . . forgot** (Verse of a song occurring also
in *Love's Labor's Lost*, 3.1.27–28. The hobbyhorse was a character made
up to resemble a horse and rider, appearing in the morris dance and
such May-game sports. This song laments the disappearance of such
customs under pressure from the Puritans.)

another man, takes off his crown, kisses it, pours
poison in the sleeper's ears, and leaves him. The
Queen returns, finds the King dead, makes
passionate action. The Poisoner with some three or
four come in again, seem to condole with her. The
dead body is carried away. The Poisoner woos the
Queen with gifts; she seems harsh awhile, but in
the end accepts love.

                                        [*Exeunt players.*]

OPHELIA   What means this, my lord?

HAMLET   Marry, this' miching mallico; it means mis-   135
chief.

OPHELIA   Belike this show imports the argument of the   137
play.

    Enter Prologue.

HAMLET   We shall know by this fellow. The players cannot keep counsel; they'll tell all.   140

OPHELIA   Will 'a tell us what this show meant?

HAMLET   Ay, or any show that you will show him. Be   142
not you ashamed to show, he'll not shame to tell you   143
what it means.

OPHELIA   You are naught, you are naught. I'll mark the   145
play.

PROLOGUE
    For us, and for our tragedy,
    Here stooping to your clemency,   148
    We beg your hearing patiently.   [*Exit.*]

HAMLET   Is this a prologue, or the posy of a ring?   150

OPHELIA   'Tis brief, my lord.

HAMLET   As woman's love.

    Enter [two Players as] King and Queen.

PLAYER KING
    Full thirty times hath Phoebus' cart gone round   153

135 this' miching mallico this is sneaking mischief   **137 Belike** probably.   **argument** plot   **140 counsel** secret   **142–143 Be not you** if you are
not   **145 naught** indecent. (Ophelia is reacting to Hamlet's pointed
remarks about not being ashamed to show all.)   **148 stooping** bowing
150 posy . . . ring brief motto in verse inscribed in a ring   **153 Phoebus'
cart** the sun god's chariot, making its yearly cycle

Neptune's salt wash and Tellus' orbèd ground,   154
And thirty dozen moons with borrowed sheen   155
About the world have times twelve thirties been,
Since love our hearts and Hymen did our hands   157
Unite commutual in most sacred bands.   158

PLAYER QUEEN
So many journeys may the sun and moon
Make us again count o'er ere love be done!
But, woe is me, you are so sick of late,
So far from cheer and from your former state,
That I distrust you. Yet, though I distrust,   163
Discomfort you, my lord, it nothing must.   164
For women's fear and love hold quantity;   165
In neither aught, or in extremity.   166
Now, what my love is, proof hath made you know,   167
And as my love is sized, my fear is so.   168
Where love is great, the littlest doubts are fear;
Where little fears grow great, great love grows there.

PLAYER KING
Faith, I must leave thee, love, and shortly too;
My operant powers their functions leave to do.   172
And thou shalt live in this fair world behind,   173
Honored, beloved; and haply one as kind
For husband shalt thou—

PLAYER QUEEN   O, confound the rest!
Such love must needs be treason in my breast.
In second husband let me be accurst!
None wed the second but who killed the first.   178

HAMLET   Wormwood, wormwood.

PLAYER QUEEN
The instances that second marriage move   180
Are base respects of thrift, but none of love.   181

154 salt wash the sea. **Tellus** goddess of the earth, of the *orbèd
ground* **155 borrowed** i.e., reflected **157 Hymen** god of matrimony
158 commutual mutually. **bands** bonds **163 distrust** am anxious
about **164 nothing** not at all **165 hold quantity** keep proportion with
one another **166 In . . . extremity** i.e., women fear and love either too
little or too much, but the two, fear and love, are equal in either case
167 proof experience **168 sized** in size **172 operant powers** vital
functions. **leave to do** cease to perform **173 behind** after I have
gone **178 None** i.e., let no woman. **but who** except her who
180 instances motives. **move** motivate **181 base . . . thrift** ignoble
considerations of material prosperity

A second time I kill my husband dead
When second husband kisses me in bed.

PLAYER KING

I do believe you think what now you speak,
But what we do determine oft we break.
Purpose is but the slave to memory,   186
Of violent birth, but poor validity,   187
Which now, like fruit unripe, sticks on the tree,   188
But fall unshaken when they mellow be.
Most necessary 'tis that we forget   190
To pay ourselves what to ourselves is debt.   191
What to ourselves in passion we propose,
The passion ending, doth the purpose lose.
The violence of either grief or joy
Their own enactures with themselves destroy.   195
Where joy most revels, grief doth most lament;   196
Grief joys, joy grieves, on slender accident.   197
This world is not for aye, nor 'tis not strange   198
That even our loves should with our fortunes change;
For 'tis a question left us yet to prove,
Whether love lead fortune, or else fortune love.
The great man down, you mark his favorite flies;   202
The poor advanced makes friends of enemies.   203
And hitherto doth love on fortune tend;   204
For who not needs shall never lack a friend,   205
And who in want a hollow friend doth try   206
Directly seasons him his enemy.   207
But, orderly to end where I begun,
Our wills and fates do so contrary run   209

---

186 Purpose . . . memory i.e., our good intentions are subject to forgetfulness   **187 validity** strength, durability   **188 Which** i.e., purpose
190–191 Most . . . debt i.e., it's inevitable that in time we forget the
obligations we have imposed on ourselves   **195 enactures** fulfillments
196–197 Where . . . accident i.e., the capacity for extreme joy and grief
go together, and often one extreme is instantly changed into its opposite
on the slightest provocation   **198 aye** ever   **202 down** fallen in fortune
203 The poor . . . enemies i.e., when one of humble station is promoted,
you see his enemies suddenly becoming his friends   **204 hitherto** up to
this point in the argument, or, to this extent.   **tend** attend   **205 who not
needs** he who is not in need (of wealth)   **206 who in want** he who, being
in need.   **try** test (his generosity)   **207 seasons him** ripens him into
209 Our . . . run what we want and what we get go so contrarily

That our devices still are overthrown;   210
Our thoughts are ours, their ends none of our own.   211
So think thou wilt no second husband wed,
But die thy thoughts when thy first lord is dead.

PLAYER QUEEN
Nor earth to me give food, nor heaven light,   214
Sport and repose lock from me day and night,   215
To desperation turn my trust and hope,
An anchor's cheer in prison be my scope!   217
Each opposite that blanks the face of joy   218
Meet what I would have well and it destroy!   219
Both here and hence pursue me lasting strife   220
If, once a widow, ever I be a wife!

HAMLET   If she should break it now!

PLAYER KING
'Tis deeply sworn. Sweet, leave me here awhile;
My spirits grow dull, and fain I would beguile   224
The tedious day with sleep.

PLAYER QUEEN   Sleep rock thy brain,
And never come mischance between us twain!
                    [*He sleeps.*] *Exit* [*Player Queen*].

HAMLET   Madam, how like you this play?

QUEEN   The lady doth protest too much, methinks.   228

HAMLET   O, but she'll keep her word.

KING   Have you heard the argument? Is there no offense   230
in 't?

HAMLET   No, no, they do but jest, poison in jest. No of- 232
fense i' the world.   233

KING   What do you call the play?

HAMLET   *The Mousetrap.* Marry, how? Tropically.   235
This play is the image of a murder done in Vienna.

210 devices still intentions continually   **211 ends** results   **214 Nor** let
neither   **215 Sport . . . night** may day deny me its pastimes and night
its repose   **217 anchor's cheer** anchorite's or hermit's fare.   **my scope**
the extent of my happiness   **218–219 Each . . . destroy** may every
adverse thing that causes the face of joy to turn pale meet and destroy
everything that I desire to see prosper.   **blanks** causes to blanch or
grow pale   **220 hence** in the life hereafter   **224 spirits** vital spirits
228 doth . . . much makes too many promises and protestations
230 argument plot   **230–233 offense . . . offense** cause for objection . . .
crime   **232 jest** make believe   **235 Tropically** figuratively. (The first
quarto reading, *trapically,* suggests a pun on *trap* in *Mousetrap*.)

Gonzago is the Duke's name, his wife, Baptista. You 237
shall see anon. 'Tis a knavish piece of work, but what
of that? Your Majesty, and we that have free souls, it 239
touches us not. Let the galled jade wince, our withers 240
are unwrung.   241

    Enter Lucianus.

This is one Lucianus, nephew to the King.

OPHELIA You are as good as a chorus, my lord.   243

HAMLET I could interpret between you and your love,
if I could see the puppets dallying.   245

OPHELIA You are keen, my lord, you are keen.   246

HAMLET It would cost you a groaning to take off mine
edge.

OPHELIA Still better, and worse.   249

HAMLET So you mis-take your husbands.—Begin, mur- 250
derer; leave thy damnable faces and begin. Come, the
croaking raven doth bellow for revenge.

LUCIANUS
Thoughts black, hands apt, drugs fit, and time agreeing,
Confederate season, else no creature seeing,   254
Thou mixture rank, of midnight weeds collected,
With Hecate's ban thrice blasted, thrice infected,   256
Thy natural magic and dire property   257
On wholesome life usurp immediately.
    [He pours the poison into the sleeper's ear.]

---

237 Duke's i.e., King's. (A slip that may be due to Shakespeare's possible source, the actual murder of the Duke of Urbino by Luigi Gonzaga in 1538.) **239 free** guiltless **240 galled jade** horse whose hide is rubbed by saddle or harness. **withers** the part between the horse's shoulder blades **241 unwrung** not rubbed sore **243 chorus** (In many Elizabethan plays the forthcoming action was explained by an actor known as the "chorus"; at a puppet show the actor who spoke the dialogue was known as an "interpreter," as indicated by the lines following.) **245 puppets dallying** (With sexual suggestion, continued in *keen*, i.e., sexually aroused, *groaning*, i.e., moaning in pregnancy, and *edge*, i.e., sexual desire or impetuosity.) **246 keen** sharp, bitter
249 Still . . . worse more keen, always *bettering* what other people say with witty wordplay, but at the same time more offensive **250 So** even thus (in marriage). **mis-take** take erringly, falseheartedly. (The marriage vows say, "for better, for worse.") **254 Confederate season** the time and occasion conspiring (to assist the murderer). **else** otherwise
256 Hecate's ban the curse of Hecate, the goddess of witchcraft
257 dire property baleful quality

HAMLET   'A poisons him i' the garden for his estate. His 259
name's Gonzago. The story is extant, and written in
very choice Italian. You shall see anon how the murderer gets the love of Gonzago's wife.

[Claudius rises.]

OPHELIA   The King rises.

HAMLET   What, frighted with false fire?   264

QUEEN   How fares my lord?

POLONIUS   Give o'er the play.

KING   Give me some light. Away!

POLONIUS   Lights, lights, lights!

Exeunt all but Hamlet and Horatio.

HAMLET

"Why, let the strucken deer go weep,   269
    The hart ungallèd play.   270
For some must watch, while some must sleep;   271
    Thus runs the world away."   272
Would not this, sir, and a forest of feathers—if the rest 273
of my fortunes turn Turk with me—with two Provin- 274
cial roses on my razed shoes, get me a fellowship in a 275
cry of players?   276

HORATIO   Half a share.

HAMLET   A whole one, I.

"For thou dost know, O Damon dear,   279
    This realm dismantled was   280
Of Jove himself, and now reigns here   281
    A very, very—pajock."   282

---

259 estate i.e., the kingship. **His** i.e., the King's **264 false fire**
the blank discharge of a gun loaded with powder but no shot
269–272 Why . . . away (Probably from an old ballad, with allusion to
the popular belief that a wounded deer retires to weep and die; cf. *As
You Like It*, 2.1.66.) **270 ungallèd** unafflicted **271 watch** remain
awake **272 Thus . . . away** thus the world goes **273 this** i.e., the play.
feathers (Allusion to the plumes that Elizabethan actors were fond of
wearing.) **274 turn Turk with** turn renegade against, go back on
274–275 Provincial roses rosettes of ribbon like the roses of a part of
France **275 razed** with ornamental slashing **275–276 fellowship
. . . players** partnership in a theatrical company. **cry** pack (of
hounds) **279 Damon** the friend of Pythias, as Horatio is friend of
Hamlet; or, a traditional pastoral name **280 dismantled** stripped,
divested **281 Of Jove** (Jove, like Hamlet's father, has been taken away,
leaving only a peacock or an ass.) **282 pajock** peacock, a bird with a
bad reputation. (Here substituted for the obvious rhyme-word "ass.")
Or possibly the word is *patchock*, savage, base person.

HORATIO You might have rhymed.

HAMLET O good Horatio, I'll take the ghost's word for a thousand pound. Didst perceive?

HORATIO Very well, my lord.

HAMLET Upon the talk of the poisoning?

HORATIO I did very well note him.

Enter Rosencrantz and Guildenstern.

HAMLET Aha! Come, some music! Come, the record- 289
ers.   290
       "For if the King like not the comedy,
          Why then, belike, he likes it not, perdy."   292
Come, some music.

GUILDENSTERN Good my lord, vouchsafe me a word with you.

HAMLET Sir, a whole history.

GUILDENSTERN The King, sir—

HAMLET Ay, sir, what of him?

GUILDENSTERN Is in his retirement marvelous dis- 299
tempered.   300

HAMLET With drink, sir?

GUILDENSTERN No, my lord, with choler.   302

HAMLET Your wisdom should show itself more richer to signify this to the doctor, for for me to put him to his purgation would perhaps plunge him into more 305
choler.

GUILDENSTERN Good my lord, put your discourse into some frame and start not so wildly from my affair. 308

HAMLET I am tame, sir. Pronounce.

GUILDENSTERN The Queen, your mother, in most great affliction of spirit, hath sent me to you.

HAMLET You are welcome.

289–290 recorders wind instruments of the flute kind   **292 perdy** (A corruption of the French *par dieu,* "by God.")   **299 retirement** withdrawal to his chambers   **299–300 distempered** out of humor. (But Hamlet deliberately plays on the wider application to any illness of mind or body, as in ll. 335–336, especially to drunkenness.)   **302 choler** i.e., anger. (But Hamlet takes the word in its more basic humors sense of "bilious disorder.")   **305 purgation** (Hamlet hints at something going beyond medical treatment to bloodletting and the extraction of confession.)   **308 frame** order.   **start** shy or jump away (like a horse; the opposite of *tame* in l. 309)

GUILDENSTERN   Nay, good my lord, this courtesy is not
of the right breed. If it shall please you to make me a 314
wholesome answer, I will do your mother's commandment; if not, your pardon and my return shall be the 316
end of my business.

HAMLET   Sir, I cannot.

ROSENCRANTZ   What, my lord?

HAMLET   Make you a wholesome answer; my wit's diseased. But, sir, such answer as I can make, you shall
command, or rather, as you say, my mother. Therefore
no more, but to the matter. My mother, you say—

ROSENCRANTZ   Then thus she says: your behavior hath
struck her into amazement and admiration.   325

HAMLET   O wonderful son, that can so stonish a mother!
But is there no sequel at the heels of this mother's admiration? Impart.

ROSENCRANTZ   She desires to speak with you in her
closet ere you go to bed.   330

HAMLET   We shall obey, were she ten times our mother.
Have you any further trade with us?

ROSENCRANTZ   My lord, you once did love me.

HAMLET   And do still, by these pickers and stealers.   334

ROSENCRANTZ   Good my lord, what is your cause of distemper? You do surely bar the door upon your own
liberty if you deny your griefs to your friend.   337

HAMLET   Sir, I lack advancement.

ROSENCRANTZ   How can that be, when you have the
voice of the King himself for your succession in Denmark?

HAMLET   Ay, sir, but "While the grass grows"—the 342
proverb is something musty.   343

   Enter the Players with recorders.

O, the recorders. Let me see one. [*He takes a recorder.*]

---

314 breed (1) kind (2) breeding, manners   **316 pardon** permission
to depart   **325 admiration** wonder   **330 closet** private chamber
334 pickers and stealers i.e., hands. (So called from the catechism, "to
keep my hands from picking and stealing.")   **337 deny** refuse to share
342 While . . . grows (The rest of the proverb is "the silly horse starves";
Hamlet may not live long enough to succeed to the kingdom.)
343 something somewhat   **s.d. Players** actors

To withdraw with you: why do you go about to recover 345
the wind of me, as if you would drive me into a toil? 346

GUILDENSTERN O, my lord, if my duty be too bold, my 347
love is too unmannerly. 348

HAMLET I do not well understand that. Will you play 349
upon this pipe?

GUILDENSTERN My lord, I cannot.

HAMLET I pray you.

GUILDENSTERN Believe me, I cannot.

HAMLET I do beseech you.

GUILDENSTERN I know no touch of it, my lord.

HAMLET It is as easy as lying. Govern these ventages 356
with your fingers and thumb, give it breath with your
mouth, and it will discourse most eloquent music.
Look you, these are the stops.

GUILDENSTERN But these cannot I command to any
utterance of harmony. I have not the skill.

HAMLET Why, look you now, how unworthy a thing
you make of me! You would play upon me, you would
seem to know my stops, you would pluck out the heart
of my mystery, you would sound me from my lowest 365
note to the top of my compass, and there is much 366
music, excellent voice, in this little organ, yet cannot 367
you make it speak. 'Sblood, do you think I am easier
to be played on than a pipe? Call me what instrument
you will, though you can fret me, you cannot play 370
upon me.

Enter Polonius.

God bless you, sir!

POLONIUS My lord, the Queen would speak with you,
and presently. 374

HAMLET Do you see yonder cloud that's almost in
shape of a camel?

345 withdraw speak privately **345–346 recover the wind** get to the
windward side (thus driving the game into the toil, or net) **346 toil**
snare **347–348 if . . . unmannerly** if I am using an unmannerly boldness, it is my love that occasions it **349 I . . . that** i.e., I don't understand how genuine love can be unmannerly **356 ventages** stops of the
recorder **365 sound** (1) fathom (2) produce sound in **366 compass**
range (of voice) **367 organ** musical instrument **370 fret** irritate (with a
quibble on *fret* meaning the piece of wood, gut, or metal that regulates
the fingering on an instrument) **374 presently** at once

POLONIUS   By the Mass and 'tis, like a camel indeed.
HAMLET   Methinks it is like a weasel.
POLONIUS   It is backed like a weasel.
HAMLET   Or like a whale?
POLONIUS   Very like a whale.
HAMLET   Then I will come to my mother by and by. 382
  [*Aside.*] They fool me to the top of my bent.—I will 383
  come by and by.
POLONIUS   I will say so.   [*Exit.*]
HAMLET   "By and by" is easily said. Leave me, friends.
                  [*Exeunt all but Hamlet.*]
'Tis now the very witching time of night,   387
When churchyards yawn and hell itself breathes out
Contagion to this world. Now could I drink hot blood 389
And do such bitter business as the day
Would quake to look on. Soft, now to my mother.
O heart, lose not thy nature! Let not ever
The soul of Nero enter this firm bosom.   393
Let me be cruel, not unnatural;
I will speak daggers to her, but use none.
My tongue and soul in this be hypocrites:
How in my words soever she be shent,   397
To give them seals never my soul consent!   *Exit.* 398

❖

3.3   *Enter King, Rosencrantz, and Guildenstern.*

KING
  I like him not, nor stands it safe with us   1
  To let his madness range. Therefore prepare you.
  I your commission will forthwith dispatch,   3
  And he to England shall along with you.

---

382 by and by quite soon   **383 fool me** make me play the fool.   **top of my bent** limit of my ability or endurance. (Literally, the extent to which a bow may be bent.)   **387 witching time** time when spells are cast and evil is abroad   **389 Now could I** i.e., now I might be tempted to **393 Nero** murderer of his mother, Agrippina   **397 How . . . soever** however much by my words.   **shent** rebuked   **398 give them seals** i.e., confirm them with deeds

3.3. Location: The castle.
1 him i.e., his behavior   **3 dispatch** prepare, cause to be drawn up

The terms of our estate may not endure   5
Hazard so near 's as doth hourly grow
Out of his brows.

GUILDENSTERN   We will ourselves provide.   7
Most holy and religious fear it is   8
To keep those many many bodies safe
That live and feed upon Your Majesty.

ROSENCRANTZ
The single and peculiar life is bound   11
With all the strength and armor of the mind
To keep itself from noyance, but much more   13
That spirit upon whose weal depends and rests
The lives of many. The cess of majesty   15
Dies not alone, but like a gulf doth draw   16
What's near it with it; or it is a massy wheel   17
Fixed on the summit of the highest mount,
To whose huge spokes ten thousand lesser things
Are mortised and adjoined, which, when it falls,   20
Each small annexment, petty consequence,   21
Attends the boisterous ruin. Never alone   22
Did the King sigh, but with a general groan.

KING
Arm you, I pray you, to this speedy voyage,   24
For we will fetters put about this fear,
Which now goes too free-footed.

ROSENCRANTZ   We will haste us.
     Exeunt Gentlemen [Rosencrantz and Guildenstern].

     Enter Polonius.

POLONIUS
My lord, he's going to his mother's closet.
Behind the arras I'll convey myself   28

---

5 terms condition, circumstances.   **our estate** my royal position
7 brows i.e., effronteries, threatening frowns, or contrivances   **8 religious fear** sacred duty   **11 single and peculiar** individual and private
13 noyance harm   **15 cess** decease, cessation   **16 gulf** whirlpool
17 massy massive   **20 when it falls** i.e., when it descends, like the wheel
of Fortune, bringing a king down with it   **21 Each . . . consequence** i.e.,
every hanger-on and unimportant person or thing connected with the
King   **22 Attends** participates in   **24 Arm** prepare   **28 arras** screen
of tapestry placed around the walls of household apartments. (On the
Elizabethan stage, the arras was presumably over a door or discovery
space in the tiring-house facade.)

To hear the process. I'll warrant she'll tax him home,   29
And, as you said—and wisely was it said—
'Tis meet that some more audience than a mother,   31
Since nature makes them partial, should o'erhear
The speech, of vantage. Fare you well, my liege.   33
I'll call upon you ere you go to bed
And tell you what I know.

KING   Thanks, dear my lord.

                          Exit [*Polonius*].

O, my offense is rank, it smells to heaven;
It hath the primal eldest curse upon 't,   37
A brother's murder. Pray can I not,
Though inclination be as sharp as will;   39
My stronger guilt defeats my strong intent,
And like a man to double business bound   41
I stand in pause where I shall first begin,
And both neglect. What if this cursèd hand
Were thicker than itself with brother's blood,
Is there not rain enough in the sweet heavens
To wash it white as snow? Whereto serves mercy   46
But to confront the visage of offense?   47
And what's in prayer but this twofold force,
To be forestallèd ere we come to fall,   49
Or pardoned being down? Then I'll look up.
My fault is past. But, O, what form of prayer
Can serve my turn? "Forgive me my foul murder"?
That cannot be, since I am still possessed
Of those effects for which I did the murder:
My crown, mine own ambition, and my queen.
May one be pardoned and retain th' offense?   56
In the corrupted currents of this world   57
Offense's gilded hand may shove by justice,   58

---

29 process proceedings.   **tax him home** reprove him severely   **31 meet**
fitting   **33 of vantage** from an advantageous place, or, in addition
37 the primal eldest curse the curse of Cain, the first murderer; he killed
his brother Abel   **39 Though . . . will** though my desire is as strong as
my determination   **41 bound** (1) destined (2) obliged. (The King wants to
repent and still enjoy what he has gained.)   **46–47 Whereto . . . offense**
i.e., for what function does mercy serve other than to undo the effects
of sin   **49 forestallèd** prevented (from sinning)   **56 th' offense** i.e., the
thing for which one offended   **57 currents** courses   **58 gilded hand**
hand offering gold as a bribe.   **shove by** thrust aside

And oft 'tis seen the wicked prize itself 59
Buys out the law. But 'tis not so above.
There is no shuffling, there the action lies 61
In his true nature, and we ourselves compelled, 62
Even to the teeth and forehead of our faults, 63
To give in evidence. What then? What rests? 64
Try what repentance can. What can it not?
Yet what can it, when one cannot repent?
O wretched state! O bosom black as death!
O limèd soul, that, struggling to be free, 68
Art more engaged! Help, angels! Make assay. 69
Bow, stubborn knees, and heart with strings of steel,
Be soft as sinews of the newborn babe!
All may be well. [*He kneels.*]

   Enter Hamlet.

HAMLET
Now might I do it pat, now 'a is a-praying; 73
And now I'll do 't. [*He draws his sword.*] And so 'a
  goes to heaven,
And so am I revenged. That would be scanned: 75
A villain kills my father, and for that,
I, his sole son, do this same villain send
To heaven.
Why, this is hire and salary, not revenge.
'A took my father grossly, full of bread, 80
With all his crimes broad blown, as flush as May; 81
And how his audit stands who knows save heaven? 82
But in our circumstance and course of thought 83
'Tis heavy with him. And am I then revenged,
To take him in the purging of his soul,

59 **wicked prize** prize won by wickedness   61 **There** i.e., in heaven.
shuffling escape by trickery.   **the action lies** the accusation is made
manifest, comes up for consideration. (A legal metaphor.)   62 **his** its
63 **to the teeth and forehead** face to face, concealing nothing   64 **give in**
provide.   **rests** remains   68 **limèd** caught as with birdlime, a sticky
substance used to ensnare birds   69 **engaged** embedded.   **assay** trial.
(Said to himself.)   73 **pat** opportunely   75 **would be scanned** needs to
be looked into, or, would be interpreted as follows   80 **grossly** i.e., not
spiritually prepared.   **full of bread** i.e., enjoying his worldly pleasures.
(See Ezekiel 16:49.)   81 **crimes broad blown** sins in full bloom.   **flush**
lusty   82 **audit** account   83 **in . . . thought** as we see it from our mortal
perspective

When he is fit and seasoned for his passage?   86
No!
Up, sword, and know thou a more horrid hent.   88
                    [*He puts up his sword.*]
When he is drunk asleep, or in his rage,
Or in th' incestuous pleasure of his bed,
At game a-swearing, or about some act
That has no relish of salvation in 't—   92
Then trip him, that his heels may kick at heaven,
And that his soul may be as damned and black
As hell, whereto it goes. My mother stays.   95
This physic but prolongs thy sickly days.   *Exit.* 96
KING
  My words fly up, my thoughts remain below.
  Words without thoughts never to heaven go.   *Exit.*

✤

3.4   *Enter [Queen] Gertrude and Polonius.*

POLONIUS
  'A will come straight. Look you lay home to him.   1
  Tell him his pranks have been too broad to bear with, 2
  And that Your Grace hath screened and stood between
  Much heat and him. I'll shroud me even here.   4
  Pray you, be round with him.   5
HAMLET (*Within*)   Mother, Mother, Mother!
QUEEN   I'll warrant you, fear me not.
  Withdraw, I hear him coming.
               [*Polonius hides behind the arras.*]

  Enter Hamlet.

HAMLET   Now, Mother, what's the matter?

86 seasoned matured, readied   **88 know . . . hent** await to be grasped by
me on a more horrid occasion   **92 relish** trace, savor   **95 stays** awaits
(me)   **96 physic** purging (by prayer), or, Hamlet's postponement of the
killing

3.4. Location: The Queen's private chamber.
1 lay thrust (i.e., reprove him soundly)   **2 broad** unrestrained   **4 Much
heat** i.e., the King's anger.   **shroud** conceal (with ironic fitness to
Polonius's imminent death. The word is only in the first quarto; the
second quarto and the Folio read "silence.")   **5 round** blunt

QUEEN

    Hamlet, thou hast thy father much offended.   10

HAMLET

    Mother, you have my father much offended.

QUEEN

    Come, come, you answer with an idle tongue.   12

HAMLET

    Go, go, you question with a wicked tongue.

QUEEN

    Why, how now, Hamlet?

HAMLET   What's the matter now?

QUEEN

    Have you forgot me?

HAMLET   No, by the rood, not so: 15

    You are the Queen, your husband's brother's wife,

    And—would it were not so!—you are my mother.

QUEEN

    Nay, then, I'll set those to you that can speak.

HAMLET

    Come, come, and sit you down; you shall not budge.

    You go not till I set you up a glass

    Where you may see the inmost part of you.

QUEEN

    What wilt thou do? Thou wilt not murder me?

    Help, ho!

POLONIUS [*Behind the arras*]   What ho! Help!

HAMLET [*Drawing*]

    How now? A rat? Dead for a ducat, dead!   25

              [*He thrusts his rapier through the arras.*]

POLONIUS [*Behind the arras*]

    O, I am slain!   [*He falls and dies.*]

QUEEN   O me, what hast thou done?

HAMLET   Nay, I know not. Is it the King?

QUEEN

    O, what a rash and bloody deed is this!

HAMLET

    A bloody deed—almost as bad, good Mother,

    As kill a king and marry with his brother.

---

10 thy father i.e., your stepfather, Claudius   **12 idle** foolish   **15 forgot me** i.e., forgotten that I am your mother.   **rood** cross of Christ
25 Dead for a ducat i.e., I bet a ducat he's dead, whoever I killed; or, a ducat is his life's fee

QUEEN
  As kill a king!
HAMLET   Ay, lady, it was my word.
            [*He parts the arras and discovers Polonius.*]
  Thou wretched, rash, intruding fool, farewell!
  I took thee for thy better. Take thy fortune.
  Thou find'st to be too busy is some danger.—   34
  Leave wringing of your hands. Peace, sit you down,
  And let me wring your heart, for so I shall,
  If it be made of penetrable stuff,
  If damnèd custom have not brazed it so   38
  That it be proof and bulwark against sense.   39
QUEEN
  What have I done, that thou dar'st wag thy tongue
  In noise so rude against me?
HAMLET   Such an act
  That blurs the grace and blush of modesty,
  Calls virtue hypocrite, takes off the rose
  From the fair forehead of an innocent love
  And sets a blister there, makes marriage vows   45
  As false as dicers' oaths. O, such a deed
  As from the body of contraction plucks   47
  The very soul, and sweet religion makes   48
  A rhapsody of words. Heaven's face does glow   49
  O'er this solidity and compound mass   50
  With tristful visage, as against the doom,   51
  Is thought-sick at the act.
QUEEN   Ay me, what act,   52
  That roars so loud and thunders in the index?   53
HAMLET [*Showing her two likenesses*]
  Look here upon this picture, and on this,
  The counterfeit presentment of two brothers.   55
  See what a grace was seated on this brow:

---

34 busy playing the busybody   **38 damnèd custom** habitual wickedness. **brazed** brazened, hardened   **39 proof** armor. **sense** feeling
45 sets a blister i.e., brands as a harlot   **47 contraction** the marriage
contract   **48 sweet religion makes** i.e., makes marriage vows
49 rhapsody senseless string   **49–52 Heaven's . . . act** heaven's face
looks down upon this solid world, this compound mass, with sorrowful
face as though the day of doom were near, and is thought-sick at the
deed (i.e., Gertrude's marriage)   **53 index** table of contents, prelude or
preface   **55 counterfeit presentment** portrayed representation

Hyperion's curls, the front of Jove himself,	57
An eye like Mars to threaten and command,	
A station like the herald Mercury	59
New-lighted on a heaven-kissing hill—	60
A combination and a form indeed	
Where every god did seem to set his seal	62
To give the world assurance of a man.	
This was your husband. Look you now what follows:	
Here is your husband, like a mildewed ear,	65
Blasting his wholesome brother. Have you eyes?	66
Could you on this fair mountain leave to feed	
And batten on this moor? Ha, have you eyes?	68
You cannot call it love, for at your age	
The heyday in the blood is tame, it's humble,	70
And waits upon the judgment, and what judgment	
Would step from this to this? Sense, sure, you have,	72
Else could you not have motion, but sure that sense	
Is apoplexed, for madness would not err,	74
Nor sense to ecstasy was ne'er so thralled,	
But it reserved some quantity of choice	76
To serve in such a difference. What devil was 't	77
That thus hath cozened you at hoodman-blind?	78
Eyes without feeling, feeling without sight,	
Ears without hands or eyes, smelling sans all,	80
Or but a sickly part of one true sense	
Could not so mope. O shame, where is thy blush?	82
Rebellious hell,	
If thou canst mutine in a matron's bones,	84

57 Hyperion's the sun god's. **front** brow   **59 station** manner of standing.   **Mercury** winged messenger of the gods   **60 New-lighted** newly alighted   **62 set his seal** i.e., affix his approval   **65 ear** i.e., of grain **66 Blasting** blighting   **68 batten** gorge.   **moor** barren upland (suggesting also "dark-skinned")   **70 heyday** state of excitement.   **blood** passion   **72 Sense** perception through the five senses (the functions of the middle or sensible soul)   **74 apoplexed** paralyzed. (Hamlet goes on to explain that without such a paralysis of will, mere madness would not so err, nor would the five senses so enthrall themselves to *ecstasy* or lunacy; even such deranged states of mind would be able to make the obvious choice between Hamlet Senior and Claudius.)   **err** so err **76 But** but that   **77 To . . . difference** to help in making choice between two such men   **78 cozened** cheated.   **hoodman-blind** blindman's buff. (In this game, says Hamlet, the devil must have pushed Claudius toward Gertrude while she was blindfolded.)   **80 sans** without   **82 mope** be dazed, act aimlessly   **84 mutine** incite mutiny

To flaming youth let virtue be as wax   85
And melt in her own fire. Proclaim no shame   86
When the compulsive ardor gives the charge,   87
Since frost itself as actively doth burn,   88
And reason panders will.   89

QUEEN   O Hamlet, speak no more!
Thou turn'st my eyes into my very soul,
And there I see such black and grainèd spots   92
As will not leave their tinct.   Nay, but to live   93

HAMLET
In the rank sweat of an enseamèd bed,   94
Stewed in corruption, honeying and making love   95
Over the nasty sty!

QUEEN   O, speak to me no more!
These words like daggers enter in my ears.
No more, sweet Hamlet!

HAMLET   A murderer and a villain,
A slave that is not twentieth part the tithe   100
Of your precedent lord, a vice of kings,   101
A cutpurse of the empire and the rule,
That from a shelf the precious diadem stole
And put it in his pocket!

QUEEN   No more!

Enter Ghost [in his nightgown].

HAMLET   A king of shreds and patches—   106
Save me, and hover o'er me with your wings,
You heavenly guards! What would your gracious figure?

QUEEN   Alas, he's mad!

HAMLET
Do you not come your tardy son to chide,

85–86 be as wax . . . fire i.e., melt like a candle or stick of sealing wax held over its own flame   **86–89 Proclaim . . . will** call it no shameful business when the compelling ardor of youth delivers the attack, i.e., commits lechery, since the frost of advanced age burns with as active a fire of lust and reason perverts itself by fomenting lust rather than restraining it   **92 grainèd** dyed in grain, indelible   **93 leave their tinct** surrender their color   **94 enseamèd** saturated in the grease and filth of passionate lovemaking   **95 Stewed** soaked, bathed (with a suggestion of *stew*, brothel)   **100 tithe** tenth part   **101 precedent** former (i.e., the elder Hamlet).   **vice** buffoon. (A reference to the Vice of the morality plays.)   **106 shreds and patches** i.e., motley, the traditional costume of the clown or fool

That, lapsed in time and passion, lets go by   111
Th' important acting of your dread command?   112
O, say!

GHOST

Do not forget. This visitation
Is but to whet thy almost blunted purpose.
But look, amazement on thy mother sits.   116
O, step between her and her fighting soul!
Conceit in weakest bodies strongest works.   118
Speak to her, Hamlet.

HAMLET   How is it with you, lady?

QUEEN   Alas, how is 't with you,
That you do bend your eye on vacancy,
And with th' incorporal air do hold discourse?   122
Forth at your eyes your spirits wildly peep,
And, as the sleeping soldiers in th' alarm,   124
Your bedded hair, like life in excrements,   125
Start up and stand on end. O gentle son,
Upon the heat and flame of thy distemper
Sprinkle cool patience. Whereon do you look?

HAMLET

On him, on him! Look you how pale he glares!
His form and cause conjoined, preaching to stones,   130
Would make them capable.—Do not look upon me,   131
Lest with this piteous action you convert   132
My stern effects. Then what I have to do   133
Will want true color—tears perchance for blood.   134

QUEEN   To whom do you speak this?

HAMLET   Do you see nothing there?

---

111 lapsed in time and passion having allowed time to lapse and passion to cool, or, having lost momentum through excessive indulgence in
passion   **112 important** importunate, urgent   **116 amazement** distraction   **118 Conceit** imagination   **122 incorporal** immaterial   **124 as . . .
alarm** like soldiers called out of sleep by an alarum   **125 bedded** laid in
smooth layers.   **like life in excrements** i.e., as though hair, an out-
growth of the body, had a life of its own. (Hair was thought to be lifeless
because it lacks sensation, and so its standing on end would be unnatural and ominous.)   **130 His . . . conjoined** his appearance joined to his
cause for speaking   **131 capable** receptive   **132–133 convert . . . effects**
divert me from my stern duty   **134 want . . . blood** lack plausibility so
that (with a play on the normal sense of *color*) I shall shed colorless
tears instead of blood

QUEEN
Nothing at all, yet all that is I see.
HAMLET   Nor did you nothing hear?
QUEEN   No, nothing but ourselves.
HAMLET
Why, look you there, look how it steals away!
My father, in his habit as he lived!   141
Look where he goes even now out at the portal!
                          Exit Ghost.

QUEEN
This is the very coinage of your brain.   143
This bodiless creation ecstasy   144
Is very cunning in.   145
HAMLET   Ecstasy?
My pulse as yours doth temperately keep time,
And makes as healthful music. It is not madness
That I have uttered. Bring me to the test,
And I the matter will reword, which madness   150
Would gambol from. Mother, for love of grace,   151
Lay not that flattering unction to your soul   152
That not your trespass but my madness speaks.
It will but skin and film the ulcerous place,   154
Whiles rank corruption, mining all within,   155
Infects unseen. Confess yourself to heaven,
Repent what's past, avoid what is to come,
And do not spread the compost on the weeds   158
To make them ranker. Forgive me this my virtue;   159
For in the fatness of these pursy times   160
Virtue itself of vice must pardon beg,
Yea, curb and woo for leave to do him good.   162
QUEEN
O Hamlet, thou hast cleft my heart in twain.
HAMLET
O, throw away the worser part of it,

141 habit dress. **as** as when   **143 very** mere   **144–145 This . . . in** madness is skillful in creating this kind of hallucination   **150 reword** repeat word for word   **151 gambol** skip away   **152 unction** ointment **154 skin** grow a skin for   **155 mining** working under the surface **158 compost** manure   **159 this my virtue** my virtuous talk in reproving you   **160 fatness** grossness. **pursy** flabby, out of shape   **162 curb** bow, bend the knee. **leave** permission

And live the purer with the other half.
Good night. But go not to my uncle's bed;
Assume a virtue, if you have it not.
That monster, custom, who all sense doth eat,   168
Of habits devil, is angel yet in this,   169
That to the use of actions fair and good
He likewise gives a frock or livery   171
That aptly is put on. Refrain tonight,   172
And that shall lend a kind of easiness
To the next abstinence; the next more easy;
For use almost can change the stamp of nature,   175
And either . . . the devil, or throw him out   176
With wondrous potency. Once more, good night;
And when you are desirous to be blest,   178
I'll blessing beg of you. For this same lord,   179

                    [Pointing to Polonius]
I do repent; but heaven hath pleased it so
To punish me with this, and this with me,
That I must be their scourge and minister.   182
I will bestow him, and will answer well   183
The death I gave him. So, again, good night.
I must be cruel only to be kind.
This bad begins, and worse remains behind.   186
One word more, good lady.
QUEEN   What shall I do?
HAMLET
Not this by no means that I bid you do:
Let the bloat king tempt you again to bed,   189
Pinch wanton on your cheek, call you his mouse,   190

---

168 who . . . eat which consumes all proper or natural feeling, all
sensibility   **169 Of habits devil** devil-like in prompting evil habits
171 livery an outer appearance, a customary garb (and hence a predis-
position easily assumed in time of stress)   **172 aptly** readily   **175 use**
habit.   **the stamp of nature** our inborn traits   **176 And either** (A defective line usually emended by inserting the word *master* after *either*,
following the fourth quarto and early editors.)   **178–179 when . . . you**
i.e., when you are ready to be penitent and seek God's blessing, I will
ask your blessing as a dutiful son should (on the occasion of departure)
182 their scourge and minister i.e., agent of heavenly retribution. (By
scourge, Hamlet also suggests that he himself will eventually suffer
punishment in the process of fulfilling heaven's will.)   **183 bestow** stow,
dispose of.   **answer** account for   **186 This** i.e., the killing of Polonius.
behind to come   **189 bloat** bloated   **190 Pinch wanton** i.e., leave his
love pinches on your cheeks, branding you as wanton

And let him, for a pair of reechy kisses, 191
Or paddling in your neck with his damned fingers, 192
Make you to ravel all this matter out 193
That I essentially am not in madness,
But mad in craft. 'Twere good you let him know, 195
For who that's but a queen, fair, sober, wise,
Would from a paddock, from a bat, a gib, 197
Such dear concernings hide? Who would do so? 198
No, in despite of sense and secrecy,
Unpeg the basket on the house's top, 200
Let the birds fly, and like the famous ape, 201
To try conclusions, in the basket creep 202
And break your own neck down. 203

QUEEN
 Be thou assured, if words be made of breath,
 And breath of life, I have no life to breathe
 What thou hast said to me.

HAMLET
 I must to England. You know that?
QUEEN   Alack,
 I had forgot. 'Tis so concluded on.

HAMLET
 There's letters sealed, and my two schoolfellows,
 Whom I will trust as I will adders fanged,
 They bear the mandate; they must sweep my way 211
 And marshal me to knavery. Let it work. 212
 For 'tis the sport to have the enginer 213
 Hoist with his own petard, and 't shall go hard 214
 But I will delve one yard below their mines 215

---

191 reechy dirty, filthy **192 paddling** fingering amorously **193 ravel
. . . out** unravel, disclose **195 in craft** by cunning. **good** (Said sarcasti-
cally; also the following 8 lines.) **197 paddock** toad. **gib** tomcat
198 dear concernings important affairs **200 Unpeg the basket** open the
cage, i.e., let out the secret **201 famous ape** (in a story now lost)
202 conclusions experiments (in which the ape apparently enters a cage
from which birds have been released and then tries to fly out of the
cage as they have done, falling to his death) **203 down** in the fall;
utterly **211–212 sweep . . . knavery** sweep a path before me and conduct me to some *knavery* or treachery prepared for me **212 work**
proceed **213 enginer** maker of military contrivances **214 Hoist with
petard** blown up by. **petard** an explosive used to blow in a door or make a
breach **214–215 't shall . . . will** unless luck is against me, I will
215 mines tunnels used in warfare to undermine the enemy's emplace-
ments; Hamlet will countermine by going under their mines

And blow them at the moon. O, 'tis most sweet
When in one line two crafts directly meet.   217
This man shall set me packing.   218
I'll lug the guts into the neighbor room.
Mother, good night indeed. This counselor
Is now most still, most secret, and most grave,
Who was in life a foolish prating knave.—
Come, sir, to draw toward an end with you.—   223
Good night, Mother.

Exeunt [separately, Hamlet
dragging in Polonius].

✢

217 **in one line** i.e., mines and countermines on a collision course, or
the countermines directly below the mines. **crafts** acts of guile, plots
218 **set me packing** set me to making schemes, and set me to lugging
(him), and, also, send me off in a hurry 223 **draw . . . end** finish up
(with a pun on *draw*, pull)

4.1 *Enter King and Queen, with Rosencrantz and Guildenstern.*

KING

There's matter in these sighs, these profound heaves. 1
You must translate; 'tis fit we understand them.
Where is your son?

QUEEN

Bestow this place on us a little while.
                    [*Exeunt Rosencrantz and Guildenstern.*]
Ah, mine own lord, what have I seen tonight!

KING

What, Gertrude? How does Hamlet?

QUEEN

Mad as the sea and wind when both contend
Which is the mightier. In his lawless fit,
Behind the arras hearing something stir,
Whips out his rapier, cries, "A rat, a rat!"
And in this brainish apprehension kills 11
The unseen good old man.

KING   O heavy deed! 12
It had been so with us, had we been there. 13
His liberty is full of threats to all—
To you yourself, to us, to everyone.
Alas, how shall this bloody deed be answered? 16
It will be laid to us, whose providence 17
Should have kept short, restrained, and out of haunt 18
This mad young man. But so much was our love,
We would not understand what was most fit,
But, like the owner of a foul disease,
To keep it from divulging, let it feed 22
Even on the pith of life. Where is he gone?

4.1. Location: The castle.
s.d. Enter . . . Queen (Some editors argue that Gertrude never exits in
3.4 and that the scene is continuous here, but the second quarto marks
an entrance for her and at l. 35 Claudius speaks of Gertrude's *closet* as
though it were elsewhere. A short time has elapsed during which the
King has become aware of her highly wrought emotional state.)
1 matter significance   **11 brainish apprehension** headstrong conception   **12 heavy** grievous   **13 us** i.e., me. (The royal "we"; also in l. 15.)
16 answered explained   **17 providence** foresight   **18 short** i.e., on a
short tether.   **out of haunt** secluded   **22 divulging** becoming evident

QUEEN
  To draw apart the body he hath killed,
  O'er whom his very madness, like some ore   25
  Among a mineral of metals base,   26
  Shows itself pure: 'a weeps for what is done.
KING   O Gertrude, come away!
  The sun no sooner shall the mountains touch
  But we will ship him hence, and this vile deed
  We must with all our majesty and skill
  Both countenance and excuse.—Ho, Guildenstern!

        Enter Rosencrantz and Guildenstern.

  Friends both, go join you with some further aid.
  Hamlet in madness hath Polonius slain,
  And from his mother's closet hath he dragged him.
  Go seek him out, speak fair, and bring the body
  Into the chapel. I pray you, haste in this.
          [*Exeunt Rosencrantz and Guildenstern.*]
  Come, Gertrude, we'll call up our wisest friends
  And let them know both what we mean to do
  And what's untimely done.   40
  Whose whisper o'er the world's diameter,   41
  As level as the cannon to his blank,   42
  Transports his poisoned shot, may miss our name
  And hit the woundless air. O, come away!   44
  My soul is full of discord and dismay.   *Exeunt.*

                        ❖

4.2   *Enter Hamlet.*

HAMLET   Safely stowed.
ROSENCRANTZ, GUILDENSTERN (*Within*) Hamlet! Lord
  Hamlet!

---

25 ore vein of gold   **26 mineral** mine   **40 And . . . done** (A defective line;
conjectures as to the missing words include *So, haply, slander* [Capell
and others]; *For, haply, slander* [Theobald and others]; and *So envious
slander* [Jenkins].)   **41 diameter** extent from side to side   **42 As level**
with as direct aim.   **his blank** its target at point-blank range
44 woundless invulnerable

4.2. Location: The castle.

HAMLET   But soft, what noise? Who calls on Hamlet? O,
here they come.

Enter Rosencrantz and Guildenstern.

ROSENCRANTZ
What have you done, my lord, with the dead body?
HAMLET
Compounded it with dust, whereto 'tis kin.
ROSENCRANTZ
Tell us where 'tis, that we may take it thence
And bear it to the chapel.
HAMLET   Do not believe it.
ROSENCRANTZ   Believe what?
HAMLET   That I can keep your counsel and not mine   12
own. Besides, to be demanded of a sponge, what rep-   13
lication should be made by the son of a king?   14
ROSENCRANTZ   Take you me for a sponge, my lord?
HAMLET   Ay, sir, that soaks up the King's countenance,   16
his rewards, his authorities. But such officers do the
King best service in the end. He keeps them, like an
ape, in the corner of his jaw, first mouthed to be last
swallowed. When he needs what you have gleaned, it
is but squeezing you, and, sponge, you shall be dry
again.
ROSENCRANTZ   I understand you not, my lord.
HAMLET   I am glad of it. A knavish speech sleeps in a   24
foolish ear.
ROSENCRANTZ   My lord, you must tell us where the
body is and go with us to the King.
HAMLET   The body is with the King, but the King is not   28
with the body. The King is a thing—   29
GUILDENSTERN   A thing, my lord?

12–13 That . . . own (Perhaps Hamlet is suggesting that they have their
secrets and he has his.)   **13 demanded of** questioned by   **13–14 rep-
lication** reply   **16 countenance** favor   **24 sleeps in** has no meaning to
28–29 The . . . body (Perhaps alludes to the legal commonplace of "the
king's two bodies," which drew a distinction between the sacred office
of kingship and the particular mortal who possessed it at any given
time. Hence, although Claudius's body is necessarily a part of him, true
kingship is not contained in it. Similarly, Claudius will have Polonius's
body when it is found, but there is no kingship in this business either.)

HAMLET Of nothing. Bring me to him. Hide fox, and   31
all after!   *Exeunt.* 32

❖

4.3   *Enter King, and two or three.*

KING
I have sent to seek him, and to find the body.
How dangerous is it that this man goes loose!
Yet must not we put the strong law on him.
He's loved of the distracted multitude,   4
Who like not in their judgment, but their eyes,   5
And where 'tis so, th' offender's scourge is weighed,   6
But never the offense. To bear all smooth and even,   7
This sudden sending him away must seem
Deliberate pause. Diseases desperate grown   9
By desperate appliance are relieved,   10
Or not at all.

> *Enter Rosencrantz, [Guildenstern,] and all the
> rest.*

>   How now, what hath befall'n?
ROSENCRANTZ
Where the dead body is bestowed, my lord,
We cannot get from him.
KING   But where is he?
ROSENCRANTZ
Without, my lord; guarded, to know your pleasure.
KING
Bring him before us.
ROSENCRANTZ   Ho! Bring in the lord.

> *They enter [with Hamlet].*

31 Of nothing (1) of no account (2) lacking the essence of kingship, as
in ll. 28–29 and note   **31–32 Hide . . . after** (An old signal cry in the game
of hide-and-seek, suggesting that Hamlet now runs away from them.)

4.3. Location: The castle.
4 distracted fickle, unstable   **5 Who . . . eyes** who choose not by judgment but by appearance   **6 scourge** punishment.   **weighed** sympatheti-
cally considered   **7 To . . . even** to manage the business in an unprovoc-
ative way   **9 Deliberate pause** carefully considered action   **10 appliance** remedy, treatment

KING　Now, Hamlet, where's Polonius?

HAMLET　At supper.

KING　At supper? Where?

HAMLET　Not where he eats, but where 'a is eaten. A
certain convocation of politic worms are e'en at him. 20
Your worm is your only emperor for diet. We fat all 21
creatures else to fat us, and we fat ourselves for maggots. Your fat king and your lean beggar is but
variable service—two dishes, but to one table. That's 24
the end.

KING　Alas, alas!

HAMLET　A man may fish with the worm that hath eat 27
of a king, and eat of the fish that hath fed of that
worm.

KING　What dost thou mean by this?

HAMLET　Nothing but to show you how a king may go
a progress through the guts of a beggar. 32

KING　Where is Polonius?

HAMLET　In heaven. Send thither to see. If your messenger find him not there, seek him i' th' other place yourself. But if indeed you find him not within this month,
you shall nose him as you go up the stairs into the
lobby.

KING [*To some attendants*]　Go seek him there.

HAMLET　'A will stay till you come. [*Exeunt attendants.*]

KING

Hamlet, this deed, for thine especial safety—
Which we do tender, as we dearly grieve 42
For that which thou hast done—must send thee hence
With fiery quickness. Therefore prepare thyself.
The bark is ready, and the wind at help, 45
Th' associates tend, and everything is bent 46
For England.

HAMLET　For England!

KING　Ay, Hamlet.

20 politic worms crafty worms (suited to a master spy like Polonius).
e'en even now　**21 Your worm** your average worm. (On *your*, compare
your fat king and your lean beggar in l. 23.)　**diet** food, eating (with a
punning reference to the Diet of Worms, a famous *convocation* held in
1521)　**24 variable service** different courses of a single meal　**27 eat**
eaten. (Pronounced *et*.)　**32 progress** royal journey of state　**42 tender**
regard, hold dear.　**dearly** intensely　**45 bark** sailing vessel　**46 tend**
wait.　**bent** in readiness

HAMLET Good.

KING

So is it, if thou knew'st our purposes.

HAMLET I see a cherub that sees them. But come, for 52
England! Farewell, dear Mother.

KING Thy loving father, Hamlet.

HAMLET My mother. Father and mother is man and
wife, man and wife is one flesh, and so, my mother.
Come, for England!   *Exit.*

KING

Follow him at foot; tempt him with speed aboard.   58
Delay it not. I'll have him hence tonight.
Away! For everything is sealed and done
That else leans on th' affair. Pray you, make haste. 61
                              [*Exeunt all but the King.*]
And, England, if my love thou hold'st at aught—   62
As my great power thereof may give thee sense,   63
Since yet thy cicatrice looks raw and red   64
After the Danish sword, and thy free awe   65
Pays homage to us—thou mayst not coldly set   66
Our sovereign process, which imports at full,   67
By letters congruing to that effect,   68
The present death of Hamlet. Do it, England,   69
For like the hectic in my blood he rages,   70
And thou must cure me. Till I know 'tis done,
Howe'er my haps, my joys were ne'er begun.   *Exit.* 72

❖

4.4 *Enter Fortinbras with his army over the stage.*

FORTINBRAS

Go, Captain, from me greet the Danish king.

52 cherub (Cherubim are angels of knowledge. Hamlet hints that both
he and heaven are onto Claudius's tricks.) **58 at foot** close behind, at
heel **61 leans on** bears upon, is related to **62 England** i.e., King of
England. **at aught** at any value **63 As . . . sense** for so my great power
may give you a just appreciation of the importance of valuing my love
64 cicatrice scar **65 free awe** voluntary show of respect **66 coldly set**
regard with indifference **67 process** command. **imports at full** conveys specific directions for **68 congruing** agreeing **69 present** immediate **70 hectic** persistent fever **72 haps** fortunes

4.4. Location: The coast of Denmark.

Tell him that by his license Fortinbras   2
Craves the conveyance of a promised march   3
Over his kingdom. You know the rendezvous.
If that His Majesty would aught with us,
We shall express our duty in his eye;   6
And let him know so.

CAPTAIN I will do 't, my lord.

FORTINBRAS Go softly on. [*Exeunt all but the Captain.*] 9

Enter Hamlet, Rosencrantz, [Guildenstern,] etc.

HAMLET Good sir, whose powers are these?   10

CAPTAIN They are of Norway, sir.

HAMLET How purposed, sir, I pray you?

CAPTAIN Against some part of Poland.

HAMLET Who commands them, sir?

CAPTAIN
The nephew to old Norway, Fortinbras.

HAMLET
Goes it against the main of Poland, sir,   16
Or for some frontier?

CAPTAIN
Truly to speak, and with no addition,   18
We go to gain a little patch of ground
That hath in it no profit but the name.
To pay five ducats, five, I would not farm it;   21
Nor will it yield to Norway or the Pole
A ranker rate, should it be sold in fee.   23

HAMLET
Why, then the Polack never will defend it.

CAPTAIN
Yes, it is already garrisoned.

HAMLET
Two thousand souls and twenty thousand ducats
Will not debate the question of this straw.   27
This is th' impostume of much wealth and peace,   28

2 license permission **3 the conveyance of** escort during **6 duty** respect. **eye** presence **9 softly** slowly, circumspectly **10 powers** forces **16 main** main part **18 addition** exaggeration **21 To pay** i.e., for a yearly rental of. **farm it** take a lease of it **23 ranker** higher. **in fee** fee simple, outright **27 debate . . . straw** settle this trifling matter **28 impostume** abscess

That inward breaks, and shows no cause without
Why the man dies. I humbly thank you, sir.

CAPTAIN
    God b' wi' you, sir.   [*Exit.*]

ROSENCRANTZ   Will 't please you go, my lord?

HAMLET
    I'll be with you straight. Go a little before.
                          [*Exeunt all except Hamlet.*]
    How all occasions do inform against me   33
    And spur my dull revenge! What is a man,
    If his chief good and market of his time   35
    Be but to sleep and feed? A beast, no more.
    Sure he that made us with such large discourse,   37
    Looking before and after, gave us not
    That capability and godlike reason
    To fust in us unused. Now, whether it be   40
    Bestial oblivion, or some craven scruple   41
    Of thinking too precisely on th' event—   42
    A thought which, quartered, hath but one part wisdom
    And ever three parts coward—I do not know
    Why yet I live to say "This thing's to do,"
    Sith I have cause, and will, and strength, and means   46
    To do 't. Examples gross as earth exhort me: 47
    Witness this army of such mass and charge,   48
    Led by a delicate and tender prince,   49
    Whose spirit with divine ambition puffed
    Makes mouths at the invisible event,   51
    Exposing what is mortal and unsure
    To all that fortune, death, and danger dare,
    Even for an eggshell. Rightly to be great
    Is not to stir without great argument,
    But greatly to find quarrel in a straw
    When honor's at the stake. How stand I then,   57
    That have a father killed, a mother stained,
    Excitements of my reason and my blood,   59

33 inform against denounce, betray; take shape against   **35 market of**
profit of, compensation for   **37 discourse** power of reasoning   **40 fust**
grow moldy   **41 oblivion** forgetfulness   **42 precisely** scrupulously.
event outcome   **46 Sith** since   **47 gross** obvious   **48 charge** expense
49 delicate and tender of fine and youthful qualities   **51 Makes mouths**
makes scornful faces.   **invisible event** unforeseeable outcome   **57 at**
the stake at risk (in gambling)   **59 Excitements of** promptings by

And let all sleep, while to my shame I see
The imminent death of twenty thousand men
That for a fantasy and trick of fame   62
Go to their graves like beds, fight for a plot 63
Whereon the numbers cannot try the cause,   64
Which is not tomb enough and continent   65
To hide the slain? O, from this time forth
My thoughts be bloody or be nothing worth!   *Exit.*

✤

4.5   *Enter Horatio, [Queen] Gertrude, and a
Gentleman.*

QUEEN
   I will not speak with her.
GENTLEMAN   She is importunate,
   Indeed distract. Her mood will needs be pitied.   2
QUEEN   What would she have?
GENTLEMAN
   She speaks much of her father, says she hears
   There's tricks i' the world, and hems, and beats her
      heart,   5
   Spurns enviously at straws, speaks things in doubt 6
   That carry but half sense. Her speech is nothing,
   Yet the unshapèd use of it doth move   8
   The hearers to collection; they yawn at it,   9
   And botch the words up fit to their own thoughts, 10
   Which, as her winks and nods and gestures yield them, 11
   Indeed would make one think there might be thought, 12
   Though nothing sure, yet much unhappily.   13

62 fantasy fanciful caprice, illusion. **trick** trifle, deceit **63 plot** i.e., of
ground **64 Whereon . . . cause** i.e., on which there is insufficient room
for the soldiers needed to engage in a military contest **65 continent**
receptacle, container

4.5. Location: The castle.
2 distract distracted **5 tricks** deceptions. **heart** i.e., breast **6 Spurns
. . . straws** kicks spitefully, takes offense at trifles. **in doubt** obscurely
8 unshapèd use distracted manner **9 collection** inference, a guess at
some sort of meaning. **yawn** gape, wonder; grasp. (The Folio reading,
aim, is possible.) **10 botch** patch **11 Which** i.e., the words. **yield**
deliver, represent **12 thought** conjectured **13 much unhappily** very
unskillfully, clumsily

HORATIO
  'Twere good she were spoken with, for she may strew
  Dangerous conjectures in ill-breeding minds.   15
QUEEN   Let her come in.   [*Exit Gentleman.*]
  [*Aside.*] To my sick soul, as sin's true nature is,
  Each toy seems prologue to some great amiss.   18
  So full of artless jealousy is guilt,   19
  It spills itself in fearing to be spilt.   20

    Enter Ophelia [distracted].

OPHELIA
  Where is the beauteous majesty of Denmark?
QUEEN   How now, Ophelia?
OPHELIA (*She sings*)
      "How should I your true love know
        From another one?
      By his cockle hat and staff,   25
        And his sandal shoon."   26
QUEEN
  Alas, sweet lady, what imports this song?
OPHELIA   Say you? Nay, pray you, mark.
      "He is dead and gone, lady,   (*Song.*)
        He is dead and gone;
      At his head a grass-green turf,
        At his heels a stone."
  Oho!
QUEEN   Nay, but Ophelia—
OPHELIA   Pray you, mark.
  [*Sings.*] "White his shroud as the mountain snow"—

    Enter King.

QUEEN   Alas, look here, my lord.
OPHELIA
      "Larded with sweet flowers;   (*Song.*) 38

15 **ill-breeding** prone to suspect the worst and to make mischief 18 **toy**
trifle. **amiss** calamity   19–20 **So . . . spilt** guilt is so full of suspicion
that it unskillfully betrays itself in fearing betrayal   20 **s.d. Enter
Ophelia** (In the first quarto, Ophelia enters "playing on a lute, and her
hair down, singing.")   25 **cockle hat** hat with cockleshell stuck in it as
a sign that the wearer had been a pilgrim to the shrine of Saint James
of Compostella in Spain   26 **shoon** shoes   38 **Larded** decorated

Which bewept to the ground did not go
　　With true-love showers.'' 40

KING　How do you, pretty lady?

OPHELIA　Well, God 'ild you! They say the owl was a 42
baker's daughter. Lord, we know what we are, but
know not what we may be. God be at your table!

KING　Conceit upon her father. 45

OPHELIA　Pray let's have no words of this; but when
they ask you what it means, say you this:

　　　''Tomorrow is Saint Valentine's day, (*Song.*) 48
　　　　All in the morning betime, 49
　　　And I a maid at your window,
　　　　To be your Valentine.
　　　Then up he rose, and donned his clothes,
　　　　And dupped the chamber door, 53
　　　Let in the maid, that out a maid
　　　　Never departed more.''

KING　Pretty Ophelia—

OPHELIA　Indeed, la, without an oath, I'll make an end
on 't:

　[*Sings.*] ''By Gis and by Saint Charity, 59
　　　　Alack, and fie for shame!
　　　Young men will do 't, if they come to 't;
　　　　By Cock, they are to blame. 62
　　　Quoth she, 'Before you tumbled me,
　　　　You promised me to wed.' ''

He answers:

　　　'' 'So would I ha' done, by yonder sun,
　　　　An thou hadst not come to my bed.' '' 67

KING　How long hath she been thus?

OPHELIA　I hope all will be well. We must be patient,
but I cannot choose but weep to think they would lay
him i' the cold ground. My brother shall know of it.
And so I thank you for your good counsel. Come, my
coach! Good night, ladies, good night, sweet ladies,
good night, good night. [*Exit.*]

---

40 showers i.e., tears　**42 God 'ild** God yield or reward.　**owl** (Refers to a
legend about a baker's daughter who was turned into an owl for refusing
Jesus bread.)　**45 Conceit** brooding　**48 Valentine's** (This song alludes to
the belief that the first girl seen by a man on the morning of this day was
his valentine or truelove.)　**49 betime** early　**53 dupped** opened　**59 Gis**
Jesus　**62 Cock** (A perversion of ''God'' in oaths.)　**67 An** if

KING [*To Horatio*]
   Follow her close. Give her good watch, I pray you.
                              [*Exit Horatio.*]
   O, this is the poison of deep grief; it springs
   All from her father's death—and now behold!
   O Gertrude, Gertrude,
   When sorrows come, they come not single spies,   79
   But in battalions. First, her father slain;
   Next, your son gone, and he most violent author
   Of his own just remove; the people muddied,   82
   Thick and unwholesome in their thoughts and whispers
   For good Polonius' death—and we have done but
      greenly   84
   In hugger-mugger to inter him; poor Ophelia   85
   Divided from herself and her fair judgment,
   Without the which we are pictures or mere beasts;
   Last, and as much containing as all these,   88
   Her brother is in secret come from France,
   Feeds on his wonder, keeps himself in clouds,   90
   And wants not buzzers to infect his ear   91
   With pestilent speeches of his father's death,
   Wherein necessity, of matter beggared,   93
   Will nothing stick our person to arraign   94
   In ear and ear. O my dear Gertrude, this,   95
   Like to a murdering piece, in many places   96
   Gives me superfluous death.   *A noise within.* 97
QUEEN   Alack, what noise is this?
KING   Attend!   99
   Where are my Switzers? Let them guard the door.   100

   Enter a Messenger.

   What is the matter?
MESSENGER   Save yourself, my lord!

79 spies scouts sent in advance of the main force   **82 muddied** stirred
up, confused   **84 greenly** imprudently, foolishly   **85 hugger-mugger**
secret haste   **88 as much containing** i.e., as full of serious matter
90 in clouds i.e., of suspicion and rumor   **91 wants** lacks.   **buzzers**
gossipers, informers   **93 necessity** i.e., the need to invent some plausible explanation.   **of matter beggared** unprovided with facts
94–95 Will . . . ear will not hesitate to accuse my (royal) person in
everybody's ears   **96 murdering piece** cannon loaded so as to scatter its
shot   **97 Gives . . . death** kills me over and over   **99 Attend** i.e., guard
me   **100 Switzers** Swiss guards, mercenaries

The ocean, overpeering of his list,   102
Eats not the flats with more impetuous haste   103
Than young Laertes, in a riotous head,   104
O'erbears your officers. The rabble call him lord,
And, as the world were now but to begin,   106
Antiquity forgot, custom not known,
The ratifiers and props of every word,   108
They cry, "Choose we! Laertes shall be king!"
Caps, hands, and tongues applaud it to the clouds,   110
"Laertes shall be king, Laertes king!"   *A noise within.*

QUEEN
  How cheerfully on the false trail they cry!
  O, this is counter, you false Danish dogs!   113

        Enter Laertes with others.

KING   The doors are broke.

LAERTES
  Where is this King?—Sirs, stand you all without.

ALL   No, let's come in.

LAERTES   I pray you, give me leave.

ALL   We will, we will.

LAERTES
  I thank you. Keep the door. [*Exeunt followers.*] O thou
    vile king,
  Give me my father!

QUEEN [*Holding him*]Calmly, good Laertes.

LAERTES
  That drop of blood that's calm proclaims me bastard,
  Cries cuckold to my father, brands the harlot
  Even here, between the chaste unsmirchèd brow   123
  Of my true mother.

KING   What is the cause, Laertes,
  That thy rebellion looks so giantlike?
  Let him go, Gertrude. Do not fear our person.   126

---

102 overpeering of his list overflowing its shore, boundary   **103 flats**
i.e., flatlands near shore.   **impetuous** violent (also with the meaning of
impiteous [*impitious*, Q2], pitiless)   **104 head** armed force   **106 as** as if
108 The ratifiers . . . word i.e., *antiquity* (or tradition) and *custom* ought
to confirm (*ratify*) and underprop our every word or promise   **110 Caps**
(The caps are thrown in the air.)   **113 counter** (A hunting term meaning
to follow the trail in a direction opposite to that which the game has
taken.)   **123 between** in the middle of   **126 fear our** fear for my

There's such divinity doth hedge a king 127
That treason can but peep to what it would, 128
Acts little of his will. Tell me, Laertes, 129
Why thou art thus incensed. Let him go, Gertrude.
Speak, man.

LAERTES   Where is my father?

KING   Dead.

QUEEN
But not by him.

KING   Let him demand his fill.

LAERTES
How came he dead? I'll not be juggled with. 133
To hell, allegiance! Vows, to the blackest devil!
Conscience and grace, to the profoundest pit!
I dare damnation. To this point I stand,
That both the worlds I give to negligence, 137
Let come what comes, only I'll be revenged
Most throughly for my father. 139

KING   Who shall stay you?

LAERTES   My will, not all the world's. 141
And for my means, I'll husband them so well
They shall go far with little.

KING   Good Laertes,
If you desire to know the certainty
Of your dear father, is 't writ in your revenge
That, swoopstake, you will draw both friend and foe, 146
Winner and loser?

LAERTES   None but his enemies.

KING   Will you know them, then?

LAERTES
To his good friends thus wide I'll ope my arms,
And like the kind life-rendering pelican 151

---

127 hedge protect as with a surrounding barrier   **128 can . . . would**
can only glance, as from afar off or through a barrier, at what it would
intend   **129 Acts . . . will** (but) performs little of what it intends
133 juggled with cheated, deceived   **137 both . . . negligence** i.e., both
this world and the next are of no consequence to me   **139 throughly**
thoroughly   **141 My will . . . world's** i.e., I'll stop (*stay*) when my will is
accomplished, not for anyone else's   **146 swoopstake** (Literally, taking
all stakes on the gambling table at once, i.e., indiscriminately; *draw* is
also a gambling term.)   **151 pelican** (Refers to the belief that the female
pelican fed its young with its own blood.)

Repast them with my blood.

KING   Why, now you speak   152
Like a good child and a true gentleman.
That I am guiltless of your father's death,
And am most sensibly in grief for it,   155
It shall as level to your judgment 'pear   156
As day does to your eye.   *A noise within.*

LAERTES
How now, what noise is that?

        Enter Ophelia.

KING   Let her come in.

LAERTES
O heat, dry up my brains! Tears seven times salt
Burn out the sense and virtue of mine eye!   160
By heaven, thy madness shall be paid with weight   161
Till our scale turn the beam. O rose of May!   162
Dear maid, kind sister, sweet Ophelia!
O heavens, is 't possible a young maid's wits
Should be as mortal as an old man's life?
Nature is fine in love, and where 'tis fine   166
It sends some precious instance of itself   167
After the thing it loves.   168

OPHELIA
        "They bore him barefaced on the bier,   (*Song.*)
              Hey non nonny, nonny, hey nonny,
              And in his grave rained many a tear—"
Fare you well, my dove!

LAERTES
Hadst thou thy wits and didst persuade revenge,   173
It could not move thus.

OPHELIA   You must sing "A-down a-down," and you   175
"call him a-down-a." O, how the wheel becomes it!   176
It is the false steward that stole his master's daughter.   177

---

152 **Repast** feed   155 **sensibly** feelingly   156 **level** plain   160 **virtue**
faculty, power   161 **paid with weight** repaid, avenged equally or more
162 **beam** crossbar of a balance   166 **fine in** refined by   167 **instance**
token   168 **After . . . loves** i.e., into the grave, along with Polonius
173 **persuade** argue cogently for   175–176 **You . . . a-down-a** (Ophelia
assigns the singing of refrains, like her own "Hey non nonny," to various imaginary singers.)   176 **wheel** spinning wheel as accompaniment
to the song, or refrain   177 **false steward** (The story is unknown.)

LAERTES This nothing's more than matter.   178

OPHELIA There's rosemary, that's for remembrance; 179
pray you, love, remember. And there is pansies; that's 180
for thoughts.

LAERTES A document in madness, thoughts and re- 182
membrance fitted.

OPHELIA There's fennel for you, and columbines. 184
There's rue for you, and here's some for me; we may 185
call it herb of grace o' Sundays. You must wear your
rue with a difference. There's a daisy. I would give 187
you some violets, but they withered all when my father 188
died. They say 'a made a good end—

[*Sings.*] "For bonny sweet Robin is all my joy."

LAERTES

Thought and affliction, passion, hell itself,   191

She turns to favor and to prettiness.   192

OPHELIA

    "And will 'a not come again?   (*Song.*)

    And will 'a not come again?

      No, no, he is dead.

      Go to thy deathbed,

    He never will come again.

    "His beard was as white as snow,

    All flaxen was his poll.   199

      He is gone, he is gone.

      And we cast away moan.

    God ha' mercy on his soul!"

And of all Christian souls, I pray God. God b' wi' you.

              [*Exit.*]

LAERTES Do you see this, O God?

---

178 This . . . matter this seeming nonsense is more eloquent than sane utterance **179 rosemary** (Used as a symbol of remembrance both at weddings and at funerals.) **180 pansies** (Emblems of love and court-ship; perhaps from French *pensées*, thoughts.) **182 document** instruc-tion, lesson **184 fennel** (Emblem of flattery.) **columbines** (Emblems of unchastity or ingratitude.) **185 rue** (Emblem of repentance; when mingled with holy water, it was known as *herb of grace*.) **187 with a difference** (A device used in heraldry to distinguish one family from another on the coat of arms, here suggesting that Ophelia and the Queen have different causes of sorrow and repentance; perhaps with a play on *rue* in the sense of ruth, pity.) **daisy** (Emblem of dissembling, faithlessness.) **188 violets** (Emblems of faithfulness.) **191 Thought** melancholy **192 favor** grace, beauty **199 poll** head

KING
Laertes, I must commune with your grief,
Or you deny me right. Go but apart,
Make choice of whom your wisest friends you will,　207
And they shall hear and judge twixt you and me.
If by direct or by collateral hand　209
They find us touched, we will our kingdom give,　210
Our crown, our life, and all that we call ours
To you in satisfaction; but if not,
Be you content to lend your patience to us,
And we shall jointly labor with your soul
To give it due content.

LAERTES　　　　　　　　Let this be so.
His means of death, his obscure funeral—
No trophy, sword, nor hatchment o'er his bones,　217
No noble rite, nor formal ostentation—　218
Cry to be heard, as 'twere from heaven to earth,
That I must call 't in question.

KING　　　　　　　　　　So you shall,　220
And where th' offense is, let the great ax fall.
I pray you, go with me.　　　　　　　*Exeunt.*

✣

4.6　　*Enter Horatio and others.*

HORATIO
What are they that would speak with me?
GENTLEMAN　Seafaring men, sir. They say they have let-
ters for you.
HORATIO　Let them come in.　　　　[*Exit Gentleman.*]
I do not know from what part of the world
I should be greeted, if not from Lord Hamlet.

　　　Enter Sailors.

FIRST SAILOR　God bless you, sir.
HORATIO　Let him bless thee too.

207 whom whichever of　**209 collateral** indirect　**210 us touched** me
implicated　**217 trophy** memorial.　**hatchment** tablet displaying the
armorial bearings of a deceased person　**218 ostentation** ceremony
220 That so that.　**call 't in question** demand an explanation

4.6. Location: The castle.

FIRST SAILOR   'A shall, sir, an please him. There's a   9
   letter for you, sir—it came from th' ambassador that   10
   was bound for England—if your name be Horatio, as
   I am let to know it is.   [*He gives a letter.*]
HORATIO [*Reads*] "Horatio, when thou shalt have over-   13
   looked this, give these fellows some means to the King; 14
   they have letters for him. Ere we were two days old at
   sea, a pirate of very warlike appointment gave us   16
   chase. Finding ourselves too slow of sail, we put on a
   compelled valor, and in the grapple I boarded them.
   On the instant they got clear of our ship, so I alone
   became their prisoner. They have dealt with me like
   thieves of mercy, but they knew what they did: I am to   21
   do a good turn for them. Let the King have the letters
   I have sent, and repair thou to me with as much speed   23
   as thou wouldest fly death. I have words to speak in
   thine ear will make thee dumb, yet are they much too
   light for the bore of the matter. These good fellows will 26
   bring thee where I am. Rosencrantz and Guildenstern
   hold their course for England. Of them I have much to
   tell thee. Farewell.

                   He that thou knowest thine, Hamlet."
Come, I will give you way for these your letters,   31
And do 't the speedier that you may direct me
To him from whom you brought them.   *Exeunt.*

❖

4.7   *Enter King and Laertes.*

KING
   Now must your conscience my acquittance seal,   1
   And you must put me in your heart for friend,
   Sith you have heard, and with a knowing ear,   3

---

9 an if it   **10 th' ambassador** (Evidently Hamlet. The sailor is being circumspect.)   **13–14 overlooked** looked over   **14 means** means of access
16 appointment equipage   **21 thieves of mercy** merciful thieves   **23 repair** come   **26 bore** caliber, i.e., importance   **31 way** means of access

4.7. Location: The castle.
1 my acquittance seal confirm or acknowledge my innocence   **3 Sith**
since

That he which hath your noble father slain
Pursued my life.

LAERTES   It well appears. But tell me
   Why you proceeded not against these feats   6
   So crimeful and so capital in nature,   7
   As by your safety, greatness, wisdom, all things else,
   You mainly were stirred up.   9

KING   O, for two special reasons,
   Which may to you perhaps seem much unsinewed,   11
   But yet to me they're strong. The Queen his mother
   Lives almost by his looks, and for myself—
   My virtue or my plague, be it either which—
   She is so conjunctive to my life and soul   15
   That, as the star moves not but in his sphere,   16
   I could not but by her. The other motive
   Why to a public count I might not go   18
   Is the great love the general gender bear him,   19
   Who, dipping all his faults in their affection,
   Work like the spring that turneth wood to stone,   21
   Convert his gyves to graces, so that my arrows,   22
   Too slightly timbered for so loud a wind,   23
   Would have reverted to my bow again   24
   But not where I had aimed them.

LAERTES
   And so have I a noble father lost,
   A sister driven into desperate terms,   27
   Whose worth, if praises may go back again,   28
   Stood challenger on mount of all the age   29
   For her perfections. But my revenge will come.

KING
   Break not your sleeps for that. You must not think
   That we are made of stuff so flat and dull

---

6 feats acts   **7 capital** punishable by death   **9 mainly** greatly
11 unsinewed weak   **15 conjunctive** closely united   **16 his** its.   **sphere**
one of the hollow spheres in which, according to Ptolemaic astronomy,
the planets were supposed to move   **18 count** account, reckoning, indictment   **19 general gender** common people   **21 Work** operate, act.
spring i.e., a spring with such a concentration of lime that it coats a
piece of wood with limestone, in effect gilding it   **22 gyves** fetters
(which, gilded by the people's praise, would look like badges of honor)
23 slightly timbered light.   **loud** strong   **24 reverted** returned
27 terms state, condition   **28 go back** i.e., recall what she was   **29 on
mount** set up on high

That we can let our beard be shook with danger
And think it pastime. You shortly shall hear more.
I loved your father, and we love ourself;
And that, I hope, will teach you to imagine—

    Enter a Messenger with letters.

How now? What news?

MESSENGER   Letters, my lord, from Hamlet:
This to Your Majesty, this to the Queen.

                            [He gives letters.]

KING   From Hamlet? Who brought them?

MESSENGER
Sailors, my lord, they say. I saw them not.
They were given me by Claudio. He received them
Of him that brought them.

KING   Laertes, you shall hear them.—
Leave us.   *[Exit Messenger.]*
[Reads.] "High and mighty, you shall know I am set
naked on your kingdom. Tomorrow shall I beg leave 45
to see your kingly eyes, when I shall, first asking your
pardon, thereunto recount the occasion of my sudden 47
and more strange return.   Hamlet."
What should this mean? Are all the rest come back?
Or is it some abuse, and no such thing?   50

LAERTES
Know you the hand?

KING   'Tis Hamlet's character. "Naked!" 51
And in a postscript here he says "alone."
Can you devise me?   53

LAERTES
I am lost in it, my lord. But let him come.
It warms the very sickness in my heart
That I shall live and tell him to his teeth,
"Thus didst thou."

KING   If it be so, Laertes—   57
As how should it be so? How otherwise?—   58
Will you be ruled by me?

45 naked destitute, unarmed, without following **47 pardon** permission **50 abuse** deceit. **no such thing** no such thing has occurred
51 character handwriting **53 devise** explain to **57 Thus didst thou** i.e., here's for what you did to my father **58 As . . . otherwise** how can this (Hamlet's return) be true? Yet how otherwise than true (since we have the evidence of his letter)

LAERTES   Ay, my lord,
So you will not o'errule me to a peace.   60
KING
  To thine own peace. If he be now returned,
  As checking at his voyage, and that he means   62
  No more to undertake it, I will work him
  To an exploit, now ripe in my device,   64
  Under the which he shall not choose but fall;
  And for his death no wind of blame shall breathe,
  But even his mother shall uncharge the practice   67
  And call it accident.
LAERTES   My lord, I will be ruled,
  The rather if you could devise it so
  That I might be the organ.
KING   It falls right.   70
  You have been talked of since your travel much,
  And that in Hamlet's hearing, for a quality
  Wherein they say you shine. Your sum of parts   73
  Did not together pluck such envy from him
  As did that one, and that, in my regard,
  Of the unworthiest siege.   76
LAERTES   What part is that, my lord?
KING
  A very ribbon in the cap of youth,
  Yet needful too, for youth no less becomes   79
  The light and careless livery that it wears
  Than settled age his sables and his weeds   81
  Importing health and graveness. Two months since   82
  Here was a gentleman of Normandy.
  I have seen myself, and served against, the French,
  And they can well on horseback, but this gallant   85
  Had witchcraft in 't; he grew unto his seat,
  And to such wondrous doing brought his horse

---

60 So provided that   **62 checking at** i.e., turning aside from (like a
falcon leaving the quarry to fly at a chance bird).   **that** if   **64 device**
devising, invention   **67 uncharge the practice** acquit the stratagem of
being a plot   **70 organ** agent, instrument   **73 Your . . . parts** i.e., all
your other virtues   **76 unworthiest siege** least important rank   **79 no
less becomes** is no less suited by   **81 sables** rich robes furred with
sable.   **weeds** garments   **82 Importing health** signifying a concern for
health and dignified prosperity; also, giving an impression of comfortable prosperity   **85 can well** are skilled

As had he been incorpsed and demi-natured   88
With the brave beast. So far he topped my thought   89
That I in forgery of shapes and tricks   90
Come short of what he did.

LAERTES   A Norman was 't?

KING   A Norman.

LAERTES
Upon my life, Lamord.

KING   The very same.

LAERTES
I know him well. He is the brooch indeed   94
And gem of all the nation.

KING   He made confession of you,   96
And gave you such a masterly report
For art and exercise in your defense,   98
And for your rapier most especial,
That he cried out 'twould be a sight indeed
If one could match you. Th' escrimers of their nation, 101
He swore, had neither motion, guard, nor eye
If you opposed them. Sir, this report of his
Did Hamlet so envenom with his envy
That he could nothing do but wish and beg
Your sudden coming o'er, to play with you.   106
Now, out of this—

LAERTES   What out of this, my lord?

KING
Laertes, was your father dear to you?
Or are you like the painting of a sorrow,
A face without a heart?

LAERTES   Why ask you this?

KING
Not that I think you did not love your father,
But that I know love is begun by time,   112
And that I see, in passages of proof,   113
Time qualifies the spark and fire of it.   114

---

88 incorpsed and demi-natured of one body and nearly of one nature (like
the centaur)   **89 topped** surpassed   **90 forgery** imagining   **94 brooch** ornament   **96 confession** testimonial, admission of superiority   **98 For . . .
defense** in respect to your skill and practice with your weapon
101 escrimers fencers   **106 play** fence   **112 begun by time** i.e., created
by the right circumstance and hence subject to change   **113 passages
of proof** actual instances   **114 qualifies** weakens, moderates

There lives within the very flame of love
A kind of wick or snuff that will abate it, 116
And nothing is at a like goodness still, 117
For goodness, growing to a pleurisy, 118
Dies in his own too much. That we would do, 119
We should do when we would; for this "would" changes
And hath abatements and delays as many 121
As there are tongues, are hands, are accidents, 122
And then this "should" is like a spendthrift sigh, 123
That hurts by easing. But, to the quick o' th' ulcer: 124
Hamlet comes back. What would you undertake
To show yourself in deed your father's son
More than in words?

LAERTES   To cut his throat i' the church.

KING
No place, indeed, should murder sanctuarize; 128
Revenge should have no bounds. But good Laertes,
Will you do this, keep close within your chamber. 130
Hamlet returned shall know you are come home.
We'll put on those shall praise your excellence 132
And set a double varnish on the fame
The Frenchman gave you, bring you in fine together, 134
And wager on your heads. He, being remiss, 135
Most generous, and free from all contriving, 136
Will not peruse the foils, so that with ease,
Or with a little shuffling, you may choose
A sword unbated, and in a pass of practice 139
Requite him for your father.

LAERTES   I will do 't,
And for that purpose I'll anoint my sword.

---

116 snuff the charred part of a candlewick **117 nothing . . . still** nothing remains at a constant level of perfection **118 pleurisy** excess, plethora. (Literally, a chest inflammation.) **119 in . . . much** of its own excess. **That** that which **121 abatements** diminutions **122 accidents** occurrences, incidents **123 spendthrift sigh** (An allusion to the belief that sighs draw blood from the heart.) **124 hurts by easing** i.e., costs the heart blood even while it affords emotional relief. **quick o' th' ulcer** heart of the matter **128 sanctuarize** protect from punishment. (Alludes to the right of sanctuary with which certain religious places were invested.) **130 Will you do this** if you wish to do this **132 put on those shall** arrange for some to **134 in fine** finally **135 remiss** negligently unsuspicious **136 generous** noble-minded **139 unbated** not blunted, having no button. **pass of practice** treacherous thrust

I bought an unction of a mountebank   142
So mortal that, but dip a knife in it,
Where it draws blood no cataplasm so rare,   144
Collected from all simples that have virtue   145
Under the moon, can save the thing from death   146
That is but scratched withal. I'll touch my point
With this contagion, that if I gall him slightly,   148
It may be death.

KING   Let's further think of this,
Weigh what convenience both of time and means
May fit us to our shape. If this should fail,   151
And that our drift look through our bad performance,   152
'Twere better not assayed. Therefore this project
Should have a back or second, that might hold
If this did blast in proof. Soft, let me see.   155
We'll make a solemn wager on your cunnings—   156
I ha 't!
When in your motion you are hot and dry—
As make your bouts more violent to that end—   159
And that he calls for drink, I'll have prepared him
A chalice for the nonce, whereon but sipping,   161
If he by chance escape your venomed stuck,   162
Our purpose may hold there. [*A cry within.*] But stay,
  what noise?

        Enter Queen.

QUEEN
One woe doth tread upon another's heel,
So fast they follow. Your sister's drowned, Laertes.
LAERTES   Drowned! O, where?
QUEEN
There is a willow grows askant the brook,   167
That shows his hoar leaves in the glassy stream;   168
Therewith fantastic garlands did she make

---

142 unction ointment.   **mountebank** quack doctor   **144 cataplasm**
plaster or poultice   **145 simples** herbs   **146 Under the moon** i.e.,
anywhere   **148 gall** graze, wound   **151 shape** part we propose to act
152 drift . . . performance i.e., intention should be made visible by our
bungling   **155 blast in proof** burst in the test (like a cannon)
156 cunnings respective skills   **159 As** i.e., and you should   **161 nonce**
occasion   **162 stuck** thrust. (From *stoccado*, a fencing term.)
167 askant aslant   **168 hoar** white or gray

Of crowflowers, nettles, daisies, and long purples,   170
That liberal shepherds give a grosser name,   171
But our cold maids do dead men's fingers call them.   172
There on the pendent boughs her crownet weeds   173
Clamb'ring to hang, an envious sliver broke,   174
When down her weedy trophies and herself   175
Fell in the weeping brook. Her clothes spread wide,
And mermaidlike awhile they bore her up,
Which time she chanted snatches of old lauds,   178
As one incapable of her own distress,   179
Or like a creature native and endued   180
Unto that element. But long it could not be
Till that her garments, heavy with their drink,
Pulled the poor wretch from her melodious lay
To muddy death.

LAERTES   Alas, then she is drowned?
QUEEN   Drowned, drowned.
LAERTES
Too much of water hast thou, poor Ophelia,
And therefore I forbid my tears. But yet
It is our trick; nature her custom holds,   188
Let shame say what it will. [*He weeps.*] When these are
     gone,   189
The woman will be out. Adieu, my lord.   190
I have a speech of fire that fain would blaze,
But that this folly douts it.   *Exit.*
KING   Let's follow, Gertrude.   192
How much I had to do to calm his rage!
Now fear I this will give it start again;
Therefore let's follow.   *Exeunt.*

170 long purples early purple orchids   **171 liberal** free-spoken.   **a
grosser name** (The testicle-resembling tubers of the orchid, also in some
cases resembling *dead men's fingers*, have earned various slang names
like dogstones and cullions.)   **172 cold** chaste   **173 crownet** made into a
chaplet or coronet   **174 envious sliver** malicious branch   **175 weedy**
i.e., of plants   **178 lauds** hymns   **179 incapable** lacking capacity to
apprehend   **180 endued** adapted by nature   **188 It is our trick** i.e.,
weeping is our natural way (when sad)   **189–190 When . . . out** when
my tears are all shed, the woman in me will be expended, satisfied
192 douts extinguishes. (The second quarto reads "drowns.")

5.1   *Enter two Clowns [with spades and mattocks].*

FIRST CLOWN   Is she to be buried in Christian burial,
when she willfully seeks her own salvation?   2

SECOND CLOWN   I tell thee she is; therefore make her
grave straight. The crowner hath sat on her, and finds   4
it Christian burial.   5

FIRST CLOWN   How can that be, unless she drowned herself in her own defense?

SECOND CLOWN   Why, 'tis found so.   8

FIRST CLOWN   It must be *se offendendo*, it cannot be   9
else. For here lies the point: if I drown myself wittingly,
it argues an act, and an act hath three branches—it is
to act, to do, and to perform. Argal, she drowned her-   12
self wittingly.

SECOND CLOWN   Nay, but hear you, goodman delver—   14

FIRST CLOWN   Give me leave. Here lies the water; good.
Here stands the man; good. If the man go to this water and drown himself, it is, will he, nill he, he goes,   17
mark you that. But if the water come to him and
drown him, he drowns not himself. Argal, he that is
not guilty of his own death shortens not his own life.

SECOND CLOWN   But is this law?

FIRST CLOWN   Ay, marry, is 't—crowner's quest law.   22

SECOND CLOWN   Will you ha' the truth on 't? If this had
not been a gentlewoman, she should have been buried out o' Christian burial.

FIRST CLOWN   Why, there thou sayst. And the more   26
pity that great folk should have countenance in this   27
world to drown or hang themselves more than their

5.1. Location: A churchyard.
s.d. Clowns rustics   **2 salvation** (A blunder for "damnation," or perhaps a suggestion that Ophelia was taking her own shortcut to
heaven.)   **4 straight** straightway, immediately. (But with a pun on *strait*,
narrow.)   **crowner** coroner.   **sat on her** conducted a session on her
case   **4–5 finds it** gives his official verdict that her means of death was
consistent with   **8 found so** determined so in the coroner's verdict
9 se offendendo (A comic mistake for *se defendendo*, term used in
verdicts of justifiable homicide.)   **12 Argal** (Corruption of *ergo*, therefore.)   **14 goodman** (An honorific title often used with the name of a
profession or craft.)   **17 will he, nill he** whether he will or no, willy-
nilly   **22 quest** inquest   **26 there thou sayst** i.e., that's right
27 countenance privilege

even-Christian. Come, my spade. There is no ancient ²⁹
gentlemen but gardeners, ditchers, and grave makers.
They hold up Adam's profession. ³¹

SECOND CLOWN   Was he a gentleman?

FIRST CLOWN   'A was the first that ever bore arms. ³³

SECOND CLOWN   Why, he had none.

FIRST CLOWN   What, art a heathen? How dost thou understand the Scripture? The Scripture says Adam
digged. Could he dig without arms? I'll put another ³⁷
question to thee. If thou answerest me not to the purpose, confess thyself— ³⁹

SECOND CLOWN   Go to.

FIRST CLOWN   What is he that builds stronger than either the mason, the shipwright, or the carpenter?

SECOND CLOWN   The gallows maker, for that frame out- ⁴³
lives a thousand tenants.

FIRST CLOWN   I like thy wit well, in good faith. The gallows does well. But how does it well? It does well to ⁴⁶
those that do ill. Now thou dost ill to say the gallows
is built stronger than the church. Argal, the gallows
may do well to thee. To 't again, come.

SECOND CLOWN   "Who builds stronger than a mason, a
shipwright, or a carpenter?"

FIRST CLOWN   Ay, tell me that, and unyoke. ⁵²

SECOND CLOWN   Marry, now I can tell.

FIRST CLOWN   To 't.

SECOND CLOWN   Mass, I cannot tell. ⁵⁵

Enter Hamlet and Horatio [at a distance].

FIRST CLOWN   Cudgel thy brains no more about it, for
your dull ass will not mend his pace with beating;
and when you are asked this question next, say "a
grave maker." The houses he makes lasts till dooms-

---

29 even-Christian fellow Christians.   **ancient** going back to ancient
times   **31 hold up** maintain   **33 bore arms** (To be entitled to bear a coat
of arms would make Adam a gentleman, but as one who bore a spade
our common ancestor was an ordinary delver in the earth.)   **37 arms**
i.e., the arms of the body   **39 confess thyself** (The saying continues,
"and be hanged.")   **43 frame** (1) gallows (2) structure   **46 does well**
(1) is an apt answer (2) does a good turn   **52 unyoke** i.e., after this great
effort you may unharness the team of your wits   **55 Mass** by the Mass

day. Go get thee in and fetch me a stoup of liquor. 60
[*Exit Second Clown. First Clown digs.*]

Song.

"In youth, when I did love, did love, 61
    Methought it was very sweet,
To contract—O—the time for—a—my behove, 63
    O, methought there—a—was nothing—a—meet." 64

HAMLET Has this fellow no feeling of his business, 'a 65
sings in grave-making?

HORATIO Custom hath made it in him a property of 67
easiness. 68

HAMLET 'Tis e'en so. The hand of little employment
hath the daintier sense. 70

FIRST CLOWN   *Song.*

"But age with his stealing steps
    Hath clawed me in his clutch,
And hath shipped me into the land, 73
    As if I had never been such."

[*He throws up a skull.*]

HAMLET That skull had a tongue in it and could sing
once. How the knave jowls it to the ground, as if 76
'twere Cain's jawbone, that did the first murder! This
might be the pate of a politician, which this ass now 78
o'erreaches, one that would circumvent God, might 79
it not?

HORATIO It might, my lord.

HAMLET Or of a courtier, which could say, "Good morrow, sweet lord! How dost thou, sweet lord?" This
might be my Lord Such-a-one, that praised my Lord
Such-a-one's horse when 'a meant to beg it, might
it not?

HORATIO Ay, my lord.

---

60 stoup two-quart measure **61 In . . . love** (This and the two following
stanzas, with nonsensical variations, are from a poem attributed to Lord
Vaux and printed in *Tottel's Miscellany*, 1557. The *O* and *a* [for "ah"]
seemingly are the grunts of the digger.) **63 To contract . . . behove** i.e.,
to shorten the time for my own advantage. (Perhaps he means to
prolong it.) **64 meet** suitable, i.e., more suitable **65 'a** that he
67–68 property of easiness i.e., something he can do easily and indifferently **70 daintier sense** more delicate sense of feeling **73 into the land**
i.e., toward my grave (?) (But note the lack of rhyme in *steps*, *land*.)
76 jowls dashes **78 politician** schemer, plotter **79 o'erreaches** circum-
vents, gets the better of (with a quibble on the literal sense)

HAMLET Why, e'en so, and now my Lady Worm's,
chapless, and knocked about the mazard with a sex- 89
ton's spade. Here's fine revolution, an we had the trick 90
to see 't. Did these bones cost no more the breeding 91
but to play at loggets with them? Mine ache to think 92
on 't.

FIRST CLOWN   *Song.*

   "A pickax and a spade, a spade,
     For and a shrouding sheet;   95
  O, a pit of clay for to be made
     For such a guest is meet."

            [He throws up another skull.]

HAMLET There's another. Why may not that be the skull
of a lawyer? Where be his quiddities now, his quilli- 99
ties, his cases, his tenures, and his tricks? Why does 100
he suffer this mad knave now to knock him about the
sconce with a dirty shovel, and will not tell him of his 102
action of battery? Hum, this fellow might be in 's time 103
a great buyer of land, with his statutes, his recogni- 104
zances, his fines, his double vouchers, his recoveries. 105
Is this the fine of his fines and the recovery of his 106
recoveries, to have his fine pate full of fine dirt? Will 107
his vouchers vouch him no more of his purchases, and
double ones too, than the length and breadth of a
pair of indentures? The very conveyances of his lands 110

---

89 chapless having no lower jaw. **mazard** i.e., head. (Literally, a drinking vessel.) **90 revolution** turn of Fortune's wheel, change. **an** if
90–91 trick to see knack of seeing **91–92 cost . . . but** involve so little
expense and care in upbringing that we may **92 loggets** a game in
which pieces of hard wood shaped like Indian clubs or bowling pins are
thrown to lie as near as possible to a stake **95 For and** and moreover
99 quiddities subtleties, quibbles. (From Latin *quid*, a thing.)
99–100 quillities verbal niceties, subtle distinctions. (Variation of *quiddities.*) **100 tenures** the holding of a piece of property or office, or the
conditions or period of such holding **102 sconce** head **103 action of
battery** lawsuit about physical assault **104–105 statutes, recognizances**
legal documents guaranteeing a debt by attaching land and property
105 fines, recoveries ways of converting entailed estates into "fee simple" or freehold. **double** signed by two signatories. **vouchers** guaran-
tees of the legality of a title to real estate **106–107 fine of his fines . . .
fine pate . . . fine dirt** end of his legal maneuvers . . . elegant head . . .
minutely sifted dirt **110 pair of indentures** legal document drawn up
in duplicate on a single sheet and then cut apart on a zigzag line so that
each pair was uniquely matched. (Hamlet may refer to two rows of
teeth, or dentures.) **conveyances** deeds

will scarcely lie in this box, and must th' inheritor 111
himself have no more, ha?

HORATIO   Not a jot more, my lord.

HAMLET   Is not parchment made of sheepskins?

HORATIO   Ay, my lord, and of calves' skins too.

HAMLET   They are sheep and calves which seek out as- 116
surance in that. I will speak to this fellow.—Whose 117
grave's this, sirrah?   118

FIRST CLOWN   Mine, sir.

   [*Sings.*] "O, a pit of clay for to be made
          For such a guest is meet."

HAMLET   I think it be thine, indeed, for thou liest in 't.

FIRST CLOWN   You lie out on 't, sir, and therefore 'tis not
yours. For my part, I do not lie in 't, yet it is mine.

HAMLET   Thou dost lie in 't, to be in 't and say it is
thine. 'Tis for the dead, not for the quick; therefore 126
thou liest.

FIRST CLOWN   'Tis a quick lie, sir; 'twill away again from
me to you.

HAMLET   What man dost thou dig it for?

FIRST CLOWN   For no man, sir.

HAMLET   What woman, then?

FIRST CLOWN   For none, neither.

HAMLET   Who is to be buried in 't?

FIRST CLOWN   One that was a woman, sir, but, rest her
soul, she's dead.

HAMLET   How absolute the knave is! We must speak by 137
the card, or equivocation will undo us. By the Lord, 138
Horatio, this three years I have took note of it: the age 139
is grown so picked that the toe of the peasant comes so 140
near the heel of the courtier, he galls his kibe.—How 141
long hast thou been grave maker?

FIRST CLOWN   Of all the days i' the year, I came to 't that
day that our last king Hamlet overcame Fortinbras.

---

111 box (1) deed box (2) coffin. ("Skull" has been suggested.) **inheritor**
possessor, owner **116–117 assurance in that** safety in legal parch-
ments **118 sirrah** (A term of address to inferiors.) **126 quick** living
137 absolute strict, precise **137–138 by the card** by the mariner's card
or chart on which the points of the compass were marked, i.e., with
precision **138 equivocation** ambiguity in the use of terms **139 took**
taken **140 picked** refined, fastidious **141 galls his kibe** chafes the
courtier's chilblain

HAMLET How long is that since?

FIRST CLOWN Cannot you tell that? Every fool can tell
that. It was that very day that young Hamlet was
born—he that is mad and sent into England.

HAMLET Ay, marry, why was he sent into England?

FIRST CLOWN Why, because 'a was mad. 'A shall recover his wits there, or if 'a do not, 'tis no great matter
there.

HAMLET Why?

FIRST CLOWN 'Twill not be seen in him there. There the
men are as mad as he.

HAMLET How came he mad?

FIRST CLOWN Very strangely, they say.

HAMLET How strangely?

FIRST CLOWN Faith, e'en with losing his wits.

HAMLET Upon what ground?   160

FIRST CLOWN Why, here in Denmark. I have been sex-
ton here, man and boy, thirty years.

HAMLET How long will a man lie i' th' earth ere he rot?

FIRST CLOWN Faith, if 'a be not rotten before 'a die—as
we have many pocky corpses nowadays that will   165
scarce hold the laying in—'a will last you some eight   166
year or nine year. A tanner will last you nine year.

HAMLET Why he more than another?

FIRST CLOWN Why, sir, his hide is so tanned with his
trade that 'a will keep out water a great while, and
your water is a sore decayer of your whoreson dead   171
body. [*He picks up a skull.*] Here's a skull now hath
lien you i' th' earth three-and-twenty years.   173

HAMLET Whose was it?

FIRST CLOWN A whoreson mad fellow's it was. Whose
do you think it was?

HAMLET Nay, I know not.

FIRST CLOWN A pestilence on him for a mad rogue! 'A
poured a flagon of Rhenish on my head once. This   179
same skull, sir, was, sir, Yorick's skull, the King's jester.

---

160 ground cause. (But in the next line the gravedigger takes the word
in the sense of "land," "country.") **165 pocky** rotten, diseased. (Literally, with the pox, or syphilis.) **166 hold the laying in** hold together
long enough to be interred **171 sore** i.e., terrible, great. **whoreson** i.e.,
vile, scurvy **173 lien you** lain. (*You* is used colloquially.) **179 Rhenish**
Rhine wine

HAMLET This?

FIRST CLOWN E'en that.

HAMLET Let me see. [*He takes the skull.*] Alas, poor Yorick! I knew him, Horatio, a fellow of infinite jest, of most excellent fancy. He hath bore me on his back a 185 thousand times, and now how abhorred in my imagination it is! My gorge rises at it. Here hung those lips 187 that I have kissed I know not how oft. Where be your gibes now? Your gambols, your songs, your flashes of merriment that were wont to set the table on a roar? Not one now, to mock your own grinning? Quite 191 chopfallen? Now get you to my lady's chamber and 192 tell her, let her paint an inch thick, to this favor she 193 must come. Make her laugh at that. Prithee, Horatio, tell me one thing.

HORATIO What's that, my lord?

HAMLET Dost thou think Alexander looked o' this fashion i' th' earth?

HORATIO E'en so.

HAMLET And smelt so? Pah! [*He puts down the skull.*]

HORATIO E'en so, my lord.

HAMLET To what base uses we may return, Horatio! Why may not imagination trace the noble dust of Alexander till 'a find it stopping a bunghole? 204

HORATIO 'Twere to consider too curiously to consider 205 so.

HAMLET No, faith, not a jot, but to follow him thither with modesty enough, and likelihood to lead it. As 208 thus: Alexander died, Alexander was buried, Alexander returneth to dust, the dust is earth, of earth we make loam, and why of that loam whereto he was 211 converted might they not stop a beer barrel?
Imperious Caesar, dead and turned to clay, 213
Might stop a hole to keep the wind away.
O, that that earth which kept the world in awe
Should patch a wall t' expel the winter's flaw! 216

---

185 bore borne **187 My gorge rises** i.e., I feel nauseated **191 mock your own grinning** i.e., laugh at the faces you make **192 chopfallen** (1) lacking the lower jaw (2) dejected **193 favor** aspect, appearance **204 bunghole** hole for filling or emptying a cask **205 curiously** minutely **208 modesty** moderation **211 loam** mortar consisting chiefly of moistened clay and straw **213 Imperious** imperial **216 flaw** gust of wind

Enter King, Queen, Laertes, and the corpse [of Ophelia, in procession, with Priest, lords, etc.].

But soft, but soft awhile! Here comes the King,   217
The Queen, the courtiers. Who is this they follow?
And with such maimèd rites? This doth betoken   219
The corpse they follow did with desperate hand
Fordo its own life. 'Twas of some estate.   221
Couch we awhile and mark.   222

> [He and Horatio conceal themselves.
> Ophelia's body is taken to the grave.]

LAERTES What ceremony else?

HAMLET [*To Horatio*]
That is Laertes, a very noble youth. Mark.

LAERTES What ceremony else?

PRIEST
Her obsequies have been as far enlarged
As we have warranty. Her death was doubtful,   227
And but that great command o'ersways the order   228
She should in ground unsanctified been lodged   229
Till the last trumpet. For charitable prayers,   230
Shards, flints, and pebbles should be thrown on her.   231
Yet here she is allowed her virgin crants,   232
Her maiden strewments, and the bringing home   233
Of bell and burial.   234

LAERTES
Must there no more be done?

PRIEST   No more be done.
We should profane the service of the dead
To sing a requiem and such rest to her   237
As to peace-parted souls.

LAERTES   Lay her i' th' earth,   238
And from her fair and unpolluted flesh

---

217 soft i.e., wait, be careful   **219 maimèd** mutilated, incomplete
221 Fordo destroy.   **estate** rank   **222 Couch we** let's hide, lurk
227 warranty i.e., ecclesiastical authority   **228 great . . . order** orders
from on high overrule the prescribed procedures   **229 She should . . .
lodged** i.e., she should have been buried in unsanctified ground   **230 For**
in place of   **231 Shards** broken bits of pottery   **232 crants** garlands
betokening maidenhood   **233 strewments** flowers strewn on a coffin
233–234 bringing . . . burial laying to rest of the body in consecrated
ground, to the sound of the bell   **237 such rest** i.e., to pray for such
rest   **238 peace-parted souls** those who have died at peace with God

May violets spring! I tell thee, churlish priest,   240
A ministering angel shall my sister be
When thou liest howling.
HAMLET [*To Horatio*]   What, the fair Ophelia!   242
QUEEN [*Scattering flowers*]   Sweets to the sweet! Farewell.
I hoped thou shouldst have been my Hamlet's wife.
I thought thy bride-bed to have decked, sweet maid,
And not have strewed thy grave.
LAERTES   O, treble woe
Fall ten times treble on that cursèd head
Whose wicked deed thy most ingenious sense   248
Deprived thee of!—Hold off the earth awhile,
Till I have caught her once more in mine arms.   250
          [*He leaps into the grave and embraces Ophelia.*]
Now pile your dust upon the quick and dead,
Till of this flat a mountain you have made
T' o'ertop old Pelion or the skyish head   253
Of blue Olympus.
HAMLET [*Coming forward*]   What is he whose grief   254
Bears such an emphasis, whose phrase of sorrow   255
Conjures the wandering stars and makes them stand   256
Like wonder-wounded hearers? This is I,   257
Hamlet the Dane.   258
LAERTES [*Grappling with him*]   The devil take thy soul!   259
HAMLET   Thou pray'st not well.
I prithee, take thy fingers from my throat,
For though I am not splenitive and rash,   262
Yet have I in me something dangerous,
Which let thy wisdom fear. Hold off thy hand.
KING   Pluck them asunder.
QUEEN   Hamlet, Hamlet!
ALL   Gentlemen!

240 violets (See 4.5.188 and note.)   **242 howling** i.e., in hell
248 ingenious sense a mind that is quick, alert, of fine qualities
250 Till . . . arms (Implies an open coffin.)   **253–254 Pelion, Olympus**
mountains in the north of Thessaly; see also *Ossa*, below, at l. 286
255 emphasis i.e., rhetorical and florid emphasis. (*Phrase* has a similar
rhetorical connotation.)   **256 wandering stars** planets   **257 wonder-**
wounded struck with amazement   **258 the Dane** (This title normally
signifies the King; see 1.1.17 and note.)   **259 s.d. Grappling with him**
(Most editors think, despite the testimony of the first quarto that *"Hamlet leaps in after Laertes,"* that Laertes jumps out of the grave to attack
Hamlet.)   **262 splenitive** quick-tempered

HORATIO   Good my lord, be quiet.
                        [*Hamlet and Laertes are parted.*]

HAMLET
  Why, I will fight with him upon this theme
  Until my eyelids will no longer wag.   270

QUEEN   O my son, what theme?

HAMLET
  I loved Ophelia. Forty thousand brothers
  Could not with all their quantity of love
  Make up my sum. What wilt thou do for her?

KING   O, he is mad, Laertes.

QUEEN   For love of God, forbear him.   276

HAMLET
  'Swounds, show me what thou'lt do.   277
  Woo't weep? Woo't fight? Woo't fast? Woo't tear
    thyself?   278
  Woo't drink up eisel? Eat a crocodile?   279
  I'll do 't. Dost come here to whine?
  To outface me with leaping in her grave?
  Be buried quick with her, and so will I.   282
  And if thou prate of mountains, let them throw
  Millions of acres on us, till our ground,
  Singeing his pate against the burning zone,   285
  Make Ossa like a wart! Nay, an thou'lt mouth,   286
  I'll rant as well as thou.

QUEEN   This is mere madness,   287
  And thus awhile the fit will work on him;
  Anon, as patient as the female dove
  When that her golden couplets are disclosed,   290
  His silence will sit drooping.

HAMLET   Hear you, sir.
  What is the reason that you use me thus?

---

270 wag move. (A fluttering eyelid is a conventional sign that life has
not yet gone.)   **276 forbear him** leave him alone   **277 'Swounds** by His
(Christ's) wounds   **278 Woo't** wilt thou   **279 drink up** drink deeply.
eisel vinegar.   **crocodile** (Crocodiles were supposed to shed hypocritical
tears.)   **282 quick** alive   **285 his pate** its head, i.e., top.   **burning zone**
zone in the celestial sphere containing the sun's orbit, between the
tropics of Cancer and Capricorn   **286 Ossa** another mountain in Thessaly. (In their war against the Olympian gods, the giants attempted to
heap Ossa, Pelion, and Olympus on one another to scale heaven.)   **an**
if.   **mouth** i.e., rant   **287 mere** utter   **290 golden couplets** two baby
pigeons, covered with yellow down.   **disclosed** hatched

I loved you ever. But it is no matter.
Let Hercules himself do what he may,   294
The cat will mew, and dog will have his day.   295
KING
I pray thee, good Horatio, wait upon him.
                              Exit Hamlet and Horatio.
[*To Laertes.*] Strengthen your patience in our last night's
    speech;   297
We'll put the matter to the present push.—   298
Good Gertrude, set some watch over your son.—
This grave shall have a living monument.   300
An hour of quiet shortly shall we see;   301
Till then, in patience our proceeding be.   *Exeunt.*

❖

5.2   *Enter Hamlet and Horatio.*

HAMLET
So much for this, sir; now shall you see the other.   I
You do remember all the circumstance?
HORATIO   Remember it, my lord!
HAMLET
Sir, in my heart there was a kind of fighting
That would not let me sleep. Methought I lay
Worse than the mutines in the bilboes. Rashly,   6
And praised be rashness for it—let us know   7
Our indiscretion sometimes serves us well   8
When our deep plots do pall, and that should learn us   9
There's a divinity that shapes our ends,
Rough-hew them how we will—
HORATIO   That is most certain.   11

294–295 Let . . . day i.e., (1) even Hercules couldn't stop Laertes's theatrical rant (2) I too will have my turn; i.e., despite any blustering attempts at interference, every person will sooner or later do what he
must do   **297 in** i.e., by recalling   **298 present push** immediate test
300 living lasting; also refers (for Laertes's benefit) to the plot against
Hamlet   **301 hour of quiet** time free of conflict

5.2. Location: The castle.
1 see the other i.e., hear the other news   **6 mutines** mutineers.   **bilboes**
shackles.   **Rashly** on impulse. (This adverb goes with ll. 12ff.)   **7 know**
acknowledge   **8 indiscretion** lack of foresight and judgment (not an
indiscreet act)   **9 pall** fail, falter, go stale.   **learn** teach   **11 Rough-hew**
shape roughly, botch

HAMLET   Up from my cabin,
My sea-gown scarfed about me, in the dark   13
Groped I to find out them, had my desire,
Fingered their packet, and in fine withdrew   15
To mine own room again, making so bold,
My fears forgetting manners, to unseal
Their grand commission; where I found, Horatio—
Ah, royal knavery!—an exact command,
Larded with many several sorts of reasons   20
Importing Denmark's health and England's too,   21
With, ho! such bugs and goblins in my life,   22
That on the supervise, no leisure bated,   23
No, not to stay the grinding of the ax,   24
My head should be struck off.

HORATIO   Is 't possible?

HAMLET [*Giving a document*]
Here's the commission. Read it at more leisure.
But wilt thou hear now how I did proceed?

HORATIO   I beseech you.

HAMLET
Being thus benetted round with villainies—
Ere I could make a prologue to my brains,   30
They had begun the play—I sat me down,   31
Devised a new commission, wrote it fair.   32
I once did hold it, as our statists do,   33
A baseness to write fair, and labored much   34
How to forget that learning, but, sir, now
It did me yeoman's service. Wilt thou know   36
Th' effect of what I wrote?

HORATIO   Ay, good my lord.   37

HAMLET
An earnest conjuration from the King,   38
As England was his faithful tributary,

13 **sea-gown** seaman's coat. **scarfed** loosely wrapped   15 **Fingered**
pilfered, pinched. **in fine** finally, in conclusion   20 **Larded** garnished,
decorated   21 **Importing** relating to   22 **bugs** bugbears, hobgoblins.
in my life i.e., to be feared if I were allowed to live   23 **supervise** reading. **leisure bated** delay allowed   24 **stay** await   30–31 **Ere . . . play**
i.e., before I could consciously turn my brain to the matter, it had
started working on a plan   32 **fair** in a clear hand   33 **statists** statesmen   34 **baseness** i.e., lower-class trait   36 **yeoman's** i.e., substantial,
faithful, loyal. (In the British navy, the ship's yeoman is usually a scribe
or clerk.)   37 **effect** purport   38 **conjuration** entreaty

As love between them like the palm might flourish,
As peace should still her wheaten garland wear   41
And stand a comma 'tween their amities,   42
And many suchlike "as"es of great charge,   43
That on the view and knowing of these contents,
Without debatement further more or less,
He should those bearers put to sudden death,
Not shriving time allowed.

HORATIO   How was this sealed?   47

HAMLET
Why, even in that was heaven ordinant.   48
I had my father's signet in my purse,   49
Which was the model of that Danish seal;   50
Folded the writ up in the form of th' other,   51
Subscribed it, gave 't th' impression, placed it safely, 52
The changeling never known. Now, the next day   53
Was our sea fight, and what to this was sequent
Thou knowest already.

HORATIO
So Guildenstern and Rosencrantz go to 't.

HAMLET
Why, man, they did make love to this employment.
They are not near my conscience. Their defeat   58
Does by their own insinuation grow.   59
'Tis dangerous when the baser nature comes   60
Between the pass and fell incensèd points   61
Of mighty opposites.

HORATIO   Why, what a king is this!   62

HAMLET
Does it not, think thee, stand me now upon—   63
He that hath killed my king and whored my mother,

---

41 still always. wheaten garland (Symbolic of fruitful agriculture, of peace and plenty.) 42 comma (Indicating continuity, link.) 43 "as"es (1) the "whereases" of a formal document (2) asses. charge (1) import (2) burden (appropriate to asses) 47 shriving time time for confession and absolution 48 ordinant directing 49 signet small seal 50 model replica 51 writ writing 52 Subscribed signed (with forged signature). impression i.e., with a wax seal 53 changeling i.e., the substituted letter. (Literally, a fairy child substituted for a human one.) 58 defeat destruction 59 insinuation intrusive intervention, sticking their noses in my business 60 baser of lower social station 61 pass thrust. fell fierce 62 opposites antagonists 63 stand me now upon become incumbent on me now

Popped in between th' election and my hopes, 65
Thrown out his angle for my proper life, 66
And with such cozenage—is 't not perfect conscience 67
To quit him with this arm? And is 't not to be damned 68
To let this canker of our nature come 69
In further evil? 70

HORATIO
It must be shortly known to him from England
What is the issue of the business there.

HAMLET
It will be short. The interim is mine,
And a man's life's no more than to say "one." 74
But I am very sorry, good Horatio,
That to Laertes I forgot myself,
For by the image of my cause I see
The portraiture of his. I'll court his favors.
But, sure, the bravery of his grief did put me 79
Into a tow'ring passion.

HORATIO   Peace, who comes here?

Enter a Courtier [Osric].

OSRIC Your lordship is right welcome back to Denmark.
HAMLET I humbly thank you, sir. [*To Horatio.*] Dost
know this water fly?
HORATIO No, my good lord.
HAMLET Thy state is the more gracious, for 'tis a vice to
know him. He hath much land, and fertile. Let a beast 86
be lord of beasts, and his crib shall stand at the King's 87
mess. 'Tis a chuff, but, as I say, spacious in the pos- 88
session of dirt.
OSRIC Sweet lord, if your lordship were at leisure, I
should impart a thing to you from His Majesty.
HAMLET I will receive it, sir, with all diligence of spirit.

65 election (The Danish monarch was "elected" by a small number of
high-ranking electors.) **66 angle** fishing line. **proper** very
67 cozenage trickery **68 quit** requite, pay back **69 canker** ulcer
69–70 come In grow into **74 a man's . . . one** i.e., one's whole life
occupies such a short time, only as long as it takes to count to one
79 bravery bravado **86–88 Let . . . mess** i.e., if a man, no matter how
beastlike, is as rich in possessions as Osric, he may eat at the King's
table **88 chuff** boor, churl. (The second quarto spelling, *chough*, is a vari-
ant spelling that also suggests the meaning here of "chattering jackdaw.")

Put your bonnet to his right use; 'tis for the head.   93
OSRIC I thank your lordship, it is very hot.
HAMLET No, believe me, 'tis very cold. The wind is
  northerly.
OSRIC It is indifferent cold, my lord, indeed.   97
HAMLET But yet methinks it is very sultry and hot for
  my complexion.   99
OSRIC Exceedingly, my lord. It is very sultry, as
  'twere—I cannot tell how. My lord, His Majesty bade
  me signify to you that 'a has laid a great wager on your
  head. Sir, this is the matter—
HAMLET I beseech you, remember.
                  [*Hamlet moves him to put on his hat.*]
OSRIC Nay, good my lord; for my ease, in good faith.   105
  Sir, here is newly come to court Laertes—believe me,
  an absolute gentleman, full of most excellent differ-   107
  ences, of very soft society and great showing. Indeed, 108
  to speak feelingly of him, he is the card or calendar of 109
  gentry, for you shall find in him the continent of what 110
  part a gentleman would see.   111
HAMLET Sir, his definement suffers no perdition in   112
  you, though I know to divide him inventorially   113
  would dozy th' arithmetic of memory, and yet but yaw   114
  neither in respect of his quick sail. But, in the verity of 115
  extolment, I take him to be a soul of great article and 116
  his infusion of such dearth and rareness as, to make   117
  true diction of him, his semblable is his mirror and   118

93 bonnet any kind of cap or hat. **his** its **97 indifferent** somewhat
99 complexion temperament **105 for my ease** (A conventional reply
declining the invitation to put his hat back on.) **107 absolute** perfect
107–108 differences special qualities **108 soft society** agreeable manners. **great showing** distinguished appearance **109 feelingly** with just
perception. **card** chart, map. **calendar** guide **110 gentry** good breeding **110–111 the continent . . . part** one who contains in him all the
qualities. (A *continent* is that which contains.) **what part** whatever
part, any part which **112 definement** definition. (Hamlet proceeds to
mock Osric by using his lofty diction back at him.) **perdition** loss,
diminution **113 divide him inventorially** i.e., enumerate his graces
114 dozy dizzy. **yaw** swing unsteadily off course. (Said of a ship.)
115 neither for all that. **in respect of** in comparison with **115–116 in
. . . extolment** in true praise (of him) **116 of great article** one with
many articles in his inventory **117 infusion** essence, character infused
into him by nature. **dearth and rareness** rarity **117–118 make true
diction** speak truly **118 semblable** only true likeness

who else would trace him his umbrage, nothing 119
more.

OSRIC   Your lordship speaks most infallibly of him.

HAMLET   The concernancy, sir? Why do we wrap the 122
gentleman in our more rawer breath?   123

OSRIC   Sir?

HORATIO   Is 't not possible to understand in another 125
tongue? You will do 't, sir, really.   126

HAMLET   What imports the nomination of this gen- 127
tleman?

OSRIC   Of Laertes?

HORATIO [*To Hamlet*]   His purse is empty already; all 's
golden words are spent.

HAMLET   Of him, sir.

OSRIC   I know you are not ignorant—

HAMLET   I would you did, sir. Yet in faith if you did,
it would not much approve me. Well, sir?   135

OSRIC   You are not ignorant of what excellence Laertes
is—

HAMLET   I dare not confess that, lest I should compare 138
with him in excellence. But to know a man well were 139
to know himself.   140

OSRIC   I mean, sir, for his weapon; but in the imputa- 141
tion laid on him by them in his meed, he's unfellowed. 142

HAMLET   What's his weapon?

OSRIC   Rapier and dagger.

HAMLET   That's two of his weapons—but well.   145

OSRIC   The King, sir, hath wagered with him six Barbary

---

119 who . . . trace any other person who would wish to follow.   **umbrage** shadow   **122 concernancy** import, relevance   **123 rawer breath** i.e., speech which can only come short in praising him   **125–126 to understand . . . tongue** i.e., for you, Osric, to understand when someone else speaks your language. (Horatio twits Osric for not being able to understand the kind of flowery speech he himself uses, when Hamlet speaks in such a vein. Alternatively, all this could be said to Hamlet.) **126 You will do 't** i.e., you can if you try   **127 nomination** naming **135 approve** commend   **138–140 I dare . . . himself** i.e., I dare not boast of knowing Laertes's excellence lest I seem to compare his with my own, since to appreciate excellence in another one must possess it oneself; by the same token, it is presumptuous to claim the self-knowledge necessary to know another person well   **141 for** i.e., with **141–142 imputation . . . them** reputation given him by others   **142 meed** merit.   **unfellowed** unmatched   **145 but well** but never mind

horses, against the which he has impawned, as I take 147
it, six French rapiers and poniards, with their assigns, 148
as girdle, hangers, and so. Three of the carriages, in 149
faith, are very dear to fancy, very responsive to the 150
hilts, most delicate carriages, and of very liberal con- 151
ceit.   152

HAMLET   What call you the carriages?

HORATIO [*To Hamlet*] I knew you must be edified by
the margent ere you had done.   155

OSRIC   The carriages, sir, are the hangers.

HAMLET   The phrase would be more germane to the
matter if we could carry a cannon by our sides; I would
it might be hangers till then. But, on: six Barbary horses
against six French swords, their assigns, and three lib-
eral-conceited carriages; that's the French bet against
the Danish. Why is this impawned, as you call it?

OSRIC   The King, sir, hath laid, sir, that in a dozen 163
passes between yourself and him, he shall not exceed 164
you three hits. He hath laid on twelve for nine, and it
would come to immediate trial, if your lordship would
vouchsafe the answer.   167

HAMLET   How if I answer no?

OSRIC   I mean, my lord, the opposition of your person
in trial.

HAMLET   Sir, I will walk here in the hall. If it please His
Majesty, it is the breathing time of day with me. Let 172
the foils be brought, the gentleman willing, and the
King hold his purpose, I will win for him an I can; if
not, I will gain nothing but my shame and the odd
hits.

---

147 he i.e., Laertes.   **impawned** staked, wagered   **148 poniards** daggers.
assigns appurtenances   **149 hangers** straps on the sword belt (*girdle*) from
which the sword hung.   **and so** and so on.   **carriages** (An affected way of
saying *hangers*; literally, gun carriages.)   **150 dear to fancy** fancifully
designed, tasteful.   **responsive** corresponding closely, matching or well
adjusted   **151 delicate** (i.e., in workmanship)   **151–152 liberal conceit**
elaborate design   **155 margent** margin of a book, place for explanatory
notes   **163 laid** wagered   **164 passes** bouts. (The odds of the betting are
hard to explain. Possibly the King bets that Hamlet will win at least five out
of twelve, at which point Laertes raises the odds against himself by betting
he will win nine.)   **167 vouchsafe the answer** be so good as to accept the
challenge. (Hamlet deliberately takes the phrase in its literal sense.)
172 breathing time exercise period.   **Let** i.e., if

OSRIC Shall I deliver you so?   177

HAMLET To this effect, sir—after what flourish your nature will.

OSRIC I commend my duty to your lordship.   180

HAMLET Yours, yours. [*Exit Osric.*] 'A does well to commend it himself; there are no tongues else for 's 182
turn.   183

HORATIO This lapwing runs away with the shell on his 184
head.

HAMLET 'A did comply with his dug before 'a sucked 186
it. Thus has he—and many more of the same breed
that I know the drossy age dotes on—only got the 188
tune of the time and, out of an habit of encounter, a 189
kind of yeasty collection, which carries them through 190
and through the most fanned and winnowed opinions; 191
and do but blow them to their trial, the bubbles are 192
out.   193

    Enter a Lord.

LORD My lord, His Majesty commended him to you by
young Osric, who brings back to him that you attend
him in the hall. He sends to know if your pleasure
hold to play with Laertes, or that you will take longer 197
time.

HAMLET I am constant to my purposes; they follow the
King's pleasure. If his fitness speaks, mine is ready; 200
now or whensoever, provided I be so able as now.

LORD The King and Queen and all are coming down.

---

177 deliver report what you say   **180 commend** commit to your favor.
(A conventional salutation; but Hamlet wryly uses a more literal meaning, "recommend," in l. 182.)   **182–183 for 's turn** for his purposes, i.e.,
to do it for him   **184 lapwing** (A proverbial type of youthful forwardness. Also, a bird that draws intruders away from its nest and was
thought to run about when newly hatched with its head in the shell; a
seeming reference to Osric's hat.)   **186 comply . . . dug** observe ceremonious formality toward his nurse's or mother's teat   **188 drossy** laden
with scum and impurities, frivolous   **189 tune** temper, mood, manner
of speech.   **habit of encounter** demeanor of social intercourse
190 yeasty frothy.   **collection** i.e., of current phrases   **191 fanned and
winnowed** select and refined. (Literally, like grain separated from its
chaff. Osric is both the chaff and the bubbly froth on the surface of the
liquor that is soon blown away.)   **192–193 blow . . . out** i.e., put them to
the test, and their ignorance is exposed   **197 that** if   **200 If . . . ready** if
he declares his readiness, my convenience waits on his

HAMLET   In happy time.   203
LORD   The Queen desires you to use some gentle enter- 204
tainment to Laertes before you fall to play.   205
HAMLET   She well instructs me.   [*Exit Lord.*]
HORATIO   You will lose, my lord.
HAMLET   I do not think so. Since he went into France, I
have been in continual practice; I shall win at the
odds. But thou wouldst not think how ill all's here
about my heart; but it is no matter.
HORATIO   Nay, good my lord—
HAMLET   It is but foolery, but it is such a kind of gain-   213
giving as would perhaps trouble a woman.   214
HORATIO   If your mind dislike anything, obey it. I will
forestall their repair hither and say you are not fit.   216
HAMLET   Not a whit, we defy augury. There is special
providence in the fall of a sparrow. If it be now, 'tis
not to come; if it be not to come, it will be now; if it
be not now, yet it will come. The readiness is all. Since 220
no man of aught he leaves knows, what is 't to leave   221
betimes? Let be.   222

> *A table prepared.* [*Enter*] *trumpets, drums, and
> officers with cushions; King, Queen,* [*Osric,*] *and
> all the state; foils, daggers,* [*and wine borne in;*]
> *and Laertes.*

KING
Come, Hamlet, come and take this hand from me.
        [*The King puts Laertes's hand into Hamlet's.*]
HAMLET
Give me your pardon, sir. I have done you wrong,
But pardon 't as you are a gentleman.
This presence knows,   226
And you must needs have heard, how I am punished
With a sore distraction. What I have done
That might your nature, honor, and exception   229

203 In happy time (A phrase of courtesy indicating acceptance.)
204–205 entertainment greeting   **213–214 gaingiving** misgiving
216 repair coming   **220–222 Since . . . Let be** since no one has knowledge of what he is leaving behind, what does an early death matter after
all? Enough; don't struggle against it.   **226 presence** royal assembly
229 exception disapproval

Roughly awake, I here proclaim was madness.
Was 't Hamlet wronged Laertes? Never Hamlet.
If Hamlet from himself be ta'en away,
And when he's not himself does wrong Laertes,
Then Hamlet does it not, Hamlet denies it.
Who does it, then? His madness. If 't be so,
Hamlet is of the faction that is wronged;   236
His madness is poor Hamlet's enemy.
Sir, in this audience,
Let my disclaiming from a purposed evil
Free me so far in your most generous thoughts
That I have shot my arrow o'er the house   241
And hurt my brother.

LAERTES   I am satisfied in nature,   242
Whose motive in this case should stir me most   243
To my revenge. But in my terms of honor
I stand aloof, and will no reconcilement
Till by some elder masters of known honor
I have a voice and precedent of peace   247
To keep my name ungored. But till that time,   248
I do receive your offered love like love,
And will not wrong it.

HAMLET   I embrace it freely,
And will this brothers' wager frankly play.—   251
Give us the foils. Come on.

LAERTES   Come, one for me.

HAMLET
I'll be your foil, Laertes. In mine ignorance   253
Your skill shall, like a star i' the darkest night,
Stick fiery off indeed.

LAERTES   You mock me, sir.   255

HAMLET   No, by this hand.

KING
Give them the foils, young Osric. Cousin Hamlet,
You know the wager?

236 faction party   **241 That I have** as if I had   **242 in nature** i.e., as to my
personal feelings   **243 motive** prompting   **247 voice** authoritative pro-
nouncement.   **of peace** for reconciliation   **248 name ungored** reputation
unwounded   **251 frankly** without ill feeling or the burden of rancor
253 foil thin metal background which sets a jewel off (with pun on the
blunted rapier for fencing)   **255 Stick fiery off** stand out brilliantly

HAMLET   Very well, my lord.
  Your Grace has laid the odds o' the weaker side.   259
KING
  I do not fear it; I have seen you both.
  But since he is bettered, we have therefore odds.   261
LAERTES
  This is too heavy. Let me see another.
                [He exchanges his foil for another.]
HAMLET
  This likes me well. These foils have all a length?   263
                    [They prepare to play.]
OSRIC   Ay, my good lord.
KING
  Set me the stoups of wine upon that table.
  If Hamlet give the first or second hit,
  Or quit in answer of the third exchange,   267
  Let all the battlements their ordnance fire.
  The King shall drink to Hamlet's better breath,   269
  And in the cup an union shall he throw   270
  Richer than that which four successive kings
  In Denmark's crown have worn. Give me the cups,
  And let the kettle to the trumpet speak,   273
  The trumpet to the cannoneer without,
  The cannons to the heavens, the heaven to earth,
  "Now the King drinks to Hamlet." Come, begin.
                    Trumpets the while.
  And you, the judges, bear a wary eye.
HAMLET   Come on, sir.
LAERTES   Come, my lord. *[They play. Hamlet scores a hit.]*
HAMLET   One.
LAERTES   No.
HAMLET   Judgment.
OSRIC   A hit, a very palpable hit.
           Drum, trumpets, and shot. Flourish.
                A piece goes off.

---

259 laid the odds o' bet on, backed   **261 is bettered** has improved; is the
odds-on favorite. (Laertes's handicap is the "three hits" specified in
l. 165.)   **263 likes me** pleases me   **267 Or . . . exchange** i.e., or requites
Laertes in the third bout for having won the first two   **269 better
breath** improved vigor   **270 union** pearl. (So called, according to Pliny's
Natural History, 9, because pearls are *unique*, never identical.)
273 kettle kettledrum

LAERTES   Well, again.

KING

Stay, give me drink. Hamlet, this pearl is thine.
            [*He throws a pearl in Hamlet's cup,
                                        and drinks.*]
Here's to thy health. Give him the cup.

HAMLET

I'll play this bout first. Set it by awhile.
Come. [*They play.*] Another hit; what say you?

LAERTES   A touch, a touch, I do confess 't.

KING

Our son shall win.

QUEEN   He's fat and scant of breath.   289
    Here, Hamlet, take my napkin, rub thy brows.   290
    The Queen carouses to thy fortune, Hamlet.   291

HAMLET   Good madam!

KING   Gertrude, do not drink.

QUEEN

I will, my lord, I pray you pardon me.   [*She drinks.*]

KING [*Aside*]

It is the poisoned cup. It is too late.

HAMLET

I dare not drink yet, madam; by and by.

QUEEN   Come, let me wipe thy face.

LAERTES [*To the King*]

My lord, I'll hit him now.

KING   I do not think 't.

LAERTES [*Aside*]

And yet it is almost against my conscience.

HAMLET

Come, for the third, Laertes. You do but dally.
I pray you, pass with your best violence;   301
I am afeard you make a wanton of me.   302

LAERTES   Say you so? Come on.   [*They play.*]

OSRIC   Nothing neither way.

LAERTES

Have at you now!

---

289 fat not physically fit, out of training   **290 napkin** handkerchief
291 carouses drinks a toast   **301 pass** thrust   **302 make . . . me** i.e.,
treat me like a spoiled child, holding back to give me an advantage

[Laertes wounds Hamlet; then, in scuffling,
they change rapiers, and Hamlet wounds Laertes.]

KING   Part them! They are incensed.   305

HAMLET

Nay, come, again.   *[The Queen falls.]*

OSRIC   Look to the Queen there, ho!

HORATIO

They bleed on both sides. How is it, my lord?

OSRIC   How is 't, Laertes?

LAERTES

Why, as a woodcock to mine own springe, Osric;   309
I am justly killed with mine own treachery.

HAMLET

How does the Queen?

KING   She swoons to see them bleed.

QUEEN

No, no, the drink, the drink—O my dear Hamlet—
The drink, the drink! I am poisoned.   *[She dies.]*

HAMLET

O villainy! Ho, let the door be locked!
Treachery! Seek it out.   *[Laertes falls. Exit Osric.]*

LAERTES

It is here, Hamlet. Hamlet, thou art slain.
No med'cine in the world can do thee good;
In thee there is not half an hour's life.
The treacherous instrument is in thy hand,
Unbated and envenomed. The foul practice   320
Hath turned itself on me. Lo, here I lie,
Never to rise again. Thy mother's poisoned.
I can no more. The King, the King's to blame.

HAMLET

The point envenomed too? Then, venom, to thy work.
                    [He stabs the King.]

ALL   Treason! Treason!

KING

O, yet defend me, friends! I am but hurt.

---

305 s.d. in scuffling, they change rapiers (This stage direction occurs in
the Folio. According to a widespread stage tradition, Hamlet receives a
scratch, realizes that Laertes's sword is unbated, and accordingly forces
an exchange.)   **309 woodcock** a bird, a type of stupidity or as a decoy.
springe trap, snare   **320 Unbated** not blunted with a button.   **practice**
plot

HAMLET [*Forcing the King to drink*]
  Here, thou incestuous, murderous, damnèd Dane,
  Drink off this potion. Is thy union here?   328
  Follow my mother.   [*The King dies.*]
LAERTES   He is justly served.
  It is a poison tempered by himself.   330
  Exchange forgiveness with me, noble Hamlet.
  Mine and my father's death come not upon thee,
  Nor thine on me!   [*He dies.*]
HAMLET
  Heaven make thee free of it! I follow thee.
  I am dead, Horatio. Wretched Queen, adieu!
  You that look pale and tremble at this chance,   336
  That are but mutes or audience to this act,   337
  Had I but time—as this fell sergeant, Death,   338
  Is strict in his arrest—O, I could tell you—   339
  But let it be. Horatio, I am dead;
  Thou livest. Report me and my cause aright
  To the unsatisfied.
HORATIO   Never believe it.
  I am more an antique Roman than a Dane.   343
  Here's yet some liquor left.
          [*He attempts to drink from the poisoned cup.
                    Hamlet prevents him.*]
HAMLET   As thou'rt a man,
  Give me the cup! Let go! By heaven, I'll ha 't.
  O God, Horatio, what a wounded name,
  Things standing thus unknown, shall I leave behind me!
  If thou didst ever hold me in thy heart,
  Absent thee from felicity awhile,
  And in this harsh world draw thy breath in pain
  To tell my story. (*A march afar off* [*and a volley within*].)
      What warlike noise is this?

      Enter Osric.

OSRIC
  Young Fortinbras, with conquest come from Poland,

328 union pearl. (See l. 270; with grim puns on the word's other meanings: marriage, shared death.) **330 tempered** mixed **336 chance**
mischance **337 mutes** silent observers **338 fell** cruel. **sergeant**
sheriff's officer **339 strict** (1) severely just (2) unavoidable. **arrest**
(1) taking into custody (2) stopping my speech **343 Roman** (It was
the Roman custom to follow masters in death.)

To th' ambassadors of England gives
This warlike volley.

HAMLET   O, I die, Horatio!
The potent poison quite o'ercrows my spirit.   355
I cannot live to hear the news from England,
But I do prophesy th' election lights
On Fortinbras. He has my dying voice.   358
So tell him, with th' occurrents more and less   359
Which have solicited—the rest is silence.   [*He dies*.]   360

HORATIO
Now cracks a noble heart. Good night, sweet prince,
And flights of angels sing thee to thy rest!

                                        [*March within*.]

Why does the drum come hither?

Enter Fortinbras, with the [*English*] *Ambassadors*
[*with drum, colors, and attendants*].

FORTINBRAS
Where is this sight?

HORATIO   What is it you would see?
If aught of woe or wonder, cease your search.

FORTINBRAS
This quarry cries on havoc. O proud Death,   366
What feast is toward in thine eternal cell,   367
That thou so many princes at a shot
So bloodily hast struck?

FIRST AMBASSADOR   The sight is dismal,
And our affairs from England come too late.
The ears are senseless that should give us hearing,
To tell him his commandment is fulfilled,
That Rosencrantz and Guildenstern are dead.
Where should we have our thanks?

HORATIO   Not from his mouth,   374
Had it th' ability of life to thank you.

355 **o'ercrows** triumphs over (like the winner in a cockfight)   358 **voice**
vote   359 **occurrents** events, incidents   360 **solicited** moved, urged.
(Hamlet doesn't finish saying what the events have prompted; presumably his acts of vengeance, or his reporting those events to Fortinbras.)   366 **quarry** heap of dead.   **cries on havoc** proclaims a general
slaughter   367 **feast** i.e., Death feasting on those who have fallen.
toward in preparation   374 **his** i.e., Claudius's

He never gave commandment for their death.
But since, so jump upon this bloody question,   377
You from the Polack wars, and you from England,
Are here arrived, give order that these bodies
High on a stage be placèd to the view,   380
And let me speak to th' yet unknowing world
How these things came about. So shall you hear
Of carnal, bloody, and unnatural acts,
Of accidental judgments, casual slaughters,   384
Of deaths put on by cunning and forced cause,   385
And, in this upshot, purposes mistook
Fall'n on th' inventors' heads. All this can I
Truly deliver.

FORTINBRAS   Let us haste to hear it,
And call the noblest to the audience.
For me, with sorrow I embrace my fortune.
I have some rights of memory in this kingdom,   391
Which now to claim my vantage doth invite me.   392

HORATIO
Of that I shall have also cause to speak,
And from his mouth whose voice will draw on more.   394
But let this same be presently performed,   395
Even while men's minds are wild, lest more mischance
On plots and errors happen.

FORTINBRAS   Let four captains   397
Bear Hamlet, like a soldier, to the stage,
For he was likely, had he been put on,   399
To have proved most royal; and for his passage,   400
The soldiers' music and the rite of war
Speak loudly for him.
Take up the bodies. Such a sight as this
Becomes the field, but here shows much amiss.   404
Go bid the soldiers shoot.

            Exeunt [marching, bearing off the dead bodies;
                    a peal of ordnance is shot off].

377 **jump** precisely, immediately. **question** dispute 380 **stage** platform
384 **judgments** retributions. **casual** occurring by chance 385 **put on**
instigated 391 **of memory** traditional, remembered, unforgotten
392 **vantage** i.e., presence at this opportune moment 394 **voice . . .**
more vote will influence still others 395 **presently** immediately
397 **On** on the basis of, on top of 399 **put on** i.e., invested in royal
office, and so put to the test 400 **passage** death 404 **field** i.e., of battle

Date and Text

Like everything else about *Hamlet*, the textual problem is complicated. On July 26, 1602, James Roberts entered in the Stationers' Register, the official record book of the London Company of Stationers (booksellers and printers), "A booke called the Revenge of Hamlett Prince Denmarke as yt was latelie Acted by the Lord Chamberleyn his servantes." For some reason, however, Roberts did not print his copy of *Hamlet* until 1604, by which time had appeared the following unauthorized edition:

> THE Tragicall Historie of HAMLET *Prince of Denmarke*[.] By William Shake-speare. As it hath beene diuerse times acted by his Highnesse seruants in the Cittie of London: as also in the two Vniuersities of Cambridge and Oxford, and elsewhere At London printed for N. L. [Nicholas Ling] and Iohn Trundell. 1603.

This edition, the bad quarto of *Hamlet*, seems to have been memorially reconstructed by actors who toured the provinces (note the references to Cambridge, Oxford, etc.), with some recollection of an earlier *Hamlet* play (the *Ur-Hamlet*) written before 1589 and acted during the 1590s. The piratical actors had no recourse to an authoritative manuscript. One may have played Marcellus and possibly Lucianus and Voltimand. Their version seems to have been based on an adaptation of the company's original promptbook, which itself stood at one remove from Shakespeare's foul papers by way of an intermediate manuscript. The resulting text is very corrupt, and yet it seems to have affected the more authentic text because the compositors of the second quarto made use of it, especially when they typeset the first act.

The authorized quarto of *Hamlet* appeared in 1604. Roberts, the printer, seems to have reached some agreement with Ling, one of the publishers of the bad quarto, for their initials are now paired on the title page:

> *THE* Tragicall Historie of HAMLET, *Prince of Denmarke*. By William Shakespeare. Newly imprinted and enlarged to almost as much againe as it was, according to the true and perfect Coppie. AT LONDON, Printed by I. R. [James Roberts]

for N. L. [Nicholas Ling] and are to be sold at his shoppe
vnder Saint Dunstons Church in Fleetstreet. 1604.

Some copies of this edition are dated 1605. This text was
based seemingly on Shakespeare's own papers with the
bookkeeper's annotations, but is marred by printing errors
and is at times contaminated by the bad quarto—presumably
when the printers found Shakespeare's manuscript
unreadable. This second quarto served as copy for a third
quarto in 1611, Ling having meanwhile transferred his
rights in the play to John Smethwick. A fourth quarto, un-
dated but before 1623, was based on the third.

The First Folio text of 1623 omits more than two hundred
lines found in the second quarto. Yet it supplies some
clearly authentic passages. It seems to derive from a transcript of Shakespeare's draft in which cuts made by the
author were observed—cuts made by Shakespeare quite
possibly because he knew the draft to be too long for performance, and which had either not been marked in the second
quarto copy or had been ignored there by the compositors.
The Folio also incorporates other alterations seemingly
made for clarity or in anticipation of performance. To this
theatrically motivated transcript Shakespeare apparently
contributed some revisions. Subsequently, this version evidently was copied again by a careless scribe who took many
liberties with the text. Typesetting from this inferior manuscript, the Folio compositors occasionally consulted the
second quarto, but not often enough. Thus, even though the
Folio supplies some genuine readings, as does the first
quarto when both the Folio and the second quarto are
wrong, the second quarto remains the most authentic version of the text.

Since the text of the second quarto is too long to be ac-
commodated in the two hours' traffic of the stage and it
becomes even longer when the words found only in the Folio are added, Shakespeare must have known it would have to
be cut for performance and probably marked at least some
omissions himself. Since he may have consented to such
cuts primarily because of the constraints of time, however,
this present edition holds to the view that the passages in
question should not be excised from the text we read. The
Hamlet presented here is doubtless longer than any version

ever acted in Shakespeare's day, and thus does not represent a script for any actual performance, but it may well represent the play as Shakespeare wrote it and then somewhat expanded it; it also includes passages that he may reluctantly have consented to cut for performance. It is also possible that some cuts were artistically intended, but, in the face of real uncertainty in this matter, an editorial policy of inclusion gives to the reader those passages that would otherwise have to be excised or put in an appendix on questionable grounds of authorial "intent."

Hamlet must have been produced before the Stationers' Register entry of July 26, 1602. Francis Meres does not mention the play in 1598 in his *Palladis Tamia: Wit's Treasury* (a slender volume on contemporary literature and art; valuable because it lists most of the plays of Shakespeare that existed at that time). Gabriel Harvey attributes the "tragedy of Hamlet, Prince of Denmark" to Shakespeare in a marginal note in Harvey's copy of Speght's Chaucer; Harvey acquired the book in 1598, but could have written the note any time between then and 1601 or even 1603. More helpful in dating is Hamlet's clear reference to the so-called "War of the Theaters," the rivalry between the adult actors and the boy actors whose companies had newly revived in 1598–1599 after nearly a decade of inactivity. The Children of the Chapel Royal began acting at Blackfriars in 1598 and provided such keen competition in 1599–1601 that the adult actors were at times forced to tour the provinces (see *Hamlet*, 2.2.332–362). Revenge tragedy was also in fashion during these years: John Marston's *Antonio's Revenge*, for example, dates from 1599–1601, and *The Malcontent* is from about the same time or slightly later.

Textual Notes

These textual notes are not a historical collation, either of the early quartos and the early folios or of more recent editions; they are simply a record of departures in this edition from the copy text. The reading adopted in this edition appears in boldface, followed by the rejected reading from the copy text, i.e., the second quarto of 1604. Only major alterations in punctuation are noted. Changes in lineation are not indicated, nor are some minor and obvious typographical errors.

Abbreviations used:
F the First Folio
Q quarto
s.d. stage direction
s.p. speech prefix

Copy text: the second quarto of 1604–1605 [Q2]. The First Folio text also represents an independently authoritative text; although seemingly not the correct choice for copy text, the Folio text is considerably less marred by typographical errors than is Q2. The adopted readings in these notes are from F unless otherwise indicated; [eds.] means that the adopted reading was first proposed by some editor since the time of F. Some readings are also supplied from the pirated first quarto of 1603 [Q1].

1.1. 1 Who's Whose **19 soldier** [F, Q1] souldiers **44 off** [Q1] of **48 harrows** horrowes **67 sledded Polacks** [eds.] sleaded pollax **77 why** [F, Q1] with **cast** cost **91 heraldry** [F, Q1] heraldy **92 those** [F, Q1] these **95 returned** returne **97 covenant** comart **98 designed** [eds.] desseigne **112 e'en so** [eds.] enso **119 tenantless** tennatlesse **125 feared** [eds.] feare **142 you** [F, Q1] your **144 at it** it **181 conveniently** [F, Q1] conuenient

1.2. s.d. Gertrude Gertrad (and elsewhere; also Gertrad) **1 s.p. King** Claud **67 so** so much **77 good** coold **82 shapes** [Q3] chapes **83 denote** deuote **96 a** or **105 corpse** [eds.] course **112 you. For** you for **129 sullied** [eds.] sallied [Q2] solid [F] **132 self** seale **133 weary** wary **137 to this** thus **140 satyr** [F4] satire **143 would** [F, Q1] should **149 even she** [F; not in Q2] **175 to drink deep** [F, Q1] for to drinke **178 to see** [F, Q1] to **199 waste** [F2] wast [Q2, F] **210 Where, as** [Q5] Whereas **225 Indeed, indeed** [F, Q1] Indeede **241 Very like, very like** [F, Q1] Very like **242 hundred** hundreth **243 s.p. Marcellus, Bernardo** [eds.] Both **247 tonight** to nigh **256 fare** farre **257 eleven** a leauen **259 Exeunt** [at l. 258 in Q2] **262 Foul** [F, Q1] fonde

1.3. 3 convoy is conuay, in **12 bulk bulkes** **18** [F; not in Q2] **29 weigh** way **49 like a** a **74 Are** Or **75 be** boy **76 loan** loue **77 dulls the** dulleth **110 Running** [eds.] Wrong [Q2] Roaming [F] **116 springes** springs **126 tether** tider **130 implorators** imploratotors **131 bawds** [eds.] bonds **132 beguile** beguide

1.4. 2 is a is **6 s.d. go off** [eds.] goes of **17 revel** [Q3] reueale **36 evil** [eds.] eale [Q2] ease [Q3] **37 often dout** [eds.] of a doubt **49 inurned** interr'd [Q2, Q1] **61, 79 wafts** waues **80 off** of **82 artery** arture **86 s.d. Exeunt** Exit **87 imagination** [F, Q1] imagion

1.5. 1 Whither [eds.] Whether　**21 fretful** [F, Q1] fearfull　**44 wit** [eds.] wits
48 what a what　**56 lust** [F, Q1] but　**57 sate** [F] sort　**59 scent** [eds.] sent
68 alleys [eds.] allies　**69 posset** possesse　**96 stiffly** swiftly　**119 bird** and
128 s.p. Horatio, Marcellus Booth [also at l. 151]　**heaven, my lord**
heauen　**138 Look you, I'll** I will　**179 soe'er** so mere　**185 Well** well, well
[Q1, Q2]

2.1. s.d. man [eds.] man or two　**29 Faith, no** Fayth　**41 warrant** wit
42 sullies sallies　**43 wi' the** with　**60 o'ertook** or tooke　**64 takes** take
76 s.d. Exit Reynaldo [at l. 75 in Q2]　**107 passion** passions

2.2. 57 o'erhasty hastie　**73 three** [F, Q1] threescore　**90 since brevity**
breuitie　**125 This** [Q2 has a speech prefix: *Pol.* This]　**126 above** about
137 winking working　**143 his her** [F, Q1; not in Q2]　**148 watch** wath　**149 to a** to　**151 'tis**
[F, Q1; not in Q2]　**170 s.d. Exeunt** [eds.] Exit　**210 sanity** sanctity
212–213 and suddenly . . . him [F; not in Q2]　**213 honorable lord** lord
214 most humbly take take　**215 cannot, sir** cannot　**216 more** not more
224 excellent extent　**228–229 overhappy. On** euer happy on　**229 cap** lap
240–270 Let . . . attended [F; not in Q2]　**267 s.p. Rosencrantz, Guildenstern**
Both [F]　**273 even** euer　**288 could** can　**292 off of**　**304 What a** What
306–307 admirable, in action how . . . angel, in [F, subst.] admirable in action,
how . . . Angell in　**310 no, nor** nor　**314 you** yee　**321 of** on　**324–325 the**
clown . . . sear [F; not in Q2]　**326 blank** black　**337–362 How . . . too** [F; not in Q2]　**342 berattle** [eds.] be-ratled [F]
349 most like [eds.] like most [F]　**373 lest my** let me　**381 too** to
398–399 tragical-historical, tragical-comical-historical-pastoral [F; not in Q2]
400–401 light . . . these [eds.] light for the lawe of writ, and the liberty: these
425 By 'r by　**429 e'en to 't** ento 't　**French falconers** friendly Fankners
433 s.p. [and elsewhere] First Player Player　**443 affectation** affection
446 tale [F, Q1] talke　**454 the** th'　**456 heraldry** [F, Q1] heraldy　**dismal.**
Head dismall head　**474 Then senseless Ilium** [F; not in Q2]　**481 And, like**
Like　**495 fellies** [F4] follies [Q2] Fallies [F]　**504 "Mobled queen" is good**
[F; not in Q2; F reads "Inobled"]　**506 bisson** Bison　**514 husband's** [F, Q1]
husband　**541 or** [F, Q1] lines, or　**547 till** tell　**548 s.d. Exeunt** [F; Q2 has
"Exeunt Pol. and Players" at l. 547]　**554 his** the　**556 and** an　**559 to Hec-**
uba [F, Q1] to her　**561 the cue** that　**582 O, vengeance** [F; not in Q2]
584 father [Q1, Q3, Q4; not in Q2, F]　**588 scullion** [F] stallyon [Q2] scalion
[Q1]　**600 the devil** a deale　**the devil** the deale

3.1. 1 And An　**28 too** two　**32 lawful espials** [F; not in Q2]　**33 Will** Wee'le
46 loneliness lowlines　**56 Let's withdraw** withdraw　**56 s.d. Enter Hamlet**
[at l. 55 in Q2]　**65 wished. To** wisht to　**73 disprized** despiz'd　**84 of us all**
[F, Q1; not in Q2]　**86 sicklied** sickled　**93 well, well, well** well　**100 the**
these　**108 your honesty** you　**119 inoculate** euocutat　**122 to a** a
130 knaves all knaues　**144 paintings too** [Q1] paintings　**146 jig, you amble**
gig & amble　**147 lisp** list　**148 your ignorance** [F, Q1] ignorance　**155 Th'**
expectancy Th' expectation　**159 music** musickt　**160 that** what　**161 tune**
time　**162 feature** stature　**164** [Q2 has "Exit" at the end of this line]
191 unwatched vnmatcht

3.2. 10 tatters totters　**split** [F, Q1] spleet　**27 of the** of　**29 praise** praysd
37 sir [F; not in Q2]　**45 s.d. Enter . . . Rosencrantz** [at l. 47 in Q2]
88 detecting detected　**107 s.p. [and elsewhere] Queen** Ger　**112–113** [F; not
in Q2]　**127 devil** deule [Q2] Diuel [F]　**133 s.d. sound** [eds.] sounds　**Anon**

comes Anon come   135 miching [F, Q1] munching   140 keep counsel [F, Q1]
keepe   153 s.p. [and throughout scene] Player King King   154 orbèd orb'd
the   159 s.p. [and throughout scene] Player Queen Quee   162 your our
164 [Q2 follows here with an extraneous unrhymed line: "For women feare
too much, euen as they loue"]   165 For And   166 In Eyther none in
167 love Lord   179 Wormwood, wormwood That's wormwood   180 s.d.
Player Queen [not in Q2]   188 like the   197 joys ioy   217 An And   221 a
widow [F, Q1] I be a widow   be be a   226 s.d. Exit [F, Q1] Exeunt
240 wince [Q1] winch [Q2, F]   241 s.d. [at l. 242 in Q2]   254 Confederate
[F, Q1] Considerat   256 infected [F, Q1, Q4] inuected   258 usurp vsurps
264 [F; not in Q2]   274 with two with   288 s.d. [F; at l. 293 in Q2]   308 start
stare   317 of my of   343 s.d. [at l. 341 in Q2]   357 thumb the vmber
366 to the top of to   370 can fret me [F] fret me not [Q2] can fret me, yet
[Q1]   371 s.d. [at l. 372 in Q2]   385 s.p. Polonius [F, Q1, Q4]   386 Leave
me, friends [so F; Q2 places before "I will say so," and assigns both to
Hamlet]   388 breathes breakes   390 bitter . . . day busines as the bitter day
395 daggers [F, Q1] dagger

3.3.   19 huge hough   22 ruin raine   23 but with but   50 pardoned pardon
58 Offense's [eds.] Offences   shove showe   73 pat . . . a-praying but now a
is a praying   75 revenged reuendge   79 hire and salary base and silly

3.4.   4 shroud [Q1] [eds.] silence [Q2, F]   5–6 with him . . . Mother [F; not in
Q2]   7 warrant wait   8 s.d. Enter Hamlet [at l. 5 in Q2]   21 inmost most
43 off of   51 tristful heated   53 [assigned in Q2 to Hamlet]   60 heaven-
kissing heaue, a kissing   89 panders pardons   91 my . . . soul [eds.] my very
eyes into my soule [Q2] mine eyes into my very soul [F]   92 grainèd greeued
93 not leave leaue there   100 tithe kyth   146 Ecstasy [F; not in Q2]   150 I
the the   165 live leaue   172 Refrain tonight to refraine night   193 ravel
rouell   205 to breathe [eds.] to breath   222 a [F, Q1] a most   224 s.d. Exeunt [eds.] Exit

4.2.   s.d. [Q2: "Enter Hamlet, Rosencraus, and others."]   2 [F; not in Q2]
3 s.p. Hamlet [not in Q2]   4 s.d. [F; not in Q2]   7 Compounded Compound
19 ape apple   31–32 Hide . . . after [F; not in Q2]

4.3.   44 With fiery quickness [F; not in Q2]   56 and so so   72 were will
begun begin

4.4.   20–21 name. To name To

4.5.   16 Let . . . in [assigned in Q2 to Horatio]   20 s.d. [at l. 16 in Q2]   38 with
all with   57 Indeed, la Indeede   83 in their in   90 his this   98 [F; not in
Q2]   100 are is   100 s.d. [at l. 97 in Q2]   103 impetuous [Q3, F2] impitious
[Q2] impittious [F]   109 They The   146 swoopstake [eds.] soopstake [Q1
reads "Swoop-stake-like"]   158 Let her come in [assigned in Q2 to Laertes
and placed before "How now, what noyse is that?"]   s.d. Enter Ophelia
[after l. 157 in Q2]   162 Till Tell   165 an old [F, Q1] a poore   166–168, 170 [F;
not in Q2]   186 must [F, Q1] may   191 affliction [F, Q1] afflictions   199 All
flaxen Flaxen   203 Christian [F] Christians   souls, I pray God [F, Q1] souls
204 you see you   217 trophy, sword trophe sword

4.6.   7, 9 s.p. First Sailor Say   22 good turn turn   26 bore bord   30 He So
31 will give will

4.7.   6 proceeded proceede   7 crimeful criminall   15 conjunctive concliue

22 gyves Giues   **23 loud a wind** loued Arm'd   **25 had** haue   **37 How . . .
Hamlet** [F; not in Q2]   **38 This** These   **46–47 your pardon** you pardon
48 and more strange [F; not in Q2]   **Hamlet** [F; not in Q2]   **56 shall live**
[F, Q1] liue   **62 checking** the King   **78 ribbon** [eds.] ribaud   **89 my** me
116 wick [eds.] weeke   **123 spendthrift** [Q5] spend thirfts   **126 yourself in
deed** indeede your fathers sonne   **135 on** ore   **139 pass** pace   **141 for that**
for   **157 ha 't** hate   **160 prepared** prefard   **168 hoar** horry   **172 cold** cull-
cold   **192 douts** [F "doubts"] drownes

5.1. 1 s.p [and throughout] First Clown Clowne   **3 s.p.** [and throughout]
Second Clown Other   **9 se offendendo** so offended   **12 and to** to   **Argal** or
all   **34–37 Why . . . arms** [F; not in Q2]   **43 that** frame that   **55 s.d.** [at l. 65
in Q2]   **60 stoup** soope   **85 meant** [F, Q1, Q3] went   **89 mazard** massene
106–107 Is . . . recoveries [F; not in Q2]   **107–108 Will his** will   **109 double
ones too** doubles   **120 O** or   **121** [F; not in Q2]   **143 Of all** Of   **165 nowadays** [F; not in Q2]   **183 Let me see** [F; not in Q]   **192 chamber** [F, Q1] table
208–209 As thus [F; not in Q2]   **216 winter's** waters   **226, 235 s.p. Priest**
Doct   **231 Shards, flints** Flints   **247 treble** double   **262 and rash** rash
288 thus this   **301 shortly** thereby   **302 Till** Tell

5.2. 5 Methought my thought   **6 bilboes** bilbo   **9 pall** fall   **17 unseal** vnfold
19 Ah [eds.] A   **29 villainies** villaines   **30 Ere** Or   **43 "as"** es as sir
52 Subscribed Subscribe   **57, 68–80** [F; not in Q2]   **73 interim is** [eds.]
interim's [F]   **78 court** [eds.] count [F]   **81 s.p.** [and throughout] Osric Cour
82 humbly humble   **93 Put your** your   **98 sultry** sully   **for** or   **107 gentleman** [eds.] gentlemen   **109 feelingly** [Q4] fellingly   **114 dozy** [eds.] dazzie
yaw [eds.] raw   **141 his** [eds.] this   **149 hangers** hanger   **156 carriages**
carriage   **159 might be** be might   **162 impawned, as** [eds.] all [Q2] impon'd,
as [F]   **181 Yours, yours. 'A does** Yours doo's [Q2] impon'd   **186 comply** so   **190 yeasty**
histy   **191 fanned** [eds.] prophane [Q2] fond [F]   **winnowed** trennowed
210 But thou thou   **218 be now** be   **220 will come** well come   **238** [F; not in
Q2]   **248 To keep** To   **till all**   **252 foils. Come on** foils   **255 off** of
261 bettered better   **270 union** Vnice ["Onixe" in some copies]   **288 A touch,
a touch, I** I   **302 afeard** sure   **316 Hamlet. Hamlet** Hamlet   **319 thy** [F, Q1]
my   **327 murderous** [F; not in Q2]   **328 off** of   **thy union** [F, Q1] the Onixe
345 ha 't [eds.] hate [Q2] have 't [F]   **366 proud** prou'd   **369 s.p. First Ambassador** Embas   **373** [and some other places] **Rosencrantz** Rosencraus   **381 th'**
yet yet   **385 forced** for no   **394 on** no

Passages contained only in F and omitted from Q2 are noted in the textual
notes above. It might be useful here to list the more important instances in
which Q2 contains words, lines, and passages omitted in F.

1.1. 112–129 BERNARDO I think . . . countrymen

1.2. 58–60 wrung . . . consent

1.3. 9 perfume and

1.4. 17–38 This heavy-headed . . . scandal   **75–78** The very . . . beneath

2.1. 122 Come

2.2. 17 Whether . . . thus   **217** except my life   **363** very   **366** 'Sblood (and some other
profanity passim)   **371** then   **444–445** as wholesome . . . fine   **521–522** of this   **589** Hum

3.2. 169–170 Where . . . there   **216–217** To . . . scope

3.4. 72–77 Sense . . . difference   **79–82** Eyes . . . mope   **168–172** That monster . . . put on
174–177 the next . . . potency   **187** One word . . . lady   **209–217** There's . . . meet

4.1. 4 Bestow . . . while   **41–44** Whose . . . air

4.2. 4 But soft

4.3. 26–29 KING Alas . . . worm

4.4. 9–67 *Enter Hamlet* . . . worth

4.5. 33 Oho

4.7. 68–82 LAERTES My lord . . . graveness   **101–103** Th' escrimers . . . them
115–124 There . . . ulcer

5.1. 154 There

5.2. 106–142 here is . . . unfellowed (replaced in F by "you are not ignorant of what
excellence Laertes is at his weapon")   **154–155** HORATIO [*To Hamlet*] I knew . . . done
193–207 *Enter a Lord* . . . lose, my lord (replaced in F by "You will lose this wager, my
lord")   **222** Let be

Shakespeare's Sources

The ultimate source of the *Hamlet* story is Saxo Grammaticus's *Historia Danica* (1180–1208), the saga of one Amlothi or (as Saxo calls him) Amlethus. The outline of the story is essentially that of Shakespeare's play, even though the emphasis of the Danish saga is overwhelmingly on cunning, brutality, and bloody revenge. Amlethus' father is Horwendil, a Governor of Jutland, who bravely kills the King of Norway in single combat and thereby wins the hand in marriage of Gerutha, daughter of the King of Denmark. This good fortune goads the envious Feng into slaying his brother Horwendil and marrying Gerutha, "capping unnatural murder with incest." Though the deed is known to everyone, Feng invents excuses and soon wins the approbation of the fawning courtiers. Young Amlethus vows revenge, but, perceiving his uncle's cunning, he feigns madness. His mingled words of craft and candor awaken suspicions that he may be playing a game of deception.

Two attempts are made to lure Amlethus into revealing that he is actually sane. The first plan is to tempt him into lechery, on the theory that one who lusts for women cannot be truly insane. Feng causes an attractive woman to be placed in a forest where Amlethus will meet her as though by chance; but Amlethus, secretly warned of the trap by a kindly foster brother, spirits the young lady off to a hideaway where they can make love unobserved by Feng's agents. She confesses the plot to Amlethus. In a second stratagem, a courtier who is reported to be "gifted with more assurance than judgment" hides himself under some straw in the Queen's chamber in order to overhear her private conversations with Amlethus. The hero, suspecting just such a trap, feigns madness and begins crowing like a noisy rooster, bouncing up and down on the straw until he finds the eavesdropper. Amlethus stabs the man to death, drags him forth, cuts the body into morsels, boils them, and flings the bits "through the mouth of an open sewer for the swine to eat." Thereupon he returns to his mother to accuse her of being an infamous harlot. He wins her over to repentant virtue and even cooperation. When Feng, returning from a journey, looks around for his counselor, Amlethus jestingly (but in part truly) suggests that the man went to the sewer and fell in.

Feng now sends Amlethus to the King of Britain with secret orders for his execution. However, Amlethus finds the letter to the British King in the coffers of the two unnamed retainers accompanying him on the journey, and substitutes a new letter ordering their execution instead. The new letter, purportedly written and signed by Feng, goes on to urge that the King of Britain marry his daughter to a young Dane being sent from the Danish court. By this means Amlethus gains an English wife and rids himself of the escorts. A year later Amlethus returns to Jutland, gets the entire court drunk, flings a tapestry (knitted for him by his mother) over the prostrate courtiers, secures the tapestry with stakes, and then sets fire to the palace. Feng escapes this holocaust, but Amlethus cuts him down with the King's own sword. (Amlethus exchanges swords because his own has been nailed fast into its scabbard by his enemies.) Subsequently, Amlethus convinces the people of the justice of his cause and is chosen King of Jutland. After ruling for several years, he returns to Britain, bigamously marries a Scottish queen, fights a battle with his first father-in-law, is betrayed by his second wife, and is finally killed in battle.

In Saxo's account we thus find the prototypes of Hamlet, Claudius, Gertrude, Polonius, Ophelia, Rosencrantz, and Guildenstern. Several episodes are close in narrative detail to Shakespeare's play: the original murder and incestuous marriage, the feigned madness, the woman used as a decoy, the eavesdropping counselor, and especially the trip to England. A translation of Saxo into French by François de Belleforest, in *Histoires Tragiques* (1576 edition), adds a few details, such as Gertrude's adultery before the murder and Hamlet's melancholy. Belleforest's version is longer than Saxo's, with more psychological and moral observation and more dialogue. Shakespeare probably consulted it.

Shakespeare need not have depended extensively on these older versions of his story, however. His main source was almost certainly an old play of *Hamlet*. Much evidence testifies to the existence of such a play. The *Diary* of Philip

Henslowe, a theater owner and manager, records a performance, not marked as "new," of a *Hamlet* at Newington Butts on June 11, 1594, by "my Lord Admiral's men" or "my Lord Chamberlain's men," probably the latter. Thomas Lodge's pamphlet *Wit's Misery and the World's Madness* (1596) refers to "the vizard of the ghost which cried so miserably at the theater, like an oyster wife, 'Hamlet, revenge!'" And Thomas Nashe, in his *Epistle* prefixed to Robert Greene's romance *Menaphon* (1589), offers the following observation:

> It is a common practice nowadays amongst a sort of shifting companions, that run through every art and thrive by none, to leave the trade of noverint, whereto they were born, and busy themselves with the endeavors of art, that could scarcely Latinize their neck verse if they should have need; yet English Seneca read by candlelight yields many good sentences, as "Blood is a beggar" and so forth; and if you entreat him fair in a frosty morning, he will afford you whole *Hamlets*, I should say handfuls, of tragical speeches. But O grief! *Tempus edax rerum*, what's that will last always? The sea exhaled by drops will in continuance be dry, and Seneca, let blood line by line and page by page, at length must needs die to our stage; which makes his famished followers to imitate the Kid in Aesop, who, enamored with the Fox's newfangles, forsook all hopes of life to leap into a new occupation; and these men, renouncing all possibilities of credit or estimation, to intermeddle with Italian translations . . .

Nashe's testimonial describes a *Hamlet* play, written in the Senecan style by some person born to the trade of "noverint," or scrivener, who has turned to hack writing and translation. The description has often been fitted to Thomas Kyd, though this identification is not certain. (Nashe could be punning on Kyd's name when he refers to "the Kid in Aesop.") Certainly Thomas Kyd's *The Spanish Tragedy* (c. 1587) shows many affinities with Shakespeare's play, and provides many Senecan ingredients missing from Saxo and Belleforest: the ghost, the difficulty in ascertaining whether the ghost's words are believable, the resulting need for delay and a feigning of madness, the moral perplexities afflicting a sensitive man called upon to revenge, the play within the play, the clever reversals and ironically caused deaths in the catastrophe, the rhetoric of tragical passion. Whether or not Kyd in fact wrote the *Ur-Hamlet*, his extant play enables us to see more clearly what that lost play must have contained. The pirated first quarto of *Hamlet* (1603) also offers a few seemingly authentic details that are not found in the authoritative second quarto but are found in the earlier sources and may have been a part of the *Ur-Hamlet*. For example, after Hamlet has killed Corambis (corresponding to Polonius), the Queen vows to assist Hamlet in his strategies against the King; and later, when Hamlet has returned to England, the Queen sends him a message by Horatio warning him to be careful.

One last document sheds light on the *Ur-Hamlet*. A German play, *Der bestrafte Brudermord* (*Fratricide Punished*), from a now-lost manuscript dated 1710, seems to have been based on a text used by English actors traveling in Germany in 1586 and afterward. Though changed by translation and manuscript transmission, and too entirely different from Shakespeare's play to have been based on it, this German version may well have been based on Shakespeare's source-play. Polonius's name in this text, Corambus, is the Corambis of the first quarto of 1603. (The name may mean "cabbage cooked twice," for *coramble-bis*, a proverbially dull dish.)

Der bestrafte Brudermord begins with a prologue in the Senecan manner, followed by the appearance of the ghost to Francisco, Horatio, and sentinels of the watch. Within the palace, meanwhile, the King carouses. Hamlet joins the watch, confiding to Horatio that he is "sick at heart" over his father's death and mother's hasty remarriage. The ghost appears to Hamlet, tells him how the juice of hebona was poured into his ear, and urges revenge. When Hamlet swears Horatio and Francisco to silence, the ghost (now invisible) says several times "We swear," his voice following the men as they move from place to place. Hamlet reveals to Horatio the entire circumstance of the murder. Later, in a formal session of the court, the new King speaks hypocritically of his brother's death and explains the reasons for his marriage to the Queen. Hamlet is forbidden to return to Wittenberg, though Corambus's son Leonhardus has already set out for France.

Some time afterward, Corambus reports the news of Hamlet's madness to the King and Queen, and presumes on the basis of his own youthful passions to diagnose Hamlet's malady as lovesickness. Concealed, he and the King overhear Hamlet tell Ophelia to "go to a nunnery." When players arrive from Germany, Hamlet instructs them in the natural style of acting, and then requests them to perform a play before the King about the murder of King Pyrrus by his brother. (Death is again inflicted by hebona poured in the ear.) After the King's guilty reaction to the play, Hamlet finds him alone at prayers but postpones the killing lest the King's soul be sent to heaven. Hamlet kills Corambus behind the tapestry in the Queen's chamber, and is visited again by the ghost (who says nothing, however). Ophelia, her mind deranged, thinks herself in love with a court butterfly named Phantasmo. (This creature is also involved in a comic action to help the clown Jens with a tax problem.) The King sends Hamlet to England with two unnamed courtiers who are instructed to kill Hamlet after their arrival. A contrary wind takes them instead to an island near Dover, where Hamlet foils his two enemies by kneeling between them and asking them to shoot him on signal; at the proper moment, he ducks and they shoot each other. He finishes them off with their own swords, and discovers letters on their persons ordering Hamlet's execution by the English King if the original plot should fail. When Hamlet returns to Denmark, the King arranges a duel between him and Corambus's son Leonhardus. If Leonhardus's poisoned dagger misses its mark, a beaker of wine containing finely ground oriental diamond dust is to do the rest. Hamlet is informed of the impending duel by Phantasmo (compare Osric), whom Hamlet taunts condescendingly and calls "Signora Phantasmo." Shortly before the duel takes place, Ophelia is reported to have thrown herself off a hill to her death. The other deaths occur much as in Shakespeare's play. The dying Hamlet bids that the crown be conveyed to his cousin, Duke Fortempras of Norway, of whom we have not heard earlier.

From the extensive similarities between *Hamlet* and this German play, we can see that Shakespeare inherited his narrative material almost intact, though in a jumble and so pitifully mangled that the modern reader can only laugh at the contrast. No source study in Shakespeare reveals so clearly the extent of Shakespeare's wholesale borrowing of plot, and the incredible transformation he achieved in re-ordering his materials.

The following excerpt is from the English *The History of Hamlet*, 1608, an unacknowledged translation of Belleforest that in one or two places seems to have been influenced by Shakespeare's play—as when Hamlet beats his arms on the hangings of the Queen's apartment instead of jumping on the quilt or bed, as in Belleforest, and cries, "A rat! a rat!" It is otherwise a close translation and, although too late for Shakespeare to have used, provides an Elizabethan version of the account Shakespeare most likely used.

The History of Hamlet
Prince of Denmark

CHAPTER 1

How Horvendil and Fengon were made Governors of the Province of Ditmarse, and how Horvendil married Geruth, the daughter to Roderick, chief King of Denmark, by whom he had Hamlet; and how after his marriage his brother Fengon slew him traitorously and married his brother's wife, and what followed.

You must understand, that long time before the kingdom of Denmark received the faith of Jesus Christ and embraced the doctrine of the Christians, that the common people in those days were barbarous and uncivil and their princes cruel, without faith or loyalty, seeking nothing but murder and deposing or at the least offending each other either in honors, goods, or lives, not caring to ransom such as they took prisoners but rather sacrificing them to the cruel vengeance naturally imprinted in their hearts; in such sort that if there were sometimes a good prince or king among them who, being adorned with the most perfect gifts of nature, would addict himself to virtue and use courtesy, although the people held him in admiration (as virtue is admirable to the most wicked) yet the envy of his neighbors was so great that they never ceased until that virtuous man were dispatched out of the world.

King Roderick, as then reigning in Denmark, after he had appeased the troubles in the country and driven the Swethlanders and Slaveans from thence, he divided the kingdom into divers provinces, placing governors therein, who after (as the like happened in France) bare the names of dukes, marquesses, and earls, giving the government of Jutie (at this present called Ditmarse), lying upon the country of the Cimbrians in the straight or narrow part of land that showeth like a point or cape of ground upon the sea which northward* bordereth upon the country of Norway, to two* valiant and warlike lords, Horvendil and Fengon, sons to Gervendil, who likewise had been governor of that province.

Now the greatest honor that men of noble birth could at that time win and obtain was in exercising the art of piracy upon the seas, assailing their neighbors and the countries bordering upon them; and how much the more they used to rob, pill,[1] and spoil other provinces and islands far adjacent, so much the more their honors and reputation increased and augmented. Wherein Horvendil obtained the highest place in his time, being the most renowned pirate that in those days scoured the seas and havens of the north parts; whose great fame so moved the heart of Collere, King of Norway, that he was much grieved to hear that Horvendil surmounted*[2] him in feats of arms, thereby obscuring the glory by him already obtained upon the seas—honor more than covetousness of riches in those days being the reason that provoked those barbarian princes to overthrow and vanquish one the other, not caring[3] to be slain by the hands of a victorious person.

This valiant and hardy king having challenged Horvendil to fight with him body to body, the combat was by him accepted, with conditions that he which should be vanquished should lose all the riches he had in his ship and that the vanquisher should cause the body of the vanquished (that should be slain in the combat) to be honorably buried, death being the prize and reward of him that should lose the battle. And to conclude, Collere, King of Norway, although a valiant, hardy, and courageous prince, was in the end vanquished and slain by Horvendil, who presently caused a tomb to be erected and therein, with all honorable obsequies fit for a prince, buried the body of King Collere, according to their ancient manner and superstitions in these days and the conditions of the combat, bereaving the King's ships of all their riches; and, having slain the King's sister, a very brave and valiant warrior, and overrun all the coast of Norway and the Northern Islands, returned home again laden with much treasure, sending the most part thereof to his sovereign, King Roderick, thereby to procure

---

1 pill plunder   **2 surmounted** excelled   **3 not caring** i.e., not considering it dishonorable

his good liking and so to be accounted one of the greatest favorites about His Majesty.

The King, allured by those presents and esteeming himself happy to have so valiant a subject, sought by a great favor and courtesy to make him become bounden unto him perpetually, giving him Geruth his daughter to his wife, of whom he knew Horvendil to be already much enamored. And, the more to honor him, determined himself in person to conduct her into Jutie, where the marriage was celebrated according to the ancient manner. And, to be brief, of this marriage proceeded Hamlet, of whom I intend to speak, and for his cause have chosen to renew this present history.

Fengon, brother to this prince Horvendil, who, not only* fretting and despiting[4] in his heart at the great honor and reputation won by his brother in warlike affairs but solicited and provoked by a foolish jealousy to see him honored with royal alliance, and fearing thereby to be deposed from his part of the government—or rather desiring to be only governor, thereby to obscure the memory of the victories and conquests of his brother Horvendil—determined, whatsoever happened, to kill him; which he effected in such sort that no man once so much as suspected him, every man esteeming that from such and so firm a knot of alliance and consanguinity there could proceed no other issue than the full effects of virtue and courtesy. But, as I said before, the desire of bearing sovereign rule and authority respecteth neither blood nor amity, nor caring for virtue, as being wholly without respect of laws or majesty divine; for it is not possible that he which invadeth the country and taketh away the riches of another man without cause or reason should know or fear God. Was not this a crafty and subtle counselor? But he might have thought that the mother, knowing her husband's case, would not cast her son into the danger of death.

But Fengon, having secretly assembled certain men, and perceiving himself strong enough to execute his enterprise, Horvendil his brother being at a banquet with his friends,

4 despiting entertaining a grudge

suddenly set upon him, where he slew him as traitorously as cunningly he purged himself of so detestable a murder to his subjects; for that before he had any violent or bloody hands, or once committed parricide upon his brother, he had incestuously abused his wife, whose honor he ought as well to have sought and procured as traitorously he pursued and effected his destruction. And it is most certain that the man that abandoneth himself to any notorious and wicked action whereby he becometh a great sinner, he careth not to commit much more heinous and abominable offenses; and covered his boldness and wicked practice with so great subtlety and policy, and under a veil of mere simplicity, that, being favored for the honest love that he bare to his sister-in-law—for whose sake, he affirmed, he had in that sort murdered his brother—that his sin found excuse among the common people and of the nobility was esteemed for justice. For that Geruth, being as courteous a princess as any then living in the north parts, and one that had never once so much as offended any of her subjects, either commons or courtiers, this adulterer and infamous murderer slandered his dead brother that he would have slain his wife,[5] and that he,[6] by chance finding him upon the point ready to do it, in defense of the lady had slain him, bearing off the blows which as then he[7] struck at the innocent princess without any other cause of malice whatsoever. Wherein he wanted[8] no false witnesses to approve[9] his act, which deposed[10] in like sort as the wicked calumniator himself protested, being the same persons that had borne him company and were participants of his treason. So that instead of pursuing him as a parricide and an incestuous person, all the courtiers admired and flattered him in his good fortune, making more account of false witnesses and detestable wicked reporters, and more honoring the calumniators, than they esteemed of those that, seeking to call the matter in question and admiring the virtues of the murdered prince, would have punished the massacrers and bereavers of his life.

---

5 slandered . . . wife i.e., made the slanderous accusation that Horvendil intended to slay his wife, Geruth   **6 he** i.e., Fengon   **7 he** i.e., Horvendil   **8 he wanted** i.e., Fengon lacked   **9 approve** confirm   **10 which deposed** who testified

Which was the cause that Fengon, boldened and encouraged by such impunity, durst venture to couple himself in marriage with her whom he used as his concubine during good Horvendil's life, in that sort spotting his name with a double vice, and charging his conscience with abominable guilt and twofold impiety, as[11] incentuous adultery and parricide murder. And that[12] the unfortunate and wicked woman, that had received the honor to be the wife of one of the valiantest and wisest* princes in the north, embased[13] herself in such vile sort as to falsify her faith unto him and, which is worse, to marry him that had been the tyrannous murderer of her lawful husband; which made divers men think that she had been the causer of the murder, thereby to live in her adultery without control.

But where shall a man find a more wicked and bold woman than a great personage once having loosed the bonds of honor and honesty? This princess, who at the first for her rare virtues and courtesies was honored of all men and beloved of her husband, as soon as she once gave ear to the tyrant Fengon forgot both the rank she held among the greatest names and the duty of an honest wife on her behalf. But I will not stand to gaze and marvel at women, for that there are many which seek to blaze[14] and set them forth, in which their writings they spare not to blame them all for the faults of some one or few women. But I say that either nature ought to have bereaved[15] man of that opinion to accompany[16] with women, or else to endow them with such spirits as that they may easily support the crosses they endure without complaining so often and so strangely, seeing it is their own beastliness that overthrows them. For if it be so that a woman is so imperfect a creature as they make her to be, and that they know this beast to be so hard to be tamed as they affirm, why then are they so foolish to preserve them and so dull and brutish as to trust their deceitful and wanton embracings? But let us leave her in this extremity of lasciviousness, and proceed to show you in what sort the young Prince Hamlet behaved himself to escape the tyranny of his uncle.

---

11 **as** that is, to wit   12 **And that** i.e., and was the cause that   13 **embased** lowered, debased   14 **blaze** proclaim   15 **bereaved** deprived   16 **accompany** keep company

CHAPTER 2

How Hamlet counterfeited the madman to escape the tyranny of his uncle, and how he was tempted by a woman through his uncle's procurement, who thereby thought to undermine the Prince and by that means to find out whether he counterfeited madness or not; and how Hamlet would by no means be brought to consent unto her, and what followed.

GERUTH having, as I said before, so much forgotten herself, the Prince Hamlet, perceiving himself to be in danger of his life, as being abandoned of his own mother and forsaken of all men, and assuring himself that Fengon would not detract[1] the time to send him the same way his father Horvendil was gone, to beguile[2] the tyrant in his subtleties (that esteemed him to be of such a mind that if he once attained to man's estate[3] he would not long delay the time to revenge the death of his father), counterfeited* the madman with such craft and subtle practices that he made show as if he had utterly lost his wits, and under that veil he covered his pretense and defended his life from the treasons and practices of the tyrant his uncle. And although[4] he had been at the school of[5] the Roman prince who, because he counterfeited himself to be a fool, was called Brutus,[6] yet he imitated his fashions and his wisdom. For, every day being in the Queen's palace (who as then was more careful to please her whoremaster than ready to revenge the cruel death of her husband or to restore her son to his inheritance), he rent and tore his clothes, wallowing and lying in the dirt and mire, his face all filthy and black, running through the streets like a man distraught, not speaking one word but such as seemed to proceed of madness and mere[7] frenzy, all his actions and gestures being no other than the right countenances[8] of a man wholly deprived of all reason and understanding, in such sort that as then he

---

1 **detract** lengthen   2 **to beguile** in order to beguile   3 **man's estate** manhood   4 **although** inasmuch as   5 **been at the school of** i.e., studied the method of   6 **Brutus** (Lucius Junius Brutus assumed the disguise of idiocy in order to escape the fate of his brother, whom their uncle Tarquinius Superbus had put to death. *Brutus* means "stupid.")
7 **mere** absolute   8 **right countenances** true demeanor

seemed fit for nothing but to make sport[9] to the pages and ruffling[10] courtiers that attended in the court of his uncle and father-in-law.[11] But the young Prince noted them well enough, minding one day to be revenged in such manner that the memory thereof should remain perpetually to the world. . . .

Hamlet, in this sort counterfeiting the madman, many times did divers actions of great and deep consideration, and often made such and so fit answers that a wise man would soon have judged from what spirit so fine an invention might proceed; for that standing by the fire and sharpening sticks like poniards and pricks, one in smiling manner asked him wherefore he made those little staves so sharp at the points? "I prepare," saith he, "piercing darts and sharp arrows to revenge my father's death." Fools, as I said before, esteemed those his words as nothing; but men of quick spirits and such as had a deeper reach[12] began to suspect somewhat, esteeming that under that kind of folly there lay hidden a great and rare subtlety such as one day might be prejudicial to their prince, saying that under color of such rudeness he shadowed a crafty policy and by his devised simplicity he concealed a sharp and pregnant[13] spirit.

For which cause they counseled the King to try and know, if it were possible, how to discover the intent and meaning of the young Prince. And they could find no better nor more fit invention to entrap him than to set some fair and beautiful woman in a secret place that, with flattering speeches and all the craftiest means she could use, should purposely seek to allure his mind to have his pleasure of her. For the nature of all young men, especially such as are brought up wantonly, is so transported with the desires of the flesh, and entereth so greedily into the pleasures thereof, that it is almost impossible to cover the foul affection, neither yet to dissemble or hide the same by art or industry, much less to shun it. What cunning or subtlety soever they use to cloak their pretense, seeing occasion offered, and that in secret, especially in the most enticing sin that reigneth in man, they cannot choose,

---

9 **make sport** serve as the butt of joking   10 **ruffling** swaggering   11 **father-in-law** i.e., stepfather   12 **reach** comprehension   13 **pregnant** fertile, inventive

being constrained by voluptuousness, but fall to natural effect and working.

To this end certain courtiers were appointed to lead Hamlet into a solitary place within the woods, whither they brought the woman, inciting him to take their pleasures together and to embrace one another—but the subtle practices used in these our days,[14] not to try if men of great account be extract[15] out of their wits but rather to deprive them of strength, virtue, and wisdom by means of such devilish practitioners and infernal* spirits, their domestical servants and ministers of corruption. And surely the poor Prince at this assault had been[16] in great danger, if a gentleman (that in Horvendil's time had been nourished with him) had not shown himself more affectioned to the bringing-up he had received with Hamlet than desirous to please the tyrant who by all means sought to entangle the son in the same nets wherein the father had ended his days. This gentleman bare the courtiers (appointed as aforesaid of this treason) company, more desiring to give the Prince instruction what he should do than to entrap him, making full account that the least show of perfect sense and wisdom[17] that Hamlet should make would be sufficient to cause him to lose his life. And therefore by certain signs he gave Hamlet intelligence in what danger he was like[18] to fall, if by any means he seemed to obey or once like the wanton toys[19] and vicious provocations of the gentlewoman sent thither by his uncle. Which much abashed the Prince, as then wholly being in affection to the lady; but by her he was likewise informed of the treason, as being one that from her infancy loved and favored him and would have been exceeding sorrowful for his misfortune, and much more[20] to leave his company without enjoying the pleasure of his body, whom she loved more than herself. The Prince in this sort having both deceived the courtiers and the lady's expectation, that affirmed and swore that he never once offered to have his pleasure of the woman, although in subtlety[21] he affirmed the contrary, every man thereupon

---

14 but . . . days i.e., machinations used often enough in more recent times. but only 15 extract extracted, removed 16 had been would have been 17 the least . . . wisdom (Hamlet's yielding to the lady's blandishments would be viewed as a proof of sanity and would thus betray him to his uncle.) 18 like likely 19 toys tricks 20 much more much more sorrowful 21 in subtlety in private

assured themselves that without all doubt he was distraught of his senses, that his brains were as then wholly void of force and incapable of reasonable apprehension, so that as then[22] Fengon's practice took no effect. But for all that he left not off, still seeking by all means to find out Hamlet's subtlety, as in the next chapter you shall perceive.

CHAPTER 3

How Fengon, uncle to Hamlet, a second time to entrap him in his politic madness, caused one of his counselors to be secretly hidden in the Queen's chamber, behind the arras, to hear what speeches passed between Hamlet and the Queen; and how Hamlet killed him and escaped that danger, and what followed.

AMONG the friends of Fengon there was one that above all the rest doubted of Hamlet's practices in counterfeiting the madman, who for that cause said that it was impossible that so crafty a gallant as Hamlet, that counterfeited the fool, should be discovered with so common and unskillful practices which might easily be perceived, and that to find out his politic pretense it were necessary to invent some subtle and crafty means more attractive whereby the gallant might not have the leisure to use his accustomed dissimulation. Which to effect he said he knew a fit way and a most convenient mean[1] to effect the King's desire and thereby to entrap Hamlet in his subtleties and cause him of his own accord to fall into the net prepared for him, and thereby evidently show his secret meaning.

His devise was thus: that King Fengon should make as though he were to go some long voyage concerning affairs of great importance, and that in the meantime Hamlet should be shut up alone in a chamber with his mother, wherein some other should secretly be hidden behind the hangings, unknown either to him or his mother, there to stand and hear their speeches and the complots[2] by them to be taken[3] con-

---

22 as then as of that time

1 mean means   **2 complots** conspiracy   **3 taken** undertaken

cerning the accomplishment of the dissembling fool's pretense; assuring the King that if there were any point of wisdom and perfect sense in the gallant's spirit, that without all doubt he would easily discover[4] it to his mother, as being devoid of all fear that she would utter or make known his secret intent, being the woman that had borne him in her body and nourished him so carefully; and withal[5] offered himself to be the man that should stand to hearken and bear witness of Hamlet's speeches with his mother, that he might not be esteemed a counselor in such a case wherein he refused to be the executioner for the behoof and service of his prince.

This invention pleased the King exceeding well, esteeming it as the only and sovereign remedy to heal the Prince of his lunacy, and to that end, making a long voyage, issued out of his palace and rode to hunt in the forest.

Meantime the counselor entered secretly into the Queen's chamber and there hid himself behind the arras not long before the Queen and Hamlet came thither, who, being crafty and politic, as soon as he was within the chamber, doubting[6] some treason and fearing if he should speak severely and wisely to his mother touching his secret practices he should be understood and by that means intercepted, used his ordinary manner of dissimulation and began to come like a cock,[7] beating with his arms (in such manner as cocks use to strike with their wings) upon the hangings of the chamber. Whereby, feeling something stirring under them, he cried, "A rat, a rat!" and presently drawing his sword thrust it into the hangings, which done, pulled the counselor (half dead) out by the heels, made an end of killing him, and, being slain, cut his body in pieces, which he caused to be boiled and then cast it into an open vault or privy that so it might serve for food to the hogs.

By which means having discovered the ambush and given the inventor thereof his just reward, he came again to his mother, who in the meantime wept and tormented herself to see all her hopes frustrate, for that what fault soever she had committed yet was she sore grieved to see her only child made a mere mockery—every man reproaching her with his

---

4 discover reveal   **5 withal** in addition   **6 doubting** suspecting, fearing
7 come like a cock crow like a rooster

folly, one point whereof she had as then seen before her eyes.
Which was no small prick to her conscience, esteeming that
the gods sent her that punishment for joining incestuously in
marriage with the tyrannous murderer of her husband (who
likewise ceased not to invent all the means he could to bring
his nephew to his end), accusing her* own natural indiscretion, as being the ordinary guide of those that so much desire
the pleasures of the body, who, shutting up the way to all
reason, respect not what may ensue of their lightness and
great inconstancy, and how a pleasure of small moment is
sufficient to give them cause of repentance during their lives,
and make them curse the day and time that ever any such
apprehensions entered into their minds or that they closed
their eyes to reject the honesty requisite in ladies of her
quality. . . .

And while in this sort she sat tormenting herself, Hamlet
entered into the chamber, who, having once again searched
every corner of the same, distrusting his mother as well as
the rest, and perceiving himself to be alone, began in sober
and discreet manner to speak unto her, saying,

"What treason is this, O most infamous woman of all that
ever prostrated themselves to the will of an abominable
whoremonger, who, under the veil of a dissembling creature,
covereth the most wicked and detestable crime that man
could ever imagine or was committed! Now may I be assured
to trust you that, like a vile wanton adulteress altogether impudent and given over to her pleasure, runs spreading forth
her arms joyfully to embrace the traitorous villainous tyrant
that murdered my father, and most incestuously receivest
the villain into the lawful bed of your loyal spouse, imprudently entertaining him instead of the dear father of your
miserable and discomforted son—if the gods grant him not
the grace speedily to escape from a captivity so unworthy
the degree he holdeth and the race and noble family of his ances-
tors. Is this the part of a queen and daughter to a king? To
live like a brute beast and like a mare that yieldeth her body
to the horse that hath beaten her companion away, to follow
the pleasure of an abominable king that hath murdered a far
more honester and better man than himself in massacring
Horvendil, the honor and glory of the Danes? Who are now
esteemed of no force nor valor at all since the shining splen-

dor of knighthood was brought to an end by the most wick-
edest and cruelest villain living upon earth.

"I for my part will never account him for my kinsman nor
once know him for mine uncle, nor you my dear mother, for
not having respect to the blood that ought to have united us
so straitly together, and who neither with your honor nor
without suspicion of consent to the death of your husband
could ever have agreed to have married with his cruel enemy.
O, Queen Geruth! It is the part of a bitch to couple with
many and desire acquaintance of divers mastiffs. It is licen-
tiousness only that hath made you deface out of your mind
the memory of the valor and virtues of the good king your
husband and my father. It was an unbridled desire that
guided the daughter of Roderick to embrace the tyrant
Fengon, and not to remember Horvendil (unworthy of so
strange entertainment),[8] neither that he[9] killed his brother
traitorously, and that she being his[10] father's wife betrayed
him, although he[11] so well favored and loved her that for her
sake he utterly bereaved Norway of her riches and valiant
soldiers to augment the treasures of Roderick and make
Geruth wife to the hardiest[12] prince in Europe. It is not the
part of a woman, much less of a princess, in whom all modesty, courtesy, compassion, and love ought to abound, thus to
leave her dear child to fortune in the bloody and murderous
hands of a villain and traitor. Brute beasts do not so, for lions
tigers, ounces,[13] and leopards fight for the safety and defense
of their whelps; and birds that have beaks, claws, and wings
resist such as would ravish them of their young ones. But
you, to the contrary, expose and deliver me to death, whereas
ye should defend me. Is not this as much as if you should
betray me, when you, knowing the perverseness of the tyrant
and his intents (full of deadly counsel as touching the race
and image of his brother), have not once sought nor desired
to find the means to save your child and only son by sending
him into Swethland,[14] Norway, or England, rather than to
leave him as a prey to your infamous adulterer?

"Be not offended, I pray you, madam, if, transported with

---

8 entertainment treatment   **9 neither that he** i.e., nor to remember that he,
Fengon   **10 his** i.e., Hamlet's   **11 although he** i.e., although Horvendil
12 hardiest bravest   **13 ounces** lynxes, wildcats   **14 Swethland** Sweden

dolor and grief, I speak so boldly unto you, and that I respect you less than duty requireth; for you, having forgotten me and wholly rejected the memory of the deceased king my father, must not be abashed if I also surpass the bounds and limits of due consideration. Behold into what distress I am now fallen, and to what mischief my fortune and your over-great lightness[15] and want of wisdom have induced me, that I am constrained to play the madman to save my life instead of using and practicing arms, following adventures, and seeking all means to make myself known to be the true and undoubted heir of the valiant and virtuous King Horvendil! It was not without cause and just occasion that my gestures, countenances, and words seem all to proceed from a madman, and that I desire to have all men esteem me wholly deprived of sense and reasonable understanding, because I am well assured that he that hath made no conscience to kill his own brother (accustomed to murders and allured with desire of government without control in his treasons) will not spare to save himself with the like cruelty in the blood and flesh of the loins of his brother by him massacred. . . .

"To conclude, weep not, madam, to see my folly, but rather sigh and lament your own offense, tormenting your conscience in regard of the infamy that hath so defiled the ancient renown and glory that in times past honored Queen Geruth; for we are not to sorrow and grieve at other men's vices but for our own misdeeds and great follies. Desiring you for the surplus[16] of my proceedings, above all things, as you love your own life and welfare, that neither the King nor any other may by any means know mine intent; and let me alone with the rest, for I hope in the end to bring my purpose to effect."

[The Queen contritely asks Hamlet's understanding for a marriage that (she insists) she entered into under duress, implores his forgiveness, and declares that her fondest hope is to see her son restored to his rights as heir and monarch of Denmark. Hamlet pledges his faith to her, beseeching her to put aside her attachment to Fengon, whom Hamlet "will surely kill, or cause to be put to death, in despite of all the devils in hell," along with the flatterers who serve him. In

---

15 lightness wantonness   **16 surplus** what remains still to be done

doing so he will act as the true King of Denmark, he avers, killing a traitor, not a legitimate ruler, and crowning virtue with glory while punishing regicide with ignominious death.]

After this, Fengon, as if he had been out some long journey, came to the court again and asked for him that had received the charge to play the intelligencer to entrap Hamlet in his dissembled wisdom, was abashed to hear neither news nor tidings of him, and for that cause asked Hamlet what was become of him, naming the man. The Prince, that never used lying, and who in all the answers that ever he made during his counterfeit madness never strayed from the truth (as a generous[17] mind is a mortal enemy to untruth), answered and said that the counselor he sought for was gone down through the privy where, being choked by the filthiness of the place, the hogs meeting him had filled their bellies.

CHAPTER 4

How Fengon, the third time, devised to send Hamlet to the King of England with secret letters to have him put to death; and how Hamlet, when his companions slept, read the letters, and instead of them counterfeited others, willing the King of England to put the two messengers to death and to marry his daughter to Hamlet, which was effected; and how Hamlet escaped out of England.

A MAN would have judged anything rather than that Hamlet had committed that murder; nevertheless Fengon could not content himself, but still his mind gave him[1] that the fool would play him some trick of legerdemain, and willingly would have killed him; but he feared King Roderick, his grandfather, and further durst not offend the Queen, mother to the fool, whom she loved and much cherished, showing great grief and heaviness to see him so transported out of his wits. And in that conceit,[2] seeking to be rid of him, he

17 generous highborn, noble

1 gave him misgave him, made him apprehensive   **2 conceit** frame of mind

determined* to find the means to do it by the aid of a
stranger, making the King of England minister of his massacring resolution, choosing rather that his friend should defile his renown with so great a wickedness than himself to
fall into perpetual infamy by an exploit of so great cruelty,
to whom he purposed to send him and by letters desire him
to put him to death.

Hamlet, understanding that he should be sent into England, presently doubted[3] the occasion of his voyage, and for
that cause, speaking to the Queen, desired her not to make
any show of sorrow or grief for his departure, but rather
counterfeit a gladness as being rid of his presence whom, although she loved, yet she daily grieved to see him in so pitiful
estate, deprived of all sense and reason; desiring her further
that she should hang the hall with tapestry and make it fast
with nails upon the walls and keep the brands[4] for him which
he had sharpened at the points, then whenas[5] he said he
made arrows to revenge the death of his father. Lastly he
counseled her that, the year after his departure being accomplished, she should celebrate his funerals, assuring her that at
the same instant she should see him return with great con-
tentment and pleasure unto her from that his voyage.

Now, to bear him company were assigned two of Fengon's
faithful ministers, bearing letters engraved in wood that contained Hamlet's death, in such sort as he had advertised[6] the
King of England. But the subtle Danish Prince, being at sea,
whilst his companions slept, having read the letters and
known his uncle's great treason, with the wicked and villainous minds of the two courtiers that led him to the slaughter,
rased[7] out the letters that concerned his death and instead
thereof graved others with commission to the King of England to hang his two companions; and not content to turn
the death they had devised against him upon their own
necks, wrote further that King Fengon willed him to give
his daughter to Hamlet in marriage.

And so arriving in England, the messengers presented

---

3 presently doubted at once suspected   **4 brands** i.e., the staves or sticks
that Hamlet sharpened as though in his madness; see Chapter 2. (*A brand*
is usually a piece of wood that has been burning on the hearth or is to be
used as a torch.)   **5 then whenas** on that occasion when   **6 advertised**
given notice to, commanded   **7 rased** erased, or possibly *razed*, scraped

themselves to the King, giving him Fengon's letters, who, having read the contents, said nothing as then, but stayed[8] convenient time to effect Fengon's desire, meantime using the Danes familiarly, doing them that honor to sit at his table (for that kings as then were not so curiously nor solemnly[9] served as in these our days, for in these days mean[10] kings and lords of small revenue are as difficult and hard to be seen as in times past the monarchs of Persia used to be, or as it is reported of the great King of Ethiopia, who will not permit any man to see his face, which ordinarily he covereth with a veil). And as the messengers sat at the table with the King, subtle Hamlet was so far from being merry with them that he would not taste one bit of meat, bread, nor cup of beer whatsoever as then set upon the table, not without great wondering of the company, abashed to see a young man and a stranger not to esteem of the delicate meats and pleasant drinks served at the banquet, rejecting them as things filthy, evil of taste, and worse prepared. The King, who for that time dissembled what he thought, caused his guests to be conveyed into their chamber, willing one of his secret servants to hide himself therein and so to certify him what speeches passed among the Danes at their going to bed.

Now they were no sooner entered into the chamber, and those that were appointed to attend upon them gone out, but Hamlet's companions asked him why he refused to eat and drink of that which he found upon the table, not honoring the banquet of so great a king, that entertained them in friendly sort, with such honor and courtesy as it deserved? Saying further that he did not well but dishonored him that sent him, as if he sent men into England that feared to be poisoned by so great a king. The Prince, that had done nothing without reason and prudent consideration, answered them and said: "What, think you that I will eat bread dipped in human blood, and defile my throat with the rust of iron, and use that meat that stinketh and savoreth of man's flesh already putrified and corrupted, and that scenteth like the savor of a dead carrion long since cast into a vault? And how would you have me to respect the King that hath the countenance of a slave, and the Queen, who instead of great maj-

8 **stayed** awaited   9 **curiously nor solemnly** fastidiously or ceremoniously
10 **mean** insignificant

esty, hath done three things more like a woman of base parentage and fitter for a waiting-gentlewoman than beseeming a lady of her quality and estate?" And, having said so, used many injurious and sharp speeches as well against the King and Queen as others that had assisted at that banquet for the entertainment of the Danish ambassadors. And therein Hamlet said truth, as hereafter you shall hear, for that in those days, the north parts of the world, living as then under Satan's laws, were full of enchanters, so that there was not any young gentleman whatsoever that knew not something therein sufficient to serve his turn if need required, as yet in those days in Gotland[11] and Biarmy[12] there are many that knew not what the Christian religion permitteth, as by reading the histories of Norway and Gotland you may easily perceive. And so Hamlet, while his father lived, had been instructed in that devilish art whereby the wicked spirit abuseth mankind and advertiseth him (as he can) of things past.

[Hamlet, aided by the devilish power of magic he has learned, amazes the King of England by demonstrating the truth of the riddling and prophetic statements he has just uttered. It turns out that the King's bread is in fact defiled by human blood shed on the battlefield where the grain was grown, that his pork comes from hogs that have fed on a hanged thief, that his beer is brewed from a water supply polluted by rusty armor, and that, more distressingly, the King is the illegitimate son of a slave and the Queen of no less base parentage. The King thereupon treats Hamlet with the respect that such awesome magical powers deserve.]

The King, admiring the young Prince and beholding in him some matter of greater respect than in the common sort of men, gave him his daughter in marriage, according to the counterfeit letters by him devised, and the next day caused the two servants of Fengon to be executed, to satisfy, as he thought, the King's desire. But Hamlet, although the sport[13]

---

11 **Gotland** an area in what is now southern Sweden 12 **Biarmy** a region in northern Lapland 13 **the sport** i.e., the execution of his two companions. (Hamlet pretends to be offended at this so that the King will pacify him with a large gift, as he does.)

pleased him well, and that the King of England could not
have done him a greater favor, made as though he had been
much offended, threatening the King to be revenged; but the
King, to appease him, gave him a great sum of gold, which
Hamlet caused to be molten and put into two staves, made
hollow for the same purpose, to serve his turn therewith as
need should require. For of all the King's treasures he took
nothing with him into Denmark but only those two staves,
and as soon as the year began to be at an end, having somewhat before obtained license of the King his father-in-law to
depart, went for Denmark, then with all the speed he could to
return again into England to marry his daughter; and so set
sail for Denmark.

CHAPTER 5

*How Hamlet, having escaped out of England, arrived in
Denmark the same day that the Danes were celebrating his
funerals, supposing him to be dead in England; and how he
revenged his father's death upon his uncle and the rest of
the courtiers; and what followed.*

HAMLET in that sort sailing into Denmark, being arrived in
the country entered into the palace of his uncle the same day
that they were celebrating his funerals, and, going into the
hall, procured no small astonishment and wonder to them
all—no man thinking other but that he had been dead.
Among the which many of them rejoiced not a little for the
pleasure which they knew Fengon would conceive for so
pleasant a loss,[1] and some were sad, as remembering the
honorable King Horvendil, whose victories they could by no
means forget, much less deface out of their memories that
which appertained unto him, who[2] as then greatly rejoiced to
see a false report spread[3] of Hamlet's death and that the tyrant had not as yet obtained his will of the heir of Jutie,[4] but
rather hoped God would restore him to his senses again for

---

1 rejoiced . . . loss i.e., rejoiced greatly to think how Fengon had desired
the loss of Hamlet and how he would now be frustrated   **2 who** i.e., the
courtiers who admire Hamlet   **3 rejoiced . . . spread** i.e., rejoiced to
learn that the rumor was false   **4 Jutie** Jutland, Denmark

the good and welfare of that province. Their amazement at
the last[5] being turned into laughter, all that as then were assistant at the funeral banquet of him whom they esteemed
dead mocked each at other for having been so simply deceived, and, wondering at the Prince, that in his so long a
voyage he had not recovered any of his senses, asked what
was become of them that had borne him company into Great
Britain? To whom he made answer (showing them the two
hollow staves wherein he had put his molten gold that the
King of England had given him to appease his fury concerning the murder of his two companions) and said, "Here they
are both." Whereat many that already knew his humors
presently conjectured that he had played some trick of legerdemain, and to deliver himself out of danger had thrown
them into the pit prepared for him; so that, fearing to follow
after them and light upon some evil adventure, they went
presently out of the court. And it was well for them that they
did so, considering the tragedy acted by him the same day,
being accounted his funeral but in truth their last days that
as then rejoiced for his* overthrow.[6]

For when every man busied himself to make good cheer,
and Hamlet's arrival provoked them more to drink and carouse, the Prince himself at that time played the butler and a
gentleman attending on the tables, not suffering the pots nor
goblets to be empty, whereby he gave the noblemen such
store of liquor that all of them, being full laden with wine
and gorged with meat, were constrained to lay themselves
down in the same place where they had supped, so much
their senses were dulled and overcome with the fire of over-
great drinking (a vice common and familiar among the Almains[7] and other nations inhabiting the north parts of the
world). Which when Hamlet perceiving, and finding so good
opportunity to effect his purpose and be revenged of his enemies, and, by the means to abandon the actions, gestures,
and apparel of a madman, occasion so fitly finding his turn
and as it were effecting itself, failed not to take hold thereof,[8]
and, seeing those drunken bodies filled with wine, lying like

5 at the last finally   6 but in truth . . . overthrow i.e., a day that was
supposed to have been for Hamlet's funeral but that in truth became
the day of doom for those who had rejoiced in his overthrow
7 Almains Germans   8 take hold thereof seize the opportunity

hogs upon the ground, some sleeping, others vomiting the over-great abundance of wine which without measure they had swallowed up, made the hangings about the hall to fall down and cover them all over, which he nailed to the ground, being boarded, and at the ends thereof he stuck the brands whereof I spake before, by him sharpened, which served for pricks,[9] binding and tying the hangings in such sort that, what force soever they used to loose themselves, it was unpossible to get from under them. And presently he set fire to the four corners of the hall in such sort that all that were as then therein not one escaped away, but were forced to purge their sins by fire and dry up the great abundance of liquor by them received into their bodies, all of them dying in the inevitable[10] and merciless flames of the hot and burning fire.

Which the Prince, perceiving, became wise; and knowing that his uncle, before the end of the banquet, had withdrawn himself into his chamber, which stood apart from the place where the fire burnt, went thither and, entering into the chamber, laid hand upon the sword of his father's murderer, leaving his own in the place (which, while he was at the banquet, some of the courtiers had nailed fast into the scabbard); and going to Fengon said: "I wonder, disloyal king, how thou canst sleep here at thine ease, and all thy palace is burnt, the fire thereof having burnt the greatest part of thy courtiers and ministers of thy cruelty and detestable tyrannies. And, which is more, I cannot imagine how thou shouldst well assure thyself and thy estate[11] as now to take thy ease, seeing Hamlet so near thee armed with the shafts by him prepared long since, and at this present is ready to revenge the traitorous injury by thee done to his lord and father."

Fengon, as then knowing the truth of his nephew's subtle practice, and hearing him speak with staid[12] mind, and, which is more, perceived a sword naked in his hand which he already lifted up to deprive him of his life, leaped quickly out of the bed, taking hold of Hamlet's sword that was nailed into the scabbard, which, as he sought to pull out, Hamlet gave him such a blow upon the chine[13] of the neck that he cut his head clean from his shoulders, and, as he fell to the

9 pricks skewers **10 inevitable** irresistible **11 assure . . . estate** feel confident about your situation **12 staid** steady · **13 chine** back

ground, said, "This just and violent death is a just reward for such as thou art. Now go thy ways, and when thou comest in hell, see thou forget not to tell thy brother whom thou traitorously slewest that it was his son that sent thee thither with the message, to the end that, being comforted thereby, his soul may rest among the blessed spirits and quit[14] me of the obligation that bound me to pursue his vengeance upon mine own blood, that seeing it was by thee that I lost the chief thing that tied me to this alliance and consanguinity."

A man, to say the truth, hardy, courageous, and worthy of eternal commendation, who, arming himself with a crafty, dissembling, and strange show of being distract out of his wits, under that pretense deceived the wise, politic, and crafty, thereby not only preserving his life from the treasons and wicked practices of the tyrant, but, which is more, by a new and unexpected kind of punishment revenged his father's death many years after the act committed, in such* sort that, directing his courses with such prudence and effecting his purposes with so great boldness, and constancy, he left a judgment to be decided among men of wisdom, which[15] was more commendable in him, his constancy, or magnanimity, or his wisdom in ordering his affairs according to the premeditable determination he had conceived. . . .

Hamlet, having in this manner revenged himself, durst not presently declare his action to the people, but to the contrary determined to work by policy, so to give them intelligence what he had done and the reason that drew him thereunto; so that, being accompanied with such of his father's friends that then were rising,[16] he stayed to see what the people would do when they should hear of that sudden and fearful action. The next morning, the towns bordering thereabouts, desiring to know from whence the flames of fire proceeded the night before they had seen, came thither, and, perceiving the King's palace burnt to ashes and many bodies (most part consumed) lying among the ruins of the house, all of them were much abashed, nothing being left of the palace but the foundation. But they were much more amazed to behold the body of the King all bloody, and his head cut off lying hard by him; whereat some began to threaten revenge, yet not

---

14 quit acquit, free   **15 which** as to which   **16 rising** arising

knowing against whom; others, beholding so lamentable a spectacle, armed themselves; the rest rejoicing, yet not daring to make any show thereof, some detesting the cruelty, others lamenting the death of their prince, but the greatest part, calling Horvendil's murder to remembrance, acknowledging a just judgment from above that had thrown down the pride of the tyrant. And in this sort, the diversities of opinions among that multitude of people being many, yet every man ignorant what would be the issue of that tragedy, none stirred from thence, neither yet attempted to move[17] any tumult, every man fearing his own skin and distrusting his neighbor, esteeming each other to be consenting to the massacre.

[In the last three chapters of the story, Hamlet makes an oration to the Danes in defense of his conduct, wins the loyalty of one and all, and makes good his promise to return to England. There, threatened with a secret plot on the part of the King of England to avenge the death of Fengon, Hamlet slays the English king and returns to Denmark with two wives. He is betrayed by his second wife, Hermetrude, Queen of Scots, in league with his uncle Wiglerus, and is slain.]

Text based on *The History of Hamlet* [spelled *Hamblet* in the original]. London: Imprinted by Richard Bradocke for Thomas Pavier, and are to be sold at his shop in Cornhill near to the Royal Exchange. 1608.

In the following, departures from the original text appear in boldface; original readings are in roman.

p. 187 *northward neithward   *to two two   p. 188 *surmounted surmounting
p. 189 *not only onely   p. 191 *wisest wiseth   p. 192 *counterfeited counterfeiting
p. 194 *infernal intefernal   p. 197 *accusing her accusing his   p. 201 *he determined determined   p. 205 *his their   p. 207 *in such in no such

---

17 **move** set in motion, instigate

Further Reading

Alexander, Nigel. *Poison, Play, and Duel: A Study in "Hamlet."* London: Routledge and Kegan Paul, 1971. Alexander argues that the play's representation of complex moral and psychological problems depends upon three dominant symbols—poison, play, and duel—that structure the play's action and language. Through these powerful images, which come together in the play's final scene, Shakespeare conveys a sense of the inescapable difficulties of moral choice and action.

Bevington, David. " 'Maimed Rites': Violated Ceremony in *Hamlet.*" *Action Is Eloquence: Shakespeare's Language of Gesture.* Cambridge and London: Harvard Univ. Press, 1984. Bevington traces how Shakespeare shapes our responses to the play through visual means. *Hamlet*, he argues, is a play of "maimed rites," perversions of ceremony that reflect the moral and social disruptions in Denmark. In the final scene, the solemnity with which Hamlet is borne offstage serves to rehabilitate ceremony, restoring "some hope of perceivable meaning in the ceremonial meanings that hold together the social and moral order."

Bohannan, Laura. "Shakespeare in the Bush." *Natural History* 75 (1966): 28–33. Rpt. in *Every Man His Way: Readings in Cultural Anthropology*, ed. Alan Dundes. Englewood Cliffs, N.J.: Prentice-Hall, 1968. Bohannan, a cultural anthropologist, narrates the response of the elders of the Tiv tribe of West Africa to her retelling of the story of *Hamlet*. Her lively essay is a lesson in cultural relativity: familiar critical issues like the ghost, the incestuous marriage, Ophelia's madness, and Hamlet's revenge are freshly viewed from the perspective of a culture with non-Western ethical values and practices.

Booth, Stephen. "On the Value of *Hamlet.*" In *Reinterpretations of Elizabethan Drama*, ed. Norman Rabkin. New York: Columbia Univ. Press, 1969. Booth focuses on the audience's experience of the play. His patient analysis of the opening scene sets forth the process whereby Hamlet's frustrated desire for certainty and coherence becomes the audience's own. The result for Booth is that "*Hamlet* is a tragedy of an audience that cannot make up its mind."

Bowers, Fredson. "Hamlet as Minister and Scourge." *PMLA* 70 (1955): 740–749. When Hamlet calls himself a "scourge and minister," Bowers argues, he signals his awareness of a conflict between his roles as private avenger and agent of providential design. By locating *Hamlet* within the moral and dramatic traditions of Elizabethan revenge tragedy, Bowers discovers the cause of the hero's delay in Hamlet's desire for Heaven to define and facilitate his complex responsibility.

Bradlay, A. C. "*Hamlet.*" *Shakespearean Tragedy*, 1904. Rpt., New York: St. Martin's, 1985. Bradley explores the sources of Hamlet's delay, locating it not in a temperament characteristically resistant to action but in a "violent shock to his moral being" that produces an enervating melancholy. The Ghost's revelation and demand for revenge is "the last rivet in the melancholy which holds him bound," and the play presents "his vain efforts to fulfill this duty, his unconscious self-excuses and unavailing self-reproaches, and the tragic results of his delay."

Calderwood, James L. *To Be and Not to Be: Negation and Metadrama in "Hamlet."* New York: Columbia Univ. Press, 1983. Calderwood's metadramatic reading provocatively examines the tensions between illusion and reality, absence and presence, negation and assertion, inscribed into a play that relentlessly proliferates uncertainties and contradictions, but that, as Calderwood's title suggests, ultimately accepts and contains them.

Charney, Maurice. *Style in "Hamlet."* Princeton, N.J.: Princeton Univ. Press, 1969. Charney provides an extensive analysis of verbal and visual style in the play. He moves from an analysis of *Hamlet*'s dominant patterns of imagery to an examination of the play in performance, concluding with an extended rhetorical analysis of the characters of Polonius, Claudius, and Hamlet.

Coleridge, Samuel Taylor. "*Hamlet.*" *Coleridge's Writings on Shakespeare*, ed. Terence Hawkes. New York: G. P. Putnam's Sons, 1959. Coleridge, along with other early nineteenth-century intellectuals, was strongly drawn to Hamlet ("I have a smack of Hamlet myself") and saw him as an agonizing intellectual, endlessly reasoning and hesitating, detached from the world of events. In Coleridge's influential psychological reading, Hamlet is a man both "amiable and excellent" who is defeated by his "aversion to action, which prevails among such as have a world in themselves."

Eliot, T. S. "Hamlet and His Problems." *Selected Essays, 1917–1932.* New York: Harcourt, Brace and Co., 1932. The "problems" Eliot identifies in his influential essay are not in Hamlet's character but in the play itself. Eliot believes that *Hamlet* is Shakespeare's revision of a lost revenge play onto which Shakespeare's main theme—the effect of a mother's guilt upon her son—is unsuccessfully grafted. Hamlet's emotions are "in excess of the facts as they appear," Eliot finds; Hamlet can neither understand nor objectify them, since Shakespeare himself is unable to find any "objective correlative" in his play for Hamlet's complex psychological state.

Ewbank, Inga-Stina. "*Hamlet* and the Power of Words." *Shakespeare Survey* 30 (1977): 85–102. Rpt. in *Aspects of "Hamlet": Articles Reprinted from "Shakespeare Survey,"* ed. Kenneth Muir and Stanley Wells. Cambridge: Cambridge Univ. Press, 1979. Examining how language functions as a major thematic concern in *Hamlet,* Ewbank explores the possibilities and limitations of verbal communication in the play. Speaking is the play's dominant mode of action, as characters stretch and shape words to the mysterious realities that they confront. For Ewbank, the play's greatness rests on its ability to express so much, even if what is finally expressed is the presence of something inexpressible at its heart.

Forker, Charles. "Shakespeare's Theatrical Symbolism and Its Function in *Hamlet.*" *Shakespeare Quarterly* 14 (1963): 215–229. Rpt. in *Essays in Shakespearean Criticism,* ed. James L. Calderwood and Harold E. Toliver. Englewood Cliffs, N.J.: Prentice-Hall, 1970. Forker examines Shakespeare's complex handling of the theatrical symbolism that pervades the play. Throughout, characters alternating between the roles of spectator and actor play to each other; Hamlet emerges as the consummate performer, whose role-playing embodies all the ambiguities and paradoxes of what it means to act.

Frye, Roland Mushat. *The Renaissance "Hamlet."* Princeton, N.J.: Princeton Univ. Press, 1984. Drawing upon a rich array of historical, literary, and pictorial evidence, Frye seeks to reconstruct the challenges and excitement that *Hamlet* offered to Shakespeare's Elizabethan audience. The rich specificity of the background that Frye reconstructs acknowledges "the complex and sophisticated concerns of Elizabethan minds" and the complexity of the play itself.

Goldman, Michael. " 'To Be or Not to Be' and the Spectrum of Action." *Acting and Action in Shakespearean Tragedy.* Princeton, N.J.: Princeton Univ. Press, 1985. Goldman argues that the challenges the role of Hamlet poses to an actor are analogous to the challenges the play poses to an audience. Each must engage in an act of interpretation that will discover unity and coherence in the multiple and often contradictory evidence of language and action.

Granville-Barker, Harley. *Preface to "Hamlet."* Princeton, N.J.: Princeton Univ. Press, 1946. This book-length "Preface" draws upon Granville-Barker's insights as a theatrical director and literary critic in its focus on the structure and tone of *Hamlet*. The first half of the study contains a detailed analysis of the three distinct movements (rather than the imposed five-act structure) that govern the play's action. Granville-Barker concludes with a discussion of the characters in this "tragedy of thwarted thought and tortured spirit."

Jones, Ernest. *Hamlet and Oepidus.* New York: Norton, 1949; published in 1910 in an earlier essay form. Jones, a student of Freud, considers the personality of Hamlet from a psychoanalytic perspective and diagnoses his delay as symptomatic of an Oepidal complex. Hamlet is incapable of revenge because of his unconscious identification with Claudius, who has enacted Hamlet's unconscious wish to kill his father and marry his mother. Jones extends his provocative argument with the suggestion that the play's Oedipal aspects have their origin in

Shakespeare's own psychology in 1601, the year the play was written and in which Shakespeare's father died.

Levin, Harry. *The Question of "Hamlet."* New York: Oxford Univ. Press, 1959. Levin's rhetorical analysis of the play's tone and action focuses on three dominant figures of speech (which are simultaneously modes of thought): interrogation, doubt, and irony. These, Levin finds, are organized dialectically, with the play's and Hamlet's own pervasive irony serving as a synthesis that permits us to face—though never to solve—the contradictions that the play's questions and unexpected answers expose.

Lewis, C. S. "Hamlet: The Prince or the Poem?" *Proceedings of the British Academy* 28 (1943 for 1942): 11–18. Rpt. in *They Asked for a Paper.* London: Bles, 1962; and in part as "Death in *Hamlet*" in *Shakespeare, the Tragedies: A Collection of Critical Essays,* ed. Alfred Harbage. Englewood Cliffs, N.J.: Prentice-Hall, 1964. Lewis takes issue with the focus on Hamlet's character that has dominated critical discussion of the play since the nineteenth century. He argues that the true subject of the play is death. The fear of being dead, born of a failure to understand human nature or the nature of the universe, is, for Lewis, the source of the play's powerful presentation of doubt and dread.

Mack, Maynard. "The World of *Hamlet*." *Yale Review* 41 (1952): 502–523. Rpt. in *Shakespeare, the Tragedies: A Collection of Critical Essays,* ed. Alfred Harbage. Englewood Cliffs, N.J.: Prentice-Hall, 1964. Mack's sensitive account of the play's verbal texture establishes the "imaginative environment" of *Hamlet* that is dominated both by a deep and disabling inscrutability and by an overriding sense of morality. In the final act, Mack argues, Hamlet comes to understand what it means to live in such a world and to accept the mysterious condition of being human.

Nietzsche, Friedrich. "The Birth of Tragedy or: Hellenism and Pessimism" (1872). In *The Birth of Tragedy and the Case of Wagner,* trans. Walter Kaufmann. New York: Vintage, 1967. Nietzsche rejects the common nineteenth-century notion that Hamlet fails to act because he is paralyzed by excessive thought in favor of a view of Hamlet's "nausea" induced by looking "truly into the nature of things." What inhibits Hamlet is his tragic knowledge of the futility and folly of action in a world that is out of joint. "Knowledge kills action," Nietzsche asserts; "action requires the veil of illusion."

Prosser, Eleanor. *Hamlet and Revenge*. Stanford, Calif.: Stanford Univ. Press, 1967. Surveying Renaissance ethical codes and dramatic conventions, Prosser examines *Hamlet* in light of the Elizabethan understanding of revenge and ghosts. She contends that once we accept that the moral universe of the play (as well as of the audience) is Christian, we must see the Ghost as "demonic" and Hamlet's commitment to revenge as immoral and appalling.

OTHELLO

Introduction

Othello differs in several respects from the other three major Shakespearean tragedies with which it is usually ranked. Written seemingly about the time of its performance at court by the King's men (Shakespeare's acting company) on November 1, 1604, after *Hamlet* (c. 1599–1601) and before *King Lear* (c. 1605) and *Macbeth* (c. 1606–1607), *Othello* shares with these other plays a fascination with evil in its most virulent and universal aspect. These plays study the devastating effects of ambitious pride, ingratitude, wrath, jealousy, and vengeful hate—the deadly sins of the spirit—with only a passing interest in the political strife to which Shakespeare's Roman or classical tragedies are generally devoted. Of the four, *Othello* is the most concentrated upon one particular evil. The action concerns sexual jealousy, and although human sinfulness is such that jealousy ceaselessly touches on other forms of depravity, the center of interest always returns in *Othello* to the destruction of a love through jealousy. *Othello* is a tragic portrait of a marriage. The protagonist is not a king or prince, as in the tragedies already mentioned, but a general recently married. There are no supernatural visitations as in *Hamlet* and *Macbeth*. Ideas of divine justice, while essential to *Othello*'s portrayal of a battle between good and evil for the allegiance of the protagonist, do not encompass the wide sweep of *King Lear;* nor do we find here the same broad indictment of humanity. Social order is not seriously shaken by Othello's tragedy. The fair-minded Duke of Venice remains firmly in control, and his deputy Lodovico oversees a just conclusion on Cyprus.

By the same token, *Othello* does not offer the remorseless questioning about man's relationship to the cosmos that we find in *King Lear, Hamlet,* and *Macbeth.* The battle of good and evil is of course cosmic, but in *Othello* that battle is realized through a taut narrative of jealousy and murder. Its poetic images are accordingly focused to a large extent on the natural world. One cluster of images is domestic and animal, having to do with goats, monkeys, wolves, baboons, guinea hens, wildcats, spiders, flies, asses, dogs, copulating horses and sheep, serpents, and toads; other images, more wide-ranging in scope, include green-eyed monsters, devils, blackness, poisons, money purses, tarnished jewels, music untuned, and light extinguished. The story is immediate and direct, retaining the sensational atmosphere of its Italian prose source by Giovanni Baptista Giraldi Cinthio, in his *Hecatommithi* of 1565 (translated into French in 1584). Events move even more swiftly than in Cinthio, for Shakespeare has compressed the story into two or three nights and days (albeit with an intervening sea journey and with an elastic use of stage time to allow for the maturing of long-term plans, as when we learn that Iago has begged Emilia "a hundred times" to steal Desdemona's handkerchief, or that Iago has accused Cassio of making love to Desdemona "a thousand times"). *Othello* does not have a fully developed double plot as in *King Lear* or a comparatively large group of characters serving as foils to the protagonist as in *Hamlet*. *Othello*'s cast is small and the plot is concentrated to an unusual degree on Othello, Desdemona, and Iago. What *Othello* may lose in breadth it gains in dramatic intensity.

Daringly, Shakespeare opens this tragedy of love not with a direct and sympathetic portrayal of the lovers themselves, but with a scene of vicious insinuation about their marriage. The images employed by Iago to describe the coupling of Othello and Desdemona are revoltingly animalistic, sodomistic. "Even now, now, very now, an old black ram / Is tupping your white ewe," he taunts Desdemona's father Brabantio. ("Tupping" is a word used specifically for the copulating of sheep.) "You'll have your daughter covered with a Barbary horse; you'll have your nephews neigh to you"; "your daughter and the Moor are now making the beast with two backs"; "the devil will make a grandsire of you" (1.1.90–93, 113–120). This degraded view reduces the marriage to one of utter carnality, with repeated emphasis on the word "gross": Desdemona has yielded "to the gross clasps of a lascivious Moor," and has made "a gross revolt" against her family and society (ll. 129, 137). Iago's second theme, one that is habitual with him, is money. "What ho, Brabantio! Thieves, thieves, thieves! / Look to your house, your daughter, and your bags!" (ll. 81–82). The implication is of a sinister bond between thievery in sex and thievery in gold. Sex and money are both commodities to be protected by watchful fathers against libidinous and opportunistic children.

We as audience make plentiful allowance for Iago's bias in all this, since he has admitted to Roderigo his knavery and resentment of Othello. Even so, the carnal vision of love we confront is calculatedly disturbing, because it seems so equated with a pejorative image of blackness. Othello is unquestionably a black man, referred to disparagingly by his detractors as the "thick-lips," with a "sooty bosom" (1.1.68; 1.2.71); Elizabethan usage applied the term "Moor" to Africans without attempting to distinguish between Arabian and Negroid peoples. From the ugly start of the play, Othello and Desdemona have to prove the worth of their love in the face of preset attitudes against miscegenation. Brabantio takes refuge in the thought that Othello must have bewitched Desdemona. His basic assumption—one to be echoed later by Iago and by Othello himself—is that miscegenation is unnatural by definition. In confronting and accusing Othello he repeatedly appeals "to all things of sense" (that is, to common sense) and asks if it is not "gross in sense" (self-evident) that Othello has practiced magic on her, since nothing else could prompt human nature so to leave its natural path. "For nature so preposterously to err, / Being not deficient, blind, or lame of sense, / Sans witchcraft could not" (1.2.65, 73; 1.3.64–66). We as audience do not endorse Brabantio's view and recognize in him the type of imperious father who conventionally opposes romantic love. It is sadly ironic that he should now prefer Roderigo as a son-in-law, evidently concluding that any white Venetian would be preferable to the prince of blacks. Still, Brabantio has been hospitable to the Moor and trusting of his daughter. He is a sorrowful rather than ridiculous figure, and the charge he levels at the married pair, however much based on a priori assumptions of what is "natural" in human behavior, remains to be answered.

After all, we find ourselves wondering, what did attract Othello and Desdemona to each other? Even though he certainly did not use witchcraft, may Othello not have employed a subtler kind of enchantment in the exotic character of his travels among "the Cannibals that each other eat, / The Anthropophagi, and men whose heads / Do grow beneath their shoulders" (1.3.145–147)? These "passing strange" events fascinate Desdemona as they do everyone including the Duke of Venice ("I think this tale would win my daughter too"). Othello has not practiced unfairly on her—"This only is the witchcraft I have used" (ll. 162, 173, 171). Yet may he not represent for Desdemona a radical novelty, being a man at once less devious and more mysterious than the dissolute Venetian swaggerers such as Roderigo and the "wealthy curlèd darlings of our nation" (1.2.69) who follow her about? Was her deceiving of her father by means of the elopement a protest, an escape from conventionality? Why has she been attracted to a man so much older than herself? For his part, Othello gives the impression of being inexperienced with women, at least of Desdemona's rank and complexion, and is both intrigued and flattered by her attentions. "She loved me for the dangers I had passed, / And I loved her that she did pity them" (1.3.169–170). Desdemona fulfills a place in Othello's view of himself. Does she also represent status for him in Venetian society, where he has been employed as a military commander but treated nonetheless as something of an alien?

These subtle but impertinent ways of doubting the motivations of Othello and Desdemona are thrust upon us by the play's opening and are later crucial to Iago's strategy of breeding mistrust. Just as important, however, these insinuations are refuted by Othello and especially by Desdemona. Whatever others may think, she never gives the slightest indication of regarding her husband as different or exotic because he is black and old. In fact the images of blackness and age are significantly reversed during the play's early scenes. Othello's blackness, like that of the natives dwelling in heathen lands, could betoken to Elizabethan audiences an innocent proneness to accept Christianity, and Othello is one who has already embraced the Christian faith. His first appearance onstage, when he confronts a party of torch-bearing men coming to arrest him and bids his followers sheathe their swords, is sufficiently reminiscent of Christ's arrest in the Garden of Gethsemane to convey a fleeting comparison between Othello and the Christian God whose charity and forbearance he seeks to emulate. Othello's blackness may be used in part as an emblem of fallen man, but so are we all fallen. His age similarly strengthens our impression of his wisdom, restraint, leadership. Any suggestions of comic sexual infidelity in the marriage of an old man and an attractive young bride are confuted by what we see in Desdemona's chaste yet sensual regard for the good man she has chosen.

Desdemona is utterly fond of Othello, admiring, and faithful. We believe her when she says that she does not even know what it means to be unfaithful; the word "whore" is not in her vocabulary. She is defenseless against the charges brought against her because she does not even comprehend them, cannot believe that anyone would imagine such things. Her love, both erotic and chaste, is of that transcendent wholesomeness common to several late Shakespearean heroines such as Cordelia in *King Lear* and Hermione in *The Winter's Tale*. Her "preferring" Othello to her father, like Cordelia's placing her duty to a husband before that to a father, is not ungrateful but natural and proper. And Othello, however much he may regard Desdemona as an extension of himself (he calls her "my fair warrior"), does cherish Desdemona as she deserves. "I cannot speak enough of this content," he exclaims when he rejoins her on Cyprus. "It stops me here; it is too much of joy" (2.1.181, 196–197). The passionate intensity of his love prepares the way for his tragedy, for he knows only too well that "when I love thee not, / Chaos is come again" (3.3.99–100). Iago speaks truly when he observes that Othello "Is of a constant, loving, noble nature" (2.1.290). Othello's tragedy is not that he is easily duped, but that his strong faith can be destroyed at such terrible cost. Othello never forgets how much he is losing. The threat to his love is not an initial lack of wholesomeness, but rather the insidious assumption that Desdemona cannot love him because such a love is unnatural. The fear of being unlovable exists in Othello's mind, but the human instrument of this vicious gospel is Iago.

Iago belongs to a select group of villains in Shakespeare who, while plausibly motivated in human terms, also take delight in evil for its own sake: Aaron the Moor in *Titus Andronicus*, Richard III, Don John in *Much Ado*, Iago, Edmund in *King Lear*. They are not, like Macbeth or like Claudius in *Hamlet*, men driven by ambition to commit crimes they clearly recognize to be wrong. Although Edmund does belatedly try to make amends, these villains are essentially conscienceless, sinister, and amused at their own cunning. They are related to one another by a stage metaphor of personified evil derived from the Vice of the morality play, whose typical role is to win the Mankind figure away from virtue and to corrupt him with worldly enticements. Like that engaging tempter, Shakespeare's villains in these plays take the audience into their confidence, boast in soliloquy of their cleverness, exult in the triumph of evil, and improvise plans with daring and resourcefulness. They are all superb actors, deceiving virtually every character onstage until late in the action with their protean and hypocritical display. They take pleasure in this "sport" and amaze us by their virtuosity. The role is paradoxically comic in its use of ingenious and resourceful deception, although it is the grim and ironic comedy of vice. We know that we are to condemn morally even while we applaud the skill.

The tradition of vice comedy may best explain a puzzling feature of Iago, noted long ago and memorably phrased by Samuel Taylor Coleridge as "the motive-hunting of motiveless malignity." Iago does offer plausible motives for what he does. Despite his resemblance to the morality Vice, he is no allegorized abstraction but an ensign in the army, a junior field officer who hates being outranked by a theoretician or staff officer. As an old-school professional he also resents that he has not been promoted on the basis of seniority, the "old gradation" (1.1.38). Even his efforts at using influence with Othello have come to naught, and Iago can scarcely be blamed for supposing that Cassio's friendship with Othello has won him special favor. Thus Iago has reason to plot against Cassio as well as Othello. Nevertheless a further dimension is needed to explain the gloating, the utter lack of moral reflection, the concentration on destroying Desdemona (who has not wronged Iago), the absorption in ingenious methods of plotting, the finesse and the style. Hatred precedes any plausible motive in Iago, and ultimately does not depend on psychological causality. Probably the tradition of the stage Machiavel (another type of gloating villain based on stereotyped attitudes toward the heretical political ideas of Niccolò Machiavelli), as in

Marlowe's *Jew of Malta*, adds an ingredient; this tradition was readily assimilated with that of the Vice.

Iago's machinations yield him both "sport" and "profit" (1.3.387); that is, he enjoys his evildoing, although he is also driven by a motive. This Vice-like behavior in human garb creates a restless sense of a dark metaphysical reality lying behind his visible exterior. Even his stated motives do not always make sense. When in an outburst of hatred he soliloquizes that "I hate the Moor; / And it is thought abroad that twixt my sheets / He's done my office," Iago goes on to concede the unlikelihood of this charge. "I know not if 't be true; / But I, for mere suspicion in that kind, / Will do as if for surety" (ll. 387–391). The charge is so absurd, in fact, that we have to look into Iago himself for the origin of this jealous paranoia. The answer may be partly emblematic: as the embodiment and genius of sexual jealousy, Iago suffers with ironic appropriateness from the evil he preaches, and without external cause. Emilia understands that jealousy is not a rational affliction but a self-induced disease of the mind. Jealous persons, she tells Desdemona, "are not ever jealous for the cause, / But jealous for they're jealous. It is a monster / Begot upon itself, born on itself" (3.4.161–163). Iago's own testimonial bears this out, for his jealousy is at once wholly irrational and agonizingly self-destructive. "I do suspect the lusty Moor / Hath leaped into my seat, the thought whereof / Doth, like a poisonous mineral, gnaw my innards" (2.1.296–298). In light of this nightmare, we can see that even his seemingly plausible resentment of Cassio's promotion is jealous envy. The "daily beauty" in Cassio's life makes Iago feel "ugly" by comparison (5.1.19–20), engendering in Iago a profound sense of lack of worth from which he can temporarily find relief only by reducing Othello and others to his own miserable condition. He is adept at provoking self-hatred in others because he suffers from it himself.

Othello comes at last to regard Iago as a "demi-devil" who has tempted Othello to damn himself "beneath all depth in hell"; Lodovico speaks of Iago in the closing lines of the play as a "hellish villain" (5.2.309, 142, 379); and Iago himself boasts that "When devils will the blackest sins put on, / They do suggest at first with heavenly shows, / As I do

now" (2.3.345–347). Iago thus bears some affinity to both
Vice and devil, suggesting his relationship both to Othello's
inner temptation and to a preexistent evil force in the universe itself. Conversely, Desdemona is in Emilia's words an
"angel," purely chaste, "So come my soul to bliss as I
speak true" (5.2.134, 259). When Desdemona lands on Cyprus, she is greeted in words that echo the *Ave Maria:* "Hail
to thee, lady! And the grace of heaven . . . Enwheel thee
round!" (2.1.87–89). These images introduce metaphorically a conflict of good and evil in which Othello, typical of
fallen man, has chosen evil and destroyed the good at the
prompting of a diabolical counselor. Again we see the heri-
tage of the morality play, especially of the later morality in
which the Mankind figure was sometimes damned rather
than saved. Even so, to allegorize *Othello* is to obscure and
misread its clash of human passion. In fact, we see that the
impulse to reduce human complexity to simplistic moral
absolutes is a fatal weakness in Othello; by insisting on
viewing Desdemona as a type or abstraction, he loses
sight of her wonderful humanity. The theological issue of
salvation or damnation is not relevant in dramatic terms;
the play is not a homily on the dangers of jealousy. The
metaphysical dimensions of a homiletic tradition are
transmuted into human drama. Acknowledging these limitations, we can notwithstanding see a spiritual analogy in
Iago's devil-like method of undoing his victims.

His trick resembles that of the similarly mischief-making
Don John in *Much Ado about Nothing:* an optical illusion by
which the blameless heroine is impugned as an adulteress.
The concealed Othello must watch Cassio boasting of sexual triumphs and believe he is talking about Desdemona.
Like the devil, Iago is given power over men's frail senses,
especially the eyes. He can create illusions to induce
Othello to see what Iago wants him to see, as Don John does
with Claudio, but Othello's acceptance of the lie must be
his own responsibility, a failure of his corrupted will. Iago
practices on Othello with an a priori logic used before on
Brabantio and Roderigo, urging the proneness of all mor-
tals to sin and the unnaturalness of a black-white marriage.
All women have appetites; Desdemona is a woman; hence
Desdemona has appetites. "The wine she drinks is made of
grapes," he scoffs to Roderigo. "If she had been blessed,

she would never have loved the Moor" (2.1.253–255). She is a Venetian, and "In Venice they do let God see the pranks / They dare not show their husbands" (3.3.216–217). Therefore she too is a hypocrite; "She did deceive her father" (l. 220). Most of all, it stands to reason that she must long for a man of her own race. As Iago succeeds in getting Othello to ponder: "And yet, how nature erring from itself—" (l. 243). This proposition that Nature teaches all persons, including Desdemona, to seek a harmonious matching of "clime, complexion, and degree" strikes a responsive chord in Othello, since he knows that he is black and alien. "Haply, for I am black / And have not those soft parts of conversation / That chamberers have." Then, too, he is sensitive that he is considerably older than she, "declined / Into the vale of years" (ll. 246, 279–282), "the young affects / In me defunct" (1.3.266–267). And so, if one must conclude from the preceding that Desdemona will seek a lover, the only question is who. "This granted—as it is a most pregnant and unforced position—who stands so eminent in the degree of this fortune as Cassio does?" (2.1.237–239). Once Othello has accepted this syllogistic sequence of proofs, specious not through any lapse in logic but because the axiomatic assumptions about human nature are degraded and do not apply to Desdemona, Othello has arrived at an unshakable conclusion to which all subsequent evidence must be forced as "a foregone conclusion." "Villain, be sure thou prove my love a whore," he commissions Iago (3.3.443, 375). Desdemona's innocent pleading for Cassio only makes things look worse. Cassio's reputed muttering while asleep, like the handkerchief seen in his possession or his giddy talk about his mistress Bianca, "speaks against her [Desdemona] with the other proofs" (l. 456).

How has Othello fallen so far in so short a time? His bliss with Desdemona as they are reunited on Cyprus knows no limit. These two persons represent married love at its very best, erotic and spiritual, she enhancing his manliness, he cherishing her beauty and virtue. His blackness and age are positive images in him, despite earlier insinuations to the contrary. He is a man of public worthiness, of command, of self-assurance. Desdemona is the most domestic of Shakespeare's tragic heroines, even while she is also representative of so much that is transcendent. Husband and wife are bound happily in one of Shakespeare's few detailed portraits of serious commitment in marriage. What then gives way? We look at Iago for one important insight, but ultimately the cause must be in Othello himself. Arthur Kirsch has argued persuasively (in *Shakespeare and the Experience of Love*, 1981) that Othello's most grave failing is an insufficient regard for himself. It is in part an inability to counter the effects on him of a culture that regards him as an outsider; he is at last persuaded to see himself with the eyes of Venice, not just of Iago but of Brabantio (who gladly entertains Othello until he has the presumption to elope with Brabantio's white daughter) and others. The resulting destruction of self-regard is devastating. Othello's jealousy stems from a profound suspicion that others cannot love him because he does not deem himself lovable.

Othello has loved Desdemona as an extension of himself, and in his moments of greatest contentedness his marriage is sustained by an idealized vision of Desdemona serving as the object of his exalted romantic passion. When he destroys Desdemona, as he realizes with a terrible clarity, Othello destroys himself; the act is a prelude to his actual suicide. Iago's mode of temptation, then, is to persuade Othello to regard himself with the eyes of Venice, to accept the view that Othello is himself alien and that any woman who loves him does so perversely. In Othello's tainted state of mind, Desdemona's very sexuality becomes an unbearable threat to him, her warmth and devotion a "proof" of disloyalty. Othello's most tortured speeches (3.4.57–77, 4.2.49–66) reveal the extent to which he equates the seemingly betraying woman he has so depended on for happiness with his own mother, who gave Othello's father a handkerchief and threatened him with loss of her love if he should lose it. Othello has briefly learned and then forgotten the precious art of harmonizing erotic passion and spiritual love, and as these two great aims of love are driven apart in him, he comes to loathe and fear the sexuality that puts him so much in mind of his physical frailty and dependence on woman. The horror and pity of *Othello* rests above all in the spectacle of a love that was once so whole and noble made filthy by self-hatred.

The increasing surrender of Othello's judgment to passion can be measured in three successive trial scenes in the play: the entirely fair trial of Othello himself by the Venetian senate concerning the elopement, Othello's trial of Cassio for drinking and rioting (when, ominously, Othello's "blood begins my safer guides to rule"; 2.3.199), and finally the prejudged sentencing of Desdemona without any opportunity for her to defend herself. In a corollary decline, Othello falls from the Christian compassion of the opening scenes (he customarily confesses to heaven "the vices of my blood," 1.3.125) to the pagan savagery of his vengeful and ritualistic execution of his wife. "My heart is turned to stone" (4.1.182–183), he vows, and at the play's end he grievingly characterizes himself as a "base Indian" who "threw a pearl away / Richer than all his tribe" (5.2.357–358). (The First Folio reading of "Iudean" or "Judean" refers perhaps to Judas Iscariot or to Herod; most editors prefer the quarto reading of "Indian.") Iago knows that he must persuade Othello to sentence and execute Desdemona himself, for only by active commitment to evil will Othello damn himself. In nothing does Iago so resemble the devil as in his wish to see Othello destroy the innocence and goodness on which his happiness depends.

The fate of some of the lesser characters echoes that of Othello, for Iago's evil intent is to "enmesh them all" (2.3.356). Cassio in particular is, like Othello, an attractive man with a single but fatally vulnerable weakness, in his case a fleshly appetite for wine and women. For him, alternately idolizing and depreciating women as he does, the gap between spiritual and sensual love remains vast, but he is essentially good-natured and trustworthy. His seemingly genial flaws lead to disaster because they put him at the mercy of a remorseless enemy. Iago is, with fitting irony, the apostle of absolute self-control: "Our bodies are our gardens, to the which our wills are gardeners" (1.3.323–324). Thus, Cassio's tragedy is anything but a straightforward homily on the virtues of temperance. Similarly, Bianca is undone not through any simple cause-and-effect punishment of her sexual conduct—she is, after all, fond of Cassio and loyal to him, even if he will not marry her—but because Iago is able to turn appearances against

her. With his usual appeal to a priori logic, he builds a case
that she and Cassio are in cahoots: "I do suspect this trash /
To be a party in this injury. . . . This is the fruits of whoring"
(5.1.86–87, 118). Roderigo is another of Iago's victims, a
contemptible one, led by the nose because he too has surrendered reason to passion. Emilia cannot escape Iago's
evil influence and gives the handkerchief to him despite
knowing its value for Desdemona. Flaws are magnified into
disasters by a remorseless evil intelligence. Men must be
ceaselessly circumspect; a good reputation is sooner lost
than recovered. Emilia is a conventionally decent enough
woman—she would be faithless in marriage, she tells Desdemona, only for a very high price—and yet her one small
compromise with her conscience contributes to the murder
of her mistress. Like Othello she offers atonement too late,
by denouncing her husband. Desdemona is the only person
in the play too good to be struck down through some inner
flaw, which may explain why Iago is committed above all
else to seeing that she be destroyed.

As a tragic hero, Othello obtains self-knowledge at a terrible price. He knows finally that what he has destroyed was
ineffably good. The discovery is too late for him to make
amends, and he dies by his own hand as atonement. The
deaths of Othello and Desdemona are, in their separate
ways, equally devastating: he is in part the victim of racism,
though he nobly refuses to deny his own culpability, and
she is the victim of sexism, lapsing sadly into the stereo-
typical role of passive and silent sufferer that has been
demanded of her. Despite the loss, however, Othello's re-
affirmation of faith in Desdemona's goodness undoes what
the devil-like Iago had most hoped to achieve: the separation of Othello from a belief in goodness. In this important
sense, Othello's self-knowledge is cathartic and a compensation for the terrible price he has paid. The very existence
of a person as good as Desdemona gives the lie to Iago's
creed that everyone has his or her price. She is the sacrificial victim who must die for Othello's loss of faith and, by
dying, rekindle that faith. ("My life upon her faith!" Othello
prophetically affirms, in response to her father's warning
that she may deceive him [1.3.297].) She cannot restore him
to himself, for self-hatred has done its ugly work, but she is

the means by which he understands at last the chimerical and wantonly destructive nature of his jealousy. His greatness appears in his acknowledgment of this truth, and in the heroic struggle with which he has confronted an inner darkness we all share.

Othello
in Performance

To a remarkable extent, the history of *Othello* in performance is the history of lead actors in the roles of Othello and Iago. Desdemona occasionally captures attention, sometimes even Cassio, but the rest of the play is largely forgotten. Scenic effects are not essential. Props are at a minimum. Indeed, there are only thirteen speaking parts. The play onstage depends almost entirely on the personal magnetism of the leading player and one or two others. Small wonder that Othello's role has been coveted by most of the famous actors in every age.

Richard Burbage played Othello in Shakespeare's company, regularly at the Globe Theatre, and at court in 1604 and again in 1613. An elegy written upon Burbage's death in 1619 remembers his "grieved Moor" among his great roles. Thomas Killigrew, who obtained the rights to *Othello* after the Restoration, performed the play with his King's men at the Cockpit. Samuel Pepys saw this production on October 11, 1660, remarking in his diary: "a pretty lady that sat by me called out to see Desdemona smothered." Thomas Betterton played Othello with great intensity from 1683 to 1709, primarily after 1703 at the theater in Lincoln's Inn Fields, London. One contemporary witness testified that "his aspect was serious, venerable, and majestic." Barton Booth, James Quin, and Spranger Barry were the great Othellos after Betterton on the Restoration and eighteenth-century stage. Oddly, David Garrick was not successful in the role: he acted Othello in two seasons only, abandoning the part for Iago in 1746. Garrick's small, wiry body and his nervous emotional intensity did not match the age's preference for a heroic protagonist. John Philip Kemble first played Othello in 1785 and struggled through various productions until 1805, but had no better luck. Kemble failed because of what his biographer James Boaden has called the "philosophy in his bearing and reason in his rage." Audiences seemed to demand from Othello either the towering violent jealousy projected by Betterton or the grandeur and presence of Quin. Spranger Barry, combining something of both, was the most successful Othello of the century, fierce in his rage but so poignant in his grief that, as a reviewer noted, "the audience seemed to lose the energies of their hands, and could only thank him with their tears." Iago, played by Lacy Ryan, Colley Cibber, and Charles Macklin, among others, required melodramatic villainy, though Macklin also provided some real depth of characterization, naturalizing his performance so that (in Macklin's words) Iago's "seeming openness and concealed revenge" became a plausible, if terrifying, human response to the goodness surrounding him. Anne Bracegirdle and Susannah Cibber were the outstanding Desdemonas of the age, energetically asserting their innocence. The play was enormously popular throughout the period, no doubt because of the persuasive acting of its principals. It was staged in all but seven years of the entire eighteenth century.

The play was cut to center attention on its main figures and to enhance the tragic nobility of the protagonist. Bell's acting version of 1773 is representative of the tradition. It omits Othello's mention of anthropophagi, cannibals, and "antres vast," does away with the storm scene for the landing in Cyprus in Act 2, cuts the Clown scene (3.1) in the interests of classical unity and decorum, banishes Bianca for reasons of moral decency, takes away the scene in which Othello's jealousy is confirmed by seeing the handkerchief in Cassio's hand, and deprives Desdemona of her conversation with Emilia before her death. The death itself is accomplished by stabbing. What remains in the text is chiefly a series of lofty tragic scenes for Othello and Iago.

Othello in the nineteenth century belonged for the most part to Edmund Kean, Edwin Booth, and Tommaso Salvini; Samuel Phelps also succeeded in the role. Kean's Othello was the most celebrated, described by critic William Hazlitt as "the finest piece of acting in the world." Kean's appalling fury and final desolation moved audiences to tears. Booth describes his father as believing that "no mortal man could equal Kean in the rendering of Othello's despair and rage." Booth himself was a more noble and humane Othello, as in his production at Booth's Theatre in New York in 1869, but was perhaps more arresting in his portrayal of a gloating and demonic Iago, as at the Winter Garden Theatre in 1866. In 1881, Booth and Henry Irving appeared at London's Lyceum Theatre, alternating the roles of Othello and Iago, with Ellen Terry as Desdemona. The production was a great success, artistically and financially. Irving had played Othello only once before, in 1876, to little acclaim, and he had never played Iago. Still, he was the greatest English actor of his generation, and people flocked to see the collision of titans from England and America. As Othello, Irving could not match the power of Booth's brooding Moor. Irving's Iago, on the other hand, was more than a match for his rival, believably genial in public and savagely sardonic when alone. Yet Irving's success with Iago was not enough to compensate him for being overpowered in the role of Othello. Although the English critics applauded Irving, the measure of Booth's triumph is that Irving never again acted either part. The Italian actor Tommaso Salvini first appeared as Othello in New York at the Academy of Music in 1873 and two years later in London at the Theatre Royal, Drury Lane. His was a fiery, sensual Moor, powerful and dangerous. The theater critic William Winter, disgusted by Salvini's barbaric Othello, claimed that "only because of the excitement that it diffused throughout the nervous systems of the multitude, it possesses a worldwide renown." What Winter intended as a slight seems high praise indeed today.

Though William Charles Macready acted the part often in his career, first in 1814, he felt that he never achieved "the real pathos and terrible fury which belong to the character." Still, his Othello was powerful and dignified, and, in keeping with the attention to realistic detail for which Macready was famous, always correctly attired as a sixteenth-century Venetian officer. When, in 1816, Macready and Charles Mayne Young alternated in the two leading parts, Macready achieved greater success as Iago. Hazlitt remembered Young's Othello as "a great humming-top, and Macready, in Iago, like a mischievous boy whipping him." Samuel Phelps and Charles Fechter also acted Othello with something like Macready's dignity and restraint. Phelps alternated with Macready in the parts of Iago and Othello in 1839 at the Haymarket Theatre, with Helen Faucit as Desdemona. Once again, Macready achieved success with his

Iago, but Phelps's unfussy, gentle Othello, much to Macready's discomfort, carried the day. The *Weekly Dispatch* delightedly remarked: "He was of all things that which we have never witnessed since the death of Kean—natural." The *Sunbeam* proclaimed, even more enthusiastically, "we are now convinced that the Othello of Mr. Phelps is the Othello of Shakespeare." His productions at the Sadler's Wells Theatre, in fifteen of his eighteen years as manager, were great successes, and he continued alternating in the two male leads in seasons when he had another actor capable of performing both. Charles Fechter's Othello was more sentimental than Phelps's, intelligent and affectionate, perhaps better suited, as the *Morning Advertiser* put it, to be the hero of a "French melodrama" than of Shakespeare's agonizing tragedy.

In some remarkable way, the emotional intensity demanded in the playing of *Othello* seemed to encourage actors to carry their theatrical roles over into their private lives. Kean was correspondent in a notorious divorce trial in 1825. In 1833 Kean collapsed into the arms of his son Charles during a performance of *Othello* and died shortly thereafter. The American actor Edwin Forrest brought to his performance of Othello the experience of divorcing his wife for adultery only to be found guilty himself and ordered to pay alimony. Court appeals dragged on for years, leaving Forrest embittered and alienated. The nineteenth-century American black actor Ira Aldridge, who successfully played Othello and other tragic parts in Europe for four decades before his death in 1867, was married to a white woman. Stories such as these, at any rate, fed a popular conception of *Othello* as a shocking and sensational affair, one well suited to the savage fury and sensuality of Salvini's performance. The scene of Desdemona's murder in Salvini's rendition was especially violent, and the production took London by storm. The famous actresses of the age—Sarah Siddons, Anna Mowatt, most of all Ellen Terry—captured the sympathies of audiences by playing to the full the melodramatic role of womanly innocence traduced and overwhelmed.

Sensationalism of this kind is made for opera, and it is no coincidence that the *Othello* of the nineteenth-century stage gave rise to immortal operatic rendition. Gioachino

Rossini's *Otello* (1816) departs too widely from Shakespeare's text to allow meaningful comparison (he relied on Cinthio's story), but Giuseppe Verdi's great *Otello* (1887), the libretto by Arrigo Boito, is integrally a part of the stage history of Shakespeare's play. The omission of the first act in Venice, the concentration on the roles of Otello, Iago, and Desdemona, the ending with Otello's last kiss of his dead wife—all are comparable to those means used by actor-managers to focus the play on the intensely emotional confrontations of the tragic protagonists. Verdi eloquently interpreted the play as it was understood by his generation, and did so with such power that his operatic version remains a central formative influence in today's theater.

The twentieth century has not brought with it a major revision in the staging of *Othello*, in part perhaps because the play does not lend itself to topical appropriation as with the antiwar satire often applied to Shakespeare's histories or the disillusioning view of sex and politics often seen in productions of *Troilus and Cressida* or *Hamlet*. *Othello* does not easily adapt itself to Edwardian decor or the American frontier West, as in some productions of *All's Well That Ends Well* or *Much Ado about Nothing*. In most twentieth-century productions the text is more nearly restored to the original than in those of the previous century, and the balance of parts gives new visibility to Roderigo, Brabantio, Emilia, and Bianca, but the text was never as rearranged as it was for many other plays. Because *Othello* is a play written around a few major roles, the nineteenth century did not have to change a great deal to get what it wanted from this play.

Changes in perception of *Othello* in the twentieth century have accordingly focused on a few delicate and critical issues, most notably that of the relations of the races. For Paul Robeson, a black American actor, the central issue was not sexual jealousy but the granting of human dignity to blacks. Starring in a production with Peggy Ashcroft as Desdemona, Sybil Thorndike as Emilia, and Ralph Richardson as Roderigo at London's Savoy Theatre in 1930, Robeson brought together his personal convictions and professional ambitions in a way very different from that of Kean or Forrest. Earlier actors of Othello, excepting Ira Aldridge, had been whites who could choose to portray a black Othello or a more Arabian and Moorish Othello to suit their own acting styles. Robeson was black, a large man, sonorous of voice, commanding, magisterial. He was also a believer in a cause, and, although limited theatrically to this one role in which he must show violence and loss of emotional control (prejudices of the time did not permit him to play Iago as Booth, Kean, and Phelps had done), the very fact of his sharing the spotlight with Peggy Ashcroft (and later in 1943 with Jose Ferrer and Uta Hagen in Margaret Webster's production at the Shubert Theatre in New York) was in itself significant. He was a man of memorable dignity and presence, and his work opened the way for other blacks, especially Earle Hyman (New York, Jan Hus Auditorium, 1953, and Stratford, Connecticut, 1957), Moses Gunn (Stratford, Connecticut, 1970), and James Earl Jones (New York Shakespeare Festival, 1964, and Stratford, Connecticut, 1981), to succeed in the part. Robeson became a controversial figure and something of an outcast, whereas, when Jones played opposite Christopher Plummer in 1981 at Stratford, Connecticut (a production that in February of 1982 opened at New York's Winter Garden Theatre), his race no longer occasioned comment; Jones had by then already won considerable praise for his portrayal of King Lear.

Today, the role of Othello is available to any leading player, and has been acted by Ralph Richardson in Tyrone Guthrie's production at the Old Vic in 1938, with Laurence Olivier as Iago; by Richard Burton, again at the Old Vic, in 1956, alternating with John Neville in the parts of Othello and Iago; by Emrys James at Stratford-upon-Avon in 1971; by Raul Julia, as a passionate, tortured Othello in Wilford Leach's production for the New York Shakespeare Festival in 1979; by Anthony Hopkins, opposite Bob Hoskins's Iago, in Jonathan Miller's BBC television version in 1981; and by Ben Kingsley, who powerfully revealed the violence at the center of Othello's achieved calm, at Stratford-upon-Avon in 1985. Laurence Olivier played Othello with great success at the Old Vic for the newly established National Theatre in 1964, although he was less convincing in his film version of the production the next year, perhaps because the close-ups made too much of Oliver's West Indian mannerisms and appearance. With his virtuoso performance of an Othello both proud and self-dramatizing, Olivier demonstrated at least that the play remains what it always has been, the vehicle for an astonishing display of acting ability by one of the great actors of the age.

When we locate *Othello* on the Elizabethan stage, we see that the absence of scenery accentuates the focus on character; indeed, scenic effects have seldom played a big part in productions of this play. The Elizabethan actor needs to build the scene around him by his commanding presence and the magic of his words. Costuming and spatial arrangement are also important: in Act 1, scene 1, we know in the Elizabethan theater that we are before Brabantio's house when Desdemona's father appears in the gallery above, at his window, and then reemerges below in his nightgown *"with servants and torches."* Torches are repeatedly necessary in *Othello*, not to illuminate the stage but to signal nighttime. Theatrical signs of darkness are often intensified by violent action, as in the drinking on watch (2.3) or the killing of Roderigo and the wounding of Cassio (5.1). The latter scene, particularly, reveals how actors on the bare Elizabethan stage, in full daylight, convey a sense of darkness and dread: they grope about, look apprehensive, call for lights, and gradually come to understand what the audience, in its omniscience, has known all along.

Illusion-making of this sort is central to a play that is so concerned with deceptive appearances and overhearing. Iago is the master of illusion, and his dominance as a baleful kind of dramatist indicates how hard it is not to be deceived by show. We watch Roderigo, Othello, and indeed virtually everyone fall under the influence of his image-making ability. What are we as audience to believe? We are left in Act 5 with a stage image that focuses our attention on this problem of truth and reputation: Desdemona's bed. Thrust onstage or set in the discovery space at the rear of the stage for the play's final scene, it is a central stage property that tests the very nature of theatrical illusion. Desdemona lies slain within its bed curtains, while Emilia and others struggle to discover what has occurred. Othello, who has begun the scene believing he could snuff out the life of Desdemona as simply as snuffing out a candle, learns too late that Desdemona is not what he, in his diseased imagination, has pictured her to be. The final "tragic loading of this bed" leaves us with an unforgettable picture of Othello's failure, but also of the innocence that his doubt and Iago's slander cannot finally unsay.

OTHELLO

The Names of the Actors

OTHELLO, *the Moor*
BRABANTIO, [*a senator,*] *father to Desdemona*
CASSIO, *an honorable lieutenant* [*to Othello*]
IAGO, [*Othello's ancient,*] *a villain*
RODERIGO, *a gulled gentleman*
DUKE OF VENICE
SENATORS [*of Venice*]
MONTANO, *Governor of Cyprus*
GENTLEMEN *of Cyprus*
LODOVICO *and* GRATIANO, [*kinsmen to Brabantio,*] *two noble Venetians*
SAILORS
CLOWN

DESDEMONA, [*daughter to Brabantio and*] *wife to Othello*
EMILIA, *wife to Iago*
BIANCA, *a courtesan* [*and mistress to Cassio*]

[A MESSENGER
A HERALD
A MUSICIAN

Servants, Attendants, Officers, Senators, Musicians, Gentlemen

SCENE: *Venice; a seaport in Cyprus*]

1.1 *Enter Roderigo and Iago.*

RODERIGO
  Tush, never tell me! I take it much unkindly   1
  That thou, Iago, who hast had my purse
  As if the strings were thine, shouldst know of this.   3
IAGO 'Sblood, but you'll not hear me.   4
  If ever I did dream of such a matter,
  Abhor me.
RODERIGO
  Thou toldst me thou didst hold him in thy hate.
IAGO Despise me
  If I do not. Three great ones of the city,
  In personal suit to make me his lieutenant,
  Off-capped to him; and by the faith of man,   11
  I know my price, I am worth no worse a place.
  But he, as loving his own pride and purposes,
  Evades them with a bombast circumstance   14
  Horribly stuffed with epithets of war,   15
  And, in conclusion,
  Nonsuits my mediators. For, "Certes," says he,   17
  "I have already chose my officer."
  And what was he?
  Forsooth, a great arithmetician,   20
  One Michael Cassio, a Florentine,
  A fellow almost damned in a fair wife,   22
  That never set a squadron in the field
  Nor the division of a battle knows   24
  More than a spinster—unless the bookish theoric,   25
  Wherein the togaed consuls can propose   26
  As masterly as he. Mere prattle without practice

1.1. Location: Venice. A street.
1 never tell me don't talk to me **3 this** i.e., Desdemona's elopement
4 'Sblood by His (Christ's) blood **11 him** i.e., Othello **14 bombast
circumstance** wordy evasion. (*Bombast* is cotton padding.) **15 epithets
of war** military expressions **17 Nonsuits** rejects the petition of. **Certes**
certainly **20 arithmetician** i.e., a man whose military knowledge is
merely theoretical, based on books of tactics **22 A . . . wife** (Cassio
does not seem to be married, but his counterpart in Shakespeare's
source does have a woman in his house. See also 4.1.131.) **24 division
of a battle** disposition of a military unit **25 a spinster** i.e., a housewife,
one whose regular occupation is spinning. **theoric** theory **26 togaed**
wearing the toga. **consuls** counselors, senators. **propose** discuss

Is all his soldiership. But he, sir, had th' election;
And I, of whom his eyes had seen the proof   29
At Rhodes, at Cyprus, and on other grounds
Christened and heathen, must be beleed and calmed   31
By debitor and creditor. This countercaster,   32
He, in good time, must his lieutenant be,   33
And I—God bless the mark!—his Moorship's ancient.   34

RODERIGO
By heaven, I rather would have been his hangman.   35

IAGO
Why, there's no remedy. 'Tis the curse of service;
Preferment goes by letter and affection,   37
And not by old gradation, where each second   38
Stood heir to the first. Now, sir, be judge yourself
Whether I in any just term am affined   40
To love the Moor.

RODERIGO   I would not follow him, then.

IAGO   O sir, content you.   43
I follow him to serve my turn upon him.
We cannot all be masters, nor all masters
Cannot be truly followed. You shall mark   46
Many a duteous and knee-crooking knave
That, doting on his own obsequious bondage,
Wears out his time, much like his master's ass,
For naught but provender, and when he's old, cashiered.   50
Whip me such honest knaves. Others there are   51
Who, trimmed in forms and visages of duty,   52
Keep yet their hearts attending on themselves,
And, throwing but shows of service on their lords,

---

29 his i.e., Othello's   **31 Christened** i.e., Christian. **beleed and calmed**
left to leeward without wind, becalmed. (A sailing metaphor.)
32 debitor and creditor (A name for a system of bookkeeping, here used
as a contemptuous nickname for Cassio.)   **countercaster** i.e., bookkeeper, one who tallies with *counters* or metal disks. (Said contemptuously.)   **33 in good time** i.e., forsooth   **34 God bless the mark** (Perhaps
originally a formula to ward off evil; here an expression of impatience.)   **ancient** standard-bearer, ensign   **35 his hangman** the executioner of him   **37 Preferment** promotion.   **letter and affection** personal
influence and favoritism   **38 old gradation** step-by-step seniority, the
traditional way   **40 term** respect.   **affined** bound   **43 content you** don't
you worry about that   **46 truly** faithfully   **50 cashiered** dismissed from
service   **51 Whip me** whip, as far as I'm concerned   **52 trimmed . . .
duty** dressed up in the mere form and show of dutifulness

Do well thrive by them, and when they have lined their
   coats, 55
Do themselves homage. These fellows have some soul, 56
And such a one do I profess myself. For, sir,
It is as sure as you are Roderigo,
Were I the Moor I would not be Iago. 59
In following him, I follow but myself—
Heaven is my judge, not I for love and duty,
But seeming so for my peculiar end. 62
For when my outward action doth demonstrate
The native act and figure of my heart 64
In compliment extern, 'tis not long after 65
But I will wear my heart upon my sleeve
For daws to peck at. I am not what I am. 67

RODERIGO
What a full fortune does the thick-lips owe 68
If he can carry 't thus!

IAGO   Call up her father. 69
Rouse him, make after him, poison his delight,
Proclaim him in the streets; incense her kinsmen,
And, though he in a fertile climate dwell, 72
Plague him with flies. Though that his joy be joy, 73
Yet throw such changes of vexation on 't 74
As it may lose some color. 75

RODERIGO
Here is her father's house. I'll call aloud.

IAGO
Do, with like timorous accent and dire yell 77

---

55 lined their coats i.e., stuffed their purses **56 Do themselves homage**
i.e., attend to self-interest solely **59 Were . . . Iago** i.e., if I were able to
assume command I certainly would not choose to remain a subordi-
nate **62 peculiar** particular, personal **64 native** innate. **figure** shape,
intent **65 compliment extern** outward show (conforming in this case to
the inner workings and intention of the heart) **67 I am not what I am**
i.e., I am not one who wears his heart on his sleeve **68 full** swelling.
thick-lips (Elizabethans often applied the term "Moor" to Negroes.)
owe own **69 carry 't thus** carry this off **72–73 though . . . flies** i.e.,
though he seems prosperous and happy now, vex him with misery
73 Though . . . be joy i.e., although he seems fortunate and happy.
(Repeats the idea of l. 72.) **74 changes of vexation** vexing changes
75 As it may that may cause it to. **some color** i.e., some of its fresh
gloss **77 timorous** frightening

As when, by night and negligence, the fire   78
Is spied in populous cities.

RODERIGO

What ho, Brabantio! Signor Brabantio, ho!

IAGO

Awake! What ho, Brabantio! Thieves, thieves, thieves!
Look to your house, your daughter, and your bags!
Thieves, thieves!   83

Brabantio [enters] above [at a window].

BRABANTIO

What is the reason of this terrible summons?
What is the matter there?   85

RODERIGO

Signor, is all your family within?

IAGO

Are your doors locked?

BRABANTIO   Why, wherefore ask you this?

IAGO

Zounds, sir, you're robbed. For shame, put on your
    gown!   88
Your heart is burst; you have lost half your soul.
Even now, now, very now, an old black ram
Is tupping your white ewe. Arise, arise!   91
Awake the snorting citizens with the bell,   92
Or else the devil will make a grandsire of you.   93
Arise, I say!

BRABANTIO   What, have you lost your wits?

RODERIGO

Most reverend signor, do you know my voice?

BRABANTIO   Not I. What are you?

RODERIGO   My name is Roderigo.

BRABANTIO   The worser welcome.
I have charged thee not to haunt about my doors.
In honest plainness thou hast heard me say
My daughter is not for thee; and now, in madness,

---

78 and negligence i.e., caused by negligence   **83 s.d. at a window** (This
stage direction, from the quarto, probably calls for an appearance on
the gallery above and rearstage.)   **85 the matter** your business
88 Zounds by His (Christ's) wounds   **91 tupping** covering, copulating
with. (Said of sheep.)   **92 snorting** snoring   **93 the devil** (The devil was
conventionally pictured as black.)

Being full of supper and distempering drafts,   102
Upon malicious bravery dost thou come   103
To start my quiet.   104

RODERIGO
Sir, sir, sir—

BRABANTIO   But thou must needs be sure
My spirits and my place have in their power   106
To make this bitter to thee.

RODERIGO   Patience, good sir.

BRABANTIO
What tell'st thou me of robbing? This is Venice;
My house is not a grange.

RODERIGO   Most grave Brabantio,   109
In simple and pure soul I come to you.   110

IAGO   Zounds, sir, you are one of those that will not
serve God if the devil bid you. Because we come to do
you service and you think we are ruffians, you'll have
your daughter covered with a Barbary horse; you'll
have your nephews neigh to you; you'll have coursers   115
for cousins and jennets for germans.   116

BRABANTIO   What profane wretch art thou?

IAGO   I am one, sir, that comes to tell you your daughter
and the Moor are now making the beast with two
backs.

BRABANTIO
Thou art a villain.

IAGO   You are—a senator.

BRABANTIO
This thou shalt answer. I know thee, Roderigo.   122

RODERIGO
Sir, I will answer anything. But, I beseech you,
If 't be your pleasure and most wise consent—
As partly I find it is—that your fair daughter,
At this odd-even and dull watch o' the night,   126

102 distempering intoxicating   **103 Upon malicious bravery** with hostile intent to defy me   **104 start** startle, disrupt   **106 My spirits and my place** my temperament and my authority of office.   **have in** have it in   **109 grange** isolated farmhouse   **110 simple** sincere   **115 nephews** i.e., grandsons. **coursers** powerful horses   **116 cousins** kinsmen. **jennets** small Spanish horses. **germans** near relatives   **122 answer** be held accountable for   **126 odd-even** between one day and the next, i.e., about midnight

Transported with no worse nor better guard   127
But with a knave of common hire, a gondolier,   128
To the gross clasps of a lascivious Moor—
If this be known to you and your allowance   130
We then have done you bold and saucy wrongs.   131
But if you know not this, my manners tell me
We have your wrong rebuke. Do not believe
That, from the sense of all civility,   134
I thus would play and trifle with your reverence.   135
Your daughter, if you have not given her leave,
I say again, hath made a gross revolt,
Tying her duty, beauty, wit, and fortunes   138
In an extravagant and wheeling stranger   139
Of here and everywhere. Straight satisfy yourself.   140
If she be in her chamber or your house,
Let loose on me the justice of the state
For thus deluding you.
BRABANTIO   Strike on the tinder, ho!   144
Give me a taper! Call up all my people!
This accident is not unlike my dream.   146
Belief of it oppresses me already.
Light, I say, light!   *Exit [above].*
IAGO   Farewell, for I must leave you.
It seems not meet nor wholesome to my place
To be produced—as, if I stay, I shall—   150
Against the Moor. For I do know the state,
However this may gall him with some check,   152
Cannot with safety cast him, for he's embarked   153
With such loud reason to the Cyprus wars,   154
Which even now stands in act, that, for their souls,   155
Another of his fathom they have none   156

127 with by   **128 But with a knave** than by a low fellow, a servant
130 allowance permission   **131 saucy** insolent   **134 from** contrary to.
civility good manners, decency   **135 your reverence** the respect due to
you   **138 wit** intelligence   **139 extravagant** expatriate, wandering far
from home.   **wheeling** roving about, vagabond.   **stranger** foreigner
140 Straight straightway   **144 tinder** charred linen ignited by a spark
from flint and steel, used to light torches or *tapers* (ll. 145, 170)
146 accident occurrence, event   **150 produced** produced (as a witness)   **152 gall** rub; oppress.   **check** rebuke   **153 cast** dismiss.   **embarked** engaged   **154 loud** i.e., self-evident, boldly proclaimed
155 stands in act are going on   **156 fathom** i.e., ability, depth of
experience

To lead their business; in which regard,   157
Though I do hate him as I do hell pains,
Yet for necessity of present life   159
I must show out a flag and sign of love,
Which is indeed but sign. That you shall surely find him,
Lead to the Sagittary the raisèd search,   162
And there will I be with him. So farewell.   *Exit.* 163

> *Enter [below] Brabantio [in his nightgown] with*
> *servants and torches.*

BRABANTIO
It is too true an evil. Gone she is;
And what's to come of my despisèd time   165
Is naught but bitterness. Now, Roderigo,
Where didst thou see her?—O unhappy girl!—
With the Moor, sayst thou?—Who would be a father!—
How didst thou know 'twas she?—O, she deceives me
Past thought!—What said she to you?—Get more tapers.
Raise all my kindred.—Are they married, think you?
RODERIGO   Truly, I think they are.
BRABANTIO
O heaven! How got she out? O treason of the blood!
Fathers, from hence trust not your daughters' minds
By what you see them act. Is there not charms   175
By which the property of youth and maidhood   176
May be abused? Have you not read, Roderigo,   177
Of some such thing?
RODERIGO   Yes, sir, I have indeed.
BRABANTIO
Call up my brother.—O, would you had had her!—
Some one way, some another.—Do you know
Where we may apprehend her and the Moor?
RODERIGO
I think I can discover him, if you please   182
To get good guard and go along with me.

---

157 in which regard out of regard for which   **159 life** livelihood
162 Sagittary (An inn where Othello and Desdemona are staying.)
raisèd search search party roused out of sleep   **163 s.d. nightgown**
dressing gown. (This costuming is specified in the quarto text.)   **165 time**
i.e., remainder of life   **175 charms** spells   **176 property** special quality,
nature   **177 abused** deceived   **182 discover** reveal, uncover

BRABANTIO
  Pray you, lead on. At every house I'll call;
  I may command at most.—Get weapons, ho!   185
  And raise some special officers of night.—
  On, good Roderigo. I will deserve your pains.   187
                                              Exeunt.

❖

1.2   *Enter Othello, Iago, attendants with torches.*

IAGO
  Though in the trade of war I have slain men,
  Yet do I hold it very stuff o' the conscience   2
  To do no contrived murder. I lack iniquity   3
  Sometimes to do me service. Nine or ten times
  I had thought t' have yerked him here under the ribs.   5
OTHELLO
  'Tis better as it is.
IAGO   Nay, but he prated,
  And spoke such scurvy and provoking terms
  Against your honor
  That, with the little godliness I have,
  I did full hard forbear him. But, I pray you, sir,   10
  Are you fast married? Be assured of this,
  That the magnifico is much beloved,   12
  And hath in his effect a voice potential   13
  As double as the Duke's. He will divorce you,   14
  Or put upon you what restraint and grievance
  The law, with all his might to enforce it on,
  Will give him cable.
OTHELLO   Let him do his spite.   17
  My services which I have done the seigniory   18

185 **command** demand assistance   187 **deserve** show gratitude for

1.2. Location: Venice. Another street, before Othello's lodgings.
2 **very stuff** essence, basic material (continuing the metaphor of *trade*
from l. 1)   3 **contrived** premeditated   5 **yerked** stabbed.   **him** i.e.,
Roderigo   10 **I . . . him** I restrained myself with great difficulty from
assaulting him   12 **magnifico** Venetian grandee, i.e., Brabantio   13 **in**
his effect at his command.   **potential** powerful   14 **double** doubly
powerful (in comparison with other senators)   17 **cable** i.e., scope
18 **seigniory** Venetian government

Shall out-tongue his complaints. 'Tis yet to know— 19
Which, when I know that boasting is an honor,
I shall promulgate—I fetch my life and being
From men of royal siege, and my demerits 22
May speak unbonneted to as proud a fortune 23
As this that I have reached. For know, Iago,
But that I love the gentle Desdemona,
I would not my unhousèd free condition 26
Put into circumscription and confine 27
For the sea's worth. But look, what lights come yond? 28

Enter Cassio [and certain Officers] with torches.

IAGO
Those are the raisèd father and his friends.
You were best go in.
OTHELLO   Not I. I must be found.
My parts, my title, and my perfect soul 31
Shall manifest me rightly. Is it they?
IAGO   By Janus, I think no. 33
OTHELLO
The servants of the Duke? And my lieutenant?
The goodness of the night upon you, friends!
What is the news?
CASSIO   The Duke does greet you, General,
And he requires your haste-post-haste appearance
Even on the instant.
OTHELLO   What is the matter, think you? 38
CASSIO
Something from Cyprus, as I may divine. 39
It is a business of some heat. The galleys 40
Have sent a dozen sequent messengers 41
This very night at one another's heels,

19 **yet to know** not yet widely known   22 **siege** i.e., rank. (Literally, a *seat* used by a person of distinction.)   **demerits** deserts   23 **unbonneted** without removing the hat, i.e., on equal terms (? Or "with hat off," "in all due modesty.")   26 **unhousèd** unconfined, undomesticated   27 **circumscription and confine** restriction and confinement   28 **the sea's worth** all the riches at the bottom of the sea   **s.d. Officers** (The quarto text calls for "Cassio with lights, officers with torches.")   31 **My . . . soul** my natural gifts, my position or reputation, and my unflawed conscience   33 **Janus** Roman two-faced god of beginnings   38 **matter** business   39 **divine** guess   40 **heat** urgency   41 **sequent** successive

And many of the consuls, raised and met,   43
Are at the Duke's already. You have been hotly called for;
When, being not at your lodging to be found,
The Senate hath sent about three several quests   46
To search you out.
OTHELLO   'Tis well I am found by you.
I will but spend a word here in the house
And go with you.   [*Exit.*]
CASSIO   Ancient, what makes he here?   49
IAGO
Faith, he tonight hath boarded a land carrack.   50
If it prove lawful prize, he's made forever.   51
CASSIO
I do not understand.
IAGO   He's married.
CASSIO   To who?

       [*Enter Othello.*]

IAGO
Marry, to—Come, Captain, will you go?   53
OTHELLO   Have with you.   54
CASSIO
Here comes another troop to seek for you.   55

       Enter Brabantio, Roderigo, with officers and
       torches.

IAGO
It is Brabantio. General, be advised.   56
He comes to bad intent.
OTHELLO   Holla! Stand there!
RODERIGO
Signor, it is the Moor.
BRABANTIO   Down with him, thief!
                              [*They draw on both sides.*]
IAGO
You, Roderigo! Come, sir, I am for you.

43 consuls senators **46 several** separate **49 makes** does **50 boarded**
gone aboard and seized as an act of piracy (with sexual suggestion).
carrack large merchant ship **51 prize** booty **53 Marry** (An oath,
originally "by the Virgin Mary.") **54 Have with you** i.e., let's go
55 s.d. officers and torches (The quarto text calls for "others with lights
and weapons.") **56 be advised** be on your guard

OTHELLO
Keep up your bright swords, for the dew will rust them. 60
Good signor, you shall more command with years
Than with your weapons.

BRABANTIO
O thou foul thief, where hast thou stowed my daughter?
Damned as thou art, thou hast enchanted her!
For I'll refer me to all things of sense, 65
If she in chains of magic were not bound
Whether a maid so tender, fair, and happy,
So opposite to marriage that she shunned
The wealthy curlèd darlings of our nation,
Would ever have, t' incur a general mock,
Run from her guardage to the sooty bosom 71
Of such a thing as thou—to fear, not to delight.
Judge me the world if 'tis not gross in sense 73
That thou hast practiced on her with foul charms,
Abused her delicate youth with drugs or minerals 75
That weakens motion. I'll have 't disputed on; 76
'Tis probable, and palpable to thinking.
I therefore apprehend and do attach thee 78
For an abuser of the world, a practicer
Of arts inhibited and out of warrant.— 80
Lay hold upon him! If he do resist,
Subdue him at his peril.

OTHELLO   Hold your hands,
Both you of my inclining and the rest. 83
Were it my cue to fight, I should have known it
Without a prompter.—Whither will you that I go
To answer this your charge?

BRABANTIO   To prison, till fit time
Of law and course of direct session 88
Call thee to answer.

OTHELLO   What if I do obey?

60 Keep up i.e., sheathe   **65 refer me** submit my case.   **things of sense**
commonsense understandings, or, creatures possessing common
sense   **71 guardage** guardianship   **73 gross in sense** obvious   **75 minerals** i.e., poisons   **76 weakens motion** impair the vital faculties.
disputed on argued in court by professional counsel, discussed by
experts   **78 attach** arrest   **80 inhibited** prohibited.   **out of warrant**
illegal   **83 inclining** following, party   **88 course of direct session**
regular or specially convened legal proceedings

How may the Duke be therewith satisfied,
Whose messengers are here about my side
Upon some present business of the state
To bring me to him?
OFFICER   'Tis true, most worthy signor.
The Duke's in council, and your noble self,
I am sure, is sent for.
BRABANTIO   How? The Duke in council?
In this time of the night? Bring him away.   96
Mine's not an idle cause. The Duke himself,   97
Or any of my brothers of the state,
Cannot but feel this wrong as 'twere their own;
For if such actions may have passage free,
Bondslaves and pagans shall our statesmen be.

                                              Exeunt.

                          ❖

1.3   *Enter Duke [and] Senators [and sit at a table,*
          with lights], and Officers. [The Duke and
          Senators are reading dispatches.]

DUKE
There is no composition in these news   1
That gives them credit.
FIRST SENATOR   Indeed, they are disproportioned.   3
My letters say a hundred and seven galleys.
DUKE
And mine, a hundred forty.
SECOND SENATOR   And mine, two hundred.
But though they jump not on a just account—   6
As in these cases, where the aim reports   7
'Tis oft with difference—yet do they all confirm
A Turkish fleet, and bearing up to Cyprus.
DUKE
Nay, it is possible enough to judgment.

---

96 away right along   **97 idle** trifling

1.3. Location: Venice. A council chamber.
s.d. Enter . . . Officers (The quarto text calls for the Duke and Senators
to "sit at a table with lights and attendants.")   **1 composition** consis-
tency   **3 disproportioned** inconsistent   **6 jump** agree.   **just** exact
7 the aim conjecture

I do not so secure me in the error   11
But the main article I do approve   12
In fearful sense.

SAILOR (*Within*)   What ho, what ho, what ho!

   Enter Sailor.

OFFICER   A messenger from the galleys.

DUKE˙ Now, what's the business?

SAILOR
The Turkish preparation makes for Rhodes.   16
So was I bid report here to the state
By Signor Angelo.

DUKE
How say you by this change?

FIRST SENATOR   This cannot be   19
By no assay of reason. 'Tis a pageant   20
To keep us in false gaze. When we consider   21
Th' importancy of Cyprus to the Turk,
And let ourselves again but understand
That, as it more concerns the Turk than Rhodes,
So may he with more facile question bear it,   25
For that it stands not in such warlike brace,   26
But altogether lacks th' abilities   27
That Rhodes is dressed in—if we make thought of this,   28
We must not think the Turk is so unskillful   29
To leave that latest which concerns him first,   30
Neglecting an attempt of ease and gain
To wake and wage a danger profitless.   32

DUKE
Nay, in all confidence, he's not for Rhodes.

OFFICER   Here is more news.

   Enter a Messenger.

11–12 I do not ... approve I do not take such (false) comfort in the
discrepancies that I fail to perceive the main point, i.e., that the Turkish
fleet is threatening   **16 preparation** fleet prepared for battle   **19 by**
about   **20 assay** test.   **pageant** mere show   **21 in false gaze** looking the
wrong way   **25 may ... it** he (the Turk) can more easily capture it
(Cyprus)   **26 For that** since.   **brace** state of defense   **27 abilities** means
of self-defense   **28 dressed in** equipped with   **29 unskillful** deficient in
judgment   **30 latest** last   **32 wake** stir up.   **wage** risk

MESSENGER
  The Ottomites, reverend and gracious,
  Steering with due course toward the isle of Rhodes,
  Have there injointed them with an after fleet.   37

FIRST SENATOR
  Ay, so I thought. How many, as you guess?

MESSENGER
  Of thirty sail; and now they do restem   39
  Their backward course, bearing with frank appearance   40
  Their purposes toward Cyprus. Signor Montano,
  Your trusty and most valiant servitor,   42
  With his free duty recommends you thus,   43
  And prays you to believe him.

DUKE   'Tis certain then for Cyprus.
  Marcus Luccicos, is not he in town?

FIRST SENATOR   He's now in Florence.

DUKE
  Write from us to him, post-post-haste. Dispatch.

FIRST SENATOR
  Here comes Brabantio and the valiant Moor.

  *Enter Brabantio, Othello, Cassio, Iago, Roderigo,
  and officers.*

DUKE
  Valiant Othello, we must straight employ you   50
  Against the general enemy Ottoman.   51
  [*To Brabantio.*] I did not see you; welcome, gentle signor.   52
  We lacked your counsel and your help tonight.

BRABANTIO
  So did I yours. Good Your Grace, pardon me;
  Neither my place nor aught I heard of business   55
  Hath raised me from my bed, nor doth the general care
  Take hold on me, for my particular grief   57
  Is of so floodgate and o'erbearing nature   58

37 injointed them joined themselves.   **after** second   **39–40 restem . . .
course** retrace their original course   **40 frank appearance** i.e., undis-
guised intent   **42 servitor** officer under your command   **43 free duty**
freely given and loyal service.   **recommends** commends himself and
reports to   **50 straight** straightway   **51 general** universal, i.e., against
all Christendom   **52 gentle** noble   **55 place** official position
57 particular personal   **58 floodgate** i.e., overwhelming (as when flood-
gates are opened)

That it engluts and swallows other sorrows   59
And it is still itself.

DUKE   Why, what's the matter?   60

BRABANTIO
  My daughter! O, my daughter!

DUKE AND SENATORS   Dead?

BRABANTIO   Ay, to me.
  She is abused, stol'n from me, and corrupted   62
  By spells and medicines bought of mountebanks;
  For nature so preposterously to err,
  Being not deficient, blind, or lame of sense,   65
  Sans witchcraft could not.   66

DUKE
  Whoe'er he be that in this foul proceeding
  Hath thus beguiled your daughter of herself,
  And you of her, the bloody book of law
  You shall yourself read in the bitter letter
  After your own sense—yea, though our proper son   71
  Stood in your action.

BRABANTIO   Humbly I thank Your Grace.   72
  Here is the man, this Moor, whom now it seems
  Your special mandate for the state affairs
  Hath hither brought.

ALL   We are very sorry for 't.

DUKE [*To Othello*]
  What, in your own part, can you say to this?

BRABANTIO   Nothing, but this is so.

OTHELLO
  Most potent, grave, and reverend signors,
  My very noble and approved good masters: 79
  That I have ta'en away this old man's daughter,
  It is most true; true, I have married her.
  The very head and front of my offending   82
  Hath this extent, no more. Rude am I in my speech,   83
  And little blessed with the soft phrase of peace;
  For since these arms of mine had seven years' pith,   85

---

59 engluts engulfs   **60 is still itself** remains undiminished   **62 abused** deceived   **65 deficient** defective   **66 Sans** without   **71 After . . . sense** according to your own interpretation.   **our proper** my own   **72 Stood . . . action** were under your accusation   **79 approved** proved, esteemed   **82 head and front** height and breadth, entire extent   **83 Rude** unpolished   **85 pith** strength, vigor (i.e., since I was seven)

Till now some nine moons wasted, they have used   86
Their dearest action in the tented field;   87
And little of this great world can I speak
More than pertains to feats of broils and battle,
And therefore little shall I grace my cause
In speaking for myself. Yet, by your gracious patience,
I will a round unvarnished tale deliver   92
Of my whole course of love—what drugs, what charms,
What conjuration, and what mighty magic,
For such proceeding I am charged withal,   95
I won his daughter.

BRABANTIO   A maiden never bold;
Of spirit so still and quiet that her motion   97
Blushed at herself; and she, in spite of nature,   98
Of years, of country, credit, everything,   99
To fall in love with what she feared to look on!
It is a judgment maimed and most imperfect
That will confess perfection so could err   102
Against all rules of nature, and must be driven
To find out practices of cunning hell   104
Why this should be. I therefore vouch again   105
That with some mixtures powerful o'er the blood,   106
Or with some dram conjured to this effect,   107
He wrought upon her.

DUKE   To vouch this is no proof,
Without more wider and more overt test   109
Than these thin habits and poor likelihoods   110
Of modern seeming do prefer against him.   111

FIRST SENATOR   But, Othello, speak.
Did you by indirect and forcèd courses
Subdue and poison this young maid's affections?
Or came it by request and such fair question   115
As soul to soul affordeth?

86 Till . . . wasted until some nine months ago (since when Othello
has evidently not been on active duty, but in Venice) 87 dearest most
valuable 92 round plain 95 withal with 97–98 her . . . herself her
very emotions prompted her to blush at discovering such feelings in
herself 99 years i.e., difference in age. credit virtuous reputation
102 confess concede (that) 104 practices plots 105 vouch assert
106 blood passions 107 conjured to this effect made by magical spells
to have this effect 109 more wider fuller 110 habits garments, i.e.,
appearances 111 modern seeming commonplace assumption. prefer
bring forth 115 question conversation

OTHELLO   I do beseech you,
Send for the lady to the Sagittary
And let her speak of me before her father.
If you do find me foul in her report,
The trust, the office I do hold of you
Not only take away, but let your sentence
Even fall upon my life.

DUKE   Fetch Desdemona hither.

OTHELLO
Ancient, conduct them. You best know the place.
             [*Exeunt Iago and attendants.*]
And, till she come, as truly as to heaven
I do confess the vices of my blood,   125
So justly to your grave ears I'll present   126
How I did thrive in this fair lady's love,
And she in mine.

DUKE   Say it, Othello.

OTHELLO
Her father loved me, oft invited me,
Still questioned me the story of my life   131
From year to year—the battles, sieges, fortunes,
That I have passed.
I ran it through, even from my boyish days
To th' very moment that he bade me tell it,
Wherein I spoke of most disastrous chances,
Of moving accidents by flood and field,   137
Of hairbreadth scapes i' th' imminent deadly breach,   138
Of being taken by the insolent foe
And sold to slavery, of my redemption thence,
And portance in my travels' history,   141
Wherein of antres vast and deserts idle,   142
Rough quarries, rocks, and hills whose heads touch
    heaven,   143
It was my hint to speak—such was my process—   144
And of the Cannibals that each other eat,
The Anthropophagi, and men whose heads   146

125 blood passions, human nature   **126 justly** truthfully, accurately
131 Still continually   **137 accidents** happenings   **138 imminent . . .
breach** death-threatening gaps made in a fortification   **141 portance**
conduct   **142 antres** caverns.   **idle** barren, desolate   **143 Rough
quarries** rugged rock formations   **144 hint** occasion, opportunity
146 Anthropophagi man-eaters. (A term from Pliny's *Natural History*.)

Do grow beneath their shoulders. These things to hear
Would Desdemona seriously incline;
But still the house affairs would draw her thence,
Which ever as she could with haste dispatch
She'd come again, and with a greedy ear
Devour up my discourse. Which I, observing,
Took once a pliant hour, and found good means   153
To draw from her a prayer of earnest heart
That I would all my pilgrimage dilate,   155
Whereof by parcels she had something heard,   156
But not intentively. I did consent,   157
And often did beguile her of her tears,
When I did speak of some distressful stroke
That my youth suffered. My story being done,
She gave me for my pains a world of sighs.
She swore, in faith, 'twas strange, 'twas passing strange,   162
'Twas pitiful, 'twas wondrous pitiful.
She wished she had not heard it, yet she wished
That heaven had made her such a man. She thanked me,
And bade me, if I had a friend that loved her,
I should but teach him how to tell my story,
And that would woo her. Upon this hint I spake.   168
She loved me for the dangers I had passed,
And I loved her that she did pity them.
This only is the witchcraft I have used.
Here comes the lady. Let her witness it.

Enter Desdemona, Iago, [and] attendants.

DUKE
I think this tale would win my daughter too.
Good Brabantio,
Take up this mangled matter at the best.   175
Men do their broken weapons rather use
Than their bare hands.
BRABANTIO   I pray you, hear her speak.
If she confess that she was half the wooer,
Destruction on my head if my bad blame

---

153 **pliant** well-suiting   155 **dilate** relate in detail   156 **by parcels** piecemeal   157 **intentively** with full attention   162 **passing** exceedingly   168 **hint** opportunity   175 **Take . . . best** make the best of a bad bargain

Light on the man!—Come hither, gentle mistress.
Do you perceive in all this noble company
Where most you owe obedience?

DESDEMONA   My noble Father,
I do perceive here a divided duty.
To you I am bound for life and education;   184
My life and education both do learn me   185
How to respect you. You are the lord of duty;
I am hitherto your daughter. But here's my husband,
And so much duty as my mother showed
To you, preferring you before her father,
So much I challenge that I may profess   190
Due to the Moor my lord.

BRABANTIO   God be with you! I have done.
Please it Your Grace, on to the state affairs.
I had rather to adopt a child than get it.   194
Come hither, Moor.   [*He joins the hands of Othello
and Desdemona.*]
I here do give thee that with all my heart   196
Which, but thou hast already, with all my heart   197
I would keep from thee.—For your sake, jewel,   198
I am glad at soul I have no other child,
For thy escape would teach me tyranny,   200
To hang clogs on them.—I have done, my lord.   201

DUKE
Let me speak like yourself, and lay a sentence   202
Which, as a grece or step, may help these lovers   203
Into your favor.
When remedies are past, the griefs are ended   205
By seeing the worst, which late on hopes depended.   206
To mourn a mischief that is past and gone   207
Is the next way to draw new mischief on.   208

---

184 education upbringing   **185 learn** teach   **190 challenge** claim
194 get beget   **196 with all my heart** wherein my whole affection has
been engaged   **197 with all my heart** willingly, gladly   **198 For your
sake** on your account   **200 escape** elopement   **201 clogs** (Literally,
blocks of wood fastened to the legs of criminals or convicts to inhibit
escape.)   **202 like yourself** i.e., as you would, in your proper temper.
sentence maxim (also at l. 219)   **203 grece** step   **205 remedies** hopes of
remedy   **206 which** i.e., the griefs.   **late . . . depended** were sustained
until recently by hopeful anticipation   **207 mischief** misfortune, injury   **208 next** nearest

What cannot be preserved when fortune takes,   209
Patience her injury a mockery makes.   210
The robbed that smiles steals something from the thief;
He robs himself that spends a bootless grief.   212

BRABANTIO
So let the Turk of Cyprus us beguile,
We lose it not, so long as we can smile.
He bears the sentence well that nothing bears   215
But the free comfort which from thence he hears,   216
But he bears both the sentence and the sorrow   217
That, to pay grief, must of poor patience borrow.   218
These sentences, to sugar or to gall,   219
Being strong on both sides, are equivocal.   220
But words are words. I never yet did hear
That the bruised heart was piercèd through the ear.   222
I humbly beseech you, proceed to th' affairs of state.

DUKE   The Turk with a most mighty preparation makes
for Cyprus. Othello, the fortitude of the place is best   225
known to you; and though we have there a substitute   226
of most allowed sufficiency, yet opinion, a sovereign   227
mistress of effects, throws a more safer voice on you.   228
You must therefore be content to slubber the gloss of   229
your new fortunes with this more stubborn and   230
boisterous expedition.

OTHELLO
The tyrant custom, most grave senators,
Hath made the flinty and steel couch of war
My thrice-driven bed of down. I do agnize   234

---

209 What whatever   **210 Patience . . . makes** patience laughs at the
injury inflicted by fortune (and thus eases the pain)   **212 spends a
bootless grief** indulges in unavailing grief   **215–218 He bears . . .
borrow** i.e., a person well bears out your maxim who takes with him
only the philosophic consolation it teaches him, a comfort free from
sorrow; but anyone whose grief bankrupts his poor patience is left with
your saying and his sorrow too. (*Bears the sentence* also plays on the
meaning, "receives judicial sentence.")   **219–220 These . . . equivocal**
i.e., these fine maxims are equivocal, either sweet or bitter in their
application   **222 piercèd . . . ear** i.e., surgically lanced and cured by
mere words of advice   **225 fortitude** strength   **226 substitute** deputy
227 allowed acknowledged   **227–228 opinion . . . on you** general opinion, an important determiner of affairs, chooses you as the best man
229 slubber soil, sully   **230 stubborn** harsh, rough   **234 thrice-driven**
thrice sifted, winnowed.   **agnize** know in myself, acknowledge

A natural and prompt alacrity
I find in hardness, and do undertake   236
These present wars against the Ottomites.
Most humbly therefore bending to your state,   238
I crave fit disposition for my wife,
Due reference of place and exhibition,   240
With such accommodation and besort   241
As levels with her breeding.   242

DUKE
Why, at her father's.

BRABANTIO   I will not have it so.

OTHELLO
Nor I.

DESDEMONA   Nor I. I would not there reside,
To put my father in impatient thoughts
By being in his eye. Most gracious Duke,
To my unfolding lend your prosperous ear,   247
And let me find a charter in your voice   248
T' assist my simpleness.

DUKE   What would you, Desdemona?

DESDEMONA
That I did love the Moor to live with him,
My downright violence and storm of fortunes   252
May trumpet to the world. My heart's subdued   253
Even to the very quality of my lord.   254
I saw Othello's visage in his mind,
And to his honors and his valiant parts   256
Did I my soul and fortunes consecrate.
So that, dear lords, if I be left behind
A moth of peace, and he go to the war,   259
The rites for why I love him are bereft me,   260
And I a heavy interim shall support

236 hardness hardship   **238 bending . . . state** bowing or kneeling to
your authority   **240 reference . . . exhibition** provision of place to live
and allowance of money   **241 accommodation** suitable provision.
besort attendance   **242 levels** equals, suits   **247 unfolding** explanation,
proposal.   **prosperous** propitious   **248 charter** privilege, authorization   **252 My . . . fortunes** my plain and total breach of social custom,
taking my future by storm and disrupting my whole life   **253–254 My
heart's . . . lord** my heart is brought wholly into accord with Othello's
virtues; I love him for his virtues   **256 parts** qualities   **259 moth** i.e.,
one who consumes merely   **260 rites** rites of love (with a suggestion too
of *rights*, sharing)

By his dear absence. Let me go with him.   262
OTHELLO   Let her have your voice.   263
  Vouch with me, heaven, I therefor beg it not
  To please the palate of my appetite,
  Nor to comply with heat—the young affects   266
  In me defunct—and proper satisfaction,   267
  But to be free and bounteous to her mind.   268
  And heaven defend your good souls that you think   269
  I will your serious and great business scant
  When she is with me. No, when light-winged toys
  Of feathered Cupid seel with wanton dullness   272
  My speculative and officed instruments,   273
  That my disports corrupt and taint my business,   274
  Let huswives make a skillet of my helm,
  And all indign and base adversities   276
  Make head against my estimation!   277
DUKE
  Be it as you shall privately determine,
  Either for her stay or going. Th' affair cries haste,
  And speed must answer it.   You must away tonight.
A SENATOR   You must away tonight.
DESDEMONA
  Tonight, my lord?
DUKE   This night.
OTHELLO   With all my heart.
DUKE
  At nine i' the morning here we'll meet again.
  Othello, leave some officer behind,
  And he shall our commission bring to you,
  With such things else of quality and respect   285
  As doth import you.
OTHELLO   So please Your Grace, my ancient;   286
  A man he is of honesty and trust.

262 **dear** (1) heartfelt (2) costly   263 **voice** consent   266 **heat** sexual
passion.   **young affects** passions of youth, desires   267 **proper** personal   268 **free** generous   269 **defend** forbid.   **think** should think
272 **seel** i.e., make blind (as in falconry, by sewing up the eyes of the
hawk during training)   273 **speculative . . . instruments** i.e., perceptive
faculties used in the performance of duty   274 **That** so that.   **disports**
sexual pastimes.   **taint** impair   276 **indign** unworthy, shameful
277 **Make head** raise an army.   **estimation** reputation   285 **of quality
and respect** of importance and relevance   286 **import** concern

To his conveyance I assign my wife,
With what else needful Your Good Grace shall think
To be sent after me.

DUKE   Let it be so.
Good night to everyone. [*To Brabantio.*] And, noble
  signor,
If virtue no delighted beauty lack,   292
Your son-in-law is far more fair than black.

FIRST SENATOR
Adieu, brave Moor. Use Desdemona well.

BRABANTIO
Look to her, Moor, if thou hast eyes to see.
She has deceived her father, and may thee.
              Exeunt [Duke, Brabantio, Cassio, Senators,
                                    and Officers].

OTHELLO
My life upon her faith! Honest Iago,
My Desdemona must I leave to thee.
I prithee, let thy wife attend on her,
And bring them after in the best advantage.   300
Come, Desdemona. I have but an hour
Of love, of worldly matters and direction,   302
To spend with thee. We must obey the time.
                          Exit [with Desdemona].

RODERIGO   Iago—
IAGO   What sayst thou, noble heart?
RODERIGO   What will I do, think'st thou?
IAGO   Why, go to bed and sleep.
RODERIGO   I will incontinently drown myself.   308
IAGO   If thou dost, I shall never love thee after. Why,
  thou silly gentleman?
RODERIGO   It is silliness to live when to live is torment;
  and then have we a prescription to die when death is   312
  our physician.
IAGO   O villainous! I have looked upon the world for   314
  four times seven years, and, since I could distinguish
  betwixt a benefit and an injury, I never found man

---

292 delighted capable of delighting   **300 in . . . advantage** at the most
favorable opportunity   **302 direction** instructions   **308 incontinently**
immediately   **312 prescription** (1) right based on long-established
custom (2) doctor's prescription   **314 villainous** i.e., what perfect
nonsense

that knew how to love himself. Ere I would say I
would drown myself for the love of a guinea hen, I   318
would change my humanity with a baboon.

RODERIGO What should I do? I confess it is my shame
to be so fond, but it is not in my virtue to amend it.   321

IAGO Virtue? A fig! 'Tis in ourselves that we are thus or   322
thus. Our bodies are our gardens, to the which our
wills are gardeners; so that if we will plant nettles or
sow lettuce, set hyssop and weed up thyme, supply it   325
with one gender of herbs or distract it with many, ei-   326
ther to have it sterile with idleness or manured with   327
industry—why, the power and corrigible authority of   328
this lies in our wills. If the beam of our lives had not   329
one scale of reason to poise another of sensuality, the   330
blood and baseness of our natures would conduct us   331
to most preposterous conclusions. But we have reason
to cool our raging motions, our carnal stings, our un-   333
bitted lusts, whereof I take this that you call love to be   334
a sect or scion.   335

RODERIGO It cannot be.

IAGO It is merely a lust of the blood and a permission
of the will. Come, be a man. Drown thyself? Drown
cats and blind puppies. I have professed me thy friend,
and I confess me knit to thy deserving with cables of
perdurable toughness. I could never better stead thee   341
than now. Put money in thy purse. Follow thou the
wars; defeat thy favor with an usurped beard. I say,   343
put money in thy purse. It cannot be long that Desdemona should continue her love to the Moor—put
money in thy purse—nor he his to her. It was a vio-

---

318 guinea hen (A slang term for a prostitute.)   **321 fond** infatuated.
virtue strength, nature   **322 fig** (To give a fig is to thrust the thumb
between the first and second fingers in a vulgar and insulting gesture.)   **325 hyssop** a herb of the mint family   **326 gender** kind.
distract it with divide it among   **327 idleness** want of cultivation
328 corrigible authority power to correct   **329 beam** balance
330 poise counterbalance   **331 blood** natural passions   **333 motions**
appetites   **333–334 unbitted** unbridled, uncontrolled   **335 sect or scion**
cutting or offshoot   **341 perdurable** very durable.   **stead** assist
343 defeat thy favor disguise your face.   **usurped** (The suggestion is
that Roderigo is not man enough to have a beard of his own.)

lent commencement in her, and thou shalt see an an- 347
swerable sequestration—put but money in thy purse. 348
These Moors are changeable in their wills—fill thy 349
purse with money. The food that to him now is as
luscious as locusts shall be to him shortly as bitter as 351
coloquintida. She must change for youth; when she is 352
sated with his body, she will find the error of her
choice. She must have change, she must. Therefore
put money in thy purse. If thou wilt needs damn thyself, do it a more delicate way than drowning. Make 356
all the money thou canst. If sanctimony and a frail vow 357
betwixt an erring barbarian and a supersubtle Vene- 358
tian be not too hard for my wits and all the tribe of
hell, thou shalt enjoy her. Therefore make money. A
pox of drowning thyself! It is clean out of the way.
Seek thou rather to be hanged in compassing thy joy 362
than to be drowned and go without her.

RODERIGO Wilt thou be fast to my hopes if I depend on 364
the issue?

IAGO Thou art sure of me. Go, make money. I have
told thee often, and I retell thee again and again, I hate
the Moor. My cause is hearted; thine hath no less rea- 368
son. Let us be conjunctive in our revenge against him. 369
If thou canst cuckold him, thou dost thyself a pleasure,
me a sport. There are many events in the womb of
time which will be delivered. Traverse, go, provide thy 372
money. We will have more of this tomorrow. Adieu.

RODERIGO Where shall we meet i' the morning?

IAGO At my lodging.

RODERIGO I'll be with thee betimes. [*He starts to leave.*] 376

IAGO Go to, farewell.—Do you hear, Roderigo?

RODERIGO What say you?

IAGO No more of drowning, do you hear?

347–348 an answerable sequestration a corresponding separation or
estrangement   **349 wills** carnal appetites   **351 locusts** fruit of the carob
tree (see Matthew 3:4), or perhaps honeysuckle   **352 coloquintida**
colocynth or bitter apple, a purgative   **356 Make** raise, collect
357 sanctimony sacred ceremony   **358 erring** wandering, vagabond,
unsteady   **362 compassing** encompassing, embracing   **364 fast** true
368 hearted fixed in the heart, heartfelt   **369 conjunctive** united
372 Traverse (A military marching term.)   **376 betimes** early

RODERIGO I am changed.

IAGO Go to, farewell. Put money enough in your purse.

RODERIGO I'll sell all my land.   *Exit.*

IAGO

Thus do I ever make my fool my purse;
For I mine own gained knowledge should profane
If I would time expend with such a snipe   386
But for my sport and profit. I hate the Moor;
And it is thought abroad that twixt my sheets   388
He's done my office. I know not if 't be true;   389
But I, for mere suspicion in that kind,
Will do as if for surety. He holds me well;   391
The better shall my purpose work on him.
Cassio's a proper man. Let me see now: 393
To get his place and to plume up my will   394
In double knavery—How, how?—Let's see:
After some time, to abuse Othello's ear   396
That he is too familiar with his wife.   397
He hath a person and a smooth dispose   398
To be suspected, framed to make women false.
The Moor is of a free and open nature,   400
That thinks men honest that but seem to be so,
And will as tenderly be led by the nose   402
As asses are.
I have 't. It is engendered. Hell and night
Must bring this monstrous birth to the world's light.
                                        [*Exit.*]

♣

386 **snipe** woodcock, i.e., fool   388 **it is thought abroad** i.e., it is rumored   389 **my office** i.e., my sexual function as husband   391 **do . . . surety** act as if on certain knowledge.   **holds me well** regards me favorably   393 **proper** handsome   394 **plume up** glorify, gratify   396 **abuse** deceive   397 **he** i.e., Cassio   398 **dispose** manner, bearing   400 **free** frank, generous.   **open** unsuspicious   402 **tenderly** readily

2.1 *Enter Montano and two Gentlemen.*

MONTANO
What from the cape can you discern at sea?

FIRST GENTLEMAN
Nothing at all. It is a high-wrought flood.   2
I cannot, twixt the heaven and the main,   3
Descry a sail.

MONTANO
Methinks the wind hath spoke aloud at land;
A fuller blast ne'er shook our battlements.
If it hath ruffianed so upon the sea,   7
What ribs of oak, when mountains melt on them,   8
Can hold the mortise? What shall we hear of this?   9

SECOND GENTLEMAN
A segregation of the Turkish fleet.   10
For do but stand upon the foaming shore,
The chidden billow seems to pelt the clouds;   12
The wind-shaked surge, with high and monstrous mane,   13
Seems to cast water on the burning Bear   14
And quench the guards of th' ever-fixèd pole.
I never did like molestation view   16
On the enchafèd flood.   17

MONTANO   If that the Turkish fleet   18
Be not ensheltered and embayed, they are drowned;   19
It is impossible to bear it out.   20

Enter a [Third] Gentleman.

THIRD GENTLEMAN   News, lads! Our wars are done.

2.1. Location: A seaport in Cyprus. An open place near the quay.
2 **high-wrought flood** very agitated sea   3 **main** ocean (also at l. 41)
7 **ruffianed** raged   8 **mountains** i.e., of water   9 **hold the mortise** hold
their joints together. (A *mortise* is the socket hollowed out in fitting
timbers.)   10 **segregation** dispersion   12 **chidden** i.e., rebuked, repelled
(by the shore), and thus shot into the air   13 **monstrous mane** (The surf
is like the mane of a wild beast.)   14 **the burning Bear** i.e., the constellation Ursa Minor or the Little Bear, which includes the polestar (and
hence regarded as the *guards of th' ever-fixèd pole* in the next line;
sometimes the term *guards* is applied to the two "pointers" of the Big
Bear or Dipper, which may be intended here.)   16 **like molestation**
comparable uproar   17 **enchafèd** angry   18 **If that** if   19 **embayed**
sheltered by a bay   20 **bear it out** survive, weather the storm

The desperate tempest hath so banged the Turks
That their designment halts. A noble ship of Venice   23
Hath seen a grievous wreck and sufferance   24
On most part of their fleet.
MONTANO   How? Is this true?
THIRD GENTLEMAN   The ship is here put in,
A Veronesa; Michael Cassio,   28
Lieutenant to the warlike Moor Othello,
Is come on shore; the Moor himself at sea,
And is in full commission here for Cyprus.
MONTANO
I am glad on 't. 'Tis a worthy governor.
THIRD GENTLEMAN
But this same Cassio, though he speak of comfort
Touching the Turkish loss, yet he looks sadly   34
And prays the Moor be safe, for they were parted
With foul and violent tempest.
MONTANO   Pray heaven he be,
For I have served him, and the man commands
Like a full soldier. Let's to the seaside, ho!   38
As well to see the vessel that's come in
As to throw out our eyes for brave Othello,
Even till we make the main and th' aerial blue   41
An indistinct regard.
THIRD GENTLEMAN   Come, let's do so,   42
For every minute is expectancy   43
Of more arrivance.   44

Enter Cassio.

CASSIO
Thanks, you the valiant of this warlike isle,
That so approve the Moor! O, let the heavens   46
Give him defense against the elements,
For I have lost him on a dangerous sea.
MONTANO   Is he well shipped?

23 designment enterprise. **halts** is lame   **24 wreck** shipwreck.
sufferance disaster   **28 Veronesa** i.e., fitted out in Verona for Venetian
service, or possibly *Verennessa* (the Folio spelling), a cutter (from *ver-
rinare*, to cut through)   **34 sadly** gravely   **38 full** perfect   **41 the main
. . . blue** the sea and the sky   **42 An indistinct regard** indistinguishable
in our view   **43 is expectancy** gives expectation   **44 arrivance** arrival
46 approve admire, honor

CASSIO
  His bark is stoutly timbered, and his pilot
  Of very expert and approved allowance;   51
  Therefore my hopes, not surfeited to death,   52
  Stand in bold cure.

                    [*A cry*] *within:* "A sail, a sail, a sail!" 53

CASSIO What noise?

A GENTLEMAN
  The town is empty. On the brow o' the sea
  Stand ranks of people, and they cry "A sail!"

CASSIO
  My hopes do shape him for the governor.

                                    [*A shot within.*]

SECOND GENTLEMAN
  They do discharge their shot of courtesy;   58
  Our friends at least.

CASSIO   I pray you, sir, go forth,
  And give us truth who 'tis that is arrived.

SECOND GENTLEMAN I shall.   *Exit.*

MONTANO
  But, good Lieutenant, is your general wived?

CASSIO
  Most fortunately. He hath achieved a maid
  That paragons description and wild fame,   64
  One that excels the quirks of blazoning pens,   65
  And in th' essential vesture of creation   66
  Does tire the enginer.

        Enter [*Second*] *Gentleman.*

                    How now? Who has put in?   67

SECOND GENTLEMAN
  'Tis one Iago, ancient to the General.

---

51 approved allowance tested reputation **52 surfeited to death** i.e.,
overextended, worn thin through repeated application or delayed fulfillment **53 in bold cure** in strong hopes of fulfillment **58 discharge . . .
courtesy** fire a salute in token of respect and courtesy **64 paragons**
surpasses. **wild fame** extravagant report **65 quirks** witty conceits.
blazoning setting forth as though in heraldic language **66–67 in . . .
enginer** in her real beauty (she) defeats any attempt to praise her.
enginer engineer, i.e., poet, one who devises **s.d. Second Gentleman**
(So identified in the quarto text here and in ll. 58, 61, 68, and 96; the
Folio calls him a gentleman.) **put in** i.e., to harbor

CASSIO
  He's had most favorable and happy speed.
  Tempests themselves, high seas, and howling winds,
  The guttered rocks and congregated sands—   71
  Traitors ensteeped to clog the guiltless keel—   72
  As having sense of beauty, do omit   73
  Their mortal natures, letting go safely by   74
  The divine Desdemona.
MONTANO   What is she?
CASSIO
  She that I spake of, our great captain's captain,
  Left in the conduct of the bold Iago,
  Whose footing here anticipates our thoughts   78
  A sennight's speed. Great Jove, Othello guard,   79
  And swell his sail with thine own powerful breath,
  That he may bless this bay with his tall ship,   81
  Make love's quick pants in Desdemona's arms,
  Give renewed fire to our extinct spirits,
  And bring all Cyprus comfort!

    Enter Desdemona, Iago, Roderigo, and Emilia.

                                O, behold,
  The riches of the ship is come on shore!   [*He kneels.*]
  You men of Cyprus, let her have your knees.
  Hail to thee, lady! And the grace of heaven
  Before, behind thee, and on every hand
  Enwheel thee round!   [*He rises.*]
DESDEMONA   I thank you, valiant Cassio.
  What tidings can you tell me of my lord?
CASSIO
  He is not yet arrived, nor know I aught
  But that he's well and will be shortly here.
DESDEMONA
  O, but I fear—How lost you company?
CASSIO
  The great contention of the sea and skies
  Parted our fellowship.
                    (*Within*) "A sail, a sail!" [*A shot.*]
                    But hark. A sail!

71 **guttered** jagged, trenched   72 **ensteeped** lying under water   73 **As** as
if. **omit** forbear to exercise   74 **mortal** deadly   78 **footing** landing
79 **sennight's** week's   81 **tall** splendid, gallant

SECOND GENTLEMAN
  They give their greeting to the citadel.
  This likewise is a friend.
CASSIO   See for the news.
               [Exit Second Gentleman.]
  Good Ancient, you are welcome. *[Kissing Emilia.]*
    Welcome, mistress.
  Let it not gall your patience, good Iago,
  That I extend my manners. 'Tis my breeding   100
  That gives me this bold show of courtesy.
IAGO
  Sir, would she give you so much of her lips
  As of her tongue she oft bestows on me,
  You would have enough.
DESDEMONA   Alas, she has no speech!
IAGO   In faith, too much.
  I find it still, when I have list to sleep.   107
  Marry, before your ladyship, I grant,
  She puts her tongue a little in her heart
  And chides with thinking.
EMILIA   You have little cause to say so. 110
IAGO
  Come on, come on. You are pictures out of doors,   111
  Bells in your parlors, wildcats in your kitchens,   112
  Saints in your injuries, devils being offended,   113
  Players in your huswifery, and huswives in your beds. 114
DESDEMONA   O, fie upon thee, slanderer!
IAGO
  Nay, it is true, or else I am a Turk.
  You rise to play, and go to bed to work.
EMILIA
  You shall not write my praise.
IAGO   No, let me not.
DESDEMONA
  What wouldst write of me, if thou shouldst praise me?

---

100 extend show   **107 still** always.   **list** desire   **110 with thinking** i.e.,
in her thoughts only   **111 pictures out of doors** i.e., silent and well-
behaved in public   **112 Bells** i.e., jangling, noisy, and brazen.   **in your
kitchens** i.e., in domestic affairs. (Ladies would not do the cooking.)
113 Saints martyrs   **114 Players** idlers, triflers, or deceivers.   **huswifery** housekeeping.   **huswives** hussies (i.e., women are "busy" in bed, or
thrifty in dispensing sexual favors)

IAGO

O gentle lady, do not put me to 't,

For I am nothing if not critical.   121

DESDEMONA

Come on, assay.—There's one gone to the harbor?   122

IAGO Ay, madam.

DESDEMONA

I am not merry, but I do beguile

The thing I am by seeming otherwise.   125

Come, how wouldst thou praise me?

IAGO

I am about it, but indeed my invention

Comes from my pate as birdlime does from frieze—   128

It plucks out brains and all. But my Muse labors,   129

And thus she is delivered:

If she be fair and wise, fairness and wit,

The one's for use, the other useth it.   132

DESDEMONA

Well praised! How if she be black and witty?   133

IAGO

If she be black, and thereto have a wit,

She'll find a white that shall her blackness fit.   135

DESDEMONA

Worse and worse.

EMILIA   How if fair and foolish?

IAGO

She never yet was foolish that was fair,

For even her folly helped her to an heir.   138

DESDEMONA These are old fond paradoxes to make fools   139

laugh i' th' alehouse. What miserable praise hast thou

for her that's foul and foolish?   141

IAGO

There's none so foul and foolish thereunto,

But does foul pranks which fair and wise ones do.   143

---

121 **critical** censorious   122 **assay** try   125 **The thing I am** i.e., my
anxious self   128 **birdlime** sticky substance used to catch small birds.
frieze coarse woolen cloth   129 **labors** (1) exerts herself (2) prepares to
deliver a child (with a following pun on *delivered* in l. 130)   132 **The
one's . . . it** i.e., her cleverness will make use of her beauty   133 **black**
dark complexioned, brunette   135 **white** a fair person (with wordplay
on *wight,* a person).   **fit** (with sexual suggestion of mating)   138 **folly**
(with added meaning of "lechery, wantonness").   **to an heir** i.e., to bear
a child   139 **fond** foolish   141 **foul** ugly   143 **foul** sluttish

DESDEMONA   O heavy ignorance! Thou praisest the worst
   best. But what praise couldst thou bestow on a deserving woman indeed, one that, in the authority of her
   merit, did justly put on the vouch of very malice itself? 147

IAGO
   She that was ever fair, and never proud,
   Had tongue at will, and yet was never loud,
   Never lacked gold and yet went never gay,   150
   Fled from her wish, and yet said, "Now I may,"   151
   She that being angered, her revenge being nigh,
   Bade her wrong stay and her displeasure fly,   153
   She that in wisdom never was so frail
   To change the cod's head for the salmon's tail,   155
   She that could think and ne'er disclose her mind,
   See suitors following and not look behind,
   She was a wight, if ever such wight were—

DESDEMONA   To do what?

IAGO
   To suckle fools and chronicle small beer.   160

DESDEMONA   O most lame and impotent conclusion! Do
   not learn of him, Emilia, though he be thy husband.
   How say you, Cassio? Is he not a most profane and   163
   liberal counselor?   164

CASSIO   He speaks home, madam. You may relish him   165
   more in the soldier than in the scholar.   166

          [Cassio and Desdemona stand together,
                     conversing intimately.]

IAGO [Aside]   He takes her by the palm. Ay, well said,   167
   whisper. With as little a web as this will I ensnare as
   great a fly as Cassio. Ay, smile upon her, do; I will
   gyve thee in thine own courtship. You say true; 'tis so, 170
   indeed. If such tricks as these strip you out of your

147 put . . . vouch compel the approval   150 gay extravagantly
clothed   151 Fled . . . may avoided temptation where the choice was
hers   153 Bade . . . stay i.e., resolved to put up with her injury patiently   155 To . . . tail i.e., to exchange a lackluster husband for a
sexy lover (?) (Cod's head is slang for penis, and tail for pudendum.)
160 suckle fools breastfeed babies.   chronicle small beer i.e., keep petty
household accounts, keep track of trivial matters   163 profane irrever-
ent, ribald   164 liberal licentious, free-spoken   165 home i.e., without
reserve.   relish appreciate   166 in in the character of   167 well said
well done   170 gyve fetter, shackle.   courtship courtesy, show of
courtly manners

lieutenantry, it had been better you had not kissed
your three fingers so oft, which now again you are
most apt to play the sir in. Very good; well kissed! An 174
excellent courtesy! 'Tis so, indeed. Yet again your fingers
to your lips? Would they were clyster pipes for your 176
sake! [*Trumpet within.*] The Moor! I know his trumpet.

CASSIO 'Tis truly so.

DESDEMONA Let's meet him and receive him.

CASSIO Lo, where he comes!

Enter Othello and attendants.

OTHELLO
　O my fair warrior!

DESDEMONA　　　　　　　My dear Othello!

OTHELLO
　It gives me wonder great as my content
　To see you here before me. O my soul's joy!
　If after every tempest come such calms,
　May the winds blow till they have wakened death!
　And let the laboring bark climb hills of seas
　Olympus-high, and duck again as low
　As hell's from heaven! If it were now to die,
　'Twere now to be most happy, for I fear
　My soul hath her content so absolute
　That not another comfort like to this
　Succeeds in unknown fate.

DESDEMONA　　　　　　　　The heavens forbid　　　192
　But that our loves and comforts should increase
　Even as our days do grow!

OTHELLO　Amen to that, sweet powers!
　I cannot speak enough of this content.
　It stops me here; it is too much of joy.
　And this, and this, the greatest discords be　　　198

　　　　　　　　　　　　　　　[*They kiss*]

　That e'er our hearts shall make!

IAGO [*Aside*]　O, you are well tuned now!

---

174 the sir i.e., the fine gentleman　**176 clyster pipes** tubes used for
enemas and douches　**192 Succeeds . . . fate** i.e., can follow in the
unknown future　**198 s.d. They kiss** (The direction is from the
quarto.)

But I'll set down the pegs that make this music,   201
As honest as I am.

OTHELLO Come, let us to the castle.
News, friends! Our wars are done, the Turks are
  drowned.
How does my old acquaintance of this isle?—
Honey, you shall be well desired in Cyprus;   206
I have found great love amongst them. O my sweet,
I prattle out of fashion, and I dote   208
In mine own comforts.—I prithee, good Iago,
Go to the bay and disembark my coffers.   210
Bring thou the master to the citadel;   211
He is a good one, and his worthiness
Does challenge much respect.—Come, Desdemona.—   213
Once more, well met at Cyprus!

           Exeunt Othello and Desdemona [and all
                     but Iago and Roderigo].

IAGO [*To an attendant*] Do thou meet me presently at
the harbor. [*To Roderigo.*] Come hither. If thou be'st
valiant—as, they say, base men being in love have   217
then a nobility in their natures more than is native to
them—list me. The Lieutenant tonight watches on the   219
court of guard. First, I must tell thee this: Desdemona   220
is directly in love with him.

RODERIGO With him? Why, 'tis not possible.

IAGO Lay thy finger thus, and let thy soul be instructed. 223
Mark me with what violence she first loved the Moor,
but for bragging and telling her fantastical lies.   225
To love him still for prating? Let not thy discreet
heart think it. Her eye must be fed; and what delight
shall she have to look on the devil? When the blood is
made dull with the act of sport, there should be, again
to inflame it and to give satiety a fresh appetite, love-
liness in favor, sympathy in years, manners, and   231

201 **set down** loosen (and hence untune the instrument) **206 desired**
welcomed **208 out of fashion** irrelevantly (?) **210 coffers** chests,
baggage **211 master** ship's captain **213 challenge** lay claim to, deserve **217 base men** even lowly born men **219 list** listen to **220 court
of guard** guardhouse. (Cassio is in charge of the watch.) **223 thus** i.e.,
on your lips **225 but** only **231 favor** appearance. **sympathy** correspondence, similarity

beauties—all which the Moor is defective in. Now, for
want of these required conveniences, her delicate ten-   233
derness will find itself abused, begin to heave the   234
gorge, disrelish and abhor the Moor. Very nature will   235
instruct her in it and compel her to some second
choice. Now, sir, this granted—as it is a most preg-   237
nant and unforced position—who stands so eminent   238
in the degree of this fortune as Cassio does? A knave
very voluble, no further conscionable than in putting   240
on the mere form of civil and humane seeming for the   241
better compassing of his salt and most hidden loose   242
affection. Why, none, why, none. A slipper and subtle   243
knave, a finder out of occasions, that has an eye can   244
stamp and counterfeit advantages, though true advantage   245
never present itself; a devilish knave. Besides, the
knave is handsome, young, and hath all those requi-
sites in him that folly and green minds look after. A   248
pestilent complete knave, and the woman hath found   249
him already.   250

RODERIGO   I cannot believe that in her. She's full of most
blessed condition.   252

IAGO   Blessed fig's end! The wine she drinks is made of   253
grapes. If she had been blessed, she would never have
loved the Moor. Blessed pudding! Didst thou not see   255
her paddle with the palm of his hand? Didst not mark
that?

RODERIGO   Yes, that I did; but that was but courtesy.

IAGO   Lechery, by this hand. An index and obscure pro-   259
logue to the history of lust and foul thoughts. They
met so near with their lips that their breaths embraced
together. Villainous thoughts, Roderigo! When these
mutualities so marshal the way, hard at hand comes   263

---

233 **conveniences** compatibilities   **234–235 heave the gorge** experience
nausea   **237–238 pregnant** evident, cogent   **240 conscionable** conscien-
tious, conscience-bound   **241 humane** polite, courteous   **242 salt**
licentious   **243 affection** passion.   **slipper** slippery   **244–245 an eye
can stamp** an eye that can coin, create   **245 advantages** favorable
opportunities   **248 folly** wantonness.   **green** immature   **249–250 found
him** sized him up   **252 condition** disposition   **253 fig's end** (See 1.3.322
for the vulgar gesture of the fig.)   **255 pudding** sausage   **259 index**
table of contents.   **obscure** (i.e., the *lust and foul thoughts*, l. 260, are
secret, hidden from view)   **263 mutualities** exchanges, intimacies.
hard at hand closely following

the master and main exercise, th' incorporate conclu- 264
sion. Pish! But, sir, be you ruled by me. I have brought
you from Venice. Watch you tonight; for the com- 266
mand, I'll lay 't upon you. Cassio knows you not. I'll 267
not be far from you. Do you find some occasion to
anger Cassio, either by speaking too loud, or tainting 269
his discipline, or from what other course you please,
which the time shall more favorably minister. 271

RODERIGO Well.

IAGO Sir, he's rash and very sudden in choler, and hap- 273
ly may strike at you. Provoke him that he may, for 274
even out of that will I cause these of Cyprus to mutiny, 275
whose qualification shall come into no true taste again 276
but by the displanting of Cassio. So shall you have a
shorter journey to your desires by the means I shall
then have to prefer them, and the impediment most 279
profitably removed, without the which there were no
expectation of our prosperity.

RODERIGO I will do this, if you can bring it to any
opportunity.

IAGO I warrant thee. Meet me by and by at the citadel. 284
I must fetch his necessaries ashore. Farewell.

RODERIGO Adieu. *Exit.*

IAGO
That Cassio loves her, I do well believe 't;
That she loves him, 'tis apt and of great credit. 288
The Moor, howbeit that I endure him not,
Is of a constant, loving, noble nature,
And I dare think he'll prove to Desdemona
A most dear husband. Now, I do love her too,
Not out of absolute lust—though peradventure
I stand accountant for as great a sin— 294
But partly led to diet my revenge 295
For that I do suspect the lusty Moor
Hath leaped into my seat, the thought whereof

---

264 incorporate carnal   **266 Watch you** stand watch   **266–267 for the command . . . you** I'll arrange for you to be appointed, given orders   **269 tainting** disparaging   **271 minister** provide   **273 choler** wrath   **273–274 haply** perhaps   **275 mutiny** riot   **276 qualification** appeasement.   **true taste** acceptable state   **279 prefer** advance   **284 warrant** assure.   **by and by** immediately   **288 apt** probable.   **credit** credibility   **294 accountant** accountable   **295 diet** feed

Doth, like a poisonous mineral, gnaw my innards;
And nothing can or shall content my soul
Till I am evened with him, wife for wife,
Or failing so, yet that I put the Moor
At least into a jealousy so strong
That judgment cannot cure. Which thing to do,
If this poor trash of Venice, whom I trace   304
For his quick hunting, stand the putting on,   305
I'll have our Michael Cassio on the hip,   306
Abuse him to the Moor in the rank garb—   307
For I fear Cassio with my nightcap too—   308
Make the Moor thank me, love me, and reward me
For making him egregiously an ass
And practicing upon his peace and quiet   311
Even to madness. 'Tis here, but yet confused.
Knavery's plain face is never seen till used.   *Exit.*

❖

2.2   *Enter Othello's Herald with a proclamation.*

HERALD   It is Othello's pleasure, our noble and valiant
general, that, upon certain tidings now arrived, importing the mere perdition of the Turkish fleet, every   3
man put himself into triumph: some to dance, some
to make bonfires, each man to what sport and revels
his addiction leads him. For, besides these beneficial   6
news, it is the celebration of his nuptial. So much was
his pleasure should be proclaimed. All offices are open,   8
and there is full liberty of feasting from this present
hour of five till the bell have told eleven. Heaven bless
the isle of Cyprus and our noble general Othello!
                                                        Exit.

304 **trace** i.e., train, or follow (?), or perhaps *trash*, a hunting term,
meaning to put weights on a hunting dog in order to slow him down
305 **For** to make more eager.   **stand . . . on** respond properly when I
incite him to quarrel   306 **on the hip** at my mercy, where I can throw
him. (A wrestling term.)   307 **Abuse** slander.   **rank garb** coarse manner,
gross fashion   308 **with my nightcap** i.e., as a rival in my bed, as one
who gives me cuckold's horns   311 **practicing upon** plotting against

2.2. Location: Cyprus. A street.
3 mere perdition complete destruction   **6 addiction** inclination
8 offices rooms where food and drink are kept

2.3 *Enter Othello, Desdemona, Cassio, and attendants.*

OTHELLO
  Good Michael, look you to the guard tonight.
  Let's teach ourselves that honorable stop   2
  Not to outsport discretion.   3
CASSIO
  Iago hath direction what to do,
  But notwithstanding, with my personal eye
  Will I look to 't.
OTHELLO   Iago is most honest.
  Michael, good night. Tomorrow with your earliest   7
  Let me have speech with you. [*To Desdemona.*] Come,
    my dear love,
  The purchase made, the fruits are to ensue;   9
  That profit's yet to come 'tween me and you.—   10
  Good night.
            Exit [*Othello, with Desdemona and attendants*].

          Enter Iago.

CASSIO Welcome, Iago. We must to the watch.
IAGO Not this hour, Lieutenant; 'tis not yet ten o' the   13
  clock. Our general cast us thus early for the love of his   14
  Desdemona; who let us not therefore blame. He hath   15
  not yet made wanton the night with her, and she is
  sport for Jove.
CASSIO She's a most exquisite lady.
IAGO And, I'll warrant her, full of game.
CASSIO Indeed, she's a most fresh and delicate creature.
IAGO What an eye she has! Methinks it sounds a parley   21
  to provocation.
CASSIO An inviting eye, and yet methinks right modest.
IAGO And when she speaks, is it not an alarum to love?   24

2.3. Location: Cyprus. The citadel.
2 stop restraint **3 outsport** celebrate beyond the bounds of **7 with
your earliest** at your earliest convenience **9–10 The purchase . . . you**
i.e., though married, we haven't yet consummated our love **13 Not this
hour** not for an hour yet **14 cast** dismissed **15 who** i.e., Othello
21 sounds a parley calls for a conference, issues an invitation
24 alarum signal calling men to arms (continuing the military metaphor
of *parley,* l. 21)

CASSIO   She is indeed perfection.

IAGO   Well, happiness to their sheets! Come, Lieutenant, I have a stoup of wine, and here without are a brace 27 of Cyprus gallants that would fain have a measure to 28 the health of black Othello.

CASSIO   Not tonight, good Iago. I have very poor and unhappy brains for drinking. I could well wish courtesy would invent some other custom of entertainment.

IAGO   O, they are our friends. But one cup! I'll drink for you.   35

CASSIO   I have drunk but one cup tonight, and that was craftily qualified too, and behold what innovation it 37 makes here. I am unfortunate in the infirmity and 38 dare not task my weakness with any more.

IAGO   What, man? 'Tis a night of revels. The gallants desire it.

CASSIO   Where are they?

IAGO   Here at the door. I pray you, call them in.

CASSIO   I'll do 't, but it dislikes me.   *Exit.*   44

IAGO
If I can fasten but one cup upon him,
With that which he hath drunk tonight already,
He'll be as full of quarrel and offense
As my young mistress' dog. Now, my sick fool Roderigo,
Whom love hath turned almost the wrong side out,
To Desdemona hath tonight caroused   50
Potations pottle-deep; and he's to watch.   51
Three lads of Cyprus—noble swelling spirits,   52
That hold their honors in a wary distance,   53
The very elements of this warlike isle—   54
Have I tonight flustered with flowing cups,
And they watch too. Now, 'mongst this flock of
    drunkards   56

---

27 stoup measure of liquor, two quarts.   **without** outside.   **brace** pair
28 have a measure drink a toast   **35 for you** in your place. (Iago will do the steady drinking to keep the gallants company while Cassio has only one cup.)   **37 qualified** diluted.   **innovation** disturbance, insurrection
38 here i.e., in my head   **44 dislikes** displeases   **50 caroused** drunk off   **51 pottle-deep** to the bottom of the tankard   **52 swelling** proud
53 hold . . . distance i.e., are extremely sensitive of their honor   **54 very elements** true representatives   **56 watch** are members of the guard

Am I to put our Cassio in some action
That may offend the isle.—But here they come.

Enter Cassio, Montano, and gentlemen; [servants following with wine].

If consequence do but approve my dream,   59
My boat sails freely both with wind and stream.   60
CASSIO 'Fore God, they have given me a rouse already.   61
MONTANO Good faith, a little one; not past a pint, as I
am a soldier.
IAGO Some wine, ho!

[*Sings.*] "And let me the cannikin clink, clink,   65
     And let me the cannikin clink.
       A soldier's a man,
       O, man's life's but a span;   68
     Why, then, let a soldier drink."

Some wine, boys!
CASSIO 'Fore God, an excellent song.
IAGO I learned it in England, where indeed they are
most potent in potting. Your Dane, your German, and   73
your swag-bellied Hollander—drink, ho!—are noth-
ing to your English.
CASSIO Is your Englishman so exquisite in his drinking?
IAGO Why, he drinks you, with facility, your Dane   77
dead drunk; he sweats not to overthrow your Almain;   78
he gives your Hollander a vomit ere the next pottle can
be filled.
CASSIO To the health of our general!
MONTANO I am for it, Lieutenant, and I'll do you justice.   82
IAGO O sweet England! [*Sings.*]

     "King Stephen was and-a worthy peer,
       His breeches cost him but a crown;
     He held them sixpence all too dear;
       With that he called the tailor lown.   87

59 If . . . dream if subsequent events will only substantiate my
scheme   **60 stream** current   **61 rouse** full draft of liquor   **65 cannikin**
small drinking vessel   **68 span** i.e., brief span of time. (Compare Psalm
39:5 as rendered in the Book of Common Prayer: "Thou hast made my
days as it were a span long.")   **73 potting** drinking   **77 drinks you**
drinks.   **your Dane** your typical Dane   **78 Almain** German   **82 I'll . . .
justice** i.e., I'll drink as much as you   **87 lown** lout, rascal

> He was a wight of high renown,
>   And thou art but of low degree.
> 'Tis pride that pulls the country down;   90
>   Then take thy auld cloak about thee."   91

Some wine, ho!

CASSIO 'Fore God, this is a more exquisite song than the other.

IAGO Will you hear 't again?

CASSIO No, for I hold him to be unworthy of his place that does those things. Well, God's above all; and there be souls must be saved, and there be souls must not be saved.

IAGO It's true, good Lieutenant.

CASSIO For mine own part—no offense to the General, nor any man of quality—I hope to be saved.   102

IAGO And so do I too, Lieutenant.

CASSIO Ay, but, by your leave, not before me. The lieutenant is to be saved before the ancient. Let's have no more of this. Let's to our affairs. God forgive us our sins! Gentlemen, let's look to our business. Do not think, gentlemen, I am drunk. This is my ancient; this is my right hand, and this is my left. I am not drunk now. I can stand well enough, and speak well enough.

GENTLEMEN Excellent well.

CASSIO Why, very well then. You must not think then that I am drunk.   *Exit.*

MONTANO
To th' platform, masters. Come, let's set the watch.   114
                    [*Exeunt Gentlemen.*]

IAGO
You see this fellow that is gone before.
He's a soldier fit to stand by Caesar
And give direction; and do but see his vice.
'Tis to his virtue a just equinox,   118
The one as long as th' other. 'Tis pity of him.
I fear the trust Othello puts him in,
On some odd time of his infirmity,
Will shake this island.

---

90 pride i.e., extravagance in dress   **91 auld** old   **102 quality** rank
114 set the watch mount the guard   **118 just equinox** exact counterpart.
(*Equinox* is an equal length of days and nights.)

MONTANO   But is he often thus?
IAGO
  'Tis evermore the prologue to his sleep.
  He'll watch the horologe a double set,   124
  If drink rock not his cradle.
MONTANO   It were well
  The General were put in mind of it.
  Perhaps he sees it not, or his good nature
  Prizes the virtue that appears in Cassio
  And looks not on his evils. Is not this true?

    Enter Roderigo.

IAGO [*Aside to him*]   How now, Roderigo?
  I pray you, after the Lieutenant; go.   [*Exit Roderigo.*]
MONTANO
  And 'tis great pity that the noble Moor
  Should hazard such a place as his own second   133
  With one of an engraffed infirmity.   134
  It were an honest action to say so
  To the Moor.
IAGO   Not I, for this fair island.
  I do love Cassio well and would do much
  To cure him of this evil.   [*Cry within:* "Help! Help!"]
               But hark! What noise?   138

    Enter Cassio, pursuing Roderigo.

CASSIO   Zounds, you rogue! You rascal!
MONTANO   What's the matter, Lieutenant?
CASSIO   A knave teach me my duty? I'll beat the knave
  into a twiggen bottle.   142
RODERIGO   Beat me?
CASSIO   Dost thou prate, rogue?   [*He strikes Roderigo.*]
MONTANO   Nay, good Lieutenant. [*Staying him.*] I pray
  you, sir, hold your hand.
CASSIO   Let me go, sir, or I'll knock you o'er the maz- 147
  ard.   148

---

124 watch . . . set stay awake twice around the clock or *horologe*
133–134 hazard . . . With risk giving such an important position as his
second in command to   **134 engraffed** engrafted, inveterate   **138 s.d.**
pursuing (The quarto text reads, "driving in.")   **142 twiggen** wicker-
covered. (Cassio vows to assail Roderigo until his skin resembles
wickerwork, or until he has driven Roderigo through the holes in a
wickerwork.)   **147–148 mazard** i.e., head. (Literally, a drinking vessel.)

MONTANO Come, come, you're drunk.
CASSIO Drunk?   [*They fight.*]
IAGO [*Aside to Roderigo*]
  Away, I say. Go out and cry a mutiny. [*Exit Roderigo.*] 151
  Nay, good Lieutenant—God's will, gentlemen—
  Help, ho!—Lieutenant—sir—Montano—sir—
  Help, masters!—Here's a goodly watch indeed!   154
                            [*A bell rings.*]
  Who's that which rings the bell?—Diablo, ho!   155
  The town will rise. God's will, Lieutenant, hold!   156
  You'll be ashamed forever.

      Enter Othello and attendants [*with weapons*].

OTHELLO
  What is the matter here?
MONTANO   Zounds, I bleed still.
  I am hurt to th' death. He dies! [*He thrusts at Cassio.*]
OTHELLO   Hold, for your lives!
IAGO
  Hold, ho! Lieutenant—sir—Montano—gentlemen—
  Have you forgot all sense of place and duty?
  Hold! The General speaks to you. Hold, for shame!
OTHELLO
  Why, how now, ho! From whence ariseth this?
  Are we turned Turks, and to ourselves do that
  Which heaven hath forbid the Ottomites?   165
  For Christian shame, put by this barbarous brawl!
  He that stirs next to carve for his own rage   167
  Holds his soul light; he dies upon his motion.   168
  Silence that dreadful bell. It frights the isle
  From her propriety. What is the matter, masters?   170
  Honest Iago, that looks dead with grieving,
  Speak. Who began this? On thy love, I charge thee.
IAGO
  I do not know. Friends all but now, even now,

151 mutiny riot **154 masters** sirs **s.d. A bell rings** (This direction is
from the quarto, as are *Exit Roderigo* at l. 131, *They fight* at l. 150, and
with weapons at l. 157.) **155 Diablo** the devil **156 rise** grow riotous
165 forbid i.e., prevented, by destroying their fleet, so that the Venetians
need not fight them **167 carve for** i.e., indulge, satisfy **168 Holds . . .
light** i.e., places little value on his life. **upon his motion** if he moves
170 propriety proper state or condition

In quarter and in terms like bride and groom   174
Devesting them for bed; and then, but now—   175
As if some planet had unwitted men—
Swords out, and tilting one at other's breast
In opposition bloody. I cannot speak   178
Any beginning to this peevish odds;   179
And would in action glorious I had lost
Those legs that brought me to a part of it!

OTHELLO

How comes it, Michael, you are thus forgot?   182

CASSIO

I pray you, pardon me. I cannot speak.

OTHELLO

Worthy Montano, you were wont be civil;   184
The gravity and stillness of your youth   185
The world hath noted, and your name is great
In mouths of wisest censure. What's the matter   187
That you unlace your reputation thus   188
And spend your rich opinion for the name   189
Of a night-brawler? Give me answer to it.

MONTANO

Worthy Othello, I am hurt to danger.
Your officer, Iago, can inform you—
While I spare speech, which something now offends
    me—   193
Of all that I do know; nor know I aught
By me that's said or done amiss this night,
Unless self-charity be sometimes a vice,
And to defend ourselves it be a sin
When violence assails us.

OTHELLO   Now, by heaven,
My blood begins my safer guides to rule,   199
And passion, having my best judgment collied,   200

174 In quarter in friendly conduct, within bounds.   in terms on good
terms   175 Devesting them undressing themselves   178 speak explain   179 peevish odds childish quarrel   182 are thus forgot have
forgotten yourself thus   184 wont be accustomed to be   185 stillness
sobriety   187 censure judgment   188 unlace undo, lay open (as one
might loose the strings of a purse containing reputation)   189 opinion
reputation   193 something somewhat.   offends pains   199 blood
passion (of anger).   guides i.e., reason   200 collied darkened

Assays to lead the way. Zounds, if I stir,   201
Or do but lift this arm, the best of you
Shall sink in my rebuke. Give me to know
How this foul rout began, who set it on;   204
And he that is approved in this offense,   205
Though he had twinned with me, both at a birth,
Shall lose me. What? In a town of war
Yet wild, the people's hearts brim full of fear,
To manage private and domestic quarrel?   209
In night, and on the court and guard of safety?   210
'Tis monstrous. Iago, who began 't?

MONTANO [*To Iago*]
If partially affined, or leagued in office,   212
Thou dost deliver more or less than truth,
Thou art no soldier.

IAGO   Touch me not so near.
I had rather have this tongue cut from my mouth
Than it should do offense to Michael Cassio;
Yet, I persuade myself, to speak the truth
Shall nothing wrong him. Thus it is, General.
Montano and myself being in speech,
There comes a fellow crying out for help,
And Cassio following him with determined sword
To execute upon him. Sir, this gentleman   222
                              [*Indicating Montano*]
Steps in to Cassio and entreats his pause.
Myself the crying fellow did pursue,
Lest by his clamor—as it so fell out—
The town might fall in fright. He, swift of foot,
Outran my purpose, and I returned, the rather   227
For that I heard the clink and fall of swords
And Cassio high in oath, which till tonight
I ne'er might say before. When I came back—
For this was brief—I found them close together
At blow and thrust, even as again they were

---

201 Assays undertakes   **204 rout** riot   **205 approved in** found guilty of
209 manage undertake   **210 on . . . safety** at the main guardhouse or head-
quarters and on watch   **212 partially affined** made partial by some personal
relationship.   **leagued in office** in league as fellow officers   **222 execute**
give effect to (his anger)   **227 rather** sooner

When you yourself did part them.
More of this matter cannot I report.
But men are men; the best sometimes forget.   235
Though Cassio did some little wrong to him,
As men in rage strike those that wish them best,   237
Yet surely Cassio, I believe, received
From him that fled some strange indignity,
Which patience could not pass.

OTHELLO   I know, Iago,   240
Thy honesty and love doth mince this matter,
Making it light to Cassio. Cassio, I love thee,
But nevermore be officer of mine.

    Enter Desdemona, attended.

Look if my gentle love be not raised up.
I'll make thee an example.

DESDEMONA
What is the matter, dear?

OTHELLO   All's well now, sweeting;
Come away to bed. [*To Montano.*] Sir, for your hurts,
Myself will be your surgeon.—Lead him off.   248

                 [*Montano is led off.*]

Iago, look with care about the town
And silence those whom this vile brawl distracted.
Come, Desdemona. 'Tis the soldiers' life
To have their balmy slumbers waked with strife.

        Exit [*with all but Iago and Cassio*].

IAGO What, are you hurt, Lieutenant?

CASSIO Ay, past all surgery.

IAGO Marry, God forbid!

CASSIO Reputation, reputation, reputation! O, I have
lost my reputation! I have lost the immortal part of
myself, and what remains is bestial. My reputation,
Iago, my reputation!

IAGO As I am an honest man, I thought you had received some bodily wound; there is more sense in that
than in reputation. Reputation is an idle and most

---

235 forget forget themselves **237 those . . . best** i.e., even those who are
well disposed **240 pass** pass over, overlook **248 be your surgeon** i.e.,
make sure you receive medical attention

false imposition, oft got without merit and lost with- 263
out deserving. You have lost no reputation at all, unless you repute yourself such a loser. What, man, there
are ways to recover the General again. You are but now 266
cast in his mood—a punishment more in policy than in 267
malice, even so as one would beat his offenseless dog 268
to affright an imperious lion. Sue to him again and 269
he's yours.

CASSIO I will rather sue to be despised than to deceive
so good a commander with so slight, so drunken, and 272
so indiscreet an officer. Drunk? And speak parrot? 273
And squabble? Swagger? Swear? And discourse fustian with one's own shadow? O thou invisible spirit
of wine, if thou hast no name to be known by, let us
call thee devil!

IAGO What was he that you followed with your sword?
What had he done to you?

CASSIO I know not.

IAGO Is 't possible?

CASSIO I remember a mass of things, but nothing distinctly; a quarrel, but nothing wherefore. O God, that 283
men should put an enemy in their mouths to steal
away their brains! That we should, with joy, pleas-
ance, revel, and applause transform ourselves into
beasts!

IAGO Why, but you are now well enough. How came
you thus recovered?

CASSIO It hath pleased the devil drunkenness to give
place to the devil wrath. One unperfectness shows me
another, to make me frankly despise myself.

IAGO Come, you are too severe a moraler. As the time, 293
the place, and the condition of this country stands, I
could heartily wish this had not befallen; but since it is

---

263 **imposition** thing artificially imposed and of no real value   266 **recover** regain favor with   267 **cast in his mood** dismissed in a moment
of anger.   **in policy** done for expediency's sake and as a public gesture
268–269 **would . . . lion** i.e., would make an example of a minor offender
in order to deter more important and dangerous offenders   269 **Sue** petition   272 **slight** worthless   273 **speak parrot** talk nonsense, rant. (*Discourse
fustian*, ll. 274–275, has much the same meaning.)   283 **wherefore** why
293 **moraler** moralizer

as it is, mend it for your own good.

CASSIO   I will ask him for my place again; he shall tell me I am a drunkard! Had I as many mouths as Hydra, 298 such an answer would stop them all. To be now a sensible man, by and by a fool, and presently a beast! O, strange! Every inordinate cup is unblessed, and the ingredient is a devil.

IAGO   Come, come, good wine is a good familiar creature, if it be well used. Exclaim no more against it. And, good Lieutenant, I think you think I love you.

CASSIO   I have well approved it, sir. I drunk!   306

IAGO   You or any man living may be drunk at a time, 307 man. I'll tell you what you shall do. Our general's wife is now the general—I may say so in this respect, for 309 that he hath devoted and given up himself to the con- 310 templation, mark, and denotement of her parts and 311 graces. Confess yourself freely to her; importune her help to put you in your place again. She is of so free, 313 so kind, so apt, so blessed a disposition, she holds it a vice in her goodness not to do more than she is requested. This broken joint between you and her husband entreat her to splinter; and, my fortunes against 317 any lay worth naming, this crack of your love shall 318 grow stronger than it was before.

CASSIO   You advise me well.

IAGO   I protest, in the sincerity of love and honest kind- 321 ness.

CASSIO   I think it freely; and betimes in the morning I 323 will beseech the virtuous Desdemona to undertake for me. I am desperate of my fortunes if they check me 325 here.

IAGO   You are in the right. Good night, Lieutenant. I must to the watch.

---

298 Hydra the Lernaean Hydra, a monster with many heads and the ability to grow two heads when one was cut off; slain by Hercules as the second of his twelve labors   **306 approved** proved   **307 at a time** at one time or another   **309–310 in . . . that** in view of this fact, that **311 mark, and denotement** (Both words mean "observation.")   **parts** qualities   **313 free** generous   **317 splinter** bind with splints   **318 lay** stake, wager   **321 protest** insist, declare   **323 freely** unreservedly **325 check** repulse

CASSIO Good night, honest Iago.   *Exit Cassio.*

IAGO
And what's he then that says I play the villain,
When this advice is free I give and honest,   331
Probal to thinking, and indeed the course   332
To win the Moor again? For 'tis most easy
Th' inclining Desdemona to subdue   334
In any honest suit; she's framed as fruitful   335
As the free elements. And then for her   336
To win the Moor—were 't to renounce his baptism,
All seals and symbols of redeemèd sin—
His soul is so enfettered to her love
That she may make, unmake, do what she list,
Even as her appetite shall play the god
With his weak function. How am I then a villain,   342
To counsel Cassio to this parallel course   343
Directly to his good? Divinity of hell!   344
When devils will the blackest sins put on,   345
They do suggest at first with heavenly shows,   346
As I do now. For whiles this honest fool
Plies Desdemona to repair his fortune,
And she for him pleads strongly to the Moor,
I'll pour this pestilence into his ear,
That she repeals him for her body's lust;   351
And by how much she strives to do him good,
She shall undo her credit with the Moor.
So will I turn her virtue into pitch,
And out of her own goodness make the net
That shall enmesh them all.

    Enter Roderigo.

                    How now, Roderigo?
RODERIGO I do follow here in the chase, not like a

---

331 free (1) free from guile (2) freely given **332 Probal** probable, reasonable **334 inclining** favorably disposed. **subdue** persuade **335 fruitful** generous **336 free elements** i.e., earth, air, fire, and water, which sustain life (?) **342 function** exercise of faculties (weakened by his fondness for her) **343 parallel** corresponding to these facts and to his best interests **344 Divinity of hell** inverted theology of hell (which seduces the soul to its damnation) **345 put on** further, instigate **346 suggest** tempt **351 repeals him** i.e., attempts to get him restored

hound that hunts, but one that fills up the cry. My 358
money is almost spent; I have been tonight exceedingly well cudgeled; and I think the issue will be I
shall have so much experience for my pains, and so, 361
with no money at all and a little more wit, return again
to Venice.

IAGO
How poor are they that have not patience!
What wound did ever heal but by degrees?
Thou know'st we work by wit, and not by witchcraft,
And wit depends on dilatory time.
Does 't not go well? Cassio hath beaten thee,
And thou, by that small hurt, hast cashiered Cassio.   369
Though other things grow fair against the sun,   370
Yet fruits that blossom first will first be ripe.   371
Content thyself awhile. By the Mass, 'tis morning!
Pleasure and action make the hours seem short.
Retire thee; go where thou art billeted.
Away, I say! Thou shalt know more hereafter.
Nay, get thee gone.   *Exit Roderigo.*
            Two things are to be done.
My wife must move for Cassio to her mistress;   377
I'll set her on;
Myself the while to draw the Moor apart
And bring him jump when he may Cassio find   380
Soliciting his wife. Ay, that's the way.
Dull not device by coldness and delay.   *Exit.* 382

❖

358 **fills up the cry** merely takes part as one of the pack   361 **so
much** just so much and no more   369 **cashiered** dismissed from service
370–371 **Though . . . ripe** i.e., the first part of our plan has already ripened
to fruition, and other parts are maturing in their own good time   377 **move**
plead   380 **jump** precisely   382 **device** plot.   **coldness** lack of zeal

3.1 *Enter Cassio [and] Musicians.*

CASSIO
  Masters, play here—I will content your pains—   1
  Something that's brief, and bid "Good morrow,
    General."   [*They play.*]

    [*Enter*] *Clown.*

CLOWN Why, masters, have your instruments been in
  Naples, that they speak i' the nose thus?   4
A MUSICIAN How, sir, how?
CLOWN Are these, I pray you, wind instruments?
A MUSICIAN Ay, marry, are they, sir.
CLOWN O, thereby hangs a tail.
A MUSICIAN Whereby hangs a tale, sir?
CLOWN Marry, sir, by many a wind instrument that I 10
  know. But, masters, here's money for you. [*He gives
  money.*] And the General so likes your music that he
  desires you, for love's sake, to make no more noise 13
  with it.
A MUSICIAN Well, sir, we will not.
CLOWN If you have any music that may not be heard, 16
  to 't again; but, as they say, to hear music the General
  does not greatly care.
A MUSICIAN We have none such, sir.
CLOWN Then put up your pipes in your bag, for I'll 20
  away. Go, vanish into air, away!   *Exeunt Musicians.* 21
CASSIO Dost thou hear, mine honest friend?
CLOWN No, I hear not your honest friend; I hear you.
CASSIO Prithee, keep up thy quillets. There's a poor 24
  piece of gold for thee. [*He gives money.*] If the gentlewoman that attends the General's wife be stirring, tell

---

3.1. Location: Before the chamber of Othello and Desdemona.
1 content reward. **pains** efforts **4 speak i' the nose** (1) sound nasal
(2) sound like one whose nose has been attacked by syphilis. (Naples
was popularly supposed to have a high incidence of venereal disease.)
10 wind instrument (With a joke on flatulence. The *tail*, l. 8, that hangs
nearby the *wind instrument* suggests the penis.) **13 for love's sake**
(1) out of friendship and affection (2) for the sake of lovemaking in
Othello's marriage **16 may not** cannot **20–21 I'll away** (Possibly a
misprint, or a snatch of song?) **24 keep up** do not bring out, do not
use. **quillets** quibbles, puns

her there's one Cassio entreats her a little favor of   27
speech. Wilt thou do this?   28

CLOWN   She is stirring, sir. If she will stir hither, I shall
seem to notify unto her.   30

CASSIO
Do, good my friend.   *Exit Clown.*

    Enter Iago.

                   In happy time, Iago.   31

IAGO   You have not been abed, then?

CASSIO   Why, no. The day had broke
Before we parted. I have made bold, Iago,
To send in to your wife. My suit to her
Is that she will to virtuous Desdemona
Procure me some access.

IAGO   I'll send her to you presently;
And I'll devise a means to draw the Moor
Out of the way, that your converse and business
May be more free.

CASSIO
I humbly thank you for 't.   *Exit [Iago].*
                 I never knew
A Florentine more kind and honest.   43

    Enter Emilia.

EMILIA
Good morrow, good Lieutenant. I am sorry
For your displeasure; but all will sure be well.   45
The General and his wife are talking of it,
And she speaks for you stoutly. The Moor replies
That he you hurt is of great fame in Cyprus
And great affinity, and that in wholesome wisdom   49
He might not but refuse you; but he protests he loves you
And needs no other suitor but his likings
To take the safest occasion by the front   52
To bring you in again.

CASSIO   Yet I beseech you,

27–28 a little . . . speech the favor of a brief talk   **30 seem** deem it
good, think fit   **31 In happy time** i.e., well met   **43 Florentine** i.e.,
even a fellow Florentine. (Iago is a Venetian, Cassio a Florentine.)
45 displeasure fall from favor   **49 affinity** kindred, family connection
52 occasion . . . front opportunity by the forelock

If you think fit, or that it may be done,
Give me advantage of some brief discourse
With Desdemon alone.
EMILIA   Pray you, come in.
I will bestow you where you shall have time
To speak your bosom freely.   58
CASSIO   I am much bound to you.   [*Exeunt.*]

❖

3.2   *Enter Othello, Iago, and Gentlemen.*

OTHELLO [*Giving letters*]
These letters give, Iago, to the pilot,
And by him do my duties to the Senate.   2
That done, I will be walking on the works;   3
Repair there to me.
IAGO   Well, my good lord, I'll do 't.   4
OTHELLO
This fortification, gentlemen, shall we see 't?
GENTLEMEN   We'll wait upon your lordship.   *Exeunt.* 6

❖

3.3   *Enter Desdemona, Cassio, and Emilia.*

DESDEMONA
Be thou assured, good Cassio, I will do
All my abilities in thy behalf.
EMILIA
Good madam, do. I warrant it grieves my husband
As if the cause were his.
DESDEMONA
O, that's an honest fellow. Do not doubt, Cassio,
But I will have my lord and you again
As friendly as you were.

---

58 bosom inmost thoughts

3.2. Location: The citadel.
2 do my duties convey my respects   **3 works** breastworks, fortifica-
tions   **4 Repair** return, come   **6 wait upon** attend

3.3. Location: The garden of the citadel.

CASSIO   Bounteous madam,
Whatever shall become of Michael Cassio,
He's never anything but your true servant.

DESDEMONA
I know 't. I thank you. You do love my lord;
You have known him long, and be you well assured
He shall in strangeness stand no farther off   12
Than in a politic distance.

CASSIO   Ay, but, lady,   13
That policy may either last so long,
Or feed upon such nice and waterish diet,   15
Or breed itself so out of circumstance,   16
That, I being absent and my place supplied,   17
My general will forget my love and service.

DESDEMONA
Do not doubt that. Before Emilia here   19
I give thee warrant of thy place. Assure thee,
If I do vow a friendship I'll perform it
To the last article. My lord shall never rest.
I'll watch him tame and talk him out of patience;   23
His bed shall seem a school, his board a shrift;   24
I'll intermingle everything he does
With Cassio's suit. Therefore be merry, Cassio,
For thy solicitor shall rather die   27
Than give thy cause away.   28

      Enter Othello and Iago [at a distance].

EMILIA   Madam, here comes my lord.
CASSIO   Madam, I'll take my leave.
DESDEMONA   Why, stay, and hear me speak.
CASSIO
Madam, not now. I am very ill at ease,
Unfit for mine own purposes.
DESDEMONA   Well, do your discretion.   *Exit Cassio.* 34

---

12 strangeness aloofness   **13 politic** required by wise policy   **15 Or . . . diet** or sustain itself at length upon such a trivial and meager means of support   **16 breed . . . circumstance** continually renew itself so out of chance events, or yield so few chances for my being pardoned **17 supplied** filled by another person   **19 doubt** fear   **23 watch him tame** tame him by keeping him from sleeping. (A term from falconry.) **out of patience** past his endurance   **24 shrift** confessional   **27 solicitor** advocate   **28 away** up   **34 do your discretion** act according to your own discretion

IAGO Ha? I like not that.

OTHELLO What dost thou say?

IAGO

Nothing, my lord; or if—I know not what.

OTHELLO

Was not that Cassio parted from my wife?

IAGO

Cassio, my lord? No, sure, I cannot think it,
That he would steal away so guiltylike,
Seeing you coming.

OTHELLO I do believe 'twas he.

DESDEMONA How now, my lord?
I have been talking with a suitor here,
A man that languishes in your displeasure.

OTHELLO Who is 't you mean?

DESDEMONA

Why, your lieutenant, Cassio. Good my lord,
If I have any grace or power to move you,
His present reconciliation take;   49
For if he be not one that truly loves you,
That errs in ignorance and not in cunning,   51
I have no judgment in an honest face.
I prithee, call him back.

OTHELLO Went he hence now?

DESDEMONA Yes, faith, so humbled
That he hath left part of his grief with me
To suffer with him. Good love, call him back.

OTHELLO

Not now, sweet Desdemon. Some other time.

DESDEMONA But shall 't be shortly?

OTHELLO The sooner, sweet, for you.

DESDEMONA Shall 't be tonight at supper?

OTHELLO No, not tonight.

DESDEMONA Tomorrow dinner, then?   63

OTHELLO I shall not dine at home.
I meet the captains at the citadel.

DESDEMONA

Why, then, tomorrow night, or Tuesday morn,
On Tuesday noon, or night, on Wednesday morn.

---

49 present immediate **51 in cunning** wittingly **63 dinner** (The noon-
time meal.)

I prithee, name the time, but let it not
Exceed three days. In faith, he's penitent;
And yet his trespass, in our common reason— 70
Save that, they say, the wars must make example 71
Out of her best—is not almost a fault 72
T' incur a private check. When shall he come? 73
Tell me, Othello. I wonder in my soul
What you would ask me that I should deny,
Or stand so mammering on. What? Michael Cassio, 76
That came a-wooing with you, and so many a time,
When I have spoke of you dispraisingly,
Hath ta'en your part—to have so much to do
To bring him in! By 'r Lady, I could do much— 80

OTHELLO
Prithee, no more. Let him come when he will;
I will deny thee nothing.

DESDEMONA Why, this is not a boon.
'Tis as I should entreat you wear your gloves,
Or feed on nourishing dishes, or keep you warm,
Or sue to you to do a peculiar profit 86
To your own person. Nay, when I have a suit
Wherein I mean to touch your love indeed,
It shall be full of poise and difficult weight, 89
And fearful to be granted.

OTHELLO I will deny thee nothing.
Whereon, I do beseech thee, grant me this, 92
To leave me but a little to myself.

DESDEMONA
Shall I deny you? No. Farewell, my lord.

OTHELLO
Farewell, my Desdemona. I'll come to thee straight. 95

DESDEMONA
Emilia, come.—Be as your fancies teach you; 96
Whate'er you be, I am obedient. *Exit [with Emilia].*

---

70 common reason everyday judgments **71–72 Save . . . best** were it
not that, as the saying goes, military discipline requires making an
example of the very best men. (*Her* refers to *wars* as a singular concept.) **72 not almost** scarcely **73 a private check** even a private repri-
mand **76 mammering on** wavering about **80 bring him in** restore him
to favor **86 peculiar** particular, personal **89 poise** weight, heaviness;
or equipoise, delicate balance involving hard choice **92 Whereon** in
return for which **95 straight** straightway **96 fancies** inclinations

OTHELLO
    Excellent wretch! Perdition catch my soul   98
    But I do love thee! And when I love thee not,   99
    Chaos is come again.

IAGO   My noble lord—

OTHELLO   What dost thou say, Iago?

IAGO
    Did Michael Cassio, when you wooed my lady,
    Know of your love?

OTHELLO
    He did, from first to last. Why dost thou ask?

IAGO
    But for a satisfaction of my thought;
    No further harm.

OTHELLO   Why of thy thought, Iago?

IAGO
    I did not think he had been acquainted with her.

OTHELLO
    O, yes, and went between us very oft.

IAGO   Indeed?

OTHELLO
    Indeed? Ay, indeed. Discern'st thou aught in that?
    Is he not honest?

IAGO   Honest, my lord?

OTHELLO   Honest. Ay, honest.

IAGO   My lord, for aught I know.

OTHELLO   What dost thou think?

IAGO   Think, my lord?

OTHELLO
    "Think, my lord?" By heaven, thou echo'st me,
    As if there were some monster in thy thought
    Too hideous to be shown. Thou dost mean something.
    I heard thee say even now, thou lik'st not that,
    When Cassio left my wife. What didst not like?
    And when I told thee he was of my counsel   123
    In my whole course of wooing, thou criedst "Indeed?"
    And didst contract and purse thy brow together   125

---

98 wretch (A term of affectionate endearment.)   **99 But I do** if I do
not   **123 of my counsel** in my confidence   **125 purse** knit

As if thou then hadst shut up in thy brain
Some horrible conceit. If thou dost love me,   127
Show me thy thought.

IAGO   My lord, you know I love you.

OTHELLO   I think thou dost;
And, for I know thou'rt full of love and honesty,
And weigh'st thy words before thou giv'st them breath,
Therefore these stops of thine fright me the more;   133
For such things in a false disloyal knave
Are tricks of custom, but in a man that's just   135
They're close dilations, working from the heart   136
That passion cannot rule.

IAGO   For Michael Cassio,   137
I dare be sworn I think that he is honest.

OTHELLO
I think so too.

IAGO   Men should be what they seem;
Or those that be not, would they might seem none!   140

OTHELLO
Certain, men should be what they seem.

IAGO
Why, then, I think Cassio's an honest man.

OTHELLO   Nay, yet there's more in this.
I prithee, speak to me as to thy thinkings,
As thou dost ruminate, and give thy worst of thoughts
The worst of words.

IAGO   Good my lord, pardon me.
Though I am bound to every act of duty,
I am not bound to that all slaves are free to.   148
Utter my thoughts? Why, say they are vile and false,
As where's that palace whereinto foul things
Sometimes intrude not? Who has that breast so pure
But some uncleanly apprehensions

---

127 conceit fancy   **133 stops** pauses   **135 of custom** customary
136 close dilations secret or involuntary expressions or delays
137 That passion cannot rule i.e., that are too passionately strong to
be restrained (referring to the workings), or, that cannot rule its own
passions (referring to the heart)   **140 none** i.e., not to be men,
or not seem to be honest   **148 that** that which.   **free to** i.e.,
free with respect to

Keep leets and law days, and in sessions sit   153
With meditations lawful?   154

OTHELLO
Thou dost conspire against thy friend, Iago,   155
If thou but think'st him wronged and mak'st his ear
A stranger to thy thoughts.

IAGO   I do beseech you,
Though I perchance am vicious in my guess—   158
As I confess it is my nature's plague
To spy into abuses, and oft my jealousy   160
Shapes faults that are not—that your wisdom then,   161
From one that so imperfectly conceits,   162
Would take no notice, nor build yourself a trouble
Out of his scattering and unsure observance.   164
It were not for your quiet nor your good,
Nor for my manhood, honesty, and wisdom,
To let you know my thoughts.

OTHELLO   What dost thou mean?

IAGO
Good name in man and woman, dear my lord,
Is the immediate jewel of their souls.   169
Who steals my purse steals trash; 'tis something,
    nothing;
'Twas mine, 'tis his, and has been slave to thousands;
But he that filches from me my good name
Robs me of that which not enriches him
And makes me poor indeed.

OTHELLO   By heaven, I'll know thy thoughts.

IAGO
You cannot, if my heart were in your hand,   176
Nor shall not, whilst 'tis in my custody.

OTHELLO
Ha?

IAGO   O, beware, my lord, of jealousy!

---

153 Keep leets and law days i.e., hold court, set up their authority in
one's heart. (*Leets* are a kind of manor court; *law days* are the days
courts sit in session, or those sessions.)   **154 With** along with.   **lawful**
innocent   **155 thy friend** i.e., Othello   **158 vicious** wrong   **160 jealousy**
suspicion of evil   **161 then** on that account   **162 one** i.e., myself,
Iago.   **conceits** judges, conjectures   **164 scattering** random
169 immediate essential, most precious   **176 if** even if

It is the green-eyed monster which doth mock   179
The meat it feeds on. That cuckold lives in bliss   180
Who, certain of his fate, loves not his wronger;   181
But O, what damnèd minutes tells he o'er   182
Who dotes, yet doubts, suspects, yet fondly loves!
OTHELLO   O misery!
IAGO
Poor and content is rich, and rich enough,   185
But riches fineless is as poor as winter   186
To him that ever fears he shall be poor.
Good God, the souls of all my tribe defend
From jealousy!
OTHELLO   Why, why is this?
Think'st thou I'd make a life of jealousy,
To follow still the changes of the moon   192
With fresh suspicions? No! To be once in doubt   193
Is once to be resolved. Exchange me for a goat   194
When I shall turn the business of my soul
To such exsufflicate and blown surmises   196
Matching thy inference. 'Tis not to make me jealous   197
To say my wife is fair, feeds well, loves company,
Is free of speech, sings, plays, and dances well;
Where virtue is, these are more virtuous.
Nor from mine own weak merits will I draw
The smallest fear or doubt of her revolt,   202
For she had eyes, and chose me. No, Iago,
I'll see before I doubt; when I doubt, prove;
And on the proof, there is no more but this—
Away at once with love or jealousy.

179–180 doth mock . . . on mocks and torments the heart of its victim,
the man who suffers jealousy   **181 his wronger** i.e., his faithless wife.
(The unsuspecting cuckold is spared the misery of loving his wife only
to discover she is cheating on him.)   **182 tells** counts   **185 Poor . . .
enough** to be content with what little one has is the greatest wealth of
all. (Proverbial.)   **186 fineless** boundless   **192–193 To follow . . . suspicions** to be constantly imagining new causes for suspicion, changing
incessantly like the moon   **194 once** once and for all.   **resolved** free of
doubt, having settled the matter   **196 exsufflicate and blown** inflated
and blown up, rumored about; or, spat out and flyblown, hence, loathsome, disgusting   **197 inference** description or allegation   **202 doubt
. . . revolt** fear of her unfaithfulness

IAGO

    I am glad of this, for now I shall have reason
    To show the love and duty that I bear you
    With franker spirit. Therefore, as I am bound,
    Receive it from me. I speak not yet of proof.
    Look to your wife; observe her well with Cassio.
    Wear your eyes thus, not jealous nor secure.   212
    I would not have your free and noble nature,
    Out of self-bounty, be abused. Look to 't.   214
    I know our country disposition well;
    In Venice they do let God see the pranks
    They dare not show their husbands; their best
      conscience
    Is not to leave 't undone, but keep 't unknown.

OTHELLO   Dost thou say so?

IAGO

    She did deceive her father, marrying you;
    And when she seemed to shake and fear your looks,
    She loved them most.

OTHELLO   And so she did.

IAGO   Why, go to, then! 222
    She that, so young, could give out such a seeming, 223
    To seel her father's eyes up close as oak, 224
    He thought 'twas witchcraft! But I am much to blame.
    I humbly do beseech you of your pardon
    For too much loving you.

OTHELLO   I am bound to thee forever. 228

IAGO

    I see this hath a little dashed your spirits.

OTHELLO

    Not a jot, not a jot.

IAGO   I' faith, I fear it has.
    I hope you will consider what is spoke
    Comes from my love. But I do see you're moved.
    I am to pray you not to strain my speech

---

212 not neither. **secure** free from uncertainty **214 self-bounty** inherent or natural goodness and generosity. **abused** deceived **222 go to** (An expression of impatience.) **223 seeming** false appearance **224 seel** blind. (A term from falconry.) **oak** (A close-grained wood.) **228 bound** indebted (but perhaps with ironic sense of "tied")

To grosser issues nor to larger reach   234
Than to suspicion.
OTHELLO   I will not.
IAGO   Should you do so, my lord,
My speech should fall into such vile success   238
Which my thoughts aimed not. Cassio's my worthy
    friend.
My lord, I see you're moved.
OTHELLO   No, not much moved.
I do not think but Desdemona's honest.   241
IAGO
Long live she so! And long live you to think so!
OTHELLO
And yet, how nature erring from itself—
IAGO
Ay, there's the point! As—to be bold with you—
Not to affect many proposèd matches   245
Of her own clime, complexion, and degree,
Whereto we see in all things nature tends—
Foh! One may smell in such a will most rank,   248
Foul disproportion, thoughts unnatural.   249
But pardon me. I do not in position   250
Distinctly speak of her, though I may fear
Her will, recoiling to her better judgment,   252
May fall to match you with her country forms   253
And happily repent.
OTHELLO   Farewell, farewell!   254
If more thou dost perceive, let me know more.
Set on thy wife to observe. Leave me, Iago.
IAGO [*Going*]   My lord, I take my leave.
OTHELLO
Why did I marry? This honest creature doubtless
Sees and knows more, much more, than he unfolds.

---

234 issues significances. **reach** meaning, scope **238 success** effect,
result **241 honest** chaste **245 affect** prefer, desire **248 will** sensuality, appetite **249 disproportion** abnormality **250 position** argument,
proposition **252 recoiling** reverting. **better** i.e., more natural and
reconsidered **253 fall . . . forms** undertake to compare you with Venetian norms of handsomeness **254 happily repent** haply repent her
marriage

IAGO [*Returning*]
    My Lord, I would I might entreat your honor
    To scan this thing no farther. Leave it to time.
    Although 'tis fit that Cassio have his place—
    For, sure, he fills it up with great ability—
    Yet, if you please to hold him off awhile,
    You shall by that perceive him and his means.
    Note if your lady strain his entertainment   266
    With any strong or vehement importunity;
    Much will be seen in that. In the meantime,
    Let me be thought too busy in my fears—
    As worthy cause I have to fear I am—
    And hold her free, I do beseech your honor.   271
OTHELLO   Fear not my government.   272
IAGO   I once more take my leave.   *Exit.*
OTHELLO
    This fellow's of exceeding honesty,
    And knows all qualities, with a learnèd spirit,   275
    Of human dealings. If I do prove her haggard,   276
    Though that her jesses were my dear heartstrings,   277
    I'd whistle her off and let her down the wind   278
    To prey at fortune. Haply, for I am black   279
    And have not those soft parts of conversation   280
    That chamberers have, or for I am declined   281
    Into the vale of years—yet that's not much—
    She's gone. I am abused, and my relief   283
    Must be to loathe her. O curse of marriage,
    That we can call these delicate creatures ours
    And not their appetites! I had rather be a toad
    And live upon the vapor of a dungeon
    Than keep a corner in the thing I love
    For others' uses. Yet, 'tis the plague of great ones;
    Prerogatived are they less than the base.   290

266 strain his entertainment urge his reinstatement   **271 hold her free**
regard her as innocent   **272 government** self-control, conduct
275 qualities natures, types   **276 haggard** wild (like a wild female
hawk)   **277 jesses** straps fastened around the legs of a trained hawk
278 I'd . . . wind i.e., I'd let her go forever. (To release a hawk downwind
was to invite it not to return.)   **279 prey at fortune** fend for herself in
the wild.   **Haply, for** perhaps because   **280 soft . . . conversation**
pleasing graces of social behavior   **281 chamberers** gallants
283 abused deceived   **290 Prerogatived** privileged (to have honest
wives).   **the base** ordinary citizens

'Tis destiny unshunnable, like death.
Even then this forkèd plague is fated to us   292
When we do quicken. Look where she comes.   293

    Enter Desdemona and Emilia.

If she be false, O, then heaven mocks itself!
I'll not believe 't.
DESDEMONA   How now, my dear Othello?
Your dinner, and the generous islanders   296
By you invited, do attend your presence.   297
OTHELLO
I am to blame.
DESDEMONA   Why do you speak so faintly?
Are you not well?
OTHELLO
I have a pain upon my forehead here.
DESDEMONA
Faith, that's with watching. 'Twill away again.   301
             [*She offers her handkerchief.*]
Let me but bind it hard, within this hour
It will be well.
OTHELLO   Your napkin is too little.   303
Let it alone. Come, I'll go in with you.   304
          [*He puts the handkerchief from him,*
                      and it drops.]

DESDEMONA
I am very sorry that you are not well.
                   Exit [*with Othello*].
EMILIA [*Picking up the handkerchief*]
I am glad I have found this napkin.
This was her first remembrance from the Moor.
My wayward husband hath a hundred times   308
Wooed me to steal it, but she so loves the token—
For he conjured her she should ever keep it—
That she reserves it evermore about her

---

292 forkèd (An allusion to the horns of the cuckold.) **293 quicken**
receive life. (*Quicken* may also mean to swarm with maggots as the
body festers, as in 4.2.69, in which case ll. 292–293 suggest that *even
then*, in death, we are cuckolded by *forkèd* worms.) **296 generous**
noble **297 attend** await **301 watching** too little sleep **303 napkin**
handkerchief **304 Let it alone** i.e., never mind **308 wayward**
capricious

To kiss and talk to. I'll have the work ta'en out,   312
And give 't Iago. What he will do with it
Heaven knows, not I;
I nothing but to please his fantasy.   315

    Enter Iago.

IAGO
How now? What do you here alone?
EMILIA
Do not you chide. I have a thing for you.
IAGO
You have a thing for me? It is a common thing—   318
EMILIA Ha?
IAGO To have a foolish wife.
EMILIA
O, is that all? What will you give me now
For that same handkerchief?
IAGO What handkerchief?
EMILIA What handkerchief?
Why, that the Moor first gave to Desdemona;
That which so often you did bid me steal.
IAGO Hast stolen it from her?
EMILIA
No, faith. She let it drop by negligence,
And to th' advantage I, being here, took 't up.   329
Look, here 'tis.
IAGO   A good wench! Give it me.
EMILIA
What will you do with 't, that you have been so earnest
To have me filch it?
IAGO [*Snatching it*]   Why, what is that to you?
EMILIA
If it be not for some purpose of import,
Give 't me again. Poor lady, she'll run mad
When she shall lack it.
IAGO   Be not acknown on 't.   335
I have use for it. Go, leave me.   *Exit Emilia.*

---

312 work ta'en out design of the embroidery copied   **315 fantasy**
whim   **318 common thing** (with bawdy suggestion; *common* suggests
coarseness and availability to all comers, and *thing* is a slang term for
the pudendum)   **329 to th' advantage** taking the opportunity   **335 Be
. . . on 't** do not confess knowledge of it

I will in Cassio's lodging lose this napkin   337
And let him find it. Trifles light as air
Are to the jealous confirmations strong
As proofs of Holy Writ. This may do something.
The Moor already changes with my poison.
Dangerous conceits are in their natures poisons,   342
Which at the first are scarce found to distaste,   343
But with a little act upon the blood   344
Burn like the mines of sulfur.

    Enter Othello.

                         I did say so.
Look where he comes! Not poppy nor mandragora   346
Nor all the drowsy syrups of the world
Shall ever medicine thee to that sweet sleep
Which thou owedst yesterday.

OTHELLO   Ha, ha, false to me?   349

IAGO

  Why, how now, General? No more of that.

OTHELLO

  Avaunt! Begone! Thou hast set me on the rack.
  I swear 'tis better to be much abused
  Than but to know 't a little.

IAGO   How now, my lord?

OTHELLO

  What sense had I of her stolen hours of lust?
  I saw 't not, thought it not, it harmed not me.
  I slept the next night well, fed well, was free and merry;   356
  I found not Cassio's kisses on her lips.
  He that is robbed, not wanting what is stolen,   358
  Let him not know 't and he's not robbed at all.

IAGO I am sorry to hear this.

OTHELLO

  I had been happy if the general camp,
  Pioners and all, had tasted her sweet body,   362
  So I had nothing known. O, now, forever   363

---

337 lose (The Folio spelling, *loose,* is a normal spelling for "lose," but it
may also contain the idea of "let go," "release.") **342 conceits** fancies,
ideas **343 distaste** be distasteful **344 act** action, working **346 mandragora** an opiate made of the mandrake root **349 thou owedst** you did own
356 free carefree **358 wanting** missing **362 Pioners** diggers of mines,
the lowest grade of soldiers **363 So** provided

Farewell the tranquil mind! Farewell content!
Farewell the plumèd troops and the big wars   365
That makes ambition virtue! O, farewell!
Farewell the neighing steed and the shrill trump,
The spirit-stirring drum, th' ear-piercing fife,
The royal banner, and all quality,   369
Pride, pomp, and circumstance of glorious war!   370
And O, you mortal engines, whose rude throats   371
Th' immortal Jove's dread clamors counterfeit,   372
Farewell! Othello's occupation's gone.

IAGO   Is 't possible, my lord?

OTHELLO
Villain, be sure thou prove my love a whore!
Be sure of it. Give me the ocular proof,
Or, by the worth of mine eternal soul,
Thou hadst been better have been born a dog
Than answer my waked wrath!

IAGO   Is 't come to this?

OTHELLO
Make me to see 't, or at the least so prove it
That the probation bear no hinge nor loop   381
To hang a doubt on, or woe upon thy life!

IAGO   My noble lord—

OTHELLO
If thou dost slander her and torture me,
Never pray more; abandon all remorse;   385
On horror's head horrors accumulate;   386
Do deeds to make heaven weep, all earth amazed;   387
For nothing canst thou to damnation add
Greater than that.

IAGO   O grace! O heaven forgive me!
Are you a man? Have you a soul or sense?
God b' wi' you; take mine office. O wretched fool,   391
That lov'st to make thine honesty a vice!   392
O monstrous world! Take note, take note, O world,

---

365 big stately   **369 quality** character, essential nature   **370 Pride** rich
display.   **circumstance** pageantry   **371 mortal engines** i.e., cannon.
(*Mortal* means "deadly.")   **372 Jove's dread clamors** i.e., thunder
381 probation proof   **385 remorse** pity   **386 horrors accumulate** add
still more horrors   **387 amazed** confounded with horror   **391 O
wretched fool** (Iago addresses himself as a fool for having carried
honesty too far.)   **392 vice** failing, something overdone

To be direct and honest is not safe.
I thank you for this profit, and from hence   395
I'll love no friend, sith love breeds such offense.   396
OTHELLO   Nay, stay. Thou shouldst be honest.   397
IAGO
I should be wise, for honesty's a fool
And loses that it works for.
OTHELLO   By the world,   399
I think my wife be honest and think she is not;
I think that thou art just and think thou art not.
I'll have some proof. My name, that was as fresh
As Dian's visage, is now begrimed and black   403
As mine own face. If there be cords, or knives,
Poison, or fire, or suffocating streams,
I'll not endure it. Would I were satisfied!
IAGO
I see, sir, you are eaten up with passion.
I do repent me that I put it to you.
You would be satisfied?
OTHELLO   Would? Nay, and I will.
IAGO
And may; but how? How satisfied, my lord?
Would you, the supervisor, grossly gape on?   411
Behold her topped?
OTHELLO   Death and damnation! O!
IAGO
It were a tedious difficulty, I think,
To bring them to that prospect. Damn them then,   414
If ever mortal eyes do see them bolster   415
More than their own. What then? How then?   416
What shall I say? Where's satisfaction?
It is impossible you should see this,
Were they as prime as goats, as hot as monkeys,   419
As salt as wolves in pride, and fools as gross   420

395 profit profitable instruction.   **hence** henceforth   **396 sith** since.
offense i.e., harm to the one who offers help and friendship   **397 Thou
shouldst be** it appears that you are. (But Iago replies in the sense of
"ought to be.")   **399 that** what   **403 Dian** Diana, goddess of the moon
and of chastity   **411 supervisor** onlooker   **414 Damn them then** i.e.,
they would have to be really incorrigible   **415 bolster** go to bed together, share a bolster   **416 More** other   **419 prime** lustful   **420 salt**
wanton, sensual.   **pride** heat

As ignorance made drunk. But yet, I say,
If imputation and strong circumstances
Which lead directly to the door of truth
Will give you satisfaction, you might have 't.

OTHELLO
Give me a living reason she's disloyal.

IAGO   I do not like the office.
But sith I am entered in this cause so far,   427
Pricked to 't by foolish honesty and love,   428
I will go on. I lay with Cassio lately,
And being troubled with a raging tooth
I could not sleep. There are a kind of men
So loose of soul that in their sleeps will mutter
Their affairs. One of this kind is Cassio.
In sleep I heard him say, "Sweet Desdemona,
Let us be wary, let us hide our loves!"
And then, sir, would he grip and wring my hand,
Cry "O sweet creature!" then kiss me hard,
As if he plucked up kisses by the roots
That grew upon my lips; then laid his leg
Over my thigh, and sighed, and kissed, and then
Cried, "Cursèd fate that gave thee to the Moor!"

OTHELLO
O monstrous! Monstrous!

IAGO   Nay, this was but his dream.

OTHELLO
But this denoted a foregone conclusion.   443
'Tis a shrewd doubt, though it be but a dream.   444

IAGO
And this may help to thicken other proofs
That do demonstrate thinly.

OTHELLO   I'll tear her all to pieces.

IAGO
Nay, yet be wise. Yet we see nothing done;
She may be honest yet. Tell me but this:
Have you not sometimes seen a handkerchief
Spotted with strawberries in your wife's hand?   450

---

427 sith since   **428 Pricked** spurred   **443 foregone conclusion** concluded experience or action   **444 shrewd doubt** suspicious circumstance   **450 Spotted with strawberries** embroidered with a strawberry
pattern

OTHELLO
  I gave her such a one. 'Twas my first gift.

IAGO
  I know not that; but such a handkerchief—
  I am sure it was your wife's—did I today
  See Cassio wipe his beard with.

OTHELLO   If it be that—

IAGO
  If it be that, or any that was hers,
  It speaks against her with the other proofs.

OTHELLO
  O, that the slave had forty thousand lives!   457
  One is too poor, too weak for my revenge.
  Now do I see 'tis true. Look here, Iago,
  All my fond love thus do I blow to heaven.   460
  'Tis gone.
  Arise, black vengeance, from the hollow hell!
  Yield up, O love, thy crown and hearted throne   463
  To tyrannous hate! Swell, bosom, with thy freight,   464
  For 'tis of aspics' tongues!   465

IAGO   Yet be content.   466

OTHELLO   O, blood, blood, blood!

IAGO
  Patience, I say. Your mind perhaps may change.

OTHELLO
  Never, Iago. Like to the Pontic Sea,   469
  Whose icy current and compulsive course
  Ne'er feels retiring ebb, but keeps due on
  To the Propontic and the Hellespont,   472
  Even so my bloody thoughts with violent pace
  Shall ne'er look back, ne'er ebb to humble love,
  Till that a capable and wide revenge   475
  Swallow them up. Now, by yond marble heaven,   476
  [*Kneeling*] In the due reverence of a sacred vow
  I here engage my words.

---

457 the slave i.e., Cassio   **460 fond** foolish   **463 hearted** fixed in
the heart   **464 freight** burden   **465 aspics'** venomous serpents'
466 content calm   **469 Pontic Sea** Black Sea   **472 Propontic** body of
water between the Bosporus and Hellespont   **475 capable** comprehensive   **476 marble** i.e., gleaming like marble

IAGO   Do not rise yet.
[*He kneels.*] Witness, you ever-burning lights above,   479
You elements that clip us round about,   480
Witness that here Iago doth give up
The execution of his wit, hands, heart,   482
To wronged Othello's service! Let him command,
And to obey shall be in me remorse,   484
What bloody business ever.   [*They rise.*]
OTHELLO   I greet thy love,   485
Not with vain thanks, but with acceptance bounteous,
And will upon the instant put thee to 't.
Within these three days let me hear thee say
That Cassio's not alive.
IAGO   My friend is dead;
'Tis done at your request. But let her live.
OTHELLO
Damn her, lewd minx! O, damn her, damn her!   491
Come, go with me apart. I will withdraw
To furnish me with some swift means of death
For the fair devil. Now art thou my lieutenant.
IAGO   I am your own forever.   *Exeunt.*

❖

3.4   *Enter Desdemona, Emilia, and Clown.*

DESDEMONA   Do you know, sirrah, where Lieutenant   1
   Cassio lies?   2
CLOWN   I dare not say he lies anywhere.
DESDEMONA   Why, man?
CLOWN   He's a soldier, and for me to say a soldier lies,
   'tis stabbing.
DESDEMONA   Go to. Where lodges he?
CLOWN   To tell you where he lodges is to tell you where
   I lie.

---

479 s.d. He kneels (In the quarto text, Iago kneels here after Othello has
knelt at l. 477.)   480 clip encompass   482 execution exercise, action.
wit mind   484 remorse pity (for Othello's wrongs)   485 ever soever
491 minx wanton

3.4. Location: Before the citadel.
1 sirrah (A form of address to an inferior.)   2 lies lodges. (But the Clown
makes the obvious pun.)

DESDEMONA   Can anything be made of this?

CLOWN   I know not where he lodges, and for me to devise a lodging and say he lies here, or he lies there,
were to lie in mine own throat.   13

DESDEMONA   Can you inquire him out, and be edified
by report?

CLOWN   I will catechize the world for him; that is, make
questions, and by them answer.

DESDEMONA   Seek him, bid him come hither. Tell him I
have moved my lord on his behalf and hope all will be   19
well.

CLOWN   To do this is within the compass of man's wit,
and therefore I will attempt the doing it.   *Exit Clown.*

DESDEMONA
Where should I lose that handkerchief, Emilia?

EMILIA   I know not, madam.

DESDEMONA
Believe me, I had rather have lost my purse
Full of crusadoes; and but my noble Moor   26
Is true of mind and made of no such baseness
As jealous creatures are, it were enough
To put him to ill thinking.

EMILIA   Is he not jealous?

DESDEMONA
Who, he? I think the sun where he was born
Drew all such humors from him.

EMILIA   Look where he comes.   31

    Enter Othello.

DESDEMONA
I will not leave him now till Cassio
Be called to him.—How is 't with you, my lord?

OTHELLO
Well, my good lady. [*Aside.*] O, hardness to dissemble!—
How do you, Desdemona?

DESDEMONA   Well, my good lord.

OTHELLO
Give me your hand. [*She gives her hand.*] This hand is
moist, my lady.

13 lie . . . throat lie egregiously and deliberately   **19 moved** petitioned
26 crusadoes Portuguese gold coins   **31 humors** (Refers to the four
bodily fluids thought to determine temperament.)

DESDEMONA
  It yet hath felt no age nor known no sorrow.
OTHELLO
  This argues fruitfulness and liberal heart.   38
  Hot, hot, and moist. This hand of yours requires
  A sequester from liberty, fasting and prayer,   40
  Much castigation, exercise devout;   41
  For here's a young and sweating devil here
  That commonly rebels. 'Tis a good hand,
  A frank one.
DESDEMONA   You may indeed say so,   44
  For 'twas that hand that gave away my heart.
OTHELLO
  A liberal hand! The hearts of old gave hands,   46
  But our new heraldry is hands, not hearts.   47
DESDEMONA
  I cannot speak of this. Come now, your promise.
OTHELLO   What promise, chuck?   49
DESDEMONA
  I have sent to bid Cassio come speak with you.
OTHELLO
  I have a salt and sorry rheum offends me;   51
  Lend me thy handkerchief.
DESDEMONA   Here, my lord. [*She offers a handkerchief.*]
OTHELLO
  That which I gave you.
DESDEMONA   I have it not about me.
OTHELLO   Not?
DESDEMONA   No, faith, my lord.
OTHELLO   That's a fault. That handkerchief
  Did an Egyptian to my mother give.
  She was a charmer, and could almost read   59
  The thoughts of people. She told her, while she kept it,

---

38 argues gives evidence of.   **fruitfulness** generosity, amorousness, and
fecundity.   **liberal** generous and sexually free   **40 sequester** separation,
sequestration   **41 castigation** corrective discipline   **44 frank** generous,
open (with sexual suggestion)   **46 The hearts . . . hands** i.e., in former
times people would give their hearts when they gave their hands to
something   **47 But . . . hearts** i.e., in our decadent times the joining of
hands is no longer a badge to signify the giving of hearts   **49 chuck** (A
term of endearment.)   **51 salt . . . rheum** distressful head cold or water-
ing of the eyes   **59 charmer** sorceress

'Twould make her amiable and subdue my father   61
Entirely to her love, but if she lost it
Or made a gift of it, my father's eye
Should hold her loathèd and his spirits should hunt
After new fancies. She, dying, gave it me,   65
And bid me, when my fate would have me wived,
To give it her. I did so; and take heed on 't;   67
Make it a darling like your precious eye.
To lose 't or give 't away were such perdition   69
As nothing else could match.

DESDEMONA   Is 't possible?

OTHELLO
'Tis true. There's magic in the web of it.   71
A sibyl, that had numbered in the world
The sun to course two hundred compasses,   73
In her prophetic fury sewed the work;   74
The worms were hallowed that did breed the silk,
And it was dyed in mummy which the skillful   76
Conserved of maidens' hearts.

DESDEMONA   I' faith! Is 't true?   77

OTHELLO
Most veritable. Therefore look to 't well.

DESDEMONA
Then would to God that I had never seen 't!

OTHELLO   Ha? Wherefore?

DESDEMONA
Why do you speak so startingly and rash?   81

OTHELLO
Is 't lost? Is 't gone? Speak, is 't out o' the way?   82

DESDEMONA   Heaven bless us!

OTHELLO   Say you?

DESDEMONA
It is not lost; but what an if it were?   85

OTHELLO   How?

---

61 amiable desirable   **65 fancies** loves   **67 her** i.e., to my wife
69 perdition loss   **71 web** fabric, weaving   **73 compasses** annual cir-
clings. (The *sibyl*, or prophetess, was 200 years old.)   **74 prophetic fury**
frenzy of prophetic inspiration   **76 mummy** medicinal or magical
preparation drained from mummified bodies   **77 Conserved of** prepared or preserved out of   **81 startingly and rash** disjointedly and
impetuously, excitedly   **82 out o' the way** lost, misplaced   **85 an if** if

DESDEMONA
  I say it is not lost.
OTHELLO   Fetch 't. Let me see 't.
DESDEMONA
  Why, so I can, sir, but I will not now.
  This is a trick to put me from my suit.
  Pray you, let Cassio be received again.
OTHELLO
  Fetch me the handkerchief! My mind misgives.
DESDEMONA   Come, come,
  You'll never meet a more sufficient man.   93
OTHELLO
  The handkerchief!
DESDEMONA   I pray, talk me of Cassio.   94
OTHELLO
  The handkerchief!
DESDEMONA   A man that all his time   95
  Hath founded his good fortunes on your love,
  Shared dangers with you—
OTHELLO   The handkerchief!
DESDEMONA   I' faith, you are to blame.
OTHELLO   Zounds!   *Exit Othello.*
EMILIA   Is not this man jealous?
DESDEMONA   I ne'er saw this before.
  Sure, there's some wonder in this handkerchief.
  I am most unhappy in the loss of it.
EMILIA
  'Tis not a year or two shows us a man.   105
  They are all but stomachs, and we all but food;   106
  They eat us hungerly, and when they are full   107
  They belch us.

        Enter Iago and Cassio.

                    Look you, Cassio and my husband.
IAGO
  There is no other way; 'tis she must do 't.
  And, lo, the happiness! Go and importune her.   110

93 sufficient able, complete   **94 talk** talk to   **95 all his time** throughout
his career   **105 'Tis . . . man** i.e., you can't really know a man even
in a year or two of experience (?) or, real men come along seldom (?)
106 but nothing but   **107 hungerly** hungrily   **110 the happiness** in
happy time, fortunately met

DESDEMONA
  How now, good Cassio? What's the news with you?
CASSIO
  Madam, my former suit. I do beseech you
  That by your virtuous means I may again   112
  Exist, and be a member of his love
  Whom I with all the office of my heart   115
  Entirely honor. I would not be delayed.
  If my offense be of such mortal kind   117
  That nor my service past nor present sorrows,   118
  Nor purposed merit in futurity,
  Can ransom me into his love again,
  But to know so must be my benefit;   121
  So shall I clothe me in a forced content,
  And shut myself up in some other course,
  To fortune's alms.
DESDEMONA   Alas, thrice-gentle Cassio,   124
  My advocation is not now in tune.   125
  My lord is not my lord; nor should I know him,
  Were he in favor as in humor altered.   127
  So help me every spirit sanctified
  As I have spoken for you all my best
  And stood within the blank of his displeasure   130
  For my free speech! You must awhile be patient.
  What I can do I will, and more I will
  Than for myself I dare. Let that suffice you.
IAGO
  Is my lord angry?
EMILIA   He went hence but now,
  And certainly in strange unquietness.
IAGO
  Can he be angry? I have seen the cannon
  When it hath blown his ranks into the air,
  And like the devil from his very arm
  Puffed his own brother—and is he angry?

---

113 virtuous efficacious   **115 office** loyal service   **117 mortal** fatal
118 nor . . . nor neither . . . nor   **121 But . . . benefit** merely to know
that my case is hopeless must be all I can expect   **124 To fortune's
alms** throwing myself on the mercy of fortune   **125 advocation** advo-
cacy   **127 favor** appearance   **130 within the blank** within point-blank
range. (The *blank* is the center of the target.)

Something of moment then. I will go meet him.　140
There's matter in 't indeed, if he be angry.

DESDEMONA

I prithee, do so.　　　　　　　　　　*Exit [Iago].*

　　　　　　　　　Something, sure, of state,　142
Either from Venice, or some unhatched practice　143
Made demonstrable here in Cyprus to him,
Hath puddled his clear spirit; and in such cases　145
Men's natures wrangle with inferior things,
Though great ones are their object. 'Tis even so;
For let our finger ache, and it indues　148
Our other healthful members even to a sense
Of pain. Nay, we must think men are not gods,
Nor of them look for such observancy　151
As fits the bridal. Beshrew me much, Emilia,　152
I was, unhandsome warrior as I am,　153
Arraigning his unkindness with my soul;　154
But now I find I had suborned the witness,　155
And he's indicted falsely.

EMILIA　　　　　　　　　Pray heaven it be
State matters, as you think, and no conception
Nor no jealous toy concerning you.　158

DESDEMONA

Alas the day! I never gave him cause.

EMILIA

But jealous souls will not be answered so;
They are not ever jealous for the cause,
But jealous for they're jealous. It is a monster　162
Begot upon itself, born on itself.　163

DESDEMONA

Heaven keep that monster from Othello's mind!

EMILIA　Lady, amen.

DESDEMONA

I will go seek him. Cassio, walk hereabout.

140 of moment of immediate importance, momentous　**142 of state**
concerning state affairs　**143 unhatched practice** as yet unexecuted or
undiscovered plot　**145 puddled** muddied　**148 indues** brings to the
same condition　**151 observancy** attentiveness　**152 bridal** wedding
(when a bridegroom is newly attentive to his bride).　**Beshrew me** (A
mild oath.)　**153 unhandsome** insufficient, unskillful　**154 with** before
the bar of　**155 suborned the witness** induced the witness to give false
testimony　**158 toy** fancy　**162 for** because　**163 Begot upon itself**
generated solely from itself

If I do find him fit, I'll move your suit
And seek to effect it to my uttermost.
CASSIO   I humbly thank your ladyship.
                          Exit [Desdemona with Emilia].

          Enter Bianca.

BIANCA
Save you, friend Cassio!
CASSIO   What make you from home?   170
How is 't with you, my most fair Bianca?
I' faith, sweet love, I was coming to your house.
BIANCA
And I was going to your lodging, Cassio.
What, keep a week away? Seven days and nights?
Eightscore-eight hours? And lovers' absent hours
More tedious than the dial eightscore times?   176
O weary reckoning!
CASSIO   Pardon me, Bianca.
I have this while with leaden thoughts been pressed;
But I shall, in a more continuate time,   179
Strike off this score of absence. Sweet Bianca,   180
            [Giving her Desdemona's handkerchief]
Take me this work out.
BIANCA   O Cassio, whence came this?   181
This is some token from a newer friend.   182
To the felt absence now I feel a cause.
Is 't come to this? Well, well.
CASSIO   Go to, woman!
Throw your vile guesses in the devil's teeth,
From whence you have them. You are jealous now
That this is from some mistress, some remembrance.
No, by my faith, Bianca.
BIANCA   Why, whose is it?
CASSIO
I know not, neither. I found it in my chamber.
I like the work well. Ere it be demanded—   190
As like enough it will—I would have it copied.   191
Take it and do 't, and leave me for this time.

170 **Save** God save. **make** do   176 **the dial** a complete revolution of the
clock   179 **continuate** uninterrupted   180 **Strike . . . score** settle this
account   181 **Take . . . out** copy this embroidery for me   182 **friend**
mistress   190 **demanded** inquired for   191 **like** likely

BIANCA   Leave you? Wherefore?

CASSIO

  I do attend here on the General,
  And think it no addition, nor my wish,   195
  To have him see me womaned.

BIANCA   Why, I pray you?

CASSIO   Not that I love you not.

BIANCA   But that you do not love me.

  I pray you, bring me on the way a little,   200
  And say if I shall see you soon at night.

CASSIO

  'Tis but a little way that I can bring you,
  For I attend here; but I'll see you soon.

BIANCA

  'Tis very good. I must be circumstanced.   204

Exeunt omnes.

❧

---

195 addition i.e., addition to my reputation   **200 bring** accompany
204 be circumstanced be governed by circumstance, yield to your
conditions

4.1 *Enter Othello and Iago.*

IAGO
  Will you think so?
OTHELLO   Think so, Iago?
IAGO   What,
  To kiss in private?
OTHELLO   An unauthorized kiss!
IAGO
  Or to be naked with her friend in bed
  An hour or more, not meaning any harm?
OTHELLO
  Naked in bed, Iago, and not mean harm?
  It is hypocrisy against the devil.
  They that mean virtuously, and yet do so,
  The devil their virtue tempts, and they tempt heaven.
IAGO
  If they do nothing, 'tis a venial slip.   9
  But if I give my wife a handkerchief—
OTHELLO What then?
IAGO
  Why then, 'tis hers, my lord, and being hers,
  She may, I think, bestow 't on any man.
OTHELLO
  She is protectress of her honor too.
  May she give that?
IAGO
  Her honor is an essence that's not seen;
  They have it very oft that have it not.   17
  But, for the handkerchief—
OTHELLO
  By heaven, I would most gladly have forgot it.
  Thou saidst—O, it comes o'er my memory
  As doth the raven o'er the infectious house,   21
  Boding to all—he had my handkerchief.
IAGO
  Ay, what of that?

4.1. Location: Before the citadel.
9 venial pardonable   **17 They have it** i.e., they enjoy a reputation for
it   **21 raven . . . house** (Allusion to the belief that the raven hovered over
a house of sickness or infection, such as one visited by the plague.)

OTHELLO   That's not so good now.

IAGO   What
If I had said I had seen him do you wrong?
Or heard him say—as knaves be such abroad,   25
Who having, by their own importunate suit,
Or voluntary dotage of some mistress,   27
Convincèd or supplied them, cannot choose   28
But they must blab—

OTHELLO   Hath he said anything?

IAGO
He hath, my lord; but, be you well assured,
No more than he'll unswear.

OTHELLO   What hath he said?

IAGO
Faith, that he did—I know not what he did.

OTHELLO   What? What?

IAGO
Lie—

OTHELLO   With her?

IAGO   With her, on her; what you will.

OTHELLO   Lie with her? Lie on her? We say "lie on her"
when they belie her. Lie with her? Zounds, that's ful-   36
some.—Handkerchief—confessions—handkerchief!   37
—To confess and be hanged for his labor—first to be 38
hanged and then to confess.—I tremble at it. Nature 39
would not invest herself in such shadowing passion   40
without some instruction. It is not words that shakes 41
me thus. Pish! Noses, ears, and lips.—Is 't possible?—
Confess—handkerchief!—O devil!

                              Falls in a trance.

IAGO   Work on,
My medicine, work! Thus credulous fools are caught,
And many worthy and chaste dames even thus,

---

25 abroad around about   **27 voluntary dotage** willing infatuation
28 Convincèd or supplied seduced or gratified   **36 belie** slander
36–37 fulsome foul   **38–39 first . . . to confess** (Othello reverses the
proverbial *confess and be hanged;* Cassio is to be given no time to
confess before he dies.)   **39–41 Nature . . . instruction** i.e., without some
foundation in fact, nature would not have dressed herself in such an
overwhelming passion that comes over me now and fills my mind with
images, or in such a lifelike fantasy as Cassio had in his dream of lying
with Desdemona   **41 words** mere words

All guiltless, meet reproach.—What ho! My lord!
My lord, I say! Othello!

Enter Cassio.

                        How now, Cassio?
CASSIO   What's the matter?
IAGO
My lord is fall'n into an epilepsy.
This is his second fit. He had one yesterday.
CASSIO
Rub him about the temples.
IAGO   No, forbear.
The lethargy must have his quiet course.   53
If not, he foams at mouth, and by and by
Breaks out to savage madness. Look, he stirs.
Do you withdraw yourself a little while.
He will recover straight. When he is gone,
I would on great occasion speak with you.   58
                        [*Exit Cassio.*]
How is it, General? Have you not hurt your head?
OTHELLO
Dost thou mock me?
IAGO   I mock you not, by heaven.   60
Would you would bear your fortune like a man!
OTHELLO
A hornèd man's a monster and a beast.
IAGO
There's many a beast then in a populous city,
And many a civil monster.   64
OTHELLO   Did he confess it?
IAGO   Good sir, be a man.
Think every bearded fellow that's but yoked   67
May draw with you. There's millions now alive   68
That nightly lie in those unproper beds   69

53 lethargy coma. **his** its **58 on great occasion** on a matter of great
importance **60 mock** (Othello takes Iago's question about hurting his
head to be a mocking reference to the cuckold's horns.) **64 civil** i.e.,
dwelling in a city **67 yoked** (1) married (2) put into the yoke of infamy
and cuckoldry **68 draw with you** pull as you do like oxen who are
yoked, i.e., share your fate as cuckold **69 unproper** not exclusively
their own

Which they dare swear peculiar. Your case is better.   70
O, 'tis the spite of hell, the fiend's arch-mock,
To lip a wanton in a secure couch   72
And to suppose her chaste! No, let me know,
And knowing what I am, I know what she shall be.   74
OTHELLO O, thou art wise. 'Tis certain.
IAGO Stand you awhile apart;
Confine yourself but in a patient list.   77
Whilst you were here o'erwhelmèd with your grief—
A passion most unsuiting such a man—
Cassio came hither. I shifted him away,   80
And laid good 'scuses upon your ecstasy,   81
Bade him anon return and here speak with me,
The which he promised. Do but encave yourself   83
And mark the fleers, the gibes, and notable scorns   84
That dwell in every region of his face;
For I will make him tell the tale anew,
Where, how, how oft, how long ago, and when
He hath and is again to cope your wife.   88
I say, but mark his gesture. Marry, patience!
Or I shall say you're all-in-all in spleen,   90
And nothing of a man.
OTHELLO   Dost thou hear, Iago?
I will be found most cunning in my patience;
But—dost thou hear?—most bloody.
IAGO   That's not amiss;
But yet keep time in all. Will you withdraw?   94
                        [Othello stands apart.]
Now will I question Cassio of Bianca,
A huswife that by selling her desires   96
Buys herself bread and clothes. It is a creature
That dotes on Cassio—as 'tis the strumpet's plague
To beguile many and be beguiled by one.

---

70 peculiar private, their own.   **better** i.e., because you know the
truth   **72 lip** kiss.   **secure** free from suspicion   **74 what I am** i.e., a
cuckold.   **she shall be** i.e., an adulteress who must die   **77 in . . . list**
within the bounds of patience   **80 shifted him away** used a dodge to get
rid of him   **81 ecstasy** trance   **83 encave** conceal   **84 fleers** sneers.
notable obvious   **88 cope** encounter with, have sex with   **90 all-in-all in
spleen** utterly governed by passionate impulses   **94 keep time** keep
yourself steady (as in music)   **96 huswife** hussy

He, when he hears of her, cannot restrain   100
From the excess of laughter. Here he comes.

    Enter Cassio.

As he shall smile, Othello shall go mad;
And his unbookish jealousy must conster   103
Poor Cassio's smiles, gestures, and light behaviors
Quite in the wrong.—How do you now, Lieutenant?

CASSIO
The worser that you give me the addition   106
Whose want even kills me.

IAGO
Ply Desdemona well and you are sure on 't.
[*Speaking lower.*] Now, if this suit lay in Bianca's power,
How quickly should you speed!

CASSIO [*Laughing*]   Alas, poor caitiff!   111

OTHELLO   Look how he laughs already!

IAGO
I never knew a woman love man so.

CASSIO
Alas, poor rogue! I think, i' faith, she loves me.

OTHELLO
Now he denies it faintly, and laughs it out.

IAGO
Do you hear, Cassio?

OTHELLO   Now he importunes him
To tell it o'er. Go to! Well said, well said.   117

IAGO
She gives it out that you shall marry her.
Do you intend it?

CASSIO   Ha, ha, ha!

OTHELLO
Do you triumph, Roman? Do you triumph?   121

CASSIO   I marry her? What? A customer? Prithee, bear   122
some charity to my wit; do not think it so unwhole-   123
some. Ha, ha, ha!

100 restrain refrain   **103 unbookish** uninstructed.   **conster** construe
106 addition title   **111 caitiff** wretch   **117 Well said** well done
121 Roman (The Romans were noted for their *triumphs* or triumphal
processions.)   **122 customer** i.e., prostitute   **122–123 bear . . . wit** be
more charitable to my judgment

OTHELLO So, so, so, so! They laugh that win.   125

IAGO Faith, the cry goes that you shall marry her.   126

CASSIO Prithee, say true.

IAGO I am a very villain else.

OTHELLO Have you scored me? Well.   129

CASSIO This is the monkey's own giving out. She is
persuaded I will marry her, out of her own love and
flattery, not out of my promise.   132

OTHELLO Iago beckons me. Now he begins the story.   133

CASSIO She was here even now; she haunts me in every
place. I was the other day talking on the seabank with
certain Venetians, and thither comes the bauble, and,   136
by this hand, she falls me thus about my neck—

                              [He embraces Iago.]

OTHELLO Crying, "O dear Cassio!" as it were; his gesture imports it.

CASSIO So hangs and lolls and weeps upon me, so
shakes and pulls me. Ha, ha, ha!

OTHELLO Now he tells how she plucked him to my
chamber. O, I see that nose of yours, but not that dog
I shall throw it to.

CASSIO Well, I must leave her company.

IAGO Before me, look where she comes.   146

          Enter Bianca [with Othello's handkerchief].

CASSIO 'Tis such another fitchew! Marry, a perfumed   147
one.—What do you mean by this haunting of me?

BIANCA Let the devil and his dam haunt you! What did   149
you mean by that same handkerchief you gave me
even now? I was a fine fool to take it. I must take out
the work? A likely piece of work, that you should find   152
it in your chamber and know not who left it there!
This is some minx's token, and I must take out the

---

125 They . . . win i.e., they that laugh last laugh best   **126 cry** rumor
129 scored me scored off me, beaten me, made up my reckoning,
branded me   **132 flattery** self-flattery, self-deception   **133 beckons**
signals   **136 bauble** plaything   **146 Before me** i.e., on my soul   **147 'Tis
. . . fitchew** what a polecat she is! Just like all the others.   **fitchew**
(Polecats were often compared with prostitutes because of their rank
smell and presumed lechery.)   **149 dam** mother   **152 A likely . . . work**
a fine story

work? There; give it your hobbyhorse. [*She gives him* 155
the handkerchief.] Wheresoever you had it, I'll take out
no work on 't.

CASSIO How now, my sweet Bianca? How now? How now?

OTHELLO By heaven, that should be my handkerchief!   159

BIANCA If you'll come to supper tonight, you may; if
you will not, come when you are next prepared for.   161

Exit.

IAGO After her, after her.

CASSIO Faith, I must. She'll rail in the streets else.

IAGO Will you sup there?

CASSIO Faith, I intend so.

IAGO Well, I may chance to see you, for I would very
fain speak with you.

CASSIO Prithee, come. Will you?

IAGO Go to. Say no more.   [*Exit Cassio.*] 169

OTHELLO [*Advancing*] How shall I murder him, Iago?

IAGO Did you perceive how he laughed at his vice?

OTHELLO O, Iago!

IAGO And did you see the handkerchief?

OTHELLO Was that mine?

IAGO Yours, by this hand. And to see how he prizes
the foolish woman your wife! She gave it him, and he
hath given it his whore.

OTHELLO I would have him nine years a-killing. A fine
woman! A fair woman! A sweet woman!

IAGO Nay, you must forget that.

OTHELLO Ay, let her rot, and perish, and be damned
tonight, for she shall not live. No, my heart is turned
to stone; I strike it, and it hurts my hand. O, the world
hath not a sweeter creature! She might lie by an emperor's side and command him tasks.

IAGO Nay, that's not your way.   186

OTHELLO Hang her! I do but say what she is. So delicate
with her needle! An admirable musician! O, she will
sing the savageness out of a bear. Of so high and plenteous wit and invention!   190

---

155 hobbyhorse harlot   **159 should be** must be   **161 when . . . for** when
I'm ready for you (i.e., never)   **169 Go to** (An expression of remonstrance.)   **186 your way** i.e., the way you should think of her
190 invention imagination

IAGO   She's the worse for all this.

OTHELLO   O, a thousand, a thousand times! And then,
of so gentle a condition!   193

IAGO   Ay, too gentle.   194

OTHELLO   Nay, that's certain. But yet the pity of it, Iago!
O, Iago, the pity of it, Iago!

IAGO   If you are so fond over her iniquity, give her patent   197
to offend, for if it touch not you it comes near nobody.

OTHELLO   I will chop her into messes. Cuckold me?   199

IAGO   O, 'tis foul in her.

OTHELLO   With mine officer?

IAGO   That's fouler.

OTHELLO   Get me some poison, Iago, this night. I'll not
expostulate with her, lest her body and beauty un-   204
provide my mind again. This night, Iago.   205

IAGO   Do it not with poison. Strangle her in her bed,
even the bed she hath contaminated.

OTHELLO   Good, good! The justice of it pleases. Very good.

IAGO   And for Cassio, let me be his undertaker. You   209
shall hear more by midnight.

OTHELLO
Excellent good. [*A trumpet within.*] What trumpet is
that same?

IAGO   I warrant, something from Venice.

Enter Lodovico, Desdemona, and attendants.

'Tis Lodovico. This comes from the Duke.
See, your wife's with him.

LODOVICO
God save you, worthy General!

OTHELLO   With all my heart, sir.   215

LODOVICO [*Giving him a letter*]
The Duke and the senators of Venice greet you.

OTHELLO
I kiss the instrument of their pleasures.
                        [*He opens the letter, and reads.*]

---

193 gentle a condition wellborn and wellbred   **194 gentle** generous,
yielding (to other men)   **197 fond** foolish.   **patent** license   **199 messes**
portions of meat, i.e., bits   **204–205 unprovide** weaken, render unfit
209 be his undertaker undertake to dispatch him   **215 With all my
heart** i.e., I thank you most heartily

DESDEMONA
And what's the news, good cousin Lodovico?

IAGO
I am very glad to see you, signor.
Welcome to Cyprus.

LODOVICO
I thank you. How does Lieutenant Cassio?

IAGO   Lives, sir.

DESDEMONA
Cousin, there's fall'n between him and my lord
An unkind breach; but you shall make all well.   224

OTHELLO   Are you sure of that?

DESDEMONA   My lord?

OTHELLO [*Reads*]   "This fail you not to do, as you will—"

LODOVICO
He did not call; he's busy in the paper.
Is there division twixt my lord and Cassio?

DESDEMONA
A most unhappy one. I would do much
T' atone them, for the love I bear to Cassio.   231

OTHELLO   Fire and brimstone!

DESDEMONA   My lord?

OTHELLO   Are you wise?

DESDEMONA
What, is he angry?

LODOVICO   Maybe the letter moved him;
For, as I think, they do command him home,
Deputing Cassio in his government.   237

DESDEMONA   By my troth, I am glad on 't.   238

OTHELLO   Indeed?

DESDEMONA   My lord?

OTHELLO   I am glad to see you mad.   241

DESDEMONA   Why, sweet Othello—

OTHELLO [*Striking her*]   Devil!

DESDEMONA   I have not deserved this.

LODOVICO
My lord, this would not be believed in Venice,

---

224 unkind unnatural, contrary to their natures; hurtful   **231 atone**
reconcile   **237 government** office   **238 on 't** of it   **241 I am . . . mad**
i.e., I am glad to see that you are insane enough to rejoice in Cassio's
promotion (? Othello bitterly plays on Desdemona's *I am glad.*)

Though I should swear I saw 't. 'Tis very much.   246
Make her amends; she weeps.
OTHELLO   O devil, devil!
If that the earth could teem with woman's tears,   248
Each drop she falls would prove a crocodile.   249
Out of my sight!
DESDEMONA   I will not stay to offend you. [*Going.*]
LODOVICO   Truly, an obedient lady.
I do beseech your lordship, call her back.
OTHELLO   Mistress!
DESDEMONA [*Returning*]   My lord?
OTHELLO   What would you with her, sir?   255
LODOVICO   Who, I, my lord?
OTHELLO
Ay, you did wish that I would make her turn.
Sir, she can turn, and turn, and yet go on
And turn again; and she can weep, sir, weep;
And she's obedient, as you say, obedient,   260
Very obedient.—Proceed you in your tears.—
Concerning this, sir—O well-painted passion!—   262
I am commanded home.—Get you away;
I'll send for you anon.—Sir, I obey the mandate
And will return to Venice.—Hence, avaunt!
                              [*Exit Desdemona.*]
Cassio shall have my place. And, sir, tonight
I do entreat that we may sup together.
You are welcome, sir, to Cyprus.—Goats and monkeys! 268
                                        Exit.
LODOVICO
Is this the noble Moor whom our full Senate
Call all in all sufficient? Is this the nature
Whom passion could not shake? Whose solid virtue
The shot of accident nor dart of chance
Could neither graze nor pierce?
IAGO   He is much changed.

246 very much too much, outrageous   **248 teem** breed, be impreg-
nated   **249 falls** lets fall.   **crocodile** (Crocodiles were supposed to weep
hypocritical tears for their victims.)   **255 What . . . sir** (Othello implies
that Desdemona is pliant and will do a *turn*, ll. 257–259, for any man.)
260 obedient (with much the same sexual connotation as *turn* in
ll. 257–259)   **262 passion** i.e., grief   **268 Goats and monkeys** (See
3.3.419.)

LODOVICO
  Are his wits safe? Is he not light of brain?
IAGO
  He's that he is. I may not breathe my censure   275
  What he might be. If what he might he is not,   276
  I would to heaven he were!
LODOVICO   What, strike his wife?   277
IAGO
  Faith, that was not so well; yet would I knew
  That stroke would prove the worst!
LODOVICO   Is it his use?   279
  Or did the letters work upon his blood   280
  And new-create his fault?
IAGO   Alas, alas!
  It is not honesty in me to speak
  What I have seen and known. You shall observe him,
  And his own courses will denote him so
  That I may save my speech. Do but go after,
  And mark how he continues.
LODOVICO
  I am sorry that I am deceived in him.   *Exeunt.*

❖

4.2   *Enter Othello and Emilia.*

OTHELLO   You have seen nothing then?
EMILIA
  Nor ever heard, nor ever did suspect.
OTHELLO
  Yes, you have seen Cassio and she together.
EMILIA
  But then I saw no harm, and then I heard
  Each syllable that breath made up between them.
OTHELLO   What, did they never whisper?
EMILIA   Never, my lord.
OTHELLO   Nor send you out o' the way?

275–277 I may . . . were i.e., I dare not venture an opinion as to whether
he's of unsound mind, as you suggest; but if he isn't, then it might be
better to wish he were in fact insane, since only that could excuse his
wild behavior   **279 use** custom   **280 blood** passions

4.2. Location: The citadel.

EMILIA Never.

OTHELLO
To fetch her fan, her gloves, her mask, nor nothing?

EMILIA Never, my lord.

OTHELLO That's strange.

EMILIA
I durst, my lord, to wager she is honest,
Lay down my soul at stake. If you think other, 14
Remove your thought; it doth abuse your bosom.
If any wretch have put this in your head,
Let heaven requite it with the serpent's curse! 17
For if she be not honest, chaste, and true,
There's no man happy; the purest of their wives
Is foul as slander.

OTHELLO   Bid her come hither. Go.
          Exit Emilia.
She says enough; yet she's a simple bawd 21
That cannot say as much. This is a subtle whore, 22
A closet lock and key of villainous secrets. 23
And yet she'll kneel and pray; I have seen her do 't.

 Enter Desdemona and Emilia.

DESDEMONA My lord, what is your will?

OTHELLO Pray you, chuck, come hither.

DESDEMONA
What is your pleasure?

OTHELLO   Let me see your eyes.
Look in my face.

DESDEMONA   What horrible fancy's this?

OTHELLO [*To Emilia*] Some of your function, mistress. 29
Leave procreants alone and shut the door; 30
Cough or cry "hem" if anybody come.
Your mystery, your mystery! Nay, dispatch. 32
          Exit Emilia.

---

14 at stake as the wager **17 the serpent's curse** the curse pronounced
by God on the serpent for deceiving Eve, just as some man has done to
Othello and Desdemona. (See Genesis 3:14.) **21–22 she's . . . much** i.e.,
any procuress or go-between who couldn't make up as convincing a
story as Emilia's would have to be pretty stupid **22 This** i.e., Desdemona **23 closet lock and key** i.e., concealer **29 Some . . . function** i.e.,
practice your chosen profession, that of bawd (by guarding the door)
30 procreants mating couples **32 mystery** trade, occupation

DESDEMONA [*Kneeling*]
  Upon my knees, what doth your speech import?
  I understand a fury in your words,
  But not the words.
OTHELLO
  Why, what art thou?
DESDEMONA   Your wife, my lord, your true
  And loyal wife.
OTHELLO   Come, swear it, damn thyself,
  Lest, being like one of heaven, the devils themselves   38
  Should fear to seize thee. Therefore be double damned:
  Swear thou art honest.
DESDEMONA   Heaven doth truly know it.
OTHELLO
  Heaven truly knows that thou art false as hell.
DESDEMONA
  To whom, my lord? With whom? How am I false?
OTHELLO [*Weeping*]
  Ah, Desdemon! Away, away, away!
DESDEMONA
  Alas the heavy day! Why do you weep?
  Am I the motive of these tears, my lord?   45
  If haply you my father do suspect
  An instrument of this your calling back,
  Lay not your blame on me. If you have lost him,
  I have lost him too.
OTHELLO   Had it pleased heaven
  To try me with affliction, had they rained   50
  All kinds of sores and shames on my bare head,
  Steeped me in poverty to the very lips,
  Given to captivity me and my utmost hopes,
  I should have found in some place of my soul
  A drop of patience. But, alas, to make me
  A fixèd figure for the time of scorn   56
  To point his slow and moving finger at!   57
  Yet could I bear that too, well, very well.

---

38 being . . . heaven looking like an angel   **45 motive** cause   **50 they**
i.e., heavenly powers   **56 time of scorn** i.e., scornful world   **57 his** its.
slow and moving finger i.e., hour hand of the clock, moving so slowly it
seems hardly to move at all. (Othello envisages himself as being eternally pointed at by the scornful world as the numbers on a clock are
pointed at by the hour hand.)

But there where I have garnered up my heart,   59
Where either I must live or bear no life,
The fountain from the which my current runs   61
Or else dries up—to be discarded thence!
Or keep it as a cistern for foul toads   63
To knot and gender in! Turn thy complexion there,   64
Patience, thou young and rose-lipped cherubin—   65
Ay, there look grim as hell!   66

DESDEMONA

I hope my noble lord esteems me honest.   67

OTHELLO

O, ay, as summer flies are in the shambles,   68
That quicken even with blowing. O thou weed,   69
Who art so lovely fair and smell'st so sweet
That the sense aches at thee, would thou hadst ne'er
    been born!

DESDEMONA

Alas, what ignorant sin have I committed?   72

OTHELLO

Was this fair paper, this most goodly book,
Made to write "whore" upon? What committed?
Committed? O thou public commoner!   75
I should make very forges of my cheeks,
That would to cinders burn up modesty,
Did I but speak thy deeds. What committed?
Heaven stops the nose at it and the moon winks;   79
The bawdy wind, that kisses all it meets,   80
Is hushed within the hollow mine of earth   81
And will not hear 't. What committed?
Impudent strumpet!

DESDEMONA   By heaven, you do me wrong.

OTHELLO   Are not you a strumpet?

DESDEMONA   No, as I am a Christian.

---

59 garnered stored   **61 fountain** spring   **63 cistern** cesspool   **64 knot**
i.e., couple.   **gender** engender.   **Turn . . . there** change your color, grow
pale, at such a sight   **65–66 Patience . . . hell** (Even Patience, that rose-
lipped cherub, will look grim and pale at this spectacle.)   **67 honest**
chaste   **68 shambles** slaughterhouse   **69 quicken** come to life.   **with
blowing** i.e., with the puffing up of something rotten in which maggots
are breeding   **72 ignorant sin** sin in ignorance   **75 commoner** prostitute   **79 winks** closes her eyes. (The moon symbolizes chastity.)
80 bawdy kissing one and all   **81 mine** cave (where the winds were
thought to dwell)

If to preserve this vessel for my lord   86
From any other foul unlawful touch
Be not to be a strumpet, I am none.

OTHELLO   What, not a whore?

DESDEMONA   No, as I shall be saved.

OTHELLO   Is 't possible?

DESDEMONA
O, heaven forgive us!

OTHELLO   I cry you mercy, then.   92
I took you for that cunning whore of Venice
That married with Othello. [*Calling out.*] You, mistress,
That have the office opposite to Saint Peter
And keep the gate of hell!

      Enter Emilia.

                   You, you, ay, you!
We have done our course. There's money for your
    pains.   [*He gives money.*]   97
I pray you, turn the key and keep our counsel.   *Exit.*

EMILIA
Alas, what does this gentleman conceive?   99
How do you, madam? How do you, my good lady?

DESDEMONA   Faith, half asleep.   101

EMILIA
Good madam, what's the matter with my lord?

DESDEMONA   With who?

EMILIA   Why, with my lord, madam.

DESDEMONA
Who is thy lord?

EMILIA   He that is yours, sweet lady.

DESDEMONA
I have none. Do not talk to me, Emilia.
I cannot weep, nor answers have I none
But what should go by water. Prithee, tonight   108
Lay on my bed my wedding sheets, remember;
And call thy husband hither.

EMILIA   Here's a change indeed!   *Exit.*

---

86 vessel i.e., body   **92 cry you mercy** beg your pardon   **97 course**
business (with an indecent suggestion of "trick," turn at sex)
99 conceive suppose, think   **101 half asleep** i.e., dazed   **108 go by**
water be expressed by tears

DESDEMONA

  'Tis meet I should be used so, very meet.   112

  How have I been behaved, that he might stick   113

  The small'st opinion on my least misuse?   114

    Enter Iago and Emilia.

IAGO

  What is your pleasure, madam? How is 't with you?

DESDEMONA

  I cannot tell. Those that do teach young babes

  Do it with gentle means and easy tasks.

  He might have chid me so, for, in good faith,

  I am a child to chiding.

IAGO   What is the matter, lady?

EMILIA

  Alas, Iago, my lord hath so bewhored her,

  Thrown such despite and heavy terms upon her,

  That true hearts cannot bear it.

DESDEMONA   Am I that name, Iago?

IAGO   What name, fair lady?

DESDEMONA

  Such as she said my lord did say I was.

EMILIA

  He called her whore. A beggar in his drink

  Could not have laid such terms upon his callet.   128

IAGO   Why did he so?

DESDEMONA [*Weeping*]

  I do not know. I am sure I am none such.

IAGO   Do not weep, do not weep. Alas the day!

EMILIA

  Hath she forsook so many noble matches,

  Her father and her country and her friends,

  To be called whore? Would it not make one weep?

DESDEMONA

  It is my wretched fortune.

IAGO   Beshrew him for 't!   135

  How comes this trick upon him?

DESDEMONA   Nay, heaven doth know.   136

---

112 meet fitting   **113 stick** attach   **114 opinion** censure.   **least misuse**
slightest misconduct   **128 callet** whore   **135 Beshrew** curse   **136 trick**
strange behavior, delusion

EMILIA

I will be hanged if some eternal villain,   137
Some busy and insinuating rogue,   138
Some cogging, cozening slave, to get some office,   139
Have not devised this slander. I will be hanged else.

IAGO

Fie, there is no such man. It is impossible.

DESDEMONA

If any such there be, heaven pardon him!

EMILIA

A halter pardon him! And hell gnaw his bones!   143
Why should he call her whore? Who keeps her
  company?
What place? What time? What form? What likelihood?   145
The Moor's abused by some most villainous knave,
Some base notorious knave, some scurvy fellow.
O heavens, that such companions thou'dst unfold,   148
And put in every honest hand a whip
To lash the rascals naked through the world
Even from the east to th' west!

IAGO   Speak within door.   151

EMILIA

O, fie upon them! Some such squire he was   152
That turned your wit the seamy side without   153
And made you to suspect me with the Moor.

IAGO

You are a fool. Go to.

DESDEMONA   Alas, Iago,   155
What shall I do to win my lord again?
Good friend, go to him; for, by this light of heaven,
I know not how I lost him. Here I kneel. [*She kneels.*]
If e'er my will did trespass 'gainst his love,
Either in discourse of thought or actual deed,   160
Or that mine eyes, mine ears, or any sense   161
Delighted them in any other form;   162

137 **eternal** inveterate   138 **insinuating** ingratiating, fawning, whee-
dling   139 **cogging** cheating.   **cozening** defrauding   143 **halter** hangman's noose   145 **form** appearance, circumstance   148 **companions**
fellows.   **unfold** expose   151 **within door** i.e., not so loud   152 **squire**
fellow   153 **seamy side without** wrong side out   155 **Go to** i.e., that's
enough   160 **discourse of thought** process of thinking   161 **that** if (also
in l. 163)   162 **Delighted them** took delight

Or that I do not yet, and ever did,   163
And ever will—though he do shake me off
To beggarly divorcement—love him dearly,
Comfort forswear me! Unkindness may do much,   166
And his unkindness may defeat my life,   167
But never taint my love. I cannot say "whore."
It does abhor me now I speak the word;   169
To do the act that might the addition earn   170
Not the world's mass of vanity could make me.   171

IAGO

I pray you, be content. 'Tis but his humor.   172
The business of the state does him offense,
And he does chide with you.

DESDEMONA   If 'twere no other—

IAGO   It is but so, I warrant.   [*Trumpets within.*]
Hark, how these instruments summon you to supper!
The messengers of Venice stays the meat.   178
Go in, and weep not. All things shall be well.

                    Exeunt Desdemona and Emilia.

    Enter Roderigo.

How now, Roderigo?

RODERIGO   I do not find that thou deal'st justly with me.

IAGO   What in the contrary?

RODERIGO   Every day thou daff'st me with some device,   183
Iago, and rather, as it seems to me now, keep'st from
me all conveniency than suppliest me with the least   185
advantage of hope. I will indeed no longer endure it,   186
nor am I yet persuaded to put up in peace what al-   187
ready I have foolishly suffered.

IAGO   Will you hear me, Roderigo?

RODERIGO   Faith, I have heard too much, for your words
and performances are no kin together.

IAGO   You charge me most unjustly.

RODERIGO   With naught but truth. I have wasted myself
out of my means. The jewels you have had from me to

---

163 yet still   **166 Comfort forswear** may heavenly comfort forsake
167 defeat destroy   **169 abhor** (1) fill me with abhorrence (2) make me
whorelike   **170 addition** title   **171 vanity** showy splendor   **172 humor**
mood   **178 stays the meat** are waiting to dine   **183 thou daff'st me** you
put me off.   **device** excuse, trick   **185 conveniency** advantage, opportunity   **186 advantage** increase   **187 put up** submit to, tolerate

deliver Desdemona would half have corrupted a vo- 195
tarist. You have told me she hath received them and 196
returned me expectations and comforts of sudden re- 197
spect and acquaintance, but I find none. 198

IAGO Well, go to, very well.

RODERIGO "Very well"! "Go to"! I cannot go to, man, nor 200
'tis not very well. By this hand, I think it is scurvy, and
begin to find myself fopped in it. 202

IAGO Very well.

RODERIGO I tell you 'tis not very well. I will make myself 204
known to Desdemona. If she will return me my jewels,
I will give over my suit and repent my unlawful solic-
itation; if not, assure yourself I will seek satisfaction 207
of you.

IAGO You have said now? 209

RODERIGO Ay, and said nothing but what I protest in- 210
tendment of doing. 211

IAGO Why, now I see there's mettle in thee, and even
from this instant do build on thee a better opinion
than ever before. Give me thy hand, Roderigo. Thou
hast taken against me a most just exception; but yet I
protest I have dealt most directly in thy affair.

RODERIGO It hath not appeared.

IAGO I grant indeed it hath not appeared, and your suspicion is not without wit and judgment. But, Roderigo, if thou hast that in thee indeed which I have
greater reason to believe now than ever—I mean purpose, courage, and valor—this night show it. If thou
the next night following enjoy not Desdemona, take
me from this world with treachery and devise engines 224
for my life. 225

RODERIGO Well, what is it? Is it within reason and compass?

---

195 deliver deliver to **195–196 votarist** nun **197–198 sudden respect**
immediate consideration **200 I cannot go to** (Roderigo changes Iago's
go to, an expression urging patience, to *I cannot go to,* "I have no
opportunity for sex.") **202 fopped** fooled, duped **204 not very well**
(Roderigo changes Iago's *very well,* "all right, then," to *not very well,*
"not at all good.") **207 satisfaction** repayment. (The term normally
means the settling of accounts in a duel.) **209 You . . . now** have you
finished **210–211 intendment** intention **224–225 engines for** plots
against

IAGO   Sir, there is especial commission come from Venice to depute Cassio in Othello's place.

RODERIGO   Is that true? Why, then Othello and Desdemona return again to Venice.

IAGO   O, no; he goes into Mauritania and takes away
with him the fair Desdemona, unless his abode be
lingered here by some accident; wherein none can be
so determinate as the removing of Cassio.   235

RODERIGO   How do you mean, removing of him?

IAGO   Why, by making him uncapable of Othello's
place—knocking out his brains.

RODERIGO   And that you would have me to do?

IAGO   Ay, if you dare do yourself a profit and a right.
He sups tonight with a harlotry, and thither will I go   241
to him. He knows not yet of his honorable fortune. If
you will watch his going thence, which I will fashion
to fall out between twelve and one, you may take him   244
at your pleasure. I will be near to second your attempt,
and he shall fall between us. Come, stand not amazed
at it, but go along with me. I will show you such a
necessity in his death that you shall think yourself
bound to put it on him. It is now high suppertime,   249
and the night grows to waste. About it.   250

RODERIGO   I will hear further reason for this.

IAGO   And you shall be satisfied.   *Exeunt.*

❖

4.3   *Enter Othello, Lodovico, Desdemona, Emilia,*
           and attendants.

LODOVICO
I do beseech you, sir, trouble yourself no further.

OTHELLO
O, pardon me; 'twill do me good to walk.

LODOVICO
Madam, good night. I humbly thank your ladyship.

---

235 determinate effective   **241 harlotry** slut   **244 fall out** occur
249 high fully   **250 grows to waste** wastes away

4.3. Location: The citadel.

DESDEMONA

Your honor is most welcome.

OTHELLO   Will you walk, sir?

O, Desdemona!

DESDEMONA My lord?

OTHELLO Get you to bed on th' instant. I will be returned forthwith. Dismiss your attendant there. Look 't be done.

DESDEMONA I will, my lord.

        Exit [Othello, with Lodovico and attendants].

EMILIA How goes it now? He looks gentler than he did.

DESDEMONA

He says he will return incontinent,   12

And hath commanded me to go to bed,

And bid me to dismiss you.

EMILIA Dismiss me?

DESDEMONA

It was his bidding. Therefore, good Emilia,

Give me my nightly wearing, and adieu.

We must not now displease him.

EMILIA I would you had never seen him!

DESDEMONA

So would not I. My love doth so approve him

That even his stubbornness, his checks, his frowns— 21

Prithee, unpin me—have grace and favor in them.

        [Emilia prepares Desdemona for bed.]

EMILIA I have laid those sheets you bade me on the bed.

DESDEMONA

All's one. Good faith, how foolish are our minds!   25

If I do die before thee, prithee shroud me

In one of these same sheets.

EMILIA   Come, come, you talk.   27

DESDEMONA

My mother had a maid called Barbary.

She was in love, and he she loved proved mad   29

And did forsake her. She had a song of "Willow."

An old thing 'twas, but it expressed her fortune,

---

12 incontinent immediately **21 stubbornness** roughness. **checks** rebukes **25 All's one** all right. It doesn't really matter **27 talk** i.e., prattle **29 mad** wild, i.e., faithless

And she died singing it. That song tonight
Will not go from my mind; I have much to do   33
But to go hang my head all at one side   34
And sing it like poor Barbary. Prithee, dispatch.

EMILIA   Shall I go fetch your nightgown?   36

DESDEMONA   No, unpin me here.
This Lodovico is a proper man.   38

EMILIA   A very handsome man.

DESDEMONA   He speaks well.

EMILIA   I know a lady in Venice would have walked
barefoot to Palestine for a touch of his nether lip.

DESDEMONA [*Singing*]

> "The poor soul sat sighing by a sycamore tree,
>   Sing all a green willow;   44
> Her hand on her bosom, her head on her knee,
>   Sing willow, willow, willow.
> The fresh streams ran by her and murmured her
>   moans;
>   Sing willow, willow, willow;
> Her salt tears fell from her, and softened the
>   stones—"

Lay by these.
[*Singing.*] "Sing willow, willow, willow—"
Prithee, hie thee. He'll come anon.   52
[*Singing.*] "Sing all a green willow must be my garland.
    Let nobody blame him; his scorn I approve—"
Nay, that's not next.—Hark! Who is 't that knocks?

EMILIA   It's the wind.

DESDEMONA [*Singing*]

> "I called my love false love; but what said he then?
>   Sing willow, willow, willow;
> If I court more women, you'll couch with more
>   men."

So, get thee gone. Good night. Mine eyes do itch;
Doth that bode weeping?

EMILIA   'Tis neither here nor there.

33–34 I . . . hang I can scarcely keep myself from hanging
36 nightgown dressing gown   **38 proper** handsome   **44 willow** (A
conventional emblem of disappointed love.)   **52 hie thee** hurry.   **anon**
right away

DESDEMONA

I have heard it said so. O, these men, these men!
Dost thou in conscience think—tell me, Emilia—
That there be women do abuse their husbands 64
In such gross kind?

EMILIA   There be some such, no question.

DESDEMONA

Wouldst thou do such a deed for all the world?

EMILIA

Why, would not you?

DESDEMONA   No, by this heavenly light!

EMILIA

Nor I neither by this heavenly light;
I might do 't as well i' the dark.

DESDEMONA

Wouldst thou do such a deed for all the world?

EMILIA

The world's a huge thing. It is a great price
For a small vice. `

DESDEMONA

Good troth, I think thou wouldst not.

EMILIA   By my troth, I think I should, and undo 't when
I had done. Marry, I would not do such a thing for a
joint ring, nor for measures of lawn, nor for gowns, 76
petticoats, nor caps, nor any petty exhibition. But for 77
all the whole world! Uds pity, who would not make 78
her husband a cuckold to make him a monarch? I
should venture purgatory for 't.

DESDEMONA

Beshrew me if I would do such a wrong
For the whole world.

EMILIA   Why, the wrong is but a wrong i' the world, and
having the world for your labor, 'tis a wrong in your
own world, and you might quickly make it right.

DESDEMONA

I do not think there is any such woman.

EMILIA   Yes, a dozen, and as many

---

64 abuse deceive   **76 joint ring** a ring made in separate halves.   **lawn**
fine linen   **77 exhibition** gift   **78 Uds** i.e., God's

To th' vantage as would store the world they played for. 88
But I do think it is their husbands' faults
If wives do fall. Say that they slack their duties 90
And pour our treasures into foreign laps, 91
Or else break out in peevish jealousies,
Throwing restraint upon us? Or say they strike us, 93
Or scant our former having in despite? 94
Why, we have galls, and though we have some grace, 95
Yet have we some revenge. Let husbands know
Their wives have sense like them. They see, and smell, 97
And have their palates both for sweet and sour,
As husbands have. What is it that they do
When they change us for others? Is it sport? 100
I think it is. And doth affection breed it? 101
I think it doth. Is 't frailty that thus errs?
It is so too. And have not we affections,
Desires for sport, and frailty, as men have?
Then let them use us well; else let them know,
The ills we do, their ills instruct us so.

DESDEMONA

Good night, good night. God me such uses send 107
Not to pick bad from bad, but by bad mend! 108

                              Exeunt.

❧

---

88 To th' vantage in addition, to boot. **store** populate. **played**
(1) gambled (2) sported sexually **90 duties** marital duties **91 pour . . .
laps** i.e., are unfaithful, give what is rightfully ours (semen) to other
women **93 Throwing . . . us** i.e., jealously restricting our freedom to
see other men **94 scant . . . despite** reduce our allowance to spite us
95 have galls i.e., are capable of resenting injury and insult **97 sense**
physical sense **100 sport** sexual pastime **101 affection** passion
107 uses habit, practice **108 Not . . . mend** i.e., not to learn bad conduct from others' badness (as Emilia has suggested women learn from
men), but to mend my ways by perceiving what badness is, making
spiritual benefit out of evil and adversity

5.1   *Enter Iago and Roderigo.*

IAGO

    Here stand behind this bulk. Straight will he come.   1

    Wear thy good rapier bare, and put it home.   2

    Quick, quick! Fear nothing. I'll be at thy elbow.

    It makes us or it mars us. Think on that,

    And fix most firm thy resolution.

RODERIGO

    Be near at hand. I may miscarry in 't.

IAGO

    Here, at thy hand. Be bold, and take thy stand.

        [Iago stands aside. Roderigo conceals himself.]

RODERIGO

    I have no great devotion to the deed;

    And yet he hath given me satisfying reasons.

    'Tis but a man gone. Forth, my sword! He dies.

                        [He draws.]

IAGO

    I have rubbed this young quat almost to the sense,   11

    And he grows angry. Now, whether he kill Cassio

    Or Cassio him, or each do kill the other,

    Every way makes my gain. Live Roderigo,   14

    He calls me to a restitution large

    Of gold and jewels that I bobbed from him   16

    As gifts to Desdemona.

    It must not be. If Cassio do remain,

    He hath a daily beauty in his life

    That makes me ugly; and besides, the Moor

    May unfold me to him; there stand I in much peril.   21

    No, he must die. Be 't so. I hear him coming.

       Enter Cassio.

RODERIGO *[Coming forth]*

    I know his gait, 'tis he.—Villain, thou diest!

                [He makes a pass at Cassio.]

CASSIO

    That thrust had been mine enemy indeed,

5.1. Location: A street in Cyprus.
1 bulk framework projecting from the front of a shop   **2 bare** unsheathed   **11 quat** pimple, pustule.   **to the sense** to the quick   **14 Live Roderigo** if Roderigo live   **16 bobbed** swindled   **21 unfold** expose

But that my coat is better than thou know'st.   25
I will make proof of thine.

> [*He draws, and wounds Roderigo.*]

RODERIGO   O, I am slain!   [*He falls.*] 26
> [*Iago from behind wounds Cassio
> in the leg, and exit.*]

CASSIO
I am maimed forever. Help, ho! Murder! Murder!

Enter Othello.

OTHELLO
The voice of Cassio! Iago keeps his word.
RODERIGO   O, villain that I am!
OTHELLO   It is even so.
CASSIO   O, help, ho! Light! A surgeon!
OTHELLO
'Tis he. O brave Iago, honest and just,
That hast such noble sense of thy friend's wrong!
Thou teachest me. Minion, your dear lies dead,   34
And your unblest fate hies. Strumpet, I come.   35
Forth of my heart those charms, thine eyes, are blotted; 36
Thy bed, lust-stained, shall with lust's blood be spotted.
> *Exit Othello.*

Enter Lodovico and Gratiano.

CASSIO
What ho! No watch? No passage? Murder! Murder!   38
GRATIANO
'Tis some mischance. The voice is very direful.
CASSIO   O, help!
LODOVICO   Hark!
RODERIGO   O wretched villain!
LODOVICO
Two or three groan. 'Tis heavy night;   43
These may be counterfeits. Let's think 't unsafe
To come in to the cry without more help.   45
> [*They remain near the entrance.*]

25 coat (Possibly a garment of mail under the outer clothing, or simply
a tougher coat than Roderigo expected.) **26 proof** a test **34 Minion**
hussy (i.e., Desdemona) **35 hies** hastens on **36 Forth of** from out
38 passage people passing by **43 heavy** thick, dark **45 come in to**
approach

RODERIGO
  Nobody come? Then shall I bleed to death.

  Enter Iago [in his shirtsleeves, with a light].

LODOVICO   Hark!
GRATIANO
  Here's one comes in his shirt, with light and weapons.
IAGO
  Who's there? Whose noise is this that cries on murder? 49
LODOVICO
  We do not know.
IAGO   Did not you hear a cry?
CASSIO
  Here, here! For heaven's sake, help me!
IAGO   What's the matter?
                           [He moves toward Cassio.]
GRATIANO *[To Lodovico]*
  This is Othello's ancient, as I take it.
LODOVICO *[To Gratiano]*
  The same indeed, a very valiant fellow.
IAGO *[To Cassio]*
  What are you here that cry so grievously?   54
CASSIO
  Iago? O, I am spoiled, undone by villains!   55
  Give me some help.
IAGO
  O me, Lieutenant! What villains have done this?
CASSIO
  I think that one of them is hereabout,
  And cannot make away.
IAGO   O treacherous villains!   59
  [To Lodovico and Gratiano.] What are you there? Come
    in, and give some help.   *[They advance.]*
RODERIGO   O, help me there!
CASSIO
  That's one of them.
IAGO   O murderous slave! O villain!
                         [He stabs Roderigo.]
RODERIGO
  O damned Iago! O inhuman dog!

49 cries on cries out   **54 What** who (also at ll. 60 and 66)   **55 spoiled** ruined, done for   **59 make** get

IAGO
  Kill men i' the dark?—Where be these bloody thieves?—
  How silent is this town!—Ho! Murder, murder!—
  [*To Lodovico and Gratiano.*] What may you be? Are you
    of good or evil?
LODOVICO As you shall prove us, praise us.   67
IAGO Signor Lodovico?
LODOVICO He, sir.
IAGO
  I cry you mercy. Here's Cassio hurt by villains.   70
GRATIANO Cassio?
IAGO How is 't, brother?
CASSIO My leg is cut in two.
IAGO Marry, heaven forbid!
  Light, gentlemen! I'll bind it with my shirt.
                 [*He hands them the light, and tends*
                          to Cassio's wound.]
    Enter Bianca.

BIANCA
  What is the matter, ho? Who is 't that cried?
IAGO Who is 't that cried?
BIANCA   O my dear Cassio!
  My sweet Cassio! O Cassio, Cassio, Cassio!
IAGO
  O notable strumpet! Cassio, may you suspect
  Who they should be that have thus mangled you?
CASSIO No.
GRATIANO
  I am sorry to find you thus. I have been to seek you.
IAGO
  Lend me a garter. [*He applies a tourniquet.*] So.—O,
    for a chair,   83
  To bear him easily hence!
BIANCA
  Alas, he faints! O Cassio, Cassio, Cassio!
IAGO
  Gentlemen all, I do suspect this trash
  To be a party in this injury.—
  Patience awhile, good Cassio.—Come, come;

67 praise appraise   **70 I cry you mercy** I beg your pardon   **83 chair**
litter

Lend me a light. [*He shines the light on Roderigo.*] Know
    we this face or no?
Alas, my friend and my dear countryman
Roderigo! No.—Yes, sure.—O heaven! Roderigo!

GRATIANO   What, of Venice?

IAGO   Even he, sir. Did you know him?

GRATIANO   Know him? Ay.

IAGO
  Signor Gratiano? I cry your gentle pardon.   95
  These bloody accidents must excuse my manners   96
  That so neglected you.

GRATIANO   I am glad to see you.

IAGO
  How do you, Cassio? O, a chair, a chair!

GRATIANO   Roderigo!

IAGO
  He, he, 'tis he. [*A litter is brought in.*] O, that's well said;
    the chair.   100
  Some good man bear him carefully from hence;
  I'll fetch the General's surgeon. [*To Bianca.*] For you,
    mistress,
  Save you your labor.—He that lies slain here, Cassio,   103
  Was my dear friend. What malice was between you?   104

CASSIO
  None in the world, nor do I know the man.

IAGO [*To Bianca*]
  What, look you pale?—O, bear him out o' th' air.   106
              [*Cassio and Roderigo are borne off.*]
  Stay you, good gentlemen.—Look you pale, mistress?—   107
  Do you perceive the gastness of her eye?—   108
  Nay, if you stare, we shall hear more anon.—   109
  Behold her well; I pray you, look upon her.
  Do you see, gentlemen? Nay, guiltiness
  Will speak, though tongues were out of use.

      [*Enter Emilia.*]

---

95 gentle noble   **96 accidents** sudden events   **100 well said** well done
103 Save . . . labor i.e., never you mind tending Cassio   **104 malice**
enmity   **106 bear . . . air** (Fresh air was thought to be dangerous for a
wound.)   **107 Stay you** (Lodovico and Gratiano are evidently about to
leave.)   **108 gastness** terror   **109 stare** (Iago pretends to interpret
Bianca's wild looks as an involuntary confession of guilt.)

EMILIA

'Las, what's the matter? What's the matter, husband?

IAGO

Cassio hath here been set on in the dark
By Roderigo and fellows that are scaped.
He's almost slain, and Roderigo dead.

EMILIA

Alas, good gentleman! Alas, good Cassio!

IAGO

This is the fruits of whoring. Prithee, Emilia,
Go know of Cassio where he supped tonight.   119
[*To Bianca.*] What, do you shake at that?

BIANCA

He supped at my house, but I therefore shake not.

IAGO

O, did he so? I charge you go with me.

EMILIA   O, fie upon thee, strumpet!

BIANCA

I am no strumpet, but of life as honest   124
As you that thus abuse me.

EMILIA   As I? Faugh! Fie upon thee!

IAGO

Kind gentlemen, let's go see poor Cassio dressed.—   127
Come, mistress, you must tell 's another tale.
Emilia, run you to the citadel
And tell my lord and lady what hath happed.—
Will you go on afore? [*Aside.*] This is the night
That either makes me or fordoes me quite.   *Exeunt.* 132

❖

5.2   *Enter Othello [with a light], and Desdemona in
            her bed.*

OTHELLO

It is the cause, it is the cause, my soul.   1
Let me not name it to you, you chaste stars!
It is the cause. Yet I'll not shed her blood,

---

119 know learn   **124 honest** chaste   **127 Cassio dressed** Cassio's
wounds dressed   **132 fordoes** undoes, ruins

5.2. Location: A bedchamber in the citadel.
s.d. in her bed (The bed is presumably "thrust out" onstage as the
scene begins.)   **1 cause** i.e., cause of justice, the offense itself, which
Othello must correct as an agent of justice

Nor scar that whiter skin of hers than snow,
And smooth as monumental alabaster.　　　　　　　　5
Yet she must die, else she'll betray more men.
Put out the light, and then put out the light.　　　　7
If I quench thee, thou flaming minister,　　　　　　8
I can again thy former light restore,
Should I repent me; but once put out thy light,　　　10
Thou cunning'st pattern of excelling nature,　　　　11
I know not where is that Promethean heat　　　　　12
That can thy light relume. When I have plucked thy rose,　13
I cannot give it vital growth again;
It needs must wither. I'll smell thee on the tree.
　　　　　　　　　　　　　　　　　[*He kisses her.*]
O balmy breath, that dost almost persuade
Justice to break her sword! One more, one more.
Be thus when thou art dead, and I will kill thee,
And love thee after. One more, and that's the last.
　　　　　　　　　　　　　　　　　[*He kisses her.*]
So sweet was ne'er so fatal. I must weep,
But they are cruel tears. This sorrow's heavenly;　　21
It strikes where it doth love. She wakes.　　　　　22
DESDEMONA　Who's there? Othello?
OTHELLO　Ay, Desdemona.
DESDEMONA　Will you come to bed, my lord?
OTHELLO　Have you prayed tonight, Desdemon?
DESDEMONA　Ay, my lord.
OTHELLO
If you bethink yourself of any crime　　　　　　　28
Unreconciled as yet to heaven and grace,
Solicit for it straight.　　　　　　　　　　　　30
DESDEMONA
Alack, my lord, what may you mean by that?
OTHELLO
Well, do it, and be brief. I will walk by.

---

5 monumental i.e., used in making tombs and funeral monuments
7 the light . . . light the torch or lamp . . . Desdemona's life　**8 flaming**
minister torch or lamp that serves me　**10 repent me** change my
mind　**11 Thou . . . pattern** you skillfully wrought perfect example
12 Promethean heat divine fire. (Alluding to the theft of fire from
heaven by Prometheus.)　**13 relume** rekindle　**21 cruel** unrelenting
22 It . . . love (Compare Hebrews 12:6: "For whom the Lord loveth he
chasteneth.")　**28 crime** sin　**30 Solicit** petition, pray.　**straight**
immediately

I would not kill thy unpreparèd spirit.
No, heaven forfend! I would not kill thy soul. 34

DESDEMONA
Talk you of killing?

OTHELLO   Ay, I do.

DESDEMONA   Then heaven
Have mercy on me!

OTHELLO   Amen, with all my heart!

DESDEMONA
If you say so, I hope you will not kill me.

OTHELLO   Humh!

DESDEMONA
And yet I fear you; for you're fatal then
When your eyes roll so. Why I should fear I know not,
Since guiltiness I know not; but yet I feel I fear.

OTHELLO
Think on thy sins.

DESDEMONA   They are loves I bear to you. 42

OTHELLO   Ay, and for that thou diest.

DESDEMONA
That death's unnatural that kills for loving.
Alas, why gnaw you so your nether lip?
Some bloody passion shakes your very frame.
These are portents; but yet I hope, I hope,
They do not point on me. 48

OTHELLO   Peace, and be still!

DESDEMONA   I will so. What's the matter?

OTHELLO
That handkerchief which I so loved and gave thee
Thou gav'st to Cassio.

DESDEMONA   No, by my life and soul!
Send for the man and ask him.

OTHELLO
Sweet soul, take heed, take heed of perjury.
Thou art on thy deathbed.

DESDEMONA
Ay, but not yet to die.

OTHELLO   Yes, presently. 56

---

34 forfend forbid **42 They are . . . you** i.e., if I sinned, it was in loving you more than my father, or more than God **48 point on** point at, predict what is to happen to **56 presently** immediately

Therefore confess thee freely of thy sin;
For to deny each article with oath
Cannot remove nor choke the strong conception   59
That I do groan withal. Thou art to die.   60

DESDEMONA
Then Lord have mercy on me!

OTHELLO   I say, amen.

DESDEMONA
And have you mercy too! I never did
Offend you in my life; never loved Cassio   63
But with such general warranty of heaven   64
As I might love. I never gave him token.

OTHELLO
By heaven, I saw my handkerchief in 's hand.
O perjured woman! Thou dost stone my heart,   67
And makes me call what I intend to do
A murder, which I thought a sacrifice.
I saw the handkerchief.

DESDEMONA   He found it, then.
I never gave it him. Send for him hither;
Let him confess a truth.

OTHELLO   He hath confessed.

DESDEMONA What, my lord?

OTHELLO
That he hath used thee.

DESDEMONA   How? Unlawfully?

OTHELLO   Ay.

DESDEMONA
He will not say so.

OTHELLO   No, his mouth is stopped;
Honest Iago hath ta'en order for 't.   76

DESDEMONA
O, my fear interprets. What, is he dead?

OTHELLO
Had all his hairs been lives, my great revenge
Had stomach for them all.

DESDEMONA
Alas, he is betrayed and I undone!   [*She weeps.*]

---

59 conception (1) belief in your guilt (2) plan in my mind   **60 groan
withal** (1) groan at in sorrow (2) groan as in giving birth   **63 Offend**
wrong   **64 warranty** sanction   **67 stone** turn to stone, harden   **76 ta'en
order** taken measures

OTHELLO
  Out, strumpet! Weep'st thou for him to my face?
DESDEMONA
  O, banish me, my lord, but kill me not!
OTHELLO   Down, strumpet!
DESDEMONA
  Kill me tomorrow; let me live tonight!
OTHELLO   Nay, if you strive—
DESDEMONA
  But half an hour!
OTHELLO   Being done, there is no pause.   86
DESDEMONA
  But while I say one prayer!
OTHELLO   It is too late.
                                    Smothers her.
EMILIA (*At the door*)
  My lord, my lord! What ho! My lord, my lord!
OTHELLO
  What noise is this? Not dead? Not yet quite dead?
  I that am cruel am yet merciful;
  I would not have thee linger in thy pain.
                          [*He dispatches her.*]
  So, so.
EMILIA (*Within*)   What ho! My lord, my lord!
OTHELLO   Who's there?
EMILIA [*Within*]
  O, good my lord, I would speak a word with you!
OTHELLO
  Yes, 'tis Emilia.—By and by.—She's dead.
  'Tis like she comes to speak of Cassio's death.—   95
  The noise was here. Ha! No more moving?   96
  Still as the grave. Shall she come in? Were 't good?—
  I think she stirs again. No. What's best to do?
  If she come in, she'll sure speak to my wife.
  My wife! My wife! What wife? I have no wife.
  O, insupportable! O heavy hour!
  Methinks it should be now a huge eclipse

---

86 Being done i.e., since justice has begun its relentless course   **95 like**
likely that   **96 here** (The Folio's *high* is possible, suggesting that the
commotion of the attack on Cassio was loud.)

Of sun and moon, and that th' affrighted globe
Should yawn at alteration.

EMILIA [*Within*]   I do beseech you   104
That I may speak with you, O, good my lord!

OTHELLO
I had forgot thee. O, come in, Emilia.—
Soft, by and by. Let me the curtains draw.—   107

> [*He closes the bed-curtains and
> opens the door.*]

Where art thou?

> *Enter Emilia.*

                    What's the matter with thee now?

EMILIA
O, my good lord, yonder's foul murders done!

OTHELLO   What, now?

EMILIA   But now, my lord.

OTHELLO
It is the very error of the moon;   112
She comes more nearer earth than she was wont,
And makes men mad.

EMILIA
Cassio, my lord, hath killed a young Venetian
Called Roderigo.

OTHELLO   Roderigo killed?
And Cassio killed?

EMILIA   No, Cassio is not killed.

OTHELLO
Not Cassio killed? Then murder's out of tune,
And sweet revenge grows harsh.

DESDEMONA   O, falsely, falsely murdered!

EMILIA   O Lord, what cry is that?

OTHELLO   That? What?

EMILIA
Out and alas, that was my lady's voice.   123

> [*She opens the bed-curtains.*]

---

104 yawn gape in amazement, i.e., move in an earthquake. (According to
Pliny, earthquakes often happen during eclipses.)   **at alteration** at these
cataclysmic events in nature, well suited to express the horror of Desdemona's death   **107 Soft** wait a minute   **112 error** aberration, irregular-
ity   **123 Out** (A cry of dismay, intensifying *alas*.)

Help, help, ho, help! O lady, speak again!
Sweet Desdemona! O sweet mistress, speak!
DESDEMONA   A guiltless death I die.
EMILIA   O, who hath done this deed?
DESDEMONA   Nobody; I myself. Farewell.
Commend me to my kind lord. O, farewell! [*She dies.*]
OTHELLO
Why, how should she be murdered?
EMILIA   Alas, who knows?
OTHELLO
You heard her say herself it was not I.
EMILIA
She said so. I must needs report the truth.
OTHELLO
She's like a liar gone to burning hell!
'Twas I that killed her.
EMILIA   O, the more angel she,
And you the blacker devil!
OTHELLO
She turned to folly, and she was a whore.   136
EMILIA
Thou dost belie her, and thou art a devil.   137
OTHELLO   She was false as water.
EMILIA   Thou art rash as fire to say
That she was false. O, she was heavenly true!
OTHELLO
Cassio did top her. Ask thy husband else.   141
O, I were damned beneath all depth in hell
But that I did proceed upon just grounds
To this extremity. Thy husband knew it all.
EMILIA   My husband?
OTHELLO   Thy husband.
EMILIA   That she was false to wedlock?
OTHELLO
Ay, with Cassio. Nay, had she been true,
If heaven would make me such another world
Of one entire and perfect chrysolite,   150
I'd not have sold her for it.
EMILIA   My husband?

---

136 folly i.e., wantonness, fleshly sin   **137 belie** slander   **141 else** i.e., if
you don't believe me   **150 chrysolite** precious topaz

OTHELLO
    Ay, 'twas he that told me on her first.
    An honest man he is, and hates the slime
    That sticks on filthy deeds.
EMILIA   My husband?
OTHELLO
    What needs this iterance, woman? I say thy husband.   157
EMILIA
    O mistress, villainy hath made mocks with love!   158
    My husband say she was false?
OTHELLO   He, woman;
    I say thy husband. Dost understand the word?
    My friend, thy husband, honest, honest Iago.
EMILIA
    If he say so, may his pernicious soul
    Rot half a grain a day! He lies to th' heart.
    She was too fond of her most filthy bargain.
OTHELLO   Ha?   [*He draws.*]
EMILIA   Do thy worst!
    This deed of thine is no more worthy heaven
    Than thou wast worthy her.
OTHELLO   Peace, you were best.   168
EMILIA
    Thou hast not half that power to do me harm
    As I have to be hurt. O gull! O dolt!   170
    As ignorant as dirt! Thou hast done a deed—
    I care not for thy sword; I'll make thee known,
    Though I lost twenty lives.—Help! Help, ho, help!
    The Moor hath killed my mistress! Murder, murder!

        Enter Montano, Gratiano, and Iago.

MONTANO
    What is the matter? How now, General?
EMILIA
    O, are you come, Iago? You have done well,
    That men must lay their murders on your neck.
GRATIANO   What is the matter?
EMILIA [*To Iago*]
    Disprove this villain, if thou be'st a man.

---

157 iterance iteration, repetition   **158 made mocks with** derided, made
sport of   **168 you were best** it would be best for you   **170 to be hurt**
i.e., to endure hurt.   **gull** dupe

He says thou toldst him that his wife was false.
I know thou didst not; thou'rt not such a villain.
Speak, for my heart is full.

IAGO
I told him what I thought, and told no more
Than what he found himself was apt and true.   184

EMILIA
But did you ever tell him she was false?

IAGO   I did.

EMILIA
You told a lie, an odious, damnèd lie!
Upon my soul, a lie, a wicked lie.
She false with Cassio? Did you say with Cassio?

IAGO
With Cassio, mistress. Go to, charm your tongue.   190

EMILIA
I will not charm my tongue; I am bound to speak.
My mistress here lies murdered in her bed—

ALL   O heavens forfend!

EMILIA
And your reports have set the murder on.

OTHELLO
Nay, stare not, masters. It is true indeed.

GRATIANO   'Tis a strange truth.

MONTANO
O monstrous act!

EMILIA   Villainy, villainy, villainy!
I think upon 't—I think I smell 't! O villainy!
I thought so then—I'll kill myself for grief—   199
O villainy, villainy!

IAGO
What, are you mad? I charge you, get you home.

EMILIA
Good gentlemen, let me have leave to speak.
'Tis proper I obey him, but not now.
Perchance, Iago, I will ne'er go home.

---

184 apt plausible   **190 charm** keep silent (as though by a magic spell)
199 then (Perhaps at 3.3.331–332 and 4.2.137–154.)

OTHELLO
O! O! O!   *[Othello falls on the bed.]*

EMILIA   Nay, lay thee down and roar,   205
For thou hast killed the sweetest innocent
That e'er did lift up eye.

OTHELLO *[Rising]*   O, she was foul!   207
I scarce did know you, uncle. There lies your niece,
Whose breath indeed these hands have newly stopped.
I know this act shows horrible and grim.   210

GRATIANO
Poor Desdemon! I am glad thy father's dead.
Thy match was mortal to him, and pure grief
Shore his old thread in twain. Did he live now,   213
This sight would make him do a desperate turn,   214
Yea, curse his better angel from his side,
And fall to reprobance.   216

OTHELLO
'Tis pitiful. But yet Iago knows
That she with Cassio hath the act of shame
A thousand times committed. Cassio confessed it;
And she did gratify his amorous works   220
With that recognizance and pledge of love   221
Which I first gave her. I saw it in his hand;
It was a handkerchief, an antique token
My father gave my mother.

EMILIA   O God! O heavenly God!

IAGO
Zounds, hold your peace.

EMILIA   'Twill out, 'twill out! I peace?
No, I will speak as liberal as the north.   227
Let heaven and men and devils, let them all,
All, all, cry shame against me, yet I'll speak.

IAGO
Be wise, and get you home.

---

205 s.d. Othello . . . bed (This direction is from the quarto, as also *He kisses her* at l. 19 and *She dies* at l. 129.) **207 lift up eye** i.e., lift her eyes to heaven **210 shows** looks **213 Shore** sheared, cut **214 turn** deed **216 reprobance** damnation, i.e., suicide **220 gratify** reward **221 recognizance** token **227 liberal as the north** freely as the north wind (blows)

EMILIA   I will not.
                            [*Iago threatens Emilia.*]
GRATIANO   Fie,
   Your sword upon a woman?
EMILIA
   O thou dull Moor! That handkerchief thou speak'st of
   I found by fortune and did give my husband;
   For often, with a solemn earnestness,
   More than indeed belonged to such a trifle,   235
   He begged of me to steal 't.
IAGO   Villainous whore!
EMILIA
   She give it Cassio? No, alas! I found it,
   And I did give 't my husband.
IAGO   Filth, thou liest!
EMILIA
   By heaven, I do not, I do not, gentlemen.
   O murderous coxcomb! What should such a fool   240
   Do with so good a wife?
OTHELLO   Are there no stones in heaven   242
   But what serves for the thunder?—Precious villain! 243
           [*He runs at Iago; Montano disarms Othello.
             Iago, from behind, stabs Emilia.*]
GRATIANO
   The woman falls! Sure he hath killed his wife.
EMILIA
   Ay, ay. O, lay me by my mistress' side.
                                    [*Exit Iago.*]
GRATIANO   He's gone, but his wife's killed.
MONTANO
   'Tis a notorious villain. Take you this weapon,
   Which I have here recovered from the Moor.
   Come, guard the door without. Let him not pass,
   But kill him rather. I'll after that same villain,
   For 'tis a damnèd slave.
                   *Exit [with all but Othello and Emilia,
                    who has been laid by Desdemona's side*].

---

235 belonged was appropriate   **240 coxcomb** fool. (Addressed to
Othello.)   **242 stones** bolts, such as those used for thunderbolts
243 Precious i.e., arrant, utter   **s.d. He . . . Emilia** (The quarto text
reads, "The Moor runs at Iago. Iago kills his wife." The quarto also
specifies the exit of Iago at l. 245 and the death of Emilia at l. 260.)

OTHELLO   I am not valiant neither,
  But every puny whipster gets my sword.   253
  But why should honor outlive honesty?   254
  Let it go all.
EMILIA   What did thy song bode, lady?
  Hark, canst thou hear me? I will play the swan,
  And die in music. [*She sings.*] "Willow, willow, willow."
  Moor, she was chaste. She loved thee, cruel Moor.
  So come my soul to bliss as I speak true.
  So speaking as I think, alas, I die.   [*She dies.*]
OTHELLO
  I have another weapon in this chamber;
  It was a sword of Spain, the ice-brook's temper—   262
  O, here it is. [*He finds a sword.*] Uncle, I must come forth.
GRATIANO [*Within*]
  If thou attempt it, it will cost thee dear.
  Thou hast no weapon, and perforce must suffer.
OTHELLO
  Look in upon me then and speak with me,
  Or, naked as I am, I will assault thee.   267

        [*Enter Gratiano.*]

GRATIANO
  What is the matter?
OTHELLO   Behold, I have a weapon;
  A better never did itself sustain
  Upon a soldier's thigh. I have seen the day
  That, with this little arm and this good sword,
  I have made my way through more impediments
  Than twenty times your stop. But O, vain boast!   273
  Who can control his fate? 'Tis not so now.
  Be not afraid, though you do see me weaponed;
  Here is my journey's end, here is my butt   276
  And very seamark of my utmost sail.   277
                        [*Gratiano steps back.*]
  Do you go back dismayed? 'Tis a lost fear;   278

---

253 whipster contemptible fellow   **254 honor** i.e., the bravery for which
one enjoys a soldier's reputation.   **honesty** true integrity   **262 the ice-
brook's temper** tempered in ice-cold water   **267 naked** unarmed
273 stop power (to stop)   **276 butt** goal, limit. (An archery term.)
277 seamark beacon (marking his destination or limit)   **278 lost** wasted,
unneeded

Man but a rush against Othello's breast   279
And he retires. Where should Othello go?
                    [*He turns to Desdemona.*]
Now, how dost thou look now? O ill-starred wench!
Pale as thy smock! When we shall meet at compt,   282
This look of thine will hurl my soul from heaven,
And fiends will snatch at it. Cold, cold, my girl?
Even like thy chastity. O cursèd, cursèd slave!   285
Whip me, ye devils,
From the possession of this heavenly sight!
Blow me about in winds! Roast me in sulfur!
Wash me in steep-down gulfs of liquid fire!
O Desdemon! Dead, Desdemon! Dead! O! O!   290

    Enter Lodovico, Cassio [carried in a litter],
    Montano, and Iago [prisoner], with officers.

LODOVICO
Where is this rash and most unfortunate man?
OTHELLO
That's he that was Othello. Here I am.
LODOVICO
Where is that viper? Bring the villain forth.
                    [*Iago is led forward.*]

OTHELLO
I look down towards his feet; but that's a fable.   294
If that thou be'st a devil, I cannot kill thee.
                    [*He wounds Iago.*]
LODOVICO
Wrench his sword from him.   [*Othello is disarmed.*]
IAGO   I bleed, sir, but not killed.
OTHELLO
I am not sorry neither. I'd have thee live,
For in my sense 'tis happiness to die.   298
LODOVICO
O thou Othello, that was once so good,
Fall'n in the practice of a cursèd slave,   300
What shall be said to thee?

---

279 Man . . . rush wield no more than a reed   **282 compt** account,
judgment day   **285 slave** i.e., Othello himself   **290 s.d. in a litter** (The
quarto specifies that Cassio is "in a chair.")   **294 towards his feet** i.e.,
to see if they are cloven like the devil's   **298 in my sense** to one who
feel as I do   **300 in the practice** through the plotting.   **slave** villain

OTHELLO   Why, anything.
  An honorable murderer, if you will,
  For naught I did in hate, but all in honor.
LODOVICO
  This wretch hath part confessed his villainy.
  Did you and he consent in Cassio's death?   305
OTHELLO   Ay.
CASSIO
  Dear General, I never gave you cause.
OTHELLO
  I do believe it, and I ask your pardon.
  Will you, I pray, demand that demi-devil
  Why he hath thus ensnared my soul and body?
IAGO
  Demand me nothing. What you know, you know.
  From this time forth I never will speak word.
LODOVICO   What, not to pray?
GRATIANO   Torments will ope your lips.   314
OTHELLO   Well, thou dost best.
LODOVICO
  Sir, you shall understand what hath befall'n,
  Which, as I think, you know not. Here is a letter
  Found in the pocket of the slain Roderigo;
  And here another. [*He produces letters.*] The one of them
    imports
  The death of Cassio, to be undertook
  By Roderigo.
OTHELLO
  O villain!
CASSIO   Most heathenish and most gross!   322
LODOVICO [*Showing another paper*]
  Now here's another discontented paper   323
  Found in his pocket too. And this, it seems,
  Roderigo meant t' have sent this damnèd villain;
  But that belike Iago in the interim   326
  Came in and satisfied him.   327
OTHELLO   O thou pernicious caitiff!—
  How came you, Cassio, by that handkerchief
  That was my wife's?

305 consent agree　**314 Torments** torture　**322 gross** monstrous　**323 discontented** full of discontent　**326 belike** most likely　**327 Came in** interposed

CASSIO   I found it in my chamber;
   And he himself confessed it but even now
   That there he dropped it for a special purpose
   Which wrought to his desire.
OTHELLO   O fool, fool, fool!   333
CASSIO
   There is besides in Roderigo's letter
   How he upbraids Iago, that he made him
   Brave me upon the watch, whereon it came   336
   That I was cast; and even but now he spake,   337
   After long seeming dead, Iago hurt him,
   Iago set him on.
LODOVICO [*To Othello*]
   You must forsake this room and go with us.
   Your power and your command is taken off,   341
   And Cassio rules in Cyprus. For this slave,
   If there be any cunning cruelty
   That can torment him much and hold him long,   344
   It shall be his. You shall close prisoner rest   345
   Till that the nature of your fault be known
   To the Venetian state.—Come, bring away.
OTHELLO
   Soft you; a word or two before you go.   348
   I have done the state some service, and they know 't.
   No more of that. I pray you, in your letters,
   When you shall these unlucky deeds relate,   351
   Speak of me as I am; nothing extenuate,
   Nor set down aught in malice. Then must you speak
   Of one that loved not wisely but too well;
   Of one not easily jealous but, being wrought,   355
   Perplexed in the extreme; of one whose hand,   356
   Like the base Indian, threw a pearl away   357

---

333 wrought . . . desire worked out as he wished, fitted in with his
plan   **336 Brave** defy   **337 cast** dismissed   **341 taken off** taken away
344 hold him long keep him alive a long time (during his torture)
345 rest remain   **348 Soft you** one moment   **351 unlucky** unfortunate
355 wrought worked upon   **356 Perplexed** distraught   **357 Indian** (This
reading from the quarto pictures an ignorant savage who cannot recognize the value of a precious jewel. The Folio reading, *Iudean* or *Judean*,
i.e., infidel or disbeliever, may refer to Herod, who slew Miriamne in a
fit of jealousy, or to Judas Iscariot, the betrayer of Christ.)

Richer than all his tribe; of one whose subdued eyes,   358
Albeit unusèd to the melting mood,
Drops tears as fast as the Arabian trees
Their medicinable gum. Set you down this;   361
And say besides that in Aleppo once,
Where a malignant and a turbaned Turk
Beat a Venetian and traduced the state,
I took by th' throat the circumcisèd dog
And smote him, thus.   [*He stabs himself.*] 366
LODOVICO O bloody period!   367
GRATIANO All that is spoke is marred.
OTHELLO
  I kissed thee ere I killed thee. No way but this,
  Killing myself, to die upon a kiss.
                            [*He kisses Desdemona and*] *dies.*

CASSIO
  This did I fear, but thought he had no weapon;
  For he was great of heart.
LODOVICO [*To Iago*]   O Spartan dog,   372
  More fell than anguish, hunger, or the sea!   373
  Look on the tragic loading of this bed.
  This is thy work. The object poisons sight;
  Let it be hid. Gratiano, keep the house,   376
                      [*The bed-curtains are drawn*]
  And seize upon the fortunes of the Moor,   377
  For they succeed on you. [*To Cassio.*] To you, Lord
    Governor,   378
  Remains the censure of this hellish villain,   379
  The time, the place, the torture. O, enforce it!
  Myself will straight aboard, and to the state
  This heavy act with heavy heart relate.   *Exeunt.*

---

358 subdued i.e., overcome by grief   **361 gum** i.e., myrrh   **366 s.d. He stabs himself** (This direction is in the quarto text.)   **367 period** termination, conclusion   **372 Spartan dog** (Spartan dogs were noted for their savagery and silence.)   **373 fell** cruel   **376 Let it be hid** i.e., draw the bed-curtains. (No stage direction specifies that the dead are to be carried offstage at the end of the play.)   **keep** remain in   **377 seize upon** take legal possession of   **378 succeed on** pass as though by inheritance to   **379 censure** sentencing

Date and Text

On October 6, 1621, Thomas Walkley entered in the Stationers' Register, the official record book of the London Company of Stationers (booksellers and printers), "The Tragedie of Othello, the moore of Venice," and published the play in the following year:

> THE Tragoedy of Othello, The Moore of Venice. *As it hath beene diuerse times acted at the* Globe, and at the Black-Friers, by *his Maiesties Seruants. Written by* VVilliam Shakespeare. LONDON, Printed by *N. O.* [Nicholas Okes] for *Thomas Walkley*, and are to be sold at his shop, at the Eagle and Child, in Brittans Bursse. 1622.

The text of this quarto is a good one, based probably on a transcript of Shakespeare's foul papers (working manuscript), although it is some 160 lines shorter than the Folio text of 1623 and may have been cut in the printing house to meet the constraints of space when the printer's copy was allocated to a fixed number of pages. The Folio text may have been derived (via an intermediate transcript) from a copy of the original foul papers, one in which Shakespeare himself copied over his work and made a large number of synonymous or nearly synonymous changes as he did so. These papers, edited by someone else to remove profanity as required by law and introducing other stylistic changes in the process, seemingly became the basis of the promptbook and also of the Folio text.

The textual situation is thus complex. The Folio text appears to contain a significant number of authorial changes, but it was also worked on by one or more sophisticating scribes and by compositors whose changes are sometimes hard to distinguish from those of Shakespeare. The quarto text was printed by a printing establishment not known for careful work, but does stand close in some ways to a Shakespearean original. Editorially, then, the Folio's readings are to be preferred when the quarto is not clearly right and especially when the Folio gives us genuinely new words; but the quarto's readings demand careful consideration when the Folio text may be suspected of mechanical error (e.g., the shortening of words in full lines) or compositorial substitution of alternative forms, normalizations, and easy adjustments of meter. There are times when the Folio's compositor may have been misled by nearby words or letters in his copy. And because the Folio's stage directions are probably scribal, attention should be paid to those in the quarto.

The earliest mention of the play is on "Hallamas Day, being the first of Nouembar," 1604, when "the Kings Maiesties plaiers" performed "A Play in the Banketinge house att Whit Hall Called The Moor of Venis." The play is attributed to "Shaxberd." The authenticity of this Revels account, first printed by Peter Cunningham in 1842, was once challenged, but it is now accepted as genuine. On stylistic grounds the play is usually dated in 1603 or 1604, although arguments are sometimes presented for a date as early as 1601 or 1602.

Textual Notes

These textual notes are not a historical collation, either of the early quartos and folios or of more recent editions; they are simply a record of departures in this edition from the copy text. The reading adopted in this edition appears in boldface, followed by the rejected reading from the copy text, i.e., the First Folio. Only major alterations in punctuation are noted. Changes in lineation are not indicated, nor are some minor and obvious typographical errors.

Abbreviations used:
F the First Folio
Q1 the quarto of 1622
s.d. stage direction
s.p. speech prefix

Copy text: the First Folio. The adopted readings are from the quarto of 1622 [Q1], unless otherwise indicated; [eds.] means that the adopted reading was first proposed by some editor subsequent to the First Folio.

1.1. 1 **Tush, never** Neuer 4 **'Sblood, but** but 16 **And, in conclusion** [Q1; not in F] 26 **togaed** Tongued 30 **other** others 34 **God bless** blesse 68 **full fall** thick-lips **thick-lips** Thick-lips 74 **changes** chances 75 **[and elsewhere] lose** [eds.] loose 81 **Thieves, thieves, thieves** Theeues, Theeues 83 s.d. **Brabantio above** [in F, printed as a speech prefix to l. 84] 88 **Zounds, sir** Sir [also at l. 111] 103 **bravery** knauerie 119 **are now** are 158 **pains** apines 161 **sign. That** [eds.] signe) that 186 **night** might

1.2. 15 **and** or 34 **Duke** Dukes 50 **carrack** Carract 64 **her!** [eds.] her 69 **darlings** Deareling 89 **I do** do

1.3. 1 **There is** There's **these** this 61 s.p. **Duke and Senators** [All Q1] Sen 101 **maimed** main'd 108 s.p. **Duke** [Q1; not in F] 109 **overt** ouer 112 s.p. **[and elsewhere] First Senator** Sen 124 **till** tell 132 **battles** Battaile **fortunes** Fortune 141 **travels'** Trauellors 143 **rocks, and** Rocks **heads** head 145 **other** others 147 **Do grow** Grew 149 **thence** hence 157 **intentively** instinctiuely 161 **sighs** kisses 204 **Into your favor** [Q1; not in F] 222 **ear** eares 227 **sovereign** more soueraigne 233 **couch** [eds.] Coach [F] Cooch [Q1] 237 **These** [eds.] This 244 **Nor I. I would not** Nor would I 251 **did love** loue 267 **me** [eds.] my 273 **instruments** Instrument 281 **Desdemona. Tonight, my lord? Duke. This night** [Q1; not in F] 285 **With** And 294 s.p. **First Senator** Sen 296 s.d. **Exeunt** Exit 302 **matters** matter 303 **the** the the 329 **beam** [eds.] braine [F] ballance [Q1] 333–334 **our unbitted** or vnbitted 335 **scion** [eds.] Seyen [F] syen [Q1] 353 **error** errors 354 **She . . . she must** [Q1; not in F] 358 **a super-subtle** super-subtle 378–382 **Roderigo. What . . . purse** [Q1; not in F] 386 **a snipe** Snpe 389 **He's** [Ha's Q1] She ha's 396 **ear** eares

2.1. 35 **prays** praye 36 **heaven** Heauens 42 s.p. **Third Gentleman** Gent 44 **arrivance** Arriuancie 45 **this** the 58 s.p. **Second Gentleman** Gent [also at ll. 61, 68, and 95] 72 **clog** enclogge 84 **And . . . comfort** [Q1; not in F] 90 **tell me** tell 94 **the sea** Sea 96 **their** this 107 **list** leaue 111 **doors**

doore   156 [and elsewhere] ne'er neu'r   158 such wight such wightes
170 gyve [eds.] giue   174 An and   175 courtesy Curtsie   176 clyster pipes
Cluster-pipes   214 s.d. Exeunt [eds.] Exit   216 hither thither   229 again a
game   239 fortune Forune   242 compassing compasse   244 finder out
finder   occasions occasion   has he's   263 mutualities mutabilities
300 for wife for wift   307 rank right   308 nightcap Night-Cape

2.2. 6 addiction [eds.] addition   **10 Heaven bless** Blesse

2.3. 27 stoup [eds.] stope   **38 unfortunate** infortunate   **52 lads** else   **57 to
put** put to   **61, 71 God** heauen   **76 Englishman** Englishmen   **91 Then . . .
auld** [Then . . . owd *Q1*] And take thy awl'd   **93 'Fore God** Why   **97 God's**
heau'ns   **106 God forgive** Forgiue   **110 speak** I speake   **123 the** his
138 s.d. Cry within: Help! Help [from Q1: "Helpe, helpe, within"]
139 Zounds, you You   **152 God's will** Alas   **153 Montano—sir** Montano
156 God's will, Lieutenant, hold Fie, fie Lieutenant   **158 Zounds, I** I
161 sense of place [eds.] place of sense   **177 breast** breastes   **184 wont be**
wont to be   **201 Zounds, if I** If I once   **212 leagued** [eds.] league   **218 Thus**
This   **227 the** then   **246 well now** well   **250 vile** vil'd   **255 God** Heauen
260 thought had thought   **266 ways** more wayes   **283 O God** Oh   **308 I'll**
I   **311 denotement** [eds.] deuotement   **325–326 me here** me   **337 were 't**
were   **369 hast** hath   **372 By the Mass** Introth   **378 on;** [on, *Q1*] on   **379 the**
[eds.] a

3.1. s.d. Musicians [eds.] Musicians, and Clowne   **21 s.d. Exeunt** [eds.]
Exit   **22 hear** heare me   **26 General's wife** Generall   **31 Cassio. Do, good
my friend** [Q1; not in F]   **42 s.d. Exit** [at l. 41 in F]   **52 To . . . front** [Q1; not
in F]

3.3. 16 circumstance Circumstances   **41 you** your   **55 Yes, faith** I sooth
66 or on   **80 By'r Lady** Trust me   **103 you** he   **118 By heaven** Alas   **124 In**
Of   **148 that all** that: All   **free to** free   **152 But some** Wherein   **160 oft** of
161 wisdom then wisdome   **175 By heaven, I'll** Ile   **183 fondly** [eds.]
soundly [F] strongly [Q1]   **188 God** Heauen   **194 Is once** Is   **196 blown**
blow'd   **199 dances well** Dances   **216 God** Heauen   **218 keep 't** [eds.] keepe
[Q1] kept [F]   **230 I' faith** Trust me   **232 my** your   **249 disproportion**
disproportions   **264 to hold** to   **275 qualities** Quantities   **289 of** to   **294 O,
then heaven mocks** Heauen mock'd   **301 Faith** Why   **305 s.d. Exit** [at l. 304
in F]   **328 faith** but   **345 s.d. Enter Othello** [after "I did say so" in F]
354 of her in her   **385 remorse;** [remorce. *Q1*] remorse   **407 see, sir** see
411 supervisor super-vision   **439 then laid** laid   **440 Over** ore   **sighed**
sigh   **kissed** kisse   **441 Cried** cry   **455 any that was** [eds.] any, it was
468 mind perhaps minde   **471 Ne'er feels** [eds.] Neu'r keepes

3.4. 23 that the   **37 It yet It** yet   **56 faith** indeed   **77 I' faith** Indeed   **79 God**
Heauen   **83 Heaven bless** Blesse   **88 can, sir** can   **94–95 Desdemona. I pray
. . . Cassio. Othello. The handkerchief!** [Q1; not in F]   **99 I' faith** Insooth
100 Zounds Away   **164 that** the   **172 I' faith** Indeed   **182 friend.** [eds.]
friend,   **183 absence** [eds.] absence, [Q1] Absence: [F]   **188 by my faith** in
good troth

4.1. 32 Faith Why   **36 Zounds, that's** that's   **45 work** workes   **52 No,
forbear** [Q1; not in F]   **72 couch** [Coach *Q1*] Cowch;   **79 unsuiting** [Q1
corrected] vnfitting [Q1 uncorrected] resulting [F]   **97 clothes** Cloath
103 conster conserue   **105 you now** you   **109 power** dowre   **114 i' faith**

indeed   **121 Do you** Do ye   **122 marry her** marry   **125 win** [eds.] winnes   **126 Faith** Why   **shall marry** marry   **133 beckons** becomes   **137 by this hand, she** [Q1; not in F]   **163 Faith, I** I   **165 Faith** Yes   **212 s.d.** [at. l. 210 in F]   **215 God save** Saue   **238 By my troth** Trust me   **251 Truly, an** Truely   **284 denote** deonte [F uncorrected] deuote [F corrected]

4.2. 32 Nay May   **33 knees** knee   **35 But not the words** [Q1; not in F]   **51 kinds** kind   **56 A** The   **66 Ay, there** [eds.] I heere   **71 ne'er** neuer   **83 Impudent strumpet** [Q1; not in F]   **96 keep** [eds.] keepes   **s.d. Enter Emilia** [at l. 94 in F]   **162 them in** [eds.] them: or   **174 And . . . you** [Q1; not in F]   **177 you to** to   **190 Faith, I** I   **for** and   **201 By this hand** Nay   **232 takes** taketh   **236 of** [Q1; not in F]

4.3. 10 s.d. Exit [at l. 9 in F]   **22 favor in them** fauour   **25 faith** Father   **26 before thee** before   **43 sighing** [eds.] singing [F corrected] sining [F uncorrected]   **73 Good troth** Introth   **74 By my troth** Introth   **78 Uds pity** why   **107 God** Heauen

5.1. 1 bulk Barke   **22 Be 't** But   **hear** heard   **36 Forth** For   **50 Did** Do   **91 O heaven** Yes, 'tis   **106 out o'** o'   **113 'Las, what's . . . What's** Alas, what is . . . What is   **116 dead** quite dead   **126 Faugh!** Fie Fie

5.2. 34 heaven Heauens   **37 say so** say   **56 Yes, presently** Presently   **61 Then Lord** O Heauen   **96 here** high   **104 Should** Did   **121 O Lord** Alas   **131 heard** heare   **148 Nay, had** had   **225 O God! O heavenly God** Oh Heauen! oh heauenly Powres   **226 Zounds** Come   **248 have here** haue   **317 not. Here** [not: here *Q1*] not) heere   **357 Indian** Iudean

Shakespeare's Sources

Shakespeare's main source for *Othello* was the seventh story from the third decade of G. B. Giraldi Cinthio's *Hecatommithi* (1565). Cinthio was available in French but not in English translation during Shakespeare's lifetime. The verbal echoes in Shakespeare's play are usually closer to the Italian original than to Gabriel Chappuys's French version of 1584. Cinthio's account may have been based on an actual incident occurring in Venice around 1508.

Shakespeare is considerably indebted to Cinthio's story for the essentials of the narrative, as can be seen in the following new translation: the marriage of a Moorish captain to a Venetian lady, Disdemona, whose relatives wish her to marry someone else, the mutual attraction to noble qualities of mind in both husband and wife, their happiness together at first, the dispatching of the Moor to Cyprus to take charge of the garrison there, Disdemona's insistence on accompanying her husband through whatever dangers may occur (though the sea voyage, as it turns out, is a very calm one), the ensign's treachery and resolve to destroy the Moor's happiness with Disdemona, her begging her husband to reinstate the squadron leader whom the Moor has demoted for fighting on guard duty (although no mention is made of drunkenness or of the ensign's role in starting the trouble), the ensign's insinuations to the Moor that his wife is cuckolding him because she is becoming weary of her marriage with a black man, the ensign's difficulty in providing ocular proof, his planting of Disdemona's handkerchief in the squadron leader's quarters and his showing the Moor that the handkerchief is now in the squadron leader's possession, his arranging for the Moor to witness at a distance a conversation between the ensign and squadron leader that is in fact not about Disdemona, Disdemona's confusion when she is asked to produce the handkerchief, the attack on the squadron leader in the dark, the murder of Disdemona in her bed, the Moor's deep regret at the loss of his wife, the eventual punishment of both the Moor and the ensign, and the telling of the story publicly by the en-

sign's wife, who has heretofore kept silent because of her
fear of her husband.

Although these correspondences in the story are many,
Shakespeare has changed a great deal. He provides Desdemona with a caring and saddened father, Brabantio, out of
Cinthio's brief suggestion of family opposition to her marriage, and adds the entire opening scene in which Iago
arouses the prejudices of Brabantio. Roderigo is a brilliantly invented character used to reveal Iago's skill in ma-
nipulation. Cinthio's ensign, though thoroughly wicked,
never expresses a resentment for the squadron leader's promotion and favored treatment by the Moor; instead, the ensign lusts for Disdemona and turns against her and the
Moor only when his passion is unrequited. In his complex
portrayal of a consuming and irrational jealousy in Iago,
Shakespeare goes far beyond his source, making use as well
of the inventive villainy of the Vice in the English late medieval morality play. In Cinthio's account the ensign filches
the handkerchief from Disdemona while she is hugging the
ensign's three-year-old daughter; the ensign's wife is unin-
volved in this mischief, though she does unwillingly learn
of her husband's villainy (since he has an idea of using her
in his plot) and later feels constrained to hold her tongue
when Disdemona asks her if she knows why the Moor is
behaving so strangely. (As is usual in prose narrative, the
passage of time is much more extended than in Shakespeare's play.)

In the later portions of the story, the changes are more
marked. Cinthio relates an episode in which the squadron
leader, finding the handkerchief in his room, takes it back
to Disdemona while the Moor is out but is interrupted by
the Moor's unexpected return home; Shakespeare instead
has Cassio approach Desdemona (earlier in the story) to beg
her assistance in persuading Othello to reinstate him. Cinthio tells of a woman in the squadron leader's household
who copies the embroidery of the handkerchief before it is
returned and is seen with it at a window by the Moor; here
Shakespeare finds a suggestion for Bianca, but her role is
considerably augmented, partly with the help of a passing
remark in Cinthio that the squadron leader is attacked and
wounded as he leaves the house of a courtesan with whom
he occasionally takes his pleasure. In the absence of any

character corresponding to Roderigo, the Cinthio narrative assigns to the ensign himself the role of wounding the squadron leader. The manner in which Disdemona is murdered is strikingly different. Cinthio has nothing equivalent to the tender scene between Desdemona and Emilia as Desdemona prepares to go to bed. Cinthio's Moor hides the ensign in a dressing room next to his bedroom and commissions the ensign to bludgeon her to death with a sand-filled stocking, after which the two murderers cause the ceiling of the room to collapse on her and create the impression that a rafter has smashed her skull.

Cinthio also treats the aftermath of the murder in a very different way. The Moor, distracted with grief, turns on the ensign and demotes him, whereupon the ensign persuades the squadron commander to take vengeance on the Moor as his attacker (according to the lying ensign) and killer of Disdemona. When the squadron commander accuses the Moor before the Seigniory, the Moor keeps silent but is banished and eventually killed by Disdemona's relatives. The ensign, returning to his own country, gets in trouble by making a false accusation and dies as the result of torture. Cinthio sees this as God's retribution. The ensign's wife lives to tell her story, unlike Shakespeare's Emilia.

The changed ending is essential to Shakespeare's play. Emilia becomes a more complex figure than the ensign's wife: Shakespeare implicates her in the taking of the handkerchief but also accentuates her love for Desdemona and her brave denunciation of her husband when at last she knows the full truth. Othello's ritual slaying of Desdemona avoids the appalling butchery of the source story. Shakespeare's ending is more unified, and brings both Othello and Iago to account for the deeds they have committed in this play. Most important, Shakespeare transforms a sensational murder story into a moving tragedy of love.

Hecatommithi (A Hundred Tales)
By Giovanni Battista Giraldi Cinthio
Translated by David Bevington and Kate Bevington

THIRD DECADE, SEVENTH NOVELLA

A Moorish captain takes as his wife a woman who is a citizen of Venice. An ensign in his company accuses her to her husband of adultery. The husband undertakes to have the ensign kill the supposed adulterer. The captain kills his wife. Having been publicly accused by the ensign, the Moor does not confess but is banished nonetheless on clear evidence of guilt. The villainous ensign, thinking to harm still other persons, brings on himself a wretched death.

There once lived in Venice a Moor, a very brave man, who, by virtue of his personal qualities and by having given proof in war of great prudence and energetic ability, was highly regarded by those signors who, in rewarding honorable actions, ever advance the interests of the republic. Now it happened that a virtuous lady of marvelous beauty, called Disdemona, drawn not by a woman's appetite but the innate qualities of the Moor himself, fell in love with him. And he, vanquished by her beauty and nobleness of mind, similarly burned with love for the lady. Their love was so well-disposed and mutual that, although the lady's relatives did what they could to get her to choose some other husband, the two were united in matrimony. And they lived together in such peace and harmony, while they were in Venice, that nothing but affectionate words ever passed between them.

Now it happened that the signors of Venice made a change in the garrison they maintained on Cyprus, and they chose the Moor to command the troops they dispatched there. He, although greatly pleased by the honor thus offered him—since such a distinguished rank is conferred only on men who are noble, mighty, and loyal, and who have shown themselves to be unusually brave—was not so happy when he considered the length and dangers of the voyage, thinking that Disdemona would be distressed by it. But the lady, who had no other happiness on earth than the Moor and was greatly pleased with the testimonial to his merits that her husband had received from so powerful and noble a republic, eagerly awaited the hour when her husband, with his men, should set forth on his way, and she accompanying him to such an honorable post.

It grieved her to see the Moor troubled. And so, not knowing what the reason could be, she said to him one day as they sat at dinner: "Why is it, my Moor, that you, who have been promoted to such a distinguished rank by the Seigniory, are nevertheless so depressed?"

The Moor said to Disdemona: "The love I have for you troubles my contentedness with the honor I have received, because I see that one of two things must necessarily happen: either I must take you with me over the perils of the sea, or I must leave you in Venice to avoid this hardship. The first of these cannot help but weigh heavily on me, since every fatigue you endured and every danger we encountered would make me extremely anxious. The second of these, having to leave you behind, would be hateful to me, since in parting from you I should be parting from my very life."

Disdemona, hearing this, said: "Alas, my husband, what thoughts are these that are going through your head? Why do you give in to such vexing ideas? I want to come with you wherever you go, even if I should have to walk through fire in my chemise rather than going by sea in a perfectly safe and handsomely furnished ship. If there are going to be dangers and fatigues, I want to share them with you. I would think you didn't love me very much if you thought of leaving me in Venice rather than taking me to sea with you, or persuaded yourself that I would prefer to stay here in safety rather than be with you in such danger. I want you to get ready for the voyage with all the cheerfulness your seniority of rank deserves."

The Moor threw his arms joyfully around his wife's neck and said with an affectionate kiss: "May God keep us long in such love, my dear wife!"

Soon after that, putting on his armor and making everything ready for the expedition, he went on board the galley with his lady and all their followers, hoisted sail, and got under way, and, favored with a perfectly tranquil sea, they made their journey to Cyprus.

Among the officers of the Moor's company was an ensign, a man of handsome appearance but of the most depraved nature in the world. He was much in favor with the Moor, who didn't have the slightest idea of his wickedness. For although his mind was utterly vile, he concealed that villainy in his heart with such high-sounding and noble speech and such pleasing demeanor that he made himself out to be a veritable Hector or Achilles. This rascal had also taken his wife, a beautiful and virtuous young woman, to Cyprus, and being of Italian birth, she was much loved by the Moor's wife, who spent the greater part of the day with her.

In the same company there was also a squadron leader of whom the Moor was very fond. He went often to the Moor's house and frequently dined with him and his wife. And so the lady, knowing how much he meant to her husband, gave him proofs of the greatest kindness. This greatly pleased the Moor.

The villainous ensign, not heeding at all the vows he had made to his wife or the friendship, loyalty, and duty he owed the Moor, fell head over heels in love with Disdemona and bent all his thoughts to see if he could enjoy her, but he didn't dare show his passion openly for fear that, if the Moor should notice, he would quickly be a dead man. And so he sought various ways, as guilefully as he could, to let the lady know that he loved her. But she, who was so entirely taken up with the Moor, never gave a thought to the ensign or anyone else. Everything he did to kindle passion in her toward him had no more effect than as if he hadn't even tried.

Then he took it into his head that this neglect was the result of her being in love with the squadron leader, and he began to wonder how he might remove this person from her sight. Not only did his mind turn to this, but the love he had for the lady changed into the bitterest hatred, and he gave himself entirely to the study of how he might bring it about that, once the squadron leader had been killed, if he himself could not enjoy the lady, the Moor would not be able to enjoy her either.

Turning over in his mind various ideas, all of them villainous and evil, the ensign finally decided to accuse her of adultery to her husband and to make him believe that the adulterer was none other than the squadron leader. But, knowing the single-hearted love the Moor had for Disdemona, and the friendship he had for the squadron leader, the ensign recognized clearly that, unless he could dupe the Moor with some clever fraud, it would be impossible to get him to listen to either accusation. For which reason he set himself to wait until time and place should open up a way for him to begin his villainous project.

Not long afterward, it happened that the Moor, because the squadron leader drew his sword on a soldier while on guard duty and wounded him, demoted him in rank. This distressed Disdemona greatly. Many times she tried to bring about a reconciliation between her husband and him. At this the Moor said to the villainous ensign that his wife was putting up such a fuss on behalf of the squadron leader that he feared he would be constrained at last to reinstate the officer. The villain took this opportunity to set in motion the deception he had planned, and said: "Perhaps Disdemona has good reason to look so kindly on him."

"And why would that be?" said the Moor.

"I have no desire," answered the ensign, "to come between husband and wife, but if you keep your eyes open, you'll see for yourself."

Nothing the Moor did could persuade the ensign to go beyond what he had said. Nevertheless, his words left such a sharp, stinging thorn in the Moor's mind that he gave himself up to thinking intently what these words could mean, and he fell into a deep melancholy.

One day, when his wife was trying to soften his anger toward the squadron leader, beseeching him not to consign to oblivion the service and friendship of so many years for a mere peccadillo, especially since matters had been patched up between the squadron leader and the soldier he wounded, the Moor burst into a rage and said to her: "There must be some extraordinary reason, Disdemona, that you should take so much trouble over this man. He isn't your brother, after all, or even a kinsman, to be so near your heart."

The lady said, courteously and humbly: "Please don't be angry with me. Nothing prompts me to do this except that it saddens me to see you deprived of such a dear friend as I know, by your own testimony, the squadron leader has been to you. He hasn't done anything to deserve so much hatred from you. But you Moors are so naturally hot-tempered that every little thing provokes you to anger and revenge."

The Moor, made still angrier by these words, answered: "Anyone who doesn't believe this can easily find proof that it's true! I will be revenged for the wrongs done to me! I will be satisfied!"

The lady was frightened at these words, and, seeing her husband to be inflamed with anger against her, quite beyond his usual self, she said humbly: "I have only the best of motives in speaking to you about this. But, not to give you any cause to be angry with me, I won't say another word about it from now on."

Seeing the earnestness with which his wife had pleaded anew on behalf of the squadron leader, the Moor guessed that the words which the ensign had spoken to him signified that Disdemona was in love with the squadron leader. And so, deeply depressed, he went to the villainous ensign and tried to get him to speak more frankly. The ensign, bent on doing injury to the unfortunate lady, after pretending not to want to say anything that might displease the Moor, gave the appearance of being brought around by the Moor's urging and said: "I can't deny that it pains me terribly to have to say anything to you that must disturb you extremely. But since you insist I tell you, and since the concern I ought to have for your honor as my commanding officer also spurs me on to tell you, I will not now refuse to obey your request and my own sense of duty. You must realize, then, that your lady's only reason for being unhappy to see the squadron leader out of favor with you is that she takes her pleasure with him whenever he comes to your house. That's how she consoles herself for the disgust she feels about your blackness."

These words penetrated to the very core of the Moor's heart. But, in order to know more (though he now believed what the ensign had told him to be true, through the suspicion that had already been born in his mind), he said, with a fierce expression: "I don't know what keeps me from cutting out that audacious tongue of yours, which has had the effrontery to offer such an insult to my lady."

Then the ensign said: "I didn't expect, Captain, any other reward for my friendly service. But, since the duty I owe you and the care I have for your honor have brought me thus far, let me repeat to you that matters stand just as you've heard. And if your lady, with her show of affection for you, has blinded your eyes to such an extent that you are unable to see what is right in front of you, that doesn't at all mean that I haven't been telling the truth. Believe me, this same squadron leader, being one of those people who don't think their happiness complete until they have made someone else acquainted with it, has told me everything." And he added: "If I hadn't feared your anger, I should, when he told me this, have given him the recompense he justly deserved by killing him. But since, by letting you know what concerns you more than any other person, I have earned for myself such an unbefitting reward, I wish I had kept silent and thus avoided falling into your disfavor."

Then the Moor, in torment, said: "If you do not make me see with my own eyes what you've told me, rest assured that I will give you reason to think you would have been better off to have been born without a tongue."

"It would have been easy enough," answered the scoundrel, "when he used to come to your house. But now that you have driven him away—and, I must say, not for any compelling need but for the most trivial of reasons—it's bound to be difficult for me, for, even though I feel sure that he enjoys Disdemona whenever you give him the chance, he must do so much more cautiously than before, now that he sees he has fallen into your disfavor. Still, I do not lose hope of being able to make you see what you are so unwilling to believe." And with these words they went their own ways.

The wretched Moor, as if struck by the most piercing of arrows, went home to await the day when the ensign would make him see that which would make him forever unhappy. But the ensign meanwhile was no less troubled by the chaste behavior with which he knew the lady to govern herself, since it seemed to him impossible to discover a way of making the Moor believe what he had falsely told him. And so, turning this over in his mind in every possible direction, the scoundrel hit at last on a new piece of cunning.

As I have told you, the Moor's wife often went to the house

of the ensign's wife and spent the better part of the day with her. Whereupon the ensign, seeing that she sometimes carried with her a handkerchief which, he knew, the Moor had given her, and which had been embroidered with an intricate Moorish design, and which was especially dear to the lady and no less so to the Moor, he devised a scheme to take it from her by stealth and thereby prepare her final ruin. He had a young daughter, three years old, and much beloved of Disdemona. One day, when the poor lady had gone to pass the time of day at the villain's house, he took up the little girl in his arms and presented her to the lady, who took the child and hugged her to her breast. The traitor, who was very quick in sleight of hand, lifted the handkerchief from her sash so adroitly that she took no notice. And so, glad at heart, he took his leave of her.

Disdemona, unaware of what had happened, went home and, busy with other considerations, never gave a thought to the handkerchief. But a few days afterward, when she went to look for it and couldn't find it, she was terribly afraid that the Moor would ask her for it as he often did.

Meantime the villainous ensign, taking a suitable occasion, visited the squadron leader in his room and, with crafty malice, left the handkerchief at the head of the bed in such a way that the squadron leader took no notice until the following morning when, as he got out of bed, and the handkerchief by this time having fallen to the floor, he put his foot on it. Not being able to imagine how it had gotten into his house, knowing it to be Disdemona's, he determined to give it back to her. And so, waiting until the Moor had gone out, he went to the back door and knocked.

Fortune seemed to have conspired with the ensign to bring about the death of the poor woman, for at that very moment the Moor came back home. Hearing a knock at the door, he went to a window and very angrily shouted: "Who is knocking?" The squadron leader, hearing the Moor's voice and fearing that he would come downstairs and do him some harm, without answering a word took to his heels. The Moor ran downstairs and, opening the door, went out into the street and looked around but found no one. Then, going back inside, filled with spite, he demanded of his wife who it was that had knocked at the downstairs door. The lady answered truthfully that she didn't know. But the Moor said: "To me it looked like the squadron leader." "I don't know," she said, "whether it was he or someone else." The Moor held in his fury, though he burned with wrath.

He didn't want to do anything before he had spoken with the ensign, and so he went to him immediately and told him what had happened, and begged him to find out from the squadron leader what he could about the business. He, delighted with the way things were going, readily agreed to do so.

And so one day he spoke with the squadron leader while the Moor was standing in a place where he could see the two of them in conversation. As they talked of all sorts of things having nothing to do with the lady, the ensign laughed with huge gusto and made as if to show great surprise, gesturing a lot with his head and hands as if he heard some incredible tale. The Moor went to the ensign as soon as he saw the two separate, in order to know what the other had told him. The ensign, after making the Moor beg for a long time, finally said to him: "He hasn't hidden a thing from me. He says that he has enjoyed your wife every time that you've given him opportunity by being away. And, he says, on the last such time he was with her, she gave him the handkerchief which you gave her as a gift when you married her." The Moor thanked the ensign, and it seemed to him obvious that if the lady no longer had the handkerchief in her possession, all must be as the ensign had said.

And so one day, after they had dined, as he discussed various things with his lady, the Moor asked for the handkerchief. The poor woman, who had been so afraid of this question, turned all red in the face, and, in order to hide her blushes, which the Moor had already taken good notice of, she ran to her chest and pretended to look for it. After she had searched a good deal, she said: "I don't know why I can't find it now. Do you have it, by any chance?" "If I had it," he said, "why would I be asking you for it? But you will look for it more easily and comfortably some other time."

And, leaving her, the Moor began to think how he might kill his lady and the squadron leader at the same time in such a way that the guilt for her death would not be laid at his door. Thinking of this day and night, he couldn't prevent his lady from noticing that he was not the same toward her as before. She said to him several times: "What thing is bothering you? What is troubling you? You, who used to be the merriest person on earth, are now the most melancholy person alive." The Moor found various excuses in replying to his lady, but she was not at all easy in her mind.

Even though she knew that no misconduct on her part could have troubled the Moor so greatly, she feared nonetheless that through the excessive amount of lovemaking he engaged in with her, he had become bored. Sometimes she would say to the ensign's wife: "I don't know what to make of the Moor. He used to be so loving to me, and now, in I don't know how short a time, he's become quite another person. I'm greatly worried that I shall prove a warning to young women not to marry against their parents' wishes, and that Italian ladies will learn by my example not to be linked in marriage with the kind of man who is separated from us by nature, Heaven itself, and an entire way of life. But because I know he is on good terms with your husband and shares with him his most private affairs, I beg of you that, if you've learned anything from him that you can tell me about, you won't fail to help me." And as she said all this she wept uncontrollably.

The ensign's wife, who knew everything (since her husband wished to use her as a means to the death of the lady, though she had never willingly consented), did not dare, for the fear she had of her husband, to say a word of this thing to Disdemona. She said only: "Take care not to give your husband the least suspicion, and strive as hard as you can to make him realize your love and loyalty to him." "Why, so I do," Disdemona said, "but nothing helps."

The Moor, meanwhile, sought every way of confirming more certainly the very thing he did not want to discover. He begged the ensign to arrange matters in such a way that he could see the handkerchief in the squadron leader's possession, and, although this request put the scoundrel rather on the spot, he promised the Moor nonetheless to make every effort to give him the proof he desired.

The squadron leader had a woman in the house who made the most marvelous embroidery on fine linen. She, seeing the handkerchief and hearing that it belonged to the Moor's wife and that it was to be given back to her, undertook to make a copy of it before it was returned. While she was doing this, it struck the ensign that she had placed herself next to a window from which she could be seen by whoever passed by in the street. He made sure that the Moor saw this, who accordingly held it for certain that his utterly chaste lady was in fact an adulteress.

The Moor came to an agreement with the ensign to kill her and the squadron leader, and as the two of them discussed between them how it was to be done, the Moor implored the ensign that he would agree to be the one to kill the squadron leader, promising to remain eternally obliged to him for doing so. Although the ensign at first refused to undertake such a difficult and exceedingly dangerous thing, since the squadron leader was no less skillful than valorous, after having been begged repeatedly and bribed with a sufficient quantity of money, he was at length induced to say that he would undertake to tempt fortune.

One evening after these matters had been settled, as the squadron leader was leaving the house of a courtesan with whom he liked to solace himself, the night being dark, the ensign accosted him with sword in hand and directed a blow at his legs to cause him to fall, and in so doing cut the right thigh entirely through so that the poor man did indeed fall to the ground. The ensign was instantly upon him to finish him off. But the squadron leader, who was brave and accustomed to blood and death, drew his own sword and, wounded though he was, put himself on guard to defend his life and shouted in a loud voice: "Help! Murder!"

At this the ensign, hearing people running toward him, and among them some soldiers who were billeted in the neighborhood, took to his heels so as not to be taken there, and then, doubling back on his tracks, made it appear that he also was running toward the noise. Blending in among the others, and seeing the leg that had been lopped off, he judged that the squadron leader, if not virtually dead already, would die in any case of such a wound. And, although he rejoiced to himself at this, he nevertheless offered condolences to the squadron leader as if he had been his brother.

Next morning the news was all over the city, and came too

to the ears of Disdemona. She, loving as always, and not thinking that she might suffer harm from it, showed the greatest sorrow for what had happened. The Moor put the worst possible construction on her behavior. He went to find the ensign and said to him: "Do you know that my fool of a wife is in such a state about what has happened to the squadron leader that she is very nearly out of her mind?"

"What else could you expect," said the ensign, "since he is her very heart and soul?"

"Heart and soul, you say?" answered the Moor. "I'll tear her heart and soul right out of her body! I couldn't think myself a man if I didn't rid the world of such a depraved creature."

As they went on discussing alternatives, whether the lady should die by poison or the knife, and not coming to an agreement between them on one or the other, the ensign said: "A way has come into my head that should satisfy you and lead to no suspicion. Here it is. The house you occupy is very old, and the ceiling in your room is full of cracks. My idea is that we pummel Disdemona with a stocking filled with sand until she dies, since this way there will appear on her body no sign of a beating. Once she is dead we can cause part of the ceiling to cave in, and we can break the lady's head in such a way as to make it appear that a falling rafter smashed her skull and killed her. This way no one will suspect you, supposing instead that her death came about by accident."

This cruel advice pleased the Moor, and he waited only for a convenient opportunity, some night when he would share his bed with Disdemona. First he concealed the ensign in a dressing room that opened off their bedroom. Then the ensign, according to the plan they had made between them, made some sort of noise in the dressing room. Hearing this, the Moor said very suddenly to his wife: "Did you hear that noise?"

"Yes, I did," she said.

"Get up and see what it is," the Moor rejoined.

Poor Disdemona got up. As soon as she had come close to the dressing room, the ensign rushed out and, being strong and muscular, gave her a terrible blow in the small of her back with the stocking he had ready, so that the lady fell immediately, hardly able to draw her breath. With the little voice she had left she called on the Moor to help her. But he, leaping out of bed, said to her: "You most wicked of women! This is the reward for your unchastity. This is what they get who, pretending to love their husbands, put horns on their heads instead."

The poor lady, hearing this and sensing that her end was near—since the ensign had landed another blow—said that she called on divine justice to attest to her fidelity, since earthly justice failed to come to her aid. And as she called on God to help her, she was struck by a third blow and lay dead, slain by the impious ensign.

Then, putting her on the bed and smashing her skull, he and the Moor caused the ceiling of the room to cave in as they had planned between them, whereupon the Moor began to cry for help, that the house was falling down. At which cry the neighbors came running, and discovered the bed, and found the lady dead under the rafters. All were amazed and grieved at this, because her life had been so good.

On the following day Disdemona was buried with deep grieving on everybody's part. But God, the just examiner of all human souls, did not wish that such monstrous evil should go without suitable punishment. He decreed that the Moor, who had loved the lady more than his own life, seeing himself deprived of her, should begin to have such an intense longing for her that he went about like one who was out of his mind, searching for her in every imaginable place in the house. And coming to the conclusion that it was the ensign who had caused him to lose, along with the lady, every joy of his life and indeed his very being, he came to loathe the villain so intensely that he couldn't even bear to look at him. If he had not been afraid of the inviolable justice of the Venetian Seigniory, the Moor would have killed him right out in the open. But since he couldn't do so safely, he instead demoted the ensign and refused to let him serve any longer in his company, whereupon was born such a bitter enmity between them that it would be impossible to imagine one more immense or deadly.

On this score the ensign, that worst of all villains, turned all his thoughts to doing harm to the Moor. Seeking out the squadron leader, who had recovered by now and who got about on a wooden leg in place of the one that had been cut off, the ensign said to him: "The time has come for you to be revenged for your cut-off leg. If you'll come with me to Venice, I will tell you who the malefactor was. I don't dare talk about it here for many reasons. And I will testify for you in court."

The squadron leader, knowing himself to have been deeply wronged but not understanding the real truth of the matter, thanked the ensign and accompanied him to Venice. When they had arrived, the ensign told him that the Moor was the one who had cut off his leg because of an idea he had gotten into his head that he, the squadron leader, had lain with Disdemona, and that for this same reason the Moor had killed her and afterward spread the report of her having been killed by the falling ceiling.

The squadron leader, hearing this, accused the Moor before the Seigniory of having cut off his leg and of having killed the lady, and he called as his witness the ensign, who said that both things were true, which he knew because the Moor had told him everything and had tried to induce him to commit both crimes; and that, having then killed his wife, impelled by the bestial jealousy that had come into his head, the Moor had told to the ensign the manner in which he had done her in.

The Venetian Seigniory, upon learning of this cruel deed perpetrated by a barbarian foreigner on a Venetian citizen, issued orders for the Moor to be arrested in Cyprus and brought back to Venice, where through numerous tortures they tried to find out the truth. But he was able to endure all the tortures with his mightiness of spirit and denied everything so steadfastly that they could not get anything out of him. And although by his steadfastness he escaped death, he was, after being confined many days in prison, condemned to perpetual exile. There he was finally put to death by Disdemona's relatives, as he deserved.

The ensign went back to his own country, and, not being inclined to change his ways, accused a companion of his of having tried to get him, the ensign, to kill one of this fellow's enemies, a person of good birth. On the basis of this accusation the fellow was taken and put to the torture.

When he denied the truth of what his accuser had said, the
ensign too was put to the torture in order that their stories
might be compared. There he was so badly tortured that his
internal organs ruptured. Afterward he was released from
prison and taken home, where he died a miserable death.
Thus did God avenge the innocence of Disdemona. And now
that he was dead, the ensign's wife, who knew the whole
story, told what had happened just as I have told you.

Gli Hecatommithi by Giovanni Battista Giraldi Cinthio was first published in
Italy in 1565. This new translation is based on the edition of 1566.

Further Reading

Adamson, Jane. *"Othello" as Tragedy: Some Problems of Judgment and Feeling*. Cambridge and New York: Cambridge Univ. Press, 1980. Adamson finds the unity of *Othello* in the similarities between the problems of judgment and feeling that characters confront and those experienced by an audience of the play. We are made uncomfortable with our own desire for certainty as we see characters who, in theirs, urgently construe and misconstrue actions and personalities.

Bayley, John. "Love and Identity." *The Characters of Love: A Study in the Literature of Personality*. London: Constable, 1960. Examining the psychological and philosophical implications of Shakespeare's revision of G. B. Giraldi Cinthio's novella, Bayley sees the play as an intensely personal tragedy rooted in the difficulties of truly knowing another being. Both Desdemona and Othello reveal powerful conceptions of love but are tragically incapable of understanding any other kind of love or of being separated from their own sense of identity.

Boose, Lynda E. "Othello's Handkerchief: 'The Recognizance and Pledge of Love.'" *English Literary Renaissance* 5 (1975): 360–374. Boose discovers in the "strawberry spotted handkerchief" the motive forces of the play itself: the concerns with fidelity and justice. Examining Shakespeare's transformation of his source material and exploring Renaissance marriage customs, Boose finds that the handkerchief functions as an emblem of marital consummation, and that Othello's chosen role as judicial executioner derives from marriage laws and rituals that prescribe the death of a wife whose wedding sheets fail to provide proof of her bridal virginity.

Bradley, A. C. *"Othello." Shakespearean Tragedy*, 1904. Rpt., New York: St. Martin's Press, 1985. Bradley's deservedly influential study focuses on character: Othello is heroic, noble, not innately jealous but unreflective; Desdemona is passive, armed with nothing to oppose evil except endurance and forgiveness; and Iago is a liar, supremely evil, motivated by an unconscious longing for power and superiority.

Cavell, Stanley. "Literature as the Knowledge of the Outsider." *The Claim of Reason: Wittgenstein, Scepticism, Morality, and Tragedy.* New York: Oxford Univ. Press, 1979. Rpt. as "On *Othello*," in *Shakespeare, the Tragedies: New Perspectives*, ed. Robert B. Heilman. Englewood Cliffs, N.J.: Prentice-Hall, 1984. Cavell sees the play enacting the tragic implications of the individual's need for the existence of—and acknowledgment by—another. Othello needs Desdemona to confirm his image of himself but simultaneously has to reject Desdemona for exposing his need. Othello's tragedy is then not the tragedy of a man who lacks certainty but of one who knows too much—about himself as dependent and imperfect—and is unable to confront that knowledge.

Coleridge, Samuel Taylor. *"Othello." Coleridge's Writings on Shakespeare*, ed. Terence Hawkes. New York: G. P. Putnam's Sons, 1959. Coleridge regards Othello as a noble and majestic figure, not jealous by nature but aroused by offended honor, moral indignation, and regret at his discovery that Desdemona's virtue is apparently impure and worthless. Coleridge views Iago as a "passionless character, all *will* and intellect," and, in a famous phrase, characterizes Iago's rationalizations of his hatred for Othello as "the motive-hunting of motiveless malignity."

Doran, Madeleine. "Iago's 'If': An Essay on the Syntax of *Othello*." In *The Drama of the Renaissance: Essays for Leicester Bradner*, ed. Elmer M. Blistein. Providence, R.I.: Brown Univ. Press, 1970. Rpt. and rev. as "Iago's 'If—': Conditional and Subjunctive in *Othello*." *Shakespeare's Dramatic Language*. Madison: Univ. of Wisconsin Press, 1976. Analyzing Shakespeare's use of syntax to inform the dramatic structure of *Othello*, Doran discovers two dominant syntactic patterns counterpointed in the play: conditional and declarative sentences. The conditionals (which initiate every significant phase of the tragic action) disrupt and finally destroy the world of Othello's assurance. His absolutism and ultimately his whole being fall victim to the terrifying ambiguities released by Iago's "if."

Empson, William. "'Honest' in *Othello.*" *The Structure of Complex Words.* New York: New Directions, 1951. Empson argues that Shakespeare's complex handling of the words "honest" and "honesty" (which appear over fifty times in the play) is central to an understanding of Iago's character and motivation. Shakespeare exploits the words' various possibilities of meaning, and a Renaissance audience, alert to the ironies and ambiguities of the words, would necessarily see Iago as less purely evil and more complexly human than most twentieth-century critics have allowed.

Gardner, Helen. "The Noble Moor." In *Proceedings of the British Academy* 41 (1956 for 1955): 189–205. Rpt. in *Shakespeare Criticism, 1935–60,* ed. Anne Ridler. London and New York: Oxford Univ. Press, 1963. As her title suggests, Gardner sees Othello as a noble and heroic figure in a play of poetic, intellectual, and moral beauty. The play's subject is not pride, egoism, or self-deception, but is, rather, loss of faith stemming from sexual jealousy. In *Othello* we are presented with the fall of a noble man from a great happiness to ruin, but a fall that affirms the value of the life and love that have been lost.

Garner, S. N. "Shakespeare's Desdemona." *Shakespeare Studies* 9 (1976): 233–252. Finding *Othello* to be among the "bleakest" of the tragedies, Garner traces Desdemona's tragic trajectory from her initial courage and confidence to her "appalling innocence" and passivity of the last two acts. Exactly like Othello, she never fully knows herself or her spouse, and both fail to "understand the way the world fosters their misperceptions."

Greenblatt, Stephen. "The Improvisation of Power." *Renaissance Self-Fashioning.* Chicago: Univ. of Chicago Press, 1980. In Greenblatt's suggestive cultural anthropology, *Othello* emerges as a play expressing the central social and psychic realities of the Renaissance. Iago's understanding that the self is something "fashioned" permits him the improvisational freedom to enter into the psychic structure of another and turn it to his advantage. Playing upon the ambivalence of Othello's relationship to Venetian society, Iago activates Othello's terrifying sexual anxieties and mistrust.

Heilman, Robert B. *Magic in the Web: Action and Language in "Othello."* Lexington, Ky.: Univ. of Kentucky Press, 1956. *Othello*, Heilman argues in his account of the play's imagery and dramatic action, is a "dramatic poem" about love. Othello's tragedy stems from his failure to recognize the transformative power of Desdemona's love. His histrionic bent, his self-pity, and his self-love allow him to be seduced by Iago's wit and reason, and he dies never knowing the true value of what he has lost.

Johnson, Samuel. *"Othello." Johnson on Shakespeare*, ed. Arthur Sherbo. *The Yale Edition of the Works of Samuel Johnson*, vol. 8. New Haven and London: Yale Univ. Press, 1969. Johnson praises the play for its moral qualities, its dramatic construction, and its vivid characterization. Othello is "boundless in his confidence, ardent in his affection, inflexible in his resolution, and obdurate in his revenge." Johnson also admires Desdemona's "soft simplicity" and finds her murder unbearable: "I am glad that I have ended my revisal of this dreadful scene. It is not to be endured."

Jones, Eldred. *Othello's Countrymen: The African in English Renaissance Drama*. London: Oxford Univ. Press, 1965. Jones surveys the Elizabethan knowledge of Africans and their representation on the stage and finds that *Othello* marks a significant departure from the traditional dramatic treatment of Moors: Shakespeare endows Othello with noble, human qualities, though the play invokes—in order to reject—racial stereotypes in the prejudice of Iago and Brabantio.

Kirsch, Arthur. "The Polarization of Erotic Love in *Othello.*" *Modern Language Review* 73 (1978): 721–740. Rpt. as *"Othello." Shakespeare and the Experience of Love*. Cambridge and New York: Cambridge Univ. Press, 1981. According to Kirsch, Shakespeare in the play, and most deeply in Othello's character, explores the powerful and often paradoxical forces of erotic love. Drawing on both Christian and Freudian theories of desire, Kirsch understands *Othello* not as a tragedy of moral or psychological failure but as an enactment of the tragic potential of a human love born necessarily in vulnerability and need.

Knight, G. Wilson. "The *Othello* Music." *The Wheel of Fire: Interpretation of Shakespeare's Tragedy*, 1930. Rev. and enl., New York: Meridian, 1957. Iago's corrosive cynicism represents for Knight a "spirit of negation" that would destroy "the domesticity, the romance, the idealized humanity of the *Othello* world." But, while Iago succeeds in destroying the love and beauty of that world, his triumph is not complete. At the end Othello recovers his former dignity, rising above the chaos into which he has sunk and denying Iago an absolute victory.

Leavis, F. R. "Diabolic Intellect and the Noble Hero: A Note on *Othello*." *Scrutiny* 6 (1937): 259–283. Rpt. in *The Common Pursuit*. London: Chatto and Windus, 1952; New York: New York Univ. Press, 1964. Leavis attacks what he calls the "Sentimentalists' Othello," promulgated by Coleridge, Johnson, and Bradley (see above). In place of their heroic and noble figure seduced by a supremely evil villain, he argues for an Othello driven by pride, sentimentality, and a lack of self-knowledge that makes him succumb "with an extraordinary promptness to suggestion."

Neely, Carol Thomas. "Women and Men in *Othello*: 'What Should Such a Fool / Do With So Good a Woman?'" *Shakespeare Studies* 10 (1977): 133–158. Rpt. in *The Woman's Part: Feminist Criticism of Shakespeare*, ed. Carolyn Ruth Swift Lenz, Gayle Greene, and Carol Thomas Neely. Urbana, Chicago, and London: Univ. of Illinois Press, 1980. Neely proposes that the play's central conflict is not between good and evil but between men and women. Unlike Shakespeare's comedies, where witty heroines are able to dispel male folly, *Othello* defines a world where male fantasies remain tragically unaffected by female wit and energy. Here the conflicts are never resolved, and at the end we do not celebrate the pairing of lovers but can only look at the dead bodies of Emilia, Desdemona, and Othello.

Orkin, Martin. "Othello and the 'Plain Face' of Racism." *Shakespeare Quarterly* 38 (1987): 166–188. Orkin traces attitudes toward race and color in Renaissance England and ways in which a "racist mythology inscribes critical responses to the play." In a final section, Orkin examines the specific case of the play as it is treated in the academic criticism of South Africa.

Rosenberg, Marvin. *The Masks of "Othello": The Search for the Identity of Othello, Iago, and Desdemona by Three Centuries of Actors and Critics.* Berkeley and Los Angeles: Univ. of California Press, 1961. Rosenberg's subtitle indicates the contents of his book. He examines the play on the stage from the eighteenth through the twentieth centuries, provides an overview of critical approaches, and attends to the ways in which the text has been reshaped for performance. In the two concluding chapters he argues against either symbolic or skeptical approaches to *Othello*, maintaining that *Othello*'s deep and complex humanity is most powerfully realized in the theater.

Synder, Susan. "Beyond Comedy: *Romeo and Juliet* and *Othello.*" *The Comic Matrix of Shakespeare's Tragedies,* esp. pp. 70–90. Princeton, N.J.: Princeton Univ. Press, 1979. Responding to the play's movement from an initial comic design to a fully developed tragic action, Snyder maintains that the power of *Othello* derives from Shakespeare's radical questioning of the fundamental assumption of romantic comedy: that self-definition and fulfillment can be achieved through union with another. The play enacts and explores the tragic implications of emotional ties that necessarily reveal the dependency and vulnerability that Iago exploits.

Spivack, Bernard. "Iago Revisited." *Shakespeare and the Allegory of Evil.* New York: Columbia Univ. Press, 1958. Finding no plausible motivation within the play for Iago's exuberant evil, Spivack discovers an explanation for his behavior not in Iago's psychology but in his literary ancestry in the medieval drama. Iago's logic and energy derive from the allegorical Vice of the morality plays, and Spivack explores the implications of this legacy for the moral dynamics of the play.

Stoll, E. E. *"Othello": An Historical and Comparative Study,* 1915. Rpt., New York: Haskell House, 1964. Stoll responds sharply to the psychological critics (notably Bradley, see above) who discuss the play's characters as if they were real people. Instead, Stoll argues for the primacy of plot, language, and stage conventions, and invites us to reconsider the play in light of the expectations and values of an Elizabethan audience.

KING LEAR

Introduction

In *King Lear*, Shakespeare pushes to its limit the hypothesis of a malign or at least indifferent universe in which man's life is meaningless and brutal. Few plays other than *Hamlet* and *Macbeth* approach *King Lear* in evoking the wretchedness of human existence, and even they cannot match the devastating spectacle of Gloucester blinded or Cordelia dead in Lear's arms. The responses of the chief characters are correspondingly searing. "Is man no more than this?" rages Lear. "Unaccommodated man is no more but such a poor, bare, forked animal as thou art" (3.4.101–107). Life he calls a "great stage of fools," an endless torment: "the first time that we smell the air / We wawl and cry" (4.6.183, 179–180). Gloucester's despair takes the form of accusing the gods of gleeful malice toward humanity: "As flies to wanton boys are we to the gods; / They kill us for their sport" (4.1.36–37). Gloucester's ministering son Edgar can offer him no greater consolation than stoic resolve: "Men must endure / Their going hence, even as their coming hither; / Ripeness is all" (5.2.9–11). These statements need not be read as choric expressions of meaning for the play as a whole, but they do attest to the depth of suffering. In no other Shakespearean play does injustice appear to triumph so ferociously, for so long, and with such impunity. Will the heavens countenance this reign of injustice on earth? Retribution is late in coming and is not certainly the work of the heavens themselves. For, at the last, we must confront the wanton death of the innocent Cordelia, a death no longer willed even by the villain who arranged her execution. "Is this the promised end?" (5.3.268), asks Kent, stressing the unparalleled horror of the catastrophe.

Throughout its earlier history, the ancient story of King Lear had always ended happily. In the popular folktale of Cinderella, to which the legend of Lear's daughters bears a significant resemblance, the youngest and virtuous daughter triumphs over her two older wicked sisters and is married to her princely wooer. Geoffrey of Monmouth's *Historia Regum Britanniae* (c. 1136), the earliest known version of the Lear story, records that after Lear is overthrown by his sons-in-law (more than by his daughters), he is restored to his throne by the intervention of the French King and is allowed to enjoy his kingdom and Cordelia's love until his natural death. (Cordelia, as his successor, is later dethroned and murdered by her wicked nephews, but that is another story.) Sixteenth-century Tudor versions of the Lear story with which Shakespeare was familiar—John Higgins's account in *The First Part of the Mirror for Magistrates* (1574), Raphael Holinshed's *Chronicles* (1587), Edmund Spenser's *The Faerie Queene*, 2.10.27–32, and a play called *The True Chronicle History of King Leir* (by 1594, published 1605)—all retain the happy ending. The tragic pattern may have been suggested instead by Shakespeare's probable source for the Gloucester-Edgar-Edmund plot, Sir Philip Sidney's *Arcadia*, 2.10, in which the Paphlagonian King is the victim of filial ingratitude and deceit.

Yet even Shakespeare's authority was not sufficient to put down the craving for a happy resolution. Nahum Tate's adaptation (1681), which banished the Fool as indecorous for a tragedy and united Edgar and Cordelia in marriage, placing Lear once again on his throne, held the English stage for about 150 years. One of Shakespeare's editors, Dr. Samuel Johnson, evidently spoke for most eighteenth-century audiences when he confessed that he could not bring himself to read Shakespeare's text. Cordelia's slaughter violated that age's longing for "poetic justice." Her death implied a wanton universe and so counseled philosophic despair. Today, Shakespeare's relentless honesty and refusal to accept easy answers convince us that he was right to defy the conventions of his source, though no doubt we too distort the play to conform with our supposed toughness of vision.

Shakespeare evidently wrote *King Lear* some time before it was performed at court in December of 1606, probably in 1605 and certainly no earlier than 1603–1604; Edgar's speeches as Tom o' Bedlam contain references to Samuel Harsnett's *Declaration of Egregious Popish Impostures*, which was registered for publication in March of 1603. Thus *King Lear* was probably written between *Othello* (c. 1603–1604) and *Macbeth* (c. 1606–1607), when Shakespeare was at the height of his tragic power.

When we look at the play in formal terms, we are apt to be

struck first by its complex double plot. Nowhere else in Shakespearean tragedy do we find anything approaching the rich orchestration of the double plotting in *King Lear*. The links and parallels between the two plots are established on a narrative level early in the play and continue to the end. King Lear misjudges his children and disinherits his loving daughter Cordelia in favor of her duplicitous sisters, whereas Gloucester falls prey to Edmund's deceptions and disinherits his loyal son Edgar; Lear is turned out into the storm by his false daughters, while Gloucester is branded as a traitor by Edmund and deprived of his eyesight; Lear in his madness realizes his fault against Cordelia, while the blind Gloucester "sees" at last the truth about Edgar; both fathers are cared for by their loving children and are belatedly reconciled to them, but die brokenhearted. As recent criticism has noted, these narrative parallels are not especially significant in themselves; we are moved not by the mere repetition of event but by the enlargement of tragic vision that results from the counterpointing of two such actions. When we see juxtaposed to each other two scenes of trial, Lear's mad arraignment of the absent Goneril and Regan and then the cruel imposition of the mere "form of justice" on the pinioned Gloucester (3.6 and 3.7), we begin to measure the extent to which justice and injustice are inverted by cruelty. When at last the two old men come together, during the storm scenes and especially at Dover, the sad comfort they derive from sharing the wreckage of their lives calls forth piercing eloquence against the stench of mortality. The sight is "most pitiful in the meanest wretch, / Past speaking of in a king" (4.6.204–205).

The play's double structure suggests another duality central to *King Lear*, an opposition of parable and realism, in which "divided and distinguished worlds" are bound together for instructive contrast. (These terms are Maynard Mack's, in his *King Lear in Our Time*, 1965.) To a remarkable degree, this play derives its story from folklore and legend, with many of the wondrous and implausible circumstances of popular romance. A prose rendition might almost begin, "Once upon a time there was a king who had three daughters. . . ." Yet Shakespeare arouses romantic expectation only to crush it by aborting the conventional happy ending, setting up a dramatic tension between an idealized world of make-believe and the actual world of disappointed hopes. We are aware of artifice and convention and yet are deeply moved by the "truth" of suffering, love, and hatred. The characters pull us two ways at once; we regard them as types with universalized characteristics, a king and father, his cruel daughters, his loving daughter, and the like, and yet we scrutinize them for psychological motivation because they seem so real and individual.

This duality appears in both the central and the secondary characters. The King of France is in part a hero out of romance, one who makes selfless choices and rescues the heroine Cordelia from her distress; yet his motive must also be appraised in the context of a bitter struggle for power. Why does he leave the English court "in choler," and why does he return to England with an army? Is it only to aid his wife and her beleaguered father, or is he negotiating for military advantage? Certainly a French invasion of England on behalf of Lear complicates the issue of loyalty for the well-meaning Duke of Albany (and perhaps as well for an English Renaissance audience, with its habitual mistrust of the French). The dual focus of the play invites conflicting interpretation. Similarly, Edgar is presented to us on the one hand as the traduced victim in a starkly pessimistic story, dominated by his rationalistic brother, Edmund, who scoffs at religion and undertakes to manipulate those around him for personal gain; on the other hand, Edgar's story grows increasingly improbable as he undertakes a series of disguises and emerges finally as an anonymous champion of chivalry, challenging his brother in the lists like a knight-errant out of Arthurian romance. Edgar's motives are hard to follow. Is he the hero of a fabulous story whose disguises and contriving of illusions for his father are simply part of that storytelling tradition, or is he, in more realistic terms, a man whose disguises are a defensive mask and whose elaborate contrivances defeat themselves? Edmund, his brother, is no less complex. Onstage today he is usually interpreted as smooth and plausible, well motivated by his father's condescending attitude and by the arbitrariness of the law that has excluded him from legitimacy and inheritance. Yet parable elevates Edmund into something monstrous. He becomes an embodiment of gleeful villainy, like Iago in *Othello*, malignantly evil simply because the evil that is in the universe must find a human form through which to express itself. Edmund's belated attempt to do some good adds to our difficulties in appraising his character, but the restless power of the dual conception supplies a vitality not to be found in pure fable or in realistic literature.

What we see then in Edmund and in others is the union of the universal and the particular, making *King Lear* at once parable and compellingly real. The parable or folktale element is prominent at the beginning of the play and focuses attention on the archetypal situations with which the story is concerned: rivalry between siblings, fear of parental rejection, and, at the same time, parental fear of children's callousness. The "unrealistic" contrast between Cordelia and her wicked sisters, or between Edgar and Edmund, is something we accept as a convention of storytelling because it expresses vividly the psychic truth of rivalry between brothers and sisters. We identify with Cordelia and Edgar as virtuous children whose worth is misjudged and who are losing to wicked siblings the contest for parental approval. (In folklore the rejecting parent is usually a stepparent, which signifies our conviction that he or she is not a true parent at all.) Similarly, we accept as a meaningful convention of storytelling the equally "unrealistic" device by which Lear tests the love of his daughters. Like any parent, he wishes to be loved and appreciated in response to the kindnesses he has performed. The tension between fathers and their marriageable daughters is a recurrent pattern in Shakespeare's late plays, as in *Othello* (where Brabantio accuses Desdemona of deceiving and deserting him), in *Pericles, Cymbeline,* and *The Winter's Tale,* and in *The Tempest,* where the pattern is best resolved. In *King Lear,* Shakespeare explores the inherently explosive situation of an imperious father, who, having provided for his children and grown old, assumes he has a right to expect that those children will express their love and gratitude by looking after him.

The difficulty is that the parable of Lear and his children presents two contrasting viewpoints, that of the unappreciated child and that of the unwanted aging parent. Tragic misunderstanding is inevitable, and it outweighs the question of assessing blame. From Lear's point of view, Cordelia's silence is a truculent scanting of obedience. What he has devised is, after all, only a prearranged formality, with Cordelia to receive the richest third of England. Cannot such a ceremony be answered with the conventional hyperbole of courtly language, to which the King's ear is attuned? Don't parents have a right to be verbally reassured of their children's love? How can children be so laconic about such a precious matter? For her part, however, Cordelia senses that Lear is demanding love as payment for his parental kindliness, quid pro quo. Genuine love ought rather to be selfless, as the King of France tells Burgundy: "Love's not love / When it is mingled with regards that stands / Aloof from th' entire point" (1.1.242–244). Is Cordelia being asked to prefer Lear before her own husband-to-be? Is this the price she must pay for her upbringing? Lear's ego seems fully capable of demanding this sacrifice from his daughters, especially from his favorite, Cordelia; he has given them his whole kingdom, now let them care for him as befits his royal rank and patriarchal role. The "second childishness" of his old age brings with it a self-centered longing to monopolize the lives of his children and to be a child again. Besides, as king, Lear has long grown accustomed to flattery and absolute obedience. Goneril and Regan are content to flatter and promise obedience, knowing they will turn him out once he has relinquished his authority. Cordelia refuses to lie in this fashion, but she also will not yield to Lear's implicit request for her undivided affection. Part of her must be loyal to her own husband and her children, in the natural cycle of the generations. "Haply, when I shall wed, / That lord whose hand must take my plight shall carry / Half my love with him, half my care and duty" (1.1.100–102). Marriage will not prevent her from obeying, loving and honoring her father as is fit, but will establish a new priority. To Lear, as to other fathers contemplating a daughter's marriage in late Shakespearean plays, this savors of desertion.

Lear is sadly deficient in self-knowledge. As Regan dryly observes, "he hath ever but slenderly known himself" (1.1.296–297), and has grown ever more changeable and imperious with age. By dividing his kingdom in three, ostensibly so that "future strife / May be prevented now" (ll. 44–45), he instead sets in motion a civil war and French invasion. His intention of putting aside his regal authority while still retaining "The name and all th' addition to a king" (l. 136) perhaps betrays a lack of comprehension of the realities of power, although Lear may also have plausible political reasons for what he does, in view of the restive ambitions of Cornwall, Albany, and Burgundy. In any case, he welcomes poisoned flattery but interprets well-intended criticism, whether from Cordelia or Kent, as treason. These failures in no sense justify what Lear's ungrateful children do to him; as he later says, just before going mad, "I am a man / More sinned against than sinning" (3.2.59–60). His failures are, however, tokens of his worldly insolence for which he must fall. The process is a painful one, but since it brings self-discovery it is not without its compensations. Indeed a central paradox of the play is that by no other way could Lear have learned what human suffering and need are all about.

Lear's Fool is instrumental in elucidating this paradox. The Fool offers Lear advice in palatable form as mere foolery or entertainment, and thus obtains a hearing when Kent and Cordelia have been angrily dismissed. Beneath his seemingly innocent jibes, however, are plain warnings of the looming disaster Lear blindly refuses to acknowledge. The Fool knows, as indeed any fool could tell, that Goneril and Regan are remorseless and unnatural. The real fool, therefore, is Lear himself, for having placed himself in their power. In a paradox familiar to Renaissance audiences—as in Erasmus's *In Praise of Folly*, Cervantes's *Don Quixote*, and Shakespeare's own earlier *As You Like It* and *Twelfth Night*—folly and wisdom exchange places. By a similar inversion of logic, the Fool offers his coxcomb to Kent for siding with Lear in his exile, "For taking one's part that's out of favor" (1.4.97). Worldly wisdom suggests that we serve those whose fortunes are on the rise, as the obsequious and servile Oswald does. Indeed, the sinister progress of the first half of the play seems to confirm the Fool's contention that kindness and love are a sure way to exile and poverty. "Let go thy hold when a great wheel runs down a hill lest it break thy neck with following; but the great one that goes upward, let him draw thee after" (2.4.70–73). Yet the Fool resolves to ignore his own cynical advice; "I would have

none but knaves follow it, since a fool gives it" (ll. 74–75).
Beneath his mocking, the Fool expresses the deeper truth
that it is better to be a "fool" and suffer than to win on the
cynical world's terms. The greatest fools truly are those
who prosper through cruelty and become hardened in sin.
As the Fool puts it, deriving a seemingly contrary lesson
from Lear's rejection of Cordelia: "Why, this fellow has
banished two on 's daughters and did the third a blessing
against his will" (1.4.99–101).

These inversions find a parallel in Christian teaching, although the play is nominally pagan in setting. (The lack of
explicit Christian reference may be in part the result of a
recent parliamentary order banning references to "God"
onstage as blasphemous.) Christianity does not hold a monopoly on the idea that one must lose the world in order to
win a better world, but its expressions of that idea were
plentifully available to Shakespeare: "Blessed are the
meek, for they shall inherit the earth" (the Sermon on the
Mount); "Go and sell that thou hast, and give to the poor,
and thou shalt have treasure in heaven" (Matthew 19:21);
"He hath put down the mighty from their seats, and exalted
them of low degree" (Luke 1:52). Cordelia's vision of genuine love is of this exalted spiritual order. She is, as the King
of France extols her, "most rich being poor, / Most choice,
forsaken, and most loved, despised" (1.1.254–255). This is
the sense in which Lear has bestowed on her an unintended
blessing, by exiling her from a worldly prosperity that is
inherently pernicious. Now, with poetic fitness, Lear must
learn the same lesson himself. He does so, paradoxically, at
the very moment he goes mad, parting ways with the conventional truths of the corrupted world. "My wits begin to
turn" (3.2.67), he says, and then speaks his first kind words
to the Fool, who is his companion in the storm. Lear senses
companionship with a fellow mortal who is cold and outcast as he is. In his madness he perceives both the worth of
this insight and the need for suffering to attain it: "The art
of our necessities is strange, / And can make vile things precious" (ll. 70–71). Misery teaches Lear things he never
could know as king about other "Poor naked wretches"
who "bide the pelting of this pitiless storm." How are such
poor persons to be fed and clothed? "O, I have ta'en / Too
little care of this! Take physic, pomp; / Expose thyself to feel

what wretches feel, / That thou mayst shake the superflux to them / And show the heavens more just" (3.4.28–36). This vision of perfect justice is visionary and utopian, utterly mad in fact, but it is also spiritual wisdom dearly bought.

Gloucester learns a similar truth and expresses it in much the same way. Like Lear he has driven into exile a virtuous child and has placed himself in the power of the wicked. Enlightenment comes only through suffering. Just as Lear achieves spiritual wisdom when he goes mad, Gloucester achieves spiritual vision when he is physically blinded. His eyes having been ground out by the heel of Cornwall's boot, Gloucester asks for Edmund only to learn that Edmund has betrayed him in return for siding with Lear in the approaching civil war. Gloucester's response, however, is not to accuse Edmund of treachery but to beg forgiveness of the wronged Edgar. No longer does Gloucester need eyes to see this truth; "I stumbled when I saw." Although the discovery is shattering, Gloucester perceives, as does Lear, that adversity is paradoxically of some benefit, since prosperity had previously caused him to be so spiritually blind. "Full oft 'tis seen / Our means secure us, and our mere defects / Prove our commodities" (4.1.19–21). And this realization leads him, as it does Lear, to express a longing for utopian social justice in which arrogant men will be humbled and the poor raised up by redistributed wealth. "Heavens, deal so still! / Let the superfluous and lust-dieted man, / That slaves your ordinance, that will not see / Because he does not feel, feel your pow'r quickly! / So distribution should undo excess / And each man have enough" (ll. 65–70).

To say that Lear and Gloucester learn something precious is not, however, to deny that they are also devastated and broken by their savage humiliation. Indeed, Gloucester is driven to a despairing attempt at suicide, and Lear remains obsessed with the rotten stench of his own mortality, "bound / Upon a wheel of fire" (4.7.47–48). Every decent value that we like to associate with civilization is grotesquely inverted during the storm scenes. Justice, for example, is portrayed in two sharply contrasting scenes: the mere "form of justice" (3.7.26) by which Cornwall condemns Gloucester for treason, and the earnestly playacted trial by which the mad Lear arraigns Goneril and Regan of

filial ingratitude (3.6). The appearance and the reality of
justice have exchanged places, as have folly and wisdom or
blindness and seeing. The trial of Gloucester is outwardly
correct, for Cornwall possesses the legal authority to try
his subjects, and at least goes through the motions of inter-
rogating his prisoner. The outcome is, however, cruelly predetermined. In the playacting trial concurrently taking
place in a wretched hovel, the outward appearance of justice is pathetically absurd. Here justice on earth is personified by a madman (Lear), Edgar disguised as another
madman (Tom o' Bedlam), and a Fool, the latter two addressed by Lear as "Thou robèd man of justice" and "thou,
his yokefellow of equity" (ll. 36–37). They are caught up in a
pastime of illusion, using a footstool to represent Lear's ungrateful daughters. Yet true justice is here and not inside
the manor house.

Similar contrasts invert the values of loyalty, obedience,
and family bonds. Edmund becomes, in the language of the
villains, the "loyal" son whose loyalty is demonstrated by
turning on his own "traitorous" father. Cornwall becomes a
new father to Edmund ("thou shalt find a dearer father in
my love," 3.5.25–26). Conversely, a servant who tries to restrain Cornwall from blinding Gloucester is, in Regan's
eyes, monstrously insubordinate. "A peasant stand up
thus?" (3.7.83). Personal and sexual relationships betray
signs of the universal malaise. The explicitly sexual ties in
the play, notably those of Goneril, Regan, and Edmund, are
grossly carnal and lead to jealousy and murder, while in
Cordelia's wifely role the sensual is underplayed. The relationships we cherish—those of Cordelia, Kent, the Fool, and
Gloucester to King Lear, and Edgar to Gloucester—are filial or are characterized by loyal service, both pointedly non-
sexual. Nowhere do we find an embodiment of love that is
both sensual and spiritual, as in Desdemona in *Othello* or
Hermione in *The Winter's Tale*. The Fool's and Tom o' Bedlam's (i.e., Edgar's) gibes about codpieces and plackets
(3.2.27–40, 3.4.96) anticipate Lear's towering indictment of
carnality, in which his fear of woman's insatiable appetite
and his revulsion at what she resembles "Down from the
waist" ("there is the sulfurous pit, burning, scalding,
stench, consumption. Fie, fie, fie! Pah, pah!") combine
with a destructive self-hatred (4.6.124–130).

All these inversions and polarizations are subsumed in the inversion of the word "natural." Edmund is the "natural" son of Gloucester, meaning literally that he is illegitimate. Figuratively he therefore represents a violation of traditional moral order. In appearance he is smooth and plausible, but in reality he is an archdeceiver like the Vice in a morality play, a superb actor who boasts to the audience in soliloquy of his protean villainy. "Nature" is Edmund's goddess, and by this he means something like a naturalistic universe in which the race goes to the swiftest and in which conscience, morality, and religion are empty myths. Whereas Lear invokes Nature as a goddess who will punish ungrateful daughters and defend rejected fathers (1.4.274–288), and whereas Gloucester believes in a cosmic correspondence between eclipses of the moon or sun and mutinous discords among men (1.2.106–117), Edmund scoffs at all such metaphysical speculations. He spurns, in other words, the Boethian conception of a divine harmony uniting the cosmos and man, with man at the center of the universe. As a rationalist, Edmund echoes Jacobean disruptions of the older world order in politics and religion as well as in science. He is a Machiavellian, atheist, Epicurean, everything inimical to traditional Elizabethan ideals of order. To him, "natural" means precisely what Lear and Gloucester call "unnatural."

His creed provides the play with its supreme test. Which definition of "natural" is true? Does heaven exist, and will it let Edmund and the other villainous persons get away with their evil? The question is frequently asked, but the answers are ambiguous. "If you do love old men," Lear implores the gods, "if your sweet sway / Allow obedience, if you yourselves are old, / Make it your cause" (2.4.191–193). His exhortations mount into frenzied rant, until finally the heavens do send down a terrible storm—on Lear himself. Witnesses agree that the absence of divine order in the universe would have the gravest consequences. "If that the heavens do not their visible spirits / Send quickly down to tame these vile offenses," says Albany of Lear's ordeal, "It will come, / Humanity must perforce prey on itself, / Like monsters of the deep" (4.2.47–51). And Cornwall's servants have perceived earlier the dire implications of their masters' evil deeds. "I'll never care what wickedness I do, / If this man come to good," says one, and his fellow agrees: "If she [Regan] live long, / And in the end meet the old course of death, / Women will all turn monsters" (3.7.102–105; quarto text only). Yet these servants do in fact obey their own best instincts, turning on Cornwall and ministering to Gloucester despite danger to themselves. Similarly, Albany abandons his mild attempts to conciliate his domineering wife and instead uses his power for good. The crimes of the villains are punished, and Albany sees divine cause in this. Just as plausibly, however, one can postulate an innate decency in humankind that has at last asserted itself, horrified by what it has seen. In part, too, villainy destroys itself, for Edmund's insatiable ambition extends past Cornwall to the English throne, and Goneril and Regan would each willingly kill the other to be Edmund's queen. Even in Cordelia's capture and death we can find affirmation of the human spirit, in her ability to forgive and cherish her father; and Edgar's comparable ministering to Gloucester gives the lie to Edmund's "natural" or amoral view of humanity. Certain it is that whatever force oversees the restoration of at least some semblance of justice cannot or will not prevent the death of Cordelia. The last tableau is a vision of doomsday, with Cordelia strangled, Lear dying of heartbreak, and the "gored state" (5.3.326) in such disarray that we cannot be sure what restoration can occur. Indeed, the political question of order is dwarfed by the enormity of Lear's disaster. No one wishes longer life for the King: "He hates him / That would upon the rack of this tough world / Stretch him out longer." He is dead; "The wonder is he hath endured so long" (ll. 319–322). Lear's view of life's terrible corruption, pronounced in his madness, seems confirmed in his end, but so is his greatness of heart confirmed. Overwhelmed as we are by the testimonial before us of mankind's vicious capacity for self-destruction, we are stirred too by the ability of some men and women to confront their fearful destiny with probity, adhering to what they believe to be good. The power of love, though learned too late to avert catastrophe, is at last discovered in its very defeat.

King Lear
in Performance

The history of *King Lear* onstage amply confirms a view of
the play as almost unbearably distressing. It was acted during Shakespeare's lifetime at the Globe Theatre, before
King James at the palace at Whitehall on December 26,
1606, in Yorkshire in 1610 by a group of strolling players,
and probably on other occasions; at least two revivals took
place during the 1660s and 1670s, with Thomas Betterton
as Lear. When Nahum Tate introduced a happily ending
History of King Lear at the theater at Dorset Garden, London, in 1681, however, the appeal of his sentimentalized adaptation was so powerful that Shakespeare's play simply
disappeared from the theater for a century and a half. Tate
was, after all, restoring the reunion of Lear and Cordelia
contained in all the accounts of the historical Lear (or Leir)
before Shakespeare: in Geoffrey of Monmouth's twelfth-
century *Historia Regum Britanniae*, in *The First Part of
the Mirror for Magistrates* (1574 edition), in the anonymous
play called *The True Chronicle History of King Leir*
(c. 1588–1594), and others. Shakespeare's vision of an unrelenting tragedy in which injustice is not always righted had
to await a modern and disillusioned world in order to be
adequately comprehended.

Tate was responding to the same discomfort later felt by
Samuel Johnson, who confessed that he found *Lear* so un-
endurably painful that he could read Shakespeare's text
only in the line of duty as an editor. Ideas of poetic justice
demanded that, as Tate put it in his concluding lines,
"Truth and virtue shall at last succeed." "Regularity" and
"probability," thought to be lacking in Shakespeare's plot,
were needed in order to confirm that the gods are benefi-
cent providers for human destiny. The slaughter of Cordelia, which seemed to imply a wanton universe and to
counsel philosophical despair, could not be allowed to
stand. Accordingly, Tate not only reunited father and
daughter at the play's end, but also provided a love interest
throughout between Edgar and Cordelia (leaving out

France and Burgundy entirely). The love story gave the play a much-desired romantic titillation. It also, in Tate's view, gave a better motivation for Edgar: his disguise was no longer merely "a poor shift to save his life" but rather a "generous design" to aid Cordelia. Tate also eliminated the Fool, motivated presumably by a desire to fulfill neoclassical standards of decorum that eschewed low comedy in a tragedy. Tate's revisions had a political point to make as well: by eliminating the King of France and the French invasion of England, he transformed the military conflict in *Lear* into one of horrifying civil war and joyful reestablishment of royal authority—an object lesson not easily missed by Restoration audiences with vivid memories of their own civil war.

Tate's *Lear* enjoyed a remarkable success. It was acted in all but nine of the years in the eighteenth century. Thomas Betterton played Tate's Lear every year until his death in 1710 and was succeeded by (among others) Barton Booth, James Quin, and, beginning in 1742, David Garrick. Anne Bracegirdle, Peg Woffington, Susannah Cibber, and George Anne Bellamy were notable Cordelias of the century. There were, to be sure, some attempts to resist the awesome popularity of Tate's version. Garrick restored a good deal of Shakespeare's language in 1756, especially at the start of the play, fitting Edmund's soliloquy in its usual place (1.2) instead of at the beginning and presenting most of Lear's scene of the division of the kingdom; nevertheless, Garrick still omitted the King of France and the Fool and retained the love of Edgar and Cordelia, leading up to the happy ending. George Colman the elder suffered a serious failure in 1768 at the Theatre Royal, Covent Garden, when he dared to remove the love story, even though he retained the happy reunion of father and daughter, arranged matters so that Gloucester was blinded offstage, and prevented Gloucester's too-improbable suicide by the timely arrival of Lear.

John Philip Kemble (with his sister, Sarah Siddons, as Cordelia, and later his brother Charles as Edmund and then as Edgar) began with Garrick's *Lear* in 1788 but reverted to a slightly restored version of Tate in 1792. This version still had Gloucester speak from offstage during his blinding and brought on Lear in time to forestall the unpalatable "fall" of Gloucester from Dover cliff. Edmund Kean, after doing well with Tate's *Lear* (or something close to it) in a production in 1820 that emphasized spectacular scenic effects, summoned up the courage to restore the tragic ending at the Theatre Royal, Drury Lane, in 1823 and in subsequent productions until his retirement. Yet even Kean retained the love story of Edgar and Cordelia and banished the Fool. Literary critics such as Joseph Addison, William Hazlitt, and Charles Lamb, long dissatisfied with the stage *Lear*, were not mollified; Hazlitt in particular was disappointed with Kean's halfhearted attempts at restoration. *Lear* had become, in the view of many nineteenth-century readers, a play incapable of being staged adequately; it existed most powerfully on the page and in the imagination.

William Charles Macready first acted Lear at Swansea in 1833, still in Tate's version. Prompted, however, by a newspaper article by John Forster urging the return of the Shakespeare play to the stage, he successfully presented a cut version of Shakespeare's text at Covent Garden in 1834, though he still excluded the Fool. Even when Macready finally restored the Fool, in 1838 at Covent Garden, he did so only after great hesitation and then assigning the part to a young actress, Priscilla Horton—the first of many actresses to play the role. Macready also eliminated the blinding of Gloucester, even when spoken from the wings, and the imaginary fall from Dover cliff. So too did Samuel Phelps at the Sadler's Wells Theatre in 1845 and afterward. Although *Bell's Weekly Messenger* rejoiced that Phelps "produced the entire play as it came from the mind of its immortal author," in fact the production made many of the same cuts as had Macready's. Later in the century, at the Lyceum Theatre in 1892, Henry Irving eliminated Gloucester's blinding and nine other scenes, leaving the play "considerably reduced," though for the most part, according to *The Times*, "in the condition in which it left the author's hand."

All these actor-managers cut extensively, though preserving in the main the ordering of Shakespeare's scenes, and provided instead a spectacular array of storm effects and monumental scenery. (Anyone who has seen Albert Finney and Tom Courtenay in the film *The Dresser* has taken a hilarious, albeit exaggerated, backstage tour of the contraptions needed to generate wind, rain, thunder, and lightning for a proscenium-arch performance, with Lear onstage doing his best to be heard over the din.) Macready's *Lear* concentrated visually on solid, warlike castles, processions, marches, druid circles on the heath, and lightning flashes that alternately lit up the stage and left it in darkness while the winds howled. Phelps sumptuously decorated his stage in the idiom of Saxon Britain. Irving set the play at the end of the Roman occupation of Britain, providing period costumes and historically accurate architectural details. Though Irving did not bestow the scenic effort on this play he had just given to *Henry VIII* (1892), he impressively produced for the storm scene a desolate heath, swept, as *The Times* reviewer wrote, "by furious blasts and beating rain, and illumined by coruscating lightning as dazzling in its brilliancy as the rolling thunder that accompanies it is terrifying." Through such effects, which took precedence over the text, nineteenth-century theater managers attempted to play up the tragic grandeur of Lear, while still ducking such apparently intractable material as the blinding of Gloucester.

The twentieth century has embraced the bitterness of *Lear* as if discovering in it a way of newly comprehending a world filled with wanton evil and uncertain justice. Restoration of the text to a virtual whole (in fact to a conflation of Folio and quarto texts that was probably never staged in Shakespeare's day) has enabled audiences to see the distressing scenes that had so long remained unknown in the theater. Harcourt Williams's production at the Old Vic in 1931, with John Gielgud as Lear and Ralph Richardson as Kent, and another by Lewis Casson and Harley Granville-Barker at the Old Vic in 1940, did much to let the play be seen as it was written, preserving its unity and rhythm. Unlocalized setting, employed for example by Nugent Monck in 1926 at the Maddermarket Theatre in Norwich and by Theodore Komisarjevsky in 1936 at Stratford-upon-Avon, permitted a new kind of fluidity in staging that recaptured some hitherto lost staging effects of Shakespeare's original.

Donald Wolfit acted Lear powerfully at London's Scala Theatre in 1944, a performance that James Agate proclaimed "the greatest piece of Shakespearean acting I have seen since I have been privileged to write for the *Sunday*

Times." Laurence Olivier directed and starred in the play at London's New Theatre in 1946, describing his Lear as "bad tempered arrogance with a crown perched on top." With Olivier's selfish and inconsiderate Lear and Alec Guinness's wry and vindictive Fool, the production emphasized the damage Lear inflicts as much as what he suffers. With greater emphasis upon the pathos of Lear's suffering, Gielgud returned to the role in 1950 and 1955, first at Stratford-upon-Avon in a production he directed with Anthony Quayle, and then at London's Palace Theatre, directed by George Devine.

One modern tendency has been to see the play in as bleak and unforgiving terms as possible. The Polish critic Jan Kott's distorted but compelling view of the play as speaking to our existential gloom (published in English in 1964 as "King Lear, or Endgame," in *Shakespeare Our Contemporary*) influenced what has been perhaps the most important twentieth-century interpretation of the play, Peter Brook's production at Stratford-upon-Avon in 1962 and the subsequent film (1970), with Paul Scofield as Lear. In this version Cordelia's role is reduced and devastatingly offset by the horrors of what Lear and Gloucester must suffer. The setting is wintry throughout. Lear's followers, crowding into Goneril's hall in Scotland, are rowdy enough to give plausibility to Goneril's impatience with her father. Cuts and rearrangement of some speeches are calculated to add to rather than relieve the horror. Lear and Gloucester, together on the beach at Dover in Act 4, scene 6, splendidly invoke a spectacle of ruin as these two old men cling together and behold their world crumble around them. Brook sees little reason to believe that Lear and Gloucester have learned much from their suffering beyond what suffering is like.

The uncompromisingly tragic vision of Brook's *Lear*, derived as much from Jan Kott, Bertolt Brecht, and Samuel Beckett as from Shakespeare, gained much of its shocking power of relevance from the disillusionment of the 1960s and 1970s. Other directors have continued to explore and at the same time qualify Brook's nihilism in ways that are sometimes more complex and less sensational in their view of the play's emotional dynamics. Trevor Nunn lessened the radical pessimism of Brook's version in his production on a virtually bare stage in 1968 at Stratford-upon-Avon, capturing the agony of Lear's experience and allowing an audience to share his suffering. In New York in 1973, Edwin Sherin directed James Earl Jones in a production at the Delacorte Theater, in which Lear, for all his arrogance, was, according to *The New York Times*, the victim of "a compassionless society, in which everything is usurped by the young." Donald Sinden's Lear, in a production directed by Nunn in collaboration with John Barton and Barry Kyle at Stratford-upon-Avon in 1976, displayed the cruelty and self-indulgence of a spoiled child, and, if the performance lacked the tragic dignity that earlier generations associated with the role, it effectively revealed the dangers of unchecked power. David Hare's production of *King Lear* at London's National Theatre in 1986 starred Anthony Hopkins as a man helpless before the brutality his own actions have released.

On film *King Lear* shows the richness and variety of perspective from which the play can be understood in our time. Brook's movie version is bleakly pessimistic. A brilliant *Lear* directed by Grigori Kozintsev (1970) sees the story from a Russian perspective, one in which individuals are caught up in larger forces of history. Peasants wordlessly behold the goings-on of their social masters and wait for deliverance; massive armies determine the outcome of battle. Yuri Yarvet's Lear is small and frail, at once pathetic and heroic as he stands defenseless against loneliness and brutality. The visual effects in this black-and-white film are, as in Brook's version, stark and uncompromising, but, unlike Brook, Kozintsev has tried, as he has said, "to strengthen the voice of Good, even in those instances when it has no words to speak." Most recently, the Japanese director Akira Kurosawa has adapted the *Lear* story in his film *Ran* (1985). Set in feudal Japan against a background of grass-covered hills, fallen castles, and a sky whose swirling clouds testify to the elemental powers that have been unleashed, Kurosawa's *Ran* ("chaos") reworks *King Lear* into the story of Lord Hidetora, the aging patriarch of the Ichimonja clan, who desperately tries to contain the passions of his family and the legacy of his own brutality.

Perhaps Laurence Olivier's television *King Lear* (1983) best sums up what the twentieth century has been able to contribute to the interpretation of this play in performance. Olivier's Lear is very frail and old—indeed, like Olivier himself when he shot this film. He is seen at first as deeply fond of Cordelia, but also accustomed to mastery of his kingdom and susceptible to the flattery plentifully bestowed upon him by his courtiers. He is thus understandably outraged at what he takes to be a betrayal of him by Cordelia and Kent. Goneril and Regan (Dorothy Tutin and Diana Rigg) are suave in their flattery, outwardly attractive, plausibly motivated, yet vicious. Edmund (Robert Lindsay) betrays his villainy with his restless and glistening eyes, well caught by the camera in close-ups. The Fool (John Hurt) is solicitous, distressed beneath his clowning, aware of the disaster to come. Gloucester (Leo McKern) is a fleshy and gullible but well-meaning old man whose ordeal of blinding and attempted suicide leaves him broken, knowing too late his folly. Lear's restoration to Cordelia is touchingly tender, all the more so because of its certain brevity. The contrast between vicious and virtuous behavior is unbridgeable; the victimization of Lear and Cordelia is heartbreaking. Olivier presents us with a *Lear* that causes pain and offers no false hopes, and yet makes the case for some kind of survival of human dignity and compassion. Olivier confronts human brutality in its full extent but provides a meaningfully tragic response as well.

On Shakespeare's stage, the effect of certain scenes in *Lear* must have been particularly suited to the theater for which they were designed. For example, the unlocalized setting enabled Shakespeare to place Kent in the stocks in the course of Act 2, scene 2, and leave him there until scene 4 when Lear arrives in Gloucestershire to find him still enfettered; in the interim, scene 3, Kent has slumbered while Edgar comes onstage in a presumably different though nearby location. Visual conventions encourage this kind of theatrical juxtaposition: Edgar ponders the danger of his being arrested and resolves to disguise himself, while simultaneously onstage another disguised outcast sleeps or meditates on his ruined fortune. The two figures are not "literally" a part of the same scene; staging flexibility in the absence of scenery makes possible such a visual pairing.

Later (4.6), Gloucester's attempted suicide makes similarly imaginative use of stage space. He and the disguised Edgar are on the bare platform stage of the Elizabethan playhouse (or at King James's court). In this theatrical environment, Edgar then conjures up for his blind father a scene of cliffs, vast heights, and a ship far below bobbing on the waves like a toy boat. What is the audience to believe? This sort of verbal scene-setting is the way Elizabethan actors regularly establish a sense of place around them onstage. Only when Gloucester falls forward and is not killed after all can the audience be sure that Edgar is playing a role, acting as director or dramatist, making up a little play for his father that is supposed to cure his despair. Edgar's theatricality, his changes of costume and voice, his commenting in soliloquy on his own performance, are only a few of the ways in which *King Lear* is fitted to the theater where it was originally performed, a theater in which the play's unsurpassed power can be fully experienced.

KING LEAR

1.1   *Enter Kent, Gloucester, and Edmund.*

KENT   I thought the King had more affected the Duke of 1
Albany than Cornwall. 2

GLOUCESTER   It did always seem so to us; but now in
the division of the kingdom it appears not which of
the dukes he values most, for equalities are so weighed 5
that curiosity in neither can make choice of either's 6
moiety. 7

KENT   Is not this your son, my lord?

GLOUCESTER   His breeding, sir, hath been at my charge. 9
I have so often blushed to acknowledge him that now
I am brazed to 't. 11

KENT   I cannot conceive you. 12

GLOUCESTER   Sir, this young fellow's mother could;
whereupon she grew round-wombed and had indeed, sir, a son for her cradle ere she had a husband
for her bed. Do you smell a fault? 16

KENT   I cannot wish the fault undone, the issue of it 17
being so proper. 18

GLOUCESTER   But I have a son, sir, by order of law, some 19
year elder than this, who yet is no dearer in my ac- 20
count. Though this knave came something saucily to 21
the world before he was sent for, yet was his mother
fair, there was good sport at his making, and the
whoreson must be acknowledged.—Do you know this 24
noble gentleman, Edmund?

EDMUND   No, my lord.

GLOUCESTER   My lord of Kent. Remember him hereafter
as my honorable friend.

EDMUND   My services to your lordship. 29

1.1. Location: King Lear's palace.
1 more affected better liked   **2 Albany** i.e., Scotland   **5–7 equalities . . .
moiety** the shares balance so equally that close scrutiny cannot find
advantage in either's portion   **9 breeding** raising, care.   **charge** expense   **11 brazed** hardened   **12 conceive** understand. (But Gloucester
puns in the sense of "become pregnant.")   **16 fault** (1) sin (2) loss of
scent by the hounds   **17 issue** (1) result (2) offspring   **18 proper**
(1) excellent (2) handsome   **19 by order of law** legitimate   **19–20 some
year** about a year   **20–21 account** estimation   **21 knave** young fellow
(not said disapprovingly, though the word is ironic).   **something** somewhat   **24 whoreson** low fellow; suggesting bastardy, but (like *knave*
above) used with affectionate condescension   **29 services** duty

KENT   I must love you, and sue to know you better.   30
EDMUND   Sir, I shall study deserving.   31
GLOUCESTER   He hath been out nine years, and away he   32
  shall again. The King is coming.   33

> *Sennet. Enter [one bearing a coronet, then] King*
> *Lear, Cornwall, Albany, Goneril, Regan, Cordelia,*
> *and attendants.*

LEAR
Attend the lords of France and Burgundy, Gloucester.   34
GLOUCESTER   I shall, my liege.   *Exit.*
LEAR
Meantime we shall express our darker purpose.   36
Give me the map there. [*He takes a map.*] Know that
  we have divided
In three our kingdom; and 'tis our fast intent   38
To shake all cares and business from our age,
Conferring them on younger strengths while we
Unburdened crawl toward death. Our son of Cornwall,
And you, our no less loving son of Albany,
We have this hour a constant will to publish   43
Our daughters' several dowers, that future strife   44
May be prevented now. The princes, France and
  Burgundy,   45
Great rivals in our youngest daughter's love,
Long in our court have made their amorous sojourn
And here are to be answered. Tell me, my daughters—
Since now we will divest us both of rule,
Interest of territory, cares of state—   50
Which of you shall we say doth love us most,
That we our largest bounty may extend
Where nature doth with merit challenge? Goneril,   53

---

30 sue petition, beg   **31 study deserving** strive to be worthy (of your
esteem)   **32 out** i.e., abroad, absent   **33 s.d. Sennet** trumpet signal
heralding a procession.   **one . . . then** (This direction is from the
quarto. The *coronet* is perhaps intended for Cordelia or her betrothed.
A coronet signifies nobility below the rank of king.)   **34 Attend** i.e., wait
on them ceremonially, usher them into our presence   **36 we, our** (The
royal plural; also in ll. 37–44, etc.)   **darker purpose** undeclared intention   **38 fast** firm   **43 constant . . . publish** firm resolve to proclaim
44 several individual   **45 prevented** forestalled   **50 Interest** possession   **53 Where . . . challenge** where both natural affection and merit
claim it as due

Our eldest born, speak first.

GONERIL

Sir, I love you more than words can wield the matter,
Dearer than eyesight, space, and liberty,   56
Beyond what can be valued, rich or rare,   57
No less than life, with grace, health, beauty, honor;
As much as child e'er loved, or father found;   59
A love that makes breath poor and speech unable.   60
Beyond all manner of so much I love you.

CORDELIA [*Aside*]

What shall Cordelia speak? Love and be silent.

LEAR [*Indicating on map*]

Of all these bounds, even from this line to this,
With shadowy forests and with champains riched,   64
With plenteous rivers and wide-skirted meads,   65
We make thee lady. To thine and Albany's issue
Be this perpetual.—What says our second daughter,
Our dearest Regan, wife of Cornwall? Speak.

REGAN

I am made of that self mettle as my sister,   69
And prize me at her worth. In my true heart   70
I find she names my very deed of love;   71
Only she comes too short, that I profess   72
Myself an enemy to all other joys
Which the most precious square of sense possesses,   74
And find I am alone felicitate   75
In your dear Highness' love.

CORDELIA [*Aside*]   Then poor Cordelia!
And yet not so, since I am sure my love's
More ponderous than my tongue.   78

LEAR

To thee and thine hereditary ever

---

56 space freedom from confinement.   **liberty** freedom of action
57 valued estimated   **59 found** i.e., found himself to be loved
60 breath voice, speech.   **unable** incompetent, inadequate   **64 shadowy**
shady.   **champains riched** fertile plains   **65 wide-skirted meads** extensive, spread out meadows   **69 self** same.   **mettle** spirit, temperament.
(But with the meaning also of *metal*, substance, continued in the metaphor of *prize* and *worth*, l. 70.)   **70 prize . . . worth** value myself as her
equal (in love for you). (*Prize* suggests "price.")   **71 names . . . love**
describes my love in very deed   **72 that** in that   **74 most . . . possesses**
most delicate test of my sensibility, most delicately sensitive part of my
nature, can enjoy   **75 felicitate** made happy   **78 ponderous** weighty

Remain this ample third of our fair kingdom,
No less in space, validity, and pleasure   81
Than that conferred on Goneril.—Now, our joy,
Although our last and least, to whose young love   83
The vines of France and milk of Burgundy   84
Strive to be interessed, what can you say to draw   85
A third more opulent than your sisters'? Speak.

CORDELIA Nothing, my lord.

LEAR   Nothing?

CORDELIA Nothing.

LEAR
Nothing will come of nothing. Speak again.

CORDELIA
Unhappy that I am, I cannot heave
My heart into my mouth. I love Your Majesty
According to my bond, no more nor less.   93

LEAR
How, how, Cordelia? Mend your speech a little,
Lest you may mar your fortunes.

CORDELIA   Good my lord,
You have begot me, bred me, loved me. I
Return those duties back as are right fit,   97
Obey you, love you, and most honor you.
Why have my sisters husbands if they say
They love you all? Haply, when I shall wed,   100
That lord whose hand must take my plight shall carry 101
Half my love with him, half my care and duty.
Sure I shall never marry like my sisters,
To love my father all.

LEAR
But goes thy heart with this?

CORDELIA   Ay, my good lord.

LEAR So young, and so untender?

CORDELIA So young, my lord, and true.

LEAR
Let it be so! Thy truth then be thy dower!

---

81 validity value.   **pleasure** pleasing features   **83 least** youngest
84 vines vineyards.   **milk** pastures (?)   **85 be interessed** be affiliated,
establish a claim, be admitted as to a privilege.   **draw** win   **93 bond**
filial obligation   **97 right fit** proper and fitting   **100 all** exclusively, and
with all of themselves.   **Haply** perhaps   **101 plight** troth-plight, pledge

For, by the sacred radiance of the sun,
The mysteries of Hecate and the night,   110
By all the operation of the orbs   111
From whom we do exist and cease to be,   112
Here I disclaim all my paternal care,
Propinquity, and property of blood,   114
And as a stranger to my heart and me
Hold thee from this forever. The barbarous Scythian,   116
Or he that makes his generation messes   117
To gorge his appetite, shall to my bosom
Be as well neighbored, pitied, and relieved
As thou my sometime daughter.

KENT   Good my liege—   120
LEAR   Peace, Kent!
Come not between the dragon and his wrath.
I loved her most, and thought to set my rest   123
On her kind nursery. [*To Cordelia.*] Hence, and avoid my
     sight!—   124
So be my grave my peace, as here I give   125
Her father's heart from her! Call France. Who stirs?   126
Call Burgundy. [*Exit one.*] Cornwall and Albany,
With my two daughters' dowers digest the third.   128
Let pride, which she calls plainness, marry her.   129
I do invest you jointly with my power,
Preeminence, and all the large effects   131
That troop with majesty. Ourself by monthly course,   132
With reservation of an hundred knights   133
By you to be sustained, shall our abode
Make with you by due turns. Only we shall retain

110 **mysteries** secret rites. **Hecate** goddess of witchcraft and the
moon 111 **operation** influence. **orbs** heavenly bodies 112 **From
whom** under whose influence 114 **Propinquity . . . blood** intimacy and
close kinship 116 **this** this time forth. **Scythian** (Scythians were
famous in antiquity for savagery.) 117 **makes . . . messes** makes meals
of his children or parents 120 **sometime** former 123 **set my rest**
repose myself. (A phrase from a game of cards meaning "to stake
all.") 124 **nursery** nursing, care. **avoid** leave 125 **So . . . peace, as** as
I hope to rest peacefully in my grave 126 **Who stirs?** i.e., somebody do
something; don't just stand there 128 **digest** assimilate, incorporate
129 **Let . . . her** let her pride be her dowry and get her a husband
131 **effects** outward shows 132 **troop with** accompany, serve. **Ourself**
(The royal "we.") 133 **With reservation of** reserving to myself the right
to be attended by

The name and all th' addition to a king.   136
The sway, revenue, execution of the rest,
Belovèd sons, be yours, which to confirm,
This coronet part between you.

KENT   Royal Lear,   139
Whom I have ever honored as my king,
Loved as my father, as my master followed,
As my great patron thought on in my prayers—

LEAR
The bow is bent and drawn. Make from the shaft.   143

KENT
Let it fall rather, though the fork invade   144
The region of my heart. Be Kent unmannerly   145
When Lear is mad. What wouldst thou do, old man?   146
Think'st thou that duty shall have dread to speak
When power to flattery bows?
To plainness honor's bound   149
When majesty falls to folly. Reserve thy state,   150
And in thy best consideration check   151
This hideous rashness. Answer my life my judgment,   152
Thy youngest daughter does not love thee least,
Nor are those emptyhearted whose low sounds
Reverb no hollowness.

LEAR   Kent, on thy life, no more.   155

KENT
My life I never held but as a pawn   156
To wage against thine enemies, nor fear to lose it,   157
Thy safety being motive.

LEAR   Out of my sight!   158

---

136 addition honors and prerogatives **139 coronet** (Perhaps Lear
gestures toward this coronet that was to have symbolized Cordelia's
dowry and marriage, or hands it to his sons-in-law, or actually attempts
to divide it.) **143 Make from** get out of the way of **144 fall** strike.
fork barbed head of an arrow **145–146 Be . . . mad** i.e., I must be
unmannerly when you behave so madly **149 To . . . bound** allegiance
demands frankness **150 Reserve thy state** retain your royal authority
151 in . . . consideration with wise deliberation. **check** restrain, with-
hold **152 Answer . . . judgment** I wager my life on my judgment that
155 Reverb no hollowness i.e., do not reverberate like a hollow drum,
insincerely **156 held** regarded. **pawn** stake, chess piece **157 wage**
wager, hazard in warfare **158 motive** that which prompts me to act

KENT
See better, Lear, and let me still remain 159
The true blank of thine eye. 160

LEAR   Now, by Apollo—

KENT   Now, by Apollo, King,
Thou swear'st thy gods in vain.

LEAR   O, vassal! Miscreant! 164

[*Laying his hand on his sword.*]

ALBANY, CORNWALL   Dear sir, forbear.

KENT
Kill thy physician, and the fee bestow
Upon the foul disease. Revoke thy gift,
Or whilst I can vent clamor from my throat
I'll tell thee thou dost evil.

LEAR
Hear me, recreant, on thine allegiance hear me! 170
That thou hast sought to make us break our vows, 171
Which we durst never yet, and with strained pride 172
To come betwixt our sentence and our power, 173
Which nor our nature nor our place can bear, 174
Our potency made good, take thy reward. 175
Five days we do allot thee for provision
To shield thee from disasters of the world, 177
And on the sixth to turn thy hated back
Upon our kingdom. If on the tenth day following
Thy banished trunk be found in our dominions, 180
The moment is thy death. Away! By Jupiter,
This shall not be revoked.

KENT
Fare thee well, King. Sith thus thou wilt appear, 183
Freedom lives hence and banishment is here.

159 still always   **160 The true . . . eye** i.e., the means to enable you to
see better. (*Blank* means the white center of the target, or, more probably, the true direct aim, as in "point-blank," traveling in a straight
line.)   **164 vassal** i.e., wretch.   **Miscreant** (Literally, infidel; hence, villain, rascal.)   **170 recreant** traitor   **171 That** in that, since   **172 strained**
excessive   **173 To . . . power** i.e., to block my power to give sentence
174 Which . . . place which neither my temperament nor my office as
king   **175 Our . . . good** my potency now being validated, to show that
I am not merely threatening   **177 disasters** misfortunes   **180 trunk**
body   **183 Sith** since

[*To Cordelia.*] The gods to their dear shelter take thee,
  maid,
That justly think'st and hast most rightly said!
[*To Regan and Goneril.*] And your large speeches may
  your deeds approve,   187
That good effects may spring from words of love.
Thus Kent, O princes, bids you all adieu.
He'll shape his old course in a country new.   *Exit.* 190

    Flourish. Enter Gloucester, with France and
    Burgundy; attendants.

GLOUCESTER
Here's France and Burgundy, my noble lord.
LEAR   My lord of Burgundy,
We first address toward you, who with this king   193
Hath rivaled for our daughter. What in the least   194
Will you require in present dower with her
Or cease your quest of love?
BURGUNDY   Most royal Majesty,
I crave no more than hath Your Highness offered,
Nor will you tender less.
LEAR   Right noble Burgundy,   198
When she was dear to us we did hold her so,   199
But now her price is fallen. Sir, there she stands.
If aught within that little-seeming substance,   201
Or all of it, with our displeasure pieced,   202
And nothing more, may fitly like Your Grace,   203
She's there, and she is yours.
BURGUNDY   I know no answer.
LEAR
Will you, with those infirmities she owes,   205
Unfriended, new-adopted to our hate,
Dowered with our curse and strangered with our oath, 207
Take her, or leave her?

---

187 your . . . approve may your deeds confirm your speeches with their
vast claims **190 shape . . . course** follow his traditional plainspoken
ways **193 address** address myself **194 rivaled** competed **198 tender**
offer **199 so** i.e., *dear*, beloved and valued at a high price **201 little-
seeming substance** one who seems substantial but whose substance is
in fact little; or, one who refuses to flatter **202 pieced** added, joined
203 like please **205 owes** owns **207 strangered with** made a
stranger by

BURGUNDY   Pardon me, royal sir.
  Election makes not up in such conditions.   209
LEAR
  Then leave her, sir, for by the power that made me,
  I tell you all her wealth. [*To France.*] For you, great King,   211
  I would not from your love make such a stray   212
  To match you where I hate; therefore beseech you   213
  T' avert your liking a more worthier way   214
  Than on a wretch whom Nature is ashamed
  Almost t' acknowledge hers.
FRANCE   This is most strange,
  That she whom even but now was your best object,   217
  The argument of your praise, balm of your age,   218
  The best, the dearest, should in this trice of time
  Commit a thing so monstrous to dismantle   220
  So many folds of favor. Sure her offense
  Must be of such unnatural degree
  That monsters it, or your forevouched affection   223
  Fall into taint, which to believe of her   224
  Must be a faith that reason without miracle
  Should never plant in me.   226
CORDELIA   I yet beseech Your Majesty—
  If for I want that glib and oily art   228
  To speak and purpose not, since what I well intend   229
  I'll do 't before I speak—that you make known
  It is no vicious blot, murder, or foulness,
  No unchaste action or dishonored step
  That hath deprived me of your grace and favor,
  But even for want of that for which I am richer: 234
  A still-soliciting eye and such a tongue   235

209 Election . . . conditions no choice is possible under such conditions   **211 tell you** (1) inform you of (2) enumerate for you.   **For** as
for   **212 make such a stray** stray so far   **213 To** as to.   **beseech** I
beseech   **214 avert your liking** turn your affections   **217 whom** who.
best object main object of love   **218 argument** theme   **220 to** as to
223 monsters it makes it monstrous   **223–224 or . . . taint** or else the
affection for her you have hitherto affirmed (*forevouched*) must fall into
suspicion (*taint*); or, before (ere, *or*) your hitherto-proclaimed affection
could have fallen into decay   **224 which** i.e., that her offense is monstrous   **226 Should** could   **228 for I want** because I lack   **229 purpose
not** not intend to do what I say   **234 for which** for want of which
235 still-soliciting ever-begging

That I am glad I have not, though not to have it
Hath lost me in your liking.

LEAR   Better thou
Hadst not been born than not t' have pleased me better.

FRANCE
Is it but this? A tardiness in nature
Which often leaves the history unspoke   240
That it intends to do? My lord of Burgundy,
What say you to the lady? Love's not love
When it is mingled with regards that stands   243
Aloof from th' entire point. Will you have her?   244
She is herself a dowry.

BURGUNDY   Royal King,
Give but that portion which yourself proposed,
And here I take Cordelia by the hand,
Duchess of Burgundy.

LEAR
Nothing. I have sworn. I am firm.

BURGUNDY [*To Cordelia*]
I am sorry, then, you have so lost a father
That you must lose a husband.

CORDELIA   Peace be with Burgundy!
Since that respects of fortune are his love,   252
I shall not be his wife.

FRANCE
Fairest Cordelia, that art most rich being poor,
Most choice, forsaken, and most loved, despised,
Thee and thy virtues here I seize upon,
Be it lawful I take up what's cast away.   257
                    [*He takes her hand.*]
Gods, gods! 'Tis strange that from their cold'st neglect 258
My love should kindle to inflamed respect.—   259
Thy dowerless daughter, King, thrown to my chance,   260
Is queen of us, of ours, and our fair France.
Not all the dukes of waterish Burgundy   262

---

240 leaves . . . unspoke does not speak aloud the action **243–244 regards
. . . point** irrelevant considerations **252 Since that** since. **respects of
fortune** concern for wealth and position **257 Be it lawful** if it be lawful
that **258 from . . . neglect** i.e., because the gods seem to have deserted
Cordelia **259 inflamed respect** ardent affection **260 chance** lot
262 waterish (1) well-watered with rivers (2) feeble, watery

Can buy this unprized precious maid of me.—   263
Bid them farewell, Cordelia, though unkind.   264
Thou losest here, a better where to find.   265

LEAR
Thou hast her, France. Let her be thine, for we
Have no such daughter, nor shall ever see
That face of hers again. Therefore begone   268
Without our grace, our love, our benison.   269
Come, noble Burgundy.

Flourish. Exeunt [all but France, Goneril,
                              Regan, and Cordelia].

FRANCE   Bid farewell to your sisters.

CORDELIA
The jewels of our father, with washed eyes   272
Cordelia leaves you. I know you what you are,
And like a sister am most loath to call   274
Your faults as they are named. Love well our father.   275
To your professèd bosoms I commit him.   276
But yet, alas, stood I within his grace,
I would prefer him to a better place.   278
So, farewell to you both.

REGAN
Prescribe not us our duty.

GONERIL   Let your study
Be to content your lord, who hath received you
At Fortune's alms. You have obedience scanted,   282
And well are worth the want that you have wanted.   283

CORDELIA
Time shall unfold what plighted cunning hides;   284

263 unprized not appreciated (with perhaps a sense also of "priceless")   **264 though unkind** though they have behaved unnaturally   **265 here** this place.   **where** place elsewhere   **268–269 Therefore . . . benison** (Said perhaps to Cordelia and to the King of France.) **benison** blessing   **272 The** you, the.   **washed** tear-washed   **274 like a sister** i.e., because I am your sister   **275 as . . . named** by their true names   **276 professèd bosoms** publicly avowed love   **278 prefer** advance, recommend   **282 At . . . alms** as a pittance or dole from Fortune.   **scanted** stinted   **283 well . . . wanted** well deserve the lack of affection which you yourself have shown. (*Want* may also refer to her dowry.)   **284 plighted** pleated, enfolded

Who covers faults, at last shame them derides.   285
Well may you prosper!
'RANCE   Come, my fair Cordelia.
                              Exeunt France and Cordelia.
GONERIL   Sister, it is not little I have to say of what most
nearly appertains to us both. I think our father will
hence tonight.
REGAN   That's most certain, and with you; next month
with us.
GONERIL   You see how full of changes his age is; the
observation we have made of it hath not been little.
He always loved our sister most, and with what poor
judgment he hath now cast her off appears too grossly. 295
REGAN   'Tis the infirmity of his age. Yet he hath ever but
slenderly known himself.
GONERIL   The best and soundest of his time hath been 298
but rash. Then must we look from his age to receive 299
not alone the imperfections of long-ingraffed condi- 300
tion, but therewithal the unruly waywardness that in- 301
firm and choleric years bring with them.
REGAN   Such unconstant starts are we like to have from 303
him as this of Kent's banishment.
GONERIL   There is further compliment of leave-taking 305
between France and him. Pray you, let us hit together. 306
If our father carry authority with such disposition as
he bears, this last surrender of his will but offend us. 308
REGAN   We shall further think of it.
GONERIL   We must do something, and i' the heat.   310
                                              Exeunt.

❧

285 Who . . . derides i.e., time, who may conceal faults for a while, at
last exposes and derides them shamefully   **295 grossly** obviously
298–299 The best . . . rash i.e., even in the prime of his life, he was
stormy and unpredictable   **300–301 long-ingraffed condition** long-
implanted habit   **301 therewithal** added thereto   **303 unconstant starts**
impulsive acts.   **like** likely   **305 compliment** ceremony   **306 hit**
agree   **308 last surrender** latest abdication.   **offend** harm, injure
310 i' the heat i.e., while the iron is hot

1.2   *Enter Bastard [Edmund, with a letter].*

EDMUND
Thou, Nature, art my goddess; to thy law   1
My services are bound. Wherefore should I
Stand in the plague of custom and permit   3
The curiosity of nations to deprive me,   4
For that I am some twelve or fourteen moonshines   5
Lag of a brother? Why bastard? Wherefore base?   6
When my dimensions are as well compact,   7
My mind as generous, and my shape as true,   8
As honest madam's issue? Why brand they us   9
With base? With baseness? Bastardy? Base, base?
Who in the lusty stealth of nature take   11
More composition and fierce quality   12
Than doth within a dull, stale, tirèd bed
Go to th' creating a whole tribe of fops   14
Got 'tween asleep and wake? Well then,   15
Legitimate Edgar, I must have your land.
Our father's love is to the bastard Edmund
As to th' legitimate. Fine word, "legitimate"!
Well, my legitimate, if this letter speed   19
And my invention thrive, Edmund the base   20
Shall top th' legitimate. I grow, I prosper.
Now, gods, stand up for bastards!

    Enter Gloucester.

GLOUCESTER
Kent banished thus? And France in choler parted?
And the King gone tonight? Prescribed his power,   24
Confined to exhibition? All this done   25
Upon the gad? Edmund, how now? What news?   26

1.2. Location: The Earl of Gloucester's house.
1 Nature i.e., the material world, governed solely by mechanistic amoral
forces   **3 Stand . . . custom** submit to the vexatious injustice of convention   **4 curiosity** fastidious distinctions.   **nations** societies   **5 For that**
because.   **moonshines** months   **6 Lag of** younger than   **7 compact**
knit together, fitted   **8 generous** noble, refined   **9 honest** chaste
11–12 take . . . quality acquire greater completeness and energetic
force   **14 fops** fools   **15 Got** begotten   **19 speed** succeed, prosper
20 invention thrive scheme prosper   **24 tonight** last night.   **Prescribed**
limited   **25 exhibition** an allowance, pension   **26 Upon the gad** suddenly, as if pricked by a gad or spur

EDMUND   So please your lordship, none.

[*Putting up the letter.*]

GLOUCESTER   Why so earnestly seek you to put up that letter?

EDMUND   I know no news, my lord.

GLOUCESTER   What paper were you reading?

EDMUND   Nothing, my lord.

GLOUCESTER   No? What needed then that terrible dis- 33
patch of it into your pocket? The quality of nothing 34
hath not such need to hide itself. Let's see. Come, if it
be nothing I shall not need spectacles.

EDMUND   I beseech you, sir, pardon me. It is a letter
from my brother, that I have not all o'erread; and for
so much as I have perused, I find it not fit for your
o'erlooking.   40

GLOUCESTER   Give me the letter, sir.

EDMUND   I shall offend either to detain or give it. The
contents, as in part I understand them, are to blame.   43

GLOUCESTER   Let's see, let's see.

[*Edmund gives the letter.*]

EDMUND   I hope for my brother's justification he wrote
this but as an essay or taste of my virtue.   46

GLOUCESTER (*Reads*)   "This policy and reverence of age 47
makes the world bitter to the best of our times, keeps 48
our fortunes from us till our oldness cannot relish
them. I begin to find an idle and fond bondage in the 50
oppression of aged tyranny, who sways not as it hath 51
power but as it is suffered. Come to me, that of this I 52
may speak more. If our father would sleep till I waked
him, you should enjoy half his revenue forever and
live the beloved of your brother,   Edgar."
Hum! Conspiracy! "Sleep till I waked him, you
should enjoy half his revenue." My son Edgar! Had he
a hand to write this? A heart and brain to breed it

33–34 terrible dispatch fearful haste   **40 o'erlooking** perusal   **43 to
blame** (The Folio reading, *too blame,* "too blameworthy to be shown,"
may be correct.)   **46 essay or taste** i.e., assay, test   **47 policy and reverence of** i.e., policy of reverencing   **48 the best . . . times** the best years
of our lives, i.e., our youth   **50 idle** useless. **fond** foolish   **51 who
sways** which rules   **52 suffered** permitted (by the young, who could
seize power if they wished)

in? When came you to this? Who brought it?   59

EDMUND   It was not brought me, my lord; there's the
cunning of it. I found it thrown in at the casement of   61
my closet.   62

GLOUCESTER   You know the character to be your broth-   63
er's?

EDMUND   If the matter were good, my lord, I drust   65
swear it were his; but in respect of that I would fain   66
think it were not.

GLOUCESTER   It is his.

EDMUND   It is his hand, my lord, but I hope his heart is
not in the contents.

GLOUCESTER   Has he never before sounded you in this
business?

EDMUND   Never, my lord. But I have heard him oft
maintain it to be fit that, sons at perfect age and fathers   74
declined, the father should be as ward to the son, and   75
the son manage his revenue.

GLOUCESTER   O villain, villain! His very opinion in the   77
letter! Abhorred villain! Unnatural, detested, brutish   78
villain! Worse than brutish! Go, sirrah, seek him. I'll   79
apprehend him. Abominable villain! Where is he?

EDMUND   I do not well know, my lord. If it shall please
you to suspend your indignation against my brother
till you can derive from him better testimony of his
intent, you should run a certain course; where, if you   84
violently proceed against him, mistaking his purpose,
it would make a great gap in your own honor and
shake in pieces the heart of his obedience. I dare pawn   87
down my life for him that he hath writ this to feel my   88
affection to your honor, and to no other pretense of   89
danger.   90

---

59 to this upon this (letter)   **61 casement** window   **62 closet** private
room   **63 character** handwriting   **65 matter** contents   **66 in . . . that**
considering what the contents are.   **fain** gladly   **74 fit** fitting, appropriate.   **perfect age** full maturity   **75 declined** having become feeble
77 villain i.e., vile wretch, diabolical schemer   **78 Abhorred** abhor-
rent.   **detested** detestable   **79 sirrah** (Form of address used to inferiors
or children.)   **84 run a certain course** proceed with safety and certainty.   **where** whereas   **87–88 pawn down** stake   **88 feel** feel out
89–90 pretense of danger dangerous purpose

GLOUCESTER Think you so?

EDMUND If your honor judge it meet, I will place you 92
where you shall hear us confer of this, and by an au-
ricular assurance have your satisfaction, and that without any further delay than this very evening.

GLOUCESTER He cannot be such a monster—

EDMUND Nor is not, sure.

GLOUCESTER To his father, that so tenderly and entirely
loves him. Heaven and earth! Edmund, seek him out;
wind me into him, I pray you. Frame the business 100
after your own wisdom. I would unstate myself to be 101
in a due resolution. 102

EDMUND I will seek him, sir, presently, convey the 103
business as I shall find means, and acquaint you
withal. 105

GLOUCESTER These late eclipses in the sun and moon 106
portend no good to us. Though the wisdom of nature 107
can reason it thus and thus, yet nature finds itself
scourged by the sequent effects. Love cools, friendship 109
falls off, brothers divide; in cities, mutinies; in countries, discord; in palaces, treason; and the bond
cracked twixt son and father. This villain of mine
comes under the prediction; there's son against father.
The King falls from bias of nature; there's father 114
against child. We have seen the best of our time.
Machinations, hollowness, treachery, and all ruinous
disorders follow us disquietly to our graves. Find out
this villain, Edmund; it shall lose thee nothing. Do it
carefully. And the noble and truehearted Kent banished! His offense, honesty! 'Tis strange.   *Exit*.

EDMUND This is the excellent foppery of the world, that 121
when we are sick in fortune—often the surfeits of our
own behavior—we make guilty of our disasters the
sun, the moon, and stars, as if we were villains on 124
necessity, fools by heavenly compulsion, knaves,

---

92 meet fitting, proper   **100 wind me into him** insinuate yourself into
his confidence. (*Me* is used colloquially.)   **Frame** arrange   **101 after
your own wisdom** as you think best   **101–102 unstate . . . resolution** suffer loss of all to know the truth, have my doubts resolved
103 presently immediately.   **convey** manage   **105 withal** therewith
106 late recent   **107 the wisdom of nature** natural science   **109 sequent
effects** i.e., devastating consequences   **114 bias of nature** natural inclination   **121 foppery** foolishness   **124 on** by

thieves, and treachers by spherical predominance, 126
drunkards, liars, and adulterers by an enforced obedience of planetary influence, and all that we are evil
in, by a divine thrusting on. An admirable evasion of 129
whoremaster man, to lay his goatish disposition on 130
the charge of a star! My father compounded with my 131
mother under the Dragon's tail and my nativity was 132
under Ursa Major, so that it follows I am rough and 133
lecherous. Fut, I should have been that I am, had the 134
maidenliest star in the firmament twinkled on my bas-
tardizing. Edgar—

    Enter Edgar.

and pat he comes like the catastrophe of the old com- 137
edy. My cue is villainous melancholy, with a sigh like
Tom o' Bedlam.—O, these eclipses do portend these 139
divisions! Fa, sol, la, mi.

EDGAR How now, brother Edmund, what serious con-
templation are you in?

EDMUND I am thinking, brother, of a prediction I read
this other day, what should follow these eclipses.   144

EDGAR Do you busy yourself with that?

EDMUND I promise you, the effects he writes of succeed 146
unhappily, as of unnaturalness between the child and 147
the parent, death, dearth, dissolutions of ancient amities, divisions in state, menaces and maledictions
against king and nobles, needless diffidences, banish- 150
ment of friends, dissipation of cohorts, nuptial 151
breaches, and I know not what.

EDGAR How long have you been a sectary astronom- 153
ical?   154

EDMUND Come, come, when saw you my father last?

---

126 treachers traitors. **spherical predominance** astrological determi-
nism; because a certain planet was ascendant at the hour of our birth
129 divine supernatural **130 goatish** lecherous **131–132 compounded
. . . Dragon's tail** had sex with my mother under the constellation
Draco **133 Ursa Major** the big bear **134 Fut** i.e., 'sfoot, by Christ's
foot. **that** what **137 catastrophe** conclusion, resolution (of a play)
139 Tom o' Bedlam a lunatic patient of Bethlehem Hospital in London
turned out to beg for his bread **144 this other day** the other day
146–147 succeed unhappily follow unluckily **150 needless diffidences**
groundless distrust of others **151 dissipation of cohorts** breaking up of
military companies, large-scale desertions **153–154 sectary astronomi-
cal** believer in astrology

EDGAR The night gone by.

EDMUND Spake you with him?

EDGAR Ay, two hours together.

EDMUND Parted you in good terms? Found you no displeasure in him by word nor countenance?   160

EDGAR None at all.

EDMUND Bethink yourself wherein you may have offended him, and at my entreaty forbear his presence 163
until some little time hath qualified the heat of his dis- 164
pleasure, which at this instant so rageth in him that
with the mischief of your person it would scarcely 166
allay.   167

EDGAR Some villain hath done me wrong.

EDMUND That's my fear. I pray you, have a continent 169
forbearance till the speed of his rage goes slower; and, 170
as I say, retire with me to my lodging, from whence I
will fitly bring you to hear my lord speak. Pray ye, go! 172
There's my key. [*He gives a key.*] If you do stir abroad,
go armed.

EDGAR Armed, brother?

EDMUND Brother, I advise you to the best. I am no honest man if there be any good meaning toward you. I 177
have told you what I have seen and heard, but faintly,
nothing like the image and horror of it. Pray you, 179
away.

EDGAR Shall I hear from you anon?

EDMUND

I do serve you in this business.   *Exit [Edgar].*
A credulous father and a brother noble,
Whose nature is so far from doing harms
That he suspects none; on whose foolish honesty
My practices ride easy. I see the business.   186
Let me, if not by birth, have lands by wit.   187
All with me's meet that I can fashion fit.   *Exit.* 188

160 **countenance** demeanor   163 **forbear his presence** avoid meeting him
164 **qualified** moderated   166 **with . . . person** with the harmful effect of
your presence; or, even if there were injury done to you   167 **allay** be
allayed   169–170 **have . . . forbearance** keep a wary distance   172 **fitly** at a
fit time   177 **meaning** intention   179 **image and horror** horrid reality
186 **practices** plots. **the business** i.e., how my plots should proceed
187 **wit** intelligence   188 **meet** justifiable. **fit** i.e., to my purpose

1.3   *Enter Goneril, and [Oswald, her] steward.*

GONERIL   Did my father strike my gentleman for chiding of his fool?

OSWALD   Ay, madam.

GONERIL

By day and night he wrongs me! Every hour
He flashes into one gross crime or other   5
That sets us all at odds. I'll not endure it.
His knights grow riotous, and himself upbraids us
On every trifle. When he returns from hunting
I will not speak with him. Say I am sick.
If you come slack of former services   10
You shall do well; the fault of it I'll answer.

                     [*Horns within.*]

OSWALD   He's coming, madam. I hear him.

GONERIL

Put on what weary negligence you please,
You and your fellows. I'd have it come to question.   14
If he distaste it, let him to my sister,   15
Whose mind and mine, I know, in that are one,
Not to be overruled. Idle old man,   17
That still would manage those authorities   18
That he hath given away! Now, by my life,
Old fools are babes again, and must be used
With checks as flatteries, when they are seen abused.   21
Remember what I have said.

OSWALD   Well, madam.

GONERIL

And let his knights have colder looks among you.
What grows of it, no matter. Advise your fellows so.
I would breed from hence occasions, and I shall,   26
That I may speak. I'll write straight to my sister   27
To hold my very course. Prepare for dinner.   *Exeunt.*

1.3. Location: The Duke of Albany's palace.
5 crime offense   **10 come slack** fall short   **14 come to question** be
made an issue   **15 distaste** dislike   **17 Idle** foolish   **18 manage those
authorities** i.e., assert those prerogatives   **21 With . . . abused** with
rebukes instead of flattery, when they (old men) act unselfknowingly (as
Lear does)   **26–27 I would . . . speak** I wish to create from these incidents the opportunity to speak out   **27 straight** immediately

1.4   *Enter Kent [disguised].*

KENT
   If but as well I other accents borrow   1
   That can my speech diffuse, my good intent   2
   May carry through itself to that full issue   3
   For which I rased my likeness. Now, banished Kent,   4
   If thou canst serve where thou dost stand condemned,
   So may it come thy master, whom thou lov'st,   6
   Shall find thee full of labors.

    Horns within. Enter Lear, [Knights,] and
    attendants.

LEAR Let me not stay a jot for dinner. Go get it ready. 8
  [*Exit an Attendant.*] How now, what art thou?   9
KENT A man, sir.
LEAR What dost thou profess? What wouldst thou 11
  with us?
KENT I do profess to be no less than I seem: to serve
  him truly that will put me in trust, to love him that is
  honest, to converse with him that is wise and says 15
  little, to fear judgment, to fight when I cannot choose, 16
  and to eat no fish.   17
LEAR What art thou?
KENT A very honest-hearted fellow, and as poor as the
  King.
LEAR If thou be'st as poor for a subject as he's for a
  king, thou'rt poor enough. What wouldst thou?
KENT Service.
LEAR Who wouldst thou serve?
KENT You.

**1.4. Location: The Duke of Albany's palace still. The sense of time is
virtually continuous.**
1 as well i.e., as well as I have disguised myself by means of costume
2 diffuse i.e., disguise   **3 carry . . . issue** succeed to that perfect result
4 rased my likeness erased my outward appearance (perhaps with a
sense also of having *razed* or scraped off his beard)   **6 come** come to
pass that   **8 stay** wait   **9 s.d. Attendant** (This attendant may be a
knight; certainly the one who speaks at l. 50 is a knight.)   **11 What . . .
profess** what is your special calling. (But Kent puns in his answer on
profess meaning to "claim.")   **15 honest** honorable.   **converse** associate   **16 judgment** i.e., God's judgment.   **choose** i.e., choose but to
fight   **17 eat no fish** i.e., eat a manly diet (?), be a good Protestant (?)

LEAR   Dost thou know me, fellow?

KENT   No, sir, but you have that in your countenance 27
which I would fain call master.

LEAR   What's that?

KENT   Authority.

LEAR   What services canst thou do?

KENT   I can keep honest counsel, ride, run, mar a curi- 32
ous tale in telling it, and deliver a plain message 33
bluntly. That which ordinary men are fit for I am
qualified in, and the best of me is diligence.

LEAR   How old art thou?

KENT   Not so young, sir, to love a woman for singing, 37
nor so old to dote on her for anything. I have years on
my back forty-eight.

LEAR   Follow me; thou shalt serve me. If I like thee no
worse after dinner, I will not part from thee yet. Dinner, ho, dinner! Where's my knave, my fool? Go you
and call my fool hither.   [*Exit one.*]

    Enter steward [*Oswald*].

You! You, sirrah, where's my daughter?

OSWALD   So please you—   *Exit.*

LEAR   What says the fellow there? Call the clodpoll back. 46
[*Exit a Knight.*] Where's my fool, ho? I think the
world's asleep.

    [*Enter Knight.*]

How now? Where's that mongrel?

KNIGHT   He says, my lord, your daughter is not well.

LEAR   Why came not the slave back to me when I called
him?

KNIGHT   Sir, he answered me in the roundest manner, 53
he would not.

LEAR   He would not?

KNIGHT   My lord, I know not what the matter is, but to
my judgment Your Highness is not entertained with 57
that ceremonious affection as you were wont. There's
a great abatement of kindness appears as well in the

27 countenance face and bearing   **32 keep honest counsel** respect
confidences   **32–33 curious** ornate, elaborate   **37 to love** as to love
46 clodpoll blockhead   **53 roundest** bluntest   **57 entertained** treated

general dependents as in the Duke himself also and
your daughter.

LEAR   Ha? Sayst thou so?

KNIGHT   I beseech you, pardon me, my lord, if I be mis-
taken, for my duty cannot be silent when I think Your
Highness wronged.

LEAR   Thou but rememberest me of mine own concep-   66
tion. I have perceived a most faint neglect of late,   67
which I have rather blamed as mine own jealous curi-   68
osity than as a very pretense and purpose of unkind-   69
ness. I will look further into 't. But where's my fool? I
have not seen him this two days.   71

KNIGHT   Since my young lady's going into France, sir,
the Fool hath much pined away.

LEAR   No more of that. I have noted it well. Go you and
tell my daughter I would speak with her. [*Exit one.*]
Go you call hither my fool.   [*Exit one.*]

   Enter steward [Oswald].

O, you, sir, you, come you hither, sir. Who am I, sir?

OSWALD   My lady's father.

LEAR   "My lady's father"? My lord's knave! You whoreson dog, you slave, you cur!

OSWALD   I am none of these, my lord, I beseech your
pardon.

LEAR   Do you bandy looks with me, you rascal?   83
                            [*He strikes Oswald.*]

OSWALD   I'll not be strucken, my lord.   84

KENT   Nor tripped neither, you base football player.   85
                      [*He trips up Oswald's heels.*]

LEAR   I thank thee, fellow. Thou serv'st me, and I'll love
thee.

KENT   Come, sir, arise, away! I'll teach you differences.   88

---

66 rememberest remind   **66–67 conception** idea, thought   **67 faint**
halfhearted   **68–69 jealous curiosity** overscrupulous regard for matters
of etiquette   **69 very pretense** true intention   **71 this** these   **83 bandy**
volley, exchange (as in tennis)   **84 strucken** struck   **85 football** (A
raucous street game played by the lower classes.)   **88 differences**
distinctions in rank

Away, away! If you will measure your lubber's length 89
again, tarry; but away! Go to. Have you wisdom? So. 90
                         [*He pushes Oswald out.*]

LEAR Now, my friendly knave, I thank thee. There's
earnest of thy service.   [*He gives Kent money.*] 92

          Enter Fool.

FOOL Let me hire him too. Here's my coxcomb. 93
                         [*Offering Kent his cap.*]

LEAR How now, my pretty knave, how dost thou?

FOOL [*To Kent*] Sirrah, you were best take my coxcomb. 95

KENT Why, Fool?

FOOL Why? For taking one's part that's out of favor.
Nay, an thou canst not smile as the wind sits, thou'lt 98
catch cold shortly. There, take my coxcomb. Why, this 99
fellow has banished two on 's daughters and did the 100
third a blessing against his will. If thou follow him, thou 101
must needs wear my coxcomb.—How now, nuncle? 102
Would I had two coxcombs and two daughters.

LEAR Why, my boy?

FOOL If I gave them all my living, I'd keep my cox- 105
combs myself. There's mine; beg another of thy
daughters.

LEAR Take heed, sirrah—the whip.

FOOL Truth's a dog must to kennel. He must be
whipped out, when the Lady Brach may stand by the 110
fire and stink.

LEAR A pestilent gall to me! 112

FOOL Sirrah, I'll teach thee a speech.

LEAR Do.

FOOL Mark it, nuncle:

89–90 If . . . again i.e., if you want to be laid out flat again, you clumsy
ox **90 Have you wisdom** i.e., are you smart enough to make a quick
retreat **92 earnest** partial advance payment **93 coxcomb** fool's cap,
crested with a red comb **95 you were best** you had better **98 an . . .
sits** i.e., if you can't play along with those in power **99 catch cold** i.e.,
find yourself out in the cold **100 banished** (i.e., paradoxically, by giving
Goneril and Regan his kingdom, Lear has lost them, given them power
over him). **on 's** of his **101 blessing** i.e., bestowing Cordelia on
France **102 nuncle** (Contraction of "mine uncle," the Fool's way of
addressing Lear.) **105 living** property **110 Brach** hound bitch (here
suggesting flattery) **112 gall** irritation

Have more than thou showest,
Speak less than thou knowest,
Lend less than thou owest,   118
Ride more than thou goest,   119
Learn more than thou trowest,   120
Set less than thou throwest;   121
Leave thy drink and thy whore,
And keep in-a-door,   123
And thou shalt have more   124
Than two tens to a score.   125

KENT   This is nothing, Fool.

FOOL   Then 'tis like the breath of an unfee'd lawyer; you   127
gave me nothing for 't. Can you make no use of nothing, nuncle?

LEAR   Why, no, boy. Nothing can be made out of
nothing.

FOOL [*To Kent*]   Prithee, tell him; so much the rent of his   132
land comes to. He will not believe a fool.

LEAR   A bitter fool!   134

FOOL   Dost thou know the difference, my boy, between
a bitter fool and a sweet one?

LEAR   No, lad. Teach me.

FOOL

That lord that counseled thee
   To give away thy land,
Come place him here by me;
   Do thou for him stand.   141
The sweet and bitter fool
   Will presently appear: 143
The one in motley here,   144
   The other found out there.   145

LEAR   Dost thou call me fool, boy?

118 owest own   **119 goest** i.e., on foot. (Travel prudently on horseback,
not afoot.)   **120 Learn** i.e., listen to.   **trowest** believe   **121 Set . . .
throwest** stake less at dice than you have a chance to throw, i.e., don't
bet all you can   **123 in-a-door** indoors, at home   **124–125 shalt . . .
score** i.e., will do better than break even (since a *score* equals two tens,
or 20)   **127 breath** speech, counsel   **132 rent** (Lear has no land, hence
no rent.)   **134 bitter** satirical   **141 for him stand** impersonate him
143 presently immediately   **144 motley** the particolored dress of the
professional fool. (The Fool identifies himself as the sweet fool, Lear as
the bitter fool who counseled himself to give away his kingdom.)
145 there (The Fool points at Lear.)

FOOL   All thy other titles thou hast given away; that thou wast born with.

KENT   This is not altogether fool, my lord.

FOOL   No, faith, lords and great men will not let me; if 150
I had a monopoly out, they would have part on 't. And 151
ladies too, they will not let me have all the fool to myself; they'll be snatching. Nuncle, give me an egg and 153
I'll give thee two crowns.

LEAR   What two crowns shall they be?

FOOL   Why, after I have cut the egg i' the middle and eat 156
up the meat, the two crowns of the egg. When thou 157
clovest thy crown i' the middle and gav'st away both
parts, thou bor'st thine ass on thy back o'er the dirt. 159
Thou hadst little wit in thy bald crown when thou
gav'st thy golden one away. If I speak like myself in 161
this, let him be whipped that first finds it so. 162
[*Sings.*] "Fools had ne'er less grace in a year, 163
    For wise men are grown foppish 164
  And know not how their wits to wear, 165
    Their manners are so apish."

LEAR   When were you wont to be so full of songs, sirrah?

FOOL   I have used it, nuncle, e'er since thou mad'st thy 169
daughters thy mothers; for when thou gav'st them the
rod and putt'st down thine own breeches,
[*Sings*] "Then they for sudden joy did weep,
    And I for sorrow sung,
  That such a king should play bo-peep 174
    And go the fools among."

Prithee, nuncle, keep a schoolmaster that can teach thy fool to lie. I would fain learn to lie.

---

150 No . . . let me i.e., great persons at court will not let me monopolize folly; I am not *altogether fool* in the sense of being "all the fool there is"   **151 a monopoly out** a corner on the market. (The granting of monopolies was a common abuse under King James and Queen Elizabeth.)   **on 't** of it   **153 snatching** i.e., at the Fool's phallic bauble
156 eat eaten, et   **157 the meat** the edible part   **159 bor'st . . . dirt** i.e., bore the ass instead of letting the ass bear you   **161 like myself** i.e., like a fool   **162 whipped** i.e., as a fool.   **finds it so** discovers from his experience that it is true (as Lear is now discovering)   **163 Fools . . . year** fools have never enjoyed less favor; i.e., they are made obsolete by the folly of supposed wise men   **164 foppish** foolish, vain   **165 wear** use   **169 used** practiced   **174 bo-peep** a child's game

LEAR   An you lie, sirrah, we'll have you whipped.   178
FOOL   I marvel what kin thou and thy daughters are.
They'll have me whipped for speaking true, thou'lt
have me whipped for lying, and sometimes I am
whipped for holding my peace. I had rather be any
kind o' thing than a fool. And yet I would not be thee,
nuncle. Thou hast pared thy wit o' both sides and left
nothing i' the middle. Here comes one o' the parings.

   Enter Goneril.

LEAR
How now, daughter? What makes that frontlet on?   186
You are too much of late i' the frown.
FOOL   Thou wast a pretty fellow when thou hadst no
need to care for her frowning; now thou art an O with-   189
out a figure. I am better than thou art now; I am a fool,   190
thou art nothing. [*To Goneril.*] Yes, forsooth, I will
hold my tongue; so your face bids me, though you say
nothing.
   Mum, mum,
   He that keeps nor crust nor crumb,   195
   Weary of all, shall want some.   196
[*Pointing to Lear.*] That's a shelled peascod.   197
GONERIL
Not only, sir, this your all-licensed fool,   198
But other of your insolent retinue
Do hourly carp and quarrel, breaking forth   200
In rank and not-to-be-endurèd riots. Sir,   201
I had thought by making this well known unto you
To have found a safe redress, but now grow fearful,   203
By what yourself too late have spoke and done,   204
That you protect this course and put it on   205
By your allowance; which if you should, the fault   206

178 An if   186 frontlet a band worn on the forehead; here, frown
189–190 O without a figure cipher of no value unless preceded by a
digit   195–196 He . . . some i.e., that person who gives away all his
possessions, having wearied of them, will find himself in need of
part of what is gone.   nor . . . nor either . . . nor   196 want lack
197 shelled peascod shelled pea pod, i.e., nothing, empty   198 all-
licensed authorized to speak or act freely   200 carp find fault
201 rank gross, excessive   203 safe certain   204 too late all too recently   205 put it on encourage it   206 allowance approval

Would not scape censure, nor the redresses sleep 207
Which in the tender of a wholesome weal 208
Might in their working do you that offense,
Which else were shame, that then necessity 210
Will call discreet proceeding. 211

FOOL   For you know, nuncle,
     "The hedge sparrow fed the cuckoo so long 213
     That it had its head bit off by its young." 214
So, out went the candle, and we were left darkling. 215

LEAR   Are you our daughter?

GONERIL
I would you would make use of your good wisdom,
Whereof I know you are fraught, and put away 218
These dispositions which of late transport you 219
From what you rightly are.

FOOL   May not an ass know when the cart draws the 221
horse? Whoop, Jug! I love thee. 222

LEAR
Does any here know me? This is not Lear.
Does Lear walk thus, speak thus? Where are his eyes?
Either his notion weakens, his discernings 225
Are lethargied—Ha! Waking? 'Tis not so. 226
Who is it that can tell me who I am?

FOOL   Lear's shadow.

LEAR
I would learn that; for, by the marks of sovereignty, 229
Knowledge, and reason, I should be false persuaded 230
I had daughters. 231

---

207 redresses sleep punishments (for the riotous conduct of Lear's
attendants) lie dormant   **208 tender . . . weal** care for preservation of
the peace of the state   **210 else were** in other circumstances would be
regarded as.   **then necessity** the necessity of the times   **211 discreet**
prudent   **213 cuckoo** a bird that lays its eggs in other birds' nests
214 its young i.e., the young cuckoo   **215 darkling** in the dark
218 fraught freighted, laden   **219 dispositions** states of mind, moods
221–222 May . . . horse i.e., may not even a fool see that matters are
backwards when a daughter lectures her father   **222 Jug** i.e., Joan. (The
origin of this phrase is uncertain.)   **225 notion** intellectual power
225–226 discernings Are lethargied faculties are asleep   **226 Waking**
i.e., am I really awake   **229 that** i.e., who I am.   **marks of sovereignty**
outward and visible evidence of being king   **230–231 I should . . .
daughters** i.e., all these outward signs of sanity and status would seem
to suggest (falsely) that I am the king who had obedient daughters

FOOL   Which they will make an obedient father.   232
LEAR   Your name, fair gentlewoman?
GONERIL
  This admiration, sir, is much o' the savor   234
  Of other your new pranks. I do beseech you   235
  To understand my purposes aright.
  As you are old and reverend, should be wise.   237
  Here do you keep a hundred knights and squires,
  Men so disordered, so debauched and bold,   239
  That this our court, infected with their manners,
  Shows like a riotous inn. Epicurism and lust   241
  Makes it more like a tavern or a brothel
  Than a graced palace. The shame itself doth speak   243
  For instant remedy. Be then desired,   244
  By her that else will take the thing she begs,
  A little to disquantity your train,   246
  And the remainders that shall still depend   247
  To be such men as may besort your age,   248
  Which know themselves and you.
LEAR   Darkness and devils!
  Saddle my horses! Call my train together! *[Exit one.]*
  Degenerate bastard, I'll not trouble thee.
  Yet have I left a daughter.
GONERIL
  You strike my people, and your disordered rabble
  Make servants of their betters.

          Enter Albany.

LEAR
  Woe, that too late repents!—O, sir, are you come?   255
  Is it your will? Speak, sir.—Prepare my horses.
                              [Exit one.]
  Ingratitude, thou marble-hearted fiend,
  More hideous when thou show'st thee in a child
  Than the sea monster!
ALBANY   Pray, sir, be patient.

232 Which whom   **234 admiration** (guise of) wonderment   **235 other**
other of   **237 should** i.e., you should   **239 disordered** disorderly
241 Shows appears.   **Epicurism** luxury   **243 graced** honorable
244 desired requested   **246 disquantity your train** diminish the number
of your attendants   **247 the remainders . . . depend** those who remain
to attend you   **248 besort** befit   **255 Woe, that** woe to the person who

LEAR [*To Goneril*]   Detested kite, thou liest!   261
  My train are men of choice and rarest parts,   262
  That all particulars of duty know
  And in the most exact regard support   264
  The worships of their name. O most small fault,   265
  How ugly didst thou in Cordelia show!
  Which, like an engine, wrenched my frame of nature   267
  From the fixed place, drew from my heart all love,
  And added to the gall. O Lear, Lear, Lear!
  Beat at this gate [*Striking his head*] that let thy folly in
  And thy dear judgment out! Go, go, my people.   271
                              [*Exeunt some.*]

ALBANY
  My lord, I am guiltless as I am ignorant
  Of what hath moved you.

LEAR   It may be so, my lord.
  Hear, Nature, hear! Dear goddess, hear!
  Suspend thy purpose if thou didst intend
  To make this creature fruitful!
  Into her womb convey sterility;
  Dry up in her the organs of increase,
  And from her derogate body never spring   279
  A babe to honor her! If she must teem,   280
  Create her child of spleen, that it may live   281
  And be a thwart disnatured torment to her!   282
  Let it stamp wrinkles in her brow of youth,
  With cadent tears fret channels in her cheeks,   284
  Turn all her mother's pains and benefits   285
  To laughter and contempt, that she may feel
  How sharper than a serpent's tooth it is
  To have a thankless child! Away, away!
                     Exit [with Kent and the rest
                          of Lear's followers].

261 kite bird of prey   **262 parts** qualities   **264 in . . . regard** with
extreme care   **265 worships** honors, reputations   **267 engine** powerful
mechanical contrivance, able to wrench Lear's *frame of nature* or
natural self from his *fixed place* or foundation like a building being torn
from its foundation   **271 dear** precious   **279 derogate** debased
280 teem increase the species   **281 of spleen** consisting only of malice   **282 thwart disnatured** obstinate, perverse, and unnatural, unfil-
ial   **284 cadent** falling.   **fret** wear   **285 mother's** motherly.   **benefits**
kind offerings

ALBANY
   Now, gods that we adore, whereof comes this?
GONERIL
   Never afflict yourself to know more of it,
   But let his disposition have that scope   291
   As dotage gives it.   292

       Enter Lear.

LEAR
   What, fifty of my followers at a clap?
   Within a fortnight?
ALBANY   What's the matter, sir?
LEAR
   I'll tell thee. [*To Goneril.*] Life and death! I am ashamed
   That thou hast power to shake my manhood thus,
   That these hot tears, which break from me perforce,
   Should make thee worth them. Blasts and fogs upon
       thee!
   Th' untented woundings of a father's curse   299
   Pierce every sense about thee! Old fond eyes,   300
   Beweep this cause again, I'll pluck ye out   301
   And cast you, with the waters that you loose,   302
   To temper clay. Yea, is 't come to this?   303
   Ha! Let it be so. I have another daughter,
   Who, I am sure, is kind and comfortable.   305
   When she shall hear this of thee, with her nails
   She'll flay thy wolvish visage. Thou shalt find
   That I'll resume the shape which thou dost think
   I have cast off forever.   *Exit.*
GONERIL   Do you mark that?
ALBANY
   I cannot be so partial, Goneril,
   To the great love I bear you—   311
GONERIL
   Pray you, content.—What, Oswald, ho!
   [*To the Fool.*] You, sir, more knave than fool, after your
       master.

---

291 disposition humor, mood   **292 As** which   **299 untented** too deep to
be probed and cleansed   **300 fond** foolish   **301 Beweep** if you weep
for   **302 loose** let loose   **303 temper** soften   **305 comfortable** willing to
comfort   **311 To** because of

FOOL   Nuncle Lear, nuncle Lear! Tarry, take the Fool with   314
  thee.   315

    A fox, when one has caught her,
    And such a daughter
    Should sure to the slaughter,   318
    If my cap would buy a halter.
    So the Fool follows after.   *Exit.*

GONERIL
  This man hath had good counsel. A hundred knights?
  'Tis politic and safe to let him keep   322
  At point a hundred knights—yes, that on every dream,   323
  Each buzz, each fancy, each complaint, dislike,   324
  He may enguard his dotage with their powers
  And hold our lives in mercy.—Oswald, I say!   326
ALBANY   Well, you may fear too far.   327
GONERIL   Safer than trust too far.
  Let me still take away the harms I fear,   329
  Not fear still to be taken. I know his heart.   330
  What he hath uttered I have writ my sister.
  If she sustain him and his hundred knights
  When I have showed th' unfitness—

    Enter steward [*Oswald*].

                          How now, Oswald?
  What, have you writ that letter to my sister?
OSWALD   Ay, madam.
GONERIL
  Take you some company and away to horse.
  Inform her full of my particular fear,
  And thereto add such reasons of your own
  As may compact it more. Get you gone,   339
  And hasten your return. [*Exit Oswald.*] No, no, my lord,
  This milky gentleness and course of yours   341
  Though I condemn not, yet, under pardon,   342

314–315 take . . . thee (1) take me with you (2) take the name "fool" with
you. (A stock phrase of taunting farewell.)   **318 Should sure** should
certainly be sent   **322 politic** prudent. (Said ironically.)   **323 At point**
under arms   **324 buzz** idle rumor   **326 in mercy** at his mercy   **327 fear
too far** overestimate the danger   **329 take away** remove   **329, 330 still**
always   **330 taken** overtaken (by the *harms*)   **339 compact** confirm
341 milky . . . course humane and gentle way   **342 under pardon** if
you'll excuse my saying so

You're much more attasked for want of wisdom   343
Than praised for harmful mildness.   344

ALBANY

How far your eyes may pierce I cannot tell.   345
Striving to better, oft we mar what's well.

GONERIL   Nay, then—

ALBANY   Well, well, th' event.   *Exeunt.* 348

❖

1.5   *Enter Lear, Kent [disguised as Caius], and Fool.*

LEAR [*Giving a letter to Kent*]   Go you before to Gloucester   1
with these letters. Acquaint my daughter no further   2
with anything you know than comes from her demand   3
out of the letter. If your diligence be not speedy, I shall   4
be there afore you.

KENT   I will not sleep, my lord, till I have delivered your
letter.   *Exit.*

FOOL   If a man's brains were in 's heels, were 't not in
danger of kibes?   9

LEAR   Ay, boy.

FOOL   Then, I prithee, be merry. Thy wit shall not go
slipshod.   12

LEAR   Ha, ha, ha!

FOOL   Shalt see thy other daughter will use thee kindly,   14
for though she's as like this as a crab's like an apple,   15
yet I can tell what I can tell.

LEAR   What canst tell, boy?

FOOL   She will taste as like this as a crab does to a crab.
Thou canst tell why one's nose stands i' the middle
on 's face?   20

343 attasked taken to task for, blamed   **344 harmful mildness** mildness
that causes harm   **345 pierce** i.e., see into matters   **348 th' event** i.e.,
time will show

1.5. Location: Before Albany's palace.
1 Gloucester i.e., the place in Gloucestershire   **2 these letters** this
letter   **3 demand** inquiry   **4 out of** prompted by   **9 kibes** chilblains
12 slipshod in slippers, worn because of chilblains. (There are no
brains, thinks the Fool, in Lear's heels when they are on their way to
visit Regan.)   **14 Shalt** thou shalt.   **kindly** (1) according to filial nature.
(Said ironically.) (2) according to her own nature   **15 crab** crab apple
20 on 's of his

LEAR   No.

FOOL   Why, to keep one's eyes of either side 's nose, 22
that what a man cannot smell out he may spy into.

LEAR   I did her wrong.   24

FOOL   Canst tell how an oyster makes his shell?

LEAR   No.

FOOL   Nor I neither. But I can tell why a snail has a house.

LEAR   Why?

FOOL   Why, to put 's head in, not to give it away to his
daughters and leave his horns without a case.   31

LEAR   I will forget my nature. So kind a father!—Be my 32
horses ready?

FOOL   Thy asses are gone about 'em. The reason why 34
the seven stars are no more than seven is a pretty 35
reason.

LEAR   Because they are not eight.

FOOL   Yes, indeed. Thou wouldst make a good fool.

LEAR   To take 't again perforce! Monster ingratitude!   39

FOOL   If thou wert my fool, nuncle, I'd have thee beaten
for being old before thy time.

LEAR   How's that?

FOOL   Thou shouldst not have been old till thou hadst
been wise.

LEAR

O, let me not be mad, not mad, sweet heaven!
Keep me in temper; I would not be mad!

[*Enter Gentleman.*]

How now, are the horses ready?

GENTLEMAN   Ready, my lord.

LEAR   Come, boy.   [*Exeunt all except the Fool.*]

---

22 of either side 's on either side of his   **24 her** i.e., Cordelia   **31 horns**
(Suggests cuckold's horns, as though Lear were figuratively not the
father of Goneril and Regan.)   **32 forget my nature** (Compare 1.4.227:
"Who is it that can tell me who I am?" Lear can no longer recognize
the kind, beloved father he thought himself to be.)   **34 Thy ... 'em** i.e.,
your servants (who labor like asses) have gone about readying the
horses   **35 seven stars** Pleiades   **39 To take ... perforce** i.e., to think
that Goneril would forcibly take back again the privileges guaranteed to
me. (Some editors suggest, less persuasively, that Lear is meditating an
armed restoration of his monarchy.)

FOOL
> She that's a maid now, and laughs at my departure,
> Shall not be a maid long, unless things be cut shorter. 51
>   *Exit.*

✤

---

51 things i.e., penises.   **cut shorter** (A bawdy joke addressed to the
audience.)

2.1 *Enter Bastard [Edmund] and Curan, severally.*

EDMUND Save thee, Curan. 1

CURAN And you, sir. I have been with your father and given him notice that the Duke of Cornwall and Regan his duchess will be here with him this night.

EDMUND How comes that?

CURAN Nay, I know not. You have heard of the news abroad—I mean the whispered ones, for they are yet 7 but ear-kissing arguments? 8

EDMUND Not I. Pray you, what are they?

CURAN Have you heard of no likely wars toward twixt 10 the Dukes of Cornwall and Albany?

EDMUND Not a word.

CURAN You may do, then, in time. Fare you well, sir.

Exit.

EDMUND
The Duke be here tonight? The better! Best! 14
This weaves itself perforce into my business.
My father hath set guard to take my brother,
And I have one thing, of a queasy question, 17
Which I must act. Briefness and fortune, work!— 18
Brother, a word. Descend. Brother, I say!

Enter Edgar.

My father watches. O sir, fly this place!
Intelligence is given where you are hid.
You have now the good advantage of the night.
Have you not spoken 'gainst the Duke of Cornwall?
He's coming hither, now, i' the night, i' the haste, 24
And Regan with him. Have you nothing said
Upon his party 'gainst the Duke of Albany? 26
Advise yourself.

EDGAR   I am sure on 't, not a word. 27

2.1. Location: The Earl of Gloucester's house.
s.d. severally separately 1 Save God save 7 ones i.e., the news, regarded as plural 8 ear-kissing arguments lightly whispered topics
10 toward impending 14 The better! Best so much the better; in fact, the best that could happen 17 queasy question hazardous or ticklish nature 18 Briefness and fortune expeditious dispatch and good luck
24 i' the haste in great haste 26 Upon his party 'gainst i.e., on Cornwall's side, reflecting on his feud with 27 Advise yourself think it over carefully. on 't of it

EDMUND
   I hear my father coming. Pardon me;
   In cunning I must draw my sword upon you.
   Draw. Seem to defend yourself. Now, quit you well.— 30
                            [*They draw.*]
   Yield! Come before my father!—Light, ho, here!— 31
   Fly, brother.—Torches, torches!—So, farewell. 32
                                    Exit Edgar.
   Some blood drawn on me would beget opinion 33
   Of my more fierce endeavor. I have seen drunkards 34
   Do more than this in sport. [*He wounds himself in the
      arm.*] Father, Father!
   Stop, stop! No help?

      Enter Gloucester, and servants with torches.

GLOUCESTER   Now, Edmund, where's the villain?
EDMUND
   Here stood he in the dark, his sharp sword out,
   Mumbling of wicked charms, conjuring the moon
   To stand 's auspicious mistress.
GLOUCESTER   But where is he? 39
EDMUND
   Look, sir, I bleed.
GLOUCESTER   Where is the villain, Edmund?
EDMUND
   Fled this way, sir. When by no means he could—
GLOUCESTER
   Pursue him, ho! Go after. [*Exeunt some servants.*] By
      no means what?
EDMUND
   Persuade me to the murder of your lordship,
   But that I told him the revenging gods 44
   'Gainst parricides did all the thunder bend, 45
   Spoke with how manifold and strong a bond
   The child was bound to the father; sir, in fine, 47
   Seeing how loathly opposite I stood 48

30 quit you defend, acquit yourself   **31–32 Yield . . . farewell** (Edmund
speaks loudly as though trying to arrest Edgar, calls for others to help,
and privately bids Edgar to flee.)   **33–34 beget . . . endeavor** create an
impression of my having fought fiercely   **39 stand 's** stand his, act as
his   **44 that** when   **45 bend** aim   **47 in fine** in conclusion   **48 loathly
opposite** loathingly opposed

To his unnatural purpose, in fell motion   49
With his preparèd sword he charges home   50
My unprovided body, latched mine arm;   51
And when he saw my best alarumed spirits,   52
Bold in the quarrel's right, roused to th' encounter,   53
Or whether gasted by the noise I made,   54
Full suddenly he fled.

GLOUCESTER   Let him fly far.   55
Not in this land shall he remain uncaught;
And found—dispatch. The noble Duke my master,   57
My worthy arch and patron, comes tonight.   58
By his authority I will proclaim it.
That he which finds him shall deserve our thanks,
Bringing the murderous coward to the stake;   61
He that conceals him, death.

EDMUND
When I dissuaded him from his intent
And found him pight to do it, with curst speech   64
I threatened to discover him. He replied,   65
"Thou unpossessing bastard, dost thou think,   66
If I would stand against thee, would the reposal   67
Of any trust, virtue, or worth in thee
Make thy words faithed? No. What I should deny—   69
As this I would, ay, though thou didst produce
My very character—I'd turn it all   71
To thy suggestion, plot, and damnèd practice;   72
And thou must make a dullard of the world   73
If they not thought the profits of my death   74
Were very pregnant and potential spirits   75
To make thee seek it."

49 fell motion deadly thrust   **50 preparèd** unsheathed and ready.
home to the very heart   **51 unprovided** unprotected.   **latched** nicked,
lanced   **52 best alarumed** thoroughly aroused to action as by a trumpet   **53 quarrel's right** justice of the cause   **54 gasted** frightened
55 Let him fly far i.e., any fleeing, no matter how far, will be in vain
57 dispatch i.e., that will be the end for him   **58 arch and patron** chief
patron   **61 to the stake** i.e., to reckoning   **64 pight** determined.   **curst**
angry   **65 discover** expose   **66 unpossessing** unable to inherit, beggarly   **67 reposal** placing   **69 faithed** believed   **71 character** written
testimony, handwriting   **72 suggestion** instigation.   **practice** plot
73 make . . . world think everyone idiotic   **74 not thought** did not
think.   **of my death** i.e., that Edmund would gain through Edgar's
death   **75 pregnant . . . spirits** fertile and potent tempters

GLOUCESTER   O strange and fastened villain! 76
Would he deny his letter, said he?
I never got him.   *Tucket within.* 78
Hark, the Duke's trumpets! I know not why he comes.
All ports I'll bar; the villain shall not scape. 80
The Duke must grant me that. Besides, his picture
I will send far and near, that all the kingdom
May have due note of him; and of my land,
Loyal and natural boy, I'll work the means 84
To make thee capable. 85

Enter Cornwall, Regan, and attendants.

CORNWALL
How now, my noble friend? Since I came hither,
Which I can call but now, I have heard strange news.
REGAN
If it be true, all vengeance comes too short
Which can pursue th' offender. How dost, my lord?
GLOUCESTER
O madam, my old heart is cracked, it's cracked!
REGAN
What, did my father's godson seek your life?
He whom my father named? Your Edgar?
GLOUCESTER
O, lady, lady, shame would have it hid!
REGAN
Was he not companion with the riotous knights
That tended upon my father?
GLOUCESTER
I know not, madam. 'Tis too bad, too bad.
EDMUND
Yes, madam, he was of that consort. 97
REGAN
No marvel, then, though he were ill affected. 98

76 strange unnatural. **fastened** hardened **78 got** begot **s.d. Tucket**
series of notes on the trumpet, here indicating Cornwall's arrival
80 ports seaports, or gateways **84 natural** (1) prompted by natural
feelings of loyalty and affection (2) bastard **85 capable** legally able to
become the inheritor **97 consort** set, company **98 though** if. **ill
affected** ill disposed, disloyal

'Tis they have put him on the old man's death,   99
To have th' expense and waste of his revenues.   100
I have this present evening from my sister
Been well informed of them, and with such cautions
That if they come to sojourn at my house
I'll not be there.

CORNWALL   Nor I, assure thee, Regan.
Edmund, I hear that you have shown your father
A childlike office.

EDMUND   It was my duty, sir.   106

GLOUCESTER [*To Cornwall*]
He did bewray his practice, and received   107
This hurt you see striving to apprehend him.   108

CORNWALL   Is he pursued?

GLOUCESTER   Ay, my good lord.

CORNWALL
If he be taken, he shall never more
Be feared of doing harm. Make your own purpose,   112
How in my strength you please. For you, Edmund,   113
Whose virtue and obedience doth this instant
So much commend itself, you shall be ours.
Natures of such deep trust we shall much need;
You we first seize on.

EDMUND   I shall serve you, sir,
Truly, however else.   118

GLOUCESTER   For him I thank Your Grace.

CORNWALL
You know not why we came to visit you—

REGAN
—Thus out of season, threading dark-eyed night:
Occasions, noble Gloucester, of some prize,   122
Wherein we must have use of your advice.
Our father he hath writ, so hath our sister,
Of differences, which I best thought it fit   125

---

99 put him on incited him to   **100 expense and waste** squandering
106 childlike filial   **107 bewray his practice** expose his (Edgar's) plot
108 apprehend arrest   **112–113 Make . . . please** form your plans,
making free use of my authority and resources   **113 For** as for
118 however else i.e., whether capably or not   **122 prize** significance
125 differences quarrels.   **which** i.e., Lear's and Goneril's letters

To answer from our home; the several messengers   126
From hence attend dispatch. Our good old friend,   127
Lay comforts to your bosom, and bestow
Your needful counsel to our businesses,   129
Which craves the instant use.
GLOUCESTER   I serve you, madam.   130
Your Graces are right welcome.
                              Flourish. Exeunt.

                              ❖

2.2   *Enter Kent [disguised as Caius] and steward
           [Oswald], severally.*

OSWALD Good dawning to thee, friend. Art of this   1
  house?
KENT Ay.
OSWALD Where may we set our horses?
KENT I' the mire.
OSWALD Prithee, if thou lov'st me, tell me.   6
KENT I love thee not.
OSWALD Why then, I care not for thee.   8
KENT If I had thee in Lipsbury pinfold, I would make   9
  thee care for me.   10
OSWALD Why dost thou use me thus? I know thee not.   11
KENT Fellow, I know thee.   12
OSWALD What dost thou know me for?
KENT A knave, a rascal, an eater of broken meats;   14
  a base, proud, shallow, beggarly, three-suited,   15

126 **from** away from   127 **attend dispatch** wait to be dispatched
129 **needful** necessary   130 **the instant use** immediate attention

2.2. Location: Before Gloucester's house.
s.d. severally at separate doors   **1 dawning** (It is not yet day.)   **6 if thou
lov'st me** i.e., if you bear good will toward me. (But Kent deliberately
takes the phrase in its literal, not courtly, sense.)   **8–10 care not for . . .
care for** do not like . . . have an anxious regard for   **9 Lipsbury pinfold**
i.e., within the pinfold of the lips, between my teeth. (A *pinfold* is a
pound for stray animals.)   **11–12 know thee not . . . know thee** am
unacquainted with you . . . can see through you   **14 broken meats**
scraps of food (such as were passed out to the most lowly)   **15 three-
suited** (Three suits a year were allowed to servants.)

hundred-pound, filthy worsted-stocking knave; a   16
lily-livered, action-taking, whoreson, glass-gazing,   17
superserviceable, finical rogue; one-trunk-inheriting   18
slave; one that wouldst be a bawd in way of good ser-   19
vice, and art nothing but the composition of a knave,   20
beggar, coward, pander, and the son and heir of a
mongrel bitch; one whom I will beat into clamorous
whining if thou deny'st the least syllable of thy addi-   23
tion.   24

OSWALD   Why, what a monstrous fellow art thou thus
to rail on one that is neither known of thee nor knows
thee!

KENT   What a brazen-faced varlet art thou to deny thou
knowest me! Is it two days since I tripped up thy heels
and beat thee before the King? Draw, you rogue, for
though it be night, yet the moon shines. I'll make a
sop o' the moonshine of you, you whoreson cullionly   32
barbermonger. Draw!   [*He brandishes his sword.*]   33

OSWALD   Away! I have nothing to do with thee.

KENT   Draw, you rascal! You come with letters against
the King, and take Vanity the puppet's part against   36
the royalty of her father. Draw, you rogue, or I'll so
carbonado your shanks—draw, you rascal! Come your   38
ways.   39

OSWALD   Help, ho! Murder! Help!

KENT   Strike, you slave! Stand, rogue, stand, you neat   41
slave, strike!   [*He beats him.*]

---

16 hundred-pound (Possible allusion to the minimum property qualification for the status of gentleman.)   **worsted-stocking** i.e., too poor and menial to wear silk stockings   **17 lily-livered** cowardly (the liver being pale through lack of blood).   **action-taking** settling quarrels by resort to law instead of arms, cowardly.   **glass-gazing** fond of looking in the mirror   **18 superserviceable** officious.   **finical** foppish, fastidious. **one-trunk-inheriting** possessing effects sufficient for one trunk only **19–20 bawd . . . service** i.e., pimp or pander as a way of providing good service   **20 composition** compound   **23–24 addition** titles   **32 sop o' the moonshine** something so perforated that it will soak up moonshine as a sop (floating piece of toast) soaks up liquor   **32–33 cullionly barbermonger** base frequenter of barber shops, fop. (*Cullion* originally meant "testicle.")   **36 Vanity . . . part** i.e., the part of Goneril (here personified as a character in a morality play)   **38 carbonado** cut crosswise like meat for broiling   **38–39 Come your ways** come on   **41 neat** (1) foppish (2) calflike. (*Neat* means "horned cattle.")

OSWALD Help, ho! Murder! Murder!

Enter Bastard [Edmund, with his rapier drawn],
Cornwall, Regan, Gloucester, servants.

EDMUND How now, what's the matter? Part! 44

KENT With you, goodman boy, an you please! Come, I'll 45
flesh ye. Come on, young master. 46

GLOUCESTER Weapons? Arms? What's the matter here?

CORNWALL Keep peace, upon your lives! [*Kent and Os-*
wald are parted.] He dies that strikes again. What is
the matter?

REGAN The messengers from our sister and the King.

CORNWALL What's your difference? Speak. 52

OSWALD I am scarce in breath, my lord.

KENT No marvel, you have so bestirred your valor. You
cowardly rascal, nature disclaims in thee. A tailor 55
made thee.

CORNWALL Thou art a strange fellow. A tailor make
a man?

KENT A tailor, sir. A stonecutter or a painter could not
have made him so ill, though they had been but two
years o' the trade.

CORNWALL Speak yet, how grew your quarrel?

OSWALD This ancient ruffian, sir, whose life I have
spared at suit of his gray beard—

KENT Thou whoreson zed! Thou unnecessary letter!—My 65
lord, if you'll give me leave, I will tread this un- 66
bolted villain into mortar and daub the wall of a jakes 67
with him.—Spare my gray beard, you wagtail? 68

CORNWALL Peace, sirrah!
You beastly knave, know you no reverence?

KENT
Yes, sir, but anger hath a privilege.

CORNWALL Why art thou angry?

---

44 matter i.e., trouble. (But Kent takes the meaning "cause for quarrel.")
45 With you I'll fight with you; my quarrel is with you. **goodman boy** (A
contemptuous epithet, a title of mock respect, addressed seemingly to
Edmund.) **an** if **46 flesh** initiate into combat **52 difference** quarrel
55 disclaims in disowns **65 zed** the letter *z*, regarded as unnecessary and
often not included in dictionaries of the time **66–67 unbolted** unsifted;
hence, coarse **67 daub** plaster. **jakes** privy **68 wagtail** i.e., bird wagging
its tail feathers in pert obsequiousness

KENT

That such a slave as this should wear a sword,
Who wears no honesty. Such smiling rogues as these,
Like rats, oft bite the holy cords atwain   75
Which are t' intrinse t' unloose; smooth every passion   76
That in the natures of their lords rebel,
Bring oil to fire, snow to their colder moods,   78
Renege, affirm, and turn their halcyon beaks   79
With every gale and vary of their masters,   80
Knowing naught, like dogs, but following.—
A plague upon your epileptic visage!   82
Smile you my speeches, as I were a fool?   83
Goose, an I had you upon Sarum plain,   84
I'd drive ye cackling home to Camelot.   85

CORNWALL What, art thou mad, old fellow?

GLOUCESTER How fell you out? Say that.

KENT

No contraries hold more antipathy
Than I and such a knave.

CORNWALL

Why dost thou call him knave? What is his fault?

KENT His countenance likes me not.   91

CORNWALL

No more, perchance, does mine, nor his, nor hers.

KENT

Sir, 'tis my occupation to be plain:
I have seen better faces in my time
Than stands on any shoulder that I see
Before me at this instant.

CORNWALL   This is some fellow
Who, having been praised for bluntness, doth affect

---

75 holy cords sacred bonds of affection and order   **76 t' intrinse** too
intrinsicate, tightly knotted.   **smooth** flatter, humor   **78 Bring oil to
fire** i.e., flattering servants fuel the flame of their masters' angry passions   **79 Renege** deny.   **halcyon beaks** (The halcyon or kingfisher, if
hung up, would supposedly turn its beak against the wind.)   **80 gale
and vary** variation in the wind   **82 epileptic** i.e., trembling and pale
with fright and distorted with a grin   **83 Smile you** do you smile at.
as as if   **84–85 Goose . . . Camelot** (The reference is obscure, but the
general sense is that Kent scorns Oswald as a cackling goose.)   **an**
if.   **Sarum** Salisbury.   **Camelot** legendary seat of King Arthur and
his Round Table, said to have been at Cadbury and at Winchester and
hence in the general vicinity of Salisbury and Gloucester   **91 likes**
pleases

A saucy roughness, and constrains the garb   98
Quite from his nature. He cannot flatter, he;   99
An honest mind and plain, he must speak truth!
An they will take 't, so; if not, he's plain.   101
These kind of knaves I know, which in this plainness
Harbor more craft and more corrupter ends
Than twenty silly-ducking observants   104
That stretch their duties nicely.   105

KENT
Sir, in good faith, in sincere verity,   106
Under th' allowance of your great aspect,   107
Whose influence, like the wreath of radiant fire   108
On flickering Phoebus' front—

CORNWALL   What mean'st by this?   109

KENT To go out of my dialect, which you discommend
so much. I know, sir, I am no flatterer. He that be- 111
guiled you in a plain accent was a plain knave, which 112
for my part I will not be, though I should win your   113
displeasure to entreat me to 't.   114

CORNWALL [To Oswald] What was th' offense you gave him?

OSWALD I never gave him any.

It pleased the King his master very late   117
To strike at me, upon his misconstruction;   118
When he, compact, and flattering his displeasure,   119

98–99 constrains . . . nature i.e., distorts plainness to the point of carica-
ture, away from its true purpose   **101 An . . . plain** if people will take
his rudeness, fine; if not, his excuse is that he speaks plain truth
104 silly-ducking observants foolishly bowing, obsequious attendants
105 stretch . . . nicely exert themselves in their courtly duties punctiliously   **106 Sir, in good faith,** etc. (Kent assumes the wordy mannerisms
of courtly flattery.)   **107 allowance** approval.   **aspect** (1) countenance
(2) astrological position   **108 influence** astrological might   **109 Phoebus
front** i.e., the sun's forehead   **111–112 He . . . accent** i.e., the man who
used plain speech to you craftily (see ll. 102–105) and thereby taught
you to suspect plain speakers of deceit   **112–114 which . . . me to 't** i.e.,
I will no longer use plain speech, despite the incentive of incurring your
displeasure by doing so. (Kent prefers to displease Cornwall, since Cornwall is pleased only by flatterers, and Kent has assumed until now that
plain speech was the best way to offend; but he now argues mockingly
that he can no longer speak plainly, since his honest utterance will be
interpreted as duplicity.)   **117 late** recently   **118 upon his misconstruction** as a result of the King's misunderstanding (me)   **119 he** i.e.,
Kent.   **compact** joined, united with the King.   **flattering his displeasure** gratifying the King's anger (at me)

Tripped me behind; being down, insulted, railed,   120
And put upon him such a deal of man   121
That worthied him, got praises of the King   122
For him attempting who was self-subdued;   123
And, in the fleshment of this dread exploit,   124
Drew on me here again.

KENT   None of these rogues and cowards   126
But Ajax is their fool.

CORNWALL   Fetch forth the stocks!   127
You stubborn ancient knave, you reverend braggart,   128
We'll teach you.

KENT   Sir, I am too old to learn.
Call not your stocks for me. I serve the King,
On whose employment I was sent to you.
You shall do small respect, show too bold malice
Against the grace and person of my master,   133
Stocking his messenger.

CORNWALL
Fetch forth the stocks! As I have life and honor,
There shall he sit till noon.

REGAN
Till noon? Till night, my lord, and all night too.

KENT
Why, madam, if I were your father's dog
You should not use me so.   139

REGAN   Sir, being his knave, I will.   140

CORNWALL
This is a fellow of the selfsame color   141
Our sister speaks of.—Come, bring away the stocks!   142
                              Stocks brought out.

GLOUCESTER
Let me beseech Your Grace not to do so.
His fault is much, and the good King his master

---

120 being down, insulted i.e., when I was down, he exulted over me
121 put . . . man acted like such a hero   **122 worthied** won reputation
for   **123 For . . . self-subdued** for assailing one (i.e., myself) who chose
not to resist   **124 fleshment** excitement resulting from a first success.
dread exploit (Said ironically.)   **126–127 None . . . fool** i.e., you never
find any rogues and cowards of this sort who do not outdo the blustering Ajax in their boasting   **128 reverend** (because old)   **133 grace**
sovereignty   **139 should** would   **140 being** since you are   **141 color**
complexion, character   **142 away** along

Will check him for 't. Your purposed low correction   145
Is such as basest and contemned'st wretches   146
For pilferings and most common trespasses
Are punished with. The King must take it ill
That he, so slightly valued in his messenger,
Should have him thus restrained.

CORNWALL   I'll answer that.   150

REGAN
My sister may receive it much more worse
To have her gentleman abused, assaulted,
For following her affairs. Put in his legs.

                    [*Kent is put in the stocks.*]
Come, my good lord, away.
                    Exeunt [all but Gloucester and Kent].

GLOUCESTER
I am sorry for thee, friend. 'Tis the Duke's pleasure,
Whose disposition, all the world well knows,
Will not be rubbed nor stopped. I'll entreat for thee.   157

KENT
Pray, do not, sir. I have watched and traveled hard.   158
Some time I shall sleep out; the rest I'll whistle.
A good man's fortune may grow out at heels.   160
Give you good morrow!   161

GLOUCESTER
The Duke's to blame in this. 'Twill be ill taken.   *Exit.*

KENT
Good King, that must approve the common saw,   163
Thou out of heaven's benediction com'st
To the warm sun!   [*He takes out a letter.*]
Approach, thou beacon to this under globe,   166
That by thy comfortable beams I may   167

---

145 check rebuke, correct   **146 contemned'st** most despised
150 answer be answerable for   **157 rubbed** hindered, obstructed. (A
term from bowls.)   **158 watched** gone sleepless   **160 A . . . heels** i.e.,
even good men suffer decline in fortune at times   **161 Give you** i.e., God
give you   **163 approve** prove true.   **saw** proverb (i.e., "To run out of
God's blessing into the warm sun," meaning "to go from better to
worse")   **166 beacon . . . globe** i.e., the sun (?) (Some editors believe that
Kent means the moon, since it is night at ll. 31 and 176, but he probably
is saying that he hopes for daylight soon in order that he can read the
letter from Cordelia.)   **167 comfortable** useful, aiding

Peruse this letter. Nothing almost sees miracles   168
But misery. I know 'tis from Cordelia,   169
Who hath most fortunately been informed
Of my obscurèd course, and shall find time   171
From this enormous state, seeking to give   172
Losses their remedies. All weary and o'erwatched,   173
Take vantage, heavy eyes, not to behold   174
This shameful lodging.   175
Fortune, good night. Smile once more; turn thy
    wheel!   [*He sleeps.*] 176

2.3   *Enter Edgar.*

EDGAR   I heard myself proclaimed,
    And by the happy hollow of a tree   2
    Escaped the hunt. No port is free, no place   3
    That guard and most unusual vigilance   4
    Does not attend my taking. Whiles I may scape   5
    I will preserve myself, and am bethought   6
    To take the basest and most poorest shape
    That ever penury, in contempt of man,   8
    Brought near to beast. My face I'll grime with filth,
    Blanket my loins, elf all my hairs in knots,   10
    And with presented nakedness outface   11
    The winds and persecutions of the sky.

168–169 Nothing . . . misery i.e., scarcely anything can make one appreciate miracles like being in a state of misery; miracles are most often experienced by those who suffer misfortune   **171 obscurèd** disguised. **shall** she shall   **171–173 and . . . remedies** (This seemingly incoherent passage may be textually corrupt or may be meant to represent fragments from the letter Kent is reading.)   **172 From** i.e., to provide relief from (?)   **enormous state** monstrous state of affairs, enormity **173 Losses** reversals of fortune.   **o'erwatched** exhausted with staying awake   **174 vantage** advantage (of sleep)   **175 lodging** i.e., the stocks **176 wheel** (Since Kent is at the bottom of Fortune's wheel, any turning will improve his situation.)

2.3. Location: Scene continues. Kent is dozing in the stocks. **2 happy** luckily found   **3 port** (See 2.1.80 and note.)   **4 That** in which **5 attend** watch, wait for   **6 bethought** resolved   **8 in . . . man** in order to show how contemptible humankind is   **10 elf** tangle into elflocks **11 presented** exposed to view, displayed

The country gives me proof and precedent   13
Of Bedlam beggars who with roaring voices   14
Strike in their numbed and mortified arms   15
Pins, wooden pricks, nails, sprigs of rosemary;   16
And with this horrible object, from low farms,   17
Poor pelting villages, sheepcotes, and mills,   18
Sometimes with lunatic bans, sometimes with prayers,   19
Enforce their charity. Poor Turlygod! Poor Tom!   20
That's something yet. Edgar I nothing am.   *Exit.*   21

2.4   *Enter Lear, Fool, and Gentleman.*

LEAR
'Tis strange that they should so depart from home
And not send back my messenger.
GENTLEMAN   As I learned,
The night before there was no purpose in them
Of this remove.
KENT   Hail to thee, noble master!   4
LEAR   Ha?
Mak'st thou this shame thy pastime?
KENT   No, my lord.
FOOL   Ha, ha, he wears cruel garters. Horses are tied by   7
the heads, dogs and bears by the neck, monkeys by the
loins, and men by the legs. When a man's overlusty at   9
legs, then he wears wooden netherstocks.   10
LEAR
What's he that hath so much thy place mistook
To set thee here?
KENT   It is both he and she: 12
Your son and daughter.

13 **proof** example   14 **Bedlam** (See note to 1.2.139.)   15 **Strike** stick.   **mortified** deadened   16 **wooden pricks** skewers   17 **object** spectacle.   **low** lowly   18 **pelting** paltry   19 **bans** curses   20 **Poor . . . Tom** (Edgar practices the begging role he is about to adopt. Beggars were known as poor Toms.)   **Turlygod** (Meaning unknown.)   21 **That's something yet** there's some kind of existence still for me as poor Tom.   **Edgar** i.e., as Edgar

2.4. Location: Scene continues before Gloucester's house. Kent still dozing in the stocks.
4 **remove** change of residence   7 **cruel** (In the quarto: *crewell*, a double meaning [1] unkind [2] crewel, a thin yarn of which garters were made.)   9–10 **overlusty at legs** given to running away   10 **netherstocks** stockings   12 **To** as to

LEAR No.
KENT Yes.
LEAR No, I say.
KENT I say yea.
LEAR No, no, they would not.
KENT Yes, they have.
LEAR By Jupiter, I swear no.
KENT By Juno, I swear ay.
LEAR   They durst not do 't!
  They could not, would not do 't. 'Tis worse than murder
  To do upon respect such violent outrage.   23
  Resolve me with all modest haste which way   24
  Thou mightst deserve, or they impose, this usage,
  Coming from us.
KENT   My lord, when at their home   26
  I did commend Your Highness' letters to them,   27
  Ere I was risen from the place that showed   28
  My duty kneeling, came there a reeking post,   29
  Stewed in his haste, half breathless, panting forth   30
  From Goneril his mistress salutations;
  Delivered letters, spite of intermission,   32
  Which presently they read; on whose contents   33
  They summoned up their meiny, straight took horse,   34
  Commanded me to follow and attend
  The leisure of their answer, gave me cold looks;
  And meeting here the other messenger,
  Whose welcome, I perceived, had poisoned mine—
  Being the very fellow which of late
  Displayed so saucily against Your Highness—   40
  Having more man than wit about me, drew.   41
  He raised the house with loud and coward cries.

---

23 upon respect i.e., against my delegates (who deserve respect)
24 Resolve enlighten. **modest** moderate **26 their home** (Kent and
Oswald went first to Cornwall's palace after leaving Albany's palace.)
27 commend deliver **28–29 from . . . kneeling** from the kneeling pos-
ture that showed my duty **29 reeking** steaming (with heat of travel)
30 Stewed i.e., thoroughly heated, soaked **32 spite of intermission**
in disregard of interrupting me; or, in spite of the interruptions caused
by his being out of breath **33 presently** instantly. **on** on the basis
of **34 meiny** retinue of servants, household **40 Displayed so saucily**
behaved so insolently **41 man** manhood, courage. **wit** discretion,
sense

Your son and daughter found this trespass worth
The shame which here it suffers.

FOOL Winter's not gone yet if the wild geese fly that 45
way. 46
          Fathers that wear rags
              Do make their children blind, 48
          But fathers that bear bags 49
              Shall see their children kind.
          Fortune, that arrant whore,
              Ne'er turns the key to the poor. 52
But, for all this, thou shalt have as many dolors for thy 53
daughters as thou canst tell in a year. 54

LEAR
O, how this mother swells up toward my heart! 55
Hysterica passio, down, thou climbing sorrow! 56
Thy element's below.—Where is this daughter? 57

KENT With the Earl, sir, here within.

LEAR Follow me not. Stay here.   *Exit.*

GENTLEMAN
Made you no more offense but what you speak of?

KENT None.
How chance the King comes with so small a number? 62

FOOL An thou hadst been set i' the stocks for that ques- 63
tion, thou'dst well deserved it.

KENT Why, Fool?

FOOL We'll set thee to school to an ant to teach thee 66
there's no laboring i' the winter. All that follow their 67
noses are led by their eyes but blind men, and there's 68
not a nose among twenty but can smell him that's 69
stinking. Let go thy hold when a great wheel runs 70
down a hill lest it break thy neck with following; but 71

45–46 Winter's . . . way i.e., the signs still point to continued and wors-
ening fortune; the wild geese are still flying south **48 blind** i.e., indifferent to their father's needs **49 bags** i.e., of gold **52 turns the key**
opens the door **53 dolors** griefs (with pun on *dollars,* English word
for an Austrian or Spanish coin). **for** on account of **54 tell** (1) relate
(2) count **55, 56 mother, Hysterica passio** i.e., hysteria, giving the sensation of choking or suffocating **57 element's** proper place is. (Hysteria
was thought to be produced by vapors ascending from the abdomen.)
62 chance chances it **63 An** if **66–67 We'll . . . winter** i.e., just as the
ant knows not to labor in the winter, the wise man knows not to labor
for one whose fortunes are fallen **67–70 All . . . stinking** i.e., one who is
out of favor can be easily detected (he smells of misfortune), and so is
easily avoided by timeservers

the great one that goes upward, let him draw thee after. When a wise man gives thee better counsel, give
me mine again. I would have none but knaves follow
it, since a fool gives it.

> That sir which serves and seeks for gain,
>> And follows but for form,
> Will pack when it begins to rain   78
>> And leave thee in the storm.
> But I will tarry; the fool will stay,
>> And let the wise man fly.
> The knave turns fool that runs away;   82
>> The fool no knave, pardie.   83

Enter Lear and Gloucester.

KENT   Where learned you this, Fool?

FOOL   Not i' the stocks, fool.

LEAR
Deny to speak with me? They are sick? They are weary?
They have traveled all the night? Mere fetches,   87
The images of revolt and flying off.   88
Fetch me a better answer.

GLOUCESTER   My dear lord,
You know the fiery quality of the Duke,
How unremovable and fixed he is
In his own course.

LEAR
Vengeance! Plague! Death! Confusion!   93
Fiery? What quality? Why, Gloucester, Gloucester,
I'd speak with the Duke of Cornwall and his wife.

GLOUCESTER
Well, my good lord, I have informed them so.

LEAR
Informed them? Dost thou understand me, man?

GLOUCESTER   Ay, my good lord.

LEAR
The King would speak with Cornwall. The dear father
Would with his daughter speak, commands, tends,
    service.   100

---

78 pack be off   **82 The knave . . . away** i.e., deserting one's master is
the greatest folly   **83 pardie** *par Dieu* (French), by God   **87 fetches**
pretexts, dodges   **88 images** signs.   **flying off** desertion   **93 Confusion**
destruction   **100 tends** attends, waits for

Are they informed of this? My breath and blood!
Fiery? The fiery Duke? Tell the hot Duke that—
No, but not yet. Maybe he is not well.
Infirmity doth still neglect all office   104
Whereto our health is bound; we are not ourselves   105
When nature, being oppressed, commands the mind
To suffer with the body. I'll forbear,
And am fallen out with my more headier will,   108
To take the indisposed and sickly fit   109
For the sound man. [*Looking at Kent.*] Death on my
    state! Wherefore   110
Should he sit here? This act persuades me
That this remotion of the Duke and her   112
Is practice only. Give me my servant forth.   113
Go tell the Duke and 's wife I'd speak with them,
Now, presently. Bid them come forth and hear me,   115
Or at their chamber door I'll beat the drum
Till it cry sleep to death.   117

GLOUCESTER   I would have all well betwixt you.   *Exit.*
LEAR
O me, my heart, my rising heart! But down!
FOOL   Cry to it, nuncle, as the cockney did to the eels   120
when she put 'em i' the paste alive. She knapped 'em   121
o' the coxcombs with a stick and cried, "Down, wan-   122
tons, down!" 'Twas her brother that, in pure kindness   123
to his horse, buttered his hay.   124

*Enter Cornwall, Regan, Gloucester, [and]
servants.*

104 still always   **104–105 all . . . bound** duties which in good health we
are bound to perform   **108–109 am . . . take** now disapprove of my
more impetuous will in having rashly taken   **110 Death on my state**
may death come to my royal authority. (An oath with ironic appropriateness.)   **112 remotion** removal, inaccessibility   **113 practice** deception.
forth out of the stocks   **115 presently** at once   **117 cry sleep to death**
i.e., put an end to sleep by the noise   **120 cockney** i.e., a Londoner,
ignorant of ways of cooking eels   **121 paste** pastry pie.   **knapped**
rapped   **122 coxcombs** heads   **122–123 wantons** playful creatures,
promiscuous things   **123–124 'Twas . . . hay** (Another city ignorance;
the act is well-intended, but horses do not like greasy hay. As with Lear,
good intentions are not enough.)   **brother** i.e., fellow creature, foolishly
tender-hearted in the same way

LEAR Good morrow to you both.
CORNWALL Hail to Your Grace!
                       Kent here set at liberty.
REGAN I am glad to see Your Highness.
LEAR
  Regan, I think you are. I know what reason
  I have to think so. If thou shouldst not be glad,
  I would divorce me from thy mother's tomb,   130
  Sepulch'ring an adult'ress. [*To Kent.*] O, are you free? 131
  Some other time for that.—Belovèd Regan,
  Thy sister's naught. O Regan, she hath tied   133
  Sharp-toothed unkindness, like a vulture, here.
                 [*He lays his hand on his heart.*]
  I can scarce speak to thee. Thou'lt not believe
  With how depraved a quality—O Regan!   136
REGAN
  I pray you, sir, take patience. I have hope   137
  You less know how to value her desert   138
  Than she to scant her duty.
LEAR   Say? How is that?   139
REGAN
  I cannot think my sister in the least
  Would fail her obligation. If, sir, perchance
  She have restrained the riots of your followers,
  'Tis on such ground and to such wholesome end
  As clears her from all blame.
LEAR My curses on her!
REGAN O, sir, you are old;
  Nature in you stands on the very verge   147
  Of his confine. You should be ruled and led   148
  By some discretion that discerns your state   149
  Better than you yourself. Therefore, I pray you,
  That to our sister you do make return.
  Say you have wronged her.

130 divorce me from i.e., refuse to be buried beside   **131 Sepulch'ring**
i.e., since it would surely contain the dead body of   **133 naught** wicked
136 quality disposition   **137–139 I have . . . duty** i.e., I trust this is more
a matter of your undervaluing her merit than of her falling slack in her
duty to you   **147–148 Nature . . . confine** i.e., your life has almost com-
pleted its allotted scope   **149 discretion** discreet person. **discerns your
state** understands your dependent situation and aged condition

LEAR   Ask her forgiveness?
Do you but mark how this becomes the house: 153
                              [*He kneels.*]
"Dear daughter, I confess that I am old;
Age is unnecessary. On my knees I beg   155
That you'll vouchsafe me raiment, bed, and food."

REGAN
Good sir, no more. These are unsightly tricks.
Return you to my sister.

LEAR [*Rising*]   Never, Regan.
She hath abated me of half my train,   159
Looked black upon me, struck me with her tongue
Most serpentlike upon the very heart.
All the stored vengeances of heaven fall
On her ingrateful top! Strike her young bones,   163
You taking airs, with lameness!

CORNWALL   Fie, sir, fie!   164

LEAR
You nimble lightnings, dart your blinding flames
Into her scornful eyes! Infect her beauty,
You fen-sucked fogs drawn by the powerful sun   167
To fall and blister!   168

REGAN
O the blest gods! So will you wish on me
When the rash mood is on.

LEAR
No, Regan, thou shalt never have my curse.
Thy tender-hafted nature shall not give   172
Thee o'er to harshness. Her eyes are fierce, but thine
Do comfort and not burn. 'Tis not in thee
To grudge my pleasures, to cut off my train,
To bandy hasty words, to scant my sizes,   176
And, in conclusion, to oppose the bolt   177

153 becomes the house suits domestic decorum, is suited to the family
or household and its dutiful relationships   **155 Age is unnecessary** old
people are useless   **159 abated** deprived   **163 ingrateful top** ungrateful
head.   **her young bones** i.e., of her not-yet-born progeny (?)   **164 taking**
infectious   **167 fen-sucked** (It was supposed that the sun sucked up
poisons from fens or marshes.)   **168 To fall and blister** to fall upon her
and blister her beauty   **172 tender-hafted** set in a tender *haft*, i.e.,
handle or frame; moved by a tender feeling, gently disposed   **176 bandy**
volley, exchange.   **scant my sizes** diminish my allowances   **177 oppose
the bolt** lock the door

Against my coming in. Thou better know'st
The offices of nature, bond of childhood,   179
Effects of courtesy, dues of gratitude.   180
Thy half o' the kingdom hast thou not forgot,
Wherein I thee endowed.

REGAN   Good sir, to the purpose.   182

LEAR
Who put my man i' the stocks?   *Tucket within.*

CORNWALL   What trumpet's that?

REGAN
I know 't—my sister's. This approves her letter,   184
That she would soon be here.

     Enter steward [Oswald].

                   Is your lady come?

LEAR
This is a slave, whose easy-borrowed pride   186
Dwells in the fickle grace of her he follows.   187
Out, varlet, from my sight!

CORNWALL   What means Your Grace?   188

LEAR
Who stocked my servant? Regan, I have good hope
Thou didst not know on 't.

     Enter Goneril.

              Who comes here? O heavens,
If you do love old men, if your sweet sway
Allow obedience, if you yourselves are old,   192
Make it your cause; send down, and take my part!
[*To Goneril.*] Art not ashamed to look upon this
    beard?   [*Goneril and Regan join hands.*]
O Regan, will you take her by the hand?

GONERIL
Why not by the hand, sir? How have I offended?
All's not offense that indiscretion finds   197
And dotage terms so.

---

179 offices of nature natural duties. **bond of childhood** filial obligations due to parents   **180 Effects** actions, manifestations   **182 purpose**
point   **184 approves** confirms   **186 easy-borrowed** i.e., acquired with
little effort at deserving and with weak commitment   **187 grace** favor
188 varlet worthless fellow   **192 Allow** approve, sanction
197 indiscretion finds poor judgment deems to be so

LEAR   O sides, you are too tough!   198
   Will you yet hold?—How came my man i' the stocks?
CORNWALL
   I set him there, sir; but his own disorders
   Deserved much less advancement.
LEAR   You? Did you?   201
REGAN
   I pray you, Father, being weak, seem so.   202
   If till the expiration of your month
   You will return and sojourn with my sister,
   Dismissing half your train, come then to me.
   I am now from home, and out of that provision
   Which shall be needful for your entertainment.   207
LEAR
   Return to her? And fifty men dismissed?
   No! Rather I abjure all roofs, and choose
   To wage against the enmity o' th' air,   210
   To be a comrade with the wolf and owl—
   Necessity's sharp pinch. Return with her?
   Why, the hot-blooded France, that dowerless took   213
   Our youngest born—I could as well be brought
   To knee his throne and, squirelike, pension beg   215
   To keep base life afoot. Return with her?
   Persuade me rather to be slave and sumpter   217
   To this detested groom.   [*He points to Oswald.*]
GONERIL   At your choice, sir.
LEAR
   I prithee, daughter, do not make me mad.
   I will not trouble thee, my child. Farewell.
   We'll no more meet, no more see one another.
   But yet thou art my flesh, my blood, my daughter—
   Or rather a disease that's in my flesh,
   Which I must needs call mine. Thou art a boil,
   A plague-sore, or embossèd carbuncle   225
   In my corrupted blood. But I'll not chide thee;
   Let shame come when it will, I do not call it.   227

198 sides i.e., sides of the chest (stretched by the swelling heart)
201 much less advancement far less honor, i.e., far worse treatment
202 seem so i.e., don't act as if you were strong   **207 entertainment**
proper reception   **210 wage** wage war   **213 hot-blooded** choleric. (Cf.
1.2.23.)   **215 knee** fall on my knees before   **217 sumpter** packhorse;
hence, drudge   **225 embossèd** swollen, tumid   **227 call** summon

I do not bid the thunder-bearer shoot,   228
Nor tell tales of thee to high-judging Jove.   229
Mend when thou canst; be better at thy leisure.
I can be patient. I can stay with Regan,
I and my hundred knights.

REGAN   Not altogether so.

I looked not for you yet, nor am provided   234
For your fit welcome. Give ear, sir, to my sister;
For those that mingle reason with your passion   236
Must be content to think you old, and so—
But she knows what she does.

LEAR   Is this well spoken?

REGAN

I dare avouch it, sir. What, fifty followers?   239
Is it not well? What should you need of more?
Yea, or so many, sith that both charge and danger   241
Speak 'gainst so great a number? How in one house
Should many people under two commands
Hold amity? 'Tis hard, almost impossible.

GONERIL

Why might not you, my lord, receive attendance
From those that she calls servants, or from mine?

REGAN

Why not, my lord? If then they chanced to slack ye,   247
We could control them. If you will come to me—   248
For now I spy a danger—I entreat you
To bring but five-and-twenty. To no more
Will I give place or notice.   251

LEAR

I gave you all—

REGAN   And in good time you gave it.

LEAR

Made you my guardians, my depositaries,   253
But kept a reservation to be followed   254
With such a number. What, must I come to you
With five-and-twenty? Regan, said you so?

---

228 the thunder-bearer i.e., Jove   **229 high-judging** judging from on high   **234 looked not for** did not expect   **236 mingle . . . passion** consider your passionate behavior reasonably   **239 avouch** vouch for **241 sith that** since.   **charge** expense   **247 slack** neglect   **248 control** correct   **251 notice** recognition, acknowledgment   **253 depositaries** trustees   **254 kept a reservation** reserved a right

REGAN
    And speak 't again, my lord. No more with me.
LEAR
    Those wicked creatures yet do look well-favored   258
    When others are more wicked; not being the worst
    Stands in some rank of praise. [*To Goneril.*] I'll go
        with thee.   260
    Thy fifty yet doth double five-and-twenty,
    And thou art twice her love.
GONERIL   Hear me, my lord:
    What need you five-and-twenty, ten, or five,
    To follow in a house where twice so many   264
    Have a command to tend you?
REGAN   What need one?
LEAR
    O, reason not the need! Our basest beggars   266
    Are in the poorest thing superfluous.   267
    Allow not nature more than nature needs,   268
    Man's life is cheap as beast's. Thou art a lady;
    If only to go warm were gorgeous,   270
    Why, nature needs not what thou gorgeous wear'st,   271
    Which scarcely keeps thee warm. But, for true need—   272
    You heavens, give me that patience, patience I need!
    You see me here, you gods, a poor old man,
    As full of grief as age, wretched in both.
    If it be you that stirs these daughters' hearts
    Against their father, fool me not so much   277
    To bear it tamely; touch me with noble anger,   278
    And let not women's weapons, water drops,
    Stain my man's cheeks! No, you unnatural hags,
    I will have such revenges on you both
    That all the world shall—I will do such things—
    What they are yet I know not, but they shall be

258 **well-favored** attractive, fair of feature 260 **Stands . . . praise**
achieves, by necessity, some relative deserving of praise 264 **follow** be
your attendants 266 **reason not** do not dispassionately analyze. **Our
basest** even our most wretched 267 **Are . . . superfluous** have some
wretched possession they can dispense with 268 **Allow not** if you do
not allow. **needs** i.e., to survive 270–272 **If . . . warm** i.e., if fashions
in clothes were determined only by the need for warmth, this natural
standard wouldn't justify the rich robes you wear to be gorgeous—
which don't serve well for warmth in any case 272 **for** as for
277–278 **fool . . . To** do not make me so foolish as to

The terrors of the earth. You think I'll weep;
No, I'll not weep.   *Storm and tempest.*
I have full cause of weeping; but this heart
Shall break into a hundred thousand flaws   287
Or ere I'll weep. O Fool, I shall go mad!   288
                    Exeunt [Lear, Gloucester, Kent, and Fool].

CORNWALL
Let us withdraw. 'Twill be a storm.

REGAN
This house is little. The old man and 's people
Cannot be well bestowed.   291

GONERIL
'Tis his own blame hath put himself from rest,   292
And must needs taste his folly.   293

REGAN
For his particular, I'll receive him gladly,   294
But not one follower.

GONERIL
So am I purposed. Where is my lord of Gloucester?

CORNWALL
Followed the old man forth.

        Enter Gloucester.

                        He is returned.

GLOUCESTER
The King is in high rage.

CORNWALL   Whither is he going?

GLOUCESTER
He calls to horse, but will I know not whither.

CORNWALL
'Tis best to give him way. He leads himself.   300

GONERIL
My lord, entreat him by no means to stay.

GLOUCESTER
Alack, the night comes on, and the bleak winds
Do sorely ruffle. For many miles about   303
There's scarce a bush.

287 **flaws** fragments   288 **Or ere** before   291 **bestowed** lodged
292 **blame** fault.   **hath** that he has, or, that has.   **from rest** i.e., out of
the house; also, lacking peace of mind   293 **taste** experience   294 **For
his particular** as for him individually   300 **give . . . himself** give him his
own way. He is guided only by his own willfulness.   303 **ruffle** bluster

REGAN   O, sir, to willful men
   The injuries that they themselves procure
   Must be their schoolmasters. Shut up your doors.
   He is attended with a desperate train,
   And what they may incense him to, being apt   308
   To have his ear abused, wisdom bids fear.   309
CORNWALL
   Shut up your doors, my lord; 'tis a wild night.
   My Regan counsels well. Come out o' the storm.
                              Exeunt.

❖

308–309 being . . . abused (he) being inclined to hearken to wild counsel

3.1　　*Storm still. Enter Kent [disguised as Caius] and*
　　　　　a Gentleman, severally.

KENT　Who's there, besides foul weather?

GENTLEMAN
　One minded like the weather, most unquietly.

KENT　I know you. Where's the King?

GENTLEMAN
　Contending with the fretful elements;
　Bids the wind blow the earth into the sea
　Or swell the curlèd waters 'bove the main,　　　　　　6
　That things might change or cease; tears his white hair,
　Which the impetuous blasts with eyeless rage
　Catch in their fury and make nothing of;　　　　　　　9
　Strives in his little world of man to outstorm　　　　10
　The to-and-fro-conflicting wind and rain.
　This night, wherein the cub-drawn bear would couch,　12
　The lion and the belly-pinchèd wolf
　Keep their fur dry, unbonneted he runs
　And bids what will take all.

KENT　　　　　　　　　　　But who is with him?　　15

GENTLEMAN
　None but the Fool, who labors to outjest　　　　　　16
　His heart-struck injuries.

KENT　　　　　　　　　　Sir, I do know you,
　And dare upon the warrant of my note　　　　　　　18
　Commend a dear thing to you. There is division,　　19
　Although as yet the face of it is covered
　With mutual cunning, twixt Albany and Cornwall;
　Who have—as who have not, that their great stars　22
　Throned and set high?—servants, who seem no less,　23

3.1. Location: An open place in Gloucestershire.
s.d. severally at separate doors　**6 main** mainland　**9 make nothing of**
treat disrespectfully　**10 little world of man** i.e., the microcosm, which
is an epitome of the macrocosm or universe　**12 cub-drawn** famished,
with udders sucked dry (and hence ravenous).　**couch** lie close in its
den　**15 take all** (A cry of desperate defiance, said by a gambler in
staking his last.)　**16 outjest** exorcise or relieve by jesting　**18 upon . . .
note** on the strength of what I know (about you)　**19 Commend . . .
thing** entrust a precious undertaking　**22 that** whom.　**stars** destinies
23 no less i.e., no other than servants

Which are to France the spies and speculations   24
Intelligent of our state. What hath been seen,   25
Either in snuffs and packings of the Dukes,   26
Or the hard rein which both of them hath borne
Against the old kind King, or something deeper,
Whereof perchance these are but furnishings—   29
But true it is, from France there comes a power   30
Into this scattered kingdom, who already,   31
Wise in our negligence, have secret feet   32
In some of our best ports and are at point   33
To show their open banner. Now to you:
If on my credit you dare build so far   35
To make your speed to Dover, you shall find
Some that will thank you, making just report   37
Of how unnatural and bemadding sorrow
The King hath cause to plain.   39
I am a gentleman of blood and breeding,
And from some knowledge and assurance offer
This office to you.   42

GENTLEMAN
I will talk further with you.

KENT   No, do not.
For confirmation that I am much more
Than my outwall, open this purse and take   45
What it contains. [*He gives a purse and a ring.*] If
    you shall see Cordelia—
As fear not but you shall—show her this ring,
And she will tell you who that fellow is   48
That yet you do not know. Fie on this storm!
I will go seek the King.

GENTLEMAN
Give me your hand. Have you no more to say?

KENT
Few words, but, to effect, more than all yet: 52

24 speculations scouts, spies   **25 Intelligent of** supplying intelligence
pertinent to   **26 snuffs** quarrels.   **packings** intrigues   **29 furnishings**
outward shows   **30 power** army   **31 scattered** divided   **32 Wise in**
taking advantage of.   **feet** i.e., foothold   **33 at point** ready   **35 credit**
trustworthiness.   **so far** so far as   **37 making just report** for making an
accurate report   **39 plain** complain   **42 office** assignment   **45 outwall**
exterior appearance   **48 fellow** i.e., Kent   **52 to effect** in their consequences

That when we have found the King—in which your pain 53
That way, I'll this—he that first lights on him   54
Holla the other.   *Exeunt [separately].*

✤

3.2   *Storm still. Enter Lear and Fool.*

LEAR
Blow, winds, and crack your cheeks! Rage, blow!
You cataracts and hurricanoes, spout   2
Till you have drenched our steeples, drowned the cocks! 3
You sulfurous and thought-executing fires,   4
Vaunt-couriers of oak-cleaving thunderbolts,   5
Singe my white head! And thou, all-shaking thunder,
Strike flat the thick rotundity o' the world!
Crack nature's molds, all germens spill at once   8
That makes ingrateful man!
FOOL   O nuncle, court holy water in a dry house is bet- 10
ter than this rainwater out o' door. Good nuncle, in,
ask thy daughters' blessing. Here's a night pities   12
neither wise men nor fools.
LEAR
Rumble thy bellyful! Spit, fire! Spout, rain!
Nor rain, wind, thunder, fire, are my daughters.
I tax not you, you elements, with unkindness;   16
I never gave you kingdom, called you children.
You owe me no subscription. Then let fall   18
Your horrible pleasure. Here I stand your slave,
A poor, infirm, weak, and despised old man.
But yet I call you servile ministers,   21

53–54 in which . . . this in which task, you search in that direction while
I go this way

3.2. Location: An open place, as before.
2 hurricanoes waterspouts   **3 drenched** drowned.   **cocks** weather-
cocks   **4 thought-executing** acting with the quickness of thought.   **fires**
i.e., lightning   **5 Vaunt-couriers** forerunners   **8 nature's molds** the
molds in which nature makes men.   **germens** germs, seeds.   **spill**
destroy   **10 court holy water** flattery   **12 ask . . . blessing** (For Lear to
do so would be to acknowledge their authority.)   **16 tax** accuse.   **with**
of   **18 subscription** allegiance   **21 ministers** agents

That will with two pernicious daughters join
Your high-engendered battles 'gainst a head   23
So old and white as this. O, ho! 'Tis foul!
FOOL   He that has a house to put 's head in has a good
headpiece.   26
    The codpiece that will house   27
      Before the head has any,   28
    The head and he shall louse;   29
      So beggars marry many.   30
    The man that makes his toe   31
      What he his heart should make   32
    Shall of a corn cry woe,   33
      And turn his sleep to wake.   34
For there was never yet fair woman but she made   35
mouths in a glass.   36
LEAR
No, I will be the pattern of all patience;
I will say nothing.

     Enter Kent, [disguised as Caius].

KENT   Who's there?
FOOL   Marry, here's grace and a codpiece; that's a wise   40
man and a fool.
KENT
Alas, sir, are you here? Things that love night
Love not such nights as these. The wrathful skies
Gallow the very wanderers of the dark   44

---

23 high-engendered battles battalions engendered in the heavens
26 headpiece (1) helmetlike covering for the head (2) head for common
sense   **27–34 The codpiece . . . wake** i.e., a man who houses his genitals
in a sexual embrace before he provides a roof for his head can expect
lice-infested penury; and one who elevates what is base above what is
noble (as Lear has done with his daughters) can expect misery and
wakeful tossing also. If he values the toe more than the heart, his
reward will be that the toe will cause him suffering.   **codpiece** covering for the genitals worn by men with their close-fitting hose; here
representing the genitals themselves   **35–36 made . . . glass** practiced
making attractive faces in a mirror   **40 Marry** (An oath, originally "by
the Virgin Mary.")   **grace** royal grace.   **codpiece** (Often prominent in
the Fool's costume.)   **44 Gallow** i.e., gally, frighten.   **wanderers of the
dark** wild beasts

And make them keep their caves. Since I was man,   45
Such sheets of fire, such bursts of horrid thunder,
Such groans of roaring wind and rain I never
Remember to have heard. Man's nature cannot carry   48
Th' affliction nor the fear.

LEAR   Let the great gods,   49
That keep this dreadful pother o'er our heads,   50
Find out their enemies now. Tremble, thou wretch,   51
That hast within thee undivulgèd crimes
Unwhipped of justice! Hide thee, thou bloody hand,   53
Thou perjured, and thou simular of virtue   54
That art incestuous! Caitiff, to pieces shake,   55
That under covert and convenient seeming   56
Has practiced on man's life! Close pent-up guilts,   57
Rive your concealing continents and cry   58
These dreadful summoners grace! I am a man   59
More sinned against than sinning.

KENT   Alack, bareheaded?
Gracious my lord, hard by here is a hovel;
Some friendship will it lend you 'gainst the tempest.
Repose you there while I to this hard house—
More harder than the stones whereof 'tis raised,
Which even but now, demanding after you,   65
Denied me to come in—return and force
Their scanted courtesy.

LEAR   My wits begin to turn.   67
Come on, my boy. How dost, my boy? Art cold?
I am cold myself.—Where is this straw, my fellow?
The art of our necessities is strange,
And can make vile things precious. Come, your hovel.—
Poor fool and knave, I have one part in my heart
That's sorry yet for thee.

---

45 keep occupy, remain inside   **48 carry** endure   **49 affliction** physical
affliction   **50 pother** hubbub, turmoil   **51 Find . . . now** i.e., expose
criminals (by their display of fear)   **53 of** by   **54 perjured** perjurer.
similar pretender   **55 Caitiff** wretch   **56 seeming** hypocrisy   **57 practiced on** plotted against.   **Close** secret   **58 Rive** split.   **continents**
covering, containers   **58–59 cry . . . grace** pray for mercy at the hands
of the officers of divine justice. (A *summoner* was the police officer
of an ecclesiastical court.)   **65 Which** i.e., the occupants of the house.
demanding I inquiring   **67 scanted** stinted

FOOL [*Sings*]
>   "He that has and a little tiny wit,   74
>   With heigh-ho, the wind and the rain,
>   Must make content with his fortunes fit,
>   Though the rain it raineth every day."   77

LEAR
True, boy.—Come, bring us to this hovel.

Exit [with Kent].

FOOL   This is a brave night to cool a courtesan. I'll speak   79
a prophecy ere I go:

>   When priests are more in word than matter;   81
>   When brewers mar their malt with water;   82
>   When nobles are their tailors' tutors,   83
>   No heretics burned but wenches' suitors,   84
>   Then shall the realm of Albion   85
>   Come to great confusion.

>   When every case in law is right,   87
>   No squire in debt, nor no poor knight;
>   When slanders do not live in tongues,
>   Nor cutpurses come not to throngs;
>   When usurers tell their gold i' the field,   91
>   And bawds and whores do churches build,
>   Then comes the time, who lives to see 't,
>   That going shall be used with feet.   94

This prophecy Merlin shall make, for I live before his   95
time.   *Exit.*

74–77 (Derived from the popular song that Feste sings in *Twelfth Night*,
5.1.389ff.)   **79 This . . . courtesan** i.e., this wretched night might at least
damp the fires of lust (?)   **brave** fine   **81 more . . . matter** better in speech
than in substance or Gospel truth. (This and the next three lines satirize
the present state of affairs.)   **82 mar** adulterate   **83 are . . . tutors** i.e.,
know more than their tailors about fashion   **84 No . . . suitors** i.e., when
heresy is a matter not of religious faith but of perjured lovers (whose
burning is not at the stake but in catching venereal disease)   **85 realm of
Albion** kingdom of England. (The Fool is parodying a pseudo-Chaucerian
prophetic verse.)   **87 right** just. (This and the next five lines offer a utopian
vision of justice and charity that will never be realized in this corrupted
world.)   **91 tell** count.   **i' the field** i.e., openly, without fear   **94 going . . .
feet** walking will be done on foot   **95 Merlin** (A great wizard of the court
of King Arthur, who came after Lear.)

3.3   *Enter Gloucester and Edmund [with lights].*

GLOUCESTER   Alack, alack, Edmund, I like not this unnatural dealing. When I desired their leave that I might
pity him, they took from me the use of mine own ³
house, charged me on pain of perpetual displeasure
neither to speak of him, entreat for him, or any way
sustain him.

EDMUND   Most savage and unnatural!

GLOUCESTER   Go to; say you nothing. There is division
between the Dukes, and a worse matter than that. I
have received a letter this night; 'tis dangerous to be
spoken; I have locked the letter in my closet. These in- ¹¹
juries the King now bears will be revenged home; ¹²
there is part of a power already footed. We must in- ¹³
cline to the King. I will look him and privily relieve ¹⁴
him. Go you and maintain talk with the Duke, that
my charity be not of him perceived. If he ask for me, I ¹⁶
am ill and gone to bed. If I die for 't, as no less is
threatened me, the King my old master must be relieved. There is strange things toward, Edmund. Pray ¹⁹
you, be careful.   *Exit.*

EDMUND
This courtesy forbid thee shall the Duke   ²¹
Instantly know, and of that letter too.
This seems a fair deserving, and must draw me   ²³
That which my father loses—no less than all.
The younger rises when the old doth fall.   *Exit.*

3.4   *Enter Lear, Kent [disguised as Caius], and Fool.*

KENT
Here is the place, my lord. Good my lord, enter.

3.3. Location: Gloucester's house.
3 pity be merciful to, relieve   **11 closet** private chamber   **12 home**
thoroughly   **13 power** armed force.   **footed** landed   **13–14 incline**
to side with   **14 look** look for   **16 of** by   **19 toward** impending
21 courtesy forbid thee kindness (to Lear) which you were forbidden
to show   **23 fair deserving** meritorious action

3.4. Location: An open place. Before a hovel.

The tyranny of the open night's too rough
For nature to endure.   *Storm still.*

LEAR   Let me alone.

KENT
Good my lord, enter here.

LEAR   Wilt break my heart?   4

KENT
I had rather break mine own. Good my lord, enter.

LEAR
Thou think'st 'tis much that this contentious storm
Invades us to the skin. So 'tis to thee,
But where the greater malady is fixed   8
The lesser is scarce felt. Thou'dst shun a bear,
But if thy flight lay toward the roaring sea
Thou'dst meet the bear i' the mouth. When the
    mind's free,   11
The body's delicate. This tempest in my mind   12
Doth from my senses take all feeling else
Save what beats there. Filial ingratitude!
Is it not as this mouth should tear this hand   15
For lifting food to 't? But I will punish home.   16
No, I will weep no more. In such a night
To shut me out? Pour on; I will endure.
In such a night as this? O Regan, Goneril,
Your old kind father, whose frank heart gave all—   20
O, that way madness lies; let me shun that!
No more of that.

KENT   Good my lord, enter here.

LEAR
Prithee, go in thyself; seek thine own ease.
This tempest will not give me leave to ponder   24
On things would hurt me more. But I'll go in.   25
[*To the Fool.*] In, boy; go first. You houseless poverty—
Nay, get thee in. I'll pray, and then I'll sleep.

                              Exit [Fool into the hovel].

---

4 break my heart i.e., cause me anguish by relieving my physical wants
and thus forcing me to confront again my *greater malady* (l. 8)   **8 fixed**
lodged, implanted   **11 i' the mouth** i.e., head-on.   **free** free of anxiety
12 The body's delicate i.e., the body's importunate needs can assert
themselves   **15 as** as if   **16 home** fully   **20 frank** liberal   **24 will . . .
leave** i.e., keeps me too preoccupied   **25 things would** things (such as
filial ingratitude) that would

Poor naked wretches, wheresoe'er you are,
That bide the pelting of this pitiless storm,   29
How shall your houseless heads and unfed sides,
Your looped and windowed raggedness, defend you   31
From seasons such as these? O, I have ta'en
Too little care of this! Take physic, pomp;   33
Expose thyself to feel what wretches feel,
That thou mayst shake the superflux to them   35
And show the heavens more just.

EDGAR [*Within*] Fathom and half, fathom and half! 37
    Poor Tom!

      Enter Fool [from the hovel].

FOOL   Come not in here, nuncle; here's a spirit. Help
    me, help me!
KENT   Give me thy hand. Who's there?
FOOL   A spirit, a spirit! He says his name's poor Tom.
KENT
What art thou that dost grumble there i' the straw?
Come forth.

      Enter Edgar [disguised as a madman].

EDGAR   Away! The foul fiend follows me! Through the 45
    sharp hawthorn blows the cold wind. Hum! Go to thy 46
    bed and warm thee.
LEAR   Didst thou give all to thy daughters? And art
    thou come to this?
EDGAR   Who gives anything to poor Tom? Whom the
    foul fiend hath led through fire and through flame,
    through ford and whirlpool, o'er bog and quagmire;
    that hath laid knives under his pillow and halters in 53
    his pew, set ratsbane by his porridge, made him 54

---

29 bide endure   **31 looped and windowed** full of openings like windows
and loopholes   **33 Take physic, pomp** cure yourself, O distempered
great ones   **35 superflux** superfluity (with suggestion of *flux*, "bodily
discharge," introduced by *physic*, "purgative," in l. 33)   **37 Fathom and
half** (A sailor's cry while taking soundings, hence appropriate to a
deluge.)   **45 Away** keep away   **45–46 Through . . . wind** (Possibly a line
from a ballad.)   **53–54 knives, halters, ratsbane** (Tempting means to
commit suicide and hence be damned.)   **54 pew** gallery, place (?)
porridge soup

proud of heart, to ride on a bay trotting horse over 55
four-inched bridges to course his own shadow for a 56
traitor. Bless thy five wits! Tom's a-cold. O, do de, 57
do de, do de. Bless thee from whirlwinds, star-blast- 58
ing, and taking! Do poor Tom some charity, whom the 59
foul fiend vexes. There could I have him now—and 60
there—and there again—and there.   *Storm still.*

LEAR

Has his daughters brought him to this pass?   62
Couldst thou save nothing? Wouldst thou give 'em all?

FOOL   Nay, he reserved a blanket, else we had been all 64
shamed.

LEAR

Now, all the plagues that in the pendulous air   66
Hang fated o'er men's faults light on thy daughters!   67

KENT   He hath no daughters, sir.

LEAR

Death, traitor! Nothing could have subdued nature
To such a lowness but his unkind daughters.
Is it the fashion that discarded fathers
Should have thus little mercy on their flesh?   72
Judicious punishment! 'Twas this flesh begot   73
Those pelican daughters.   ·   74

EDGAR   Pillicock sat on Pillicock Hill. Alow, alow, loo, 75
loo!

FOOL   This cold night will turn us all to fools and madmen.

EDGAR   Take heed o' the foul fiend. Obey thy parents;

55–56 over four-inched bridges i.e., taking mad risks on narrow bridges
with the devil's assistance   **56 course** chase.   **for** as   **57 five wits**
either the five senses, or common wit, imagination, fantasy, estimation,
and memory   **58–59 star-blasting** being blighted by influence of the
stars   **59 taking** pestilence; or witchcraft   **60 There** (Perhaps he slaps
at lice and other vermin as if they were devils.)   **62 pass** miserable
plight   **64 reserved a blanket** kept a wrap (for his nakedness)
66 pendulous suspended, overhanging   **67 fated** having the power of
fate   **72 have . . . flesh** i.e., punish themselves, as Edgar has done
(probably with pins and thorns stuck in his flesh)   **73 Judicious** appropriate to the crime   **74 pelican** greedy. (Young pelicans supposedly
smote their parents and fed on the blood of their mothers' breasts.)
75 Pillicock (From an old rhyme, suggested by the sound of *pelican*.
Pillicock in nursery rhyme seems to have been a euphemism for penis,
Pillicock Hill for the Mount of Venus.)

keep thy word's justice; swear not; commit not with 80
man's sworn spouse; set not thy sweet heart on proud
array. Tom's a-cold.

LEAR   What hast thou been?

EDGAR   A servingman, proud in heart and mind, that 84
curled my hair, wore gloves in my cap, served the lust 85
of my mistress' heart, and did the act of darkness with
her; swore as many oaths as I spake words, and broke
them in the sweet face of heaven. One that slept in the
contriving of lust and waked to do it. Wine loved I
deeply, dice dearly, and in woman out-paramoured 90
the Turk. False of heart, light of ear, bloody of hand; 91
hog in sloth, fox in stealth, wolf in greediness, dog in
madness, lion in prey. Let not the creaking of shoes 93
nor the rustling of silks betray thy poor heart to
woman. Keep thy foot out of brothels, thy hand out of
plackets, thy pen from lenders' books, and defy the 96
foul fiend. Still through the hawthorn blows the cold
wind; says suum, mun, nonny. Dolphin my boy, boy, 98
sessa! Let him trot by.   *Storm still.* 99

LEAR   Thou wert better in a grave than to answer with
thy uncovered body this extremity of the skies. Is man
no more than this? Consider him well. Thou ow'st the 102
worm no silk, the beast no hide, the sheep no wool,
the cat no perfume. Ha! Here's three on 's are sophis- 104
ticated. Thou art the thing itself; unaccommodated 105
man is no more but such a poor, bare, forked animal
as thou art. Off, off, you lendings! Come, unbutton
here.   *[Tearing off his clothes.]*

FOOL   Prithee, nuncle, be contented; 'tis a naughty night 109

---

80 justice integrity.   **commit not** i.e., do not commit adultery. (Edgar's
mad catechism contains fragments of the Ten Commandments.)
84 servingman either a "servant" in the language of courtly love or an
ambitious servant in a household   **85 gloves** i.e., my mistress's favors
90–91 out-paramoured the Turk outdid the Sultan in keeping mis-
tresses   **91 light of ear** foolishly credulous; frivolous   **93 prey** preying   **96 plackets** slits in skirts or petticoats.   **thy pen . . . books** i.e., do
not sign a contract for a loan   **98 suum . . . nonny** (Imitative of the
wind?)   **Dolphin my boy** (A slang phrase, or bit of song?)   **99 sessa** i.e.,
away, cease (?)   **102 ow'st** have borrowed from   **104 çat** civet cat
104–105 sophisticated clad in the trappings of civilized life; adulter-
ated   **105 unaccommodated** unfurnished with the trappings of civilization   **109 naughty** bad

to swim in. Now a little fire in a wild field were like 110
an old lecher's heart—a small spark, all the rest on 's 111
body cold.

    Enter Gloucester, with a torch.

Look, here comes a walking fire.

EDGAR This is the foul fiend Flibbertigibbet! He begins 114
at curfew and walks till the first cock; he gives the web 115
and the pin, squinnies the eye and makes the harelip, 116
mildews the white wheat, and hurts the poor creature 117
of earth.

    Swithold footed thrice the 'old; 119
    He met the nightmare and her ninefold; 120
        Bid her alight,
        And her troth plight,
    And aroint thee, witch, aroint thee! 123

KENT How fares Your Grace?

LEAR What's he?

KENT Who's there? What is 't you seek?

GLOUCESTER What are you there? Your names?

EDGAR Poor Tom, that eats the swimming frog, the
toad, the tadpole, the wall newt and the water; that in 129
the fury of his heart, when the foul fiend rages, eats
cow dung for salads, swallows the old rat and the
ditch-dog, drinks the green mantle of the standing 132
pool; who is whipped from tithing to tithing and 133
stock-punished and imprisoned; who hath had three 134
suits to his back, six shirts to his body, 135
    Horse to ride, and weapon to wear;
    But mice and rats and such small deer 137

110 wild barren, uncultivated **111 on 's** of his **114 Flibbertigibbet**
(A devil from Elizabethan folklore whose name appears in Samuel
Harsnett's *Declaration* of 1603 and elsewhere.) **115 first cock** midnight **115–116 web and the pin** cataract of the eye **116 squinnies**
causes to squint **117 white** ripening **119 Swithold** Saint Withold, a
famous Anglo-Saxon exorcist, who here provides defense against the
nightmare, or demon thought to afflict sleepers, by commanding the
nightmare to *alight*, i.e., stop riding over the sleeper, and *plight* her
troth, i.e., vow true faith, promise to do no harm. **footed . . . 'old** thrice
traversed the wold (tract of hilly upland) **120 ninefold** nine offspring
(with possible pun on *fold, foal*) **123 aroint thee** begone **129 water** i.e.,
water newt **132 ditch-dog** i.e., dead dog in a ditch. **mantle** scum.
standing stagnant **133 tithing to tithing** i.e., one ward or parish to
another **134 stock-punished** placed in the stocks **134–135 three suits**
(Like the menial servant at 2.2.15.) **137 deer** animals

Have been Tom's food for seven long year.
Beware my follower. Peace, Smulkin! Peace, thou fiend! 139

GLOUCESTER
What, hath Your Grace no better company?

EDGAR   The Prince of Darkness is a gentleman. Modo 141
he's called, and Mahu.   142

GLOUCESTER
Our flesh and blood, my lord, is grown so vile
That it doth hate what gets it.   144

EDGAR   Poor Tom's a-cold.

GLOUCESTER
Go in with me. My duty cannot suffer   146
T' obey in all your daughters' hard commands.
Though their injunction be to bar my doors
And let this tyrannous night take hold upon you,
Yet have I ventured to come seek you out
And bring you where both fire and food is ready.

LEAR
First let me talk with this philosopher.
[*To Edgar.*] What is the cause of thunder?

KENT   Good my lord,
Take his offer. Go into the house.

LEAR
I'll talk a word with this same learnèd Theban.   155
[*To Edgar.*] What is your study?   156

EDGAR   How to prevent the fiend, and to kill vermin.   157

LEAR   Let me ask you one word in private.

                        [*Lear and Edgar talk apart.*]

KENT [*To Gloucester*]
Importune him once more to go, my lord.
His wits begin t' unsettle.

GLOUCESTER   Canst thou blame him?
                                        Storm still.
His daughters seek his death. Ah, that good Kent!
He said it would be thus, poor banished man.
Thou sayest the King grows mad; I'll tell thee, friend,
I am almost mad myself. I had a son,

---

139 follower familiar, attendant devil   **139, 141–142 Smulkin, Modo,
Mahu** (Shakespeare found these Elizabethan devils in Samuel
Harsnett's *Declaration.*)   **144 gets** begets   **146 suffer** permit me
155 Theban i.e., one deeply versed in "philosophy" or natural science
156 study special competence   **157 prevent** thwart

Now outlawed from my blood; he sought my life   165
But lately, very late. I loved him, friend,
No father his son dearer. True to tell thee,
The grief hath crazed my wits. What a night's this!—
I do beseech Your Grace—

LEAR   O, cry you mercy, sir.   170
[*To Edgar.*] Noble philosopher, your company.

EDGAR   Tom's a-cold.

GLOUCESTER [*To Edgar*]   In, fellow, there, into the hovel.
Keep thee warm.

LEAR [*Starting toward the hovel*]
Come, let's in all.

KENT   This way, my lord.

LEAR   With him!
I will keep still with my philosopher.

KENT [*To Gloucester*]
Good my lord, soothe him. Let him take the fellow.   177

GLOUCESTER [*To Kent*]   Take him you on.   178

KENT [*To Edgar*]
Sirrah, come on. Go along with us.

LEAR   Come, good Athenian.   180

GLOUCESTER   No words, no words! Hush.

EDGAR
Child Rowland to the dark tower came;   182
His word was still, "Fie, foh, and fum,   183
   I smell the blood of a British man."   *Exeunt.* 184

✱

3.5   *Enter Cornwall and Edmund [with a letter].*

CORNWALL   I will have my revenge ere I depart his
house.

EDMUND   How, my lord, I may be censured, that nature ³

---

165 outlawed . . . blood exiled from kinship with me and legally outlawed   **170 cry you mercy** I beg your pardon   **177 soothe** humor
178 Take . . . on i.e., take Edgar along with you   **180 Athenian** i.e.,
philosopher   **182 Child Rowland,** etc. (Probably a fragment of a ballad
about the hero of the Charlemagne legends. A *child* is a candidate for
knighthood.)   **183 word** watchword.   **still** always   **183–184 Fie . . . man**
(This is essentially what the Giant says in "Jack, the Giant Killer.")

3.5. Location: Gloucester's house.
3 censured judged

thus gives way to loyalty, something fears me to 4
think of.

CORNWALL   I now perceive it was not altogether your
brother's evil disposition made him seek his death, 7
but a provoking merit set awork by a reprovable 8
badness in himself.   9

EDMUND   How malicious is my fortune that I must repent to be just! This is the letter he spoke of, which 11
approves him an intelligent party to the advantages 12
of France. O heavens! That this treason were not, or
not I the detector!

CORNWALL   Go with me to the Duchess.

EDMUND   If the matter of this paper be certain, you have
mighty business in hand.

CORNWALL   True or false, it hath made thee Earl of
Gloucester. Seek out where thy father is, that he may
be ready for our apprehension.   20

EDMUND [*Aside*]   If I find him comforting the King, it 21
will stuff his suspicion more fully.—I will persevere in 22
my course of loyalty, though the conflict be sore between that and my blood.   24

CORNWALL   I will lay trust upon thee, and thou shalt
find a dearer father in my love.   *Exeunt.*

❖

3.6   *Enter Kent [disguised as Caius] and Gloucester.*

GLOUCESTER   Here is better than the open air; take it
thankfully. I will piece out the comfort with what ad- 2
dition I can. I will not be long from you.

---

4 something fears somewhat frightens   **7 his** i.e., his father's   **8–9 a
provoking . . . himself** i.e., the badness of Gloucester which deserved
punishment, set awork by an evil propensity in Edgar himself   **11 to be
just** that I am righteous in my duty (to Cornwall)   **12 approves**
proves.   **an intelligent . . . advantages** a spy in the service   **20 apprehension** arrest   **21 him** i.e., Gloucester.   **comforting** offering aid and
comfort to, helping   **22 his** i.e., Cornwall's or, *his suspicion* may mean
"suspicion of him, Gloucester"   **24 blood** family loyalty, filial instincts

3.6. Location: Within a building on Gloucester's estate, near or adjoin-
ing his house; or part of the house itself. See 3.4.146–154. Cushions are
provided, and stools.
2 piece eke

KENT   All the power of his wits have given way to his
impatience. The gods reward your kindness!   5
                                   Exit [Gloucester].

Enter Lear, Edgar [as poor Tom], and Fool.

EDGAR   Frateretto calls me, and tells me Nero is an an-   6
gler in the lake of darkness. Pray, innocent, and be-   7
ware the foul fiend.

FOOL   Prithee, nuncle, tell me whether a madman be a
gentleman or a yeoman?

LEAR   A king, a king!

FOOL   No, he's a yeoman that has a gentleman to his
son; for he's a mad yeoman that sees his son a gentleman before him.

LEAR
To have a thousand with red burning spits
Come hizzing in upon 'em—   16

EDGAR   The foul fiend bites my back.

FOOL   He's mad that trusts in the tameness of a wolf, a
horse's health, a boy's love, or a whore's oath.

LEAR
It shall be done; I will arraign them straight.
[*To Edgar.*] Come, sit thou here, most learnèd justicer.   21
[*To the Fool.*] Thou, sapient sir, sit here. Now, you
she-foxes!

EDGAR   Look where he stands and glares! Want'st thou   23
eyes at trial, madam?   24
[*Sings.*] "Come o'er the burn, Bessy, to me—"   25

FOOL [*Sings*]
          Her boat hath a leak,
          And she must not speak
Why she dares not come over to thee.

5 impatience rage, inability to endure more   **6 Frateretto** (Another of the
fiends from Harsnett.)   **6–7 Nero is an angler** (See Chaucer's "Monk's
Tale," ll. 485–486; in Rabelais, 2.30, Nero is described as a fiddler and
Trajan an angler in the underworld.)   **7 innocent** simpleton, fool (i.e., the
Fool)   **16 hizzing** hissing   **21 justicer** judge, justice   **23 he** (Probably one
of Edgar's devils; or Lear.)   **23–24 Want'st . . . trial** do you lack spectators
at your trial, or do you want to have them   **25 Come . . . me** (First line of
a ballad by William Birche, 1558. A *burn* is a brook. The Fool makes a
ribald reply, in which the *leaky boat* suggests her easy virtue or perhaps
her menstrual period.)

EDGAR   The foul fiend haunts poor Tom in the voice of
a nightingale. Hoppedance cries in Tom's belly for two 30
white herring. Croak not, black angel; I have no food 31
for thee.

KENT
How do you, sir? Stand you not so amazed.   33
Will you lie down and rest upon the cushions?

LEAR
I'll see their trial first. Bring in their evidence.   35
[*To Edgar.*] Thou robèd man of justice, take thy place; 36
[*To the Fool.*] And thou, his yokefellow of equity,   37
Bench by his side. [*To Kent.*] You are o' the commission; 38
Sit you too.   [*They sit.*]

EDGAR   Let us deal justly.   [*He sings.*]
    Sleepest or wakest thou, jolly shepherd?
      Thy sheep be in the corn;   42
    And for one blast of thy minikin mouth,   43
      Thy sheep shall take no harm.   44
Purr the cat is gray.   45

LEAR   Arraign her first; 'tis Goneril, I here take my oath
before this honorable assembly, kicked the poor King 47
her father.

FOOL   Come hither, mistress. Is your name Goneril?

LEAR   She cannot deny it.

FOOL   Cry you mercy, I took you for a joint stool.   51

LEAR
And here's another, whose warped looks proclaim
What store her heart is made on. Stop her there!   53

---

30 Hoppedance (Harsnett mentions "Hoberdidance.")   **31 white** un-
smoked (contrasted with *black angel*).   **Croak** (Refers to the rumbling in
Edgar's stomach denoting hunger.)   **33 amazed** bewildered   **35 their
evidence** the witnesses against them   **36 robèd man** i.e., Edgar, with his
blanket   **37 yokefellow of equity** partner in the law   **38 Bench** take
your place on the bench.   **o' the commission** one commissioned to be a
justice   **42 corn** grain field   **43–44 And . . . harm** (This may mean that
if the shepherd recalls his sheep by piping to them before they consume
the grainfield, they will not be put in the pound.)   **43 minikin** dainty,
pretty   **45 Purr the cat** (A devil or familiar from Harsnett; see 3.4.114,
note. *Purr* may be the sound the familiar makes.)   **47 kicked** who
kicked   **51 joint stool** low stool made by a joiner, or maker of furniture
with joined parts. (Proverbially the phrase "I took . . . stool" meant "I
beg your pardon for failing to notice you." The reference is also presumably to a real stool onstage.)   **53 store** material.   **on** of

Arms, arms, sword, fire! Corruption in the place!   54
False justicer, why hast thou let her scape?

EDGAR   Bless thy five wits!

KENT

O, pity! Sir, where is the patience now
That you so oft have boasted to retain?

EDGAR [*Aside*]

My tears begin to take his part so much
They mar my counterfeiting.

LEAR   The little dogs and all,
Tray, Blanch, and Sweetheart, see, they bark at me.

EDGAR   Tom will throw his head at them. Avaunt, you   63
curs!

    Be thy mouth or black or white,
    Tooth that poisons if it bite,
    Mastiff, greyhound, mongrel grim,
    Hound or spaniel, brach or lym,   68
    Or bobtail tike or trundle-tail,   69
    Tom will make him weep and wail;
    For, with throwing thus my head,
    Dogs leapt the hatch, and all are fled.   72

Do de, de, de. Sessa! Come, march to wakes and fairs   73
and market towns. Poor Tom, thy horn is dry.   74

LEAR   Then let them anatomize Regan; see what breeds   75
about her heart. Is there any cause in nature that make
these hard hearts? [*To Edgar.*] You, sir, I entertain for   77
one of my hundred; only I do not like the fashion of
your garments. You will say they are Persian; but let   79
them be changed.

KENT

Now, good my lord, lie here and rest awhile.

LEAR [*Lying on cushions*]   Make no noise, make no
noise. Draw the curtains. So, so. We'll go to supper i'   83
the morning.   [*He sleeps.*]

---

54 Corruption in the place i.e., there is iniquity or bribery in this court
63 throw his head at i.e., threaten   **68 brach** hound bitch.   **lym** blood-
hound   **69 bobtail** short-tailed small dog, cur.   **trundle-tail** long-tailed
dog   **72 hatch** lower half of a divided door   **73 Sessa** i.e., away, cease (?)
wakes (Here, parish festivals.)   **74 horn** i.e., horn bottle used by beggars to beg for drinks   **75 anatomize** dissect   **77 entertain** take into
my service   **79 Persian** i.e., gorgeous intricate attire   **83 curtains** bed-
curtains. (They presumably exist only in Lear's mad imagination.)

FOOL   And I'll go to bed at noon.

Enter Gloucester.

GLOUCESTER
Come hither, friend. Where is the King my master?
KENT
Here, sir, but trouble him not. His wits are gone.
GLOUCESTER
Good friend, I prithee, take him in thy arms.
I have o'erheard a plot of death upon him.   89
There is a litter ready; lay him in 't
And drive toward Dover, friend, where thou shalt meet
Both welcome and protection. Take up thy master.
If thou shouldst dally half an hour, his life,
With thine and all that offer to defend him,
Stand in assurèd loss. Take up, take up,   95
And follow me, that will to some provision   96
Give thee quick conduct.
KENT   Oppressèd nature sleeps.   97
This rest might yet have balmed thy broken sinews,   98
Which, if convenience will not allow,   99
Stand in hard cure. [*To the Fool.*] Come, help to bear
   thy master.   100
Thou must not stay behind.   [*They pick up Lear.*]
GLOUCESTER   Come, come, away!
                         Exeunt [all but Edgar].
EDGAR
When we our betters see bearing our woes,   102
We scarcely think our miseries our foes.   103
Who alone suffers suffers most i' the mind,   104
Leaving free things and happy shows behind;   105
But then the mind much sufferance doth o'erskip   106
When grief hath mates, and bearing fellowship.   107

89 upon against   **95 Stand . . . loss** will assuredly be lost   **96 provision**
supplies; or, means of providing for safety   **97 conduct** guidance
98 balmed cured, healed.   **sinews** nerves   **99 convenience** fortunate
circumstances   **100 Stand . . . cure** will be hard to cure   **102 our woes**
woes like ours   **103 our foes** i.e., hostile toward us alone (since we see how
human suffering afflicts even the great)   **104 Who . . . mind** i.e., he who
suffers alone suffers mental agonies greater than those who perceive they
have companions in misery   **105 free** carefree.   **shows** scenes   **106 sufferance** suffering   **107 bearing fellowship** tribulation (has) company

How light and portable my pain seems now,   108
When that which makes me bend makes the King bow—
He childed as I fathered. Tom, away!   110
Mark the high noises, and thyself bewray   111
When false opinion, whose wrong thoughts defile thee,
In thy just proof repeals and reconciles thee.   113
What will hap more tonight, safe scape the King!   114
Lurk, lurk.   [*Exit.*]

❖

3.7   *Enter Cornwall, Regan, Goneril, Bastard*
          [*Edmund*], *and Servants.*

CORNWALL [*To Goneril*]   Post speedily to my lord your hus-   1
band; show him this letter. [*He gives a letter.*] The army
of France is landed.—Seek out the traitor Gloucester.
                              [*Exeunt some Servants.*]
REGAN   Hang him instantly.
GONERIL   Pluck out his eyes.
CORNWALL   Leave him to my displeasure. Edmund,
keep you our sister company. The revenges we are   7
bound to take upon your traitorous father are not fit   8
for your beholding. Advise the Duke, where you are   9
going, to a most festinate preparation; we are bound   10
to the like. Our posts shall be swift and intelligent be-   11
twixt us. Farewell, dear sister; farewell, my lord of   12
Gloucester.   13

          Enter steward [*Oswald*].

How now? Where's the King?

108 **portable** bearable, endurable   110 **He . . . fathered** i.e., he suffering
cruelty from his children as I from my father   111 **Mark . . . noises** i.e.,
observe what is being said about those in high places, or about great
events.   **bewray** reveal   113 **In . . . thee** upon your being proved innocent recalls you and restores you to favor   114 **What . . . King** whatever
else happens tonight, may the King escape safely

3.7. Location: Gloucester's house.
1 **Post speedily** hurry   7 **sister** i.e., sister-in-law, Goneril   8 **bound** intend-
ing; obliged   9 **the Duke** i.e., Albany   10 **festinate** hasty.   **are bound**
intend, are committed   11 **posts** messengers.   **intelligent** serviceable in
bearing information, knowledgeable   12–13 **my . . . Gloucester** i.e., Edmund, the recipient now of his father's forfeited estate and title. (Two lines
later, Oswald uses the same title to refer to Edmund's father.)

OSWALD

My lord of Gloucester hath conveyed him hence.
Some five- or six-and-thirty of his knights,   16
Hot questrists after him, met him at gate,   17
Who, with some other of the lord's dependents,   18
Are gone with him toward Dover, where they boast
To have well-armèd friends.

CORNWALL   Get horses for your mistress. [*Exit Oswald.*]
GONERIL   Farewell, sweet lord, and sister.
CORNWALL

Edmund, farewell.   *Exeunt* [*Goneril and Edmund*].
                  Go seek the traitor Gloucester.
Pinion him like a thief; bring him before us.
                              [*Exeunt Servants.*]
Though well we may not pass upon his life   25
Without the form of justice, yet our power
Shall do a court'sy to our wrath, which men   27
May blame but not control.

    Enter Gloucester, and Servants [*leading him*].

                  Who's there? The traitor?
REGAN   Ingrateful fox! 'Tis he.
CORNWALL   Bind fast his corky arms.   30
GLOUCESTER

What means Your Graces? Good my friends, consider
You are my guests. Do me no foul play, friends.
CORNWALL

Bind him, I say.   [*Servants bind him.*]
REGAN   Hard, hard. O filthy traitor!
GLOUCESTER

Unmerciful lady as you are, I'm none.
CORNWALL

To this chair bind him.—Villain, thou shalt find—
                  [*Regan plucks Gloucester's beard.*]
GLOUCESTER

By the kind gods, 'tis most ignobly done
To pluck me by the beard.

16–17 his, him i.e., Lear's, Lear   **17 questrists** searchers   **18 the lord's**
i.e., Gloucester's   **25 pass upon his life** pass the death sentence upon
him   **27 do a court'sy** i.e., bow before, yield precedence   **30 corky**
withered with age

REGAN
So white, and such a traitor?

GLOUCESTER   Naughty lady,   38
These hairs which thou dost ravish from my chin
Will quicken and accuse thee. I am your host.   40
With robbers' hands my hospitable favors   41
You should not ruffle thus. What will you do?   42

CORNWALL
Come, sir, what letters had you late from France?   43

REGAN
Be simple-answered, for we know the truth.   44

CORNWALL
And what confederacy have you with the traitors
Late footed in the kingdom?

REGAN   To whose hands   46
You have sent the lunatic King. Speak.

GLOUCESTER
I have a letter guessingly set down,   48
Which came from one that's of a neutral heart,
And not from one opposed.

CORNWALL   Cunning.

REGAN   And false.

CORNWALL   Where hast thou sent the King?

GLOUCESTER   To Dover.

REGAN
Wherefore to Dover? Wast thou not charged at peril—   55

CORNWALL
Wherefore to Dover? Let him answer that.

GLOUCESTER
I am tied to the stake, and I must stand the course.   57

REGAN   Wherefore to Dover?

GLOUCESTER
Because I would not see thy cruel nails
Pluck out his poor old eyes, nor thy fierce sister

---

38 white i.e., white-haired, venerable. **Naughty** wicked **40 quicken**
come to life **41 my hospitable favors** the features of me, your host
42 ruffle tear or snatch at, treat with such violence **43 late** lately
44 simple-answered straightforward in your answers **46 footed**
landed **48 guessingly set down** which was tentatively stated **55 charged
at peril** commanded on peril of your life **57 tied to the stake** i.e., like a
bear to be baited with dogs. **the course** the dogs' attack

In his anointed flesh rash boarish fangs.   61
The sea, with such a storm as his bare head
In hell-black night endured, would have buoyed up   63
And quenched the stellèd fires;   64
Yet, poor old heart, he holp the heavens to rain.   65
If wolves had at thy gate howled that dern time,   66
Thou shouldst have said, "Good porter, turn the key."   67
All cruels else subscribe. But I shall see   68
The wingèd Vengeance overtake such children.   69

CORNWALL
See 't shalt thou never. Fellows, hold the chair.
Upon these eyes of thine I'll set my foot.

GLOUCESTER
He that will think to live till he be old,   72
Give me some help!

> [*Servants hold the chair as Cornwall grinds
> out one of Gloucester's eyes with his boot.*]
>   O cruel! O you gods!

REGAN
One side will mock another. Th' other too.

CORNWALL
If you see Vengeance—

FIRST SERVANT   Hold your hand, my lord!
I have served you ever since I was a child;
But better service have I never done you
Than now to bid you hold.

REGAN   How now, you dog?

FIRST SERVANT [*To Regan*]
If you did wear a beard upon your chin,
I'd shake it on this quarrel.—What do you mean?   80

CORNWALL   My villain?   [*He draws his sword.*] 81

---

61 anointed consecrated with holy oil.   **rash** slash sideways
63–64 would . . . fires i.e., would have swelled high enough to quench
the stars. (The storm was monstrous in its scope and in its assault on
order.)   **buoyed** lifted itself.   **stellèd fires** stars   **65 holp** helped
66 dern dire, dread   **67 turn the key** i.e., let them in   **68 All . . . subscribe** all other cruel creatures would show forgiveness except you; this
cruelty is unparalleled   **69 The wingèd Vengeance** the swift vengeance
of the avenging angel of divine wrath   **72 will think** hopes   **80 I'd . . .
quarrel** i.e., I'd pull your beard in vehement defiance in this cause.
What do you mean i.e., what are you thinking of, what do you think
you're doing. (Said perhaps to Cornwall.)   **81 villain** servant, bondman.
(Cornwall's question implies, "How dare you do such a thing?")

FIRST SERVANT [*Drawing*]
　Nay, then, come on, and take the chance of anger.   82
　　　　　　[*They fight. Cornwall is wounded.*]
REGAN [*To another Servant*]
　Give me thy sword. A peasant stand up thus?   83
　　　　　　[*She takes a sword and runs at him behind.*]
FIRST SERVANT
　O, I am slain! My lord, you have one eye left
　To see some mischief on him. O!   [*He dies.*] 85
CORNWALL
　Lest it see more, prevent it. Out, vile jelly!
　　　　　　[*He puts out Gloucester's other eye.*]
　Where is thy luster now?
GLOUCESTER
　All dark and comfortless. Where's my son Edmund?
　Edmund, enkindle all the sparks of nature   89
　To quit this horrid act.
REGAN   Out, treacherous villain!   90
　Thou call'st on him that hates thee. It was he
　That made the overture of thy treasons to us,   92
　Who is too good to pity thee.
GLOUCESTER
　O my follies! Then Edgar was abused.   94
　Kind gods, forgive me that, and prosper him!
REGAN
　Go thrust him out at gates and let him smell
　His way to Dover. *Exit* [*a Servant*] *with Gloucester.*
　How is 't, my lord? How look you?   97
CORNWALL
　I have received a hurt. Follow me, lady.—
　Turn out that eyeless villain. Throw this slave
　Upon the dunghill.—Regan, I bleed apace.
　Untimely comes this hurt. Give me your arm.
　　　　　Exit [*Cornwall, supported by Regan*].

---

82 the chance of anger the risks of an angry encounter   **83 s.d. She . . .
behind** (This stage direction appears in the quarto.)   **85 mischief** injury
89 nature i.e., filial love   **90 quit** requite.   **Out** (An exclamation of anger
or impatience.)   **92 overture** disclosure   **94 abused** wronged   **97 How
look you** how is it with you

SECOND SERVANT
  I'll never care what wickedness I do,
  If this man come to good.

THIRD SERVANT   If she live long,
  And in the end meet the old course of death,   104
  Women will all turn monsters.

SECOND SERVANT
  Let's follow the old Earl, and get the Bedlam
  To lead him where he would. His roguish madness   107
  Allows itself to anything.   108

THIRD SERVANT
  Go thou. I'll fetch some flax and whites of eggs
  To apply to his bleeding face. Now, heaven help him!   110
                               Exeunt [separately].

❖

104 old customary, natural   **107–108 His . . . anything** i.e., his being a madman and derelict allows him to do anything   **110 s.d. Exeunt** (At some point after ll. 99–100 the body of the slain First Servant must be removed.)

4.1   *Enter Edgar [as poor Tom].*

EDGAR

Yet better thus, and known to be contemned,   1
Than still contemned and flattered. To be worst,   2
The lowest and most dejected thing of fortune,   3
Stands still in esperance, lives not in fear.   4
The lamentable change is from the best;   5
The worst returns to laughter. Welcome, then,   6
Thou unsubstantial air that I embrace!
The wretch that thou hast blown unto the worst
Owes nothing to thy blasts.

   Enter Gloucester, and an Old Man [leading him].

                              But who comes here?   9
My father, poorly led? World, world, O world!
But that thy strange mutations make us hate thee,   11
Life would not yield to age.   12

OLD MAN

O, my good lord, I have been your tenant
And your father's tenant these fourscore years.

GLOUCESTER

Away, get thee away! Good friend, begone.
Thy comforts can do me no good at all;   16
Thee they may hurt.

OLD MAN   You cannot see your way.

GLOUCESTER

I have no way and therefore want no eyes;
I stumbled when I saw. Full oft 'tis seen
Our means secure us, and our mere defects   20
Prove our commodities. O dear son Edgar,   21

4.1. Location: An open place.
1 Yet better thus i.e., it is better to be a beggar.   **known** know what it
is.   **contemned** despised   **2 contemned and flattered** despised behind
your back and flattered to your face   **3 dejected . . . of** debased or
humbled by   **4 esperance** hope.   **fear** i.e., of something worse happening   **5–6 The lamentable . . . laughter** i.e., any change from the best
is grievous, just as any change from the worst is bound to be for
the better   **9 Owes nothing** can pay no more, is free of obligation
11–12 But . . . age i.e., if it were not for your hateful inconstancy, we
would never be reconciled to old age and death   **16 comforts** kindnesses   **20 Our means secure us** our prosperity makes us overconfi-
dent.   **mere defects** sheer afflictions   **21 commodities** benefits

The food of thy abusèd father's wrath!   22
Might I but live to see thee in my touch,   23
I'd say I had eyes again!
OLD MAN   How now? Who's there?
EDGAR [*Aside*]
    O gods! Who is 't can say, "I am at the worst"?
    I am worse than e'er I was.
OLD MAN   'Tis poor mad Tom.
EDGAR [*Aside*]
    And worse I may be yet. The worst is not   27
    So long as we can say, "This is the worst."   28
OLD MAN
    Fellow, where goest?
GLOUCESTER   Is it a beggar-man?
OLD MAN   Madman and beggar too.
GLOUCESTER
    He has some reason, else he could not beg.   31
    I' the last night's storm I such a fellow saw,
    Which made me think a man a worm. My son
    Came then into my mind, and yet my mind
    Was then scarce friends with him. I have heard more
       since.
    As flies to wanton boys are we to the gods;   36
    They kill us for their sport.
EDGAR [*Aside*]   How should this be?   37
    Bad is the trade that must play fool to sorrow,   38
    Ang'ring itself and others.—Bless thee, master!   39
GLOUCESTER
    Is that the naked fellow?
OLD MAN   Ay, my lord.
GLOUCESTER
    Then, prithee, get thee gone. If for my sake
    Thou wilt o'ertake us hence a mile or twain   42

22 The . . . wrath on whom thy deceived father's wrath fed, the object of
his anger   **23 in** i.e., by means of   **27–28 The worst . . . worst** so long as
we can speak and act and delude ourselves with false hopes, our fortunes can in fact grow worse   **31 reason** power of reason   **36 wanton**
playful   **37 How . . . be** i.e., how can he have suffered so much, changed
so much   **38 Bad . . . sorrow** i.e., it's a bad business to have to play
the fool to my sorrowing father   **39 Ang'ring** offending, distressing
42 o'ertake us catch up to us (after you have found clothing for Tom o'
Bedlam)

I' the way toward Dover, do it for ancient love,   43
And bring some covering for this naked soul,
Which I'll entreat to lead me.
OLD MAN   Alack, sir, he is mad.
GLOUCESTER
'Tis the time's plague, when madmen lead the blind.   46
Do as I bid thee, or rather do thy pleasure;
Above the rest, begone.   48
OLD MAN
I'll bring him the best 'parel that I have,
Come on 't what will.   *Exit.*
GLOUCESTER   Sirrah, naked fellow—   50
EDGAR
Poor Tom's a-cold. [*Aside.*] I cannot daub it further.   51
GLOUCESTER   Come hither, fellow.
EDGAR [*Aside*]
And yet I must.—Bless thy sweet eyes, they bleed.
GLOUCESTER   Know'st thou the way to Dover?
EDGAR   Both stile and gate, horseway and footpath.
Poor Tom hath been scared out of his good wits. Bless
thee, good man's son, from the foul fiend! Five fiends
have been in poor Tom at once: of lust, as Obidicut; 58
Hobbididance, prince of dumbness; Mahu, of steal- 59
ing; Modo, of murder; Flibbertigibbet, of mopping 60
and mowing, who since possesses chambermaids and 61
waiting-women. So, bless thee, master!
GLOUCESTER [*Giving a purse*]
Here, take this purse, thou whom the heavens' plagues
Have humbled to all strokes. That I am wretched   64
Makes thee the happier. Heavens, deal so still!
Let the superfluous and lust-dieted man,   66
That slaves your ordinance, that will not see   67

---

43 ancient love i.e., the mutually trusting relationship of master and
tenant that Gloucester and the Old Man have long enjoyed   **46 'Tis the
times' plague** i.e., it well expresses the spreading sickness of our
present state   **48 the rest** all   **50 on 't** of it   **51 daub it further**
i.e., keep up this pretense   **58–60 Obidicut . . . Flibbertigibbet** (Fiends
borrowed, as before in 3.4.139–142, from Harsnett.)   **60–61 mopping
and mowing** making grimaces and mouths   **61 since** since that time
64 Have . . . strokes have brought so low as to be prepared to accept
every blow of Fortune   **66 superfluous** having a superfluity.   **lust-
dieted** feeding luxuriously   **67 slaves your ordinance** i.e., makes the
laws of heaven his slaves

Because he does not feel, feel your pow'r quickly!   68
So distribution should undo excess
And each man have enough. Dost thou know Dover?

EDGAR   Ay, master.

GLOUCESTER

There is a cliff, whose high and bending head   72
Looks fearfully in the confinèd deep.   73
Bring me but to the very brim of it
And I'll repair the misery thou dost bear
With something rich about me. From that place
I shall no leading need.

EDGAR   Give me thy arm.
Poor Tom shall lead thee.   *Exeunt.*

❖

4.2   *Enter Goneril [and] Bastard [Edmund].*

GONERIL

Welcome, my lord. I marvel our mild husband   1
Not met us on the way.

          [Enter] Steward [Oswald].

                              Now, where's your master?   2

OSWALD

Madam, within, but never man so changed.
I told him of the army that was landed;
He smiled at it. I told him you were coming;
His answer was "The worse." Of Gloucester's treachery
And of the loyal service of his son
When I informed him, then he called me sot   8
And told me I had turned the wrong side out.
What most he should dislike seems pleasant to him;
What like, offensive.

GONERIL [*To Edmund*] Then shall you go no further.

68 feel feel sympathy or fellow feeling; suffer   **72 bending** overhanging   **73 in . . . deep** i.e., into the sea below, which is confined by its
shores

4.2. Location: Before the Duke of Albany's palace.
1 Welcome (Goneril, who has just arrived home from Gloucestershire
escorted by Edmund, bids him brief welcome before he must return.)
2 Not met has not met   **8 sot** fool

It is the cowish terror of his spirit,   12
That dares not undertake. He'll not feel wrongs   13
Which tie him to an answer. Our wishes on the way   14
May prove effects. Back, Edmund, to my brother;   15
Hasten his musters and conduct his powers.   16
I must change names at home and give the distaff   17
Into my husband's hands. This trusty servant
Shall pass between us. Ere long you are like to hear,   19
If you dare venture in your own behalf,
A mistress's command. Wear this; spare speech.   21
                          [*She gives him a favor.*]
Decline your head. [*She kisses him.*] This kiss, if it
   durst speak,
Would stretch thy spirits up into the air.
Conceive, and fare thee well.   24

EDMUND
Yours in the ranks of death.   *Exit.*
GONERIL   My most dear Gloucester!
O, the difference of man and man!
To thee a woman's services are due;
My fool usurps my body.   28
OSWALD   Madam, here comes my lord.   [*Exit.*]   29

   Enter Albany.

GONERIL
I have been worth the whistling.
ALBANY   O Goneril,   30
You are not worth the dust which the rude wind

---

12 cowish cowardly   **13 undertake** venture   **13–14 He'll . . . answer** he
will ignore insults that, if he took notice, would oblige him to respond, to
fight   **14–15 Our . . . effects** i.e., the hopes we discussed on our journey
here (presumably concerning the supplanting of Albany by Edmund) may
come to pass   **15 brother** i.e., brother-in-law, Cornwall   **16 musters**
assembling of troops.   **powers** armed forces   **17 change names** i.e.,
exchange the roles of master and mistress of the household, and exchange
the insignia of man and woman: the sword and the *distaff.*   **distaff**
spinning staff, symbolizing the wife's role   **19 like** likely   **21 mistress's**
(with sexual double meaning)   **24 Conceive** understand, take my meaning
(with sexual double entendre, continuing from *stretch thy spirits* in the
previous line and continued in *death,* l. 25)   **28 My fool . . . body** i.e., my
husband claims possession of me but is unfitted to do so   **29 s.d. Exit**
(Oswald could exit later with Goneril, at l. 88.)   **30 worth the whistling**
i.e., worth the attentions of men. (Alludes to the proverb, "It is a poor dog
that is not worth the whistling.")

Blows in your face. I fear your disposition;   32
That nature which contemns its origin   33
Cannot be bordered certain in itself.   34
She that herself will sliver and disbranch   35
From her material sap perforce must wither   36
And come to deadly use.   37
GONERIL   No more. The text is foolish.   38
ALBANY
Wisdom and goodness to the vile seem vile;
Filths savor but themselves. What have you done?   40
Tigers, not daughters, what have you performed?
A father, and a gracious agèd man,
Whose reverence even the head-lugged bear would lick,   43
Most barbarous, most degenerate, have you madded.   44
Could my good brother suffer you to do it?   45
A man, a prince, by him so benefited?
If that the heavens do not their visible spirits   47
Send quickly down to tame these vile offenses,
It will come,
Humanity must perforce prey on itself,
Like monsters of the deep.
GONERIL   Milk-livered man,   51
That bear'st a cheek for blows, a head for wrongs,
Who hast not in thy brows an eye discerning   53
Thine honor from thy suffering, that not know'st   54
Fools do those villains pity who are punished   55
Ere they have done their mischief. Where's thy drum?   56
France spreads his banners in our noiseless land,   57

---

32 fear your disposition mistrust your nature   **33 contemns** despises
34 bordered certain safely restrained, kept within bounds   **35 sliver**
tear off   **36 material sap** nourishing substance, the stock from which
she grew   **37 to deadly use** to destruction, like firewood   **38 The text**
i.e., on which you have been preaching   **40 savor but themselves** i.e.,
hunger only for that which is filthy   **43 head-lugged** dragged by the
head (or by the ring in its nose) and infuriated   **44 madded** driven
mad   **45 brother** brother-in-law (Cornwall)   **47 visible** made visible
51 Milk-livered white-livered, cowardly   **53–54 discerning . . . suffering**
able to tell the difference between an insult to your honor and something you should tolerate   **55 Fools** i.e., only fools. (Goneril goes on to
say that only fools are so tenderhearted as to worry about injustices to
potential troublemakers, like Lear and Gloucester, instead of applaud-
ing measures taken to insure order.)   **56 thy drum** i.e., your military
preparations   **57 noiseless** peaceful, having none of the bustle of war

With plumèd helm thy state begins to threat,	58
Whilst thou, a moral fool, sits still and cries,	59

"Alack, why does he so?"

ALBANY   See thyself, devil!   60

Proper deformity shows not in the fiend   61

So horrid as in woman.

GONERIL   O vain fool!

ALBANY

Thou changèd and self-covered thing, for shame,   63

Bemonster not thy feature. Were 't my fitness   64

To let these hands obey my blood,   65

They are apt enough to dislocate and tear   66

Thy flesh and bones. Howe'er thou art a fiend,   67

A woman's shape doth shield thee.   68

GONERIL   Marry, your manhood! Mew!   69

Enter a Messenger.

ALBANY   What news?

MESSENGER

O, my good lord, the Duke of Cornwall's dead,

Slain by his servant, going to put out

The other eye of Gloucester.

ALBANY   Gloucester's eyes!

MESSENGER

A servant that he bred, thrilled with remorse,   74

Opposed against the act, bending his sword   75

To his great master, who, thereat enraged,   76

Flew on him and amongst them felled him dead,   77

58 thy state . . . threat i.e., France begins to threaten your kingdom
59 moral moralizing   **60 why does he so** i.e., why does the King of
France invade England   **61 Proper deformity** i.e., the deformity appropriate to the fiend. (Such deformity seems even uglier in a woman's
features than in a fiend's, since it is appropriate in a fiend's.)
63 changèd transformed.   **self-covered** having the true nature concealed   **64 Bemonster . . . feature** i.e., do not, however evil you are, take
on the outward form of a monster or fiend.   **my fitness** suitable for
me   **65 blood** passion   **66 apt** ready   **67 Howe'er . . . fiend** however
much you may be a fiend in reality   **68 shield** (Since I, as a gentleman,
cannot lay violent hands on a lady.)   **69 Mew** (An exclamation of disgust, a derisive catcall: You speak of manhood in shielding me as a
woman. Some manhood!)   **74 bred** kept in his household.   **thrilled with
remorse** deeply moved with pity   **75 Opposed** opposed himself
75–76 bending . . . To directing his sword against   **77 amongst them**
together with the others (?) in their midst (?) out of their number (?)

But not without that harmful stroke which since
Hath plucked him after.
ALBANY   This shows you are above,   79
You justicers, that these our nether crimes   80
So speedily can venge! But, O poor Gloucester!
Lost he his other eye?
MESSENGER   Both, both, my lord.—
This letter, madam, craves a speedy answer;
'Tis from your sister.   [*He gives her a letter.*]
GONERIL [*Aside*]   One way I like this well;   84
But being widow, and my Gloucester with her,
May all the building in my fancy pluck   86
Upon my hateful life. Another way   87
The news is not so tart.—I'll read, and answer.   88
                              [*Exit.*]

ALBANY
Where was his son when they did take his eyes?
MESSENGER
Come with my lady hither.
ALBANY   He is not here.
MESSENGER
No, my good lord. I met him back again.   91
ALBANY   Knows he the wickedness?
MESSENGER
Ay, my good lord. 'Twas he informed against him,
And quit the house on purpose that their punishment
Might have the freer course.
ALBANY   Gloucester, I live
To thank thee for the love thou show'dst the King
And to revenge thine eyes.—Come hither, friend.
Tell me what more thou know'st.   *Exeunt.*

❖

79 **after** along (to death)   80 **justicers** (heavenly) judges.   **nether** i.e.,
committed here below, on earth   84 **One way** i.e., because Edmund is
now Duke of Gloucester, and Cornwall, a dangerous rival for the throne,
is dead   86–87 **May . . . life** i.e., may pull down my imagined happiness
(of possessing the entire kingdom with Edmund) and make hateful my
life   88 **tart** bitter, sour   91 **back** going back

4.3   *Enter Kent and a Gentleman.*

KENT   Why the King of France is so suddenly gone back
  know you no reason?

GENTLEMAN   Something he left imperfect in the state,   3
  which since his coming forth is thought of, which im-   4
  ports to the kingdom so much fear and danger that his   5
  personal return was most required and necessary.

KENT
  Who hath he left behind him general?

GENTLEMAN
  The Marshal of France, Monsieur La Far.

KENT   Did your letters pierce the Queen to any demon-
  stration of grief?

GENTLEMAN
  Ay, sir. She took them, read them in my presence,
  And now and then an ample tear trilled down   12
  Her delicate cheek. It seemed she was a queen
  Over her passion, who, most rebel-like,   14
  Sought to be king o'er her.

KENT   O, then it moved her?

GENTLEMAN
  Not to a rage. Patience and sorrow strove
  Who should express her goodliest. You have seen   17
  Sunshine and rain at once. Her smiles and tears
  Were like a better way; those happy smilets   19
  That played on her ripe lip seemed not to know
  What guests were in her eyes, which parted thence   21
  As pearls from diamonds dropped. In brief,
  Sorrow would be a rarity most beloved   23
  If all could so become it.   24

KENT   Made she no verbal question?   25

GENTLEMAN
  Faith, once or twice she heaved the name of "father"   26

4.3. Location: The French camp near Dover.
3 imperfect in the state unsettled in state affairs   **4–5 imports** por-
tends   **12 trilled** trickled   **14 passion, who** emotion, which   **17 Who
. . . goodliest** which of the two could make her appear more lovely
19 like a better way better than that, though similar   **21 which** i.e., the
guests or tears   **23 a rarity** i.e., a precious thing, like a jewel   **24 If . . .
it** i.e., if all persons were as attractive in sorrow as she   **25 verbal** i.e.,
as distinguished from her tears and looks   **26 heaved** breathed out
with difficulty

Pantingly forth, as if it pressed her heart;
Cried, "Sisters, sisters! Shame of ladies, sisters!
Kent! Father! Sisters! What, i' the storm, i' the night?
Let pity not be believed!" There she shook   30
The holy water from her heavenly eyes,
And, clamor-moistened, then away she started   32
To deal with grief alone.

KENT   It is the stars,
The stars above us, govern our conditions,   34
Else one self mate and make could not beget   35
Such different issues. You spoke not with her since?   36

GENTLEMAN   No.

KENT
Was this before the King returned?

GENTLEMAN   No, since.   38

KENT
Well, sir, the poor distressèd Lear's i' the town,
Who sometimes in his better tune remembers   40
What we are come about, and by no means
Will yield to see his daughter.

GENTLEMAN   Why, good sir?

KENT
A sovereign shame so elbows him—his own unkindness   43
That stripped her from his benediction, turned her   44
To foreign casualties, gave her dear rights   45
To his dog-hearted daughters—these things sting
His mind so venomously that burning shame
Detains him from Cordelia.

GENTLEMAN   Alack, poor gentleman!

KENT
Of Albany's and Cornwall's powers you heard not?   50

GENTLEMAN   'Tis so. They are afoot.   51

KENT
Well, sir, I'll bring you to our master Lear

---

30 believed i.e., believed to be extant   **32 clamor-moistened** i.e., her outcry of grief assuaged by tears.   **started** i.e., went   **34 conditions** characters   **35 Else . . . make** otherwise, one couple (husband and wife)   **36 issues** offspring   **38 the King** the King of France   **40 better tune** more composed state   **43 sovereign** overruling.   **elbows him** i.e., prods his memory, jostles him, thrusts him back   **44 turned her** turned her out   **45 foreign casualties** chances of fortune abroad   **50 powers** troops, armies   **51 afoot** on the march

And leave you to attend him. Some dear cause   53
Will in concealment wrap me up awhile.
When I am known aright, you shall not grieve   55
Lending me this acquaintance. I pray you, go   56
Along with me.   *Exeunt.*

❧

4.4   *Enter, with drum and colors, Cordelia, Doctor,*
        and soldiers.

CORDELIA
  Alack, 'tis he! Why, he was met even now
  As mad as the vexed sea, singing aloud,
  Crowned with rank fumiter and furrow weeds,   3
  With hardocks, hemlock, nettles, cuckooflowers,   4
  Darnel, and all the idle weeds that grow   5
  In our sustaining corn. A century send forth!   6
  Search every acre in the high-grown field
  And bring him to our eye. [*Exit a soldier or soldiers.*]
    What can man's wisdom   8
  In the restoring his bereavèd sense?
  He that helps him take all my outward worth.   10
DOCTOR   There is means, madam.
  Our foster nurse of nature is repose,
  The which he lacks. That to provoke in him   13
  Are many simples operative, whose power   14
  Will close the eye of anguish.
CORDELIA   All blest secrets,
  All you unpublished virtues of the earth,   16
  Spring with my tears! Be aidant and remediate   17
  In the good man's distress! Seek, seek for him,

53 dear cause important purpose   **55–56 grieve . . . acquaintance** regret
having made my acquaintance

4.4. Location: The French camp.
3 fumiter i.e., fumitory, a weed or herb   **4 hardocks** i.e., burdocks or
hoardocks, white-leaved (?) (Identity uncertain.)   **5 Darnel** (A weed of
the grass kind.)   **idle** worthless   **6 sustaining** giving sustenance.   **corn**
grain.   **century** troop of 100 men   **8 What . . . wisdom** i.e., what can
medical knowledge accomplish   **10 outward** material   **13 That to
provoke** to induce that   **14 simples** medicinal plants.   **operative** effective   **16 unpublished virtues** little-known benign herbs   **17 Spring**
grow.   **aidant and remediate** helpful and remedial

Lest his ungoverned rage dissolve the life   19
That wants the means to lead it.

    Enter Messenger.

MESSENGER   News, madam.   20
  The British powers are marching hitherward.   21
CORDELIA
  'Tis known before. Our preparation stands
  In expectation of them. O dear Father,
  It is thy business that I go about;
  Therefore great France
  My mourning and importuned tears hath pitied.   26
  No blown ambition doth our arms incite,   27
  But love, dear love, and our aged father's right.
  Soon may I hear and see him!   *Exeunt.*

❖

4.5   *Enter Regan and steward [Oswald].*

REGAN   But are my brother's powers set forth?   1
OSWALD   Ay, madam.
REGAN   Himself in person there?
OSWALD   Madam, with much ado.   4
  Your sister is the better soldier.
REGAN
  Lord Edmund spake not with your lord at home?
OSWALD   No, madam.
REGAN
  What might import my sister's letter to him?   8
OSWALD   I know not, lady.
REGAN
  Faith, he is posted hence on serious matter.   10
  It was great ignorance, Gloucester's eyes being out,   11
  To let him live. Where he arrives he moves
  All hearts against us. Edmund, I think, is gone,

19 rage frenzy   **20 wants** lacks.   **means** i.e., his reason   **21 powers** armies   **26 importuned** importunate   **27 blown** puffed up with pride

4.5. Location: Gloucester's house.
1 my brother's powers i.e., Albany's forces   **4 with much ado** after much fuss and persuasion   **8 import** bear as its purport, express   **10 is posted** has hurried   **11 ignorance** error, folly

In pity of his misery, to dispatch
His nighted life; moreover to descry   15
The strength o' th' enemy.

OSWALD
I must needs after him, madam, with my letter.

REGAN
Our troops set forth tomorrow. Stay with us;
The ways are dangerous.

OSWALD   I may not, madam.
My lady charged my duty in this business.   20

REGAN
Why should she write to Edmund? Might not you
Transport her purposes by word? Belike   22
Something—I know not what. I'll love thee much;
Let me unseal the letter.

OSWALD   Madam, I had rather—

REGAN
I know your lady does not love her husband,
I am sure of that; and at her late being here   26
She gave strange oeillades and most speaking looks   27
To noble Edmund. I know you are of her bosom.   28

OSWALD   I, madam?

REGAN
I speak in understanding; y' are, I know 't.   30
Therefore I do advise you, take this note: 31
My lord is dead; Edmund and I have talked,   32
And more convenient is he for my hand   33
Than for your lady's. You may gather more.   34
If you do find him, pray you, give him this;   35
And when your mistress hears thus much from you,   36
I pray, desire her call her wisdom to her.   37
So, fare you well.
If you do chance to hear of that blind traitor,
Preferment falls on him that cuts him off.   40

---

15 nighted benighted, blinded   **20 charged** ordered strictly   **22 Belike**
it may be   **26 late** recently   **27 oeillades** amorous glances   **28 of her
bosom** in her confidence   **30 y' are** you are   **31 take this note** i.e.,
mark this advice   **32 have talked** have come to an understanding
33 convenient fitting   **34 gather more** i.e., infer what I am trying to
suggest   **35 this** i.e., this information, or possibly a letter (though only
one letter, Goneril's, is found on his dead body at 4.6.262)   **36 thus
much** what I have told you   **37 call . . . to her** recall her to her senses
40 Preferment advancement

OSWALD
  Would I could meet him, madam! I should show
  What party I do follow.
REGAN   Fare thee well.
                              Exeunt [separately].

4.6   *Enter Gloucester, and Edgar [in peasant's
          clothes, leading his father].*

GLOUCESTER
  When shall I come to the top of that same hill?   1
EDGAR
  You do climb up it now. Look how we labor.
GLOUCESTER
  Methinks the ground is even.
EDGAR   Horrible steep.
  Hark, do you hear the sea?
GLOUCESTER   No, truly.
EDGAR
  Why, then, your other senses grow imperfect
  By your eyes' anguish.
GLOUCESTER   So may it be, indeed.
  Methinks thy voice is altered, and thou speak'st
  In better phrase and matter than thou didst.
EDGAR
  You're much deceived. In nothing am I changed
  But in my garments.
GLOUCESTER   Methinks you're better spoken.
EDGAR
  Come on, sir, here's the place. Stand still. How fearful
  And dizzy 'tis to cast one's eyes so low!
  The crows and choughs that wing the midway air   13
  Show scarce so gross as beetles. Halfway down   14
  Hangs one that gathers samphire—dreadful trade!   15
  Methinks he seems no bigger than his head.
  The fishermen that walk upon the beach
  Appear like mice, and yond tall anchoring bark

4.6. Location: Open place near Dover.
1 that same hill i.e., the cliff we talked about (4.1.72–74)   **13 choughs**
jackdaws.   **midway** halfway down   **14 gross** large   **15 samphire** (A
herb used in pickling.)

Diminished to her cock; her cock, a buoy   19
Almost too small for sight. The murmuring surge,
That on th' unnumbered idle pebble chafes,   21
Cannot be heard so high. I'll look no more,
Lest my brain turn, and the deficient sight   23
Topple down headlong.

GLOUCESTER   Set me where you stand.   24

EDGAR
Give me your hand. You are now within a foot
Of th' extreme verge. For all beneath the moon
Would I not leap upright.

GLOUCESTER   Let go my hand.   27
Here, friend, 's another purse; in it a jewel
Well worth a poor man's taking. [*He gives a purse.*]
     Fairies and gods   29
Prosper it with thee! Go thou further off.   30
Bid me farewell, and let me hear thee going.

EDGAR [*Moving away*]
Now fare ye well, good sir.

GLOUCESTER   With all my heart.

EDGAR [*Aside*]
Why I do trifle thus with his despair
Is done to cure it.

GLOUCESTER [*Kneeling*]   O you mighty gods!
This world I do renounce, and in your sights
Shake patiently my great affliction off.
If I could bear it longer, and not fall
To quarrel with your great opposeless wills,   38
My snuff and loathèd part of nature should   39
Burn itself out. If Edgar live, O, bless him!
Now, fellow, fare thee well.   [*He falls forward.*]

EDGAR   Gone, sir. Farewell.—
And yet I know not how conceit may rob   42

---

19 Diminished . . . cock reduced to the size of her cockboat, small ship's
boat   **21 unnumbered** innumerable.   **idle** randomly shifting.   **pebble**
pebbles   **23–24 the deficient sight Topple** my failing sight topple me
27 upright i.e., up and down, much less forward   **29–30 Fairies . . . thee**
i.e., may the fairies and gods who guard hidden treasure cause this to
multiply in your possession   **38 To quarrel with** into rebellion
against.   **opposeless** irresistible   **39 snuff** i.e., useless residue. (Literally, the smoking wick of a candle.)   **of nature** i.e., of my life
42 conceit imagination

The treasury of life, when life itself
Yields to the theft. Had he been where he thought,　　44
By this had thought been past. Alive or dead?—
Ho, you, sir! Friend! Hear you, sir! Speak!—
Thus might he pass indeed; yet he revives.—　　47
What are you, sir?

GLOUCESTER　　　　　Away, and let me die.　　48

EDGAR
Hadst thou been aught but gossamer, feathers, air,
So many fathom down precipitating,
Thou'dst shivered like an egg; but thou dost breathe,
Hast heavy substance, bleed'st not, speak'st, art sound. 52
Ten masts at each make not the altitude　　53
Which thou hast perpendicularly fell.
Thy life's a miracle. Speak yet again.

GLOUCESTER　　But have I fallen or no?

EDGAR
From the dread summit of this chalky bourn.　　57
Look up aheight; the shrill-gorged lark so far　　58
Cannot be seen or heard. Do but look up.

GLOUCESTER　　Alack, I have no eyes.
Is wretchedness deprived that benefit
To end itself by death? 'Twas yet some comfort
When misery could beguile the tyrant's rage　　63
And frustrate his proud will.

EDGAR　　　　　　　　　　　Give me your arm.
　　　　　　　　　　　　　[*He lifts him up.*]
Up—so. How is 't? Feel you your legs? You stand.

GLOUCESTER
Too well, too well.

EDGAR　　　　　This is above all strangeness.
Upon the crown o' the cliff what thing was that
Which parted from you?

GLOUCESTER　　　　　A poor unfortunate beggar.

EDGAR
As I stood here below, methought his eyes

44 Yields consents　**47 pass** die　**48 What** who. (Edgar now speaks in a new voice, differing from that of "poor Tom" and also from the "altered" voice he used at the start of this scene; see ll. 7–10.)　**52 heavy substance** the substance of the flesh　**53 at each** end to end　**57 bourn** limit, boundary (i.e., the edge of the sea)　**58 aheight** on high.　**shrill-gorged** shrill-throated　**63 beguile** outwit

Were two full moons; he had a thousand noses,
Horns whelked and waved like the enridgèd sea.   71
It was some fiend. Therefore, thou happy father,   72
Think that the clearest gods, who make them honors   73
Of men's impossibilities, have preserved thee.   74

GLOUCESTER
I do remember now. Henceforth I'll bear
Affliction till it do cry out itself   76
"Enough, enough," and die. That thing you speak of,   77
I took it for a man; often 'twould say
"The fiend, the fiend." He led me to that place.

EDGAR
Bear free and patient thoughts.

Enter Lear [mad, fantastically dressed with wild flowers].

                              But who comes here?   80
The safer sense will ne'er accommodate   81
His master thus.   82

LEAR   No, they cannot touch me for coining. I am the   83
King himself.

EDGAR   O thou side-piercing sight!   85

LEAR   Nature's above art in that respect. There's your   86
press money. That fellow handles his bow like a crow-   87
keeper. Draw me a clothier's yard. Look, look, a   88
mouse! Peace, peace; this piece of toasted cheese will
do 't. There's my gauntlet; I'll prove it on a giant. Bring   90

---

71 whelked twisted, convoluted.   **enridgèd** furrowed (by the wind)
72 happy father lucky old man   **73 clearest** purest, most righteous
73–74 who ... impossibilities who win our awe and reverence by doing
things impossible to men   **76–77 till ... die** i.e., until affliction itself has
had enough, or until I die   **80 free** i.e., free from despair   **81–82 The safer
... thus** i.e., a person in his right senses would never dress himself in such
a fashion.   **His master** the owner of the *safer sense* or sane mind. (*His*
means "its.")   **83 touch** arrest, prosecute.   **coining** minting coins. (A royal
prerogative; the King wants money for his imaginary soldiers, ll. 86–87.)
85 side-piercing heartrending (with a suggestion also of Christ's suffering
on the cross)   **86 Nature's ... respect** i.e., a born king is proof against any
counterfeiting; his coinage is superior to that of the counterfeiter (?)
87 press money enlistment bonus   **87–88 crowkeeper** laborer hired to
scare away the crows   **88 me** for me.   **clothier's yard** arrow the length of
a cloth yard   **90 do 't** i.e., capture the mouse, an imagined enemy.
gauntlet armored glove thrown down as a challenge.   **prove it on** maintain
it against

up the brown bills. O, well flown, bird! I' the clout, i' 91
the clout—hewgh! Give the word.   92
EDGAR Sweet marjoram.   93
LEAR Pass.
GLOUCESTER I know that voice.
LEAR Ha! Goneril with a white beard? They flattered
me like a dog and told me I had white hairs in my   97
beard ere the black ones were there. To say ay and   98
no to everything that I said ay and no to was   99
no good divinity. When the rain came to wet me   100
once and the wind to make me chatter, when the
thunder would not peace at my bidding, there I found   102
'em, there I smelt 'em out. Go to, they are not men o'   103
their words. They told me I was everything. 'Tis a lie;
I am not ague-proof.

GLOUCESTER
The trick of that voice I do well remember.   106
Is 't not the King?
LEAR   Ay, every inch a king.
When I do stare, see how the subject quakes.
I pardon that man's life. What was thy cause?   109
Adultery?
Thou shalt not die. Die for adultery? No.
The wren goes to 't, and the small gilded fly
Does lecher in my sight.
Let copulation thrive; for Gloucester's bastard son
Was kinder to his father than my daughters
Got 'tween the lawful sheets.
To 't, luxury, pell-mell, for I lack soldiers.   117
Behold yond simpering dame,
Whose face between her forks presages snow,   119

---

91 brown bills soldiers carrying pikes (painted brown), or the pikes
themselves.   **well flown, bird** (Lear uses the language of hawking to
describe the flight of an arrow.)   **clout** target, bull's-eye   **92 hewgh**
(The arrow's noise.)   **word** password   **93 Sweet marjoram** (A herb used
to cure madness.)   **97 like a dog** i.e., as a dog fawns   **97–98 had . . .
beard** i.e., had wisdom   **98–99 To . . . no to** i.e., to agree flatteringly
with   **100 no good divinity** not good theology, contrary to biblical
teaching. (See 2 Cor. 1:18 and James 5:12.)   **102–103 found 'em** found
them out   **103 Go to** (An expression of impatience.)   **106 trick** peculiar
characteristic   **109 cause** offense   **117 luxury** lechery   **119 Whose . . .
snow** whose frosty countenance seems to suggest frigidity between
her legs

That minces virtue and does shake the head   120
To hear of pleasure's name;   121
The fitchew nor the soilèd horse goes to 't   122
With a more riotous appetite.
Down from the waist they are centaurs,   124
Though women all above.
But to the girdle do the gods inherit;   126
Beneath is all the fiends'.
There's hell, there's darkness, there is the sulfurous pit,
burning, scalding, stench, consumption. Fie, fie, fie!
Pah, pah! Give me an ounce of civet, good apothecary, 130
sweeten my imagination. There's money for thee.

GLOUCESTER   O, let me kiss that hand!

LEAR   Let me wipe it first; it smells of mortality.

GLOUCESTER
O ruined piece of nature! This great world   134
Shall so wear out to naught. Dost thou know me?   135

LEAR   I remember thine eyes well enough. Dost thou
squinny at me? No, do thy worst, blind Cupid; I'll not 137
love. Read thou this challenge. Mark but the penning
of it.

GLOUCESTER
Were all thy letters suns, I could not see.

EDGAR [*Aside*]
I would not take this from report. It is,   141
And my heart breaks at it.

LEAR   Read.

GLOUCESTER   What, with the case of eyes?   144

LEAR   Oho, are you there with me? No eyes in your 145
head, nor no money in your purse? Your eyes are in a
heavy case, your purse in a light, yet you see how this 147
world goes.

120 minces affects, mimics   **121 pleasure's name** i.e., any talk of sexual
pleasure   **122 fitchew** polecat.   **soilèd horse** horse turned out to grass,
well-fed and hence wanton   **124 centaurs** incontinent monsters, half man,
half horse   **126 But** only.   **girdle** waist.   **inherit** possess   **130 civet** musk
perfume   **134 piece** masterpiece.   **This great world** i.e., the macrocosm, of
which man, the masterpiece of nature, is the microcosm   **135 so** similarly   **137 squinny** squint   **141 take** believe, credit.   **It is** it is taking place,
incredibly enough   **144 case** mere sockets   **145 are . . . me** is that your
meaning, the point you are making, or your situation   **147 heavy case** sad
plight (with pun on *case* in l. 144)

GLOUCESTER I see it feelingly.   149

LEAR What, art mad? A man may see how this world
goes with no eyes. Look with thine ears. See how
yond justice rails upon yond simple thief. Hark in 152
thine ear: change places and, handy-dandy, which is 153
the justice, which is the thief? Thou hast seen a
farmer's dog bark at a beggar?

GLOUCESTER Ay, sir.

LEAR And the creature run from the cur? There thou 157
mightst behold the great image of authority: a dog's 158
obeyed in office.   159
Thou rascal beadle, hold thy bloody hand!   160
Why dost thou lash that whore? Strip thine own back;
Thou hotly lusts to use her in that kind   162
For which thou whip'st her. The usurer hangs the
   cozener.   163
Through tattered clothes small vices do appear;
Robes and furred gowns hide all. Plate sin with gold, 165
And the strong lance of justice hurtless breaks; 166
Arm it in rags, a pygmy's straw does pierce it.
None does offend, none, I say, none. I'll able 'em. 168
Take that of me, my friend, who have the power 169
To seal th' accuser's lips. Get thee glass eyes, 170
And like a scurvy politician seem
To see the things thou dost not. Now, now, now, now!
Pull off my boots. Harder, harder! So.

EDGAR [*Aside*]
O, matter and impertinency mixed,   174
Reason in madness!

---

149 feelingly (1) by touch (2) keenly, painfully   **152 simple** of humble
station   **153 handy-dandy** take your choice of hands (as in a well-known
child's game)   **157 creature** poor fellow   **158–159 a dog's . . . office** i.e.,
even currish power commands submission   **160 beadle** parish officer,
responsible for giving whippings   **162 kind** way   **163 The usurer** i.e., a
judge guilty of lending money at usurious rates.   **cozener** petty
cheater   **165 Plate** arm in plate armor   **166 hurtless breaks** splinters
harmlessly   **168 able** give warrant to   **169 that** i.e., a guarantee of
immunity   **170 glass eyes** (With glass eyes, possibly spectacles, Gloucester could pretend to see or understand what he does not comprehend,
like a vile *politician* governing through opportunism and trickery,
hiding his blindness behind his glass eyes.)   **174 matter and impertinency** sense and nonsense

LEAR
    If thou wilt weep my fortunes, take my eyes.
    I know thee well enough; thy name is Gloucester.
    Thou must be patient. We came crying hither.
    Thou know'st the first time that we smell the air
    We wawl and cry. I will preach to thee. Mark.
GLOUCESTER   Alack, alack the day!
LEAR
    When we are born, we cry that we are come
    To this great stage of fools.—This' a good block.   183
    It were a delicate stratagem to shoe   184
    A troop of horse with felt. I'll put 't in proof,   185
    And when I have stolen upon these son-in-laws,
    Then, kill, kill, kill, kill, kill, kill!

        Enter a Gentleman [with attendants].

GENTLEMAN
    O, here he is. Lay hand upon him.—Sir,
    Your most dear daughter—
LEAR
    No rescue? What, a prisoner? I am even
    The natural fool of fortune. Use me well;   191
    You shall have ransom. Let me have surgeons;
    I am cut to the brains.
GENTLEMAN   You shall have anything.   193
LEAR   No seconds? All myself?   194
    Why, this would make a man a man of salt   195
    To use his eyes for garden waterpots,
    Ay, and laying autumn's dust.
    I will die bravely, like a smug bridegroom. What?   198
    I will be jovial. Come, come, I am a king,
    Masters, know you that?
GENTLEMAN
    You are a royal one, and we obey you.

---

183 This' this is.   **block** felt hat (?) (Lear may refer to the weeds strewn
in his hair, which he removes as though doffing a hat before preaching a
sermon.)   **184 delicate** subtle   **185 in proof** to the test   **191 natural fool**
born plaything   **193 cut** wounded   **194 seconds** supporters   **195 of salt**
of salt tears   **198 bravely** (1) courageously (2) splendidly attired.   **smug**
trimly dressed. (*Bridegroom* continues the punning sexual suggestion of
die bravely, have sex successfully.)

LEAR   Then there's life in 't. Come, an you get it, you 202
shall get it by running. Sa, sa, sa, sa.   203

Exit [running, followed by attendants].

GENTLEMAN
A sight most pitiful in the meanest wretch,
Past speaking of in a king! Thou hast one daughter
Who redeems nature from the general curse   206
Which twain have brought her to.

EDGAR   Hail, gentle sir.   208

GENTLEMAN   Sir, speed you. What's your will?   209

EDGAR
Do you hear aught, sir, of a battle toward?   210

GENTLEMAN
Most sure and vulgar. Everyone hears that   211
Which can distinguish sound.

EDGAR   But, by your favor,   212
How near's the other army?

GENTLEMAN
Near and on speedy foot. The main descry   214
Stands on the hourly thought.   215

EDGAR   I thank you, sir; that's all.

GENTLEMAN
Though that the Queen on special cause is here,   217
Her army is moved on.

EDGAR   I thank you, sir.

Exit [Gentleman].

GLOUCESTER
You ever-gentle gods, take my breath from me;
Let not my worser spirit tempt me again   220
To die before you please!

EDGAR   Well pray you, father.

GLOUCESTER   Now, good sir, what are you?   223

---

202 life i.e., hope still. **an** if   **203 Sa . . . sa** (A hunting cry.)
206 general curse universal damnation   **208 gentle** noble   **209 speed**
God speed   **210 toward** imminent   **211 vulgar** in everyone's mouth,
generally known   **212 Which** who   **214–215 The main . . . thought** the
full view of the main body is expected every hour   **217 on special cause**
for a special reason, i.e., to minister to Lear   **220 worser spirit** bad
angel, or ill thoughts   **223 what** who. (Again, Edgar alters his voice to
personate a new stranger assisting Gloucester. See l. 48, above, and
note.)

EDGAR
A most poor man, made tame to fortune's blows,   224
Who, by the art of known and feeling sorrows,   225
Am pregnant to good pity. Give me your hand.   226
I'll lead you to some biding.   [*He offers his arm.*]
GLOUCESTER   Hearty thanks.   227
The bounty and the benison of heaven   228
To boot, and boot!

      Enter steward [Oswald].

OSWALD   A proclaimed prize! Most happy!   229
                    [*He draws his sword.*]
That eyeless head of thine was first framed flesh   230
To raise my fortunes. Thou old unhappy traitor,
Briefly thyself remember. The sword is out   232
That must destroy thee.
GLOUCESTER   Now let thy friendly hand   233
Put strength enough to 't.   [*Edgar intervenes.*]
OSWALD   Wherefore, bold peasant,
Durst thou support a published traitor? Hence,   235
Lest that th' infection of his fortune take   236
Like hold on thee. Let go his arm.   237
EDGAR   'Chill not let go, zir, without vurther 'cagion.   238
OSWALD   Let go, slave, or thou diest!
EDGAR   Good gentleman, go your gait, and let poor volk   240
pass. An 'chud ha' bin zwaggered out of my life,   241
'twould not ha' bin zo long as 'tis by a vortnight. Nay,
come not near th' old man; keep out, 'che vor ye, or   243
Ise try whether your costard or my ballow be the   244
harder. 'Chill be plain with you.
OSWALD   Out, dunghill!

224 tame submissive   **225 known** personally experienced.   **feeling**
heartfelt, deep   **226 pregnant** prone   **227 biding** abiding place
228–229 The bounty . . . and boot i.e., in addition to my thanks, I wish
you the bounty and blessings of heaven   **229 proclaimed prize** one with
a price on his head.   **happy** fortunate   **230 framed flesh** born
232 thyself remember i.e., confess your sins   **233 friendly** i.e., welcome,
since I desire death   **235 published** proclaimed   **236 Lest that** lest
237 Like similar   **238 'Chill** I will. (Literally, a contraction of *Ich will.*
Edgar adopts Somerset dialect, a stage convention regularly used for
peasants.)   **vurther 'cagion** further occasion   **240 go your gait** go your
own way   **241 An 'chud** if I could.   **zwaggered** swaggered, bluffed
243 'che vor ye I warrant you   **244 Ise** I shall.   **costard** head. (Literally,
an apple.)   **ballow** cudgel

EDGAR   'Chill pick your teeth, zir. Come, no matter vor
  your foins. [*They fight. Edgar fells him with his cudgel.*]   248
OSWALD
  Slave, thou hast slain me. Villain, take my purse.   249
  If ever thou wilt thrive, bury my body
  And give the letters which thou find'st about me   251
  To Edmund, Earl of Gloucester. Seek him out
  Upon the English party. O, untimely death!   253
  Death!   [*He dies.*]
EDGAR
  I know thee well: a serviceable villain,   255
  As duteous to the vices of thy mistress
  As badness would desire.
GLOUCESTER   What, is he dead?
EDGAR   Sit you down, father. Rest you. [*Gloucester sits.*]
  Let's see these pockets; the letters that he speaks of
  May be my friends. He's dead; I am only sorry
  He had no other deathsman. Let us see.   262
                    [*He finds a letter, and opens it.*]
  Leave, gentle wax, and, manners, blame us not.   263
  To know our enemies' minds we rip their hearts;
  Their papers is more lawful.   (*Reads the letter.*)
      "Let our reciprocal vows be remembered. You have
  many opportunities to cut him off; if your will want   267
  not, time and place will be fruitfully offered. There is   268
  nothing done if he return the conqueror. Then am I   269
  the prisoner, and his bed my jail, from the loathed
  warmth whereof deliver me and supply the place for   271
  your labor.   272
      Your—wife, so I would say—
                        Affectionate servant,   Goneril."
  O indistinguished space of woman's will!   275
  A plot upon her virtuous husband's life,
  And the exchange my brother! Here in the sands

248 **foins** thrusts   249 **Villain** serf   251 **letters** letter.   **about me** upon
my person   253 **Upon** on.   **party** side   255 **serviceable** officious
262 **deathsman** executioner   263 **Leave** by your leave.   **wax** wax seal on
the letter   267–268 **want not** is not lacking   268 **fruitfully** plentifully and
with results   268–269 **There is nothing done** i.e., we will have accomplished nothing   271–272 **for your labor** (1) as recompense for your
efforts (2) as a place for your amorous labors   275 **indistinguished ...
will** limitless and incalculable range of woman's appetite

Thee I'll rake up, the post unsanctified   278
Of murderous lechers; and in the mature time   279
With this ungracious paper strike the sight   280
Of the death-practiced Duke. For him 'tis well   281
That of thy death and business I can tell.

GLOUCESTER
The King is mad. How stiff is my vile sense,   283
That I stand up and have ingenious feeling   284
Of my huge sorrows! Better I were distract;   285
So should my thoughts be severed from my griefs,
And woes by wrong imaginations lose   287
The knowledge of themselves.   *Drum afar off.*

EDGAR   Give me your hand.
Far off, methinks, I hear the beaten drum.
Come, father, I'll bestow you with a friend.   *Exeunt.* 290

❖

4.7   *Enter Cordelia, Kent [dressed still in his
           disguise costume, and Doctor].*

CORDELIA
O thou good Kent, how shall I live and work
To match thy goodness? My life will be too short,
And every measure fail me.   3

KENT
To be acknowledged, madam, is o'erpaid.
All my reports go with the modest truth,   5
Nor more nor clipped, but so.

CORDELIA   Be better suited.   6

---

278 rake up cover up.   **post unsanctified** unholy messenger   **279 in . . .
time** when the time is ripe   **280 ungracious** wicked.   **strike** blast
281 death-practiced whose death is plotted   **283 stiff** obstinate.   **sense**
consciousness, sane mental powers   **284 ingenious** conscious. (Gloucester
laments that he remains sane and hence fully conscious of his troubles,
unlike Lear.)   **285 distract** distracted, crazy   **287 wrong imaginations**
delusions   **290 bestow** lodge. (At the scene's end, Edgar leads off Gloucester; presumably he also disposes of Oswald's body, which must be removed
from the stage or somehow concealed.)

4.7. Location: The French camp.
3 every . . . me i.e., every attempt to match your goodness will fall short
5 All my reports go i.e., let all reports (of my service as Caius to Lear)
conform   **6 Nor . . . clipped** i.e., neither more nor less.   **suited** dressed

These weeds are memories of those worser hours;   7
I prithee, put them off.

KENT   Pardon, dear madam;
Yet to be known shortens my made intent.   9
My boon I make it that you know me not   10
Till time and I think meet.   11

CORDELIA
Then be 't so, my good lord. [*To the Doctor.*] How does
the King?

DOCTOR   Madam, sleeps still.

CORDELIA   O you kind gods,
Cure this great breach in his abusèd nature!
Th' untuned and jarring senses, O, wind up   16
Of this child-changèd father!   17

DOCTOR   So please Your Majesty
That we may wake the King? He hath slept long.

CORDELIA
Be governed by your knowledge, and proceed
I' the sway of your own will.—Is he arrayed?   21

> *Enter Lear in a chair carried by servants,*
> [*attended by a Gentleman*].

GENTLEMAN
Ay, madam. In the heaviness of sleep
We put fresh garments on him.

DOCTOR
Be by, good madam, when we do awake him.
I doubt not of his temperance.

CORDELIA   Very well.   [*Music.*] 25

DOCTOR
Please you, draw near.—Louder the music there!

CORDELIA [*Kissing him*]
O my dear Father! Restoration hang
Thy medicine on my lips, and let this kiss

---

7 weeds garments. **memories** remembrances **9 Yet . . . intent** i.e.,
to reveal my true identity now would alter my carefully made plan
10 My . . . it the reward I seek is. **know** acknowledge **11 meet** appropriate **16 wind up** tune (as by winding the slackened string of an
instrument) **17 child-changèd** changed (in mind) by children's cruelty
21 I' the sway under the direction **25 temperance** self-control, calm
behavior

Repair those violent harms that my two sisters
Have in thy reverence made!

KENT   Kind and dear princess!

CORDELIA

Had you not been their father, these white flakes   31
Did challenge pity of them. Was this a face   32
To be opposed against the warring winds?
To stand against the deep dread-bolted thunder   34
In the most terrible and nimble stroke
Of quick cross lightning? To watch—poor perdu!—   36
With this thin helm? Mine enemy's dog,   37
Though he had bit me, should have stood that night
Against my fire; and wast thou fain, poor Father,   39
To hovel thee with swine and rogues forlorn   40
In short and musty straw? Alack, alack!   41
'Tis wonder that thy life and wits at once
Had not concluded all.—He wakes! Speak to him.   43

DOCTOR   Madam, do you; 'tis fittest.

CORDELIA

How does my royal lord? How fares Your Majesty?

LEAR

You do me wrong to take me out o' the grave.
Thou art a soul in bliss; but I am bound
Upon a wheel of fire, that mine own tears   48
Do scald like molten lead.

CORDELIA   Sir, do you know me?

LEAR

You are a spirit, I know. When did you die?

CORDELIA   Still, still, far wide!   51

DOCTOR

He's scarce awake. Let him alone awhile.

LEAR

Where have I been? Where am I? Fair daylight?

---

31 Had you even if you had. **flakes** locks of hair **32 Did challenge**
would have demanded **34 deep** bass-voiced. **dread-bolted** furnished
with the dreadful thunderstone **36 cross** zigzag. **watch** stay awake
(like a sentry on duty). **perdu** soldier placed in a position of peculiar
danger **37 helm** helmet, i.e., his scanty hair **39 Against** before, in
front of. **fain** glad, constrained **40 rogues forlorn** abandoned vaga-
bonds **41 short** broken up and hence uncomfortable **43 concluded
all** come to an end altogether **48 wheel of fire** (A hellish torment
for the eternally damned.) **that** so that **51 wide** wide of the mark,
wandering

I am mightily abused. I should ev'n die with pity   54
To see another thus. I know not what to say.   55
I will not swear these are my hands. Let's see;
I feel this pinprick. Would I were assured
Of my condition!
CORDELIA   O, look upon me, sir,
And hold your hand in benediction o'er me.
                              [*He attempts to kneel.*]
No, sir, you must not kneel.
LEAR   Pray, do not mock me.
I am a very foolish fond old man,   61
Fourscore and upward, not an hour more nor less;
And, to deal plainly,
I fear I am not in my perfect mind.
Methinks I should know you, and know this man,
Yet I am doubtful; for I am mainly ignorant   66
What place this is, and all the skill I have
Remembers not these garments, nor I know not
Where I did lodge last night. Do not laugh at me,
For, as I am a man, I think this lady
To be my child Cordelia.
CORDELIA [*Weeping*]   And so I am, I am.
LEAR
Be your tears wet? Yes, faith. I pray, weep not.
If you have poison for me I will drink it.
I know you do not love me, for your sisters
Have, as I do remember, done me wrong.
You have some cause, they have not.
CORDELIA   No cause, no cause.
LEAR   Am I in France?
KENT   In your own kingdom, sir.
LEAR   Do not abuse me.   81
DOCTOR
Be comforted, good madam. The great rage,   82
You see, is killed in him, and yet it is danger
To make him even o'er the time he has lost.   84
Desire him to go in. Trouble him no more
Till further settling.   86

54 abused confused, deluded   **55 thus** i.e., thus confused, bewildered
61 fond foolish   **66 mainly** perfectly   **81 abuse** deceive   **82 rage**
frenzy   **84 even o'er** fill in, go over in his mind   **86 settling** composing
of his mind

CORDELIA Will 't please Your Highness walk?   87
LEAR You must bear with me.
  Pray you now, forget and forgive.
  I am old and foolish.
                    Exeunt [*all but Kent and Gentleman*].
GENTLEMAN Holds it true, sir, that the Duke of Corn- 91
  wall was so slain?
KENT Most certain, sir.
GENTLEMAN Who is conductor of his people?   94
KENT As 'tis said, the bastard son of Gloucester.
GENTLEMAN They say Edgar, his banished son, is with
  the Earl of Kent in Germany.
KENT Report is changeable. 'Tis time to look about; the 98
  powers of the kingdom approach apace.   99
GENTLEMAN The arbitrament is like to be bloody. Fare 100
  you well, sir.   [*Exit.*]
KENT
  My point and period will be throughly wrought,   102
  Or well or ill, as this day's battle's fought.   *Exit.* 103

❖

<hr>

87 walk withdraw   **91 Holds it true** is it still held to be true
94 conductor leader, general   **98 look about** i.e., be wary   **99 powers of
the kingdom** British armies (marching against the French invaders)
100 arbitrament decision by arms, decisive encounter   **102 My . . .
wrought** i.e., the conclusion of my destiny (literally, the full stop at the
end of my life's sentence) will be thoroughly brought about   **103 Or**
either.   **as** according as

5.1 *Enter, with drum and colors, Edmund, Regan,*
Gentlemen, and soldiers.

EDMUND [*To a Gentleman*]
  Know of the Duke if his last purpose hold,　　　　　1
  Or whether since he is advised by aught　　　　　2
  To change the course. He's full of alteration　　　3
  And self-reproving. Bring his constant pleasure.　4
　　　　　　　　　　　　　　　[*Exit Gentleman.*]

REGAN
  Our sister's man is certainly miscarried.　　　　　5

EDMUND
  'Tis to be doubted, madam.

REGAN　　　　　　　　　　Now, sweet lord,　　　6
  You know the goodness I intend upon you.　　　　7
  Tell me, but truly—but then speak the truth—
  Do you not love my sister?

EDMUND　　　　　　　　　In honored love.　　　9

REGAN
  But have you never found my brother's way
  To the forfended place?　　　　　　　　　　　11

EDMUND　　That thought abuses you.　　　　　　12

REGAN
  I am doubtful that you have been conjunct　　　13
  And bosomed with her, as far as we call hers.　14

EDMUND　　No, by mine honor, madam.

REGAN
  I never shall endure her. Dear my lord,
  Be not familiar with her.　　　　　　　　　　17

EDMUND
  Fear me not.—She and the Duke her husband!　18

    Enter, with drum and colors, Albany, Goneril,
    [*and*] *soldiers.*

5.1. Location: The British camp near Dover.
1 Know inquire. **last purpose hold** most recent intention (to fight)
remain firm **2 since** since then. **advised by aught** persuaded by any
consideration **3 alteration** vacillation **4 constant pleasure** settled
decision **5 man** i.e., Oswald. **miscarried** lost, perished **6 doubted**
feared **7 intend** intend to confer **9 honored** honorable **11 forfended**
forbidden (by the commandment against adultery) **12 abuses** degrades,
wrongs **13–14 I am . . . hers** I suspect that you have been coupled and
intimate with her in the fullest manner **17 familiar** intimate **18 Fear
me not** don't worry about me on that score

GONERIL [*Aside*]
　I had rather lose the battle than that sister
　Should loosen him and me.

ALBANY
　Our very loving sister, well bemet.   21
　Sir, this I heard: the King is come to his daughter,
　With others whom the rigor of our state   23
　Forced to cry out. Where I could not be honest,   24
　I never yet was valiant. For this business,   25
　It touches us as France invades our land,   26
　Not bolds the King, with others whom, I fear,   27
　Most just and heavy causes make oppose.   28

EDMUND　Sir, you speak nobly.

REGAN　Why is this reasoned?   30

GONERIL
　Combine together 'gainst the enemy;
　For these domestic and particular broils   32
　Are not the question here.

ALBANY　　　　　　　Let's then determine
　With th' ancient of war on our proceeding.   34

EDMUND
　I shall attend you presently at your tent.   35

REGAN　Sister, you'll go with us?

GONERIL　No.

REGAN
　'Tis most convenient. Pray, go with us.   38

GONERIL [*Aside*]
　Oho, I know the riddle.—I will go.   39

　　　[*As they are going out,*] enter Edgar [*disguised*].

EDGAR [*To Albany*]
　If e'er Your Grace had speech with man so poor,

21 bemet met　23 rigor of our state harshness of our rule　24 Where in a case where. honest honorable　25 For as for　26 touches us as concerns us insofar as　27–28 Not . . . oppose not because France encourages the King and others who, I fear, are driven into opposition by just and weighty grievances. bolds emboldens by offering encouragement and support　30 reasoned argued (i.e., why are we arguing about reasons for fighting, instead of fighting)　32 particular broils private quarrels　34 ancient of war veteran officers　35 presently at once　38 convenient proper, befitting　39 know the riddle i.e., understand Regan's enigmatic demand that Goneril accompany her, which is that Regan wants to keep Goneril from Edmund

Hear me one word.
ALBANY [*To the others*] I'll overtake you.
                              Exeunt both the armies.
                                     Speak.
EDGAR [*Giving a letter*]
  Before you fight the battle, ope this letter.
  If you have victory, let the trumpet sound   43
  For him that brought it. Wretched though I seem,
  I can produce a champion that will prove   45
  What is avouchèd there. If you miscarry,   46
  Your business of the world hath so an end,
  And machination ceases. Fortune love you!   48
ALBANY   Stay till I have read the letter.
EDGAR   I was forbid it.
  When time shall serve, let but the herald cry
  And I'll appear again.   *Exit* [*Edgar*].
ALBANY
  Why, fare thee well. I will o'erlook thy paper.   53
     Enter Edmund.

EDMUND
  The enemy's in view. Draw up your powers.
                      [*He offers Albany a paper.*]
  Here is the guess of their true strength and forces   55
  By diligent discovery, but your haste   56
  Is now urged on you.
ALBANY   We will greet the time.   *Exit.*   57
EDMUND
  To both these sisters have I sworn my love,
  Each jealous of the other, as the stung   59
  Are of the adder. Which of them shall I take?
  Both? One? Or neither? Neither can be enjoyed
  If both remain alive. To take the widow
  Exasperates, makes mad her sister Goneril,
  And hardly shall I carry out my side,   64
  Her husband being alive. Now then, we'll use
  His countenance for the battle, which being done,   66

43 sound sound a summons   **45 prove** i.e., in trial by combat
46 avouchèd maintained.   **miscarry** perish, come to destruction
48 machination plotting (against your life)   **53 o'erlook** peruse   **55 guess**
estimate   **56 discovery** reconnoitering   **57 greet the time** meet the occasion   **59 jealous** suspicious   **64 carry out my side** fulfill my ambition, and
satisfy her (Goneril)   **66 countenance** backing, authority of his name

Let her who would be rid of him devise
His speedy taking off. As for the mercy   68
Which he intends to Lear and to Cordelia,
The battle done and they within our power,
Shall never see his pardon, for my state   71
Stands on me to defend, not to debate.   72

Exit.

❖

5.2   *Alarum within. Enter, with drum and colors,*
          Lear, Cordelia, and soldiers, over the stage; and
          exeunt.

     Enter Edgar and Gloucester.

EDGAR
Here, father, take the shadow of this tree
For your good host. Pray that the right may thrive.   2
If ever I return to you again,
I'll bring you comfort.
GLOUCESTER   Grace go with you, sir!   4
                        Exit [Edgar].

     Alarum and retreat within. Enter Edgar.

EDGAR
Away, old man! Give me thy hand, away!
King Lear hath lost, he and his daughter ta'en.
Give me thy hand. Come on.
GLOUCESTER
No further, sir. A man may rot even here.
EDGAR
What, in ill thoughts again? Men must endure
Their going hence, even as their coming hither;
Ripeness is all. Come on.
GLOUCESTER   And that's true too.   11
                         Exeunt.

❖

68 taking off killing   **71 Shall** they shall   **71–72 my state . . . debate** my
position depends upon maintenance by force, not by talk

5.2. Location: The battlefield.
s.d. Alarum trumpet call to arms   **2 host** shelterer   **4 s.d. retreat**
trumpet signal for withdrawal   **11 Ripeness** i.e., fulfillment of one's
allotted years and readiness for death when it comes

5.3   *Enter, in conquest, with drum and colors,*
            Edmund; Lear and Cordelia, as prisoners;
            soldiers, Captain.

EDMUND
  Some officers take them away. Good guard,   1
  Until their greater pleasures first be known   2
  That are to censure them.
CORDELIA [*To Lear*]   We are not the first   3
  Who with best meaning have incurred the worst.   4
  For thee, oppressèd King, I am cast down;
  Myself could else outfrown false Fortune's frown.
  Shall we not see these daughters and these sisters?   7
LEAR
  No, no, no, no! Come, let's away to prison.
  We two alone will sing like birds i' the cage.
  When thou dost ask me blessing, I'll kneel down
  And ask of thee forgiveness. So we'll live,
  And pray, and sing, and tell old tales, and laugh
  At gilded butterflies, and hear poor rogues   13
  Talk of court news; and we'll talk with them too—
  Who loses and who wins; who's in, who's out—
  And take upon 's the mystery of things,   16
  As if we were God's spies; and we'll wear out,   17
  In a walled prison, packs and sects of great ones,   18
  That ebb and flow by the moon.
EDMUND   Take them away.   19
LEAR
  Upon such sacrifices, my Cordelia,
  The gods themselves throw incense. Have I caught thee? 21

5.3. Location: The British camp.
1 Good guard guard them well   **2 their greater pleasures** i.e., the
wishes of those in command   **3 censure** judge   **4 meaning** intentions
7 Shall . . . sisters i.e., aren't we even allowed to speak to Goneril and
Regan before they order to prison their own father and sister
13 gilded butterflies i.e., gaily dressed courtiers and other ephemeral
types, or perhaps actual butterflies   **16 take upon 's** assume the burden
of, or profess to understand   **17 God's spies** i.e., detached observers
surveying the deeds of mankind from an eternal vantage point.   **wear
out** outlast   **18–19 packs . . . moon** i.e., followers and cliques attached
to persons of high station, whose fortunes change erratically and constantly   **21 throw incense** participate as celebrants

He that parts us shall bring a brand from heaven   22
And fire us hence like foxes. Wipe thine eyes;   23
The goodyears shall devour them, flesh and fell,   24
Ere they shall make us weep. We'll see 'em starved first.
Come.   *Exit [with Cordelia, guarded].*

EDMUND   Come hither, Captain. Hark.
Take thou this note [*Giving a paper*]; go follow them
   to prison.
One step I have advanced thee; if thou dost
As this instructs thee, thou dost make thy way
To noble fortunes. Know thou this: that men
Are as the time is. To be tender-minded
Does not become a sword. Thy great employment   33
Will not bear question; either say thou'lt do 't   34
Or thrive by other means.

CAPTAIN   I'll do 't, my lord.

EDMUND
About it, and write "happy" when th' hast done.   36
Mark, I say, instantly, and carry it so   37
As I have set it down.

CAPTAIN
I cannot draw a cart, nor eat dried oats;
If it be man's work, I'll do 't.   *Exit Captain.*

   *Flourish. Enter Albany, Goneril, Regan, [another
   Captain, and] soldiers.*

ALBANY
Sir, you have showed today your valiant strain,
And fortune led you well. You have the captives
Who were the opposites of this day's strife;   43
I do require them of you, so to use them
As we shall find their merits and our safety
May equally determine.

EDMUND   Sir, I thought it fit

22–23 He . . . foxes i.e., anyone seeking to part us will have to employ a
heavenly firebrand to drive us out of our prison refuge as foxes are
driven out of their holes by fire and smoke. (Suggests that only death
will part them.)   **24 goodyears** (Apparently a word connoting evil or
conceivably the passage of time.)   **flesh and fell** flesh and skin, completely   **33 become a sword** i.e., suit a warrior   **34 bear question** admit
of discussion   **36 write "happy"** call yourself fortunate.   **th'** thou
37 carry it arrange it   **43 opposites** enemies

To send the old and miserable King
To some retention and appointed guard,   49
Whose age had charms in it, whose title more,   50
To pluck the common bosom on his side   51
And turn our impressed lances in our eyes   52
Which do command them. With him I sent the Queen,   53
My reason all the same; and they are ready
Tomorrow, or at further space, t' appear   55
Where you shall hold your session. At this time
We sweat and bleed; the friend hath lost his friend,
And the best quarrels in the heat are cursed   58
By those that feel their sharpness.   59
The question of Cordelia and her father
Requires a fitter place.
ALBANY   Sir, by your patience,
I hold you but a subject of this war,   62
Not as a brother.
REGAN   That's as we list to grace him.   63
Methinks our pleasure might have been demanded   64
Ere you had spoke so far. He led our powers,
Bore the commission of my place and person,
The which immediacy may well stand up   67
And call itself your brother.
GONERIL   Not so hot!
In his own grace he doth exalt himself
More than in your addition.
REGAN   In my rights,   70
By me invested, he compeers the best.   71
GONERIL
That were the most if he should husband you.   72

---

49 retention confinement   **50 Whose** i.e., the King's   **51 common
bosom** affection of the multitude   **52 turn . . . eyes** i.e., turn against us
the weapons of those very troops whom we impressed into service
53 Which we who   **55 space** interval of time   **58–59 And . . . sharpness**
i.e., and even the best of causes, at this moment when the passions of
battle have not cooled, are viewed with hatred by those who have suffered the painful consequences. (Edmund pretends to worry that
Lear and Cordelia would not receive a fair trial.)   **quarrels** causes.
sharpness keenness, painful consequences   **62 subject of** subordi-
nate in   **63 list** please   **64 pleasure** wish.   **demanded** asked about
67 immediacy nearness of connection   **70 your addition** the titles you
confer   **71 compeers** is equal with   **72 That . . . most** that investiture
would be most complete

REGAN
  Jesters do oft prove prophets.
GONERIL   Holla, holla!   73
  That eye that told you so looked but asquint.   74
REGAN
  Lady, I am not well, else I should answer
  From a full-flowing stomach. [*To Edmund*.] General,   76
  Take thou my soldiers, prisoners, patrimony;   77
  Dispose of them, of me; the walls is thine.   78
  Witness the world that I create thee here
  My lord and master.
GONERIL   Mean you to enjoy him?
ALBANY
  The let-alone lies not in your good will.   81
EDMUND
  Nor in thine, lord.
ALBANY   Half-blooded fellow, yes.   82
REGAN [*To Edmund*]
  Let the drum strike and prove my title thine.   83
ALBANY
  Stay yet; hear reason. Edmund, I arrest thee
  On capital treason; and, in thy attaint   85
                              [*Pointing to Goneril*]
  This gilded serpent. For your claim, fair sister,
  I bar it in the interest of my wife;
  'Tis she is subcontracted to this lord,
  And I, her husband, contradict your banns.   89
  If you will marry, make your loves to me;
  My lady is bespoke.
GONERIL   An interlude!   91
ALBANY
  Thou art armed, Gloucester. Let the trumpet sound.

---

73 prove turn out to be   **74 asquint** (Jealousy proverbially makes the
eye look *asquint*, furtively, suspiciously.)   **76 full-flowing stomach** full
tide of angry rejoinder   **77 patrimony** inheritance   **78 the walls is thine**
i.e., the citadel of my heart and body surrenders completely to you
81 let-alone preventing, denying   **82 Half-blooded** only partly of noble
blood, bastard   **83 Let . . . strike** i.e., let there be a public announcement (?) a battle (?)   **85 in thy attaint** i.e., as partner in your corruption
and as one who has (unwittingly) provided the *attaint* or impeachment
against you   **89 banns** public announcement of a proposed marriage
91 An interlude a play; i.e., you are being melodramatic; or, what a farce
this is

If none appear to prove upon thy person
Thy heinous, manifest, and many treasons,
There is my pledge. [*He throws down a glove.*] I'll make
   it on thy heart,   95
Ere I taste bread, thou art in nothing less   96
Than I have here proclaimed thee.

REGAN   Sick, O, sick!

GONERIL [*Aside*]   If not, I'll ne'er trust medicine.   99

EDMUND [*Throwing down a glove*]
There's my exchange. What in the world he is   100
That names me traitor, villain-like he lies.
Call by the trumpet. He that dares approach,
On him, on you—who not?—I will maintain
My truth and honor firmly.

ALBANY
A herald, ho!

EDMUND   A herald, ho, a herald!

    Enter a Herald.

ALBANY
Trust to thy single virtue; for thy soldiers,   106
All levied in my name, have in my name
Took their discharge.

REGAN   My sickness grows upon me.

ALBANY
She is not well. Convey her to my tent.
                [*Exit Regan, supported.*]
Come hither, herald. Let the trumpet sound,
And read out this.   [*He gives a paper.*]

CAPTAIN   Sound, trumpet!   *A trumpet sounds.*

HERALD (*Reads*)   "If any man of quality or degree within   113
the lists of the army will maintain upon Edmund, supposed Earl of Gloucester, that he is a manifold traitor,
let him appear by the third sound of the trumpet. He
is bold in his defense."

EDMUND   Sound!   *First trumpet.*
HERALD   Again!   *Second trumpet.*
HERALD   Again!   *Third trumpet.*
                Trumpet answers within.

---

95 make prove   **96 in nothing less** in no respect less guilty
99 medicine i.e., poison   **100 What** whoever   **106 single virtue** unaided
prowess   **113 degree** rank

Enter Edgar, armed, [with a trumpeter before him].

ALBANY
  Ask him his purposes, why he appears
  Upon this call o' the trumpet.

HERALD   What are you?   122
  Your name, your quality, and why you answer
  This present summons?

EDGAR   Know my name is lost,
  By treason's tooth bare-gnawn and canker-bit.   125
  Yet am I noble as the adversary
  I come to cope.

ALBANY   Which is that adversary?   127

EDGAR
  What's he that speaks for Edmund, Earl of Gloucester?

EDMUND
  Himself. What sayst thou to him?

EDGAR   Draw thy sword,
  That, if my speech offend a noble heart,
  Thy arm may do thee justice. Here is mine.
                   [He draws his sword.]
  Behold, it is the privilege of mine honors,   132
  My oath, and my profession. I protest,   133
  Maugre thy strength, place, youth, and eminence,   134
  Despite thy victor sword and fire-new fortune,   135
  Thy valor, and thy heart, thou art a traitor—   136
  False to thy gods, thy brother, and thy father,
  Conspirant 'gainst this high-illustrious prince,
  And from th' extremest upward of thy head   139
  To the descent and dust below thy foot   140
  A most toad-spotted traitor. Say thou no,   141
  This sword, this arm, and my best spirits are bent   142
  To prove upon thy heart, whereto I speak,
  Thou liest.

EDMUND   In wisdom I should ask thy name.   144
  But since thy outside looks so fair and warlike,

122 What who **125 canker-bit** eaten as by the caterpillar **127 cope**
encounter **132 of mine honors** i.e., of my knighthood **133 profession** i.e.,
knighthood **134 Maugre** in spite of **135 victor** victorious. **fire-new**
newly minted **136 heart** courage **139 upward** top **140 descent** lowest
extreme **141 toad-spotted** venomous, or having spots of infamy. **Say
thou** if you say **142 bent** prepared **144 wisdom** prudence

And that thy tongue some say of breeding breathes,   146
What safe and nicely I might well delay   147
By rule of knighthood, I disdain and spurn.   148
Back do I toss these treasons to thy head,   149
With the hell-hated lie o'erwhelm thy heart,   150
Which—for they yet glance by and scarcely bruise—   151
This sword of mine shall give them instant way,   152
Where they shall rest forever. Trumpets, speak!   153
      [*He draws.*] *Alarums. Fight.* [*Edmund falls.*]

ALBANY [*To Edgar*]
   Save him, save him!

GONERIL   This is practice, Gloucester.   154
   By th' law of war thou wast not bound to answer
   An unknown opposite. Thou art not vanquished,
   But cozened and beguiled.

ALBANY   Shut your mouth, dame,   157
   Or with this paper shall I stopple it.—Hold, sir.—   158
   [*To Goneril.*] Thou worse than any name, read thine own
     evil.   [*He shows her the letter.*]
   No tearing, lady; I perceive you know it.

GONERIL
   Say if I do, the laws are mine, not thine.
   Who can arraign me for 't?

ALBANY   Most monstrous! O!
   Know'st thou this paper?

GONERIL   Ask me not what I know.
                                    Exit.

ALBANY
   Go after her. She's desperate; govern her.   164
                    [*Exit a Soldier.*]

---

146 say smack, taste, indication   **147 safe and nicely** prudently and
punctiliously   **148 I . . . spurn** i.e., I disdain to insist on my right to
refuse combat with one of lower rank   **149 treasons . . . head** i.e.,
accusations of treason in your teeth   **150 hell-hated** hated as hell is
hated   **151 Which . . . bruise** i.e., which charges of treason—since they
merely glance off your armor and do no harm.   **for** since.   **yet** as yet
152 give . . . way i.e., provide them an immediate pathway to your
heart   **153 Where . . . forever** i.e., my victory in trial by combat will
prove forever that the charges of treason apply to you   **154 Save** spare.
(Albany wishes to spare Edmund's life so that he may confess and be
found guilty.)   **practice** trickery; or (said sardonically) astute management   **157 cozened** tricked   **158 stopple** stop up.   **Hold, sir** (Perhaps
addressed to Edgar; see l. 154 and note.)   **164 govern** restrain

EDMUND
  What you have charged me with, that have I done,
  And more, much more. The time will bring it out.
  'Tis past, and so am I. But what art thou
  That hast this fortune on me? If thou'rt noble,   168
  I do forgive thee.
EDGAR   Let's exchange charity.   169
  I am no less in blood than thou art, Edmund;
  If more, the more th' hast wronged me.   171
  My name is Edgar, and thy father's son.
  The gods are just, and of our pleasant vices   173
  Make instruments to plague us.
  The dark and vicious place where thee he got   175
  Cost him his eyes.
EDMUND   Th' hast spoken right. 'Tis true.
  The wheel is come full circle; I am here.   177
ALBANY [To Edgar]
  Methought thy very gait did prophesy
  A royal nobleness. I must embrace thee.

                                        [They embrace.]
  Let sorrow split my heart if ever I
  Did hate thee or thy father!
EDGAR   Worthy prince, I know 't.
ALBANY   Where have you hid yourself?
  How have you known the miseries of your father?
EDGAR
  By nursing them, my lord. List a brief tale,
  And when 'tis told, O, that my heart would burst!
  The bloody proclamation to escape   187
  That followed me so near—O, our lives' sweetness,
  That we the pain of death would hourly die
  Rather than die at once!—taught me to shift
  Into a madman's rags, t' assume a semblance
  That very dogs disdained; and in this habit
  Met I my father with his bleeding rings,   193
  Their precious stones new lost; became his guide,

168 fortune on victory over   **169 charity** forgiveness (for Edmund's
wickedness toward Edgar and Edgar's having slain Edmund)   **171 th'**
thou   **173 pleasant** pleasurable   **175 got** begot   **177 wheel** i.e., wheel of
fortune.   **here** i.e., at its bottom   **187 The . . . escape** in order to escape the
death-threatening proclamation   **193 rings** sockets

Led him, begged for him, saved him from despair;
Never—O fault!—revealed myself unto him   196
Until some half hour past, when I was armed.
Not sure, though hoping, of this good success,   198
I asked his blessing, and from first to last
Told him our pilgrimage. But his flawed heart—   200
Alack, too weak the conflict to support—
Twixt two extremes of passion, joy and grief,
Burst smilingly.
EDMUND   This speech of yours hath moved me,
And shall perchance do good. But speak you on;
You look as you had something more to say.

ALBANY
If there be more, more woeful, hold it in,
For I am almost ready to dissolve,   207
Hearing of this.
EDGAR   This would have seemed a period   208
To such as love not sorrow; but another,   209
To amplify too much, would make much more   210
And top extremity. Whilst I   211
Was big in clamor, came there in a man   212
Who, having seen me in my worst estate,
Shunned my abhorred society; but then, finding
Who 'twas that so endured, with his strong arms
He fastened on my neck and bellowed out
As he'd burst heaven, threw him on my father,   217
Told the most piteous tale of Lear and him
That ever ear received, which in recounting
His grief grew puissant, and the strings of life   220
Began to crack. Twice then the trumpets sounded,
And there I left him tranced.
ALBANY   But who was this?   222
EDGAR
Kent, sir, the banished Kent, who in disguise

---

196 fault mistake   **198 success** outcome   **200 flawed** cracked
207 dissolve i.e., in tears   **208 a period** the limit   **209 love not** are not in
love with   **209–211 but . . . extremity** i.e., another sorrowful circumstance,
adding to what is already too much, would increase it and exceed the
limit   **212 big in clamor** loud in my lamenting   **217 As** as if.   **threw . . .
father** threw himself on my father's body   **220 His** i.e., Kent's.   **puissant**
powerful.   **strings of life** heartstrings   **222 tranced** entranced, senseless

Followed his enemy king and did him service   224
Improper for a slave.

    Enter a Gentleman [with a bloody knife].

GENTLEMAN
  Help, help, O, help!
EDGAR   What kind of help?
ALBANY   Speak, man.
EDGAR
  What means this bloody knife?
GENTLEMAN   'Tis hot, it smokes.   227
  It came even from the heart of—O, she's dead!
ALBANY Who dead? Speak, man.
GENTLEMAN
  Your lady, sir, your lady! And her sister
  By her is poisoned; she confesses it.
EDMUND
  I was contracted to them both. All three
  Now marry in an instant.
EDGAR   Here comes Kent.

    Enter Kent.

ALBANY
  Produce the bodies, be they alive or dead.
                     [Exit Gentleman.]
  This judgment of the heavens, that makes us tremble,
  Touches us not with pity.—O, is this he?
  [To Kent.] The time will not allow the compliment   237
  Which very manners urges.
KENT   I am come   238
  To bid my king and master aye good night.   239
  Is he not here?
ALBANY   Great thing of us forgot!
  Speak, Edmund, where's the King? And where's
    Cordelia?
        Goneril's and Regan's bodies [are] brought out.
  Seest thou this object, Kent?   242

224 **his enemy king** i.e., the king who had rejected and banished him
227 **smokes** steams   237 **compliment** ceremony   238 **very manners
urges** mere decency requires   239 **aye good night** farewell forever. (Kent
believes he himself is near death, his heartstrings having begun to
crack.)   242 **object** sight

KENT   Alack, why thus?

EDMUND   Yet Edmund was beloved.   244
  The one the other poisoned for my sake
  And after slew herself.   246

ALBANY   Even so. Cover their faces.

EDMUND
  I pant for life. Some good I mean to do,
  Despite of mine own nature. Quickly send—
  Be brief in it—to the castle, for my writ
  Is on the life of Lear and on Cordelia.
  Nay, send in time.

ALBANY   Run, run, O, run!

EDGAR
  To who, my lord? Who has the office? Send   253
  Thy token of reprieve.

EDMUND   Well thought on. Take my sword.
  Give it the Captain.

EDGAR   Haste thee, for thy life.
                 [*Exit one with Edmund's sword.*]

EDMUND
  He hath commission from thy wife and me
  To hang Cordelia in the prison and
  To lay the blame upon her own despair,
  That she fordid herself.   260

ALBANY
  The gods defend her! Bear him hence awhile.
                 [*Edmund is borne off.*]

  Enter Lear, with Cordelia in his arms; [Captain].

LEAR
  Howl, howl, howl! O, you are men of stones!
  Had I your tongues and eyes, I'd use them so
  That heaven's vault should crack. She's gone forever.
  I know when one is dead and when one lives;
  She's dead as earth. Lend me a looking glass;
  If that her breath will mist or stain the stone,   267
  Why, then she lives.

KENT   Is this the promised end?   268

---

244 Yet despite everything   **246 after** afterwards   **253 office** commission   **260 fordid** destroyed   **267 stone** crystal or polished stone of which the mirror is made   **268 promised end** i.e., Last Judgment

EDGAR
  Or image of that horror?

ALBANY   Fall and cease!   269

LEAR
  This feather stirs; she lives! If it be so,
  It is a chance which does redeem all sorrows
  That ever I have felt.

KENT [*Kneeling*]   O my good master!

LEAR
  Prithee, away.

EDGAR   'Tis noble Kent, your friend.

LEAR
  A plague upon you, murderers, traitors all!
  I might have saved her; now she's gone forever!
  Cordelia, Cordelia! Stay a little. Ha?
  What is 't thou sayst? Her voice was ever soft,
  Gentle, and low, an excellent thing in woman.
  I killed the slave that was a-hanging thee.

CAPTAIN
  'Tis true, my lords, he did.

LEAR   Did I not, fellow?
  I have seen the day, with my good biting falchion   281
  I would have made them skip. I am old now,
  And these same crosses spoil me.—Who are you?   283
  Mine eyes are not o' the best; I'll tell you straight.   284

KENT
  If Fortune brag of two she loved and hated,   285
  One of them we behold.

LEAR
  This is a dull sight. Are you not Kent?

KENT   The same,   287
  Your servant Kent. Where is your servant Caius?   288

LEAR
  He's a good fellow, I can tell you that;
  He'll strike, and quickly too. He's dead and rotten.

---

269 image representation.   **Fall and cease** i.e., let heavens fall and all
things cease   **281 falchion** light sword   **283 crosses spoil me** adversities take away my strength   **284 I'll . . . straight** I'll recognize you in a
moment   **285 two** i.e., Lear, and a hypothetical individual whose misfortunes are without parallel.   **loved and hated** i.e., first raised and then
lowered   **287 This . . . sight** i.e., my vision is clouding; or, this is a
dismal spectacle   **288 Caius** (Kent's disguise name)

KENT
  No, my good lord, I am the very man—
LEAR   I'll see that straight.   292
KENT
  That from your first of difference and decay   293
  Have followed your sad steps—
LEAR   You are welcome hither.
KENT
  Nor no man else. All's cheerless, dark, and deadly.   295
  Your eldest daughters have fordone themselves,   296
  And desperately are dead.
LEAR   Ay, so I think.   297
ALBANY
  He knows not what he says, and vain is it
  That we present us to him.
EDGAR   Very bootless.   299

    Enter a Messenger.

MESSENGER   Edmund is dead, my lord.
ALBANY   That's but a trifle here.
  You lords and noble friends, know our intent:
  What comfort to this great decay may come   303
  Shall be applied. For us, we will resign,
  During the life of this old majesty,
  To him our absolute power; [*To Edgar and Kent*] you,
    to your rights,
  With boot and such addition as your honors   307
  Have more than merited. All friends shall taste
  The wages of their virtue, and all foes
  The cup of their deservings.—O, see, see!
LEAR
  And my poor fool is hanged! No, no, no life?   311
  Why should a dog, a horse, a rat, have life,
  And thou no breath at all? Thou'lt come no more,

---

292 see that straight attend to that in a moment; or, comprehend that
soon   **293 first of difference** beginning of your change for the worse
295 Nor . . . else no, not I nor anyone else; or, I am *the very man* (l. 291),
him and no one else.   **deadly** deathlike   **296 fordone** destroyed
297 desperately in despair   **299 bootless** in vain   **303 What . . . come** i.e.,
whatever means of comforting this ruined king may present themselves
307 boot advantage, good measure.   **addition** titles, further distinctions
311 poor fool i.e., Cordelia. (*Fool* is here a term of endearment.)

Never, never, never, never, never!
Pray you, undo this button. Thank you, sir.
Do you see this? Look on her, look, her lips,
Look there, look there!   *He dies.*

EDGAR   He faints. My lord, my lord!

KENT
Break, heart, I prithee, break!

EDGAR   Look up, my lord.

KENT
Vex not his ghost. O, let him pass! He hates him   319
That would upon the rack of this tough world   320
Stretch him out longer.

EDGAR   He is gone indeed.

KENT
The wonder is he hath endured so long.
He but usurped his life.

ALBANY
Bear them from hence. Our present business
Is general woe. [*To Kent and Edgar.*] Friends of my
    soul, you twain
Rule in this realm, and the gored state sustain.

KENT
I have a journey, sir, shortly to go.   327
My master calls me; I must not say no.

EDGAR
The weight of this sad time we must obey;
Speak what we feel, not what we ought to say.
The oldest hath borne most; we that are young
Shall never see so much nor live so long.   332

                    Exeunt, with a dead march.

---

319 ghost departing spirit   **320 rack** torture rack (with suggestion, in
the Folio and quarto spelling *wracke,* of shipwreck, disaster)
327 journey i.e., to another world   **332 s.d. Exeunt** (Presumably the
dead bodies are borne out in procession.)

Date and Text

On November 26, 1607, Nathaniel Butter and John Busby entered on the Stationers' Register, the official record book of the London Company of Stationers (booksellers and printers), "A booke called. Master William Shakespeare his historye of Kinge Lear, as yt was played before the Kinges maiestie at Whitehall vppon Sainct Stephens night at Christmas Last, by his maiesties servantes playinge vsually at the Globe on the Banksyde." Next year appeared the following quarto:

> M. William Shak-speare: *HIS* True Chronicle Historie of the life and death of King LEAR and his three Daughters. *With the vnfortunate life of* Edgar, *sonne* and heire to the Earle of Gloster, and his sullen and assumed humor of TOM of Bedlam: *As it was played before the Kings Maiestie at Whitehall vpon S.* Stephans *night in Christmas Hollidayes.* By his Maiesties seruants playing vsually at the Gloabe on the Bancke-side. *LONDON,* Printed for *Nathaniel Butter,* and are to be sold at his shop in *Pauls* Church-yard at the signe of the Pide Bull neere St. *Austins* Gate. 1608.

This quarto is often called the "Pied Bull" quarto in reference to its place of sale. Twelve copies exist today, in ten different "states," because proofreading was being carried on while the sheets were being run off in the press; the copies variously combine corrected and uncorrected sheets. A second quarto, printed in 1619 by William Jaggard for Thomas Pavier with the fraudulent date of 1608, was based on a copy of the first quarto combining corrected and uncorrected sheets.

The First Folio text of 1623 may have been typeset from a promptbook cut for performance or from a transcript of such a manuscript, and the promptbook in its turn appears to have been based on Shakespeare's fair copy of his first draft. The Folio compositors also pretty certainly consulted a copy of the second quarto from time to time, or may have typeset directly from this quarto as annotated with reference to Shakespeare's fair copy. In writing the fair copy Shakespeare may have marked some 300 lines for deletion, but it is possible that he did so chiefly to shorten time of performance. He also seems to have added some 100 lines, an apparent contradiction in view of the need for cutting but possibly dictated by Shakespeare's developing sense of his play. It is also possible that the cuts were carried out by someone else in the preparation of the promptbook.

The first quarto, on the other hand, appears in some fashion to have descended from Shakespeare's unrevised and evidently very untidy foul or working papers. It is often corrupt. Still, in some matters—especially variants indifferent in meaning (such as *an/if* or *thine/thy*)—it may be closer to Shakespeare's preferences than the Folio, behind which are several stages of transmission.

This edition agrees with most recent students of the *Lear* text that the Folio represents a theatrical revision in which the cuts were devised for performance by Shakespeare's company, quite possibly made by Shakespeare himself as a member of that company. The case for artistic preference in the making of those cuts, on the other hand, is less certain and may have been overstated. Many of the cuts have the effect of shortening scenes, especially in the latter half of the play. Some scenes, like 3.6, show open gaps as a result of the cutting: Lear's "Then let them anatomize Regan" (l. 75) implies the trial of Goneril as it is dramatized in the first quarto but cut from the Folio. Other omissions as well read like expedients, although they can also be explained by a hypothesis of literary and theatrical rewriting; if Shakespeare himself undertook the cutting, he would presumably do so as expertly as possible. The fact that the Folio text gives no rewritten speeches may suggest that the large cuts were motivated by the need for shortening. This edition holds to the principle that it is unwise to omit the material cut from the Folio text, since we cannot be sure that Shakespeare would have shortened the text had there been no external constraints. At the same time, the added material in the Folio is clearly his and belongs in his conception of the play. The resulting text is a conflation, but one that avoids cutting material that Shakespeare may well have regretted having to excise.

The Stationers' Register entry for November 26, 1607, describes a performance at court on the previous St. Stephen's night, December 26, 1606. The title page of the first quarto confirms this performance on St. Stephen's night. Such a performance at court was not likely to have been the first, however. Shakespeare's repeated use of Samuel Harsnett's *Declaration of Egregious Popish Impostures*, registered on March 16, 1603, sets an early limit for composition of the play. Other circumstances point to the existence of the play by May of 1605. In that month, an old play called *The True Chronicle History of King Leir* was entered in the Stationers' Register as a "Tragecall historie," a phrase suggesting the influence of Shakespeare's play, since the old *King Leir* does not end tragically. Moreover, the title page of the old *King Leir*, issued in 1605, proclaims the text to be "as it hath bene diuers and sundry times lately acted." In view of the unlikelihood that such an old play (written before 1594) would be revived in 1605, scholars have suggested that the title page was the publisher's way of trying to capitalize on the recent popularity of Shakespeare's play. In this case, the likeliest date for the composition of Shakespeare's *King Lear* would be in the winter of 1604–1605. Shakespeare certainly used the old *King Leir* as a chief source, but he need not have waited for its publication in 1605 if, as seems perfectly plausible, his company owned the promptbook. On the other hand, Gloucester's mentioning of "These late eclipses in the sun and moon" (1.2.106) seems to refer to an eclipse of the moon in September and of the sun in October of 1605, and we are left wondering if Shakespeare was so foresighted as to have anticipated these events.

Textual Notes

These textual notes are not a historical collation, either of the early quartos and folios or of more recent editions; they are simply a record of departures in this edition from the copy text. The reading adopted in this edition appears in boldface, followed by the rejected reading from the copy text, i.e., the First Folio. Only major alterations in punctuation are noted. Changes in lineation are not indicated, nor are some minor and obvious typographical errors.

Abbreviations used:
F the First Folio
Q quarto
s.d. stage direction
s.p. speech prefix

Copy text: the First Folio, except for those 300 or so lines found only in the first quarto of 1608 [Q1]. Unless otherwise indicated, adopted readings are from the corrected state of Q1. A few readings are supplied from the second quarto of 1619 [Q2]. All readings subsequent to 1619 are marked as supplied by "eds."

1.1. 5 equalities qualities   **20–22 account . . . yet** [eds.] account, though . . . for: yet   **35 liege** Lord   **55 words** word   **66 issue** issues   **68 Speak** [Q1; not in F]   **74 possesses** professes   **85 interessed** [eds.] interest   **104** [Q1; not in F]   **110 mysteries** [eds.] miseries [F] mistresse [Q1]   **135 turns** turne   **156 as a** as   **157 nor** nere   **161 s.p. Lear** Kear   **162 s.p. Kent** Lent   **165 s.p. Cornwall** [eds.] Cor   **166 the** thy   **173 sentence** sentences   **191 s.p. Gloucester** Cor   **217 best object** obiect   **229 well** will   **252 respects of fortune** respect and Fortunes   **285 shame them** with shame   **286 s.d. Exeunt** [eds.] Exit   **293 hath not** hath   **306 hit** sit

1.2. 1 s.p. [and elsewhere] Edmund Bast   **21 top** [eds.] to'   **56 waked** wake   **97–99 Edmund. Nor . . . earth** [Q1; not in F]   **134 Fut, I** I   **136 Edgar** [Q1; not in F]   **137 and pat** [eds.] Pat [F] and out [Q1]   **147–155 as . . . come,** [Q1; not in F]   **182 s.d.** [at l. 181 in F]

1.3. 3 s.p. [and elsewhere] Oswald [eds.] Ste   **17–21** [Q1; not in F]   **26–27 I would . . . speak** [Q1; not in F]   **28 very** [Q1; not in F]

1.4. 1 well will   **43 s.d. Enter steward** [at l. 44 in F]   **50 daughter** Daughters   **76 s.d. Enter steward** [eds.; after l. 77 in F]   **96 s.p. Kent** Lear   **Fool my boy**   **138–153 Fool. That . . . snatching** [Q1; not in F]   **158 crown** Crownes   **175 fools** Foole   **195 nor crumb** not crum   **214 it had** it's had   **229–232** [Q1; not in F]   **255 O . . . come** [Q1; not in F]   **303 Yea . . . this** [Q1; not in F]   **343 You're** Your   **attasked** at task

1.5. s.d. Kent Kent, Gentleman   **51 s.d. Exit** Exeunt

2.1. 2 you your   **19 s.d.** [at l. 18 in F]   **39 stand 's** stand   **69 I should** should I   **70 ay, though** though   **78 I never got him** [Q1; not in F]   **78 s.d.** [at l. 77 in F]   **79 why** wher   **87 strange news** strangenesse   **125 thought** though

2.2. 22 clamorous clamours   **45 an** if   **52 What's** What is   **66 you'll** you
will   **78 Bring . . . their** Being . . . the   **79 Renege** Reuenge   **80 gale** gall
84 an if   **101 take 't** take it   **109 flickering** flicking   **124 dread** dead
127 their there   **132 respect** respects   **142 s.d.** [at l. 140 in F]   **144–148 His
. . . with** [Q1; not in F]   **146 contemnèd'st** [eds.] temnest [Q1]   **148 King**
King his Master, needs   **153** [Q1; not in F]   **154 Come . . . away** [assigned
in F to Cornwall   **good** [Q1; not in F]   **s.d. Exeunt** [eds.] Exit   **155 Duke's**
Duke

2.3. 18 sheepcotes Sheeps-Coates

2.4. 2 messenger Messengers   **9 man's** man   **18–19** [Q1; not in F]
30 panting painting   **33 whose** those   **56 Hysterica** [eds.] Historica   **62 the**
the the   **74 have** hause   **128 you** your   **130 mother's** Mother   **185 s.d.** [at
l. 183 in F]   **187 fickle** fickly   **190 s.d.** [at l. 188 in F]   **213 hot-blooded** hot-
bloodied   **297 s.d.** [after l. 295 in F]   **302 bleak** high

3.1. 7–15 tears . . . all [Q1; not in F]   **10 outstorm** [eds.] outscorne [Q1]
30–42 [Q1; not in F]

3.2. 3 drowned drown   **38 s.d.** [at l. 36 in F]   **85–86** [these lines follow l. 91
in F]

3.3. 17 for 't for it

3.4. 10 thy they   **12 This** the   **27 s.d.** [at l. 26 in F]   **31 looped** lop'd   **38 s.d.
Enter Fool** [F, at l. 36: "Enter Edgar, and Foole"]   **46 blows the cold wind**
blow the windes   **51 through fire** though Fire   **52 ford** Sword   **57, 58 Bless**
Blisse   **90 deeply** deerely   **99 sessa** [eds.] Sesey   **112 s.d.** [at l. 109 in F]
114 fiend [Q1; not in F]   **115 till the** at   **116 squinnies** [eds.] squints [F]
squemes [Q1]   **134 stock-punished** stockt, punish'd   **hath had** hath

3.5. 11 he which hee   **26 dearer** deere

3.6. 5 s.d. Exit [at l. 3 in F]   **17–55** [Q1; not in F]   **21 justicer** [eds.] Iustice
[Q1]   **22 Now** [Q2] No [Q1]   **25 burn** [eds.] broome [Q1]   **34 cushions** [eds.]
cushings [Q1]   **51 joint** [eds.] ioyne [Q1]   **53 on** [eds.] an [Q1]   **68 lym** [eds.]
Hym   **69 tike** tight   **trundle-tail** Troudle taile   **85 s.d.** [at l. 80 in F]
97–101 Oppressèd . . . behind [Q1; not in F]   **101 s.p. Gloucester** [not in F]
102–115 [Q1; not in F]

3.7. 10 festinate [eds.] festiuate   **18 lord's dependents** Lords, dependants
23 s.d. Exeunt [eds.] Exit   **61 rash** sticke   **66 dern** sterne   **75 s.p. First
Servant** Seru [also at ll. 79, 82, 84]   **83** [F provides a stage direction: "Killes
him"]   **102–110** [Q1; not in F]   **102 s.p. Second Servant** Seruant [and called
"1 Ser" at l. 106 in Q1]   **103, 109 s.p. Third Servant** 2 Seruant [Q1]
107 roguish [Q2; not in Q1]   **110 s.d. Exeunt** Exit

4.1. 41 Then . . . gone Get thee away   **57–62 Five . . . master** [Q1; not in F]
60 Flibbertigibbet [eds.] Stiberdigebit [Q]   **60–61 mopping and mowing**
[eds.] Mobing, & Mohing [Q]

4.2. s.d. Bastard Bastard, and Steward   **2 s.d. Steward** [Q1; placed at beginning in F]   **30 whistling** whistle   **32–51 I fear . . . deep** [Q1; not in F]   **33 its**
[eds.] ith [Q1]   **48 these** [eds.] this [Q1]   **54–60 that . . . so** [Q1; not
in F]   **58 to threat** thereat [Q1]   **61 shows** seemes   **63–69, 70** [Q1; not
in F]   **76 threat** threat   **80 justicers** [Q1 corrected] Iustices

4.3. 1–57 [scene omitted in F]   **11 sir** [eds.] say [Q1]   **16 strove** [eds.] streme [Q1]   **20 seemed** [eds.] seeme [Q1]   **22 dropped. In** dropt in   **32 then** her, then   **44 benediction, turned her** benediction turnd her,   **57 s.d. Exeunt** [eds.] Exit [Q1]

4.4 [F reads "Scena Tertia"]   **s.d. Doctor** Gentlemen   **3 fumiter** [eds.] femiter [Q1] Fenitar [F]   **6 century** Centery   **11 s.p. Doctor** Gent   **18 distress** desires   **28 right** Rite

4.5 [F reads "Scena Quarta"]   **23 Something** Some things   **27 oeillades** [eds.] Eliads   **41 meet him** meet

4.6 [F reads "Scena Quinta"]   **17 walk** walk'd   **57 summit** Somnet   **66–67 strangeness. / Upon . . . cliff what** [eds.] strangenesse, / Vpon . . . Cliffe. What   **71 enridgèd** enraged   **83 coining** crying   **97 white** the white   **161 thine** thy   **164 Through** Thorough   **small** great   **165 Plate sin** [eds.] Place sinnes   **197 Ay . . . dust** [Q1; not in F]   **205 one** a   **218 s.d. Exit** [after "moved on" in l. 218 in F]   **235 Durst** Dar'st   **238 'cagion** 'casion   **269 done if . . . conqueror. Then** [eds.] done. If . . . Conqueror then   **275 indistinguished** indinguish'd   **288 s.d. Drum afar off** [after l. 286 in F]

4.7. 13 s.p. Doctor Gent [also at ll. 18, 44, 52, 82]   **24 s.p. Doctor** [Q1; not in F]   **25 doubt not** doubt   **25–26 Cordelia. Very . . . there** [Q1; not in F]   **33 warring** iarring   **34–37 To stand . . . helm** [Q1; not in F]   **50 When** where   **60 No, sir** [Q1; not in F]   **83–84 and . . . lost** [Q1; not in F]   **91–103** [Q1; not in F]

5.1. 12–14 [Q1; not in F]   **18 me not** not   **19–20** [Q1; not in F]   **24–29 Where . . . nobly** [Q1; not in F]   **35** [Q1; not in F]   **41 s.d. Exeunt . . . armies** [at l. 39 in F]   **48 love** loues

5.3. 39–40 [Q1; not in F]   **49 and appointed guard** [Q1 corrected; not in F]   **56–61 At . . . place** [Q1; not in F]   **57 We** [Q1 corrected] mee [Q1 uncorrected]   **59 sharpness** [Q1 corrected] sharpes [Q1 uncorrected]   **72 s.p. Goneril** Alb   **85 attaint** arrest   **86 sister** Sisters   **87 bar** [eds.] bare   **100 he is** hes   **105 Edmund. A herald, ho, a herald** [Q1; not in F]   **106 s.p. Albany** [not in F]   **112, 118** [Q1; not in F]   **132 the** my priuiledge, The   **135 Despite** Despise   **151 scarcely** scarely   **153 s.d. Fight** [eds.] Fights   **158 stopple** stop   **163 s.p. Goneril** Bast   **163 s.d. Exit** [at l. 162 after "for 't" in F]   **208–225 This . . . slave** [Q1; not in F]   **217 him** [eds.] me [Q1]   **241 s.d.** [at l. 234 in F; F reads "Gonerill"]   **262 you** your   **280 s.p. Captain** Gent   **282 them** him   **294 You are** [eds.] Your are [F] You'r [Q1]   **299 s.d.** [after "to him" in l. 299 in F]

The above textual notes list all instances in which material not in F is included from Q1. To enable the reader to compare further the F and Q1 texts, a list is here provided of material not in Q1 that is to be found in F. There are some 100 lines in all.

1.1. 40–45 while . . . now   49–50 Since . . . state   64–65 and . . . rivers   83–85 to whose . . . interested   88–89 LEAR Nothing? **CORDELIA** Nothing   **165 ALBANY, CORNWALL.** Dear sir, forbear.

1.2. 112–117 This . . . graves   **169–175** I pray . . . brother

1.4. 260 ALBANY Pray . . . patient   **273** Of . . . you   **321–333** This . . . unfitness

2.4. 6 KENT No, my lord   **21** KENT By Juno . . . ay   **45–54** FOOL Winter's . . . year
96–97 GLOUCESTER Well . . . man   **101–102** Are they . . . Fiery? The   **139–144** LEAR
Say . . . blame   **298–299** CORNWALL Whither . . . horse

3.1. 22–29 Who . . . furnishings

3.2. 79–96 FOOL This . . . time. Exit

3.4. 17–18 In . . . endure   **26–27** In . . . sleep   **37–38** Fathom . . . Tom

3.6. 12–14 FOOL No . . . him   **85** FOOL And . . . noon

4.1. 6–9 Welcome . . . blasts

4.2. 26 O, the . . . man

4.6. 165–170 Plate . . . lips

5.2 11 GLOUCESTER And . . . too

5.3. 78 Dispose . . . thine   **91** GONERIL. An interlude   **147** What . . . delay   **226** ALBANY
Speak, man   **316–317** Do you . . . look there

Shakespeare's Sources

The story of Lear goes back into ancient legend. The motif of two wicked sisters and a virtuous youngest sister reminds us of Cinderella. Lear himself appears to come from Celtic mythology. Geoffrey of Monmouth, a Welshman in close contact with Celtic legend, included a Lear or Leir as one of the pseudo-historical kings in his *Historia Regum Britanniae* (c. 1136). This fanciful mixture of history and legend traces a supposed line of descent from Brut, great-grandson of Aeneas of Troy, through Locrine, Bladud, Leir, Gorboduc, Ferrex and Porrex, Lud, Cymbeline, Bonduca, Vortigern, Arthur, to the historical kings of England. The Tudor monarchs made much of their purported claim to such an ancient dynasty, and in Shakespeare's day this mythology had a quasi-official status demanding a certain reverential suspension of disbelief.

King Leir, according to Geoffrey, is the father of three daughters, Gonorilla, Regan, and Cordeilla, among whom he intends to divide his kingdom. To determine who deserves most, he asks them who loves him most. The two eldest sisters protest undying devotion; but Cordeilla, perceiving how the others flatter and deceive him, renounces hyperbole and promises only to love him as a daughter should love a father. Furious, the King denies Cordeilla her third of the kingdom but permits her to marry Aganippus, King of the Franks, without dowry. Thereafter Leir bestows his two eldest daughters on the Dukes of Albania and Cornubia (Albany and Cornwall), together with half the island during his lifetime and the possession of the remainder after his death. In due course his two sons-in-law rebel against Leir and seize his power. Thereafter Maglaunus, Duke of Albania, agrees to maintain Leir with sixty retainers, but after two years of chafing at this arrangement Gonorilla insists that the number be reduced to thirty. Angrily the King goes to Henvin, Duke of Cornubia, where all goes well for a time; within a year, however, Regan demands that Leir reduce his retinue to five knights. When Gonorilla refuses to take him back with more than one retainer, Leir crosses into France and is generously received by Cordeilla and Aganippus. An invasion restores Leir to his throne. Three years later he and Aganippus die, after which Cordeilla rules successfully for five years until overthrown by the sons of Maglaunus and Henvin. In prison she commits suicide.

This story, as part of England's mythic genealogy, was repeated in various Tudor versions such as *The First Part of the Mirror for Magistrates* (1574), William Warner's *Albion's England* (1586), and Raphael Holinshed's *Chronicles* (second edition, 1587; see the first of the following selections). Warner refers to the King's sons-in-law as "the Prince of Albany" and "the Cornish prince"; Holinshed refers to them as "the Duke of Albania" and "the Duke of Cornwall," but reports that it is Cornwall who marries the eldest daughter Gonorilla. *The Mirror*, closer to Shakespeare in these details, speaks of "Gonerell" as married to "Albany" and of "Cordila" as married to "the King of France." Edmund Spenser's *The Faerie Queene* (2.10.27–32) reports that "Cordeill" or "Cordelia" ends her life by hanging herself. Other retellings appear in Gerard Legh's *Accidence of Armory* and William Camden's *Remains*. All of these accounts leave the story virtually unchanged.

Shakespeare's immediate source for *King Lear* was an old play called *The True Chronicle History of King Leir*. It was published in 1605 but plainly is much earlier in style. The Stationers' Register, the official record of the London Company of Stationers (booksellers and printers), for May 14, 1594, lists "A booke called the Tragecall historie of kinge Leir and his Three Daughters &c.," and a short time earlier Philip Henslowe's *Diary* records the performance of a "Kinge Leare" at the Rose Theatre on April 6 and 8, 1594. The actors were either the Queen's or the Earl of Sussex's men (two acting companies), though probably the Queen's. The play may have been written as early as 1588. George Peele, Robert Greene, Thomas Lodge, and Thomas Kyd have all been suggested as possible authors. Shakespeare probably knew the play before its publication in 1605.

This play of *Leir* ends happily, with the restoration of Leir to his throne. Essentially the play is a legendary history with a strong element of romance. (Some similarities and differences between the anonymous play and Shakespeare's *King Lear* can be seen in the second of the following selections, containing the first three scenes.) The two wicked sisters are warned of the King's plans for dividing his kingdom by an obsequious courtier named Skalliger (cf. Oswald). It is Skalliger, in fact, who proposes the idea of apportioning the kingdom in accord with the lovingness of the daughters' responses. Cordella receives the ineffectual support of an honest courtier, Perillus (cf. Kent), but is disinherited by her angry father. In subsequent scenes not included in this selection, Cordella, trusting herself to God's mercy and setting forth alone to live by her own labor, is found by the Gallian King and his bluff companion Mumford, who have come to England disguised as palmers to see if the English King's daughters are as beautiful as reported. The King hears Cordella's sad story, falls in love with her, and woos her (still wearing his disguise) in the name of the Gallian King. When she virtuously suggests the palmer woo for himself, he throws off his disguise and marries her forthwith.

Meanwhile the other sons-in-law, Cornwall and Cambria (cf. Albany), draw lots for their shares of the kingdom. Leir announces that he will sojourn with Cornwall and Gonorill first. Cornwall treats the King with genuine solicitude, but Gonorill, abetted by Skalliger, tauntingly drives her father away. The King acknowledges to his loyal companion Perillus that he has wronged Cordella. Regan, who rules her mild husband as she pleases, receives the King with seeming tenderness but secretly hires an assassin to end his life. (Gonorill is partner in this plot.) The suborned agent, frightened into remorse by a providentially sent thunderstorm, shows his intended victim the letter ordering the assassination.

The Gallian King and Cordella, who have previously sent ambassadors to Leir urging him to come to France, now decide to journey with Mumford into Britain disguised as countryfolk. Before they can do so, however, Leir and Perillus arrive in France, in mariners' garb, where they encounter Cordella and her party dressed as countryfolk. Cordella recognizes Leir's voice, and father and daughter are tearfully reunited. The Gallian King invades England and restores Leir to his throne.

Shakespeare has changed much in the narrative of his source. He discards not only the happy ending but the attempted assassination and the numerous romancelike uses of disguise (although Tom o' Bedlam, in an added plot, repeatedly uses disguise). Shakespeare eliminates the humorous Mumford and replaces Perillus with both Kent and the Fool. He turns Cornwall into a villain and Albany into a belated champion of justice. He creates the storm scene out of a mere suggestion of such an event, serving a very different purpose, in his source.

Most of all, he adds the parallel plot of Gloucester, Edgar, and Edmund. Here Shakespeare derived some of his material from Sir Philip Sidney's *Arcadia* (1590). In Book 2, chapter 10, of this greatest of all Elizabethan prose romances, presented in the third of the following selections, the two heroes Pyrocles and Musidorus encounter a son leading his blind old father. The old man tells his pitiful tale. He is the deposed King of Paphlagonia, father of a bastard son named Plexirtus who, he now bitterly realizes, turned the King against his true son Leonatus—the very son who is now his guide and guardian. The true son, having managed to escape his father's order of execution, has been forced to live poorly as a soldier, while the bastard son has proceeded to usurp his father's throne. In his wretchedness, the King has been succored by his forgiving true son and has been prevented from casting himself off the top of a hill. At the conclusion of this narrative, the villain Plexirtus arrives and attacks Leonatus; reinforcements arrive on both sides, but eventually Plexirtus is driven off, enabling the King to return to his court and bestow the crown on Leonatus. The old King thereupon dies, his heart having been stretched beyond the limits of endurance.

Other parts of the *Arcadia* may have given Shakespeare further suggestions; for example, the disguises adopted by Kent and Edgar are like those of Zelmane and Pyrocles in Sidney's prose work, and Albany's speeches about anarchy and the monstrosity that results from assaults on the rule of law recall one of Sidney's deepest concerns. Edmund is decidedly indebted to the allegorical Vice figure of the late medieval morality play tradition. For Tom o' Bedlam's mad language, Shakespeare consulted Samuel Harsnett's *Decla-*

ration of Egregious Popish Impostures, 1603. (See Kenneth Muir's Arden edition of *King Lear*, pp. 253–256, for an extensive comparison.)

The First and Second Volumes
of Chronicles (1587 edition)
Compiled by Raphael Holinshed

VOLUME 1, THE HISTORY OF ENGLAND,
THE SECOND BOOK: LEIR, THE TENTH RULER

Leir, the son of Bladud, was admitted ruler over the Britons in the year of the world 3105, at what time Joas reigned in Judah. This Leir was a prince of right noble demeanor, governing his land and subjects in great wealth. He made the town of Caerleir, now called Leicester, which standeth upon the river of Soar. It is written that he had by his wife three daughters, without other issue, whose names were Gonorilla, Regan, and Cordeilla, which daughters he greatly loved, but specially Cordeilla, the youngest, far above the two elder. When this Leir therefore was come to great years and began to wax unwieldy through age, he thought to understand the affections of his daughters towards him and prefer[1] her whom he best loved to the succession over the kingdom. Whereupon he first asked Gonorilla, the eldest, how well she loved him; who, calling her gods to record, protested that she loved him more than her own life, which by right and reason should be most dear unto her. With which answer the father, being well pleased, turned to the second and demanded of her how well she loved him; who answered, confirming her sayings with great oaths, that she loved him more than tongue could express and far above all other creatures of the world.

Then called he his youngest daughter Cordeilla before him and asked of her what account she made of him, unto whom she made this answer as followeth: "Knowing the great love and fatherly zeal that you have always borne towards me, for the which I may not answer you otherwise

1 **prefer** advance

than[2] I think and as my conscience leadeth me, I protest unto you that I have loved you ever and will continually while I live love you as my natural father. And if you would more understand of the love that I bear you, ascertain[3] yourself that so much as you have, so much you are worth, and so much I love you and no more." The father, being nothing content with this answer, married his two eldest daughters, the one unto Henninus, the Duke of Cornwall, and the other unto Maglanus, the Duke of Albania, betwixt whom he willed and ordained that his land should be divided after his death, and the one half thereof immediately should be assigned to them in hand; but for the third daughter, Cordeilla, he reserved nothing.

Nevertheless it fortuned that one of the princes of Gallia (which now is called France), whose name was Aganippus, hearing of the beauty, womanhood, and good conditions of the said Cordeilla, desired to have her in marriage and sent over to her father requiring[4] that he might have her to wife; to whom answer was made that he might have his daughter, but as for any dower he could have none, for all was promised and assured to her other sisters already. Aganippus, notwithstanding this answer of denial to receive anything by way of dower with Cordeilla, took her to wife, only moved thereto (I say) for respect of her person and amiable virtues. This Aganippus was one of the twelve kings that ruled Gallia in those days, as in the British history it is recorded. But to proceed.

After that[5] Leir was fallen into age, the two dukes that had married his two eldest daughters, thinking it long ere the government of the land did come to their hands, arose against him in armor and reft[6] from him the governance of the land upon conditions to be continued for term of life, by the which he was put to his portion, that is, to live after a rate assigned to him for the maintenance of his estate, which in process of time was diminished as well by Maglanus as by Henninus. But the greatest grief that Leir took was to see the unkindness[7] of his daughters, which[8] seemed to think that all was too much which their father

---

2 than than as   **3 ascertain** assure   **4 requiring** requesting   **5 After that** after   **6 reft** stripped, took   **7 unkindness** (with meaning also of "unnaturalness")   **8 which** who

had, the same being never so little; insomuch that, going from the one to the other, he was brought to that misery that scarcely they would allow him one servant to wait upon him.

In the end, such was the unkindness or (as I may say) the unnaturalness which he found in his two daughters, notwithstanding their fair and pleasant words uttered in time past, that, being constrained of necessity, he fled the land and sailed into Gallia, there to seek some comfort of his youngest daughter Cordeilla whom beforetime he hated. The Lady Cordeilla, hearing that he was arrived in poor estate, she first sent to him privily[9] a certain sum of money to apparel himself withal[10] and to retain a certain number of servants that might attend upon him in honorable wise, as appertained to the estate which he had borne. And then, so accompanied,[11] she appointed him[12] to come to the court, which he did, and was so joyfully, honorably, and lovingly received, both by his son-in-law Aganippus and also by his daughter Cordeilla, that his heart was greatly comforted, for he was no less honored than if he had been king of the whole country himself.

Now, when he had informed his son-in-law and his daughter in what sort he had been used by his other daughters, Aganippus caused a mighty army to be put in a readiness, and likewise a great navy of ships to be rigged, to pass over into Britain with Leir, his father-in-law, to see him again restored to his kingdom. It was accorded that Cordeilla should also go with him to take possession of the land, the which he promised to leave unto her as the rightful inheritor after his decease, notwithstanding any former grant made to her sisters or to their husbands in any manner of wise.

Hereupon, when this army and navy of ships were ready, Leir and his daughter Cordeilla with her husband took the sea and, arriving in Britain, fought with their enemies and discomfited[13] them in battle, in the which Maglanus and Henninus were slain. And then was Leir restored to his kingdom, which he ruled after this by the space of two

---

9 privily secretly　**10 withal** with　**11 so accompanied** he being so accompanied　**12 appointed him** arranged for him　**13 discomfited** overthrew

years, and then died, forty years after he first began to reign. His body was buried at Leicester, in a vault under the channel of the river of Soar, beneath the town.

THE GUNARCHY[14] OF QUEEN CORDEILLA

Cordeilla, the youngest daughter of Leir, was admitted Queen and supreme Governess of Britain in the year of the world 3155, before the building of Rome 54,[15] Uzia then reigning in Judah and Jeroboam over Israel. This Cordeilla, after her father's decease, ruled the land of Britain right worthily during the space of five years, in which meantime her husband died; and then, about the end of those five years, her two nephews Margan and Cunedag, sons to her aforesaid sisters, disdaining to be under the government of a woman, levied war against her and destroyed a great part of the land, and finally took her prisoner and laid her fast in ward,[16] wherewith she took such grief, being a woman of a manly courage, and despairing to recover liberty, there she slew herself, when she had reigned (as before is mentioned) the term of five years.

The second edition of Raphael Holinshed's *Chronicles* was published in 1587. This selection is based on that edition, Volume 1, The History of England, folios 12–13.

14 Gunarchy government by a woman ruler   **15 3155, 54** (The beginning of Cordeilla's reign is reckoned to be 3155 years after God's creation of the world as recorded in Genesis and 54 years before the building of Rome, or c. 822–817 B.C. *Jeroboam* did actually reign over Israel c. 931.) **16 ward** prison

The True Chronicle History of King Leir and His Three Daughters

[*Dramatis Personae*

LEIR, *King of Brittany*
GONORILL,
RAGAN,   } *daughters of Leir*
CORDELLA,
KING OF GALLIA
KING OF CORNWALL
KING OF CAMBRIA
PERILLUS, *a nobleman*
MUMFORD, *a knight*
SKALLIGER, *a courtier*
A LORD
A MESSENGER
THE GALLIAN AMBASSADOR

Nobles, Mariners, Captains, Watchmen, Attendants, Soldiers,
    etc.

SCENE: *Brittany and Gallia*]

1.1   *Enter King Leir and Nobles.*

LEIR
    Thus to our grief the obsequies performed   1
    Of our too late deceased and dearest queen,   2
    Whose soul, I hope, possessed of heavenly joys
    Doth ride in triumph 'mongst the cherubins,
    Let us request your grave advice, my lords,
    For the disposing of our princely daughters,   6
    For whom our care is specially employed,
    As nature bindeth, to advance their states   8
    In royal marriage with some princely mates.

1.1. Location: The court of Britain.
1 performed having been performed   **2 our** i.e., my. (The royal plural.)   **too late** all too recently   **6 For** about   **8 bindeth** ties with obligations of family feeling.   **states** estates

For, wanting now their mother's good advice, 10
Under whose government they have received
A perfect pattern of a virtuous life,
Left as it were a ship without a stern 13
Or silly sheep without a pastor's care, 14
Although ourselves do dearly tender them, 15
Yet are we ignorant of their affairs.
For fathers best do know to govern sons,
But daughters' steps the mother's counsel turns. 18
A son we want for to succeed our crown, 19
And course of time hath cancellèd the date 20
Of further issue from our withered loins; 21
One foot already hangeth in the grave,
And age hath made deep furrows in my face.
The world of me, I of the world, am weary,
And I would fain resign these earthly cares 25
And think upon the welfare of my soul,
Which by no better means may be effected
Than by resigning up the crown from me
In equal dowry to my daughters three.

SKALLIGER

A worthy care, my liege, which well declares
The zeal you bare unto our quondam queen. 31
And since Your Grace hath licensed me to speak,
I censure thus: Your Majesty, knowing well 33
What several suitors your princely daughters have, 34
To make them each a jointure, more or less 35
As is their worth, to them that love profess.

LEIR

No more nor less, but even all alike
My zeal is fixed, all fashioned in one mold.
Wherefore unpartial shall my censure be? 39
Both old and young shall have alike for me.

A NOBLE

My gracious lord, I heartily do wish

---

10 wanting lacking **13 stern** rudder and helm **14 silly** innocent
15 tender cherish **18 turns** directs **19 want for to succeed** lack to
inherit **20 date** season, period of time **21 further issue** any more
children **25 fain** gladly **31 bare** bore. **quondam** former **33 censure**
pronounce judgment **33–35 Your Majesty . . . To make** that Your
Majesty . . . make **34 several** various **35 jointure** dowry; property for
the joint use of husband and wife **39 censure** judgment

That God had lent you an heir indubitate   42
Which might have set upon your royal throne
When fates should loose the prison of your life,   44
By whose succession all this doubt might cease,
And, as by you, by him we might have peace.
But after-wishes ever come too late,
And nothing can revoke the course of fate.
Wherefore, my liege, my censure deems it best
To match them with some of your neighbor kings
Bordering within the bounds of Albion,   51
By whose united friendship this our state
May be protected 'gainst all foreign hate.

LEIR

Herein, my lords, your wishes sort with mine,   54
And mine, I hope, do sort with heavenly powers.
For at this instant two near neighboring kings,
Of Cornwall and of Cambria, motion love   57
To my two daughters, Gonorill and Ragan.
My youngest daughter, fair Cordella, vows
No liking to a monarch unless love allows.
She is solicited by divers peers,
But none of them her partial fancy hears.   62
Yet if my policy may her beguile,   63
I'll match her to some king within this isle,
And so establish such a perfect peace
As fortune's force shall ne'er prevail to cease.   66

PERILLUS

Of us and ours, your gracious care, my lord,   67
Deserves an everlasting memory,   68
To be enrolled in chronicles of fame
By never-dying perpetuity.   70
Yet to become so provident a prince,
Lose not the title of a loving father.

---

42 indubitate undoubted, certain   **44 When . . . life** i.e., when the Fates, the three sisters of destiny, should set loose your soul from the prison of your body   **51 Albion** England   **54 sort** accord   **57 Cambria** i.e., the mountainous area of Wales. (Shakespeare's equivalent character is the Duke of Albany, in Scotland.)   **motion** propose   **62 partial fancy** inclination in love   **63 policy may her beguile** plan can win her over   **66 As** that.   **to cease** i.e., to end this peace   **67–68 Of . . . memory** your gracious care of your kingdom, my lord, deserves from us and our posterity an everlasting remembrance   **70 By** i.e., in

Do not force love where fancy cannot dwell,   73
Lest streams, being stopped, above the banks do swell.   74

LEIR

I am resolved, and even now my mind
Doth meditate a sudden stratagem
To try which of my daughters loves me best,
Which, till I know, I cannot be in rest.
This granted, when they jointly shall contend   79
Each to exceed the other in their love,
Then at the vantage will I take Cordella: 81
Even as she doth protest she loves me best,
I'll say, "Then, daughter, grant me one request.
To show thou lovest me as thy sisters do,
Accept a husband, whom myself will woo."   85
This said, she cannot well deny my suit,
Although, poor soul, her senses will be mute.   87
Then will I triumph in my policy
And match her with a king of Brittany.

SKALLIGER [*Aside*]

I'll to them before and bewray your secrecy.   90
                    [*Exeunt all but Perillus.*]

PERILLUS

Thus fathers think their children to beguile,
And oftentimes themselves do first repent
When heavenly powers do frustrate their intent. *Exit.*

❧

1.2   *Enter Gonorill and Ragan.*

GONORILL

I marvel, Ragan, how you can endure
To see that proud pert peat, our youngest sister,   2
So slightly to account of us, her elders,   3

73 fancy love   **74 stopped** dammed up   **79 This granted** this having
been undertaken   **81 at the vantage** with this advantage or superior
position.   **take** (As in a game of chess.)   **85 woo** solicit for marriage
(with Cordella)   **87 her senses . . . mute** i.e., she will be stricken silent
90 I'll . . . secrecy i.e., I'll go first to Gonorill and Ragan and reveal your
confidential plan

1.2. Location: The court of Britain.
2 peat spoiled girl   **3 account of** esteem, value

As if we were no better than herself!
We cannot have a quaint device so soon,   5
Or new-made fashion of our choice invention,   6
But, if she like it, she will have the same,
Or study newer to exceed us both.   8
Besides, she is so nice and so demure,   9
So sober, courteous, modest, and precise,   10
That all the court hath work enough to do
To talk how she exceedeth me and you.

RAGAN
What should I do? Would it were in my power
To find a cure for this contagious ill!
Some desperate medicine must be soon applied
To dim the glory of her mounting fame;
Else, ere 't be long, she'll have both prick and praise,   17
And we must be set by for working days.   18
Do you not see what several choice of suitors   19
She daily hath, and of the best degree?
Say, amongst all, she hap to fancy one   21
And have a husband whenas we have none.   22
Why, then, by right to her we must give place,
Though it be ne'er so much to our disgrace.

GONORILL
By my virginity, rather than she shall have
A husband before me,
I'll marry one or other in his shirt!   27
And yet I have made half a grant already
Of my good will unto the King of Cornwall.

RAGAN   Swear not so deeply, sister. Here cometh my lord
Skalliger.
Something his hasty coming doth import.   32

    Enter Skalliger.

---

5 We . . . soon we no sooner have something (clothing, jewelry, etc.) that
is artistically or ingeniously devised   **6 of our choice invention** of our
own well-chosen devising   **8 study newer** i.e., apply her mind to divis-
ing newer fashions   **9 nice** fastidious, refined   **10 precise** scrupulous
17 prick and praise success and its acknowledgment   **18 set by . . . days**
i.e., treated as ordinary creatures for everyday use   **19 several** various
21 Say suppose.   **hap to fancy** happen to love   **22 whenas** when,
whereas   **27 in his shirt** i.e., half unready, in great haste   **32 import**
signify

SKALLIGER
   Sweet princesses, I am glad I met you here so luckily,
   Having good news which doth concern you both
   And craveth speedy expedition.   35

RAGAN
   For God's sake, tell us what it is, my lord.
   I am with child until you utter it.   37

SKALLIGER
   Madam, to save your longing, this it is:
   Your father in great secrecy today
   Told me he means to marry you out of hand   40
   Unto the noble Prince of Cambria;
   [*To Gonorill*] You, madam, to the King of Cornwall's
     Grace.
   Your younger sister he would fain bestow
   Upon the rich King of Hibernia,   44
   But that he doubts she hardly will consent,
   For hitherto she ne'er could fancy him.
   If she do yield, why then, between you three
   He will divide his kingdom for your dowries.
   But yet there is further mystery,
   Which, so you will conceal, I will disclose.   50

GONORILL
   Whate'er thou speak'st to us, kind Skalliger,
   Think that thou speak'st it only to thyself.

SKALLIGER
   He earnestly desireth for to know   53
   Which of you three do bear most love to him,
   And on your loves he so extremely dotes
   As never any did, I think, before.
   He presently doth mean to send for you   57
   To be resolved of this tormenting doubt;
   And look whose answer pleaseth him the best,   59
   They shall have most unto their marriages.

RAGAN
   O, that I had some pleasing mermaid's voice
   For to enchant his senseless senses with!   62

35 expedition speed   **37 with child** i.e., eager, yearning (to know)
40 out of hand at once   **44 Hibernia** Ireland   **50 so** provided   **53 for
to know** to know   **57 presently** immediately   **59 look whose answer**
whoever it is whose answer   **62 For to** to.   **senseless** incapable of
sensation (owing to old age)

SKALLIGER

For he supposeth that Cordella will,
Striving to go beyond you in her love,
Promise to do whatever he desires.
Then will he straight enjoin her for his sake   66
The Hibernian King in marriage for to take.
This is the sum of all I have to say,
Which being done, I humbly take my leave,
Not doubting but your wisdoms will foresee
What course will best unto your good agree.   71

GONORILL

Thanks, gentle Skalliger. Thy kindness, undeserved,
Shall not be unrequited if we live.   *Exit Skalliger.*

RAGAN

Now have we fit occasion offered us
To be revenged upon her unperceived.

GONORILL

Nay, our revenge we will inflict on her
Shall be accounted piety in us.
I will so flatter with my doting father   78
As he was ne'er so flattered in his life.
Nay, I will say that if it be his pleasure
To match me to a beggar, I will yield,
Forwhy I know whatever I do say   82
He means to match me with the Cornwall King.

RAGAN

I'll say the like, for I am well assured,
Whate'er I say to please the old man's mind,
Who dotes as if he were a child again,
I shall enjoy the noble Cambrian prince.
Only to feed his humor will suffice   88
To say I am content with anyone
Whom he'll appoint me; this will please him more
Than e'er Apollo's music pleasèd Jove.

GONORILL

I smile to think in what a woeful plight

---

66 straight at once   **71 agree** serve   **78 flatter with** speak flatteringly
to, fawn upon   **82 Forwhy** because.   **whatever I do say** i.e., whatever I
say of a flattering kind, however I vary my outrageous flattery. (Compare Ragan in l. 85.)   **88 Only . . . suffice** it will suffice to feed his
whimsical mood

Cordella will be when we answer thus,
For she will rather die than give consent
To join in marriage with the Irish King.
So will our father think she loveth him not,
Because she will not grant to his desire,
Which we will aggravate in such bitter terms
That he will soon convert his love to hate.
For he, you know, is always in extremes.

RAGAN
Not all the world could lay a better plot.
I long till it be put in practice.   *Exeunt.*

❖

1.3   *Enter Leir and Perillus.*

LEIR   Perillus, go seek my daughters.
Will them immediately come and speak with me.
PERILLUS   I will, my gracious lord.   *Exit.*
LEIR
O, what a combat feels my panting heart
Twixt children's love and care of commonweal!
How dear my daughters are unto my soul
None knows but he that knows my thoughts and secret
    deeds.
Ah, little do they know the dear regard
Wherein I hold their future state to come!
When they securely sleep on beds of down,
These aged eyes do watch for their behalf.   11
While they like wantons sport in youthful toys,   12
This throbbing heart is pierced with dire annoys.   13
As doth the sun exceed the smallest star,
So much the father's love exceeds the child's.
Yet my complaints are causeless, for the world
Affords not children more conformable.   17
And yet methinks my mind presageth still
I know not what; and yet I fear some ill.

1.3. Location: The court of Britain.
11 **watch for** stay awake on   12 **While . . . toys** while they, like pam-
pered children, frolic in idle youthful pastimes   13 **annoys** vexations
17 **conformable** tractable, submissive

Enter Perillus, with the three daughters.

Well, here my daughters come. I have found out
A present means to rid me of this doubt.

GONORILL

Our royal lord and father, in all duty
We come to know the tenor of your will,
Why you so hastily have sent for us.

LEIR

Dear Gonorill, kind Ragan, sweet Cordella,
Ye flourishing branches of a kingly stock
Sprung from a tree that once did flourish green,
Whose blossoms now are nipped with winter's frost,
And pale grim Death doth wait upon my steps
And summons me unto his next assizes.   30
Therefore, dear daughters, as ye tender the safety
Of him that was the cause of your first being,
Resolve a doubt which much molests my mind:
Which of you three to me would prove most kind,
Which loves me most, and which at my request
Will soonest yield unto their father's hest.   36

GONORILL

I hope, my gracious father makes no doubt
Of any of his daughters' love to him.
Yet for my part, to show my zeal to you,
Which cannot be in windy words rehearsed,   40
I prize my love to you at such a rate
I think my life inferior to my love.
Should you enjoin me for to tie a millstone
About my neck and leap into the sea,
At your command I willingly would do it.
Yea, for to do you good I would ascend
The highest turret in all Brittany
And from the top leap headlong to the ground.
Nay, more, should you appoint me for to marry   49
The meanest vassal in the spacious world,   50
Without reply I would accomplish it.
In brief, command whatever you desire,
And, if I fail, no favor I require.

---

30 assizes court session   **36 hest** behest   **40 rehearsed** recited, told
49 appoint me arrange for me   **50 meanest** most lowly born

LEIR
  O, how thy words revive my dying soul!
CORDELLA [*Aside*]
  O, how I do abhor this flattery!
LEIR
  But what saith Ragan to her father's will?
RAGAN
  O, that my simple utterance could suffice
  To tell the true intention of my heart,
  Which burns in zeal of duty to Your Grace
  And never can be quenched but by desire   60
  To show the same in outward forwardness!   61
  O, that there were some other maid that durst
  But make a challenge of her love with me!
  I'd make her soon confess she never loved
  Her father half so well as I do you.
  Ay, then my deeds should prove in plainer case
  How much my zeal aboundeth to Your Grace.
  But for them all, let this one mean suffice   68
  To ratify my love before your eyes:
  I have right noble suitors to my love,
  No worse than kings, and happily I love one;
  Yet, would you have me make my choice anew,
  I'd bridle fancy and be ruled by you.
LEIR
  Did never Philomel sing so sweet a note.   74
CORDELLA [*Aside*]
  Did never flatterer tell so false a tale.
LEIR
  Speak now, Cordella. Make my joys at full
  And drop down nectar from thy honey lips.
CORDELLA
  I cannot paint my duty forth in words.
  I hope my deeds shall make report for me.
  But look what love the child doth owe the father,   80
  The same to you I bear, my gracious lord.

60–61 And never . . . forwardness and can be quenched only by continual striving to display my ardent love in openly displayed zeal and
attentiveness **68 for them all** to stand for all my zealous deeds. **let
this one mean** let this humble and insufficient one **74 Philomel** the
nightingale **80 look what** whatever

GONORILL

    Here is an answer answerless indeed.
    Were you my daughter, I should scarcely brook it.   83

RAGAN

    Dost thou not blush, proud peacock as thou art,
    To make our father such a slight reply?

LEIR

    Why how now, minion, are you grown so proud?
    Doth our dear love make you thus peremptory?
    What, is your love become so small to us
    As that you scorn to tell us what it is?
    Do you love us as every child doth love
    Their father? True indeed, as some
    Who by disobedience short their father's days,   92
    And so would you. Some are so father-sick
    That they make means to rid them from the world,
    And so would you. Some are indifferent
    Whether their aged parents live or die,
    And so are you. But didst thou know, proud girl,
    What care I had to foster thee to this,
    Ah, then thou wouldst say as thy sisters do.
    Our life is less than love we owe to you.   100

CORDELLA

    Dear Father, do not so mistake my words
    Nor my plain meaning be misconstrued.   102
    My tongue was never used to flattery.

GONORILL

    You were not best say I flatter. If you do,   104
    My deeds shall show I flatter not with you.   105
    I love my father better than thou canst.

CORDELLA

    The praise were great, spoke from another's mouth;   107
    But it should seem your neighbors dwell far off.   108

---

83 brook endure   **92 short** shorten   **100 Our life . . . to you** i.e., my very life cannot equal the sum of the love I owe to you   **102 Nor** i.e., nor let   **104 You were not best say** you had better not say. (Perhaps the text should read, *You were best not say*.)   **105 I flatter not with you** I do not flatter as you do   **107 The praise . . . mouth** that would be great praise indeed if spoken by another (i.e., by one who could speak sincerely)   **108 But . . . far off** i.e., but it's obvious that you have no near competitors in this business of flattery

RAGAN
   Nay, here is one that will confirm as much   109
   As she hath said, both for myself and her.
   I say thou dost not wish my father's good.

CORDELLA   Dear Father—

LEIR
   Peace, bastard imp, no issue of King Leir!
   I will not hear thee speak one tittle more.   114
   Call not me father, if thou love thy life,
   Nor these thy sisters once presume to name.   116
   Look for no help henceforth from me nor mine;
   Shift as thou wilt and trust unto thyself.   118
   My kingdom will I equally divide
   Twixt thy two sisters to their royal dower,   120
   And will bestow them worthy their deserts.   121
   This done, because thou shalt not have the hope   122
   To have a child's part in the time to come,
   I presently will dispossess myself   124
   And set up these upon my princely throne.

GONORILL
   I ever thought that pride would have a fall.

RAGAN
   Plain-dealing sister, your beauty is so sheen   127
   You need no dowry to make you be a queen.
                   Exeunt Leir, Gonorill, Ragan.

CORDELLA
   Now whither, poor forsaken, shall I go
   When mine own sisters triumph in my woe
   But unto Him which doth protect the just?
   In Him will poor Cordella put her trust.
   These hands shall labor for to get my spending,   133
   And so I'll live until my days have ending.   [*Exit.*]

PERILLUS
   O, how I grieve to see my lord thus fond   135
   To dote so much upon vain flattering words!

---

109 here is one that i.e., I too am one who **114 tittle** bit **116 Nor . . . name** i.e., nor presume to claim a sisterly relationship to Gonorill and Ragan **118 Shift** manage, get on **120 to** as **121 bestow them** i.e., settle them in marriages **122 because** so that **124 presently** at once **127 sheen** fair, beautiful. (Cf. German *schön*.) **133 for to get my spending** to earn my livelihood **135 fond** foolish

Ah, if he but with good advice had weighed   137
The hidden tenor of her humble speech,
Reason to rage should not have given place
Nor poor Cordella suffer such disgrace.   *Exit.*

Text based on *The True Chronicle History of King Leir and His Three Daughters, Gonorill, Ragan, and Cordella. As it hath been divers and sundry times lately acted. London: Printed by Simon Stafford for John Wright. . . . 1605.*

In the following, the departure from the original text appears in boldface; the original reading is in roman.

1.1. 93 s.d. Exit Exeunt

Arcadia (1590)
By Sir Philip Sidney
BOOK 2, CHAPTER 10

The pitiful state and story of the Paphlagonian unkind[1] King and his kind son, first related by the son, then by the blind father.

It was in the kingdom of Galatia, the season being, as in the depth of winter, very cold, and as then suddenly grown to so extreme and foul a storm that never any winter, I think, brought forth a fouler child; so that the princes[2] were even compelled by the hail that the pride[3] of the wind blew into their faces to seek some shrouding place within.[4] A certain hollow rock offering it[5] unto them, they made it their shield

---

137 advice wisdom

1 unkind (With meaning also of "unnatural") **2 the princes** i.e., Pyrocles and Mucidorus, son and nephew of the King of Macedon, gallant knights and close friends, whose shipwreck and subsequent adventures in Arcadia form the main plot of *Arcadia*. (The present story is a digression from the main narrative.) **3 pride** imperiousness **4 shrouding place within** shelter out of the storm **5 it** itself

against the tempest's fury. And so, staying there till the violence thereof was past, they heard the speech of a couple[6] who, not perceiving them (being hid[7] within that rude canopy), held a strange and pitiful disputation, which made them step out,[8] yet in such sort as they might see unseen.

There they perceived an aged man and a young scarcely come to the age of a man, both poorly arrayed, extremely weather-beaten; the old man blind, the young man leading him. And yet through all those miseries, in both these[9] seemed to appear a kind of nobleness not suitable[10] to that affliction. But the first words they heard were these of the old man.

"Well, Leonatus," said he, "since I cannot persuade thee to lead me to that which should end my grief and thy trouble,[11] let me now entreat thee to leave me. Fear not; my misery cannot be greater than it is, and nothing doth become me[12] but misery. Fear not the danger of my blind steps. I cannot fall worse than I am. And do not, I pray thee, do not obstinately continue to infect thee[13] with my wretchedness. But fly, fly from this region only worthy of me."[14]

"Dear Father," answered he, "do not take away from me the only remnant of my happiness! While I have power to do you service, I am not wholly miserable."

"Ah, my son," said he, and with that he groaned as if sorrow strave to break his heart, "how evil fits it me[15] to have such a son, and how much doth thy kindness upbraid my wickedness!"

These doleful speeches and some others to like purpose, well showing they had not been born to the fortune they were in, moved the princes to go out unto them and ask the younger what[16] they were.

"Sirs," answered he with a good grace, and made the more agreeable by a certain noble kind of piteousness, "I see well you are strangers that know not our misery, so well

---

6 a couple i.e., two men   **7 being hid** i.e., the princes being hid   **8 them step out** i.e., the princes leave their shelter somewhat   **9 both these** both of them   **10 suitable** corresponding. (Their noble bearing seemed well above their wretched appearance.)   **11 to that which . . . trouble** i.e., to my suicide   **12 become me** suit me (in my present sad condition)   **13 thee** thyself   **14 only worthy of me** worthy only of (wretched) me   **15 how evil fits it me** i.e., how little do I deserve   **16 what** who

here known that no man dare know but that we must be miserable.[17] Indeed our state is such as though nothing is so needful unto us as pity, yet nothing is more dangerous unto us than to make ourselves so known as may stir pity. But your presence promiseth that cruelty shall not overrun hate.[18] And if it did,[19] in truth our state is sunk below the degree of fear.

"This old man whom I lead was lately rightful prince of this country of Paphlagonia, by the hard-hearted ungratefulness of a son of his deprived[20] not only of his kingdom (whereof no foreign forces were ever able to spoil[21] him) but of his sight, the riches which Nature grants to the poorest creatures. Whereby, and by other his[22] unnatural dealings, he hath been driven to such grief as even now he would have had me to have led him to the top of this rock, thence to cast himself headlong to death. And so would have made me, who received my life of him, to be the worker of his destruction. But, noble gentlemen," said he, "if either of you have a father and feel what dutiful affection is engraffed[23] in a son's heart, let me entreat you to convey this afflicted prince to some place of rest and security. Amongst your worthy acts it shall be none of the least that a king of such might and fame, and so unjustly oppressed, is in any sort by you relieved."

But before they could make him answer, his father began to speak. "Ah, my son," said he, "how evil an historian are you, that leave out the chief knot of all the discourse: my wickedness, my wickedness! And if thou dost it to spare my ears, the only sense now left me proper for knowledge,[24] assure thyself thou dost mistake me. And I take witness of that sun which you see"—with that he cast up his blind eyes as if he would hunt for light—"and wish myself in worse case than I do wish myself, which is as evil as may be, if I speak untruly: that nothing is so welcome to my thoughts as the publishing of my shame.

17 **that no man . . . miserable** i.e., that no one dare inquire about us (as fugitives from justice) other than to know we are wretched 18 **that cruelty . . . hate** i.e., that you will not cruelly turn against us in your hatred of what you must hear 19 **if it did** i.e., even if you did 20 **by . . . deprived** i.e., who, by . . . was deprived 21 **spoil** despoil, plunder 22 **other his** his other, the ungrateful son's other 23 **engraffed** engrafted 24 **proper for knowledge** suited to the acquiring of knowledge

"Therefore know you, gentlemen, to whom from my heart I wish that it may not prove ominous foretoken of misfortune to have met with such a miser[25] as I am, that whatsoever my son (O God, that truth binds me to reproach him with the name of my son!) hath said is true. But besides those truths this also is true: that, having had[26] in lawful marriage, of a mother fit to bear royal children, this son[27] (such one as partly you see and better shall know by my short declaration),[28] and so enjoyed the expectations in the world of him[29] till he was grown to justify their expectations, so as[30] I needed envy no father for the chief comfort of mortality to leave another oneself after me,[31] I was carried[32] by a bastard son of mine (if at least I be bound to believe[33] the words of that base woman my concubine, his mother) first to mislike, then to hate, lastly to destroy, to do my best to destroy, this son I think you think undeserving[34] destruction.

"What ways he used to bring me to it, if I should tell you, I should tediously trouble you with as much poisonous hypocrisy, desperate fraud, smooth malice, hidden ambition, and smiling envy as in any living person could be harbored. But I list it not.[35] No remembrance—no, of naughtiness[36]— delights me but mine own, and methinks the accusing his trains[37] might in some manner excuse my fault, which certainly I loathe to do. But the conclusion is that I gave order to some servants of mine, whom I thought as apt for such charities[38] as myself, to lead him out into a forest and there to kill him.

"But those thieves, better natured to my son than myself,

---

25 miser miserable, wretched person   **26 had** begotten, sired   **27 of a mother . . . son** this son, the child of a mother worthy to bear royal children   **28 better . . . declaration** shall know better soon by my story   **29 and so enjoyed . . . of him** i.e., and took such pleasure in people's high hopes for his success   **30 was grown . . . so as** had grown up justifying everyone's expectations so fully that   **31 for the chief . . . after me** i.e., as to the chief comfort a man has in the face of death, that of leaving an image of himself behind   **32 carried** influenced, swayed   **33 to believe** i.e., to believe that this bastard was mine and not some other man's   **34 I think you think undeserving** whom I believe you must consider undeserving of   **35 list it not** do not wish to do that   **36 no, of naughtiness** no, not of any conceivable wickedness whatsoever   **37 trains** treachery   **38 charities** charitable, loving deeds. (Said with deep irony.)

spared his life, letting him go to learn to live poorly; which he did, giving himself to be[39] a private soldier in a country hereby.[40] But as he was ready to be greatly advanced for some noble pieces of service which he did, he heard news of me—who, drunk in my affection to that unlawful and unnatural son of mine, suffered[41] myself so to be governed by him that all favors and punishments passed by him, all offices and places of importance distributed to his favorites; so that, ere I was aware, I had left myself nothing but the name of a king. Which he shortly weary of too,[42] with many indignities (if anything may be called an indignity[43] which was laid upon me) threw me out of my seat[44] and put out my eyes; and then, proud in his tyranny, let me go, neither imprisoning nor killing me, but rather delighting to make me feel my misery. Misery indeed, if ever there were any! Full of wretchedness, fuller of disgrace, and fullest of guiltiness.

"And as he came to the crown by so unjust means, as unjustly he kept it, by force of stranger[45] soldiers in citadels, the nests of tyranny and murderers of liberty, disarming all his own countrymen, that no man durst show himself a well-willer of mine—to say the truth I think few of them being so, considering my cruel folly to my good son and foolish kindness to my unkind bastard. But if there were any who fell to pity of so great a fall and had yet any sparks of unstained duty left in them towards me, yet durst they not show it, scarcely with giving me alms at their doors—which yet was the only sustenance of my distressed life, nobody daring to show so much charity as to lend me a hand to guide my dark steps.

"Till this son of mine (God knows, worthy of a more virtuous and more fortunate father), forgetting my abominable wrongs, not recking[46] danger, and neglecting the present good way he was in doing himself good, came hither to do this kind office you see him perform towards me, to my un-

---

39 giving himself to be enlisting as   **40 hereby** nearby   **41 suffered** allowed   **42 Which he . . . too** i.e., and he, the bastard, soon impatient with my having even that   **43 may . . . an indignity** (The old King considers himself deserving of every punishment, so that no affliction laid on him can properly be called an *indignity* or undeserved blow.)   **44 seat** throne   **45 stranger** foreign (and mercenary)   **46 recking** heeding

speakable grief—not only because his kindness is a glass[47] even to my blind eyes of my naughtiness,[48] but that above all griefs it grieves me he should desperately adventure the loss of his soul-deserving life for mine, that yet owe more to fortune for my deserts,[49] as if he would carry mud in a chest[50] of crystal. For well I know, he that now reigneth, how much soever (and with good reason) he despiseth me, of all men despised,[51] yet he will not let slip any advantage to make away him whose just title, ennobled by courage and goodness,[52] may one day shake the seat of a never secure tyranny.

"And for this cause I craved of him to lead me to the top of this rock, indeed, I must confess, with meaning[53] to free him from so serpentine[54] a companion as I am. But he, finding what I purposed, only therein since[55] he was born showed himself disobedient unto me. And now, gentlemen, you have the true story, which I pray you publish to the world, that my mischievous[56] proceedings may be the glory of his filial piety, the only reward now left for so great a merit. And if it may be, let me obtain that of you which my son denies me.[57] For never was there more pity in saving any than in ending me,[58] both because therein my agonies shall end, and so shall you preserve this excellent young man who else willfully follows his own ruin."

The matter, in itself lamentable, lamentably expressed by the old prince (which[59] needed not take to himself[60] the gestures of pity, since his face could not put off[61] the marks thereof) greatly moved the two princes to compassion,

---

47 glass mirror   **48 naughtiness** wickedness   **49 that yet . . . deserts** I who must repay still more to fortune for my wicked deservings (and am likely therefore to poison my virtuous son's life with my evil fortune) **50 chest** coffer to contain valuables   **51 of all men despised** I who am despised by one and all   **52 ennobled . . . goodness** i.e., strengthened by the virtuous qualities of my son. (The bastard mercilessly kicked his blind father out of doors, contemptuously allowing him to live in wretchedness, but now that the father is joined by his son and legitimate heir to the crown he is a threat.)   **53 meaning** intention **54 serpentine** i.e., wicked   **55 only therein since** for the first time since **56 mischievous** wicked, poisonous   **57 obtain . . . me** obtain by your means that which my son denies me, i.e., the chance to kill myself **58 For . . . ending me** i.e., allowing me to die will be a more pitying and charitable act than the saving of someone else   **59 which** who   **60 take to himself** adopt, put on   **61 put off** efface, conceal

which could not stay in such hearts as theirs without seeking remedy. But by and by the occasion was presented. For Plexirtus (so was the bastard called) came thither with forty horse, only of purpose[62] to murder this brother; of whose coming he had soon advertisement,[63] and thought no eyes of sufficient credit[64] in such a matter but his own, and therefore came himself to be actor and spectator.

And as soon as he came, not regarding[65] the weak (as he thought) guard of but two men, commanded[66] some of his followers to set their hands to his[67] in the killing of Leonatus. But the young Prince, though not otherwise armed but with a sword, how falsely soever he was dealt with by others, would not betray himself;[68] but bravely drawing it[69] out, made the death of the first that assaulted him warn[70] his fellows to come more warily after him. But then Pyrocles and Musidorus were quickly become parties[71] (so just a defense deserving as much as old friendship) and so did behave them among that company (more injurious[72] than valiant) that many of them lost their lives for their wicked master.

Yet perhaps had the number of them at last prevailed if the King of Pontus (lately by them[73] made so) had not come unlooked-for to their succor. Who, having had a dream which had fixed his imagination vehemently upon some great danger presently[74] to follow those two Princes whom he most dearly loved, was come in all haste, following as well as he could their track with a hundred horses[75] in that country, which he thought (considering who then reigned) a fit place enough to make the stage[76] of any tragedy.

But then the match had been so ill made for Plexirtus that his ill-led life and worse-gotten honor should have tumbled together to destruction, had there not come in Tydeus and

---

62 horse, only of purpose horsemen, solely in order   **63 he had soon advertisement** i.e., Leonatus soon had warning, notice   **64 of sufficient credit** worthy to be believed   **65 not regarding** not having a proper respect or fear for   **66 commanded** he commanded   **67 set . . . to his** give him a helping hand   **68 betray himself** i.e., behave in cowardly fashion   **69 it** i.e., his sword   **70 warn** i.e., give warning to   **71 were . . . parties** quickly became participants   **72 injurious** intent on inflicting wrongful injury   **73 lately by them** i.e., recently by Musidorus and Pyrocles   **74 presently** immediately   **75 horses** horsemen   **76 stage** place where an action occurs

Telenor, with forty or fifty in their suit,[77] to the defense of Plexirtus. These two were brothers of the noblest house of that country, brought up from their infancy with Plexirtus—men of such prowess as not to know fear in themselves and yet to teach it others that should deal with them. For they had often made their lives triumph over most terrible dangers, never dismayed and ever fortunate, and truly no more settled[78] in their valor than disposed to goodness and justice, if either they had lighted on a better friend or could have learned to make friendship a child and not the father of virtue.[79] But bringing up rather than choice[80] having first knit their minds unto him (indeed crafty enough[81] either to hide his faults or never to show them but when they might pay home),[82] they willingly held out the course[83] rather to satisfy him than all the world, and rather to be good friends than good men. So as[84] though they did not like the evil he did, yet they liked him that did the evil, and though not councilors of the offense, yet protectors of the offender.

Now they, having heard of this sudden going out[85] with so small a company, in a country full of evil-wishing minds toward him (though they knew not the cause), followed him, till they found him in such case as they were to venture their lives or else he to lose his; which they did with such force of mind and body that truly I may justly say, Pyrocles and Musidorus had never till then found any that could make them so well repeat their hardest lesson in the feats of arms. And briefly so they[86] did that, if they overcame not, yet were they not overcome, but carried away that ungrateful master of theirs to a place of security howsoever the princes labored to the contrary. But this matter being thus far begun, it became not the constancy of[87] the princes so to

---

77 suit entourage   **78 settled** steadfast   **79 or could have learned . . . virtue** i.e., if they, Tydeus and Telenor, had not allowed their friendship with Plexirtus to dominate over their otherwise virtuous impulses **80 But . . . choice** i.e., but the circumstances in which they were reared rather than their own deliberate choosing   **81 indeed crafty enough** he (Plexirtus) indeed being crafty enough   **82 pay home** i.e., seem thoroughly to justify themselves by the results   **83 held out the course** stuck to their determination   **84 So as** so that   **85 going out** excursion   **86 they** i.e., Tydeus and Telenor   **87 it became . . . of** it was not fitting to the knightly resolution and oaths of

leave it; but in all haste making forces both in Pontus and Phrygia, they had in few days left him[88] but only that one strong place where he was. For, fear having been the only knot that had fastened his people unto him, that once untied by a greater force, they all scattered from him like so many birds whose cage had been broken.

In which season the blind King, having in the chief city of his realm set the crown upon his son Leonatus' head, with many tears both of joy and sorrow setting forth to the whole people his own fault and his son's virtue, after he had kissed him and forced his son to accept honor of him as of his new-become subject, even in a moment died, as it should seem his heart, broken with unkindness and affliction, stretched so far beyond his[89] limits with this excess of comfort as it was able no longer to keep safe his royal spirits. But the new king, having no less lovingly performed all duties to him dead than alive, pursued on[90] the siege of his unnatural brother, as much for the revenge of his father as for the establishing of his own quiet. In which siege truly I cannot but acknowledge the prowess of those two brothers,[91] than whom the princes never found in all their travel two men of greater ability to perform nor of abler skill for conduct.

But Plexirtus, finding that, if nothing else, famine[92] would at last bring him to destruction, thought better by humbleness to creep where by pride he could not march. For certainly so had nature formed him, and the exercise of craft conformed him to all turnings of sleights,[93] that though no man had less goodness in his soul than he, no man could better find the places[94] whence arguments[95] might grow of goodness to another; though no man felt less pity, no man could tell better how to stir pity; no man more impudent to deny where proofs were not manifest, no man more ready to confess with a repenting manner of aggravating his own evil where denial would but make the fault fouler. Now he took this way that, having gotten a passport[96] for one that pre-

---

88 him i.e., Plexirtus   **89 his** its   **90 pursued on** pursued, carried on   **91 two brothers** i.e., Tydeus and Telenor   **92 famine** i.e., being starved out in a siege   **93 turnings of sleights** fashioning of deceitful stratagems   **94 places** logical positions or topics   **95 arguments** proofs, manifestations   **96 passport** i.e., pass through the enemy lines, from the besieged city to the camp of Leonatus

tended he would put Plexirtus alive into his[97] hands, to speak with the King his brother, he himself (though much against the minds of the valiant brothers, who rather wished to die in brave defense), with a rope about his neck, barefooted, came to offer himself to the discretion of Leonatus. Where what submission he used, how cunningly in making greater the fault he made the faultiness the less, how artificially he could set out the torments of his own conscience with the burdensome cumber he had found of his ambitious desires, how finely—seeming to desire nothing but death, as ashamed[98] to live—he begged life in the refusing it,[99] I am not cunning enough to be able to express. But so fell out of it that, though at first sight Leonatus saw him with no other eye than as the murderer of his father, and anger already began to paint revenge in many colors, ere long he had not only gotten pity but pardon, and, if not an excuse of the fault past, yet an opinion of future amendment; while the poor villains[100] (chief ministers of his wickedness, now betrayed by the author thereof) were delivered to many cruel sorts of death, he so handling it that it rather seemed he had rather come into the defense of an unremediable mischief already committed than that they had done it at first by his consent.

Text based on *The Countess of Pembroke's Arcadia. Written by Sir Philip Sidney.* London: Printed for William Ponsonbie, Anno Domini, 1590. Book 2, chapter 10.

---

97 his i.e., Leonatus's. (Plexirtus obtains a passport ostensibly for one who will turn Plexirtus over to Leonatus, and then uses the passport himself to go to Leonatus and beg for mercy.) **98 as ashamed** as if he were ashamed **99 in the refusing it** even as he seemed to be asking for death **100 the poor villains** the poor wretches, i.e., his chief officers and allies

Further Reading

Adelman, Janet. ed. *Twentieth Century Interpretations of "King Lear."* Englewood Cliffs, N.J.: Prentice-Hall, 1978. Adelman offers a useful anthology of modern criticism of the play, including commentary by C. L. Barber, L. C. Knights, Kenneth Muir, Phyllis Rackin, and her own valuable introductory essay, as well as interpretations, considered below, by Booth, Bradley, Cavell, Danby, Mack, and Rosenberg.

Alpers, Paul. "*King Lear* and the Theory of the 'Sight Pattern.'" In *In Defense of Reading: A Reader's Approach to Literary Criticism*, ed. Reuben A. Brower and Richard Poirier. New York: E. P. Dutton, 1962. Responding to the critical commonplace that the play's pattern of "sight imagery" traces a movement toward moral insight, Alpers argues that the recurring language of vision is used not metaphorically but literally to suggest human relationships and moral obligations. Eyes are important in *King Lear* because they permit recognition, because they weep, and because in their fragility they reveal the human vulnerability that is preyed upon in the play.

Booth, Stephen. "On the Greatness of *King Lear*." *"King Lear," "Macbeth," Indefinition, and Tragedy*. New Haven, Conn.: Yale Univ. Press, 1983. For Booth the play's "greatness" lies as much in its length onstage as in the depth and power of its artistic vision. *King Lear* forces an audience to experience the play in ways that reflect the characters' experience of events, as a shocking confrontation with cruelty in the face of the persistent promise—and failure—of order and resolution.

Bradley, A. C. *"King Lear." Shakespearean Tragedy*, 1904. Rpt., New York: St. Martin's Press, 1985. In a seminal essay, Bradley finds that the play confronts us with the rending image of the destruction of good by evil, a pattern true to the tragic facts of life but balanced by the assertion that adversity purges and purifies. Evil is powerful in the play but it is "*merely* destructive," Bradley says, as the play suggests that life is valuable and must be faced patiently.

Brooke, Nicholas. *Shakespeare: "King Lear."* London: Edward Arnold; Great Neck, N.Y.: Barron's Educational Series, 1963. Brooke's monograph contends that *King Lear* is our culture's bleakest literary experience, resisting all efforts to escape, contain, or compensate the tragic facts it presents. His act-by-act analysis traces the trajectory of Lear's emotional and moral development from arrogance through isolation, suffering, and reconciliation to final defeat.

Cavell, Stanley. "The Avoidance of Love: A Reading of *King Lear." Must We Mean What We Say? A Book of Essays.* New York: Scribner's, 1969. Cavell's richly suggestive essay argues that the play's tragic action is motivated by characters' efforts to evade the threat of exposure and self-revelation. Lear's elaborate ritual in Act 1, Cornwall's blinding of Gloucester, Edgar's disguise and delay in abandoning it, and Lear's renunciation in Act 5 are each modulations of the play's characteristic action: the avoidance of recognition that is for Cavell the essence of the tragic experience.

Colie, Rosalie L., and F. T. Flahiff, eds. *Some Facets of "King Lear": Essays in Prismatic Criticism.* Toronto: Univ. of Toronto Press, 1974. This collection of twelve essays on *King Lear* is designed, as its title suggests, to respond to various aspects of a play that resists any single critical approach. Among the interesting contributions are Bridget Gellert Lyons's study of the subplot "as simplification" of the mystery of Lear's experience; Rosalie Colie's account of the contemporary social tensions articulated by the play; and Sheldon P. Zitner's analysis of language itself as one of *King Lear*'s central thematic concerns.

Danby, John F. *Shakespeare's Doctrine of Nature: A Study of "King Lear."* London: Faber and Faber, 1949. *King Lear*, according to Danby, dramatizes the conflict between opposing concepts of nature: one, articulated by Elizabethans such as Richard Hooker, assumes that nature is orderly, rational, and benign; the other, voiced in the play by Edmund, envisions nature as amoral, aggressive, and unrelated to any providential plan. Danby's intellectual history and his tracing of the theme of nature through the play and through Shakespeare's career discover behind the play's tragic tension an ultimately Christian view of the world and society.

Dollimore, Jonathan. *"King Lear* (c. 1605–6) and Essentialist Humanism." *Radical Tragedy: Religion, Ideology, and Power in the Drama of Shakespeare and his Contemporaries.* Chicago: Univ. of Chicago Press, 1984. Arguing against responses to *King Lear* that find the experience of suffering redemptive, Dollimore believes the play's tragedy stems from the fact that human values (such as pity or justice) are dependent upon material realities (such as power and property). Only through his powerlessness does Lear come to feel the deprivations of others, but, Dollimore argues, pity born of powerlessness cannot redeem either Lear or his society.

Doran, Madeleine. " 'Give Me the Map There!': Command, Question, and Assertion in *King Lear.*" In *Shakespeare's Art: Seven Essays,* ed. Milton Crane. Chicago: Univ. of Chicago Press, 1973. Rpt. in *Shakespeare's Dramatic Language.* Madison: Univ. of Wisconsin Press, 1976. Doran examines the characteristic syntactic patterns of Lear's speech and explores how the grammatical structures, like other verbal resources, help create the universe of the play. She identifies recurring patterns of command, question, and assertion, and by tracing their modulation shows how they articulate Lear's moral and emotional growth to a full though tragic awareness of life's contingencies.

Elton, William R. *"King Lear" and the Gods.* San Marino, Calif.: Huntington Library, 1966. Challenging optimistic Christian readings of *King Lear,* Elton explores both the complex religious climate of Renaissance Europe and the play's sources and structure. Elton finds in the play a provocative ambiguity that permits spectators to discover in its grim spectacle either an example of the failure of pagan ethics or an image of the crisis of faith that marked the late Renaissance.

Empson, William. "Fool in *Lear.*" *Sewanee Review* 57 (1949): 177–214. Rpt. in *The Structure of Complex Words.* New York: New Directions, 1951. In his characteristically provocative manner, Empson explores the various meanings of the word "fool" in the play. The ambiguities that surround the word lead Empson to a sense of the play's horror: Lear makes a fool of himself but in so doing reveals the folly of God and Nature. If there is an effective religious dimension of the play, Empson would locate it in Lear's relation to the tradition of the Holy Fool defined by Erasmus and Thomas More, though it is less for Lear's wisdom than for his endurance that we admire him.

Frye, Northrop. *Fools of Time: Studies in Shakespearean Tragedy*, pp. 103–121. Toronto: Univ. of Toronto Press, 1967. *King Lear*, according to Frye, articulates two versions of tragedy. Gloucester moves through terrible suffering to serenity as the violated moral order is validated and restored. Lear's experience is less explicable: his abdication isolates him from his social context, forcing a radical questioning of identity that ends in anguish and absurdity. The play's ultimate meaning, Frye finds, rests not in what characters learn but in what we learn by participating in their experience.

Goldberg, S. L. *An Essay on "King Lear."* London and New York: Cambridge Univ. Press, 1974. Tracing the developing logic of *King Lear*, Goldberg argues that the play's meaning resides in the unfolding of its poetry and action rather than in any moral or philosophical center. The play confronts both its characters and its audience with contradictory realities that resist any comprehensive and confident judgment of their meaning, affirming only the inescapable world of violence and an irreducible humanity that is vulnerable to it.

Goldman, Michael. "The Worst of *King Lear*." *Shakespeare and the Energies of Drama*. Princeton, N.J.: Princeton Univ. Press, 1972. Goldman explores the play's relentless intensification of suffering and degradation—the succession of savage shocks that demand from characters and audience efforts to make the horror bearable. Goldman shows the failure of these attempts to rationalize and contain the suffering, while he acknowledges their necessity: *King Lear* will not allow us to turn away from its pain, permitting us only the consolation of the discovery of the bond between ourselves and suffering humanity.

Hazlitt, William. "Lear." *Characters of Shakespear's Plays*, 1817. Rpt., London: Oxford Univ. Press, 1966. Hazlitt regards *King Lear* as "the best of all Shakespeare's plays" because of its powerful presentation of the passions that are its subject. *King Lear* balances its sense of the enormity of evil by exciting a desire for the goodness that has been destroyed; but, for Hazlitt, the play's achievement finally resists formulation: "To attempt to give a description of the play itself, of its effects upon the mind, is mere impertinence: yet we must say something."

Heilman, Robert B. *This Great Stage: Image and Structure in "King Lear,"* 1948. Rpt., Seattle: Univ. of Washington Press, 1963. In a book that was the first full-length New Critical study of a Shakespearean play, Heilman explores in detail the iterative language of sight, clothing, sex, and madness. In *King Lear*'s recurring patterns of imagery Heilman discovers its complex tragic awareness of both the reality of evil and the possibilities and value of goodness.

Johnson, Samuel. *"King Lear." Johnson on Shakespeare,* ed. Arthur Sherbo. *The Yale Edition of the Works of Samuel Johnson,* vol. 8. New Haven and London: Yale Univ. Press, 1969. Johnson's justly famous comments on the play defend the double plot as part of its "chief design" and respond to the question of its excessive cruelty. Johnson justifies the behavior of Regan and Goneril as "historical fact" but, approving Tate's revision (see below), he finds the death of Cordelia shocking: "I know not whether I ever endured to read again the last scenes of the play till I undertook to revise them as an editor."

Kott, Jan. "King Lear or Endgame." *Shakespeare Our Contemporary,* trans. Boleslaw Taborski. Garden City, N.Y.: Doubleday, 1964. Kott argues that the play is "grotesque" rather than tragic, since the tragic experience is located in an absurd universe where choice is irrelevant and defeat unavoidable. The play dramatizes the decay of the social order and offers no hope of healing or consolation. Only the Fool, in Kott's view, fully sees the absurdity of the world, and Lear comes finally to share his disillusioned vision.

Mack, Maynard. *"King Lear" in Our Time.* Berkeley and Los Angeles: Univ. of California Press, 1965. Mack, in a brief but influential study, considers *King Lear*'s stage history, its literary and imaginative sources, and its modernity. Mack's analysis reveals that *King Lear* resists the sentimentality either of Christian readings that would transfigure the play's suffering or of the nihilism that finds only imbecility in the play's world. For Mack, Lear's tragic experience agonizingly measures what human beings can both lose and win.

Reibetanz, John. *The "Lear" World: A Study of "King Lear" in Its Dramatic Context.* Toronto: Univ. of Toronto Press, 1977. Examining the relationship of *King Lear* to the dramatic traditions of Jacobean England, Reibetanz explores the dramaturgy of the play, especially how the play is designed to force spectators to confront and respond compassionately to the image of suffering. He discovers the play's unity not in narrative continuity but in emblematic and scenic juxtapositions that gradually reveal the emotional and moral issues of the play.

Rosenberg, Marvin. *The Masks of "King Lear."* Berkeley, Calif.: Univ. of California Press, 1972. Proceeding through the play scene by scene, Rosenberg combines critical analysis and theatrical history to explore the possibilities of meaning presented by the play. By surveying the interpretations of actors, directors, and critics, Rosenberg discovers that only in the theater is the full complexity of the play's design organized and experienced.

Tate, Nahum. *The History of King Lear* (1681), ed. James Black. Lincoln, Neb.: Univ. of Nebraska Press, 1975. Tate's Restoration adaptation of *King Lear* rejects Shakespeare's tragic denouement in favor of a happy ending in which Lear survives and Cordelia lives to marry Edgar. The play's commitment to poetic justice, as virtue is rewarded and vice punished, has been derided, but its theatrical success (keeping Shakespeare's original version off the stage until 1823) reveals something profound both about changes in taste and about the horrific power of Shakespeare's tragic design.

Taylor, Gary, and Michael Warren, eds. *The Division of the Kingdoms: Shakespeare's Two Versions of "King Lear."* Oxford: Clarendon Press; New York: Oxford Univ. Press, 1983. The essays here are devoted to the thesis that the text of *King Lear* in the First Folio of 1623 represents Shakespeare's revision of an earlier design rather than an imperfect version that must be corrected and supplemented by readings from the 1608 quarto. Contributors examine both the bibliographic and critical evidence for the theory that the two texts of *King Lear* are each unified and coherent versions of the play.

MACBETH

Introduction

Macbeth is seemingly the last of four great Shakespearean tragedies—*Hamlet* (c. 1599–1601), *Othello* (c. 1603–1604), *King Lear* (c. 1605), and *Macbeth* (c. 1606–1607)—that examine the dimensions of spiritual evil, as distinguished from the political strife of Roman tragedies such as *Julius Caesar*, *Antony and Cleopatra*, and *Coriolanus*. Whether or not Shakespeare intended *Macbeth* as a culmination of a series of tragedies on evil, the play does offer a particularly terse and gloomy view of humanity's encounter with the powers of darkness. Macbeth, more consciously than any other of Shakespeare's major tragic protagonists, has to face the temptation of committing what he knows to be a monstrous crime. Like Doctor Faustus in Christopher Marlowe's play *The Tragedy of Doctor Faustus* (c. 1588–1592), and to a lesser extent like Adam in John Milton's *Paradise Lost* (1667), Macbeth understands the reasons for resisting evil and yet goes ahead with his disastrous plan. His awareness of and sensitivity to moral issues, together with his conscious choice of evil, produce an unnerving account of human failure, all the more distressing because Macbeth is so representatively human. He seems to possess freedom of will and accepts personal responsibility for his fate, and yet his tragic doom seems unavoidable. Nor is there eventual salvation to be hoped for, as there is in *Paradise Lost*, since Macbeth's crime is too heinous and his heart too hardened. He is more like Doctor Faustus, damned and in despair.

To an extent not found in the other tragedies, the issue is stated in terms of salvation versus damnation. Macbeth knows before he acts that Duncan's virtues "Will plead like angels, trumpet-tongued, against / The deep damnation of his taking-off" (1.7.19–20). After the murder, he is equally aware that he has "Put rancors in the vessel of my peace . . . and mine eternal jewel / Given to the common enemy of man" (3.1.68–70). His enemies later describe him as a devil and a "hellhound" (5.8.3). He, like Marlowe's Doctor Faustus before him, has knowingly sold his soul for gain. And although as a mortal he still has time to repent his crimes, horrible as they are, Macbeth cannot find the words to be

penitent. "Wherefore could not I pronounce 'Amen'?" he
implores his wife after they have committed the murder. "I
had most need of blessing, and 'Amen' / Stuck in my throat"
(2.2.35–37). Macbeth's own answer seems to be that he has
committed himself so inexorably to evil that he cannot
turn back. Sentence has been pronounced: "Glamis hath
murdered sleep, and therefore Cawdor / Shall sleep no more;
Macbeth shall sleep no more" (ll. 46–47).

Macbeth is not a conventional morality play (even less so
than *Doctor Faustus*) and is not concerned primarily with
preaching against sinfulness or demonstrating that Macbeth is finally damned for what he does. A tradition of
moral and religious drama has been transformed into an
intensely human study of the psychological effects of evil
on a particular man and, to a lesser extent, on his wife. That
moral tradition nevertheless provides as its legacy a perspective on the operation of evil in human affairs. A perverse ambition seemingly inborn in Macbeth himself is
abetted by dark forces dwelling in the universe, waiting to
catch him off guard. Among Shakespeare's tragedies, indeed, *Macbeth* is remarkable for its focus on evil in the protagonist, and on his relationship to the sinister forces
tempting him. In no other Shakespearean play do we identify to such an extent with the evildoer himself. *Richard III*
also focuses on an evil protagonist, but in that play we are
distanced by the character's gloating and are not partakers
in the introspective soliloquies of a man confronting his
own ambition. Macbeth is more like us. We share Macbeth's
inclination toward brutality, as well as his humane resistance of that urge. We witness and struggle to understand
his downfall through two phases: the spiritual struggle before he actually commits the crime, and the despairing
aftermath with its vain quest for security through continued violence. Evil is thus presented in two aspects, first as
insidious suggestion leading us on toward an illusory promise of gain, and then as frenzied addiction to the hated thing
by which we are possessed.

In the first phase, before the commission of the crime, we
wonder to what extent the powers of darkness are a deter-
mining factor in what Macbeth does. Can he avoid the fate
the witches proclaim? Evidently he and Lady Macbeth have
previously considered murdering Duncan; the witches ap-

pear after the thought, not before. Lady Macbeth reminds her wavering husband that he was the first to "break this enterprise" to her, on some previous occasion when "Nor time nor place / Did then adhere, and yet you would make both" (1.7.49–53). Elizabethans would understand that evil spirits such as witches appear when summoned, whether by our conscious or unconscious minds. Macbeth is ripe for their insinuations. A mind free of taint would see no sinister invitation in their prophecy of greatness to come. And in a saner moment Macbeth knows that his restless desire to interfere with destiny is arrogant and useless. "If chance will have me king, why, chance may crown me / Without my stir" (1.3.145–146). Banquo, his companion, serves as his dramatic opposite by consistently displaying the correct attitude toward the witches. "Speak then to me," he addresses them, "who neither beg nor fear / Your favors nor your hate" (ll. 60–61). Like Horatio in *Hamlet*, Banquo strongly resists the blandishments of fortune as well as its buffets, though not without an agonizing night of moral struggle. Indeed, promises of success are often more ruinous than setbacks—as in the seemingly paradoxical instance of the farmer, cited by Macbeth's porter, who "hanged himself on th' expectation of plenty" (2.3.4–5). It is by showing Macbeth that he is two-thirds of his way to the throne that the witches tempt him to seize the last third at whatever cost. "Glamis, and Thane of Cawdor! / The greatest is behind"(1.3.116–117).

Banquo comprehends the nature of temptation. "To win us to our harm," he observes, "The instruments of darkness tell us truths, / Win us with honest trifles, to betray 's / In deepest consequence" (1.3.123–126). The devil can speak true, and his strategy is to invite us into a trap we help prepare. Without our active consent in evil (as Othello also learns) we cannot fall. Yet in what sense are the witches trifling with Macbeth, or prevaricating? When they address him as one "that shalt be king hereafter" (l. 50), they are stating a certainty, for they can "look into the seeds of time / And say which grain will grow and which will not," as Banquo says (ll. 58–59). They know that Banquo will be "Lesser than Macbeth, and greater, / Not so happy, yet much happier" (ll. 65–66), since Banquo will beget a race of kings and Macbeth will not. How then do they know that

Macbeth will be king? If we consider the hypothetical question, what if Macbeth does *not* murder Duncan, we can gain some understanding of the relationship between character and fate; for the only valid answer is that the question remains hypothetical, Macbeth *does* kill Duncan, the witches are right in their prediction. It is idle to speculate that providence would have found another way to make Macbeth king, for the witches' prophecy is self-fulfilling in the very way they foresee. Character is fate; they know Macbeth's fatal weakness and know they can "enkindle" him to seize the crown by laying irresistible temptations before him. This does not mean that they determine his choice, but rather that Macbeth's choice is predictable and therefore unavoidable, even though not preordained. He has free choice, but that choice will in fact go only one way—as with Adam and Eve in Milton's *Paradise Lost* and in the medieval tradition from which this poem was derived.

Although the powers of evil cannot determine Macbeth's choice, they can influence the external conditions affecting that choice. By a series of apparently circumstantial events, well timed in their effect, they can repeatedly assail him just when he is about to rally to the call of conscience. The witches, armed with supernatural knowledge, inform Macbeth of his new title shortly before the King's ambassadors confirm that he is to be the Thane of Cawdor. Duncan chooses this night to lodge under Macbeth's roof. And just when Macbeth resolves to abandon even this unparalleled opportunity, his wife intervenes on the side of the witches. Macbeth commits the murder in part to keep his word to her and to prove he is no coward (like Donwald, the slayer of King Duff in one of Shakespeare's chief sources, Raphael Holinshed's *Chronicles*). Not only the opportunities presented to Macbeth but the obstacles put in his way are cannily timed to overwhelm his conscience. When King Duncan announces that his son Malcolm is now Prince of Cumberland and official heir to the throne (1.4), the unintended threat deflects Macbeth's mood from one of gratitude and acceptance to one of hostility. These are mitigating circumstances that affect our judgment of Macbeth, and even though they cannot excuse him they certainly increase our sympathetic identification.

We are moved too by the poetic intensity of Macbeth's

moral vision. His soliloquies are memorable as poetry, not merely because Shakespeare wrote them, but because Macbeth is sensitive and aware. The horror, indeed, of his crime is that his cultivated self is revolted by what he cannot prevent himself from doing. He understands with a terrible clarity not only the moral wrong of what he is about to do, but also the inescapably destructive consequences for himself. He is as reluctant as we to see the crime committed, and yet he goes to it with a sad and rational deliberateness rather than in a self-blinding fury. For Macbeth there is no seeming loss of perspective, and yet there is total alienation of the act from his moral consciousness. The arguments for and against murdering Duncan, as Macbeth pictures them in his acutely visual imagination, when weighed are overwhelmingly opposed to the deed. Duncan is his king and his guest, deserving Macbeth's duty and hospitality. The King is virtuous and able. He has shown every favor to Macbeth, thereby removing any sane motive for striving after further promotion. All human history shows that murders of this sort "return / To plague th' inventor" (1.7.9–10)—that is, provide only guilt and punishment rather than satisfaction. Finally, judgment in "the life to come" includes the prospect of eternal torment. On the other side of the argument is nothing but Macbeth's "Vaulting ambition, which o'erleaps itself" (l. 27)—a perverse refusal to be content with his present good fortune because there is more that beckons. Who could weigh the issues so dispassionately and still choose the wrong? The answer apparently is that we all could, for Macbeth strikes us as typically human both in his understanding and in his perverse ambition.

Macbeth's clarity of moral imagination is contrasted with his wife's imperceptiveness. He is always seeing visions or hearing voices—a dagger in the air, the ghost of Banquo, a voice crying "Sleep no more!"—and she is always denying them. "The sleeping and the dead / Are but as pictures," she insists. He knows that "all great Neptune's ocean" cannot wash the blood from his hands; "No, this my hand will rather / The multitudinous seas incarnadine, / Making the green one red." To Lady Macbeth, contrastingly, "A little water clears us of this deed. / How easy is it, then!" (2.2.57–72). Macbeth knows that the murder of Duncan is but the beginning: "We have scorched the snake,

not killed it." Lady Macbeth would prefer to believe that
"What's done is done" (3.2.14–15). Ironically, it is she finally who must endure visions of the most agonizing sort,
sleepwalking in her madness and trying to rub away the
"damned spot" that before seemed so easy to remove. "All
the perfumes of Arabia will not sweeten this little hand,"
she laments (5.1.34–51). This relationship between Macbeth
and Lady Macbeth owes much to traditional contrasts between male and female principles. As in the pairing of
Adam and Eve, the man is the more rational of the two but
knowingly shares his wife's sin through fondness for her.
She has failed to foresee the long-range consequences of
sinful ambition and so becomes a temptress to her husband. The fall of man takes place in an incongruous atmosphere of domestic intimacy and mutual concern; Lady
Macbeth is motivated by ambition for her husband in much
the same way that he sins to win her approbation.

The fatal disharmony flawing this domestic accord is
conveyed through images of sexual inversion. Lady Macbeth prepares for her ordeal with the incantation, "Come,
you spirits / That tend on mortal thoughts, unsex me here
. . . Come to my woman's breasts / And take my milk for
gall" (1.5.40–48). When she accuses her husband of unmanly cowardice and vows she would dash out the brains of
her own infant for such effeminacy as he has displayed, he
extols her with "Bring forth men-children only! / For thy
undaunted mettle should compose / Nothing but males"
(1.7.73–75). She takes the initiative, devising and then carrying out the plan to drug Duncan's chamber-guards with
wine. This assumption of the dominant male role by the
woman would again bring to the Elizabethan mind numerous biblical, medieval, and classical parallels deploring the
ascendancy of passion over reason: Eve choosing for Adam,
Noah's wife taking command of the ark, the Wife of Bath
dominating her husbands, Venus emasculating Mars, and
others.

In *Macbeth* sexual inversion also allies Lady Macbeth
with the witches or weird sisters, the bearded women.
Their unnaturalness betokens disorder in nature, for they
can sail in a sieve and "look not like th' inhabitants o' th'
earth / And yet are on 't" (1.3.41–42). Characteristically they
speak in paradoxes: "When the battle's lost and won,"

"Fair is foul, and foul is fair" (1.1.4,11). Shakespeare probably drew on numerous sources to depict the witches: Holinshed's *Chronicles* (in which he conflated two accounts, one of Duncan and Macbeth, and the other of King Duff slain by Donwald with the help of his wife), King James's writings on witchcraft, Samuel Harsnett's *Declaration of Egregious Popish Impostures* (used also for *King Lear*), and the accounts of the Scottish witch trials published around 1590. In the last, particularly, Shakespeare could have found mention of witches raising storms and sailing in sieves to endanger vessels at sea, performing threefold rituals blaspheming the Trinity, and brewing witches' broth. Holinshed's *Chronicles* refer to the weird sisters as "goddesses of destiny," associating them with the three fates, Clotho, Lachesis, and Atropos, who spin, pull, and cut the thread of life. In *Macbeth* the weird sisters' power to control fortune is curtailed, and they are portrayed as witches according to popular contemporary understanding rather than as goddesses of destiny; nonetheless, witches were thought to be servants of the devil (Banquo wonders if the devil can speak true in their utterances, 1.3.107), and through them Macbeth has made an ominous pact with evil itself. His visit to their seething cauldron in Act 4, scene 1, brings him to the witches' masters, those unknown powers that know his very thought and who tempt him with those equivocations of which Banquo has warned Macbeth. The popularity of witchlore tempted Shakespeare's acting company to expand the witches' scenes with spectacles of song and dance; even the Folio text we have evidently contains interpolations derived in part from Thomas Middleton's *The Witch* (see especially 3.5 and part of 4.1 containing mention of Middleton's songs "Come away" and "Black spirits"). Nevertheless, Shakespeare's original theme of a disharmony in nature remains clearly visible.

Patterns of imagery throughout the play point to the same disorder in nature and in man. The murder of Duncan, like that of Caesar in *Julius Caesar,* is accompanied by signs of the heavens' anger. Various observers report that chimneys blow down during the unruly night, that owls clamor and attack falcons, that the earth shakes, and that Duncan's horses devour each other. (Some of these portents are from Holinshed.) Banquo's ghost returns from the dead

to haunt his murderer, prompting Macbeth to speak in metaphors of charnel houses and graves that send back their
dead and of birds of prey that devour the corpses. The
drunken porter who opens the gate to Macduff and Lennox
after the murder (2.3) invokes images of judgment and everlasting bonfire through which the scene takes on the semblance of hell gate and the Harrowing of Hell. Owls appear
repeatedly in the imagery, along with other creatures associated with nighttime and horror: wolves, serpents, scorpions, bats, toads, beetles, crows, rooks. Darkness itself
assumes tangible and menacing shapes of hidden stars or
extinguished candles, a thick blanket shrouded "in the dunnest smoke of hell" (1.5.51), an entombment of the earth in
place of "living light" (2.4.10), a scarf to hoodwink the eye
of "pitiful day" (3.2.50), and a bloody and invisible hand to
tear to pieces the lives of virtuous men. Sleep is transformed from "great nature's second course" and a "nourisher" of life that "knits up the raveled sleave of care"
(2.2.41–44) into "death's counterfeit" (2.3.77) and a living
hell for Lady Macbeth. Life becomes sterile for Macbeth, a
denial of harvest, the lees or dregs of the wine and "the
sere, the yellow leaf" (5.3.23). In a theatrical metaphor life
becomes for him unreal, "a walking shadow, a poor player /
That struts and frets his hour upon the stage / And then is
heard no more" (5.5.24–26). This theme of empty illusion
carries over into the recurring image of borrowed or ill-
fitting garments that belie the wearer. Macbeth is an actor,
a hypocrite, whose "False face must hide what the false
heart doth know" (1.7.83) and who must "Look like th' innocent flower, / But be the serpent under 't" (1.5.65–66).
Even the show of grief is an assumed mask whereby evil-
doers deceive the virtuous, so much so that Malcolm,
Donalbain, and Macduff learn to conceal their true feeling
rather than be thought to "show an unfelt sorrow" (2.3.138).

Blood is not only a literal sign of disorder but an emblem
of Macbeth's remorseless butchery, a "damned spot" on
the conscience, and a promise of divine vengeance: "It will
have blood, they say; blood will have blood" (3.4.123). The
emphasis on corrupted blood also suggests disease, in
which Macbeth's tyranny is a sickness to his country as
well as to himself. Scotland bleeds (4.3.32), needing a physician; Macduff and his allies call themselves "the medicine

of the sickly weal" (5.2.27). Lady Macbeth's disease is incurable, something spiritually corrupt wherein "the patient / Must minister to himself" (5.3.47–48). Conversely, the English King Edward is renowned for his divine gift of curing what was called the king's evil, or scrofula.

Throughout, the defenders of righteousness are associated with positive images of natural order. Duncan rewards his subjects by saying, "I have begun to plant thee, and will labor / To make thee full of growing" (1.4.28–29). His arrival at Inverness Castle is heralded by signs of summer, sweet air, and "the temple-haunting martlet" (1.6.4). He is a fatherly figure, so much so that even Lady Macbeth balks at an act so like patricide. Macduff too is a father and husband whose family is butchered. The forest of Birnam marching to confront Macbeth, although rationally explainable as a device of camouflage for Macduff's army, is emblematic of the natural order itself rising up against the monstrosity of Macbeth's crimes. Banquo is above all a patriarchal figure, ancestor of the royal line governing Scotland and England at the time the play was written. These harmonies are to an extent restorative. Even the witches' riddling prophecies, "th' equivocation of the fiend" (5.5.43) luring Macbeth into further atrocities with the vain promise of security, anticipate a just retribution.

Nonetheless, the play's vision of evil shakes us deeply. Scotland's peace has been violated, so much so that "to do harm / Is often laudable, to do good sometimes / Accounted dangerous folly" (4.2.76–78). Lady Macduff and her son, along with young Siward, have had to pay with their innocent lives the terrible price of Scotland's tyranny; in his frenzied attempt to prevent the fulfillment of the prophecy about Banquo's lineage inheriting the kingdom, Macbeth has, like King Herod, slaughtered much of the younger generation on whom the future depends. We can only hope that the stability to which Scotland returns after his death will be lasting. Banquo's line is to rule eventually and to produce a line of kings reaching down to the royal occupant to whom Shakespeare will present his play, but when *Macbeth* ends, it is Malcolm who is king. The killing of a traitor (Macbeth) and the placing of his head on a pole replicate the play's beginning in the treason and beheading of the Thane of Cawdor—a gentleman on whom Duncan built "An absolute trust" (1.4.14). Most troublingly, the humanly representative nature of Macbeth's crime leaves us with little assurance that we could resist his temptation. The most that can be said is that wise and good men such as Banquo and Macduff have learned to know the evil in themselves and to resist it as nobly as they can.

Macbeth
in Performance

Theater managers have too often been unwilling to leave *Macbeth* as Shakespeare wrote it. The tampering began even during Shakespeare's lifetime or shortly thereafter. Added music and business for the witches must have been included in performances prior to 1623, since interpolations of this sort are found in the original Folio text published in that year. Act 3, scene 5, consisting chiefly of an unnecessary appearance by the witch Hecate, is probably by another author, and the song "Black Spirits" in Act 4, scene 1, is from a play by Thomas Middleton.

To be sure, Simon Forman's description of his visit to the Globe Theatre on April 20, 1611, suggests that he saw something close to what Shakespeare wrote. Forman, an astrologer and quack doctor, tells of Macbeth and Banquo "riding through a wood" (were Richard Burbage and a fellow actor on horseback?) where they encountered "three women fairies or nymphs" who saluted Macbeth, "saying three times to him, 'Hail, Macbeth, King of Codon'" (i.e., Thane of Cawdor). Forman goes on to describe a banquet at which Macbeth "began to speak of noble Banquo, and to wish that he were there. And as he thus did, standing up to drink a carouse to him, the ghost of Banquo came and sat down in his chair beside him. And he, turning about to sit down again, saw the ghost of Banquo, which fronted [affronted] him so that he fell into a great passion of fear and fury." All this sounds close to Shakespeare's text, as one would expect of a performance some three or four years after Shakespeare wrote the play and while he was still an active member of his acting company, the King's men. *Macbeth* probably remained in repertory during those years. Richard Burbage is likely to have played Macbeth, and John Rice, a boy actor in the company, may have played Lady Macbeth in 1611 when Forman saw the play. But fidelity to Shakespeare's intention was not to continue for long.

The play that diarist Samuel Pepys saw and enjoyed in the 1660s had already been expanded to include a good deal of new spectacle. Pepys marveled, on April 19, 1667: "Here we saw *Macbeth*, which, though I have seen it often, yet it is one of the best plays for a stage, and variety of dancing and music, that ever I saw." Earlier, in January of the same year, Pepys especially liked the "divertissement," that is to say the song and dance. William Davenant provided the altered and augmented script for this production, not only amplifying the original through operatic and scenic splendor, but also symmetrically balancing the play with an enlarged role for Lady Macduff so that her invincible virtue might offset the wickedness of Lady Macbeth. A production of Davenant's version in 1672 at the Dorset Garden Theatre, according to John Downes, showed the play "being dressed in all its finery, as new clothes, new scenes, machines, as flyings for the witches, with all the swinging and dancing in it." Music was provided by Matthew Locke and others. Thomas Betterton enjoyed one of his great successes as Macbeth, and continued to play the part until 1707. The witches flew, danced, sang, and otherwise amused the spectators; their parts were taken by comic actors, and their costumes were meant to invite laughter.

Macbeth had become something of an opera. The scenic effects and additional stage business were simply irresistible, and audiences continued to demand more than Shakespeare had provided. The operatic tradition continued well into the eighteenth century after Betterton had been succeeded as Macbeth by John Mills and James Quin, and Mary Porter had emerged as the most remarkable Lady Macbeth of the era—even better than Hannah Pritchard, according to the actor Charles Macklin.

David Garrick made an attempt to restore Shakespeare's play in 1744, though at the last minute, afraid of an adverse reaction, he partly backed down. He did reintroduce some of Shakespeare's language, permitted the witches to rise from under the stage rather than enter in flight, and cut away the platitudinous moralisms that Davenant had supplied for Lady Macduff. On the other hand he omitted the murder of Lady Macduff and her son (4.2), left out the drunken Porter (2.3) as a blatant violation of classical strictures against including comic material in a tragedy, and then, somewhat incongruously perhaps, continued to provide the diverting song and dance of the witches to which audiences had grown so accustomed. Despite these unreformed accretions, Garrick's interpretation of the lead role contributed to a new understanding of Shakespeare's artistry. Garrick's thoughtful soliloquies, intimately shared with the audience in the small Theatre Royal, Drury Lane, presented Macbeth as a sensitive and poetic man caught up in the horrid deed he could not resist. Hannah Pritchard, physically towering over Garrick as Lady Macbeth, was, in Thomas Davies's words, "insensible to compunction and inflexibly bent to cruelty" as she shamed Macbeth into action with her ferocious strength of spirit. Together, this famous pair performed so compellingly that they lent authority and impetus to the new movement in literary criticism toward the study of character as the central feature of Shakespearean drama.

Garrick performed *Macbeth* in contemporary eighteenth-century dress. The movement toward naturalistic and authentic setting and costume, with which the nineteenth century was to be increasingly fascinated, seems to have begun with West Digges at Edinburgh in 1757 and then Charles Macklin at Covent Garden in 1773, both of whom dressed in historical Scottish garb. (Garrick considered the idea in 1772 but finally rejected it.) Macklin's costumes and sets were as yet far from accurate—he included cannon for Macbeth's castle in a presumably eleventh-century Scottish setting long before the discovery of gunpowder, dressed Lady Macbeth in modern robes, and indeed wore a tunic himself that reflected early sixteenth- rather than eleventh-century fashion—but his attempt at least attested to a growing interest in historical realism.

John Philip Kemble's production at Drury Lane in 1794 was, according to theater historian and producer W. C. Oulton, distinguished by its realistic attention to the appearance of the witches: they were no longer dressed in "mittens, plaited caps, laced aprons, red stomachers, ruffs, etc., which was the dress of those weird sisters when Mesdames Beard, Champness, etc. represented them with Garrick's *Macbeth*," but appeared as "preternatural beings, distinguished only by the fellness of their purposes and the fatality of their delusions." In the cauldron scene, serpents writhed around the evil spirits. Kemble was the first to treat Banquo's ghost as a phantasm seen only by Macbeth.

Kemble's famous leading lady (and sister), Sarah Siddons, offered an intensely psychological portrayal of Lady Macbeth in the great tradition of Mary Porter and Hannah Pritchard. With her "turbulent and inhuman strength of spirit," so much admired by William Hazlitt, Siddons was also able, especially in the sleepwalking scene, to move audiences with the suggestion of a desolate and tortured soul. She and Kemble did much to further Garrick's and Pritchard's exploitation of character as the essence of Shakespearean tragedy, further humanizing the portraits that they had developed. Yet Kemble did little to take away Davenant's spectacle; Matthew Locke's music was still to be heard, and scenic extravagance was abetted by the large size of the Drury Lane theater after it was renovated in 1794 and by the capacity of the Theatre Royal, Covent Garden (where Kemble and Siddons performed in 1800, 1803, 1809, and afterward).

Still greater magnificence was on its way. Edmund Kean, a fierce devotee of visual authenticity, produced a version of *Macbeth* in 1814 that, along with the music of Locke, provided new scenery of a splendidly romantic cast: a rocky pass and a bridge, a gallery and banquet hall in Macbeth's castle, a cavern and "car of clouds," Hecate's cave, and much more. The ascent of Hecate in her chariot was particularly admired. Kean wore kilts over an armored breastplate in the first acts, as Kemble had done. William Charles Macready, who played Macbeth over a period of some thirty years (starting in 1820 at Covent Garden, and thereafter chiefly at Drury Lane opposite the brilliant Helen Faucit), devised striking atmospheric effects for his production at Drury Lane in 1837 in order to evoke the dark visionary realm that Macbeth inhabits. These effects included a mist that rose slowly in Act 1 to reveal a barren heath and highland landscape, a rustic bridge, later a royal march for Duncan, a castle interior at Dunsinane with torches and with servants carrying food, a walled courtyard of the same castle in Act 2, an opulent banquet scene, and a ghost entering through a trapdoor hidden from the audience by a cluster of servants. At Birnam Wood, each soldier was completely screened by the huge bough he carried, while the illusion of the forested army receded into the infinite distance of a diorama. To accommodate the scenic elaboration Macready could not play Shakespeare's complete text, omitting, among others, the Porter scene while preserving many of Davenant's hoary alterations.

Not until Samuel Phelps's production of 1847 at the Sadler's Wells Theatre, in fact, did a theater manager summon the resolution to do away with the witch scenes of Davenant and limit the music to between acts. Phelps went on to restore the Porter (though cutting the second half of his speech), the killing of Lady Macduff and her son onstage, and the killing of Macbeth offstage, as in Shakespeare's original. Objection was raised to the horror of some of Phelps's restorations, and in later productions he eliminated the murder of Macduff's young son and Macduff's entry with Macbeth's head on a pole. Phelps provided some striking effects of "darkness visible" by means of gauze screens and imaginative lighting. His own acting of Macbeth was rugged and energetic, less poetic and haunted than Macready's or Edwin Booth's, but, as one critic wrote, "robust and terrible, and, to my mind, closer to the spirit of Shakespeare."

Phelps's courageous restoration was almost immediately undone, however, by Charles Kean, who resuscitated Locke and Davenant in an especially magnificent spectacle at the Princess's Theatre in 1853. Gone once again was the scene of Lady Macduff and her son and the slaying of Macbeth offstage. Instead of striving for textual accuracy, Kean lavished all his attention on what he took to be an authentic reproduction of eleventh-century Scotland. Reasoning that the era in question was one of Danish invasion, Kean devised tunics, mantles, and cross-gartering of Danish and Anglo-Saxon style, along with feathered helmets, particolored woolens, and iron mail sewn on cloth or leather. His sets aimed at architectural reconstruction as well, with sloping roofs supported by Saxon pillars and the like. The Victorian age, besotted by the delights of scenic splendor in the theater, simply was not ready to give up the opportunities that Davenant and Locke had provided for visual and musical elaboration. Kean's production did not, to be sure, delight everyone: *Lloyd's Weekly* complained that "in Garrick's day we had a Macbeth without the costume, and now we have the costume without Macbeth." If the lavish spectacle, the inclusion of music, and the focus on the main characters at the expense of lesser figures threatened to overwhelm Shakespeare's play, it did provide the cultural matrix in which Giuseppe Verdi could write his Italian opera, *Macbeth* (first performed in 1847, revised in 1865).

Late nineteenth-century theater managers gave full expression to the prevailing taste in opulent historical realism. Henry Irving, at the Lyceum Theatre in 1875 and 1888, chose to revive eleventh-century Scotland once again while banishing Lady Macduff and her son and including songs from stage tradition, though he did restore the drunken Porter. Ellen Terry excelled in his 1888 production as Lady Macbeth: she was, as one critic wrote, "the stormy dominant woman of the eleventh century equipped with the capricious emotional subtlety of the nineteenth century." Sarah Bernhardt startled audiences in 1884 at the Gaiety Theatre by coming onstage in the sleepwalking scene barefoot and in a clinging nightdress. Tommaso Salvini (1884, Covent Garden) and Johnston Forbes-Robertson (1898, Lyceum Theatre) continued the tradition of bulky and nearly unmovable sets. Herbert Beerbohm Tree (1911, His Majesty's Theatre) paid particular attention to beautiful stage pictures—Lady Macbeth (Violet Vanbrugh) in a long scarf of crimson silk or veiled in black, Lady Macbeth ascending and descending a staircase in defiance of the requirements of Shakespeare's text for the sleepwalking scene, torches glowing in the dark, an exquisite set for the murder of Duncan—which inevitably required extensive cutting and reduction of the number of scenes. Frank Benson, who directed the play in nine different seasons between 1896 and 1911 at Stratford-upon-Avon, summed up in his own way what nineteenth-century staging and interpretation had to offer.

A new direction manifested itself in William Poel's return to the original Folio text in a performance by the Shakespeare Reading Society in 1895. Though anticipated by Garrick and especially Phelps in regard to textual restoration, Poel went beyond them in staging the play as an Elizabethan drama, not as a Scottish one, using Elizabethan dress and a thrust apron stage. Change was in the air, and by 1915 and 1918 Sybil Thorndike at the Old Vic played Lady Macbeth as though she and her husband were " 'big capitalists' in a tragic partnership" (Dennis Bartholomeusz, *Mac-*

beth and the Players, p. 226, quoting Thorndike). Lewis Casson, at the Prince's Theatre in 1926, tried to reconcile the scenic realism of Tree and Kean with Casson's interest in the staging theories of Poel and Harley Granville-Barker. Sybil Thorndike again played Lady Macbeth. Harcourt Williams, at the Old Vic in 1930, provided simple sets and swift-paced action for John Gielgud's subtle portrait of Macbeth's moral isolation. Tyrone Guthrie dropped the witches from the opening scene of his Old Vic production of 1934, arguing that they should not be allowed to govern the entire tragedy; his Macbeth, played by Charles Laughton with Flora Robson as Lady Macbeth, was a man caught in conflict between his noble qualities and the destructive ambition that those very qualities seemed to generate.

Innovation encouraged further experiment. Theodore Komisarjevsky used modern dress against a backdrop of the howitzers and field uniforms of World War I for his *Macbeth* at Stratford-upon-Avon in 1933. Komisarjevsky's witches were old hags who rifled the corpses of soldiers slain in battle and used palmistry to tell the fortunes of Macbeth and Banquo. John Gielgud directed Ralph Richardson as Macbeth at Stratford-upon-Avon in 1952 on an abstract set of menacing dark masses lit only by torchlight. In Glen Byam Shaw's memorable production at Stratford-upon-Avon three years later, with Laurence Olivier and Vivien Leigh as Macbeth and Lady Macbeth, the brutality of the murder of Lady Macduff and her son was in keeping with the production's bleakly formidable set and unsparing confrontation with uncontrollable evil. Interpretations have ranged from Guthrie's excision of the witches in Act 1, scene 1, to more predetermined views of Macbeth's tragedy, as in Stratford, Ontario's *Macbeth* of 1983, in which the witches hovered everywhere and even took the part of the third murderer of Banquo so that they could enable Fleance to escape as predicted, or the Kabuki *Macbeth* of Chicago's Wisdom Bridge Theatre, 1983, in which the witches were puppetmasters guiding the players in their drama by invisible wires.

The twentieth century has been a time, then, of experimentation in nonrepresentational staging and of candid exploration of evil in the context of modern experience with war and terror. Orson Welles directed a *Macbeth* with an all black cast at New York's Lafayette Theater in 1936, with the witches replaced by voodoo practitioners. Peter Hall's production at Stratford-upon-Avon in 1967 consciously explored what Hall termed "the metaphysics of evil," opening with a large white sheet that fluttered away at the approach of the witches to reveal a bloodred carpet. At Stratford, Ontario, in 1971, Peter Gill directed a *Macbeth* centered on the idea of tyranny, with throngs of "poor people" present as the silent victims of the powerful. In 1974, at the height of interest in the Watergate scandal, Edward Berkeley directed the play for the New York Shakespeare Festival, on a grim set composed of subway grates, as a study of public corruption and the inner wastage it involves. The following year, at Stratford-upon-Avon, Trevor Nunn produced a dark, brooding version of the play, with Nicol Williamson playing Macbeth, in the words of drama critic Irving Wardle, as "a secretive man who becomes more and more unreachable until by the end events are happening only in his head." Two years later, at The Other Place in Stratford, Nunn brilliantly directed Ian McKellen and Judi Dench on a small, bare stage with a few crates as props, emphasizing the claustrophobic world created by Macbeth's manic evil. Adrian Noble's *Macbeth*, starring Jonathan Pryce, at Stratford-upon-Avon in 1986, was domestic and introverted, all the more terrifying for being so, finding the tragedy in Macbeth's inability to live with the consequences of his actions and their ramifications. In whatever guise, and in spite of its notoriety for being bad luck in the theater, *Macbeth* has attracted a remarkable roster of great performers in recent years: Judith Anderson, Alec Guinness, Pamela Brown, Donald Wolfit, Michael Redgrave, Godfrey Tearle, Diana Wynyard, Paul Rogers, Albert Finney, Simone Signoret, Michael Hordern, Christopher Plummer, Eric Porter, Jason Robards, Jr., Christopher Walken, F. Murray Abraham, Janet Suzman, and Peter O'Toole, to name only some.

Macbeth has also attracted the attention of gifted filmmakers. Orson Welles's *Macbeth* (1948), though marred by a low budget and some uneven acting, makes bold use of the film medium to support the psychological proposition that much of Macbeth's imagining is unreal. The camera is permitted to see—or not see—things from Macbeth's point of view by literally peering over his shoulder. Roman Polanski's *Macbeth* (1971) revels in the kind of graphic and sensational violence that film can exploit, establishing the deep pessimism of Polanski's vision. Macbeth's defeat does not signal a renewed order: Macduff's victory is achieved with a random blow, and the play ends with Donalbain now in search of the witches and his own crown. Beyond doubt the greatest film version of *Macbeth* is Akira Kurosawa's *Throne of Blood* (1957), in which the story of Macbeth is retold in terms of Japanese warlord history, with arresting images of mist-shrouded forests and mysteriously disappearing witches, and spare oriental interiors intensifying the loneliness of the murdering protagonists. Whenever it is performed, *Macbeth*'s desolating story of crime and tragic failure remains essentially timeless, even while it enables the performers to gather around them the particular forms of human gesture and experience through which succeeding generations of actors and playgoers have striven to understand Shakespeare's masterful play.

MACBETH

[Dramatis Personae

DUNCAN, *King of Scotland*
MALCOLM,
DONALBAIN, } *his sons*

MACBETH, *Thane of Glamis, later of Cawdor, later King of Scotland*
LADY MACBETH

BANQUO, *a thane of Scotland*
FLEANCE, *his son*
MACDUFF, *Thane of Fife*
LADY MACDUFF
SON *of Macduff and Lady Macduff*

LENNOX,
ROSS,
MENTEITH, } *thanes and noblemen of Scotland*
ANGUS,
CAITHNESS,

SIWARD, *Earl of Northumberland*
YOUNG SIWARD, *his son*
SEYTON, *an officer attending Macbeth*
Another LORD
ENGLISH DOCTOR
SCOTTISH DOCTOR
GENTLEWOMAN *attending Lady Macbeth*
CAPTAIN *serving Duncan*
PORTER
OLD MAN
Three MURDERERS *of Banquo*
FIRST MURDERER *at Macduff's castle*
MESSENGER *to Lady Macbeth*
MESSENGER *to Lady Macduff*
SERVANT *to Macbeth*
SERVANT *to Lady Macbeth*

Three WITCHES *or* WEIRD SISTERS
HECATE
Three APPARITIONS

*Lords, Gentlemen, Officers, Soldiers, Murderers, and
  Attendants*

SCENE: *Scotland; England*]

1.1   *Thunder and lightning. Enter three Witches.*

FIRST WITCH
  When shall we three meet again?
  In thunder, lightning, or in rain?   2
SECOND WITCH
  When the hurlyburly's done,   3
  When the battle's lost and won.
THIRD WITCH
  That will be ere the set of sun.
FIRST WITCH
  Where the place?
SECOND WITCH   Upon the heath.
THIRD WITCH
  There to meet with Macbeth.
FIRST WITCH   I come, Grimalkin!   8
SECOND WITCH   Paddock calls.   9
THIRD WITCH   Anon.   10
ALL
  Fair is foul, and foul is fair.
  Hover through the fog and filthy air.   *Exeunt.*

❖

1.2   *Alarum within. Enter King [Duncan], Malcolm,*
Donalbain, Lennox, with attendants, meeting a
bleeding Captain.

DUNCAN
  What bloody man is that? He can report,
  As seemeth by his plight, of the revolt
  The newest state.
MALCOLM   This is the sergeant   3

1.1. Location: An open place.
2 In thunder . . . rain (Witches were thought able to choose and localize
the storms about them.)   **3 hurlyburly** tumult   **8 Grimalkin** i.e., gray
cat, name of the witch's familiar spirit   **9 Paddock** toad; also a familiar   **10 Anon** at once, right away

1.2. Location: A camp near Forres.
s.d. Alarum trumpet call to arms   **3 sergeant** i.e., staff officer. (There
may be no inconsistency with his rank of "captain" in the stage direction and speech prefixes in the Folio.)

Who like a good and hardy soldier fought
'Gainst my captivity. Hail, brave friend!
Say to the King the knowledge of the broil   6
As thou didst leave it.

CAPTAIN   Doubtful it stood,
As two spent swimmers that do cling together   8
And choke their art. The merciless Macdonwald—   9
Worthy to be a rebel, for to that   10
The multiplying villainies of nature   11
Do swarm upon him—from the Western Isles   12
Of kerns and gallowglasses is supplied;   13
And Fortune, on his damnèd quarrel smiling,   14
Showed like a rebel's whore. But all's too weak;   15
For brave Macbeth—well he deserves that name—   16
Disdaining Fortune, with his brandished steel,
Which smoked with bloody execution,
Like valor's minion carved out his passage   19
Till he faced the slave,   20
Which ne'er shook hands nor bade farewell to him   21
Till he unseamed him from the nave to the chops,   22
And fixed his head upon our battlements.

DUNCAN

O valiant cousin, worthy gentleman!   24

CAPTAIN

As whence the sun 'gins his reflection   25
Shipwrecking storms and direful thunders break,   26
So from that spring whence comfort seemed to come   27
Discomfort swells. Mark, King of Scotland, mark.   28
No sooner justice had, with valor armed,

---

6 broil battle **8 spent** tired out **9 choke their art** render their skill in
swimming useless **10 to that** as if to that end or purpose **11–12 The
multiplying . . . him** i.e., ever-increasing numbers of villainous rebels
swarm about him like vermin **12 Western Isles** islands to the west of
Scotland, the Hebrides and perhaps Ireland **13 Of kerns** with light-
armed Irish foot soldiers. **gallowglasses** horsemen armed with axes
14 quarrel cause, claim **15 Showed** appeared **16 name** i.e., "brave"
19 minion darling **20 the slave** i.e., Macdonwald **21 Which** who, i.e.,
Macbeth. **ne'er . . . to him** i.e., proffered no polite salutation or farewell, acted without ceremony **22 nave** navel. **chops** jaws **24 cousin**
kinsman **25 As whence** just as from the place where. **'gins his reflection** begins its turning back (from its southward progression during
winter) **26 break** break forth, emanate **27 spring** (1) the season of
spring (2) source **28 swells** wells up

Compelled these skipping kerns to trust their heels   30
But the Norweyan lord, surveying vantage,   31
With furbished arms and new supplies of men,
Began a fresh assault.

DUNCAN
Dismayed not this our captains, Macbeth and Banquo?

CAPTAIN
Yes, as sparrows eagles, or the hare the lion.
If I say sooth, I must report they were   36
As cannons overcharged with double cracks,   37
So they doubly redoubled strokes upon the foe.   38
Except they meant to bathe in reeking wounds   39
Or memorize another Golgotha,   40
I cannot tell.
But I am faint. My gashes cry for help.

DUNCAN
So well thy words become thee as thy wounds;
They smack of honor both.—Go get him surgeons.
                              [*Exit Captain, attended.*]

    Enter Ross and Angus.

Who comes here?
MALCOLM   The worthy Thane of Ross.   45
LENNOX   What a haste looks through his eyes!
So should he look that seems to speak things strange.   47
ROSS   God save the King!
DUNCAN   Whence cam'st thou, worthy thane?
ROSS   From Fife, great King,
Where the Norweyan banners flout the sky   51
And fan our people cold.   52
Norway himself, with terrible numbers,   53
Assisted by that most disloyal traitor,
The Thane of Cawdor, began a dismal conflict,   55

30 skipping (1) lightly armed, quick at maneuvering (2) skittish
31 surveying vantage seeing an opportunity   **36 say sooth** tell the
truth   **37 cracks** charges of explosive   **38 So** in such a way that
39 Except unless   **40 memorize** make memorable or famous.   **Golgotha**
"place of a skull," where Christ was crucified. (Mark 15:22.)   **45 Thane**
Scottish title of honor, roughly equivalent to "Earl"   **47 seems to** seems
about to   **51 flout** mock, insult   **52 fan . . . cold** fan cold fear into our
troops   **53 Norway** the King of Norway   **55 dismal** ominous

Till that Bellona's bridegroom, lapped in proof,   56
Confronted him with self-comparisons,   57
Point against point, rebellious arm 'gainst arm,
Curbing his lavish spirit; and to conclude,   59
The victory fell on us.
DUNCAN   Great happiness!
ROSS   That now
Sweno, the Norways' king, craves composition;   62
Nor would we deign him burial of his men
Till he disbursèd at Saint Colme's Inch   64
Ten thousand dollars to our general use.   65
DUNCAN
No more that Thane of Cawdor shall deceive
Our bosom interest. Go pronounce his present death,   67
And with his former title greet Macbeth.
ROSS   I'll see it done.
DUNCAN
What he hath lost noble Macbeth hath won.

                                              Exeunt.

                            ❖

1.3   *Thunder. Enter the three Witches.*

FIRST WITCH   Where hast thou been, sister?
SECOND WITCH   Killing swine.
THIRD WITCH   Sister, where thou?
FIRST WITCH
A sailor's wife had chestnuts in her lap,
And munched, and munched, and munched. "Give me,"
    quoth I.
"Aroint thee, witch!" the rump-fed runnion cries.   6

---

56 Till . . . proof i.e., until Macbeth, clad in well-tested armor. (Bellona
was the Roman goddess of war.) **57 him** i.e., the King of Norway. **self-
comparisons** i.e., matching counterthrusts **59 lavish** insolent, unrestrained **62 Norways'** Norwegians'. **composition** agreement, treaty of
peace **64 Saint Colme's Inch** Inchcolm, the Isle of St. Columba in the
Firth of Forth **65 dollars** Spanish or Dutch coins **67 Our** (The royal
"we.") **bosom** close and affectionate. **present** immediate

1.3. Location: A heath near Forres.
6 Aroint thee avaunt, begone. **rump-fed** fed on refuse, or fat-rumped.
runnion mangy creature, scabby woman

Her husband's to Aleppo gone, master o' the *Tiger;*   7
But in a sieve I'll thither sail,
And like a rat without a tail   9
I'll do, I'll do, and I'll do.

SECOND WITCH
  I'll give thee a wind.

FIRST WITCH
  Thou'rt kind.

THIRD WITCH
  And I another.

FIRST WITCH
  I myself have all the other,
  And the very ports they blow,   15
  All the quarters that they know
  I' the shipman's card.   17
  I'll drain him dry as hay.
  Sleep shall neither night nor day
  Hang upon his penthouse lid.   20
  He shall live a man forbid.   21
  Weary sev'nnights nine times nine   22
  Shall he dwindle, peak, and pine.   23
  Though his bark cannot be lost,
  Yet it shall be tempest-tossed.
  Look what I have.

SECOND WITCH   Show me, show me.

FIRST WITCH
  Here I have a pilot's thumb,
  Wrecked as homeward he did come.   *Drum within.*

THIRD WITCH
  A drum, a drum!
  Macbeth doth come.

ALL [*Dancing in a circle*]
  The Weird Sisters, hand in hand,   32

---

7 Tiger (A ship's name.)   **9 like** in the shape of.   **without a tail** (A familiar, or transformed witch, was thought to be recognizable by some bodily defect. The missing tail here, suggestive of a generative defect and hence of futility, introduces a sexual pun on *do,* l. 10.)   **15 they blow** i.e., from which the winds blow. (The witches can prevent a ship from entering port this way.)   **17 shipman's card** compass card, or a chart   **20 penthouse lid** i.e., eyelid (which projects out over the eye like a *penthouse* or slope-roofed structure)   **21 forbid** accursed   **22 sev'nnights** weeks   **23 peak** grow peaked or thin   **32 Weird** connected with fate

Posters of the sea and land,   33
Thus do go about, about,
Thrice to thine, and thrice to mine,
And thrice again, to make up nine.
Peace! The charm's wound up.

Enter Macbeth and Banquo.

MACBETH
So foul and fair a day I have not seen.
BANQUO
How far is 't called to Forres?—What are these,   39
So withered and so wild in their attire,
That look not like th' inhabitants o' th' earth
And yet are on 't?—Live you? Or are you aught
That man may question? You seem to understand me
By each at once her chappy finger laying   44
Upon her skinny lips. You should be women,
And yet your beards forbid me to interpret
That you are so.
MACBETH   Speak, if you can. What are you?
FIRST WITCH
All hail, Macbeth! Hail to thee, Thane of Glamis!
SECOND WITCH
All hail, Macbeth! Hail to thee, Thane of Cawdor!
THIRD WITCH
All hail, Macbeth, that shalt be king hereafter!
BANQUO
Good sir, why do you start and seem to fear
Things that do sound so fair?—I' the name of truth,
Are ye fantastical or that indeed   53
Which outwardly ye show? My noble partner   54
You greet with present grace and great prediction   55
Of noble having and of royal hope,
That he seems rapt withal. To me you speak not.   57
If you can look into the seeds of time
And say which grain will grow and which will not,

---

33 Posters of swift travelers over   **39 is 't called** is it said to be
44 chappy chapped   **53 fantastical** creatures of fantasy or imagination   **54 show** appear   **55 grace** honor   **57 rapt** carried away (by
thought).   **withal** with it, by it

Speak then to me, who neither beg nor fear   60
Your favors nor your hate.   61

FIRST WITCH   Hail!

SECOND WITCH   Hail!

THIRD WITCH   Hail!

FIRST WITCH
Lesser than Macbeth, and greater.

SECOND WITCH
Not so happy, yet much happier.   66

THIRD WITCH
Thou shalt get kings, though thou be none.   67
So all hail, Macbeth and Banquo!

FIRST WITCH
Banquo and Macbeth, all hail!

MACBETH
Stay, you imperfect speakers, tell me more!   70
By Sinel's death I know I am Thane of Glamis,   71
But how of Cawdor? The Thane of Cawdor lives
A prosperous gentleman; and to be king
Stands not within the prospect of belief,
No more than to be Cawdor. Say from whence
You owe this strange intelligence, or why   76
Upon this blasted heath you stop our way   77
With such prophetic greeting? Speak, I charge you.
                             Witches vanish.

BANQUO
The earth hath bubbles, as the water has,
And these are of them. Whither are they vanished?

MACBETH
Into the air; and what seemed corporal melted,   81
As breath into the wind. Would they had stayed!

BANQUO
Were such things here as we do speak about?
Or have we eaten on the insane root   84
That takes the reason prisoner?

60–61 beg . . . hate beg your favors nor fear your hate   **66 happy** fortunate   **67 get** beget   **70 imperfect** incomplete   **71 Sinel's** (Sinel was Macbeth's father.)   **76 owe** own, possess.   **strange** (1) unusual (2) unnatural, frighteningly alien to human experience (as often elsewhere in this play).   **intelligence** news   **77 blasted** blighted   **81 corporal** bodily   **84 on** of.   **insane root** root causing insanity; variously identified

MACBETH
　Your children shall be kings.

BANQUO　　　　　　　　　　　You shall be king.

MACBETH
　And Thane of Cawdor too. Went it not so?

BANQUO
　To th' selfsame tune and words.—Who's here?

　　Enter Ross and Angus.

ROSS
　The King hath happily received, Macbeth,
　The news of thy success; and when he reads　　　90
　Thy personal venture in the rebels' sight,　　　91
　His wonders and his praises do contend　　　92
　Which should be thine or his. Silenced with that,　　93
　In viewing o'er the rest o' the selfsame day
　He finds thee in the stout Norweyan ranks,
　Nothing afeard of what thyself didst make,　　　96
　Strange images of death. As thick as tale　　　97
　Came post with post, and every one did bear　　98
　Thy praises in his kingdom's great defense,
　And poured them down before him.

ANGUS　　　　　　　　　　　We are sent
　To give thee from our royal master thanks,
　Only to herald thee into his sight,
　Not pay thee.

ROSS
　And, for an earnest of a greater honor,　　　104
　He bade me, from him, call thee Thane of Cawdor;
　In which addition, hail, most worthy thane,　　106
　For it is thine.

BANQUO　　　　　What, can the devil speak true?

MACBETH
　The Thane of Cawdor lives. Why do you dress me
　In borrowed robes?

ANGUS　　　　　　　　　Who was the thane lives yet,　　109

---

90 reads i.e., considers　**91 Thy . . . sight** your endangering yourself
before the very eyes of the rebels　**92–93 His . . . that** i.e., your wondrous deeds so outdo any praise he could offer that he is silenced
96 Nothing not at all　**97–98 As . . . with post** as fast as could be told,
i.e., counted, came messenger after messenger　**104 earnest** token
payment　**106 addition** title　**109 Who** he who

But under heavy judgment bears that life
Which he deserves to lose. Whether he was combined 111
With those of Norway, or did line the rebel   112
With hidden help and vantage, or that with both
He labored in his country's wrack, I know not;   114
But treasons capital, confessed and proved,   115
Have overthrown him.

MACBETH [*Aside*]   Glamis, and Thane of Cawdor!
The greatest is behind. [*To Ross and Angus.*] Thanks for
    your pains.   117
[*Aside to Banquo.*] Do you not hope your children shall
    be kings
When those that gave the Thane of Cawdor to me
Promised no less to them?

BANQUO [*To Macbeth*]   That, trusted home,   120
Might yet enkindle you unto the crown,
Besides the Thane of Cawdor. But 'tis strange;
And oftentimes to win us to our harm
The instruments of darkness tell us truths,   124
Win us with honest trifles, to betray 's
In deepest consequence.—   126
Cousins, a word, I pray you.   127
            [*He converses apart with Ross and Angus.*]

MACBETH [*Aside*] Two truths are told,
As happy prologues to the swelling act   129
Of the imperial theme.—I thank you, gentlemen.
[*Aside.*] This supernatural soliciting   131
Cannot be ill, cannot be good. If ill,
Why hath it given me earnest of success
Commencing in a truth? I am Thane of Cawdor.
If good, why do I yield to that suggestion
Whose horrid image doth unfix my hair   136
And make my seated heart knock at my ribs,
Against the use of nature? Present fears   138

---

111 combined confederate **112 line** strengthen. **the rebel** i.e., Macdonwald **114 in** i.e., to bring about. **wrack** ruin **115 capital** deserving death **117 behind** to come **120 home** all the way **124 darkness**
(Indicates the demonic beyond the witches.) **126 In deepest consequence** in the profoundly important sequel **127 Cousins** i.e., fellow
lords **129 swelling act** stately drama **131 soliciting** tempting
136 horrid literally, "bristling," like Macbeth's hair **138 use** custom.
fears things feared

Are less than horrible imaginings.
My thought, whose murder yet is but fantastical,   140
Shakes so my single state of man   141
That function is smothered in surmise,   142
And nothing is but what is not.   143

BANQUO   Look how our partner's rapt.

MACBETH [*Aside*]
If chance will have me king, why, chance may crown me
Without my stir.

BANQUO   New honors come upon him,   146
Like our strange garments, cleave not to their mold   147
But with the aid of use.

MACBETH [*Aside*]   Come what come may,
Time and the hour runs through the roughest day.   149

BANQUO
Worthy Macbeth, we stay upon your leisure.   150

MACBETH
Give me your favor. My dull brain was wrought   151
With things forgotten. Kind gentlemen, your pains
Are registered where every day I turn   153
The leaf to read them. Let us toward the King.
[*Aside to Banquo.*] Think upon what hath chanced, and
     at more time,   155
The interim having weighed it, let us speak
Our free hearts each to other.   157

BANQUO [*To Macbeth*]   Very gladly.

MACBETH [*To Banquo*]   Till then, enough.—Come, friends.
                                        Exeunt.

❦

140 **whose** in which.   **but fantastical** merely imagined   141 **single . . .
man** weak human condition   142 **function** normal power of action.
surmise speculation, imaginings   143 **nothing . . . not** only unreal
imaginings have (for me) any reality   146 **stir** bestirring (myself).   **come**
i.e., which have come   147 **strange** unaccustomed (with an ironical
glance at "alien").   **their mold** i.e., the shape of the person within
them   149 **Time . . . day** i.e., what must happen will happen one way or
another   150 **stay** wait   151 **favor** pardon   153 **registered** recorded (in
my memory)   155 **at more time** at a time of greater leisure   157 **Our
free hearts** our hearts freely

1.4   *Flourish. Enter King [Duncan], Lennox,*
       Malcolm, Donalbain, and attendants.

DUNCAN
  Is execution done on Cawdor? Are not
  Those in commission yet returned?
MALCOLM   My liege,   2
  They are not yet come back. But I have spoke
  With one that saw him die, who did report
  That very frankly he confessed his treasons,
  Implored Your Highness' pardon, and set forth
  A deep repentance. Nothing in his life
  Became him like the leaving it. He died
  As one that had been studied in his death   9
  To throw away the dearest thing he owed   10
  As 'twere a careless trifle.
DUNCAN   There's no art   11
  To find the mind's construction in the face.
  He was a gentleman on whom I built
  An absolute trust.

       Enter Macbeth, Banquo, Ross, and Angus.

            O worthiest cousin!
  The sin of my ingratitude even now
  Was heavy on me. Thou art so far before   16
  That swiftest wing of recompense is slow
  To overtake thee. Would thou hadst less deserved,
  That the proportion both of thanks and payment   19
  Might have been mine! Only I have left to say,   20
  More is thy due than more than all can pay.
MACBETH
  The service and the loyalty I owe,
  In doing it, pays itself. Your Highness' part
  Is to receive our duties; and our duties
  Are to your throne and state children and servants,   25

1.4. Location: Forres. The palace.
2 in commission having warrant (to see to the execution of Cawdor)
9 been studied made it his study   **10 owed** owned   **11 careless** uncared
for   **16 before** ahead (in deserving)   **19–20 That . . . mine** i.e., that I
might have thanked and rewarded you in ample proportion to your
worth   **25 Are . . . servants** i.e., are like children and servants in relation
to your throne and dignity, existing only to serve you

Which do but what they should by doing everything
Safe toward your love and honor.

DUNCAN   Welcome hither!   27
I have begun to plant thee, and will labor
To make thee full of growing. Noble Banquo,
That hast no less deserved, nor must be known
No less to have done so, let me infold thee
And hold thee to my heart.

BANQUO   There if I grow,
The harvest is your own.

DUNCAN   My plenteous joys,
Wanton in fullness, seek to hide themselves   34
In drops of sorrow.—Sons, kinsmen, thanes,
And you whose places are the nearest, know
We will establish our estate upon   37
Our eldest, Malcolm, whom we name hereafter
The Prince of Cumberland; which honor must   39
Not unaccompanied invest him only,   40
But signs of nobleness, like stars, shall shine
On all deservers.—From hence to Inverness,   42
And bind us further to you.   43

MACBETH
The rest is labor which is not used for you.   44
I'll be myself the harbinger and make joyful   45
The hearing of my wife with your approach;
So humbly take my leave.

DUNCAN   My worthy Cawdor!

MACBETH [*Aside*]
The Prince of Cumberland! That is a step
On which I must fall down or else o'erleap,
For in my way it lies. Stars, hide your fires;   50

---

27 Safe toward to safeguard   **34 Wanton** unrestrained   **37 We** (The royal
"we.")   **establish our estate** fix the succession of our state   **39 Prince
of Cumberland** title of the heir apparent to the Scottish throne   **40 Not
. . . only** i.e., not be bestowed on Malcolm alone; other deserving nobles
are to share honors   **42 Inverness** the seat or location of Macbeth's
castle, Dunsinane   **43 bind . . . you** i.e., put me further in your (Macbeth's) obligation by your hospitality   **44 The . . . you** i.e., even repose,
when not devoted to your service, becomes tedious and wearisome
45 harbinger forerunner, messenger to arrange royal lodging   **50 in my
way it lies** (The monarchy was not hereditary, and Macbeth had a right
to believe that he himself might be chosen as Duncan's successor; he
here questions whether he will interfere with the course of events.)

Let not light see my black and deep desires.
The eye wink at the hand; yet let that be   52
Which the eye fears, when it is done, to see.   *Exit.*

DUNCAN
True, worthy Banquo. He is full so valiant,   54
And in his commendations I am fed;
It is a banquet to me. Let's after him,
Whose care is gone before to bid us welcome.
It is a peerless kinsman.   *Flourish. Exeunt.*

❖

1.5 *Enter Macbeth's Wife, alone, with a letter.*

LADY MACBETH [*Reads*] "They met me in the day of
success; and I have learned by the perfect'st report they   2
have more in them than mortal knowledge. When I
burnt in desire to question them further, they made
themselves air, into which they vanished. Whiles I
stood rapt in the wonder of it came missives from the   6
King, who all-hailed me 'Thane of Cawdor,' by which
title, before, these Weird Sisters saluted me, and referred me to the coming on of time with 'Hail, king
that shalt be!' This have I thought good to deliver thee,   10
my dearest partner of greatness, that thou mightst not
lose the dues of rejoicing by being ignorant of what
greatness is promised thee. Lay it to thy heart, and
farewell."
Glamis thou art, and Cawdor, and shalt be
What thou art promised. Yet do I fear thy nature;   16
It is too full o' the milk of human kindness
To catch the nearest way. Thou wouldst be great,
Art not without ambition, but without
The illness should attend it. What thou wouldst highly,   20
That wouldst thou holily; wouldst not play false,
And yet wouldst wrongly win. Thou'dst have, great
   Glamis,

---

52 wink . . . hand blind itself to the hand's deed. **let that be** may that
thing come to pass **54 full so valiant** fully as valiant as you say

1.5. Location: Inverness. Macbeth's castle.
2 perfect'st most accurate **6 missives** messengers **10 deliver** inform
16 fear am anxious about, mistrust **20 illness** evil (which). **highly** greatly

That which cries "Thus thou must do," if thou have it, 23
And that which rather thou dost fear to do   24
Than wishest should be undone. Hie thee hither,   25
That I may pour my spirits in thine ear
And chastise with the valor of my tongue
All that impedes thee from the golden round   28
Which fate and metaphysical aid doth seem   29
To have thee crowned withal.

    Enter Messenger.

                          What is your tidings?   30

MESSENGER
The King comes here tonight.

LADY MACBETH   Thou'rt mad to say it!
Is not thy master with him, who, were 't so,
Would have informed for preparation?   33

MESSENGER
So please you, it is true. Our thane is coming.
One of my fellows had the speed of him,   35
Who, almost dead for breath, had scarcely more
Than would make up his message.

LADY MACBETH   Give him tending;   37
He brings great news.   *Exit Messenger.*
                The raven himself is hoarse
That croaks the fatal entrance of Duncan
Under my battlements. Come, you spirits
That tend on mortal thoughts, unsex me here   41
And fill me from the crown to the toe top-full
Of direst cruelty! Make thick my blood;
Stop up th' access and passage to remorse,   44
That no compunctious visitings of nature   45
Shake my fell purpose, nor keep peace between   46

---

23 have are to have, want to have   **24–25 And that . . . undone** i.e., and
the thing you ambitiously crave frightens you more in terms of the
means needed to achieve it than in the idea of having it; if you could
have it without those means, you certainly wouldn't wish it undone
25 Hie hasten   **28 round** crown   **29 metaphysical** supernatural
30 withal with   **33 informed for preparation** i.e., sent me word so that I
might get things ready   **35 had . . . of** outstripped   **37 tending** attendance   **41 tend . . . thoughts** attend on, act as the instruments of deadly
or murderous thoughts   **44 remorse** pity   **45 nature** natural feelings
46 fell fierce, cruel.   **keep peace** intervene

Th' effect and it! Come to my woman's breasts   47
And take my milk for gall, you murdering ministers,   48
Wherever in your sightless substances   49
You wait on nature's mischief! Come, thick night,   50
And pall thee in the dunnest smoke of hell,   51
That my keen knife see not the wound it makes,
Nor heaven peep through the blanket of the dark
To cry "Hold, hold!"

     Enter Macbeth.

             Great Glamis! Worthy Cawdor!
Greater than both by the all-hail hereafter!
Thy letters have transported me beyond   56
This ignorant present, and I feel now
The future in the instant.
MACBETH   My dearest love,
Duncan comes here tonight.
LADY MACBETH   And when goes hence?
MACBETH
Tomorrow, as he purposes.
LADY MACBETH   O, never
Shall sun that morrow see!
Your face, my thane, is as a book where men
May read strange matters. To beguile the time,   63
Look like the time; bear welcome in your eye,   64
Your hand, your tongue. Look like th' innocent flower,
But be the serpent under 't. He that's coming
Must be provided for; and you shall put
This night's great business into my dispatch,   68
Which shall to all our nights and days to come
Give solely sovereign sway and masterdom.
MACBETH
We will speak further.
LADY MACBETH   Only look up clear.   71

---

47 Th' effect and it i.e., my *fell purpose* and its accomplishment   **48 for gall** in exchange for gall.   **ministers** agents   **49 sightless** invisible **50 wait on** attend, assist.   **nature's mischief** evil done to nature, or within the realm of nature   **51 pall** envelop.   **dunnest** darkest **56 letters have** i.e., letter has   **63 beguile the time** i.e., deceive all observers   **64 Look like the time** look the way people expect you to look   **68 dispatch** management   **71 look up clear** give the appearance of being untroubled

To alter favor ever is to fear.   72
Leave all the rest to me.   *Exeunt.*

❖

1.6   *Hautboys and torches. Enter King [Duncan],*
          Malcolm, Donalbain, Banquo, Lennox,
          Macduff, Ross, Angus, and attendants.

DUNCAN
  This castle hath a pleasant seat. The air   1
  Nimbly and sweetly recommends itself
  Unto our gentle senses.
BANQUO   This guest of summer,   3
  The temple-haunting martlet, does approve   4
  By his loved mansionry that the heaven's breath   5
  Smells wooingly here. No jutty, frieze,   6
  Buttress, nor coign of vantage but this bird   7
  Hath made his pendent bed and procreant cradle.   8
  Where they most breed and haunt, I have observed
  The air is delicate.

          Enter Lady [Macbeth].

DUNCAN   See, see, our honored hostess!
  The love that follows us sometimes is our trouble,   11
  Which still we thank as love. Herein I teach you   12
  How you shall bid God 'ild us for your pains,   13
  And thank us for your trouble.
LADY MACBETH   All our service
  In every point twice done, and then done double,

---

72 To . . . fear to show a troubled countenance is to arouse suspicion

1.6. Location: Before Macbeth's castle.
s.d. Hautboys oboelike instruments   1 seat site   3 gentle (1) noble
(2) delicate (applied to the air)   4 temple-haunting nesting in
churches.   martlet house martin.   approve prove   5 mansionry nest-
building   6 jutty projection of wall or building   7 coign of vantage
convenient corner, i.e., for nesting   8 procreant for breeding
11–12 The love . . . love i.e., the love that sometimes forces itself incon-
veniently upon us we still appreciate, since it is meant as love. (Duncan
is graciously suggesting that his visit is a bother, but, he hopes, a
welcome one.)   13 bid . . . pains ask God to reward me for the trouble
I'm giving you. (This is said in the same gently jocose spirit as ll. 11–12.)

Were poor and single business to contend   16
Against those honors deep and broad wherewith   17
Your Majesty loads our house. For those of old,   18
And the late dignities heaped up to them,   19
We rest your hermits.
DUNCAN   Where's the Thane of Cawdor?   20
We coursed him at the heels, and had a purpose   21
To be his purveyor; but he rides well,   22
And his great love, sharp as his spur, hath holp him   23
To his home before us. Fair and noble hostess,
We are your guest tonight.
LADY MACBETH   Your servants ever
Have theirs, themselves, and what is theirs in compt   26
To make their audit at Your Highness' pleasure,   27
Still to return your own.
DUNCAN   Give me your hand.   28
Conduct me to mine host. We love him highly,   29
And shall continue our graces towards him.
By your leave, hostess.   *Exeunt.*

✢

1.7   *Hautboys. Torches. Enter a sewer, and divers
servants with dishes and service, [and pass]
over the stage. Then enter Macbeth.*

MACBETH
If it were done when 'tis done, then 'twere well
It were done quickly. If th' assassination

16 **single** small, inconsiderable   **16–17 contend Against** vie with
18 **those of old** i.e., honors formerly bestowed on us   **19 late** recent.
to besides, in addition to   **20 rest** remain.   **hermits** i.e., those who will
pray for you like hermits or beadsmen   **21 coursed** followed (as in a
hunt)   **22 purveyor** an officer sent ahead to provide for entertainment;
here, forerunner   **23 holp** helped   **26 Have theirs** i.e., have their servants.   **what is theirs** their wealth, possessions.   **in compt** in trust,
under obligation (to serve the King)   **27 make their audit** render their
account   **28 Still** always.   **return your own** i.e., merely render back
what is yours, since we hold it in trust from you   **29 We** (The royal
"we.")

1.7. Location: Macbeth's castle; an inner courtyard.
s.d. sewer chief waiter, butler

Could trammel up the consequence and catch   3
With his surcease success—that but this blow   4
Might be the be-all and the end-all!—here,   5
But here, upon this bank and shoal of time,
We'd jump the life to come. But in these cases   7
We still have judgment here, that we but teach   8
Bloody instructions, which, being taught, return   9
To plague th' inventor. This evenhanded justice
Commends th' ingredience of our poisoned chalice   11
To our own lips. He's here in double trust:
First, as I am his kinsman and his subject,
Strong both against the deed; then, as his host,
Who should against his murderer shut the door,
Not bear the knife myself. Besides, this Duncan
Hath borne his faculties so meek, hath been   17
So clear in his great office, that his virtues   18
Will plead like angels, trumpet-tongued, against
The deep damnation of his taking-off;   20
And Pity, like a naked newborn babe
Striding the blast, or heaven's cherubin, horsed   22
Upon the sightless couriers of the air,   23
Shall blow the horrid deed in every eye,
That tears shall drown the wind. I have no spur   25
To prick the sides of my intent, but only
Vaulting ambition, which o'erleaps itself
And falls on th' other—   28

    Enter Lady [Macbeth].

How now, what news?

LADY MACBETH
   He has almost supped. Why have you left the chamber?

---

3 trammel . . . consequence entangle in a net and prevent the resulting
events **4 his surcease** cessation (of the assassination and of Duncan's
life). **success** what succeeds, follows **5 here** in this world **7 jump**
risk. (But imaging the physical act is characteristic of Macbeth; cf.
l. 27.) **8 still have judgment** are invariably punished. **that** in that
9 instructions lessons **11 Commends** presents. **ingredience** contents
of a mixture **17 faculties** powers of office **18 clear** free of taint
20 taking-off murder **22 Striding** bestriding **23 sightless couriers**
invisible steeds or runners, i.e., the winds **25 shall drown the wind** i.e.,
will be as heavy as a downpour of rain, which is thought to still the
wind **28 other** other side. (The image is of a horseman vaulting into his
saddle and ignominiously falling on the opposite side.)

MACBETH
    Hath he asked for me?
LADY MACBETH   Know you not he has?
MACBETH
    We will proceed no further in this business.
    He hath honored me of late, and I have bought   33
    Golden opinions from all sorts of people,
    Which would be worn now in their newest gloss,   35
    Not cast aside so soon.
LADY MACBETH   Was the hope drunk
    Wherein you dressed yourself? Hath it slept since?
    And wakes it now, to look so green and pale   38
    At what it did so freely? From this time
    Such I account thy love. Art thou afeard
    To be the same in thine own act and valor
    As thou art in desire? Wouldst thou have that
    Which thou esteem'st the ornament of life,   43
    And live a coward in thine own esteem,
    Letting "I dare not" wait upon "I would,"   45
    Like the poor cat i' th' adage?
MACBETH   Prithee, peace!   46
    I dare do all that may become a man;
    Who dares do more is none.
LADY MACBETH   What beast was 't, then,
    That made you break this enterprise to me?   49
    When you durst do it, then you were a man;
    And to be more than what you were, you would
    Be so much more the man. Nor time nor place
    Did then adhere, and yet you would make both.   53
    They have made themselves, and that their fitness now 54
    Does unmake you. I have given suck, and know
    How tender 'tis to love the babe that milks me;
    I would, while it was smiling in my face,
    Have plucked my nipple from his boneless gums
    And dashed the brains out, had I so sworn as you
    Have done to this.
MACBETH   If we should fail?

---

33 bought acquired (by bravery in battle)   **35 would** ought to, want to
38 green sickly   **43 the ornament of life** i.e., the crown   **45 wait upon**
accompany, attend   **46 adage** (i.e., "The cat would eat fish, and would
not wet her feet")   **49 break** broach   **53 adhere** agree, suit.   **would**
wanted to   **54 that their fitness** their very suitability

LADY MACBETH   We fail?
But screw your courage to the sticking place   61
And we'll not fail. When Duncan is asleep—
Whereto the rather shall his day's hard journey
Soundly invite him—his two chamberlains   64
Will I with wine and wassail so convince   65
That memory, the warder of the brain,   66
Shall be a fume, and the receipt of reason   67
A limbeck only. When in swinish sleep   68
Their drenchèd natures lies as in a death,
What cannot you and I perform upon
Th' unguarded Duncan? What not put upon
His spongy officers, who shall bear the guilt   72
Of our great quell?

MACBETH   Bring forth men-children only!   73
For thy undaunted mettle should compose   74
Nothing but males. Will it not be received,   75
When we have marked with blood those sleepy two
Of his own chamber and used their very daggers,
That they have done 't?

LADY MACBETH   Who dares receive it other,   78
As we shall make our griefs and clamor roar   79
Upon his death?

MACBETH   I am settled, and bend up   80
Each corporal agent to this terrible feat.   81
Away, and mock the time with fairest show.   82
False face must hide what the false heart doth know.

                              Exeunt.

❖

61 **But** only. **the sticking place** the notch into which is fitted the string
of a crossbow cranked taut for shooting **64 chamberlains** attendants
on the bedchamber **65 wassail** carousal, drink. **convince** overpower
66–68 warder . . . only (The brain was thought to be divided into three
ventricles, imagination in front, memory at the back, and between them
the seat of reason. The fumes of wine, arising from the stomach, would
deaden memory and judgment.) **67 receipt** receptacle, ventricle
68 limbeck alembic, still **72 spongy** soaked, drunken **73 quell** murder **74 mettle** temperament **75 received** i.e., as truth **78 other**
otherwise **79 As** inasmuch as **80–81 bend . . . agent** strain every
muscle **82 mock** deceive

2.1   *Enter Banquo, and Fleance, with a torch
          before him.*

BANQUO How goes the night, boy?

FLEANCE
  The moon is down. I have not heard the clock.

BANQUO
  And she goes down at twelve.

FLEANCE   I take 't 'tis later, sir.

BANQUO
  Hold, take my sword. [*He gives him his sword.*] There's
    husbandry in heaven;   4
  Their candles are all out. Take thee that too.
                    [*He gives him his belt and dagger.*]
  A heavy summons lies like lead upon me,   6
  And yet I would not sleep. Merciful powers,   7
  Restrain in me the cursèd thoughts that nature
  Gives way to in repose!

      Enter Macbeth, and a servant with a torch.

  Give me my sword. Who's there? [*He takes his sword.*]

MACBETH A friend.

BANQUO
  What, sir, not yet at rest? The King's abed.
  He hath been in unusual pleasure,
  And sent forth great largess to your offices.   14
  This diamond he greets your wife withal,
  By the name of most kind hostess, and shut up   16
  In measureless content.   [*He gives a diamond.*]

MACBETH   Being unprepared,   17
  Our will became the servant to defect,   18
  Which else should free have wrought.   19

**2.1. Location: Inner courtyard of Macbeth's castle. Time is virtually
continuous from the previous scene.**
s.d. torch (This may mean "torchbearer," although it does not at l. 9
s.d.)   **4 husbandry** economy   **6 summons** i.e., to sleep   **7 would not** do
not wish to.   **powers** order of angels deputed by God to resist demons
14 largess gifts, gratuities.   **offices** quarters used for the household
work   **16–17 shut up In** concluded what he had to say with expressions
of; or, perhaps, he professes himself enclosed in   **18 Our . . . defect** our
good will (to entertain the King handsomely) was limited by our meager
means (at such short notice)   **19 free** freely, unrestrainedly

BANQUO All's well.
  I dreamt last night of the three Weird Sisters.
  To you they have showed some truth.
MACBETH   I think not of them.
  Yet, when we can entreat an hour to serve,
  We would spend it in some words upon that business,
  If you would grant the time.
BANQUO   At your kind'st leisure.
MACBETH
  If you shall cleave to my consent when 'tis,   26
  It shall make honor for you.
BANQUO   So I lose none   27
  In seeking to augment it, but still keep
  My bosom franchised and allegiance clear,   29
  I shall be counseled.
MACBETH   Good repose the while!   30
BANQUO Thanks, sir. The like to you.
                         Exit Banquo [with Fleance].

MACBETH
  Go bid thy mistress, when my drink is ready,   32
  She strike upon the bell. Get thee to bed.
                              Exit [Servant].
  Is this a dagger which I see before me,
  The handle toward my hand? Come, let me clutch thee.
  I have thee not, and yet I see thee still.
  Art thou not, fatal vision, sensible   37
  To feeling as to sight? Or art thou but
  A dagger of the mind, a false creation,
  Proceeding from the heat-oppressèd brain?   40
  I see thee yet, in form as palpable
  As this which now I draw.   *[He draws a dagger.]*
  Thou marshall'st me the way that I was going,   43
  And such an instrument I was to use.

26 cleave . . . 'tis give me your support when the time comes **27 So**
provided **29 franchised** free (from guilt). **clear** unstained
30 counseled receptive to suggestion **32 drink** i.e., posset or bedtime
drink of hot spiced milk curdled with ale or wine, as also at 2.2.6
37 fatal ominous. **sensible** perceivable by the senses **40 heat-**
oppressèd fevered **43 Thou . . . going** i.e., you seem to guide me toward
the destiny I intended, toward Duncan's chambers

Mine eyes are made the fools o' th' other senses,   45
Or else worth all the rest. I see thee still,   46
And on thy blade and dudgeon gouts of blood,   47
Which was not so before. There's no such thing.
It is the bloody business which informs   49
Thus to mine eyes. Now o'er the one half world
Nature seems dead, and wicked dreams abuse   51
The curtained sleep. Witchcraft celebrates   52
Pale Hecate's offerings, and withered Murder,   53
Alarumed by his sentinel, the wolf,   54
Whose howl's his watch, thus with his stealthy pace,   55
With Tarquin's ravishing strides, towards his design   56
Moves like a ghost. Thou sure and firm-set earth,
Hear not my steps which way they walk, for fear
Thy very stones prate of my whereabouts
And take the present horror from the time   60
Which now suits with it. Whiles I threat, he lives;   61
Words to the heat of deeds too cold breath gives.   62

                                        A bell rings.

I go, and it is done. The bell invites me.
Hear it not, Duncan, for it is a knell
That summons thee to heaven or to hell.   *Exit.*

2.2   *Enter Lady [Macbeth].*

LADY MACBETH
    That which hath made them drunk hath made me bold;

45–46 Mine . . . rest i.e., either this is a fantasy, deceiving me with what my eyes seem to see, or else it is a true vision expressing something that is beyond ordinary sensory experience   **47 dudgeon** hilt of a dagger.   **gouts** drops   **49 informs** creates forms or impressions **51 abuse** deceive   **52 curtained** (1) veiled by bedcurtains (2) screened from rationality and consciousness   **53 Pale Hecate's offerings** sacrificial offerings to Hecate, the goddess of night and witchcraft. (She is *pale* because she is identified with the pale moon.)   **54 Alarumed** given the signal to action   **55 watch** i.e., watchword, or cry like the hourly call of the night watchman   **56 Tarquin's** (Tarquin was a Roman tyrant who ravished Lucrece.)   **60–61 And take . . . with it** and thus imitate and augment the horror which is so suited to this evil hour (?) or, remove the present horror, the murder, by crying out and revealing Macbeth's intent (?)   **62 Words . . . gives** i.e., words give only lifeless expression to live deeds, are no substitute for deeds

2.2. Location: Scene continues.

What hath quenched them hath given me fire. Hark!
  Peace!
It was the owl that shrieked, the fatal bellman,   3
Which gives the stern'st good-night. He is about it.   4
The doors are open; and the surfeited grooms   5
Do mock their charge with snores. I have drugged their
  possets,   6
That death and nature do contend about them
Whether they live or die.

MACBETH [*Within*]   Who's there? What, ho!

LADY MACBETH
Alack, I am afraid they have awaked,
And 'tis not done. Th' attempt and not the deed
Confounds us. Hark! I laid their daggers ready;   11
He could not miss 'em. Had he not resembled
My father as he slept, I had done 't.

    Enter Macbeth, [bearing bloody daggers].

My husband!

MACBETH
I have done the deed. Didst thou not hear a noise?

LADY MACBETH
I heard the owl scream and the crickets cry.   16
Did not you speak?

MACBETH   When?

LADY MACBETH   Now.

MACBETH   As I descended?

LADY MACBETH   Ay.

MACBETH   Hark! Who lies i' the second chamber?

LADY MACBETH   Donalbain.

MACBETH   This is a sorry sight. [*He looks at his hands.*]

LADY MACBETH
A foolish thought, to say a sorry sight.

MACBETH
There's one did laugh in 's sleep, and one cried
  "Murder!"

---

3 bellman one who rings a bell to announce a death or to mark the hours
of the night   **4 stern'st good-night** i.e., notice to condemned criminals
that they are to be executed in the morning   **5 grooms** servants
6 mock their charge make a mockery of their guard duty.   **possets** hot
bedtime drinks, (as at 2.1.32)   **11 Confounds** ruins   **16 owl, crickets**
(The sounds of both could be ominous and prophetic of death.)

That they did wake each other. I stood and heard them.
But they did say their prayers, and addressed them   28
Again to sleep.

LADY MACBETH   There are two lodged together.   29

MACBETH
One cried "God bless us!" and "Amen!" the other,
As they had seen me with these hangman's hands.   31
List'ning their fear, I could not say "Amen"
When they did say "God bless us!"

LADY MACBETH   Consider it not so deeply.

MACBETH
But wherefore could not I pronounce "Amen"?
I had most need of blessing, and "Amen"
Stuck in my throat.

LADY MACBETH   These deeds must not be thought   37
After these ways; so, it will make us mad.   38

MACBETH
Methought I heard a voice cry "Sleep no more!
Macbeth does murder sleep," the innocent sleep,
Sleep that knits up the raveled sleave of care,   41
The death of each day's life, sore labor's bath,   42
Balm of hurt minds, great nature's second course,   43
Chief nourisher in life's feast—

LADY MACBETH   What do you mean?

MACBETH
Still it cried "Sleep no more!" to all the house;
"Glamis hath murdered sleep, and therefore Cawdor
Shall sleep no more; Macbeth shall sleep no more."

LADY MACBETH
Who was it that thus cried? Why, worthy thane,
You do unbend your noble strength to think   49
So brainsickly of things. Go get some water
And wash this filthy witness from your hand.   51

---

28 addressed them settled themselves   **29 two** i.e., Malcolm and Donalbain   **31 As** as if.   **hangman's hands** bloody hands (because the hangman would draw and quarter the condemned, and also executed with an
ax)   **37 thought** thought about   **38 so** if we do so   **41 raveled sleave**
tangled skein   **42 bath** i.e., to relieve the soreness   **43 second course**
(Ordinary feasts had two courses, of which the second was the *chief
nourisher;* here, sleep is seen as following eating in a restorative process.)   **49 unbend** slacken (as one would a bow; contrast "bend up" at
1.7.80)   **51 witness** evidence

Why did you bring these daggers from the place?
They must lie there. Go, carry them and smear
The sleepy grooms with blood.

MACBETH   I'll go no more.
I am afraid to think what I have done;
Look on 't again I dare not.

LADY MACBETH   Infirm of purpose!
Give me the daggers. The sleeping and the dead
Are but as pictures. 'Tis the eye of childhood
That fears a painted devil. If he do bleed,
I'll gild the faces of the grooms withal,   60
For it must seem their guilt.

> [*She takes the daggers, and*] *Exit.*
> *Knock within.*

MACBETH   Whence is that knocking?
How is 't with me, when every noise appalls me?
What hands are here? Ha! They pluck out mine eyes.
Will all great Neptune's ocean wash this blood
Clean from my hand? No, this my hand will rather
The multitudinous seas incarnadine,   66
Making the green one red.   67

Enter Lady [*Macbeth*].

LADY MACBETH
My hands are of your color, but I shame
To wear a heart so white. (*Knock.*) I hear a knocking
At the south entry. Retire we to our chamber.
A little water clears us of this deed.
How easy is it, then! Your constancy   72
Hath left you unattended. (*Knock.*) Hark! More
  knocking.   73
Get on your nightgown, lest occasion calls us   74
And show us to be watchers. Be not lost   75
So poorly in your thoughts.   76

60 gild (Gold was ordinarily spoken of as red.) **66 multitudinous**
existing in multitudes, numerous. **incarnadine** make red **67 one red**
one all-pervading red **72–73 Your . . . unattended** your firmness has
deserted you **74 nightgown** dressing gown **75 watchers** those who
have remained awake **76 poorly** dejectedly

MACBETH

To know my deed, 'twere best not know myself.   77

Knock.

Wake Duncan with thy knocking! I would thou
    couldst!   *Exeunt.*

2.3   *Knocking within. Enter a Porter.*

PORTER   Here's a knocking indeed! If a man were porter
of hell gate, he should have old turning the key. 2
(*Knock.*) Knock, knock, knock! Who's there, i' the
name of Beelzebub? Here's a farmer that hanged him- 4
self on th' expectation of plenty. Come in time! Have 5
napkins enough about you; here you'll sweat for 't. 6
(*Knock.*) Knock, knock! Who's there, in th' other
devil's name? Faith, here's an equivocator, that could 8
swear in both the scales against either scale, who committed treason enough for God's sake, yet could not
equivocate to heaven. O, come in, equivocator.
(*Knock.*) Knock, knock, knock! Who's there? Faith,
here's an English tailor come hither for stealing out of
a French hose. Come in, tailor. Here you may roast 14
your goose. (*Knock.*) Knock, knock! Never at quiet! 15

---

77 To . . . myself i.e., it were better to be lost in my thoughts than to
have consciousness of my deed; if I am to live with myself, I will have to
shut this out or be no longer the person I was

**2.3. Location: Scene continues. The knocking at the door has already
been heard in 2.2. It is not necessary to assume literally, however, that
Macbeth and Lady Macbeth have been talking near the *south entry*
(2.2.70) where the knocking is heard.**
2 old i.e., plenty of   **4–5 Here's . . . plenty** i.e., here's a farmer who
has hoarded in anticipation of a scarcity, and will be justly punished by a crop surplus and low prices   **5 Come in time** i.e., you have
come in good time   **6 napkins** handkerchiefs (to mop up the sweat)
8 equivocator (This is regarded by many editors as an allusion to the
trial of the Jesuit Henry Garnet for treason in the spring of 1606, and to
the doctrine of equivocation said to have been presented in his defense;
according to this doctrine a lie was not a lie if the utterer had in his
mind a different meaning in which the utterance was true.)   **14 French
hose** very narrow breeches and therefore hard for the tailor to steal
cloth from when he made them; or, very loose-fitting breeches, in which
case the tailor would easily be tempted to skimp on the cloth supplied
him for their manufacture   **14–15 roast your goose** heat your tailor's
smoothing iron (with an obvious pun)

What are you? But this place is too cold for hell. I'll
devil-porter it no further. I had thought to have let in
some of all professions that go the primrose way to th'
everlasting bonfire. (*Knock.*) Anon, anon! [*He opens
the gate.*] I pray you, remember the porter.

    Enter Macduff and Lennox.

MACDUFF
  Was it so late, friend, ere you went to bed,
  That you do lie so late?
PORTER Faith, sir, we were carousing till the second 23
  cock; and drink, sir, is a great provoker of three things. 24
MACDUFF What three things does drink especially provoke?
PORTER Marry, sir, nose-painting, sleep, and urine. 27
  Lechery, sir, it provokes and unprovokes: it provokes
  the desire but it takes away the performance. Therefore much drink may be said to be an equivocator
  with lechery: it makes him and it mars him; it sets him
  on and it takes him off; it persuades him and dis-
  heartens him, makes him stand to and not stand to; 33
  in conclusion, equivocates him in a sleep and, giving 34
  him the lie, leaves him. 35
MACDUFF I believe drink gave thee the lie last night. 36
PORTER That it did, sir, i' the very throat on me. But I
  requited him for his lie, and, I think, being too strong
  for him, though he took up my legs sometimes, yet I 39
  made a shift to cast him. 40
MACDUFF Is thy master stirring?

    Enter Macbeth.

  Our knocking has awaked him. Here he comes.
                       [*Exit Porter.*]

23–24 second cock i.e., 3 A.M., when the cock was thought to crow a
second time   **27 Marry** (Originally, an oath, "by the Virgin Mary.")
nose-painting i.e., reddening of the nose through drink   **33 makes . . .
stand to** stimulates him sexually but without sexual capability
34 equivocates . . . sleep (1) lulls him asleep (2) gives him an erotic
experience in dream only   **34–35 giving him the lie** (1) deceiving him
(2) laying him out flat   **35 leaves him** (1) dissipates as intoxication (2) is
passed off as urine   **36 gave thee the lie** (1) called you a liar (2) made
you unable to stand, and put you to sleep   **39 took up my legs** lifted me
as a wrestler would (with a suggestion of the drunkard's unsteadiness
on his legs, and perhaps also of lifting the leg as a dog might to urinate)
40 made a shift managed.   **cast** (1) throw as in wrestling (2) vomit

LENNOX
Good morrow, noble sir.

MACBETH   Good morrow, both.

MACDUFF
Is the King stirring, worthy thane?

MACBETH   Not yet.

MACDUFF
He did command me to call timely on him.   45
I have almost slipped the hour.

MACBETH   I'll bring you to him.   46

MACDUFF
I know this is a joyful trouble to you,
But yet 'tis one.

MACBETH
The labor we delight in physics pain.   49
This is the door.

MACDUFF   I'll make so bold to call,
For 'tis my limited service.   *Exit Macduff.* 51

LENNOX   Goes the King hence today?

MACBETH   He does; he did appoint so.

LENNOX
The night has been unruly. Where we lay,
Our chimneys were blown down, and, as they say,
Lamentings heard i' th' air, strange screams of death,
And prophesying with accents terrible   57
Of dire combustion and confused events   58
New hatched to the woeful time. The obscure bird   59
Clamored the livelong night. Some say the earth
Was feverous and did shake.

MACBETH   'Twas a rough night.

LENNOX
My young remembrance cannot parallel
A fellow to it.

     Enter Macduff.

MACDUFF   O, horror, horror, horror!
Tongue nor heart cannot conceive nor name thee!

---

45 timely betimes, early   **46 slipped** let slip   **49 physics pain** i.e., cures that labor of its troublesome aspect   **51 limited** appointed   **57 accents terrible** terrifying utterances   **58 combustion** tumult   **59 New . . . time** newly born to accompany the woeful nature of the time.   **obscure bird** owl, the bird of darkness

MACBETH AND LENNOX   What's the matter?

MACDUFF

Confusion now hath made his masterpiece!   66
Most sacrilegious murder hath broke ope
The Lord's anointed temple and stole thence
The life o' the building!

MACBETH   What is 't you say? The life?

LENNOX   Mean you His Majesty?

MACDUFF

Approach the chamber and destroy your sight
With a new Gorgon. Do not bid me speak;   73
See, and then speak yourselves.

                        Exeunt Macbeth and Lennox.
                        Awake, awake!

Ring the alarum bell. Murder and treason!
Banquo and Donalbain, Malcolm, awake!
Shake off this downy sleep, death's counterfeit,
And look on death itself! Up, up, and see
The great doom's image! Malcolm, Banquo,   79
As from your graves rise up and walk like sprites   80
To countenance this horror! Ring the bell.   *Bell rings.*   81

        Enter Lady [Macbeth].

LADY MACBETH   What's the business,
That such a hideous trumpet calls to parley   83
The sleepers of the house? Speak, speak!

MACDUFF   O gentle lady,
'Tis not for you to hear what I can speak.
The repetition in a woman's ear   87
Would murder as it fell.

        Enter Banquo.

                        O Banquo, Banquo,
Our royal master's murdered!

---

66 Confusion destruction   **73 Gorgon** one of three monsters with
hideous faces (Medusa was a Gorgon) whose look turned the beholders
to stone   **79 great doom's image** replica of Doomsday   **80 As . . . rise
up** (At the Last Judgment, the dead will rise from their graves to be
judged.)   **sprites** souls, ghosts   **81 countenance** (1) be in keeping with
(2) behold   **83 trumpet** (Another metaphorical suggestion of the Last
Judgment; the *trumpet* here is the shouting and the bell.)   **87 repetition** recital, report

LADY MACBETH   Woe, alas!
   What, in our house?
BANQUO   Too cruel anywhere.
   Dear Duff, I prithee, contradict thyself
   And say it is not so.

     Enter Macbeth, Lennox, and Ross.

MACBETH
   Had I but died an hour before this chance   93
   I had lived a blessèd time; for from this instant
   There's nothing serious in mortality.   95
   All is but toys. Renown and grace is dead;   96
   The wine of life is drawn, and the mere lees   97
   Is left this vault to brag of.   98

     Enter Malcolm and Donalbain.

DONALBAIN
   What is amiss?
MACBETH   You are, and do not know 't.   99
   The spring, the head, the fountain of your blood
   Is stopped, the very source of it is stopped.
MACDUFF
   Your royal father's murdered.
MALCOLM   O, by whom?
LENNOX
   Those of his chamber, as it seemed, had done 't.
   Their hands and faces were all badged with blood;   104
   So were their daggers, which unwiped we found
   Upon their pillows. They stared and were distracted;
   No man's life was to be trusted with them.
MACBETH
   O, yet I do repent me of my fury,
   That I did kill them.
MACDUFF   Wherefore did you so?
MACBETH
   Who can be wise, amazed, temp'rate and furious,   110
   Loyal and neutral, in a moment? No man.

93 chance occurrence (the murder of Duncan)   **95 serious in mortality**
worthwhile in mortal life   **96 toys** trifles   **97 lees** dregs   **98 vault** (1) wine-
vault (2) earth, with its vaulted sky   **99 You are** i.e., you are amiss, having suffered the murder of your father   **104 badged** marked as with a
badge or emblem   **110 amazed** bewildered

Th' expedition of my violent love   112
Outrun the pauser, reason. Here lay Duncan,
His silver skin laced with his golden blood,   114
And his gashed stabs looked like a breach in nature   115
For ruin's wasteful entrance; there the murderers,   116
Steeped in the colors of their trade, their daggers
Unmannerly breeched with gore. Who could refrain   118
That had a heart to love, and in that heart
Courage to make 's love known?

LADY MACBETH [*Fainting*]   Help me hence, ho!   120

MACDUFF
Look to the lady.

MALCOLM [*Aside to Donalbain*]
                   Why do we hold our tongues,
That most may claim this argument for ours?   122

DONALBAIN [*Aside to Malcolm*]
What should be spoken here, where our fate,
Hid in an auger hole, may rush and seize us?   124
Let's away. Our tears are not yet brewed.

MALCOLM [*Aside to Donalbain*]
Nor our strong sorrow upon the foot of motion.   126

BANQUO   Look to the lady.

                   [*Lady Macbeth is carried out.*]
And when we have our naked frailties hid,   128
That suffer in exposure, let us meet
And question this most bloody piece of work   130
To know it further. Fears and scruples shake us.   131
In the great hand of God I stand, and thence   132
Against the undivulged pretense I fight   133
Of treasonous malice.

MACDUFF   And so do I.

ALL   So all.   134

---

112 expedition haste   **114 golden** (See 2.2.60, note.)   **115 breach in
nature** gap in the defenses of life. (A metaphor of military siege.)
116 wasteful destructive   **118 breeched with gore** covered to the hilts
with gore (as with breeches)   **120 make 's love known** make manifest
his love   **122 argument** topic, business   **124 in an auger hole** i.e., in
some hiding place, in ambush   **126 upon . . . motion** yet in motion,
ready to act   **128 frailties hid** (1) bodies clothed (2) emotions con-
trolled   **130 question** discuss   **131 scruples** doubts, suspicions
132–134 thence . . . malice i.e., with God's help I will fight against the
as-yet-unknown purpose which prompted this treason   **133 pretense**
design   **134 malice** enmity

MACBETH

   Let's briefly put on manly readiness   135
   And meet i' the hall together.

ALL   Well contented.

        Exeunt [all but Malcolm and Donalbain].

MALCOLM

   What will you do? Let's not consort with them.   137
   To show an unfelt sorrow is an office
   Which the false man does easy. I'll to England.   139

DONALBAIN

   To Ireland, I. Our separated fortune
   Shall keep us both the safer. Where we are,
   There's daggers in men's smiles; the nea'er in blood,   142
   The nearer bloody.

MALCOLM   This murderous shaft that's shot   143
   Hath not yet lighted, and our safest way   144
   Is to avoid the aim. Therefore to horse,
   And let us not be dainty of leave-taking,   146
   But shift away. There's warrant in that theft   147
   Which steals itself when there's no mercy left.

                        Exeunt.

❖

2.4   *Enter Ross with an Old Man.*

OLD MAN

   Threescore and ten I can remember well,
   Within the volume of which time I have seen
   Hours dreadful and things strange, but this sore night   3
   Hath trifled former knowings.

ROSS   Ha, good father,   4
   Thou seest the heavens, as troubled with man's act,   5
   Threatens his bloody stage. By th' clock 'tis day,   6

135 briefly quickly.   **manly readiness** men's clothing, or armor
137 consort keep company, associate   **139 easy** easily   **142 nea'er**
nearer   **143 The nearer bloody** i.e., the greater the danger of being
murdered   **144 lighted** alighted, descended   **146 dainty of** particular
about   **147 shift away** disappear by stealth.   **warrant** justification

2.4. Location: Outside Macbeth's castle of Inverness.
3 sore dreadful, grievous   **4 trifled former knowings** made trivial all
former experiences.   **father** old man   **5–6 heavens, act, stage** (A theatrical metaphor; the *heavens* are the decorated roof over the *stage*.)

And yet dark night strangles the traveling lamp.   7
Is 't night's predominance or the day's shame   8
That darkness does the face of earth entomb
When living light should kiss it?

OLD MAN   'Tis unnatural,
Even like the deed that's done. On Tuesday last
A falcon, towering in her pride of place,   12
Was by a mousing owl hawked at and killed.   13

ROSS
And Duncan's horses—a thing most strange and
    certain—
Beauteous and swift, the minions of their race,   15
Turned wild in nature, broke their stalls, flung out,
Contending 'gainst obedience, as they would   17
Make war with mankind.

OLD MAN   'Tis said they eat each other. 18

ROSS
They did so, to th' amazement of mine eyes
That looked upon 't.

        Enter Macduff.

                        Here comes the good Macduff.—
How goes the world, sir, now?

MACDUFF   Why, see you not?

ROSS
Is 't known who did this more than bloody deed?

MACDUFF
Those that Macbeth hath slain.

ROSS   Alas the day,
What good could they pretend?

MACDUFF   They were suborned.   24
Malcolm and Donalbain, the King's two sons,
Are stolen away and fled, which puts upon them
Suspicion of the deed.

ROSS   'Gainst nature still!

---

7 traveling lamp i.e., sun   **8 predominance** ascendancy, superior influence (as of a heavenly body)   **12 towering** circling higher and higher. (A
term in falconry.)   **place** pitch, highest point in the falcon's flight
13 mousing i.e., ordinarily preying on mice   **15 minions** darlings   **17 as**
as if   **18 eat** ate. (Pronounced "et.")   **24 What . . . pretend** i.e., what
could they hope to gain by it.   **pretend** intend.   **suborned** bribed, hired

Thriftless ambition, that will ravin up   28
Thine own life's means! Then 'tis most like
The sovereignty will fall upon Macbeth.

MACDUFF
He is already named and gone to Scone   31
To be invested.

ROSS   Where is Duncan's body?

MACDUFF   Carried to Colmekill,   33
The sacred storehouse of his predecessors
And guardian of their bones.

ROSS   Will you to Scone?

MACDUFF
No, cousin, I'll to Fife.

ROSS   Well, I will thither.   36

MACDUFF
Well, may you see things well done there. Adieu,
Lest our old robes sit easier than our new!

ROSS   Farewell, father.

OLD MAN
God's benison go with you, and with those   40
That would make good of bad, and friends of foes!

                              Exeunt omnes.

❖

---

28 Thriftless wasteful.   **ravin up** devour ravenously   **31 named** chosen.
(See 1.4.50, note.)   **Scone** ancient royal city of Scotland near Perth
33 Colmekill Icolmkill, i.e., Cell of St. Columba, the barren islet of Iona
in the Western Islands, a sacred spot where the kings were buried; here
called a *storehouse*   **36 Fife** (Of which Macduff is Thane.)   **40 benison**
blessing

3.1 *Enter Banquo.*

BANQUO
　　Thou hast it now—King, Cawdor, Glamis, all
　　As the weird women promised, and I fear
　　Thou played'st most foully for 't. Yet it was said
　　It should not stand in thy posterity,　　　　　　　4
　　But that myself should be the root and father
　　Of many kings. If there come truth from them—
　　As upon thee, Macbeth, their speeches shine—　　7
　　Why, by the verities on thee made good,
　　May they not be my oracles as well
　　And set me up in hope? But hush, no more.　　　10

　　　　Sennet sounded. Enter Macbeth as King, Lady
　　　　[Macbeth], Lennox, Ross, lords, and attendants.

MACBETH
　　Here's our chief guest.
LADY MACBETH　　　　　　　　If he had been forgotten,
　　It had been as a gap in our great feast
　　And all-thing unbecoming.　　　　　　　　　　13
MACBETH
　　Tonight we hold a solemn supper, sir,　　　　　14
　　And I'll request your presence.
BANQUO　　　　　　　　　　　Let Your Highness
　　Command upon me, to the which my duties　　16
　　Are with a most indissoluble tie
　　Forever knit.
MACBETH　　Ride you this afternoon?
BANQUO　　Ay, my good lord.
MACBETH
　　We should have else desired your good advice,
　　Which still hath been both grave and prosperous,　22
　　In this day's council; but we'll take tomorrow.
　　Is 't far you ride?

3.1. Location: Forres. The palace.
4 stand stay, remain　**7 shine** are brilliantly manifest　**10 s.d. Sennet**
trumpet call　**13 all-thing** in every way　**14 solemn** ceremonious
16 Command lay your command　**22 still** always.　**grave** weighty.
prosperous profitable

BANQUO
　As far, my lord, as will fill up the time
　Twixt this and supper. Go not my horse the better,　26
　I must become a borrower of the night
　For a dark hour or twain.
MACBETH　Fail not our feast.
BANQUO　My lord, I will not.
MACBETH
　We hear our bloody cousins are bestowed　31
　In England and in Ireland, not confessing
　Their cruel parricide, filling their hearers
　With strange invention. But of that tomorrow,　34
　When therewithal we shall have cause of state　35
　Craving us jointly. Hie you to horse. Adieu,　36
　Till you return at night. Goes Fleance with you?
BANQUO
　Ay, my good lord. Our time does call upon 's.
MACBETH
　I wish your horses swift and sure of foot,
　And so I do commend you to their backs.　40
　Farewell.　　　　　　　　　　*Exit Banquo.*
　Let every man be master of his time
　Till seven at night. To make society
　The sweeter welcome, we will keep ourself　44
　Till suppertime alone. While then, God be with you!　45
　　　　　　　　Exeunt Lords [and all but Macbeth
　　　　　　　　　　　　　　　and a Servant.]
　Sirrah, a word with you. Attend those men　46
　Our pleasure?
SERVANT
　They are, my lord, without the palace gate.
MACBETH
　Bring them before us.　　　　*Exit Servant.*
　　　　　　　　To be thus is nothing,　49
　But to be safely thus.—Our fears in Banquo　50

26 Go . . . better i.e., unless my horse makes better time than I expect
31 bestowed lodged　**34 invention** falsehood (i.e., that Macbeth was the
murderer)　**35 therewithal** besides that　**35–36 cause . . . jointly** questions
of state occupying our joint attention　**40 commend** commit, entrust
44 keep ourself keep to myself　**45 While** till　**46 Sirrah** (A form of address to a social inferior.)　**49 thus** i.e., king　**50 But** unless.　**in** concerning

Stick deep, and in his royalty of nature   51
Reigns that which would be feared. 'Tis much he dares;   52
And to that dauntless temper of his mind   53
He hath a wisdom that doth guide his valor
To act in safety. There is none but he
Whose being I do fear; and under him
My genius is rebuked, as it is said   57
Mark Antony's was by Caesar. He chid the sisters   58
When first they put the name of king upon me,
And bade them speak to him. Then, prophetlike,
They hailed him father to a line of kings.
Upon my head they placed a fruitless crown
And put a barren scepter in my grip
Thence to be wrenched with an unlineal hand,   64
No son of mine succeeding. If 't be so,
For Banquo's issue have I filed my mind;   66
For them the gracious Duncan have I murdered,
Put rancors in the vessel of my peace   68
Only for them, and mine eternal jewel   69
Given to the common enemy of man   70
To make them kings, the seeds of Banquo kings.
Rather than so, come fate into the list,   72
And champion me to th' utterance!—Who's there?   73

             Enter Servant and two Murderers.

Now go to the door, and stay there till we call.
                                          Exit Servant.
Was it not yesterday we spoke together?
MURDERERS
It was, so please Your Highness.
MACBETH   Well then, now
Have you considered of my speeches? Know
That it was he in the times past which held you

---

51 royalty of nature natural kingly bearing   **52 would be** deserves
to be   **53 to** added to   **57 genius** guardian spirit.   **rebuked** abashed,
daunted   **58 Caesar** Octavius Caesar   **64 with** by.   **unlineal** not of
lineal descent from me   **66 filed** defiled   **68 rancors** malignant enemies (here visualized as a poison added to a vessel full of wholesome drink)   **69 eternal jewel** i.e., soul   **70 common . . . man** i.e.,
devil   **72 list** lists, place of combat   **73 champion me** fight with me
in single combat.   **to th' utterance** to the last extremity (French, *à
l'outrance*)

So under fortune, which you thought had been   79
Our innocent self. This I made good to you
In our last conference, passed in probation with you   81
How you were borne in hand, how crossed, the
    instruments,   82
Who wrought with them, and all things else that might
To half a soul and to a notion crazed   84
Say, "Thus did Banquo."

FIRST MURDERER   You made it known to us.

MACBETH
I did so, and went further, which is now
Our point of second meeting. Do you find
Your patience so predominant in your nature
That you can let this go? Are you so gospeled   89
To pray for this good man and for his issue,
Whose heavy hand hath bowed you to the grave
And beggared yours forever?

FIRST MURDERER   We are men, my liege.   92

MACBETH
Ay, in the catalogue ye go for men,   93
As hounds and greyhounds, mongrels, spaniels, curs,
Shoughs, water-rugs, and demi-wolves are clept   95
All by the name of dogs. The valued file   96
Distinguishes the swift, the slow, the subtle,
The housekeeper, the hunter, every one   98
According to the gift which bounteous nature
Hath in him closed, whereby he does receive   100
Particular addition from the bill   101
That writes them all alike; and so of men.   102
Now, if you have a station in the file,   103
Not i' the worst rank of manhood, say 't,
And I will put that business in your bosoms

79 under out of favor with   **81 passed in probation** went over the
proof   **82 borne in hand** deceived by false promises.   **crossed**
thwarted.   **instruments** agents   **84 To half a soul** even to a half-wit.
notion mind   **89 gospeled** imbued with the gospel spirit   **92 yours** your
family   **93 go for** pass for, are entered for   **95 Shoughs** a kind of
shaggy dog.   **water-rugs** long-haired water dogs.   **demi-wolves** a cross-
breed with the wolf.   **clept** called   **96 valued file** list classified according to value   **98 housekeeper** watchdog   **100 in him closed** enclosed in
him, set in him like a jewel   **101–102 Particular . . . alike** particular
qualification apart from the catalog that lists them all indiscriminately   **103 file** military row, as in "rank and file"; see *rank* in l. 104

Whose execution takes your enemy off,
Grapples you to the heart and love of us,
Who wear our health but sickly in his life,   108
Which in his death were perfect.

SECOND MURDERER   I am one, my liege,
Whom the vile blows and buffets of the world
Hath so incensed that I am reckless what
I do to spite the world.

FIRST MURDERER   And I another,
So weary with disasters, tugged with fortune,   113
That I would set my life on any chance   114
To mend it or be rid on 't.

MACBETH   Both of you
Know Banquo was your enemy.

BOTH MURDERERS   True, my lord.

MACBETH
So is he mine, and in such bloody distance   117
That every minute of his being thrusts   118
Against my near'st of life. And though I could   119
With barefaced power sweep him from my sight   120
And bid my will avouch it, yet I must not,   121
For certain friends that are both his and mine,   122
Whose loves I may not drop, but wail his fall   123
Who I myself struck down. And thence it is   124
That I to your assistance do make love,   125
Masking the business from the common eye
For sundry weighty reasons.

SECOND MURDERER   We shall, my lord,
Perform what you command us.

FIRST MURDERER   Though our lives—

MACBETH
Your spirits shine through you. Within this hour at most   129
I will advise you where to plant yourselves,   130

108 **in his life** while he lives   113 **tugged with** pulled about by (as in
wrestling)   114 **set** risk, stake   117 **distance** (1) hostility, enmity
(2) interval of distance to be kept between fencers   118 **thrusts** (as in
fencing)   119 **near'st of life** most vital part, the heart   120 **With barefaced power** by open use of my supreme royal authority   121 **And . . .
avouch it** and use my mere wish as my justification   122 **For** because
of, for the sake of   123 **wail** i.e., I must lament   124 **Who** he whom
125 **to . . . make love** woo your aid   129 **Your . . . you** i.e., enough; I can
see your determination in your faces   130 **advise** instruct

Acquaint you with the perfect spy o' the time, 131
The moment on 't, for 't must be done tonight,
And something from the palace; always thought 133
That I require a clearness. And with him— 134
To leave no rubs nor botches in the work— 135
Fleance his son, that keeps him company,
Whose absence is no less material to me
Than is his father's, must embrace the fate
Of that dark hour. Resolve yourselves apart; 139
I'll come to you anon.

BOTH MURDERERS   We are resolved, my lord.

MACBETH
I'll call upon you straight. Abide within.

                              Exeunt [Murderers].

It is concluded. Banquo, thy soul's flight,
If it find heaven, must find it out tonight.   [*Exit.*]

*

3.2   *Enter Macbeth's Lady and a Servant.*

LADY MACBETH   Is Banquo gone from court?

SERVANT
Ay, madam, but returns again tonight.

LADY MACBETH
Say to the King I would attend his leisure
For a few words.

SERVANT   Madam, I will.   *Exit.*

LADY MACBETH   Naught's had, all's spent,
Where our desire is got without content. 7
'Tis safer to be that which we destroy
Than by destruction dwell in doubtful joy. 9

     Enter Macbeth.

How now, my lord? Why do you keep alone,

---

131 **perfect spy o' the time** knowledge or espial of the exact time (?)
133 **something from** some distance removed from.   **thought** being
borne in mind   134 **clearness** freedom from suspicion   135 **rubs** defects, rough spots   139 **Resolve yourselves apart** make up your minds
in private conference

3.2. Location: The palace.
7 **content** contentedness   9 **Than . . . joy** than by destroying achieve
only an apprehensive joy

Of sorriest fancies your companions making,   11
Using those thoughts which should indeed have died   12
With them they think on? Things without all remedy   13
Should be without regard. What's done is done.   14

MACBETH
We have scorched the snake, not killed it.   15
She'll close and be herself, whilst our poor malice   16
Remains in danger of her former tooth.   17
But let the frame of things disjoint, both the worlds
          suffer,   18
Ere we will eat our meal in fear and sleep
In the affliction of these terrible dreams
That shake us nightly. Better be with the dead,
Whom we, to gain our peace, have sent to peace,   22
Than on the torture of the mind to lie   23
In restless ecstasy. Duncan is in his grave;   24
After life's fitful fever he sleeps well.   25
Treason has done his worst; nor steel, nor poison,
Malice domestic, foreign levy, nothing   27
Can touch him further.

LADY MACBETH   Come on,
Gentle my lord, sleek o'er your rugged looks.   30
Be bright and jovial among your guests tonight.

MACBETH
So shall I, love, and so, I pray, be you.
Let your remembrance apply to Banquo;   33
Present him eminence, both with eye and tongue—   34
Unsafe the while, that we   35
Must lave our honors in these flattering streams   36

---

11 **sorriest** most despicable or wretched   12 **Using** keeping company
with, entertaining   13 **without** beyond   14 **without regard** not pon-
dered upon   15 **scorched** slashed, cut   16 **close** heal, close up again.
poor malice feeble hostility   17 **her former tooth** her fang, just as
before   18 **let . . . suffer** let the universe itself fall apart, both heaven
and earth perish   22 **to gain . . . peace** to gain contentedness through
satisfaction of desire, have sent to their eternal rest   23 **torture** rack
24 **ecstasy** frenzy   25 **fitful** characterized by paroxysms; or, intermit-
tent   27 **Malice domestic** civil war.   **foreign levy** levying of troops
abroad (against Scotland)   30 **Gentle . . . looks** my noble lord, smooth
over your rough looks   33 **remembrance** greetings expressive of remembrance.   **apply** be shown   34 **eminence** favor   35–36 **Unsafe . . .
streams** i.e., we are unsafe at present, and so must put on a show of
flattering cordiality to make our reputation look clean; or, we are unsafe
so long as we must flatter thus. (*Lave* means "wash.")

And make our faces vizards to our hearts,   37
Disguising what they are.

LADY MACBETH   You must leave this.

MACBETH

O, full of scorpions is my mind, dear wife!
Thou know'st that Banquo and his Fleance lives.

LADY MACBETH

But in them nature's copy's not eterne.   41

MACBETH

There's comfort yet; they are assailable.   42
Then be thou jocund. Ere the bat hath flown
His cloistered flight, ere to black Hecate's summons   44
The shard-borne beetle with his drowsy hums   45
Hath rung night's yawning peal, there shall be done   46
A deed of dreadful note.

LADY MACBETH   What's to be done?

MACBETH

Be innocent of the knowledge, dearest chuck,   48
Till thou applaud the deed. Come, seeling night,   49
Scarf up the tender eye of pitiful day,   50
And with thy bloody and invisible hand
Cancel and tear to pieces that great bond   52
Which keeps me pale! Light thickens,   53
And the crow makes wing to the rooky wood;   54
Good things of day begin to droop and drowse,
Whiles night's black agents to their preys do rouse.   56
Thou marvel'st at my words, but hold thee still.
Things bad begun make strong themselves by ill.
So, prithee, go with me.   *Exeunt.*

❖

37 **vizards** masks   41 **nature's copy** lease of life (i.e., by copyhold or
lease subject to cancellation); also, the individual man made from
nature's mold. **eterne** perpetual   42 **There's** i.e., in that thought there
is   44 **cloistered** i.e., in and among buildings   45 **shard-borne** borne on
shards, or horny wing cases; or, *shard-born*, bred in cow-droppings
(shards)   46 **yawning** drowsy   48 **chuck** (A term of endearment.)
49 **seeling** eye-closing. (Night is pictured here as a falconer sewing up
the eyes of day lest it should struggle against the deed that is to be
done.)   50 **Scarf up** blindfold. **pitiful** compassionate   52 **bond** i.e.,
Banquo's lease of life   53 **pale** pallid from fear (with a suggestion
perhaps of *paled*, fenced in). **thickens** grows opaque and dim   54 **crow**
rook. **rooky** full of rooks   56 **to . . . rouse** bestir themselves to hunt
their prey

3.3   *Enter three Murderers.*

FIRST MURDERER
But who did bid thee join with us?
THIRD MURDERER   Macbeth.
SECOND MURDERER [*To the First Murderer*]
He needs not our mistrust, since he delivers   2
Our offices and what we have to do   3
To the direction just.
FIRST MURDERER   Then stand with us.   4
The west yet glimmers with some streaks of day.
Now spurs the lated traveler apace   6
To gain the timely inn, and near approaches   7
The subject of our watch.
THIRD MURDERER   Hark, I hear horses.
BANQUO (*Within*)   Give us a light there, ho!
SECOND MURDERER   Then 'tis he. The rest
That are within the note of expectation   12
Already are i' the court.
FIRST MURDERER   His horses go about.
THIRD MURDERER
Almost a mile; but he does usually—
So all men do—from hence to the palace gate
Make it their walk.

   Enter Banquo and Fleance, with a torch.

SECOND MURDERER   A light, a light!
THIRD MURDERER   'Tis he.
FIRST MURDERER   Stand to 't.
BANQUO   It will be rain tonight.
FIRST MURDERER   Let it come down!
                              [*They attack Banquo.*]
BANQUO
O, treachery! Fly, good Fleance, fly, fly, fly!
Thou mayst revenge.—O slave!
                         [*He dies. Fleance escapes.*]

3.3. Location: A park near the palace.
2–3 He . . . offices we need not mistrust this man, since he states exactly our duties (as told us by Macbeth)   **4 To** according to.   **just** exactly. (That is, one can tell he comes from Macbeth, since he has identical instructions.)   **6 lated** belated   **7 timely** arrived at in good time   **12 note of expectation** list of those expected

THIRD MURDERER
  Who did strike out the light?
FIRST MURDERER   Was 't not the way?   25
THIRD MURDERER
  There's but one down; the son is fled.
SECOND MURDERER
  We have lost best half of our affair.
FIRST MURDERER
  Well, let's away and say how much is done.   28
                                        Exeunt.

❈

3.4   *Banquet prepared. Enter Macbeth, Lady*
       [Macbeth], Ross, Lennox, Lords, and
       attendants.

MACBETH
  You know your own degrees; sit down. At first   1
  And last, the hearty welcome.   [*They sit.*]
LORDS   Thanks to Your Majesty.   2
MACBETH
  Ourself will mingle with society   3
  And play the humble host.
  Our hostess keeps her state, but in best time   5
  We will require her welcome.   6
LADY MACBETH
  Pronounce it for me, sir, to all our friends,
  For my heart speaks they are welcome.

    Enter First Murderer [to the door].

MACBETH
  See, they encounter thee with their hearts' thanks.   9
  Both sides are even. Here I'll sit i' the midst. [*He sits.*]   10

25 way i.e., thing to do   **28 s.d. Exeunt** (Presumably the murderers drag
the body of Banquo offstage as they go.)
3.4. Location: A room of state in the palace.
1 degrees ranks (as a determinant of seating)   **1–2 At . . . last** once for
all   **3 mingle with society** i.e., leave the chair of state and circulate
among the guests   **5 keeps her state** remains in her canopied chair of
state.   **in best time** when it is most appropriate   **6 require** request
9 encounter respond to   **10 even** full, with equal numbers on both sides

Be large in mirth; anon we'll drink a measure   11
The table round. [*He rises and goes to the Murderer.*]
    There's blood upon thy face.
MURDERER 'Tis Banquo's then.
MACBETH
'Tis better thee without than he within.   14
Is he dispatched?
MURDERER
My lord, his throat is cut. That I did for him.
MACBETH Thou art the best o' the cutthroats.
Yet he's good that did the like for Fleance;
If thou didst it, thou art the nonpareil.   19
MURDERER Most royal sir, Fleance is scaped.
MACBETH
Then comes my fit again. I had else been perfect,
Whole as the marble, founded as the rock,   22
As broad and general as the casing air.   23
But now I am cabined, cribbed, confined, bound in   24
To saucy doubts and fears. But Banquo's safe?   25
MURDERER
Ay, my good lord. Safe in a ditch he bides,
With twenty trenchèd gashes on his head,
The least a death to nature.
MACBETH   Thanks for that.
There the grown serpent lies; the worm that's fled   29
Hath nature that in time will venom breed,
No teeth for the present. Get thee gone. Tomorrow
We'll hear ourselves again.   *Exit Murderer.*
LADY MACBETH   My royal lord,   32
You do not give the cheer. The feast is sold   33
That is not often vouched, while 'tis a-making,   34
'Tis given with welcome. To feed were best at home;   35

11 **large** liberal, free.   **measure** bumper   14 **'Tis . . . within** it is better
for you to have it on you than he to have it within him   19 **the nonpareil** without equal   22 **founded** firmly established   23 **broad and
general** unconfined.   **casing** encasing, enveloping   24 **cribbed** shut in
25 **saucy** sharp, impudent, importunate   29 **worm** small serpent
32 **hear ourselves** confer   33-35 **is sold . . . welcome** i.e., seems grudg-
ingly given, as if in return for money, unless it is often accompanied
with assurances of welcome while it is in progress   35 **To feed . . .
home** i.e., mere eating is best done at home

From thence, the sauce to meat is ceremony;   36
Meeting were bare without it.   37

> *Enter the Ghost of Banquo, and sits in Macbeth's
> place.*

MACBETH   Sweet remembrancer!
Now, good digestion wait on appetite,   38
And health on both!
LENNOX   May 't please Your Highness sit?
MACBETH
Here had we now our country's honor roofed   40
Were the graced person of our Banquo present,   41
Who may I rather challenge for unkindness   42
Than pity for mischance.
ROSS   His absence, sir,
Lays blame upon his promise. Please 't Your Highness
To grace us with your royal company?
MACBETH [*Seeing his place occupied*]
The table's full.
LENNOX   Here is a place reserved, sir.
MACBETH   Where?
LENNOX
Here, my good lord. What is 't that moves Your
    Highness?
MACBETH
Which of you have done this?
LORDS   What, my good lord?
MACBETH
Thou canst not say I did it. Never shake
Thy gory locks at me.
ROSS
Gentlemen, rise. His Highness is not well.
                [*They start to rise.*]
LADY MACBETH
Sit, worthy friends. My lord is often thus,
And hath been from his youth. Pray you, keep seat.

---

36 From thence i.e., away from home, dining in company.   **meat** food
37 Meeting were bare gatherings of friends would be unadorned
38 wait on attend   **40 roofed** under one roof   **41 graced** gracious
42 Who may I whom I hope I may.   **challenge for** reprove for

The fit is momentary; upon a thought   55
He will again be well. If much you note him
You shall offend him and extend his passion.   57
Feed, and regard him not.—[*She confers apart with
    Macbeth*.] Are you a man?

MACBETH
Ay, and a bold one, that dare look on that
Which might appall the devil.

LADY MACBETH   O, proper stuff!   60
This is the very painting of your fear.
This is the air-drawn dagger which, you said,   62
Led you to Duncan. O, these flaws and starts,   63
Impostors to true fear, would well become   64
A woman's story at a winter's fire,
Authorized by her grandam. Shame itself!   66
Why do you make such faces? When all's done,
You look but on a stool.

MACBETH   Prithee, see there!
Behold, look! Lo, how say you?
Why, what care I? If thou canst nod, speak too.
If charnel houses and our graves must send   71
Those that we bury back, our monuments   72
Shall be the maws of kites.   [*Exit Ghost*.] 73

LADY MACBETH   What, quite unmanned in folly?

MACBETH
If I stand here, I saw him.

LADY MACBETH   Fie, for shame!

MACBETH
Blood hath been shed ere now, i' th' olden time,
Ere humane statute purged the gentle weal;   77
Ay, and since too, murders have been performed
Too terrible for the ear. The time has been
That, when the brains were out, the man would die,

55 upon a thought in a moment   **57 offend him** make him worse.
extend prolong   **60 O, proper stuff** O, nonsense   **62 air-drawn** made of
thin air, or floating disembodied in space   **63 flaws** gusts, outbursts
64 to compared with.   **become** befit   **66 Authorized** told on the authority of   **71 charnel houses** depositories for bones or bodies   **72–73 our
. . . kites** i.e., we will have to leave the unburied bodies to scavenging
birds of prey   **77 Ere . . . weal** before the institution of law cleansed the
commonwealth of violence and made it gentle.   **humane** (This spelling,
interchangeable with *human*, carries both meanings: "appertaining to
humankind" and "befitting humanity.")

And there an end; but now they rise again
With twenty mortal murders on their crowns,   82
And push us from our stools. This is more strange   83
Than such a murder is.

LADY MACBETH   My worthy lord,
Your noble friends do lack you.

MACBETH   I do forget.
Do not muse at me, my most worthy friends;
I have a strange infirmity, which is nothing
To those that know me. Come, love and health to all!
Then I'll sit down. Give me some wine. Fill full.
                              [*He is given wine.*]

    Enter Ghost.

I drink to the general joy o' the whole table,
And to our dear friend Banquo, whom we miss.
Would he were here! To all, and him, we thirst,   92
And all to all.

LORDS   Our duties and the pledge.   93
                              [*They drink.*]

MACBETH [*Seeing the Ghost*]
Avaunt, and quit my sight! Let the earth hide thee!
Thy bones are marrowless, thy blood is cold;
Thou hast no speculation in those eyes   96
Which thou dost glare with.

LADY MACBETH   Think of this, good peers,
But as a thing of custom. 'Tis no other;
Only it spoils the pleasure of the time.

MACBETH   What man dare, I dare.
Approach thou like the rugged Russian bear,   101
The armed rhinoceros, or the Hyrcan tiger;   102
Take any shape but that, and my firm nerves   103
Shall never tremble. Or be alive again
And dare me to the desert with thy sword.   105

---

82 mortal murders deadly wounds.   **crowns** heads   **83 push . . . stools**
usurp our places at feasts (with a suggestion of usurpation of the
throne)   **92 thirst** desire to drink   **93 all to all** all good wishes to all; or,
let all drink to everyone else.   **Our . . . pledge** in drinking the toast you
just proposed, we offer our homage   **96 speculation** power of sight
101 like in the likeness of   **102 armed** armor-plated.   **Hyrcan** of Hyrcania, in ancient times a region near the Caspian Sea   **103 nerves** sinews
105 the desert some solitary place

If trembling I inhabit then, protest me 106
The baby of a girl. Hence, horrible shadow! 107
Unreal mockery, hence! [*Exit Ghost.*] Why, so; being gone,
I am a man again. Pray you, sit still.

LADY MACBETH
You have displaced the mirth, broke the good meeting
With most admired disorder.

MACBETH   Can such things be, 111
And overcome us like a summer's cloud, 112
Without our special wonder? You make me strange 113
Even to the disposition that I owe, 114
When now I think you can behold such sights
And keep the natural ruby of your cheeks
When mine is blanched with fear.

ROSS   What sights, my lord?

LADY MACBETH
I pray you, speak not. He grows worse and worse;
Question enrages him. At once, good night. 119
Stand not upon the order of your going, 120
But go at once.

LENNOX   Good night, and better health 121
Attend His Majesty!

LADY MACBETH   A kind good night to all!
                 Exeunt Lords [*and attendants*].

MACBETH
It will have blood, they say; blood will have blood.
Stones have been known to move, and trees to speak; 124
Augurs and understood relations have 125
By maggotpies and choughs and rooks brought forth 126
The secret'st man of blood. What is the night? 127

---

106 If . . . then i.e., if then I tremble. protest proclaim 107 The baby
of a girl a baby girl, or, girl's doll 111 admired wondered at. disorder
lack of self-control 112 overcome come over 113–114 You make . . .
owe you cause me to feel I do not know my own nature (which I had
presumed to be that of a brave man) 119 Question talk. At once to
you all; now 120 Stand . . . going i.e., do not take the time to leave in
ceremonious order of rank, as you entered 121 at once all together and
now 124 Stones . . . speak i.e., even inanimate nature speaks in such a
way as to reveal the unnatural act of murder 125 Augurs auguries.
understood relations comprehended reports or utterances 126 By . . .
choughs by means of magpies and jackdaws. brought forth revealed
127 man of blood murderer. the night i.e., the time of night

LADY MACBETH
  Almost at odds with morning, which is which.
MACBETH
  How sayst thou, that Macduff denies his person   129
  At our great bidding?
LADY MACBETH   Did you send to him, sir?
MACBETH
  I hear it by the way; but I will send.   131
  There's not a one of them but in his house
  I keep a servant fee'd. I will tomorrow—   133
  And betimes I will—to the Weird Sisters.   134
  More shall they speak, for now I am bent to know   135
  By the worst means the worst. For mine own good
  All causes shall give way. I am in blood   137
  Stepped in so far that, should I wade no more,   138
  Returning were as tedious as go o'er.   139
  Strange things I have in head, that will to hand,
  Which must be acted ere they may be scanned.   141
LADY MACBETH
  You lack the season of all natures, sleep.   142
MACBETH
  Come, we'll to sleep. My strange and self-abuse   143
  Is the initiate fear that wants hard use.   144
  We are yet but young in deed.   *Exeunt.*

❖

3.5   *Thunder. Enter the three Witches,*
         meeting Hecate.

FIRST WITCH
  Why, how now, Hecate? You look angerly.   1

129 How sayst thou what do you say to the fact that   **131 by the way**
indirectly   **133 fee'd** i.e., paid to spy   **134 betimes** (1) early (2) while
there is still time   **135 bent** determined   **137 All causes** all other
considerations   **138 should . . . more** even if I were to wade no farther   **139 were** would be.   **go** going   **141 ere . . . scanned** i.e., even
before thinking about them carefully, at once   **142 season** preserva-
tive   **143 strange and self-abuse** strange self-delusion   **144 initiate fear**
fear experienced by a novice.   **wants hard use** lacks toughening experience

3.5. Location: A heath. (This scene is probably by another author.)
1 angerly angrily, angry

HECATE

    Have I not reason, beldams as you are?   2
    Saucy and overbold, how did you dare
    To trade and traffic with Macbeth
    In riddles and affairs of death,
    And I, the mistress of your charms,
    The close contriver of all harms,   7
    Was never called to bear my part
    Or show the glory of our art?
    And, which is worse, all you have done
    Hath been but for a wayward son,
    Spiteful and wrathful, who, as others do,
    Loves for his own ends, not for you.
    But make amends now. Get you gone,
    And at the pit of Acheron   15
    Meet me i' the morning. Thither he
    Will come to know his destiny.
    Your vessels and your spells provide,
    Your charms and everything beside.
    I am for th' air. This night I'll spend
    Unto a dismal and a fatal end.   21
    Great business must be wrought ere noon.
    Upon the corner of the moon
    There hangs a vaporous drop profound;   24
    I'll catch it ere it come to ground,
    And that, distilled by magic sleights,
    Shall raise such artificial sprites   27
    As by the strength of their illusion
    Shall draw him on to his confusion.   29
    He shall spurn fate, scorn death, and bear
    His hopes 'bove wisdom, grace, and fear.
    And you all know, security   32
    Is mortals' chiefest enemy.   *Music and a song.*
    Hark! I am called. My little spirit, see,
    Sits in a foggy cloud and stays for me.   [*Exit.*] 35
          Sing within, "Come away, come away," *etc.*

---

2 beldams hags   **7 close** secret   **15 Acheron** the river of sorrows in Hades; here, hell itself   **21 dismal** disastrous, ill-omened   **24 profound** i.e., heavily pendent, ready to drop off   **27 artificial** produced by magical arts   **29 confusion** ruin   **32 security** overconfidence   **35 s.d. Come away** etc. (The song occurs in Thomas Middleton's *The Witch*.)

FIRST WITCH

Come, let's make haste. She'll soon be back again.

Exeunt.

❖

3.6 *Enter Lennox and another Lord.*

LENNOX

My former speeches have but hit your thoughts,   1
Which can interpret farther. Only I say   2
Things have been strangely borne. The gracious Duncan   3
Was pitied of Macbeth; marry, he was dead.   4
And the right valiant Banquo walked too late,
Whom you may say, if 't please you, Fleance killed,
For Fleance fled. Men must not walk too late.
Who cannot want the thought how monstrous   8
It was for Malcolm and for Donalbain
To kill their gracious father? Damnèd fact!   10
How it did grieve Macbeth! Did he not straight   11
In pious rage the two delinquents tear   12
That were the slaves of drink and thralls of sleep?   13
Was not that nobly done? Ay, and wisely too;
For 'twould have angered any heart alive
To hear the men deny 't. So that I say
He has borne all things well; and I do think   17
That had he Duncan's sons under his key—
As, an 't please heaven, he shall not—they should find   19
What 'twere to kill a father. So should Fleance.
But peace! For from broad words, and 'cause he failed   21
His presence at the tyrant's feast, I hear   22
Macduff lives in disgrace. Sir, can you tell
Where he bestows himself?

LORD   The son of Duncan,   24

3.6. Location: Somewhere in Scotland.
1 My former speeches what I've just said.   **hit** coincided with
2 interpret farther draw further conclusions (i.e., it is unwise for me to
say more, but you can surmise the rest)   **3 borne** carried on   **4 of** by.
marry . . . dead i.e., to be sure, this pity occurred after Duncan died, not
before   **8 cannot . . . thought** can help thinking   **10 fact** deed, crime
11 straight straightway, at once   **12 pious** holy, loyal, sonlike
13 thralls slaves   **17 borne all things well** managed everything clev-
erly   **19 an 't** if it.   **should** would be sure to   **21 from broad words** on
account of plain speech   **22 His presence** i.e., to be present   **24 bestows
himself** is quartered, has taken refuge

From whom this tyrant holds the due of birth,   25
Lives in the English court, and is received
Of the most pious Edward with such grace   27
That the malevolence of fortune nothing
Takes from his high respect. Thither Macduff   29
Is gone to pray the holy king, upon his aid,   30
To wake Northumberland and warlike Siward,
That by the help of these—with Him above
To ratify the work—we may again
Give to our tables meat, sleep to our nights,   34
Free from our feasts and banquets bloody knives,   35
Do faithful homage, and receive free honors—   36
All which we pine for now. And this report
Hath so exasperate the King that he   38
Prepares for some attempt of war.

LENNOX   Sent he to Macduff?

LORD

He did; and with an absolute "Sir, not I,"   41
The cloudy messenger turns me his back   42
And hums, as who should say, "You'll rue the time
That clogs me with this answer."

LENNOX   And that well might   44
Advise him to a caution, t' hold what distance   45
His wisdom can provide. Some holy angel   46
Fly to the court of England and unfold
His message ere he come, that a swift blessing
May soon return to this our suffering country   49
Under a hand accursed!   50

LORD   I'll send my prayers with him.   *Exeunt.*

❖

25 **holds . . . birth** withholds the birthright (i.e., the Scottish crown)   27 **Of** by.   **Edward** Edward the Confessor   29 **his high respect** high respect paid to him. (Being out of fortune has not lessened the dignity with which Malcolm is received in England.)   30 **upon his aid** i.e., in aid of Malcolm 34 **meat** food   35 **Free . . . banquets** free our feasts and banquets from 36 **free** freely bestowed; or, pertaining to freemen   38 **exasperate the King** i.e., exasperated Macbeth   41 **with . . . I** i.e., when Macduff answered the messenger curtly with a refusal   42 **cloudy** louring, scowling. **turns me** i.e., turns. (*Me* is used colloquially for emphasis.)   44 **clogs** encumbers, loads   45–46 **Advise . . . provide** warn him (Macduff) to keep what safe distance he can (from Macbeth)   49–50 **suffering country Under** country suffering under

4.1   *Thunder. Enter the three Witches.*

FIRST WITCH
　Thrice the brinded cat hath mewed.　　　　　　　　1

SECOND WITCH
　Thrice, and once the hedgepig whined.　　　　　　2

THIRD WITCH
　Harpier cries. 'Tis time, 'tis time!　　　　　　　　3

FIRST WITCH
　Round about the cauldron go;
　In the poisoned entrails throw.
　Toad, that under cold stone
　Days and nights has thirty-one　　　　　　　　　7
　Sweltered venom, sleeping got,　　　　　　　　　8
　Boil thou first i' the charmèd pot.

ALL [*As they dance round the cauldron*]
　Double, double, toil and trouble;
　Fire burn, and cauldron bubble.

SECOND WITCH
　Fillet of a fenny snake　　　　　　　　　　　　12
　In the cauldron boil and bake;
　Eye of newt and toe of frog,
　Wool of bat and tongue of dog,
　Adder's fork and blindworm's sting,　　　　　　　16
　Lizard's leg and owlet's wing,
　For a charm of powerful trouble,
　Like a hell-broth boil and bubble.

ALL
　Double, double, toil and trouble;
　Fire burn, and cauldron bubble.

THIRD WITCH
　Scale of dragon, tooth of wolf,
　Witches' mummy, maw and gulf　　　　　　　　　23

4.1. Location: A cavern (see 3.5.15). In the middle, a boiling cauldron
(provided presumably by means of the trapdoor; see 4.1.106. The trapdoor must also be used in this scene for the apparitions.)
1 brinded marked by streaks (as by fire), brindled   **2 hedgepig** hedgehog
3 Harpier (The name of a familiar spirit; probably derived from *harpy*.)
cries i.e., gives the signal to begin   **7–8 Days . . . got** for thirty-one days
and nights has exuded venom formed during sleep   **12 Fillet** slice.   **fenny**
inhabiting fens or swamps   **16 fork** forked tongue.   **blindworm** slow-
worm, a harmless burrowing lizard   **23 mummy** mummified flesh
made into a magical potion.   **maw and gulf** gullet and stomach

Of the ravined salt-sea shark,   24
Root of hemlock digged i' the dark,
Liver of blaspheming Jew,
Gall of goat, and slips of yew   27
Slivered in the moon's eclipse,   28
Nose of Turk and Tartar's lips,
Finger of birth-strangled babe
Ditch-delivered by a drab,   31
Make the gruel thick and slab.   32
Add thereto a tiger's chaudron   33
For th' ingredients of our cauldron.

ALL
Double, double, toil and trouble;
Fire burn, and cauldron bubble.

SECOND WITCH
Cool it with a baboon's blood,
Then the charm is firm and good.   38

Enter Hecate to the other three Witches.

HECATE
O, well done! I commend your pains,   39
And everyone shall share i' the gains.
And now about the cauldron sing
Like elves and fairies in a ring,
Enchanting all that you put in.   43
              Music and a song: "Black spirits," *etc.*
                                    [*Exit Hecate.*]

SECOND WITCH
By the pricking of my thumbs,
Something wicked this way comes.
      Open, locks,
      Whoever knocks!

Enter Macbeth.

---

24 ravined ravenous, glutted with prey (?) **27 slips** cuttings for grafting
or planting **28 Slivered** broken off (as a branch) **31 Ditch . . . drab**
born in a ditch of a harlot **32 slab** viscous, thick **33 chaudron** entrails **38 s.d. other** (Said because Hecate is a witch too, not because
more witches enter.) **39–43 O . . . in** (These lines are universally regarded as non-Shakespearean.) **43 s.d. Black spirits etc.** (This song is
found in Middleton's *The Witch*.)

MACBETH
  How now, you secret, black, and midnight hags?   48
  What is 't you do?
ALL   A deed without a name.
MACBETH
  I conjure you, by that which you profess,
  Howe'er you come to know it, answer me.
  Though you untie the winds and let them fight
  Against the churches, though the yeasty waves   53
  Confound and swallow navigation up,   54
  Though bladed corn be lodged and trees blown down,   55
  Though castles topple on their warders' heads,
  Though palaces and pyramids do slope   57
  Their heads to their foundations, though the treasure
  Of nature's germens tumble all together,   59
  Even till destruction sicken, answer me   60
  To what I ask you.
FIRST WITCH   Speak.
SECOND WITCH   Demand.
THIRD WITCH   We'll answer.
FIRST WITCH
  Say if thou'dst rather hear it from our mouths
  Or from our masters.
MACBETH   Call 'em. Let me see 'em.
FIRST WITCH
  Pour in sow's blood, that hath eaten
  Her nine farrow; grease that's sweaten   65
  From the murderer's gibbet throw
  Into the flame.
ALL   Come high or low,
  Thyself and office deftly show!   68

    Thunder. First Apparition, an armed Head.

MACBETH
  Tell me, thou unknown power—

---

48 black i.e., dealing in black magic   **53 yeasty** foamy   **54 Confound** destroy   **55 bladed** in the ear.   **corn** (General name for wheat and other grains.)   **lodged** thrown down, laid   **57 slope** bend   **59 nature's germens** seed or elements from which all nature operates   **60 sicken** be surfeited   **65 nine farrow** litter of nine.   **sweaten** sweated   **68 office** function   **s.d. armed Head** (Perhaps symbolizes the head of Macbeth cut off by Macduff and presented by him to Malcolm; or the rebellion of Macduff.)

FIRST WITCH   He knows thy thought.
Hear his speech, but say thou naught.

FIRST APPARITION
Macbeth! Macbeth! Macbeth! Beware Macduff,
Beware the Thane of Fife. Dismiss me. Enough.   72
                                        He descends.

MACBETH
Whate'er thou art, for thy good caution, thanks;
Thou hast harped my fear aright. But one word more— 74

FIRST WITCH
He will not be commanded. Here's another,
More potent than the first.   76

    Thunder. Second Apparition, a bloody Child.

SECOND APPARITION   Macbeth! Macbeth! Macbeth!
MACBETH   Had I three ears, I'd hear thee.
SECOND APPARITION
Be bloody, bold, and resolute; laugh to scorn
The power of man, for none of woman born
Shall harm Macbeth.   *Descends.*

MACBETH
Then live, Macduff; what need I fear of thee?
But yet I'll make assurance double sure,
And take a bond of fate. Thou shalt not live,   84
That I may tell pale-hearted fear it lies,
And sleep in spite of thunder.   86

    *Thunder. Third Apparition, a Child crowned,
    with a tree in his hand.*

                          What is this
That rises like the issue of a king   87
And wears upon his baby brow the round   88
And top of sovereignty?
ALL   Listen, but speak not to 't.   89

---

72 s.d. He descends (i.e., by means of the trap door)   **74 harped** hit,
touched (as in touching a harp to make it sound)   **76 s.d. bloody Child**
(Symbolizes Macduff untimely ripped from his mother's womb; see
5.8.15–16.)   **84 take a bond of** get a guarantee from (i.e., by killing
Macduff, to make doubly sure he can do no harm)   **86 s.d. Child . . .
hand** (Symbolizes Malcolm, the royal child; the tree anticipates the
cutting of boughs in Birnam Wood, 5.4.)   **87 like** in the likeness of
88–89 round And top crown

THIRD APPARITION

Be lion-mettled, proud, and take no care
Who chafes, who frets, or where conspirers are.
Macbeth shall never vanquished be until
Great Birnam Wood to high Dunsinane Hill
Shall come against him.   *Descends.*

MACBETH   That will never be.

Who can impress the forest, bid the tree   95
Unfix his earthbound root? Sweet bodements, good!   96
Rebellious dead, rise never till the wood   97
Of Birnam rise, and our high-placed Macbeth
Shall live the lease of nature, pay his breath   99
To time and mortal custom. Yet my heart   100
Throbs to know one thing. Tell me, if your art
Can tell so much: shall Banquo's issue ever
Reign in this kingdom?

ALL   Seek to know no more.

MACBETH

I will be satisfied. Deny me this,
And an eternal curse fall on you! Let me know.
        [*The cauldron descends.*] *Hautboys.*

Why sinks that cauldron? And what noise is this?   106

FIRST WITCH   Show!

SECOND WITCH   Show!

THIRD WITCH   Show!

ALL

Show his eyes, and grieve his heart;
Come like shadows, so depart!   111

     A show of eight Kings and Banquo last; [*the*
     eighth King] *with a glass in his hand.*

MACBETH

Thou art too like the spirit of Banquo. Down!
Thy crown does sear mine eyeballs. And thy hair,
Thou other gold-bound brow, is like the first.   114
A third is like the former. Filthy hags,
Why do you show me this? A fourth? Start, eyes!   116

---

95 impress press into service, like soldiers   **96 bodements** prophecies
97 Rebellious dead i.e., Banquo and his lineage (?)   **99 lease of nature**
natural period, full life-span   **100 mortal custom** death, the common lot
of humanity   **106 noise** music   **111 s.d. glass** (magic) mirror (also in
l. 119)   **114 other** i.e., second   **116 Start** bulge from their sockets

What, will the line stretch out to th' crack of doom?
Another yet? A seventh? I'll see no more.
And yet the eighth appears, who bears a glass
Which shows me many more; and some I see
That twofold balls and treble scepters carry.   121
Horrible sight! Now I see 'tis true,
For the blood-boltered Banquo smiles upon me   123
And points at them for his. [*The apparitions vanish.*]
     What, is this so?   124

FIRST WITCH
Ay, sir, all this is so. But why   125
Stands Macbeth thus amazedly?   126
Come, sisters, cheer we up his sprites   127
And show the best of our delights.
I'll charm the air to give a sound,
While you perform your antic round,   130
That this great king may kindly say
Our duties did his welcome pay.   132
          Music. The Witches dance, and vanish.

MACBETH
Where are they? Gone? Let this pernicious hour
Stand aye accursèd in the calendar!
Come in, without there!

     Enter Lennox.

LENNOX   What's Your Grace's will?
MACBETH
Saw you the Weird Sisters?
LENNOX   No, my lord.
MACBETH
Came they not by you?
LENNOX   No, indeed, my lord.

---

121 twofold balls (A probable reference to the double coronation of
James at Scone and Westminster, as King of England and Scotland.)
treble scepters (Probably refers to James's assumed title as King of
Great Britain, France, and Ireland.)   **123 blood-boltered** having his hair
matted with blood   **124 for his** as his descendants   **125–132 Ay . . . pay**
(These lines are held to be spurious.)   **126 amazedly** stunned
127 sprites spirits   **130 antic round** grotesque dance in a circle
132 pay repay

MACBETH

    Infected be the air whereon they ride,

    And damned all those that trust them! I did hear

    The galloping of horse. Who was 't came by?   140

LENNOX

    'Tis two or three, my lord, that bring you word

    Macduff is fled to England.

MACBETH   Fled to England!

LENNOX   Ay, my good lord.

MACBETH [*Aside*]

    Time, thou anticipat'st my dread exploits.   144

    The flighty purpose never is o'ertook   145

    Unless the deed go with it. From this moment   146

    The very firstlings of my heart shall be   147

    The firstlings of my hand. And even now,   148

    To crown my thoughts with acts, be it thought and done:

    The castle of Macduff I will surprise,   150

    Seize upon Fife, give to th' edge o' the sword

    His wife, his babes, and all unfortunate souls

    That trace him in his line. No boasting like a fool;   153

    This deed I'll do before this purpose cool.

    But no more sights!—Where are these gentlemen?

    Come, bring me where they are.   *Exeunt.*

❖

4.2   *Enter Macduff's Wife, her Son, and Ross.*

LADY MACDUFF

    What had he done to make him fly the land?

ROSS

    You must have patience, madam.

LADY MACDUFF   He had none.

---

140 horse horses **144 thou anticipat'st** you forestall. (By allowing time
to pass without my acting, I have lost an opportunity.) **145 flighty**
fleeting **146 Unless . . . it** unless the execution of the deed accompanies the conception of it immediately **147–148 The very . . . hand** i.e.,
my impulses will be acted on immediately **150 surprise** seize without
warning **153 trace him** follow his tracks. **line** family succession

4.2. Location: Fife. Macduff's castle.

His flight was madness. When our actions do not,   3
Our fears do make us traitors.

ROSS   You know not   4
Whether it was his wisdom or his fear.

LADY MACDUFF
Wisdom? To leave his wife, to leave his babes,
His mansion, and his titles in a place   7
From whence himself does fly? He loves us not,
He wants the natural touch; for the poor wren,   9
The most diminutive of birds, will fight,
Her young ones in her nest, against the owl.   11
All is the fear and nothing is the love,
As little is the wisdom, where the flight
So runs against all reason.

ROSS   My dearest coz,   14
I pray you, school yourself. But, for your husband,   15
He is noble, wise, judicious, and best knows
The fits o' the season. I dare not speak much further,   17
But cruel are the times when we are traitors   18
And do not know ourselves, when we hold rumor   19
From what we fear, yet know not what we fear,   20
But float upon a wild and violent sea
Each way and none. I take my leave of you;   22
Shall not be long but I'll be here again.   23
Things at the worst will cease, or else climb upward
To what they were before.—My pretty cousin,
Blessing upon you!

LADY MACDUFF
Fathered he is, and yet he's fatherless.

ROSS
I am so much a fool, should I stay longer

3–4 When . . . traitors i.e., even when we have committed no treasonous act, our fears of being suspected traitors make us act as if we were **7 titles** i.e., possessions to which he has title   **9 wants** lacks.   **the natural touch** i.e., the feelings natural to a husband and father   **11 Her . . . nest** when her young ones are in the nest   **14 coz** kinswoman   **15 school** control.   **for** as for   **17 fits 'o the season** violent disorders of the time   **18–19 are traitors . . . ourselves** i.e., are accused of treason without recognizing ourselves as such   **19–20 hold . . . fear** i.e., believe every fearful rumor on the basis of what we fear might be   **22 Each . . . none** i.e., being tossed this way and that without any real progress   **23 Shall** it shall.   **but** before

It would be my disgrace and your discomfort.   29
I take my leave at once.   *Exit Ross.*

LADY MACDUFF   Sirrah, your father's dead;   31
And what will you do now? How will you live?

SON
As birds do, Mother.

LADY MACDUFF   What, with worms and flies?

SON
With what I get, I mean; and so do they.

LADY MACDUFF   Poor bird! Thou'dst never fear
The net nor lime, the pitfall nor the gin.   36

SON
Why should I, Mother? Poor birds they are not set for.   37
My father is not dead, for all your saying.

LADY MACDUFF
Yes, he is dead. How wilt thou do for a father?

SON   Nay, how will you do for a husband?

LADY MACDUFF   Why, I can buy me twenty at any
market.

SON   Then you'll buy 'em to sell again.

LADY MACDUFF   Thou speak'st with all thy wit,
And yet, i' faith, with wit enough for thee.

SON   Was my father a traitor, Mother?

LADY MACDUFF   Ay, that he was.

SON   What is a traitor?

LADY MACDUFF   Why, one that swears and lies.   49

SON   And be all traitors that do so?

LADY MACDUFF
Every one that does so is a traitor,
And must be hanged.

SON
And must they all be hanged that swear and lie?

LADY MACDUFF   Every one.

SON   Who must hang them?

LADY MACDUFF   Why, the honest men.

SON   Then the liars and swearers are fools, for there are

---

29 It . . . discomfort i.e., I should disgrace my manhood by weeping, and
cause you distress   **31 Sirrah** (Here, an affectionate form of address to
a child.)   **36 lime** birdlime (a sticky substance put on branches to snare
birds).   **gin** snare   **37 Poor . . . for** i.e., traps are not set for *poor* birds,
as you call me   **49 swears and lies** i.e., swears an oath and breaks it
(though the boy may understand *swears* to mean "uses profanity")

liars and swearers enough to beat the honest men and hang up them.

LADY MACDUFF Now, God help thee, poor monkey! But how wilt thou do for a father?

SON If he were dead, you'd weep for him; if you would not, it were a good sign that I should quickly have a new father.

LADY MACDUFF Poor prattler, how thou talk'st!

Enter a Messenger.

MESSENGER
Bless you, fair dame! I am not to you known,
Though in your state of honor I am perfect.   67
I doubt some danger does approach you nearly.   68
If you will take a homely man's advice,   69
Be not found here. Hence with your little ones!
To fright you thus, methinks, I am too savage;
To do worse to you were fell cruelty,   72
Which is too nigh your person. Heaven preserve you! 73
I dare abide no longer.   *Exit Messenger.*

LADY MACDUFF   Whither should I fly?
I have done no harm. But I remember now
I am in this earthly world, where to do harm
Is often laudable, to do good sometimes
Accounted dangerous folly. Why then, alas,
Do I put up that womanly defense
To say I have done no harm?

Enter Murderers.

                              What are these faces?

FIRST MURDERER Where is your husband?

LADY MACDUFF
I hope in no place so unsanctified
Where such as thou mayst find him.

FIRST MURDERER   He's a traitor.

SON
Thou liest, thou shag-haired villain!

---

67 in . . . honor with your honorable state. **perfect** perfectly acquainted **68 doubt** fear **69 homely** plain **72 To do worse** i.e., actually to harm you. **fell** savage **73 Which . . . person** i.e., which savage cruelty is all too near at hand

FIRST MURDERER   What, you egg?
                                        [*He stabs him.*]
    Young fry of treachery!
SON   He has killed me, Mother.   85
    Run away, I pray you!   [*He dies.*]
        Exit [*Lady Macduff*] *crying* "Murder!" [*followed
            by the Murderers with the Son's body*].

❖

4.3   *Enter Malcolm and Macduff.*

MALCOLM
    Let us seek out some desolate shade, and there
    Weep our sad bosoms empty.
MACDUFF   Let us rather
    Hold fast the mortal sword, and like good men   3
    Bestride our downfall'n birthdom. Each new morn   4
    New widows howl, new orphans cry, new sorrows
    Strike heaven on the face, that it resounds   6
    As if it felt with Scotland and yelled out   7
    Like syllable of dolor.
MALCOLM   What I believe, I'll wail;   8
    What know, believe; and what I can redress,   9
    As I shall find the time to friend, I will.   10
    What you have spoke it may be so, perchance.
    This tyrant, whose sole name blisters our tongues, 12
    Was once thought honest. You have loved him well;
    He hath not touched you yet. I am young; but something 14
    You may deserve of him through me, and wisdom   15

---

85 fry spawn, progeny

4.3. Location: England. Before King Edward the Confessor's palace.
3 mortal deadly   **4 Bestride** stand over in defense.   **birthdom** native
land   **6 Strike . . . face** offer an insulting slap in the face to heaven
itself.   **that it resounds** so that it echoes   **7–8 As . . . dolor** as if heaven,
feeling itself the blow delivered to Scotland, cried out with a similar cry
of pain   **8 Like** similar   **8–9 What . . . believe** i.e., what I believe to be
amiss in Scotland I will grieve for, and anything I am certain to be true
I will believe. (But one must be cautious in these duplicitous times.)
10 to friend opportune   **12 sole** mere   **14 He . . . yet** i.e., the fact that
Macbeth hasn't hurt you yet makes me suspicious of your loyalties.
young i.e., inexperienced   **14–15 something . . . me** i.e., you may win
favor with Macbeth by delivering me to him   **15 wisdom** i.e., it would
be worldly-wise

To offer up a weak, poor, innocent lamb
T' appease an angry god.
MACDUFF   I am not treacherous.
MALCOLM   But Macbeth is.
A good and virtuous nature may recoil   20
In an imperial charge. But I shall crave your pardon.   21
That which you are my thoughts cannot transpose;   22
Angels are bright still, though the brightest fell.   23
Though all things foul would wear the brows of grace,   24
Yet grace must still look so.
MACDUFF   I have lost my hopes.   25
MALCOLM
Perchance even there where I did find my doubts.   26
Why in that rawness left you wife and child,   27
Those precious motives, those strong knots of love,   28
Without leave-taking? I pray you,
Let not my jealousies be your dishonors,   30
But mine own safeties. You may be rightly just,   31
Whatever I shall think.
MACDUFF   Bleed, bleed, poor country!
Great tyranny, lay thou thy basis sure,   33
For goodness dare not check thee; wear thou thy wrongs,   34
The title is affeered! Fare thee well, lord.   35
I would not be the villain that thou think'st
For the whole space that's in the tyrant's grasp,

---

20 recoil give way, fall back (as in the firing of a gun)   **21 In . . . charge**
under pressure from royal command. (*Charge* puns on the idea of a
quantity of powder and shot for a gun, as in *recoil*.)   **22 That . . . transpose** my suspicious thoughts cannot change you from what you are,
cannot make you evil   **23 the brightest** i.e., Lucifer   **24–25 Though . . .
so** i.e., even though evil puts on the appearance of good so often as to
cast that appearance into deep suspicion, yet goodness must go on
looking and acting like itself   **25 hopes** i.e., hopes of Malcolm's assistance in the cause against Macbeth   **26 Perchance even there** i.e.,
perhaps in that same mistrustful frame of mind.   **doubts** i.e., fears
such as that Macduff may covertly be on Macbeth's side   **27 rawness**
unprotected condition. (Malcolm suggests that Macduff's leaving his
family unprotected could be construed as more evidence of his not
having anything to fear from Macbeth.)   **28 motives** persons inspiring
you to cherish and protect them; incentives to offer strong protection
30–31 Let . . . safeties i.e., may it be true that my suspicions of your
lack of honor are founded only in my own wariness   **33 basis** foundation   **34 wrongs** wrongfully gained powers   **35 affeered** confirmed,
certified

And the rich East to boot.

MALCOLM   Be not offended.   38
  I speak not as in absolute fear of you.   39
  I think our country sinks beneath the yoke;   40
  It weeps, it bleeds, and each new day a gash
  Is added to her wounds. I think withal   42
  There would be hands uplifted in my right;   43
  And here from gracious England have I offer   44
  Of goodly thousands. But, for all this,
  When I shall tread upon the tyrant's head,
  Or wear it on my sword, yet my poor country
  Shall have more vices than it had before,
  More suffer, and more sundry ways than ever,   49
  By him that shall succeed.

MACDUFF   What should he be?   50

MALCOLM
  It is myself I mean, in whom I know
  All the particulars of vice so grafted   52
  That, when they shall be opened, black Macbeth   53
  Will seem as pure as snow, and the poor state
  Esteem him as a lamb, being compared
  With my confineless harms.

MACDUFF   Not in the legions   56
  Of horrid hell can come a devil more damned
  In evils to top Macbeth.

MALCOLM   I grant him bloody,   58
  Luxurious, avaricious, false, deceitful,   59
  Sudden, malicious, smacking of every sin   60
  That has a name. But there's no bottom, none,
  In my voluptuousness. Your wives, your daughters,
  Your matrons, and your maids could not fill up
  The cistern of my lust, and my desire
  All continent impediments would o'erbear   65
  That did oppose my will. Better Macbeth   66

---

38 to boot in addition   **39 absolute fear** complete mistrust   **40 think** am mindful that   **42 withal** in addition   **43 right** cause   **44 England** i.e., the King of England   **49 more sundry** in more various   **50 What** who   **52 particulars** varieties.   **grafted** (1) engrafted, indissolubly mixed (2) grafted like a plant that will then *open* or unfold   **53 opened** unfolded (like a bud)   **56 my confineless harms** the boundless injuries I shall inflict   **58 top** surpass   **59 Luxurious** lecherous   **60 Sudden** violent, passionate   **65 continent** (1) chaste (2) restraining, containing   **66 will** lust (also in l. 89)

Than such an one to reign.

MACDUFF   Boundless intemperance
In nature is a tyranny; it hath been   68
Th' untimely emptying of the happy throne
And fall of many kings. But fear not yet   70
To take upon you what is yours. You may
Convey your pleasures in a spacious plenty,   72
And yet seem cold; the time you may so hoodwink.   73
We have willing dames enough. There cannot be
That vulture in you to devour so many
As will to greatness dedicate themselves,
Finding it so inclined.

MALCOLM   With this there grows
In my most ill-composed affection such   78
A stanchless avarice that, were I king,   79
I should cut off the nobles for their lands,
Desire his jewels and this other's house,   81
And my more-having would be as a sauce
To make me hunger more, that I should forge   83
Quarrels unjust against the good and loyal,
Destroying them for wealth.

MACDUFF   This avarice
Sticks deeper, grows with more pernicious root
Than summer-seeming lust, and it hath been   87
The sword of our slain kings. Yet do not fear;   88
Scotland hath foisons to fill up your will   89
Of your mere own. All these are portable,   90
With other graces weighed.   91

MALCOLM
But I have none. The king-becoming graces,
As justice, verity, temperance, stableness,
Bounty, perseverance, mercy, lowliness,   94
Devotion, patience, courage, fortitude,
I have no relish of them, but abound   96

68 nature human nature **70 yet** nevertheless **72 Convey** manage with
secrecy **73 cold** chaste. **the time . . . hoodwink** you may so deceive
the age. **hoodwink** blindfold **78 ill-composed affection** evil disposition **79 stanchless** insatiable **81 his** one man's. **this other's** another's **83 that** so that **87 summer-seeming** appropriate to youth (and
lessening in later years) **88 sword** i.e., cause of overthrow **89 foisons**
resources, plenty **90 Of . . . own** i.e., in your own royal estates alone.
portable bearable **91 weighed** counterbalanced **94 lowliness** humil-
ity **96 relish** flavor or trace

In the division of each several crime,   97
Acting it many ways. Nay, had I power, I should
Pour the sweet milk of concord into hell,
Uproar the universal peace, confound   100
All unity on earth.
MACDUFF   O Scotland, Scotland!
MALCOLM
If such a one be fit to govern, speak.
I am as I have spoken.
MACDUFF   Fit to govern?
No, not to live. O nation miserable,
With an untitled tyrant bloody-sceptered,   105
When shalt thou see thy wholesome days again,
Since that the truest issue of thy throne
By his own interdiction stands accursed   108
And does blaspheme his breed? Thy royal father   109
Was a most sainted king; the queen that bore thee,
Oft'ner upon her knees than on her feet,
Died every day she lived. Fare thee well.   112
These evils thou repeat'st upon thyself
Hath banished me from Scotland. O my breast,   114
Thy hope ends here!
MALCOLM   Macduff, this noble passion,
Child of integrity, hath from my soul   116
Wiped the black scruples, reconciled my thoughts
To thy good truth and honor. Devilish Macbeth
By many of these trains hath sought to win me   119
Into his power, and modest wisdom plucks me   120
From overcredulous haste. But God above
Deal between thee and me! For even now
I put myself to thy direction and
Unspeak mine own detraction, here abjure   124
The taints and blames I laid upon myself
For strangers to my nature. I am yet   126

97 **division** subdivisions, various possible forms. **several** separate
100 **Uproar** throw into an uproar 105 **untitled** lacking rightful title,
usurping 108 **interdiction** debarring of self 109 **blaspheme** slander,
defame. **breed** breeding (i.e., he is a disgrace to his royal lineage)
112 **Died . . . lived** i.e., lived a life of daily mortification 114 **breast**
heart 116 **Child of integrity** a product of your integrity of spirit
119 **trains** plots, artifices 120 **modest . . . me** wise prudence holds me
back 124 **mine own detraction** my detraction of myself 126 **For** as

Unknown to woman, never was forsworn,   127
Scarcely have coveted what was mine own,
At no time broke my faith, would not betray
The devil to his fellow, and delight
No less in truth than life. My first false speaking
Was this upon myself. What I am truly   132
Is thine and my poor country's to command—
Whither indeed, before thy here-approach,
Old Siward with ten thousand warlike men,
Already at a point, was setting forth.   136
Now we'll together; and the chance of goodness   137
Be like our warranted quarrel! Why are you silent?   138

MACDUFF
Such welcome and unwelcome things at once
'Tis hard to reconcile.

    Enter a Doctor.

MALCOLM
Well, more anon.—Comes the King forth, I pray you?

DOCTOR
Ay, sir. There are a crew of wretched souls
That stay his cure. Their malady convinces   143
The great assay of art; but at his touch—   144
Such sanctity hath heaven given his hand—
They presently amend.

MALCOLM   I thank you, Doctor.   146

                        Exit [Doctor].

MACDUFF
What's the disease he means?

MALCOLM   'Tis called the evil.   147
A most miraculous work in this good king,
Which often, since my here-remain in England,   149
I have seen him do. How he solicits heaven   150
Himself best knows; but strangely-visited people,   151

---

127 Unknown to woman a virgin   **132 upon** against   **136 at a point**
ready, prepared   **137 the chance of goodness** may the chance of success   **138 Be . . . quarrel** be proportionate to the justice of our cause.
143 stay wait for. **convinces** conquers   **144 assay of art** efforts of
medical skill   **146 presently** immediately   **147 evil** i.e., scrofula, supposedly cured by the royal touch; James I claimed this power   **149 here-
remain** stay   **150 solicits** prevails by prayer with   **151 strangely-visited**
afflicted by strange diseases

All swoll'n and ulcerous, pitiful to the eye,
The mere despair of surgery, he cures,   153
Hanging a golden stamp about their necks   154
Put on with holy prayers; and 'tis spoken,
To the succeeding royalty he leaves
The healing benediction. With this strange virtue   157
He hath a heavenly gift of prophecy,
And sundry blessings hang about his throne
That speak him full of grace.

    Enter Ross.

MACDUFF   See who comes here.
MALCOLM
My countryman, but yet I know him not.   161
MACDUFF
My ever-gentle cousin, welcome hither.   162
MALCOLM
I know him now. Good God betimes remove   163
The means that makes us strangers!
ROSS   Sir, amen.
MACDUFF
Stands Scotland where it did?
ROSS   Alas, poor country,
Almost afraid to know itself. It cannot
Be called our mother, but our grave; where nothing   167
But who knows nothing is once seen to smile;   168
Where sighs and groans and shrieks that rend the air
Are made, not marked; where violent sorrow seems   170
A modern ecstasy. The dead man's knell   171
Is there scarce asked for who, and good men's lives
Expire before the flowers in their caps,
Dying or ere they sicken.
MACDUFF   O, relation   174
Too nice, and yet too true!
MALCOLM   What's the newest grief?   175

---

153 mere utter   **154 stamp** minted coin   **157 virtue** healing power
161 My countryman (So identified by his dress.)   **know** recognize
162 gentle noble   **163 betimes** speedily   **167 nothing** nobody   **168 But
who** except a person who.   **once** ever   **170 marked** noticed (because
they are so common)   **171 modern ecstasy** commonplace emotion
174 or ere they sicken before they have had time to fall ill.   **relation**
report   **175 nice** minutely accurate, elaborately phrased

ROSS
That of an hour's age doth hiss the speaker;   176
Each minute teems a new one.

MACDUFF   How does my wife?   177

ROSS
Why, well.

MACDUFF   And all my children?

ROSS   Well too.   178

MACDUFF
The tyrant has not battered at their peace?

ROSS
No, they were well at peace when I did leave 'em.

MACDUFF
Be not a niggard of your speech. How goes 't?

ROSS
When I came hither to transport the tidings
Which I have heavily borne, there ran a rumor   183
Of many worthy fellows that were out,   184
Which was to my belief witnessed the rather   185
For that I saw the tyrant's power afoot.   186
Now is the time of help; your eye in Scotland
Would create soldiers, make our women fight,
To doff their dire distresses.

MALCOLM   Be 't their comfort   189
We are coming thither. Gracious England hath   190
Lent us good Siward and ten thousand men;
An older and a better soldier none
That Christendom gives out.

ROSS   Would I could answer   193
This comfort with the like! But I have words
That would be howled out in the desert air,
Where hearing should not latch them.

MACDUFF   What concern they?   196
The general cause? Or is it a fee-grief   197

---

176 hiss cause to be hissed (for repeating stale news)   **177 teems** teems
with, yields   **178 Well** (Ross quibbles, in his reluctance to tell the bad
news, on the saying that "the dead are well," i.e., at rest.)   **183 heavily**
sadly   **184 out** in arms, in the field   **185 witnessed the rather** made
the more believable   **186 power** army   **189 doff** put off, get rid of
190 Gracious England i.e., Edward the Confessor   **193 gives out** tells of,
proclaims   **196 latch** catch (the sound of)   **197 fee-grief** a grief with an
individual owner, having absolute ownership

Due to some single breast?

ROSS   No mind that's honest   198
But in it shares some woe, though the main part
Pertains to you alone.

MACDUFF   If it be mine,
Keep it not from me; quickly let me have it.

ROSS
Let not your ears despise my tongue forever,
Which shall possess them with the heaviest sound   203
That ever yet they heard.

MACDUFF   Hum! I guess at it.

ROSS
Your castle is surprised, your wife and babes
Savagely slaughtered. To relate the manner
Were, on the quarry of these murdered deer,   207
To add the death of you.

MALCOLM   Merciful heaven!
What, man, ne'er pull your hat upon your brows;   209
Give sorrow words. The grief that does not speak
Whispers the o'erfraught heart and bids it break.   211

MACDUFF
My children too?

ROSS   Wife, children, servants, all
That could be found.

MACDUFF   And I must be from thence!   213
My wife killed too?

ROSS   I have said.

MALCOLM   Be comforted.
Let's make us medicines of our great revenge
To cure this deadly grief.

MACDUFF
He has no children. All my pretty ones?   217
Did you say all? O hell-kite! All?
What, all my pretty chickens and their dam
At one fell swoop?   220

198 Due to i.e., owned by   **203 possess them with** put them in possession of   **207 quarry** heap of slaughtered deer at a hunt (with a pun on
dear, deer)   **209 pull your hat** (A conventional gesture of grief.)
211 Whispers whispers to.   **o'erfraught** overburdened   **213 must** had
to   **217 He has no children** i.e., no father would do such a thing (?), or,
he (Malcolm) speaks comfort without knowing what such a loss feels
like (?)   **220 fell swoop** cruel swoop of the *hell-kite*, bird of prey from
hell (with a suggestion too of swoopstake, sweepstake)

MALCOLM   Dispute it like a man.   221
MACDUFF   I shall do so;
  But I must also feel it as a man.
  I cannot but remember such things were,
  That were most precious to me. Did heaven look on
  And would not take their part? Sinful Macduff,
  They were all struck for thee! Naught that I am,   227
  Not for their own demerits, but for mine,
  Fell slaughter on their souls. Heaven rest them now!
MALCOLM
  Be this the whetstone of your sword. Let grief
  Convert to anger; blunt not the heart, enrage it.   231
MACDUFF
  O, I could play the woman with mine eyes
  And braggart with my tongue! But, gentle heavens,
  Cut short all intermission. Front to front   234
  Bring thou this fiend of Scotland and myself;
  Within my sword's length set him. If he scape,
  Heaven forgive him too!
MALCOLM   This tune goes manly.   237
  Come, go we to the King. Our power is ready;   238
  Our lack is nothing but our leave. Macbeth   239
  Is ripe for shaking, and the powers above
  Put on their instruments. Receive what cheer you may.   241
  The night is long that never finds the day.   *Exeunt.*

❖

---

221 Dispute it i.e., fight on the issue; or, be a man, don't give in to
grief   **227 for thee** i.e., as divine punishment for your sins.   **Naught**
wicked   **231 Convert** change   **234 intermission** delay, interval.   **Front
to front** face to face   **237 too** i.e., as I would have had to forgive him
before allowing him to escape. (Macduff's point is that Macbeth will
never escape, since these conditions will never be met.)   **238 power**
army   **239 Our . . . leave** we need only to take our leave (of the English
King)   **241 Put . . . instruments** set us on as their agents; or, arm
themselves

5.1   *Enter a Doctor of Physic and a*
Waiting-Gentlewoman.

DOCTOR   I have two nights watched with you, but can
perceive no truth in your report. When was it she last
walked?

GENTLEWOMAN   Since His Majesty went into the field, I
have seen her rise from her bed, throw her nightgown
upon her, unlock her closet, take forth paper, fold it,   5
write upon 't, read it, afterwards seal it, and again return to bed; yet all this while in a most fast sleep.

DOCTOR   A great perturbation in nature, to receive at
once the benefit of sleep and do the effects of watch-   9
ing! In this slumbery agitation, besides her walking   10
and other actual performances, what, at any time,
have you heard her say?

GENTLEWOMAN   That, sir, which I will not report after her.

DOCTOR   You may to me, and 'tis most meet you should.

GENTLEWOMAN   Neither to you nor anyone, having no
witness to confirm my speech.

Enter Lady [*Macbeth*], *with a taper.*

Lo you, here she comes! This is her very guise, and,
upon my life, fast asleep. Observe her. Stand close.   19
                                [*They stand aside.*]

DOCTOR   How came she by that light?

GENTLEWOMAN   Why, it stood by her. She has light by
her continually. 'Tis her command.

DOCTOR   You see her eyes are open.

GENTLEWOMAN   Ay, but their sense are shut.

DOCTOR   What is it she does now? Look how she rubs
her hands.

GENTLEWOMAN   It is an accustomed action with her to
seem thus washing her hands. I have known her continue in this a quarter of an hour.

LADY MACBETH   Yet here's a spot.

DOCTOR   Hark, she speaks. I will set down what comes

5.1. Location: Dunsinane. Macbeth's castle.
5 closet chest or desk   **9–10 effects of watching** deeds characteristic of
waking   **10 agitation** activity   **19 close** concealed

from her, to satisfy my remembrance the more 32
strongly.

LADY MACBETH Out, damned spot! Out, I say! One—
two—why then, 'tis time to do 't. Hell is murky.—
Fie, my lord, fie, a soldier, and afeard? What need we
fear who knows it, when none can call our power to
account? Yet who would have thought the old man to
have had so much blood in him?

DOCTOR Do you mark that?

LADY MACBETH The Thane of Fife had a wife. Where is
she now?—What, will these hands ne'er be clean?—
No more o' that, my lord, no more o' that; you mar all
with this starting.   44

DOCTOR Go to, go to. You have known what you should
not.

GENTLEWOMAN She has spoke what she should not, I
am sure of that. Heaven knows what she has known.

LADY MACBETH Here's the smell of the blood still. All
the perfumes of Arabia will not sweeten this little
hand. O, O, O!

DOCTOR What a sigh is there! The heart is sorely 52
charged.   53

GENTLEWOMAN I would not have such a heart in my
bosom for the dignity of the whole body.   55

DOCTOR Well, well, well.

GENTLEWOMAN Pray God it be, sir.

DOCTOR This disease is beyond my practice. Yet I have
known those which have walked in their sleep who
have died holily in their beds.

LADY MACBETH Wash your hands, put on your nightgown; look not so pale! I tell you yet again, Banquo's
buried. He cannot come out on 's grave.   63

DOCTOR Even so?

LADY MACBETH To bed, to bed! There's knocking at the
gate. Come, come, come, come, give me your hand.
What's done cannot be undone. To bed, to bed,
to bed!   *Exit Lady.*

DOCTOR Will she go now to bed?

---

32 satisfy confirm, support **44 this starting** these startled movements **52–53 sorely charged** heavily burdened **55 dignity** worth,
value **63 on 's** of his

GENTLEWOMAN   Directly.

DOCTOR

Foul whisperings are abroad. Unnatural deeds
Do breed unnatural troubles. Infected minds
To their deaf pillows will discharge their secrets.
More needs she the divine than the physician.
God, God forgive us all! Look after her;
Remove from her the means of all annoyance,   76
And still keep eyes upon her. So, good night.   77
My mind she has mated, and amazed my sight.   78
I think, but dare not speak.

GENTLEWOMAN   Good night, good Doctor.

Exeunt.

✣

5.2   *Drum and colors. Enter Menteith, Caithness,*
Angus, Lennox, [and] soldiers.

MENTEITH

The English power is near, led on by Malcolm,
His uncle Siward, and the good Macduff.
Revenges burn in them, for their dear causes   3
Would to the bleeding and the grim alarm   4
Excite the mortified man.

ANGUS   Near Birnam Wood   5
Shall we well meet them; that way are they coming.   6

CAITHNESS

Who knows if Donalbain be with his brother?

LENNOX

For certain, sir, he is not. I have a file   8
Of all the gentry. There is Siward's son,
And many unrough youths that even now   10
Protest their first of manhood.

MENTEITH   What does the tyrant?   11

---

76 annoyance i.e., harming herself   **77 still** constantly   **78 mated**
bewildered, stupefied

5.2. Location: The country near Dunsinane.
3 dear heartfelt, grievous   **4 bleeding** bloody.   **alarm** call to battle
5 Excite . . . man awaken the dead   **6 well** no doubt   **8 file** list, roster
10 unrough beardless   **11 Protest** assert publicly

CAITHNESS
    Great Dunsinane he strongly fortifies.
    Some say he's mad, others that lesser hate him
    Do call it valiant fury; but for certain
    He cannot buckle his distempered cause   15
    Within the belt of rule.
ANGUS   Now does he feel
    His secret murders sticking on his hands;
    Now minutely revolts upbraid his faith-breach.   18
    Those he commands move only in command,   19
    Nothing in love. Now does he feel his title
    Hang loose about him, like a giant's robe
    Upon a dwarfish thief.
MENTEITH   Who then shall blame
    His pestered senses to recoil and start,   23
    When all that is within him does condemn
    Itself for being there?
CAITHNESS   Well, march we on
    To give obedience where 'tis truly owed.
    Meet we the medicine of the sickly weal,   27
    And with him pour we in our country's purge   28
    Each drop of us.
LENNOX   Or so much as it needs   29
    To dew the sovereign flower and drown the weeds.   30
    Make we our march towards Birnam.
                                Exeunt, marching.

❖

5.3   *Enter Macbeth, Doctor, and attendants.*

MACBETH
    Bring me no more reports. Let them fly all!   1
    Till Birnam Wood remove to Dunsinane,

---

15 distempered disease-swollen, dropsical **18 minutely** every minute.
upbraid censure. **faith-breach** violation of all trust and sacred vows
19 in command under orders **23 pestered** troubled, tormented
27 Meet we . . . weal i.e., let us join forces with Malcolm, the physician
of our sick land **28–29 pour . . . of us** i.e., let us shed all our blood as a
bloodletting or *purge* of our country **30 dew** bedew, water. **sovereign**
(1) royal (2) medically efficacious

5.3. Location: Dunsinane. Macbeth's castle.
1 them i.e., the thanes. **fly** desert

I cannot taint with fear. What's the boy Malcolm?   3
Was he not born of woman? The spirits that know
All mortal consequences have pronounced me thus: 5
"Fear not, Macbeth. No man that's born of woman
Shall e'er have power upon thee." Then fly, false thanes,
And mingle with the English epicures!   8
The mind I sway by and the heart I bear   9
Shall never sag with doubt nor shake with fear.   10

    Enter Servant.

The devil damn thee black, thou cream-faced loon!   11
Where gott'st thou that goose look?
SERVANT
  There is ten thousand—
MACBETH   Geese, villain?
SERVANT   Soldiers, sir.
MACBETH
  Go prick thy face and over-red thy fear,   14
  Thou lily-livered boy. What soldiers, patch?   15
  Death of thy soul! Those linen cheeks of thine   16
  Are counselors to fear. What soldiers, whey-face?   17
SERVANT   The English force, so please you.
MACBETH
  Take thy face hence. [*Exit Servant.*] Seyton!—I am sick
    at heart
  When I behold—Seyton, I say!—This push   20
  Will cheer me ever, or disseat me now.   21
  I have lived long enough. My way of life   22
  Is fall'n into the sere, the yellow leaf,   23
  And that which should accompany old age,
  As honor, love, obedience, troops of friends,   25
  I must not look to have, but in their stead

---

3 taint with become imbued or infected with, weakened by   **5 mortal consequences** what befalls humanity   **8 epicures** luxury-loving persons   **9 sway** rule myself   **10 sag** droop   **11 loon** stupid fellow   **14 Go prick . . . fear** i.e., go prick or pinch your pale cheeks to bring some color into them. (The servant's blood has all retired into his lower abdomen on account of his fear, so that he is very pale and there is no blood in his liver, where his courage should have resided—hence, *lily-livered* l. 15.)   **15 patch** domestic fool   **16 of thy** on your   **17 Are . . . fear** i.e., teach others to fear   **20 behold** (Macbeth does not finish this thought.)   **push** effort, crisis   **21 disseat** dethrone   **22 way** course   **23 sere** dry and withered   **25 As** such as

Curses, not loud but deep, mouth-honor, breath,
Which the poor heart would fain deny and dare not.
Seyton!

Enter Seyton.

SEYTON
What's your gracious pleasure?
MACBETH   What news more?
SEYTON
All is confirmed, my lord, which was reported.
MACBETH
I'll fight till from my bones my flesh be hacked.
Give me my armor.
SEYTON   'Tis not needed yet.
MACBETH   I'll put it on.
Send out more horses. Skirr the country round.   36
Hang those that talk of fear. Give me mine armor.
How does your patient, Doctor?
DOCTOR   Not so sick, my lord,
As she is troubled with thick-coming fancies
That keep her from her rest.
MACBETH   Cure her of that.
Canst thou not minister to a mind diseased,
Pluck from the memory a rooted sorrow,
Rase out the written troubles of the brain,   44
And with some sweet oblivious antidote   45
Cleanse the stuffed bosom of that perilous stuff   46
Which weighs upon the heart?
DOCTOR   Therein the patient
Must minister to himself.
MACBETH
Throw physic to the dogs! I'll none of it.   49
Come, put mine armor on. Give me my staff.   50
                              [*Attendants arm him.*]
Seyton, send out. Doctor, the thanes fly from me.—
Come, sir, dispatch.—If thou couldst, Doctor, cast   52
The water of my land, find her disease,   53

36 **Skirr** scour 44 **Rase** erase, obliterate. **written troubles of** troubles
written on 45 **oblivious** causing forgetfulness 46 **stuffed** clogged
49 **physic** medicine 50 **staff** lance or baton of office 52 **dispatch**
hurry. **cast** diagnose 53 **water** i.e., urine, used in diagnosis

And purge it to a sound and pristine health,
I would applaud thee to the very echo,
That should applaud again.—Pull 't off, I say.—   56
What rhubarb, senna, or what purgative drug   57
Would scour these English hence? Hear'st thou of
    them?   58

DOCTOR
Ay, my good lord. Your royal preparation
Makes us hear something.

MACBETH   Bring it after me.—   60
I will not be afraid of death and bane,
Till Birnam Forest come to Dunsinane.

                            Exeunt [all but the Doctor].

DOCTOR
Were I from Dunsinane away and clear,
Profit again should hardly draw me here.   [*Exit.*]

                    ❖

5.4   *Drum and colors. Enter Malcolm, Siward,*
    Macduff, Siward's Son, Menteith, Caithness,
    Angus, [Lennox, Ross,] and soldiers, marching.

MALCOLM
Cousins, I hope the days are near at hand
That chambers will be safe.

MENTEITH   We doubt it nothing.   2

SIWARD
What wood is this before us?

MENTEITH   The wood of Birnam.

MALCOLM
Let every soldier hew him down a bough
And bear 't before him. Thereby shall we shadow
The numbers of our host and make discovery   6
Err in report of us.

SOLDIERS   It shall be done.

---

56 Pull 't off (Refers to some part of the armor not properly put on.)
57 senna a purgative drug   **58 scour** purge, cleanse, rid   **60 it** i.e., the
armor not yet put on Macbeth

5.4. Location: Country near Birnam Wood.
2 chambers . . . safe i.e., we may sleep safely in our bedchambers.
nothing not at all   **6 discovery** scouting reports

SIWARD
   We learn no other but the confident tyrant
   Keeps still in Dunsinane and will endure   9
   Our setting down before 't.
MALCOLM   'Tis his main hope;   10
   For where there is advantage to be given,   11
   Both more and less have given him the revolt,   12
   And none serve with him but constrainèd things
   Whose hearts are absent too.
MACDUFF   Let our just censures   14
   Attend the true event, and put we on   15
   Industrious soldiership.
SIWARD   The time approaches
   That will with due decision make us know
   What we shall say we have and what we owe.   18
   Thoughts speculative their unsure hopes relate,   19
   But certain issue strokes must arbitrate—   20
   Towards which advance the war.   *Exeunt, marching.*   21

❧

5.5   *Enter Macbeth, Seyton, and soldiers, with
           drum and colors.*

MACBETH
   Hang out our banners on the outward walls.
   The cry is still, "They come!" Our castle's strength
   Will laugh a siege to scorn. Here let them lie

9 Keeps remains.   **endure** allow, not attempt to prevent   **10 setting
down before** laying siege to   **11 advantage** opportunity (i.e., in military
operations outside Macbeth's castle in which it is possible for would-be
deserters to slip away; in a siege, his forces will be more confined to the
castle and under his watchful eye)   **12 more and less** high and low
14–15 Let . . . event i.e., let us postpone judgment about these uncertain
matters until we've achieved our goal   **18 What . . . owe** i.e., what we
only claim to have, as distinguished from what we actually have (or
perhaps what we *owe* as duty).   **owe** own   **19–20 Thoughts . . . arbitrate** i.e., speculating can only convey our sense of hope; blows must
decide the actual outcome   **21 war** army

5.5. Location: Dunsinane. Macbeth's castle.

Till famine and the ague eat them up.
Were they not forced with those that should be ours,   5
We might have met them dareful, beard to beard,   6
And beat them backward home.

                              A cry within of women.
                              What is that noise?

SEYTON
It is the cry of women, my good lord.
                              [*He goes to the door.*]

MACBETH
I have almost forgot the taste of fears.
The time has been my senses would have cooled   10
To hear a night-shriek, and my fell of hair   11
Would at a dismal treatise rouse and stir   12
As life were in 't. I have supped full with horrors;   13
Direness, familiar to my slaughterous thoughts,
Cannot once start me.

        [*Seyton returns.*]

                              Wherefore was that cry?   15
SEYTON   The Queen, my lord, is dead.
MACBETH   She should have died hereafter;   17
There would have been a time for such a word.
Tomorrow, and tomorrow, and tomorrow   19
Creeps in this petty pace from day to day
To the last syllable of recorded time,   21
And all our yesterdays have lighted fools
The way to dusty death. Out, out, brief candle!   23
Life's but a walking shadow, a poor player
That struts and frets his hour upon the stage
And then is heard no more. It is a tale
Told by an idiot, full of sound and fury,
Signifying nothing.   28

---

5 forced reinforced   **6 dareful** boldly, in open battle   **10 cooled** felt the
chill of terror   **11 my fell of hair** the hair of my scalp   **12 dismal
treatise** sinister story   **13 As** as if   **15 start me** make me start   **17 She
. . . hereafter** she would have died someday; or, she should have died at
some more appropriate time freed from the relentless pressures of the
moment   **19–28 Tomorrow . . . nothing** (For biblical echoes in this speech,
see Psalms 18:28, 22:15, 90:9; Job 8:9, 14:1–2, 18:6.)   **21 recorded time**
the record of time   **23 dusty** (Since life, made out of dust, returns to dust.)

Enter a Messenger.

Thou com'st to use thy tongue; thy story quickly.

MESSENGER　Gracious my lord,
　I should report that which I say I saw,
　But know not how to do 't.

MACBETH　　　　　　　　　　　　Well, say, sir.

MESSENGER
　As I did stand my watch upon the hill,
　I looked toward Birnam, and anon, methought,
　The wood began to move.

MACBETH　　　　　　　　　Liar and slave!

MESSENGER
　Let me endure your wrath if 't be not so.
　Within this three mile may you see it coming;
　I say, a moving grove.

MACBETH　　　　　　　　If thou speak'st false,
　Upon the next tree shall thou hang alive
　Till famine cling thee. If thy speech be sooth,　　40
　I care not if thou dost for me as much.
　I pull in resolution, and begin　　　　　　　　　42
　To doubt th' equivocation of the fiend
　That lies like truth. "Fear not, till Birnam Wood
　Do come to Dunsinane," and now a wood
　Comes toward Dunsinane. Arm, arm, and out!
　If this which he avouches does appear,
　There is nor flying hence nor tarrying here.
　I 'gin to be aweary of the sun,
　And wish th' estate o' the world were now undone.　50
　Ring the alarum bell! Blow wind, come wrack,　　51
　At least we'll die with harness on our back.　　*Exeunt.*　52

❖

5.6　*Drum and colors. Enter Malcolm, Siward,
　　　　Macduff, and their army, with boughs.*

MALCOLM
　Now near enough. Your leafy screens throw down,

---

40 cling cause to shrivel.　**sooth** truth　**42 pull in** check, rein in
50 estate settled order　**51 wrack** ruin　**52 harness** armor

5.6. Location: Dunsinane. Before Macbeth's castle.

And show like those you are. You, worthy uncle,   2
Shall with my cousin, your right noble son,
Lead our first battle. Worthy Macduff and we   4
Shall take upon 's what else remains to do,
According to our order.
SIWARD   Fare you well.   6
Do we but find the tyrant's power tonight,   7
Let us be beaten if we cannot fight.
MACDUFF
Make all our trumpets speak! Give them all breath,
Those clamorous harbingers of blood and death.   10
               Exeunt. Alarums continued.

5.7   *Enter Macbeth.*

MACBETH
They have tied me to a stake. I cannot fly,
But bearlike I must fight the course. What's he   2
That was not born of woman? Such a one
Am I to fear, or none.

     Enter young Siward.

YOUNG SIWARD   What is thy name?
MACBETH   Thou'lt be afraid to hear it.
YOUNG SIWARD
No, though thou call'st thyself a hotter name
Than any is in hell.
MACBETH   My name's Macbeth.
YOUNG SIWARD
The devil himself could not pronounce a title
More hateful to mine ear.
MACBETH   No, nor more fearful.
YOUNG SIWARD
Thou liest, abhorrèd tyrant! With my sword

---

2 show appear   **4 battle** battalion   **6 order** plan of battle   **7 power**
army   **10 harbingers** forerunners

**5.7. Location: Before Macbeth's castle; the battle action is continuous
here.**
2 course bout or round of bearbaiting, in which the bear was tied to a
stake and dogs were set upon him

I'll prove the lie thou speak'st.

Fight, and young Siward slain.

MACBETH   Thou wast born of woman. 12
But swords I smile at, weapons laugh to scorn,
Brandished by man that's of a woman born.   *Exit.*

Alarums. Enter Macduff.

MACDUFF
That way the noise is. Tyrant, show thy face!
If thou be'st slain, and with no stroke of mine,
My wife and children's ghosts will haunt me still.
I cannot strike at wretched kerns, whose arms   18
Are hired to bear their staves. Either thou, Macbeth,   19
Or else my sword with an unbattered edge
I sheathe again undeeded. There thou shouldst be;   21
By this great clatter one of greatest note
Seems bruited. Let me find him, Fortune,   23
And more I beg not.   *Exit. Alarums.*

Enter Malcolm and Siward.

SIWARD
This way, my lord. The castle's gently rendered: 25
The tyrant's people on both sides do fight,
The noble thanes do bravely in the war,
The day almost itself professes yours,
And little is to do.
MALCOLM   We have met with foes
That strike beside us.
SIWARD   Enter, sir, the castle.   30

Exeunt. Alarum.

---

12 s.d. young Siward slain (In some unspecified way, young Siward's
body must be removed from the stage; his own father enters at l. 24 and
perceives nothing amiss, and in 5.8.38 young Siward is reported *missing*
in action. Perhaps Macbeth drags off the body, or perhaps it is removed
by soldiers during the alarums.)   **18 kerns** (Properly, Irish foot soldiers;
here applied contemptuously to the rank and file.)   **19 staves** spears.
Either thou i.e., either I find you   **21 undeeded** having seen no action
23 bruited announced   **25 rendered** surrendered   **30 strike beside us**
fight on our side, or miss us deliberately

5.8   *Enter Macbeth.*

MACBETH
Why should I play the Roman fool and die   1
On mine own sword? Whiles I see lives, the gashes   2
Do better upon them.

     Enter Macduff.

MACDUFF   Turn, hellhound, turn!
MACBETH
Of all men else I have avoided thee.
But get thee back. My soul is too much charged
With blood of thine already.
MACDUFF   I have no words;
My voice is in my sword, thou bloodier villain
Than terms can give thee out!   *Fight. Alarum.*
MACBETH   Thou losest labor.   8
As easy mayst thou the intrenchant air   9
With thy keen sword impress as make me bleed.   10
Let fall thy blade on vulnerable crests;
I bear a charmèd life, which must not yield
To one of woman born.
MACDUFF   Despair thy charm,   13
And let the angel whom thou still hast served   14
Tell thee, Macduff was from his mother's womb
Untimely ripped.   16
MACBETH
Accursèd be that tongue that tells me so,
For it hath cowed my better part of man!   18
And be these juggling fiends no more believed   19
That palter with us in a double sense,   20
That keep the word of promise to our ear
And break it to our hope. I'll not fight with thee.

**5.8. Location: Before Macbeth's castle, as the battle continues; after
l. 34, within the castle.**
1 Roman fool i.e., suicide, like Brutus, Mark Antony, and others
2 Whiles . . . lives i.e., as long as I see any enemy living   **8 give thee out**
name you, describe you   **9 intrenchant** that cannot be cut, indivisible
10 impress make an impression on   **13 Despair** despair of   **14 angel**
evil angel, Macbeth's genius.   **still** always   **16 Untimely** prematurely
18 better . . . man i.e., courage   **19 juggling** deceiving   **20 palter . . .
sense** equivocate with us

MACDUFF   Then yield thee, coward,
And live to be the show and gaze o' the time!
We'll have thee, as our rarer monsters are,
Painted upon a pole, and underwrit,   26
"Here may you see the tyrant."

MACBETH   I will not yield
To kiss the ground before young Malcolm's feet
And to be baited with the rabble's curse.
Though Birnam Wood be come to Dunsinane,
And thou opposed, being of no woman born,
Yet I will try the last. Before my body   32
I throw my warlike shield. Lay on, Macduff,
And damned be him that first cries, "Hold, enough!"   34
                                    Exeunt, fighting. Alarums.

> *Enter fighting, and Macbeth slain. [Exit Macduff
> with Macbeth's body.] Retreat, and flourish.
> Enter, with drum and colors, Malcolm, Siward,
> Ross, thanes, and soldiers.*

MALCOLM
I would the friends we miss were safe arrived.

SIWARD
Some must go off; and yet, by these I see   36
So great a day as this is cheaply bought.

MALCOLM
Macduff is missing, and your noble son.

ROSS
Your son, my lord, has paid a soldier's debt.
He only lived but till he was a man,
The which no sooner had his prowess confirmed
In the unshrinking station where he fought,   42
But like a man he died.

SIWARD   Then he is dead?

---

26 Painted . . . pole i.e., painted on a board suspended on a pole   **32 the
last** i.e., my last resort: my own strength and resolution   **34 s.d. Enter,
with drum and colors, etc.** (The remainder of the play is perhaps imagined as taking place in Macbeth's castle, and could be marked as a
separate scene. In Shakespeare's theater, however, the shift is so nonrepresentational and without scenic alteration that the action is virtually
continuous.)   **36 go off** die.   **by these** to judge by these (assembled)
42 unshrinking station post from which he did not shrink

ROSS

   Ay, and brought off the field. Your cause of sorrow
   Must not be measured by his worth, for then
   It hath no end.

SIWARD   Had he his hurts before?

ROSS

   Ay, on the front.

SIWARD   Why then, God's soldier be he!
   Had I as many sons as I have hairs
   I would not wish them to a fairer death.
   And so, his knell is knolled.

MALCOLM   He's worth more sorrow,
   And that I'll spend for him.

SIWARD   He's worth no more.
   They say he parted well and paid his score,   52
   And so, God be with him! Here comes newer comfort.

   Enter Macduff, with Macbeth's head.

MACDUFF

   Hail, King! For so thou art. Behold where stands   54
   Th' usurper's cursèd head. The time is free.   55
   I see thee compassed with thy kingdom's pearl,   56
   That speak my salutation in their minds,
   Whose voices I desire aloud with mine:
   Hail, King of Scotland!

ALL   Hail, King of Scotland!   *Flourish.*

MALCOLM

   We shall not spend a large expense of time
   Before we reckon with your several loves   62
   And make us even with you. My thanes and kinsmen,   63
   Henceforth be earls, the first that ever Scotland
   In such an honor named. What's more to do
   Which would be planted newly with the time,   66
   As calling home our exiled friends abroad
   That fled the snares of watchful tyranny,

---

52 parted departed. **score** reckoning **54 stands** i.e., on a pole **55 free**
released from tyranny **56 compassed . . . pearl** surrounded by the
nobles of your kingdom (literally, the pearls encircling a crown)
62 reckon come to a reckoning **63 make . . . you** i.e., repay your worthiness **66 would . . . time** i.e., should be established at the commencement of this new era

Producing forth the cruel ministers　　　　　　　69
Of this dead butcher and his fiendlike queen—
Who, as 'tis thought, by self and violent hands　　71
Took off her life—this, and what needful else
That calls upon us, by the grace of Grace
We will perform in measure, time, and place.
So, thanks to all at once and to each one,
Whom we invite to see us crowned at Scone.

　　　　　　　　　　　Flourish. Exeunt omnes.

69 Producing forth bringing forward to trial.　**ministers** agents
71 self and violent her own violent

Date and Text

Macbeth was first printed in the First Folio of 1623. It was set up from a promptbook or a transcript of one. The text is unusually short, and seems to have been cut for reasons of censorship or for some special performance. Moreover, all of 3.5 and parts of 4.1 (39–43, 125–132) appear to be interpolations, containing songs from Thomas Middleton's *The Witch*. Middleton may have been responsible for other alterations and additions.

An astrologer named Simon Forman, in his manuscript *The Book of Plays and Notes thereof per Formans for Common Policy*, records the first known performance of *Macbeth* on April 20, 1611, at the Globe Theatre. The play must have been in existence by 1607, however, for allusions to it seemingly occur in *Lingua* and *The Puritan* (both published in 1607) and in *The Knight of the Burning Pestle* (probably acted in 1607). On the other hand, the play itself seemingly alludes to James I's royal succession in 1603, and to the trial of the notorious Gunpowder Plot conspirators in March of 1606.

Textual Notes

These textual notes are not a historical collation, either of the early folios or of more recent editions; they are simply a record of departures in this edition from the copy text. The reading adopted in this edition appears in boldface, followed by the rejected reading from the copy text, i.e., the First Folio. Only major alterations in punctuation are noted. Changes in lineation are not indicated, nor are some minor and obvious typographical errors.

Abbreviations used:
F the First Folio
s.d. stage direction
s.p. speech prefix

Copy text: the First Folio

1.1. 9 s.p. Second Witch All **10 s.p. Third Witch** [not in F] **11 s.p. All** [at l. 9 in F]

1.2. 1 s.p. [and elsewhere] Duncan King **13 gallowglasses** Gallowgrosses **14 quarrel** Quarry **21 ne'er** neu'r **26 thunders break** Thunders

1.3. 32 Weird weyward [elsewhere in F spelled "weyward" or "weyard"] **39 Forres** Soris **98 Came** Can **111 lose** loose

1.4. 1 Are Or

1.5. 1 s.p. [and elsewhere] Lady Macbeth Lady **12 lose** loose **47 it** hit

1.6. 4 martlet Barlet **9 most** must

1.7. 6 shoal Schoole **48 do** no

2.1. 56 strides sides **57 sure** sowre **58 way they** they may

2.2. 13 s.d. [at l. 8 in F]

2.3. 41 s.d. [at l. 40 in F]

3.1. 76 s.p. Murderers Murth [also at ll. 116 and 141] **142 s.d. Exeunt** [after l. 143 in F]

3.3. 7 and end

3.4. 79 time times **122 s.d. Exeunt** Exit

3.6. 24 son Sonnes **38 the** their

4.1. 34 ingredients ingredience **38 s.d. to** and **59 germens** Germaine **93 Dunsinane** Dunsmane **94 s.d. Descends** Descend **98 Birnam** Byrnan [also spelled "Byrnam" at l. 93 and "Birnan," "Byrnane," and "Birnane" in Act 5] **119 eighth** eight

4.2. 1 s.p. [and throughout] Lady Macduff Wife **22 none** moue **70–71 ones . . . methinks** ones / To fright you thus. Me thinkes **80 s.d. Enter Murderers** [after "What are these faces" in F] **81 s.p. [and throughout scene] First Murderer** Mur **84 shag-haired** shagger-ear'd

4.3. 4 downfall'n downfall   **15 deserve** discerne   **35 Fare** Far   **108 accursed**
accust   **124 detraction, here** detraction. Heere   **134 thy** they   **237 tune** time

5.1. 37 fear who feare? who

5.3. 41 Cure her Cure   **54 pristine** pristiue   **57 senna** Cyme   **62 s.d.** [at l. 64
in F]

5.4. 16 s.p. Siward Sey

Shakespeare's Sources

Shakespeare's chief source for *Macbeth* was Raphael Holinshed's *Chronicles* (1587 edition). Holinshed had gone for most of his material to Hector Boece, *Scotorum Historiae* (1526–1527), who in turn was indebted to a fourteenth-century priest named John of Fordun and to a fifteenth-century chronicler, Andrew of Wyntoun. By the time Holinshed found it, the story of Macbeth had become more fiction than fact. The historical Macbeth, who ruled from 1040 to 1057, did take the throne by killing Duncan, but in a civil conflict between two clans contending for the kingship. Contemporary observers credit him with having been a good ruler. Although he was defeated by the Earl of Northumbria (the Siward of Shakespeare's play) at Birnam Wood in 1054, the Earl was forced by his own losses to retire, and Macbeth ruled three years longer before being slain by Duncan's son Malcolm. Banquo and Fleance are fictional characters apparently invented by Boece.

In Holinshed's telling of the story, as we see in the selection that follows, Duncan is a king of a soft and gentle nature, negligent in punishing his enemies and thereby an unwitting encourager of sedition. It falls to his cousin, Macbeth, a critic of this soft line, and to Banquo, the Thane of Lochaber, to defend Scotland against her enemies: first against Macdowald (Macdonwald in Shakespeare) with his Irish kerns and gallowglasses, and then against Sueno, King of Norway. (Shakespeare fuses these battles into one.) Shortly thereafter, Macbeth and Banquo encounter "three women in strange and wild apparel, resembling creatures of elder world," who predict their futures as in the play. Although Macbeth and Banquo jest about the matter, common opinion later maintains that "these women were either the Weird Sisters, that is (as ye would say), the goddesses of destiny, or else some nymphs or fairies endued with knowledge of prophecy." Certainly Macbeth soon becomes the Thane of Cawdor, whereupon, jestingly reminded of the three sisters' promise by Banquo, he resolves to seek the throne. His way is blocked, however, by Duncan's naming of his eldest but still underage son

Malcolm to be Prince of Cumberland and heir to the throne. Macbeth's resentment at this is understandable, since Scottish law provides that, until the King's son is of age, the "next of blood unto him"—i.e., Macbeth himself, as Duncan's cousin—should reign. Accordingly, Macbeth begins to plot with his associates how to usurp the kingdom by force. His "very ambitious" wife urges him on because of her "unquenchable desire" to be queen. Banquo is one among many trusted friends with whose support Macbeth slays the King at Inverness or at Bothgowanan. (No mention is made of a visit to Macbeth's castle.) Malcolm and Donald Bane, the dead King's sons, fly for their safety to Cumberland, where Malcolm is well received by Edward the Confessor of England; Donald Bane proceeds on to Ireland.

Holinshed's Macbeth is at first no brutal tyrant, as in Shakespeare. For some ten years he rules well, using great liberality and correcting the laxity of his predecessor's reign. (Holinshed does suggest, to be sure, that his justice is only contrived to court popularity among his subjects.) Inevitably, however, the Weird Sisters' promise of a posterity to Banquo goads Macbeth into ordering the murder of his onetime companion. Fleance escapes Macbeth's henchmen in the dark, and afterward founds the lineage of the Stuart kings. (This genealogy is fictitious.) Macbeth's vain quest for absolute power further causes him to build Dunsinane fortress. When Macduff refuses to help, the King turns against him and would kill him except that "a certain witch, whom he had in great trust," tells the King he need never fear a man born of woman nor any vanquishment till Birnam Wood come to Dunsinane. Macduff flees for his safety into England and joins Malcolm, whereupon Macbeth's agents slaughter Macduff's wife and children at Fife. Malcolm, fearing that Macduff may be an agent of Macbeth, dissemblingly professes to be a voluptuary, miser, and tyrant; but when Macduff responds as he should in righteous sorrow at Scotland's evil condition, Malcolm reveals his steadfast commitment to the cause of right. These leaders return to Scotland and defeat Macbeth at Birnam Wood, with their soldiers carrying branches before them. Macduff, proclaiming that he is a man born of no woman since he was "ripped out" of his mother's womb, slays Macbeth.

Despite extensive similarities, Shakespeare has made some significant changes. Duncan is no longer an ineffectual king. Macbeth can no longer justify his claim to the throne. Most important, Banquo is no longer partner to a broadly based though secret conspiracy against Duncan. Banquo is, after all, ancestor of James I (at least according to this legendary history), so that his hands must be kept scrupulously clean; King James disapproved of all tyrannicides, whatever the circumstances. Macbeth is no longer a just lawgiver. The return of Banquo's ghost to Macbeth's banqueting table is an added scene. Macbeth hears the prophecy about Birnam Wood and Macduff from the Weird Sisters, not, as in Holinshed, from some witch. Lady Macbeth's role is considerably enhanced, and her sleepwalking scene is original. Shakespeare compresses time, as he usually does.

In making some of these alterations, Shakespeare turned to another story in Holinshed's chronicle of Scotland: the murder of King Duff by Donwald (historically preceding the chronicle of Duncan in the following pages). King Duff, never suspecting any treachery in Donwald, often spends time at the castle of Forres, where Donwald is captain of the castle. On one occasion Donwald's wife, bearing great malice toward the King, shows Donwald (who already bears a grudge against Duff) "the means whereby he might soonest accomplish" the murder. The husband and wife ply Duff's few chamberlains with much to eat and drink. Donwald abhors the act "greatly in heart," but perseveres "through instigation of his wife." Four of Donwald's servants actually commit the murder under his instruction. Next morning, Donwald breaks into the King's chamber and slays the chamberlains as though believing them guilty. Donwald is so overzealous in his investigation of the murder that many lords begin to suspect him of having done it. For six months afterward, the sun refuses to appear by day and the moon by night.

The chronicle accounts in Holinshed of Malcolm and Edward the Confessor supplied Shakespeare with further details. A more important supplementary source may have been George Buchanan's *Rerum Scoticarum Historia* (1582), a Latin history not translated in Shakespeare's lifetime, presenting a more complex psychological portrait of the protagonist than in Holinshed. Finally, Shakespeare may have known King James I's *Daemonology* (1597), John Studley's early seventeenth-century version of Seneca's *Medea*, Samuel Harsnett's *Declaration of Egregious Popish Impostures* (1603), and accounts of the Scottish witch trials published around 1590.

The First and Second Volumes
of Chronicles (1587 edition)
Compiled by Raphael Holinshed

VOLUME 2: THE HISTORY OF SCOTLAND

DUFF

[King Duff of Scotland, having been restored to health from a sickness in which the magical practice of witches is said to have played a part, undertakes a campaign into Morayland against the rebels there. He apprehends them and brings them back to the royal castle at Forres to be hanged as traitors.]

Amongst them there were also certain young gentlemen, right beautiful and goodly personages, being near of kin unto Donwald, captain of the castle, and had been persuaded to be partakers with the other rebels more through the fraudulent counsel of divers wicked persons than of their own accord. Whereupon the foresaid Donwald, lamenting their case, made earnest labor and suit to the King to have begged their pardon; but having a plain denial, he conceived such an inward malice towards the King (though he showed it not outwardly at the first) that the same continued still boiling in his stomach[1] and ceased not till, through setting on of his wife and in revenge of such unthankfulness, he found means to murder the King within the foresaid castle of Forres where he used to sojourn. For the King, being in that country, was accustomed to lie most commonly within the same castle, having a special trust in Donwald as a man whom he never suspected.

But Donwald, not forgetting the reproach which his lineage[2] had sustained by the execution of those his kinsmen whom the King for a spectacle to the people had caused to be hanged, could not but show manifest tokens of great grief at home amongst his family, which his wife, perceiving, ceased not to travail[3] with him till she understood what

___

1 stomach i.e., bosom, innermost thoughts   **2 lineage** family   **3 travail** labor. strive

the cause was of his displeasure. Which at length when she had learned by his own relation, she, as one that bare no less malice in her heart towards the King for the like cause on her behalf than her husband did for his friends', counseled him (sith[4] the King oftentimes used to lodge in his house without any guard about him other than the garrison of the castle, which was wholly at his[5] commandment) to make him away, and showed him the means whereby he might soonest accomplish it.

Donwald, thus being the more kindled in wrath by the words of his wife, determined to follow her advice in the execution of so heinous an act. Whereupon, devising with himself for a while which way he might best accomplish his cursed intent, at length gat[6] opportunity and sped his purpose as followeth. It chanced that the King, upon the day before he purposed to depart forth of the castle, was long in his oratory[7] at his prayers and there continued till it was late in the night. At the last, coming forth, he called such afore him[8] as had faithfully served him in pursuit and apprehension of the rebels, and, giving them hearty thanks, he bestowed sundry honorable gifts amongst them, of the which number Donwald was one, as he that had been ever accounted a most faithful servant to the King.

At length, having talked with them a long time, he got him[9] into his privy chamber only with two of his chamberlains who, having brought him to bed, came forth again and then fell to banqueting with Donwald and his wife, who had prepared divers delicate dishes and sundry sorts of drinks for their rear supper or collation;[10] whereat they sat up so long till they had charged their stomachs with such full gorges[11] that their heads were no sooner got to the pillow but asleep they were so fast that a man might have removed the chamber over them sooner than to have awaked them out of their drunken sleep.

Then Donwald, though he abhorred the act greatly in heart, yet through instigation of his wife he called four of his servants unto him whom he had made privy to his

---

4 sith since   **5 his** i.e., Donwald's, as captain of the castle   **6 gat** i.e., he got   **7 oratory** small chapel   **8 such afore him** such persons before him   **9 got him** betook himself   **10 rear supper or collation** repast at the end of the day   **11 such full gorges** i.e., so much food

wicked intent before and framed[12] to his purpose with large
gifts. And now declaring[13] unto them after what sort they
should work the feat, they gladly obeyed his instructions,
and speedily going about the murder they entered* the
chamber in which the King lay a little before cock's crow,[14]
where they secretly cut his throat as he lay sleeping, without any buskling at all. And immediately, by a postern[15] gate,
they carried forth the dead body into the fields, and, throwing it upon an horse there provided ready for that purpose,
they conveyed* it unto a place about two miles distant from
the castle, where they stayed and gat certain laborers to
help them to turn the course of a little river running
through the fields there; and digging a deep hole in the
channel, they buried* the body in the same, ramming it up
with stones and gravel so closely that, setting the water in
the right course again, no man could perceive that anything
had been newly digged there. This they did by order appointed them by Donwald (as is reported), for that[16] the
body should not be found and, by bleeding when Donwald
should be present, declare him to be guilty of the murder.
For such an opinion men have that the dead corpse of any
man, being slain, will bleed abundantly if the murderer be
present. But for what consideration soever they buried him
there, they had no sooner finished the work but that they
slew them whose help they used herein, and straightways
thereupon fled into Orkney.

Donwald, about the time that the murder was in doing,[17]
got him amongst them that kept the watch[18] and so continued in company with them all the residue of the night. But
in the morning, when the noise was raised in the King's
chamber how the King was slain, his body conveyed away,
and the bed all berayed[19] with blood, he with the watch ran
thither as though he had known nothing of the matter and,
breaking into the chamber and finding cakes[20] of blood in
the bed and on the floor about the sides of it, he forthwith

---

12 framed shaped, inclined   **13 And now declaring** i.e., and he now
declaring   **14 cock's crow** (The first cock supposedly crowed at midnight.)   **15 buskling . . . postern** scuffling . . . back, private   **16 for that**
in order that   **17 in doing** being done   **18 amongst . . . watch** among
those who were standing watch. (Donwald's reason for doing so is to
have an alibi.)   **19 berayed** befouled   **20 cakes** clots

slew the chamberlains as guilty of that heinous murder. And then, like a madman, running to and fro, he ransacked every corner within the castle as though it had been to have seen if he might have found either the body or any of the murderers hid in any privy place. But at length coming to the postern gate and finding it open, he burdened the chamberlains whom he had slain with all the fault, they having the keys of the gates committed to their keeping all the night, and therefore it could not be otherwise (said he) but that they were of counsel in the committing of that most detestable murder.

Finally, such was his overearnest diligence in the severe inquisition and trial of the offenders herein that some of the lords began to mislike the matter and to smell forth shrewd tokens[21] that he should not be altogether clear himself. But forsomuch as they were in that country where he had the whole rule, what by reason of[22] his friends and authority together, they doubted[23] to utter what they thought till time and place should better serve thereunto, and hereupon got them away, every man to his home. For the space of six months together after this heinous murder thus committed, there appeared no sun by day nor moon by night in any part of the realm, but still[24] was the sky covered with continual clouds, and sometimes such outrageous winds arose, with lightnings and tempests, that the people were in great fear of present destruction. . . .

Monstrous sights also that were seen within the Scottish kingdom that year were these: Horses in Lothian, being of singular beauty and swiftness, did eat their own flesh and would in no wise taste any other meat.[25] In Angus there was a gentlewoman brought forth a child without eyes, nose, hand, or foot. There was a sparhawk[26] also strangled by an owl. Neither was it any less wonder that the sun, as before is said, was continually covered with clouds for six months' space. But all men understood that the abominable murder of King Duff was the cause hereof, which being revenged by the death of the authors[27] (in manner as before

---

21 shrewd tokens malignant or ominous indications   **22 what by reason of** i.e., what with   **23 doubted** feared   **24 still** continually   **25 meat** food   **26 sparhawk** sparrowhawk   **27 the authors** i.e., Duff's chamberlains, presumed guilty

is said), Cullen was crowned as lawful successor to the
same Duff at Scone, with all due honor and solemnity, in
the year of our Lord 972, after that Duff had ruled the Scottish kingdom about the space of four years.

[Kenneth, a brother of Duff, succeeds to the Scottish throne
after Cullen is murdered by a thane whose daughter he has
ravished. In order that his own sons might enjoy the crown,
Kenneth poisons Malcolm, son of King Duff and presumed
heir to the Scottish kingdom. Though no suspicion falls on
Kenneth, he is so tormented by his conscience that he hears
voices in the night assuring him that God knows his every
secret. After a series of bloody civil wars, another Malcolm
succeeds to the Scottish throne and rules for thirty-two
years.]

DUNCAN

After Malcolm, succeeded his nephew[1] Duncan, the son of
his daughter Beatrice. For Malcolm had two daughters. The
one, which was this Beatrice, being given in marriage unto
one Abbanath Crinen, a man of great nobility and thane of
the Isles and west parts of Scotland, bare of that marriage
the foresaid Duncan. The other, called Doada, was married
unto Sinel, the Thane of Glamis, by whom she had issue one
Macbeth, a valiant gentleman and one that, if he had not
been somewhat cruel of nature, might have been thought
most worthy the government of a realm. On the other part,
Duncan was so soft and gentle of nature that the people
wished the inclinations and manners of these two cousins
to have been so tempered[2] and interchangeably bestowed
betwixt them that, where the one had too much of clemency
and the other of cruelty, the mean virtue betwixt these two
extremities might have reigned by indifferent[3] partition in
them both; so should Duncan have proved a worthy king
and Macbeth an excellent captain. The beginning of Duncan's reign was very quiet and peaceable, without any notable trouble; but after it was perceived how negligent he was
in punishing offenders, many misruled[4] persons took occa-

---

1 nephew i.e., grandson   2 tempered mixed, blended   3 indifferent
evenhanded   4 misruled disorderly

sion thereof to trouble the peace and quiet state of the commonwealth by seditious commotions which first had their beginnings in this wise.

Banquo, the Thane of Lochaber, of whom the House of the Stuarts is descended, the which by order of lineage hath now for a long time enjoyed the crown of Scotland even till these our days, as he gathered the finances due to the King and further punished somewhat sharply such as were notorious offenders, being assailed by a number of rebels inhabiting in that country and spoiled[5] of the money and all other things, had much ado to get away with life after he had received sundry grievous wounds amongst them. Yet escaping their hands, after he was somewhat recovered of his hurts and was able to ride, he repaired[6] to the court, where, making his complaint to the King in most earnest wise, he purchased[7] at length that the offenders were sent for by a sergeant-at-arms to appear to make answer unto such matters as should be laid to their charge. But they, augmenting their mischievous act with a more wicked deed, after they had misused the messenger with sundry kinds of reproaches, they finally slew him also.

Then, doubting not but for such contemptuous demeanor against the King's regal authority they should be invaded with all the power the King could make, Macdowald, one of great estimation among them, making first a confederacy with his nearest friends and kinsmen, took upon him to be chief captain of all such rebels as would stand against the King in maintenance of their grievous offenses lately committed against him. Many slanderous words also and railing taunts this Macdowald uttered against his prince, calling him a fainthearted milksop more meet to govern a sort[8] of idle monks in some cloister than to have the rule of such valiant and hardy men-of-war as the Scots were. He used also such subtle persuasions and forged allurements that in a small time he had gotten together a mighty power[9] of men; for out of the Western Isles there came unto him a great multitude of people offering themselves to assist him in that rebellious quarrel, and out of Ireland in hope of the

5 **spoiled** plundered   6 **repaired** went, returned   7 **purchased** arranged, contrived   8 **sort** gang, bunch   9 **power** army

spoil[10] came no small number of kerns and gallowglasses,[11] offering gladly to serve under him whither[12] it should please him to lead them.

Macdowald, thus having a mighty puissance[13] about him, encountered with such of the King's people as were sent against him into Lochaber and, discomfiting them, by mere[14] force took their captain Malcolm and after the end of the battle smote off his head. This overthrow, being notified[15] to the King, did put him in wonderful[16] fear by reason of his small skill in warlike affairs. Calling therefore his nobles to a council, he asked of them their best advice for the subduing of Macdowald and other the rebels. Here in sundry heads (as ever it happeneth) were sundry opinions, which they uttered according to every man his skill. At length Macbeth, speaking much against the King's softness and overmuch slackness in punishing offenders, whereby they had such time to assemble together, he promised notwithstanding, if the charge were committed[17] unto him and unto Banquo, so to order the matter that the rebels should be shortly vanquished and quite put down, and that not so much as one of them should be found to make resistance within the country.

And even so it came to pass. For, being sent forth with a new power,[18] at his entering into Lochaber the fame of his coming put the enemies in such fear that a great number of them stale secretly away from their captain Macdowald, who nevertheless, enforced thereto, gave battle unto Macbeth with the residue which remained with him. But being overcome and fleeing for refuge into a castle (within the which his wife and children were enclosed), at length, when he saw how he could neither defend the hold[19] any longer against his enemies nor yet upon surrender be suffered to depart with life saved, he first slew his wife and children and lastly himself, lest if he had yielded simply he should have been executed in most cruel wise for an example to

---

10 **spoil** plunder   11 **kerns and gallowglasses** light-armed Irish foot soldiers and horsemen armed with axes   12 **whither** wherever 13 **puissance** power, military force   14 **discomfiting . . . mere** overthrowing . . . sheer   15 **notified** conveyed   16 **wonderful** great 17 **charge were committed** command were given   18 **power** army 19 **hold** stronghold, fortified place of defense

other.[20] Macbeth, entering into the castle by the gates as then[21] set open, found the carcass of Macdowald lying dead there amongst the residue of the slain bodies, which, when he beheld, remitting no piece of his cruel nature with that pitiful sight, he caused the head to be cut off and set upon a pole's end, and so sent it as a present to the King, who as then lay at Bertha.[22] The headless trunk he commanded to be hung up upon an high pair of gallows.

[No sooner has order been restored by Macbeth than Sueno, King of Norway, arrives in Fife "with a puissant army to subdue the whole realm of Scotland." Sueno's forces do well at first and besiege the Scots, but then let down their guard in drunken rioting and are slaughtered by Macbeth. Sueno flees. The Scots celebrate their notable victory with processions and offerings to God; but soon the Danes, acting under the orders of Canute, King of England, send another force to revenge the overthrow and subsequent death of Canute's brother, Sueno. Macbeth and Banquo, commissioned by King Duncan to meet this threat, act with great success, overwhelming the Danes to such a degree that the latter are constrained to pay Macbeth handsomely for the right to have their dead buried at Saint Colme's Inch—i.e., Inchcolm, the Isle of St. Columba in the Firth of Forth. Peace is concluded between the Scots and the Danes.]

Shortly after happened a strange and uncouth[23] wonder, which afterward was the cause of much trouble in the realm of Scotland, as ye shall after hear. It fortuned, as Macbeth and Banquo journeyed toward Forres where the King then lay, they went sporting[24] by the way together without other company save only themselves, passing thorough the woods and fields, when suddenly, in the midst of a laund,[25] there met them three women in strange and wild apparel, resembling creatures of elder world,[26] whom when they attentively beheld, wondering much at the sight, the first of them spake and said, "All hail, Macbeth, Thane

---

20 other others **21 as then** at that time **22 lay at Bertha** resided at Perth **23 uncouth** unaccustomed **24 sporting** for pleasure **25 laund** glade **26 elder world** ancient times

of Glamis!'' (for he had lately entered into that dignity and office by the death of his father Sinel). The second of them said, "Hail, Macbeth, Thane of Cawdor!" But the third said, "All hail, Macbeth, that hereafter shalt be King of Scotland!"

Then Banquo: "What manner of women," saith he, "are you, that seem so little favorable unto me, whereas to my fellow here, besides high offices, ye assign also the kingdom, appointing forth nothing for me at all?" "Yes," saith the first of them, "we promise greater benefits unto thee than unto him, for he shall reign indeed, but with an unlucky end, neither shall he leave any issue[27] behind him to succeed in his place; where, contrarily, thou indeed shalt not reign at all, but of thee those shall be born which shall govern the Scottish kingdom by long order of continual descent." Herewith the foresaid women vanished immediately out of their sight. This was reputed at the first but some vain fantastical illusion by Macbeth and Banquo, insomuch that Banquo would call Macbeth, in jest, King of Scotland, and Macbeth again would call him, in sport likewise, the father of many kings. But afterwards the common opinion was that these women were either the Weird Sisters, that is (as ye would say), the goddesses of destiny, or else some nymphs or fairies endued with knowledge of prophecy by their necromantical science, because everything came to pass as they had spoken. For shortly after, the Thane of Cawdor being condemned at Forres of treason against the King committed, his lands, livings, and offices were given of[28] the King's liberality to Macbeth.

The same night after, at supper, Banquo jested with him and said, "Now Macbeth, thou hast obtained those things which the two former sisters prophesied; there remaineth only for thee to purchase[29] that which the third said should come to pass." Whereupon Macbeth, revolving the thing in his mind, began even then to devise how he might attain to the kingdom. But yet he thought with himself that he must tarry a time which should advance him thereto by the divine providence, as it had come to pass in his former preferment.[30] But shortly after it chanced that King Duncan,

27 issue offspring   **28 of** through   **29 purchase** obtain   **30 preferment** advancement

having two sons by his wife (which was the daughter of Siward, Earl of Northumberland), he made the elder of them, called Malcolm, Prince of Cumberland, as it were thereby to appoint him his successor in the kingdom immediately after his decease. Macbeth, sore troubled herewith for that he saw by this means his hope sore hindered (where, by the old laws of the realm, the ordinance was that if he that should succeed were not of able age to take the charge upon himself, he that was next of blood unto him should be admitted), he began to take counsel how he might usurp the kingdom by force, having a just quarrel[31] so to do, as he took[32] the matter, for that Duncan did what in him lay[33] to defraud him of all manner of title and claim which he might, in time to come, pretend[34] unto the crown.

The words of the three Weird Sisters also (of whom before ye have heard) greatly encouraged him hereunto; but specially his wife lay sore upon him[35] to attempt the thing, as she that was very ambitious, burning in unquenchable desire to bear the name of a queen. At length, therefore, communicating his purposed intent with his trusty friends, amongst whom Banquo was the chiefest, upon confidence of their promised aid he slew the King at Inverness or (as some say) at Bothgowanan, in the sixth year of his reign. Then, having a company about him of such as he had made privy to his enterprise, he caused himself to be proclaimed king and forthwith went unto Scone, where by common consent he received the investure[36] of the kingdom according to the accustomed manner. The body of Duncan was first conveyed unto Elgin and there buried in kingly wise; but afterwards it was removed and conveyed unto Colmekill and there laid in a sepulture amongst his predecessors, in the year after the birth of our Saviour 1046.

Malcolm Cammore and Donald Bane, the sons of King Duncan, for fear of their lives (which they might well know that Macbeth would seek to bring to end for his more sure confirmation in the estate), fled into Cumberland, where Malcolm remained till time that Saint Edward, the son of

---

31 quarrel cause, occasion **32 took** understood **33 for that ... lay** because Duncan did all that lay in his power **34 pretend** lay claim **35 lay sore upon him** pressed him hard, nagged at him **36 investure** investiture, ceremonial robes and symbols of rule

Ethelred, recovered the dominion of England from the Danish power; the which Edward received Malcolm by way of most friendly entertainment;[37] but Donald passed over into Ireland where he was tenderly cherished by the king of that land. Macbeth, after the departure thus of Duncan's sons, used great liberality towards the nobles of the realm, thereby to win their favor; and, when he saw that no man went about to trouble him, he set his whole intention to maintain justice and to punish all enormities and abuses which had chanced through the feeble and slothful administration of Duncan. . . . Macbeth, showing himself thus a most diligent punisher of all injuries and wrongs attempted by any disordered[38] persons within his realm, was accounted the sure defense and buckler[39] of innocent people; and hereto he also applied his whole endeavor to cause young men to exercise themselves in virtuous manners, and men of the Church to attend their divine service according to their vocations.

He caused to be slain sundry thanes, as of Caithness, Sutherland, Stranaverne, and Ross, because through them and their seditious attempts much trouble daily rose in the realm. He appeased the troubled state of Galloway, and slew one Magill, a tyrant who had many years before passed nothing of[40] the regal authority or power. To be brief, such were the worthy doings and princely acts of this Macbeth in the administration of the realm that if he had attained thereunto by rightful means and continued in uprightness of justice, as he began, till the end of his reign, he might well have been numbered amongst the most noble princes that anywhere had reigned. He made many wholesome laws and statutes for the public weal of his subjects.

[Holinshed here prints the laws made by King Macbeth, according to Hector Boece's *Scotoram Historiae*.]

These and the like commendable laws Macbeth caused to be put as then in use, governing the realm for the space of ten years in equal justice. But this was but a counterfeit zeal of equity showed by him, partly against his natural in-

---

37 by way of . . . entertainment with friendly reception   **38 disordered** disorderly   **39 buckler** shield   **40 passed nothing of** paid no regard to

clination, to purchase thereby the favor of the people. Shortly after, he began to show what he was, instead of equity practicing cruelty. For the prick of conscience (as it chanceth[41] ever in tyrants and such as attain to any estate by unrighteous means) caused him ever to fear lest he should be served of the same cup as he had ministered to his predecessor. The words also of the three Weird Sisters would not out of his mind, which,[42] as they promised him the kingdom, so likewise did they promise it at the same time unto the posterity of Banquo. He willed therefore the same Banquo, with his son named Fleance, to come to a supper that he had prepared for them; which was indeed, as he had devised, present[43] death at the hands of certain murderers whom he hired to execute that deed, appointing[44] them to meet with the same Banquo and his son without[45] the palace as they returned to their lodgings and there to slay them, so that he would not have his house slandered,[46] but that in time to come he might clear himself if anything were laid to his charge upon any suspicion that might arise.

It chanced by the benefit of the dark night that, though the father were slain, yet the son, by* the help of almighty God reserving him to better fortune, escaped that danger; and afterwards having some inkling, by the admonition of some friends which he had in the court, how his life was sought no less than his father's—who was slain not by chance-medley,[47] as by the handling of the matter Macbeth would have had it to appear, but even upon a prepensed[48] device—whereupon to avoid further peril he fled into Wales. But here I think it shall not much make against my purpose if, according to the order which I find observed in the Scottish history, I shall in few words rehearse[49] the original line of those kings which have descended from the foresaid Banquo, that they which have enjoyed the kingdom by so long continuance of descent, from one to another and that even unto these our days, may be known from whence they had their first beginning.

---

41 chanceth happens **42 which** who **43 present** immediate **44 appointing** arranging for **45 without** outside of **46 so that . . . slandered** i.e., so that his royal *house* or lineage should not suffer the reproach of having committed murder **47 chance-medley** accidental homicide **48 prepensed** premeditated **49 rehearse** recite, name

[Holinshed here traces the line of descent from Fleance to James VI, King of Scotland in the late sixteenth century.]

But to return unto Macbeth in continuing the history, and to begin where I left, ye shall understand that after the contrived slaughter of Banquo, nothing prospered with the foresaid Macbeth. For in manner[50] every man began to doubt[51] his own life and durst uneath[52] appear in the King's presence; and even as there were many that stood in fear of him, so likewise stood he in fear of many, in such sort that he began to make those away by one surmised cavillation[53] or other whom he thought most able to work him any displeasure.

At length he found such sweetness by putting his nobles thus to death that his earnest thirst after blood in this behalf might in no wise be satisfied. For ye must consider he wan[54] double profit (as he thought) hereby, for first they were rid out of the way whom he feared, and then again his coffers were enriched by their goods which were forfeited to his use, whereby he might better maintain a guard of armed men about him to defend his person from injury of them whom he had in any suspicion. Further, to the end he might the more cruelly oppress his subjects with all tyrant-like wrongs, he builded a strong castle on the top of an high hill called Dunsinane, situate in Gowrie, ten miles from Perth, on such a proud height that, standing there aloft, a man might behold well near[55] all the countries of Angus, Fife, Stormont, and Earndale as it were lying underneath him. This castle, then, being founded on the top of that high hill, put the realm to great charges[56] before it was finished, for all the stuff necessary to the building could not be brought up without much toil and business. But Macbeth, being once determined to have the work go forward, caused the thanes of each shire within the realm to come and help towards that building, each man his course about.[57]

At the last, when the turn fell unto Macduff, Thane of Fife, to build his part, he sent workmen with all needful

---

50 in manner as it were, nearly 51 doubt fear for 52 uneath reluctantly, scarcely 53 make those . . . cavillation do away with those persons by one fraudulent piece of legal chicanery 54 wan won 55 well near nearly 56 charges expenses 57 his course about taking his turn

provision and commanded them to show such diligence in
every behalf that no occasion might be given for the King to
find fault with him in that he came not himself, as other had
done, which he refused to do for doubt[58] lest the King, bearing him (as he partly understood) no great good will, would
lay violent hands upon him as he had done upon divers
other. Shortly after, Macbeth coming to behold how the
work went forward and, because he found not Macduff
there, he was sore offended and said, "I perceive this man
will never obey my commandments till he be ridden with a
snaffle;[59] but I shall provide well enough for him." Neither
could he afterwards abide to look upon the said Macduff,
either for that[60] he thought his puissance[61] overgreat, either
else for that he had learned of certain wizards in whose
words he put great confidence (for that the prophecy had
happened so right which the three fairies or Weird Sisters
had declared unto him) how that he ought to take heed of
Macduff, who in time to come should seek to destroy him.

And surely hereupon had he put Macduff to death but
that a certain witch, whom he had in great trust, had told
that he should never be slain with[62] man born of any woman
nor vanquished till the wood of Birnam came to the castle
of Dunsinane. By this prophecy Macbeth put all fear out of
his heart, supposing he might do what he would, without
any fear to be punished for the same; for by the one prophecy he believed it was unpossible[63] for any man to vanquish
him, and by the other unpossible to slay him. This vain hope
caused him to do many outrageous things, to the grievous
oppression of his subjects. At length Macduff, to avoid peril
of life, purposed with himself[64] to pass into England to procure[65] Malcolm Cammore to claim the crown of Scotland.
But this was not so secretly devised by Macduff but that
Macbeth had knowledge given him thereof, for kings (as is
said) have sharp sight like unto Lynx[66] and long ears like

---

58 doubt fear   **59 ridden with a snaffle** i.e., reined in. (A *snaffle* is a bridle
bit.)   **60 for that** because   **61 puissance** power   **62 with** by   **63 unpossible** impossible   **64 purposed with himself** resolved, made up his mind
65 procure prevail upon   **66 Lynx** Lynceus, one of the Argonauts, whose
eyesight was so keen that he could see through the earth

unto Midas.[67] For Macbeth had in every nobleman's house one sly fellow or other in fee with him to reveal all that was said or done within the same, by which sleight[68] he oppressed the most part of the nobles of his realm.

Immediately, then, being advertised[69] whereabout Macduff went, he came hastily with a great power[70] into Fife and forthwith besieged the castle where Macduff dwelled, trusting to have found him therein. They that kept the house without any resistance opened the gates and suffered him to enter, mistrusting none evil. But nevertheless Macbeth most cruelly caused the wife and children of Macduff, with all other whom he found in that castle, to be slain. Also, he confiscated the goods of Macduff, proclaimed him traitor, and confined[71] him out of all the parts of his realm; but Macduff was already escaped out of danger and gotten into England unto Malcolm Cammore, to try what purchase[72] he might make by means of his support to revenge the slaughter so cruelly executed on his wife, his children, and other friends. At his coming unto Malcolm he declared into what great misery the estate of Scotland was brought by the detestable cruelties exercised by the tyrant Macbeth, having committed many horrible slaughters and murders both as well of the nobles as commons, for the which he was hated right mortally of all his liege people,[73] desiring nothing more than to be delivered of that intolerable and most heavy yoke of thralldom which they sustained at such a caitiff's[74] hands.

Malcolm, hearing Macduff's words which he uttered in very lamentable sort, for mere[75] compassion and very ruth[76] that pierced his sorrowful heart bewailing the miserable state of his country, he fetched a deep sigh, which Macduff, perceiving, began to fall most earnestly in hand with him to enterprise[77] the delivering of the Scottish people out of the

---

67 Midas semi-legendary King of Lydia whose ears were changed into ass's ears for his indiscretion in declaring Pan a better flute player than Apollo   **68 sleight** cunning device, contrivance   **69 advertised** informed   **70 power** army   **71 confined** banished   **72 purchase** advantage   **73 liege people** subjects, those who should owe him allegiance   **74 caitiff's** villain's   **75 mere** utter   **76 ruth** pity   **77 began . . . enterprise** began endeavoring to persuade him to undertake

hands of so cruel and bloody a tyrant as Macbeth by too many plain experiments[78] did show himself to be; which was an easy matter for him to bring to pass, considering not only the good title he had but also the earnest desire of the people to have some occasion ministered whereby they might be revenged of those notable injuries which they daily sustained by the outrageous cruelty of Macbeth's misgovernance. Though Malcolm was very sorrowful for the oppression of his countrymen, the Scots, in manner as Macduff had declared, yet doubting[79] whether he were come as one that meant unfeignedly as he spake or else as sent from Macbeth to betray him, he thought to have some further trial; and thereupon dissembling his mind at the first, he answered as followeth.

"I am truly very sorry for the misery chanced to my country of Scotland, but though I have never so great affection to relieve the same, yet by reason of certain incurable vices which reign in me I am nothing meet thereto.[80] First, such immoderate lust and voluptuous sensuality (the abominable fountain of all vices) followeth me that, if I were made King of Scots, I should seek to deflower your maids and matrons in such wise that mine intemperancy should be more importable[81] unto you than the bloody tyranny of Macbeth now is." Hereunto Macduff answered, "This surely is a very evil fault, for many noble princes and kings have lost both lives and kingdoms for the same. Nevertheless there are women enough in Scotland, and therefore follow my counsel. Make thyself king, and I shall convey the matter so wisely that thou shalt be so satisfied at thy pleasure in such secret wise that no man shall be aware thereof."

Then said Malcolm, "I am also the most avaricious creature on the earth, so that if I were king I should seek so many ways to get lands and goods that I would slay the most part of all the nobles of Scotland by surmised accusations,[82] to the end I might enjoy their lands, goods, and possessions. And therefore, to show you what mischief may ensue on you through mine unsatiable covetousness, I will rehearse unto you a fable. There was a fox having a sore

78 experiments trials, hard experiences   **79 doubting** mistrusting
80 nothing meet thereto not at all suitable for that role   **81 importable**
unbearable   **82 surmised accusations** false allegations

place on her* overset with a swarm of flies that continually
sucked out her blood. And when one that came by and saw
this manner demanded whether she would have the flies
driven before her, she answered: 'No, for if these flies that
are already full, and by reason thereof suck not very eagerly, should be chased away, other that are empty and felly
an-hungered[83] should light in their places and suck out the
residue of my blood far more to my grievance than these
which now, being satisfied, do not much annoy me.' Therefore," saith Malcolm, "suffer me to remain where I am, lest
if I attain to the regiment[84] of your realm, mine unquenchable avarice may prove such that ye would think the dis-
pleasures which now grieve you should seem easy in respect of the unmeasurable outrage which might ensue
through my coming amongst you."

Macduff to this made answer how it was a far worse fault
than the other. "For avarice is the root of all mischief, and
for that crime the most part of our kings have been slain
and brought to their final end. Yet notwithstanding, follow
my counsel and take upon thee the crown. There is gold and
riches enough in Scotland to satisfy thy greedy desire."
Then said Malcolm again, "I am, furthermore, inclined to
dissimulation, telling of leasings,[85] and all other kinds of
deceit, so that I naturally rejoice in nothing so much as to
betray and deceive such as put any trust or confidence in
my words. Then, sith there is nothing that more becometh a
prince than constancy, verity, truth, and justice, with the
other laudable fellowship of those fair and noble virtues
which are comprehended only in soothfastness,[86] and that
lying utterly overthroweth the same, you see how unable I
am to govern any province or region; and therefore, sith you
have remedies to cloak and hide all the rest of my other
vices, I pray you find shift to cloak this vice amongst the
residue."

Then said Macduff, "This yet is the worst of all, and there
I leave thee and therefore say: 'O ye unhappy and miserable
Scottishmen, which are thus scourged with so many and
sundry calamities, each one above other! Ye have one
cursed and wicked tyrant that now reigneth over you with-

83 felly an-hungered fiercely hungry   **84 regiment** rule   **85 lastings** lies
86 soothfastness truthfulness

out any right or title, oppressing you with his most bloody cruelty. This other, that hath the right to the crown, is so replete with the inconstant behavior and manifest vices of Englishmen that he is nothing[87] worthy to enjoy it; for by his own confession he is not only avaricious and given to unsatiable lust but so false a traitor withal[88] that no trust is to be had unto any word he speaketh. Adieu, Scotland, for now I account myself a banished man forever, without comfort or consolation.'" And with those words the brackish tears trickled down his cheeks very abundantly.

At the last, when he was ready to depart, Malcolm took him by the sleeve and said, "Be of good comfort, Macduff, for I have none of these vices before remembered,[89] but have jested with thee in this manner only to prove thy mind,[90] for divers times heretofore hath Macbeth sought by this manner of means to bring me into his hands; but the more slow I have showed myself to condescend[91] to thy motion and request, the more diligence shall I use in accomplishing the same." Incontinently[92] hereupon they embraced each other and, promising to be faithful the one to the other, they fell in consultation how they might best provide for all their business to bring the same to good effect. Soon after, Macduff, repairing[93] to the borders of Scotland, addressed his letters with secret dispatch unto the nobles of the realm, declaring how Malcolm was confederate with him to come hastily into Scotland to claim the crown; and therefore he required them, sith he[94] was right inheritor thereto, to assist him with their powers to recover the same out of the hands of the wrongful usurper.

In the meantime, Malcolm purchased such favor at King Edward's hands that old Siward, Earl of Northumberland, was appointed with ten thousand men to go with him into Scotland, to support him in this enterprise for recovery of his right. After these news were spread abroad in Scotland, the nobles drew into two several[95] factions, the one taking part with Macbeth and the other with Malcolm. Hereupon

---

87 nothing not in the least   **88 withal** in addition   **89 before remembered** already mentioned   **90 prove thy mind** test your intent   **91 condescend** agree   **92 Incontinently** immediately   **93 repairing** journeying   **94 required . . . he** requested them, since he, Malcolm   **95 several** separate

ensued oftentimes sundry bickerings and divers light skir-
mishes, for those that were of Malcolm's side would not
jeopard[96] to join with their enemies in a pight field[97] till
his coming out of England to their support. But after that[98]
Macbeth perceived his enemies' power to increase by such
aid as came to them forth of England with his adversary
Malcolm, he recoiled back into Fife, there purposing to
abide in camp fortified at the castle of Dunsinane and to
fight with his enemies if they meant to pursue him. Howbeit, some of his friends advised him that it should be best
for him either to make some agreement with Malcolm or
else to flee with all speed into the Isles, and to take his treasure with him, to the end he might wage[99] sundry great
princes of the realm to take his part, and retain strangers[100]
in whom he might better trust than in his own subjects,
which stale[101] daily from him. But he had such confidence
in his prophecies that he believed he should never be vanquished till Birnam Wood were brought to Dunsinane, nor
yet to be slain with[102] any man that should be or was born of
any woman.

Malcolm, following hastily after Macbeth, came the night
before the battle unto Birnam Wood; and when his army
had rested awhile there to refresh them, he commanded
every man to get a bough of some tree or other of that wood
in his hand, as big as he might bear, and to march forth
therewith in such wise that on the next morrow they might
come closely and without sight in this manner within view
of his enemies. On the morrow, when Macbeth beheld them
coming in this sort, he first marveled what the matter
meant, but in the end remembered himself that the prophecy which he had heard long before that time, of the coming
of Birnam Wood to Dunsinane Castle, was likely to be now
fulfilled. Nevertheless, he brought his men in order of battle and exhorted them to do valiantly. Howbeit, his enemies
had scarcely cast from them their boughs when Macbeth,
perceiving their numbers, betook him straight to flight;
whom Macduff pursued with great hatred even till he came

---

96 jeopard take the risk   **97 pight field** full battle   **98 after that** after,
as soon as   **99 wage** bribe, or engage for military service   **100 strangers**
foreign (mercenary) troops   **101 which stale** who stole   **102 with** by

unto Lunfannaine, where Macbeth, perceiving that Macduff was hard at his back, leapt beside his horse,[103] saying, "Thou traitor, what meaneth it that thou shouldst thus in vain follow me that am not appointed to be slain by any creature that is born of a woman? Come on, therefore, and receive thy reward which thou hast deserved for thy pains!" And therewithal he lifted up his sword, thinking to have slain him.

But Macduff, quickly avoiding[104] from his horse ere he came at him, answered with his naked sword in his hand, saying, "It is true, Macbeth, and now shall thine insatiable cruelty have an end, for I am even he that thy wizards have told thee of, who was never born of my mother but ripped out of her womb." Therewithal he stepped unto him and slew him in the place. Then, cutting his head from his shoulders, he set it upon a pole and brought it unto Malcolm. This was the end of Macbeth, after he had reigned seventeen years over the Scottishmen. In the beginning of his reign he accomplished many worthy acts, very profitable to the commonwealth as ye have heard; but afterward, by illusion of the devil, he defamed[105] the same with most terrible cruelty. He was slain in the year of the Incarnation 1057, and in the sixteenth year of King Edward's reign over the Englishmen.

[Malcolm Cammore is crowned at Scone on April 25, 1057, creating on that occasion many earls and others of rank. "These were the first earls that have ever been heard of amongst the Scottishmen (as their histories do make mention)." The chronicles also record the death of one of Siward's sons at the battle at Dunsinane, and mention Edward the Confessor's gift of healing the "King's Evil."]

---

103 leapt beside his horse dismounted   **104 avoiding** dismounting
105 defamed brought dishonor to

The second edition of Raphael Holinshed's *Chronicles* was published in 1587. This selection is based on that edition, Volume 2, The History of Scotland, folios 150–152 and 168–176. Some proper names have been modernized: Macbeth (Mackbeth), Banquo (Banquho), Lochaber (Lochquahaver), Duncan (Duncane), Malcolm (Malcolme), Macduff (Mackduffe), Bothgowanan (Botgosvane), Birnam (Birnane), Stormont (Stermont).

In the following, departures from the original text appear in boldface; original readings are in roman.

p. 721 ***entered** enter   ***conveyed** conuey   ***buried** burie   **p. 730** ***yet the son, by** the sonne yet by   **p. 735** ***her** him

Further Reading

Bartholomeusz, Dennis, *"Macbeth" and the Players*. London: Cambridge Univ. Press, 1969. Bartholomeusz surveys the history of the play onstage, focusing on actors' insights into and interpretations of the roles of Macbeth and Lady Macbeth, from the earliest performances at the Globe Theatre through the production at London's Mermaid Theatre in 1964.

Berger, Harry, Jr. "The Early Scenes of *Macbeth:* Preface to a New Interpretation." *ELH* 47 (1980): 1–31. Berger argues that from its first scenes the play reveals "something rotten in Scotland" more powerful than "the melodramatic wickedness" of one or two individuals." Focusing on tensions and contradictions in the rhetoric of the early scenes, Berger discovers not the natural unity of Scotland that Macbeth's villainy shatters but a culture riven by fear and anxiety that gives rise to Macbeth's fearful desires.

Booth, Stephen. "*Macbeth*, Aristotle, Definition, and Tragedy." *"King Lear," "Macbeth," Indefinition, and Tragedy*. New Haven and London: Yale Univ. Press, 1983. In the tension between the appeal of Macbeth's play of infinite possibility and the moral categories that must condemn him, Booth finds that Shakespeare's play establishes "dual contradictory allegiances" that test the audience "with mental challenges as demanding as the ones that overwhelm Macbeth." The play has a "double action": the tragic events expose "the artificiality, frailty, and ultimate impossibility of limits," and the envelope of the play itself asserts the "comforting limitation of artistic pattern."

Bradley, A. C. "*Macbeth.*" *Shakespearean Tragedy*, 1904. Rpt. New York: St. Martin's, 1985. For Bradley, *Macbeth* is Shakespeare's most concentrated and terrifying tragedy, in which an atmosphere of darkness broods over the play and is "continued" in the "souls" of Macbeth and Lady Macbeth. Bradley focuses on the psychological makeup of the protagonists and concludes, among other things, that Macbeth "never totally loses our sympathy" and that Lady Macbeth, who would have done anything "to undo what she had done," is "too great to repent."

Brooks, Cleanth. "The Naked Babe and the Cloak of Manliness." *The Well Wrought Urn*. New York: Harcourt, Brace and World, 1947. Brooks finds the central themes of the play articulated in the imagery of clothing and children. Clothing imagery testifies to the play's concern with disguising and denying one's "essential humanity"; references to children recur in the play as symbols of innocence, helplessness, and "the future which Macbeth would control and cannot control."

Brown, John Russell, ed. *Focus on "Macbeth."* London and Boston: Routledge and Kegan Paul, 1982. This wide-ranging collection of recent criticism includes a director's view of the play by Peter Hall, an account of its "language and action" by Michael Goldman, a study of visual imagery by D. J. Palmer, and an essay by Peter Stallybrass exploring the relationship of the witches to the play's social and political vision.

Calderwood, James L. *If It Were Done: "Macbeth" and Tragic Action*. Amherst, Mass.: Univ. of Massachusetts Press, 1986. Calderwood holds that *Macbeth* is "a tragedy about the nature of tragedy," self-consciously countering "Aristotelian principles of wholeness." Focusing on its rhetorical and structural resistances to completion, Calderwood traces the ways in which the play's "dismantling of the structure of action is extended into the political and social order."

De Quincey, Thomas. "On the Knocking at the Gate in *Macbeth*," 1823. Rpt. in *Shakespeare Criticism: A Selection, 1623–1840*, ed. D. Nicol Smith. London: Oxford Univ. Press, 1916. De Quincey considers the "peculiar awfulness" and "depth of solemnity" of the knocking at the gate in the Porter's scene. The knocking ends the "awful parenthesis" in which the murder takes place, and "makes known audibly that the reaction has commenced; the human has made its reflux upon the fiendish."

Felperin, Howard. "A Painted Devil: *Macbeth*." *Shakespearean Representation*. Princeton, N.J.: Princeton Univ. Press, 1977. Felperin sees the tyrant plays of the medieval religious drama as *Macbeth*'s primary literary model. Malcolm and Macduff conceive of their return to Scotland in the restorative moral patterns suggested by this drama, and Macbeth, because of his internalization of the culture's dominant ways of seeing, allows himself to be cast as tyrant. The play, however, repudiates the archaic oversimplifications of its forebears in the very complexity that its characters would deny.

Fergusson, Francis. "*Macbeth* as the Imitation of an Action." *English Institute Essays, 1951* (1952): 31–43. Rpt. in *The Human Image in Dramatic Literature*. Garden City, N.Y.: Doubleday, 1957. Drawing on Aristotle's theory of tragedy, Fergusson argues that *Macbeth* is an "imitation of an action" defined by Macbeth's desire "to outrun the pauser, reason." The play traces the virulent consequences of Macbeth's violation of reason, until we are finally returned to "the familiar world, where reason, nature, and common sense still have their validity."

Freud, Sigmund. "Some Character-Types Met with in Psycho-Analytic Work," trans. E. Coburn Mayne, in Freud's *Collected Papers*, vol. 4, pp. 326–332. London: The Hogarth Press and The Institute of Psycho-Analysis, 1925. In attempting to explain the paradox of the personality wrecked by success, Freud finds in Lady Macbeth an example of one "who collapses on attaining her aim." He speculates that her breakdown as well as Macbeth's brutalization can be attributed to their childlessness, which Lady Macbeth perceives as a sign of her impotence against Nature's decree, and which serves as the appropriate punishment for their "crimes against the sanctity of geniture."

Heilman, Robert B. "The Criminal as Tragic Hero: Dramatic Methods." *Shakespeare Survey* 19 (1966): 12–24. Heilman recognizes the play's "complexity of form" and traces its strategies of evoking sympathy for Macbeth. The play moves beyond melodrama, demanding our participation with the protagonist's "contracting personality." In spite of his brutality and our necessary identification with the forces of order, Macbeth compels our "collusion" with his fate.

Jorgensen, Paul A. *Our Naked Frailties: Sensational Art and Meaning in "Macbeth."* Berkeley and Los Angeles: Univ. of California Press, 1971. Jorgensen sets out the play's "sensational" presentation of "the terrible raw nature of evil" and its effects upon Macbeth. Focusing on the play's poetic texture and dramatic structure, Jorgensen argues that "Shakespeare disturbs us throughout our nervous system, by exposing to each of us what is within us."

Knights, L. C. "How Many Children Had Lady Macbeth? An Essay in the Theory and Practice of Shakespearean Criticism." *Explorations: Essays in Criticism, Mainly on the Literature of the Seventeenth Century.* London: Chatto and Windus, 1946; Westport, Conn.: Greenwood Press, 1975. Knights insists on the poetic nature and thematic organization of Shakespeare's drama, challenging those practitioners of "character criticism," such as A. C. Bradley, whose "mistaking the *dramatis personae* for real persons" is mocked in Knights's title. For Knights, *Macbeth* is a "statement of evil" in which three themes predominate: "the reversal of values," "unnatural disorder," and "deceitful appearance." His analysis of allegedly minor scenes reveals the coherence of "the pattern of the whole."

McElroy, Bernard. "*Macbeth*: The Torture of the Mind." *Shakespeare's Mature Tragedies.* Princeton, N.J.: Princeton Univ. Press, 1973. McElroy finds *Macbeth* the "most completely internal" of Shakespeare's plays, locating the tragedy in the discrepancy between Macbeth's moral intelligence and his amoral will. Macbeth thus becomes a tragic hero not "*in spite* of his criminality but *because* of his criminality"; in his inability to reconcile irreconcilable aspects of himself, "he assumes a tragic dimension."

Paul, Henry N. *The Royal Play of "Macbeth."* New York: Macmillan, 1950. Paul claims that Shakespeare wrote *Macbeth* for a specific performance at court on August 7, 1606, as a dramatic compliment to King James I. In composing the play for this occasion Shakespeare focused on political and cultural concerns known to be of interest to James, and in the "show of eight kings" Shakespeare represented the Stuart succession.

Rosenberg, Marvin. *The Masks of "Macbeth."* Berkeley and Los Angeles: Univ. of California Press, 1978. Seeking to know the play "from the inside, as actors do," Rosenberg uses stage history, comments by actors, directors, and spectators, and critical commentary in a scene-by-scene analysis designed to uncover the complexity of the play's characterization and action.

Sanders, Wilbur. "'An Unknown Fear': *The Tragedie of Macbeth.*" *The Dramatist and the Received Idea: Studies in the Plays of Marlowe and Shakespeare*. London: Cambridge Univ. Press, 1968. Arguing against optimistic moral readings that neutralize the power of evil, Sanders denies that Macbeth is diminished by the end of the play. He is merely defeated, fighting with remarkable energy and a scrupulous honesty about what he has become. In the face of Macbeth's "fierce brand of nihilism," Malcolm seems callow, his victory over Macbeth punitive rather than restorative and marked "with the disturbing ambivalence of all acts of violence."

Memorable Lines

Hamlet

A little more than kin, and less than kind. (HAMLET   1.2.65)

O, that this too too sullied flesh would melt . . .
(HAMLET   1.2.129)

How weary, stale, flat, and unprofitable
Seem to me all the uses of this world!
(HAMLET   1.2.133–134)

Frailty, thy name is woman!   (HAMLET   1.2.146)

'A was a man. Take him for all in all,
I shall not look upon his like again. (HAMLET   1.2.187–188)

Neither a borrower nor a lender be.   (POLONIUS   1.3.75)

This above all: to thine own self be true.   (POLONIUS   1.3.78)

But to my mind, though I am native here
And to the manner born, it is a custom
More honored in the breach than the observance.
(HAMLET   1.4.14–16)

Something is rotten in the state of Denmark.
(MARCELLUS   1.4.90)

Murder most foul, as in the best it is . . .   (GHOST   1.5.28)

O, my prophetic soul!   (HAMLET   1.5.42)

There are more things in heaven and earth, Horatio,
Than are dreamt of in your philosophy.
(HAMLET   1.5.175–176)

The time is out of joint. O cursèd spite
That ever I was born to set it right! (HAMLET 1.5.197–198)

Brevity is the soul of wit. (POLONIUS 2.2.90)

More matter, with less art. (QUEEN 2.2.95)

That he's mad, 'tis true; 'tis true 'tis pity,
And pity 'tis 'tis true. (POLONIUS 2.2.97–98)

Words, words, words. (HAMLET 2.2.193)

Though this be madness, yet there is method in 't.
(POLONIUS 2.2.205–206)

There is nothing either good or bad but thinking makes it so.
(HAMLET 2.2.250–251)

What a piece of work is a man! (HAMLET 2.2.304–305)

What's Hecuba to him, or he to Hecuba,
That he should weep for her? (HAMLET 2.2.559–560)

The play's the thing
Wherein I'll catch the conscience of the King.
(HAMLET 2.2.605–606)

To be, or not to be, that is the question. (HAMLET 3.1.57)

Whether 'tis nobler in the mind to suffer
The slings and arrows of outrageous fortune,
Or to take arms against a sea of troubles
And by opposing end them. (HAMLET 3.1.58–61)

To die, to sleep;
To sleep, perchance to dream. Ay, there's the rub.
(HAMLET 3.1.65–66)

Thus conscience does make cowards of us all.
(HAMLET 3.1.84)

Get thee to a nunnery. (HAMLET 3.1.122)

The glass of fashion and the mold of form,
Th' observed of all observers . . .   (OPHELIA   3.1.156–157)

I would have such a fellow whipped for o'erdoing Termagant.
It out-Herods Herod.   (HAMLET   3.2.12–14)

Suit the action to the word, the word to the action, with this
special observance, that you o'erstep not the modesty of nature.   (HAMLET   3.2.17–19)

. . . the purpose of playing, whose end, both at the first and
now, was and is to hold as 'twere the mirror up to nature.
          (HAMLET   3.2.20–22)

. . . for thou hast been
As one, in suffering all, that suffers nothing,
A man that Fortune's buffets and rewards
Hast ta'en with equal thanks.   (HAMLET   3.2.64–67)

OPHELIA   'Tis brief, my lord.
HAMLET   As woman's love.   (3.2.151–152)

The lady doth protest too much, methinks.   (QUEEN   3.2.228)

'Tis now the very witching time of night.   (HAMLET   3.2.387)

The cess of majesty
Dies not alone, but like a gulf doth draw
What's near it with it.   (ROSENCRANTZ   3.3.15–17)

For 'tis the sport to have the enginer
Hoist with his own petard.   (HAMLET   3.4.213–214)

How all occasions do inform against me
And spur my dull revenge!   (HAMLET   4.4.33–34)

Rightly to be great
Is not to stir without great argument,
But greatly to find quarrel in a straw
When honor's at the stake.   (HAMLET   4.4.54–57)

When sorrows come, they come not single spies,
But in battalions.   (KING   4.5.79–80)

There's rosemary, that's for remembrance . . . And there is
pansies; that's for thoughts.   (OPHELIA   4.5.179–181)

Alas, poor Yorick! I knew him, Horatio, a fellow of infinite
jest, of most excellent fancy.   (HAMLET   5.1.183–185)

The cat will mew, and dog will have his day.
                                      (HAMLET   5.1.295)

There's a divinity that shapes our ends,
Rough-hew them how we will.   (HAMLET   5.2.10–11)

Not a whit, we defy augury. There is special providence in
the fall of a sparrow. If it be now, 'tis not to come; if it be not
to come, it will be now; if it be not now, yet it will come. The
readiness is all.   (HAMLET   5.2.217–220)

A hit, a very palpable hit.   (OSRIC   5.2.282)

          Good night, sweet prince,
And flights of angels sing thee to thy rest!
                                      (HORATIO   5.2.361–362)

Memorable Lines

Othello

A fellow almost damned in a fair wife.   (IAGO   1.1.22)

But I will wear my heart upon my sleeve
For daws to peck at.   (IAGO   1.1.66–67)

Keep up your bright swords, for the dew will rust them.
     (OTHELLO   1.2.60)

Rude am I in my speech,
And little blessed with the soft phrase of peace . . .
     (OTHELLO   1.3.83–84)

Wherein of antres vast and deserts idle,
Rough quarries, rocks, and hills whose heads touch
   heaven . . .   (OTHELLO   1.3.142–143)

She swore, in faith, 'twas strange, 'twas passing strange,
'Twas pitiful, 'twas wondrous pitiful.
     (OTHELLO   1.3.162–163)

She loved me for the dangers I had passed,
And I loved her that she did pity them.
     (OTHELLO   1.3.169–170)

My noble Father,
I do perceive here a divided duty.
     (DESDEMONA   1.3.182–183)

Virtue? A fig! 'Tis in ourselves that we are thus or thus. Our
bodies are our gardens, to the which our wills are gardeners.
     (IAGO   1.3.322–324)

For I am nothing if not critical.   (IAGO   2.1.121)

To suckle fools and chronicle small beer.   (IAGO   2.1.160)

RODERIGO She's full of most blessed condition.
IAGO Blessed fig's end! The wine she drinks is made of
grapes.   (2.1.251–254)

I do suspect the lusty Moor
Hath leaped into my seat, the thought whereof
Doth, like a poisonous mineral, gnaw my innards.
                                (IAGO 2.1.296–298)

But men are men; the best sometimes forget. (IAGO 2.3.235)

Reputation, reputation, reputation! O, I have lost my reputation!   (CASSIO 2.3.256–257)

Divinity of hell!
When devils will the blackest sins put on,
They do suggest at first with heavenly shows,
As I do now.   (IAGO 2.3.344–347)

How poor are they that have not patience!
What wound did ever heal but by degrees?
                                (IAGO 2.3.364–365)

Good name in man and woman, dear my lord,
Is the immediate jewel of their souls.
Who steals my purse steals trash.   (IAGO 3.3.168–170)

O, beware, my lord, of jealousy!
It is the green-eyed monster which doth mock
The meat it feeds on.   (IAGO 3.3.178–180)

Poor and content is rich, and rich enough.   (IAGO 3.3.185)

To be once in doubt
Is once to be resolved.   (OTHELLO 3.3.193–194)

And yet, how nature erring from itself— (OTHELLO 3.3.243)

I'd whistle her off and let her down the wind
To prey at fortune.   (OTHELLO 3.3.278–279)

Trifles light as air
Are to the jealous confirmations strong
As proofs of Holy Writ.　　　(IAGO　3.3.338–340)

O, now, forever
Farewell the tranquil mind! Farewell content!
　　　　　　　(OTHELLO　3.3.363–364)

On horror's head horrors accumulate.　　(OTHELLO　3.3.386)

Take note, take note, O world,
To be direct and honest is not safe.　　(IAGO　3.3.393–394)

There's magic in the web of it.　　　(OTHELLO　3.4.71)

O, she will sing the savageness out of a bear.
　　　　　　　(OTHELLO　4.1.188–189)

But yet the pity of it, Iago! O, Iago, the pity of it, Iago!
　　　　　　　(OTHELLO　4.1.195–196)

It makes us or it mars us.　　　　(IAGO　5.1.4)

It is the cause, it is the cause, my soul.　　(OTHELLO　5.2.1)

Put out the light, and then put out the light.
　　　　　　　(OTHELLO　5.2.7)

Here is my journey's end, here is my butt
And very seamark of my utmost sail.
　　　　　　　(OTHELLO　5.2.276–277)

Cold, cold, my girl?
Even like thy chastity.　　　(OTHELLO　5.2.284–285)

I have done the state some service, and they know 't.
　　　　　　　(OTHELLO　5.2.349)

Then must you speak
Of one that loved not wisely but too well. . . .
　　　　　　　(OTHELLO　5.2.353–354)

. . . of one whose hand,
Like the base Indian, threw a pearl away
Richer than all his tribe. (OTHELLO 5.2.356–358)

Memorable Lines

King Lear

Nothing will come of nothing.   (LEAR   1.1.90)

Fairest Cordelia, that art most rich being poor,
Most choice, forsaken, and most loved, despised . . .
   (FRANCE   1.1.254–255)

Thou, Nature, art my goddess.   (EDMUND   1.2.1)

Now, gods, stand up for bastards!   (EDMUND   1.2.22)

Have more than thou showest,
Speak less than thou knowest,
Lend less than thou owest.   (FOOL   1.4.116–118)

Ingratitude, thou marble-hearted fiend . . .   (LEAR   1.4.257)

Hear, Nature, hear! Dear goddess, hear!
Suspend thy purpose if thou didst intend
To make this creature fruitful!   (LEAR   1.4.274–276)

How sharper than a serpent's tooth it is
To have a thankless child!   (LEAR   1.4.287–288)

You see me here, you gods, a poor old man,
As full of grief as age, wretched in both.   (LEAR   2.4.274–275)

Blow, winds, and crack your cheeks! Rage, blow!
   (LEAR   3.2.1)

Here I stand your slave,
A poor, infirm, weak, and despised old man.
   (LEAR   3.2.19–20)

Let the great gods,
That keep this dreadful pother o'er our heads,
Find out their enemies now.   (LEAR   3.2.49–51)

> I am a man
> More sinned against than sinning.　　(LEAR　3.2.59–60)

> The art of our necessities is strange,
> And can make vile things precious.　　(LEAR　3.2.70–71)

> Poor naked wretches, wheresoe'er you are,
> That bide the pelting of this pitiless storm,
> How shall your houseless heads and unfed sides,
> Your looped and windowed raggedness, defend you
> From seasons such as these?　　(LEAR　3.4.28–32)

> O, I have ta'en
> Too little care of this! Take physic, pomp;
> Expose thyself to feel what wretches feel.　　(LEAR　3.4.32–34)

> Is man no more than this?　　(LEAR　3.4.101–102)

> Unaccommodated man is no more but such a poor, bare,
> forked animal as thou art.　　(LEAR　3.4.105–107)

> 'Tis a naughty night to swim in.　　(FOOL　3.4.109–110)

> Child Rowland to the dark tower came.　　(EDGAR　3.4.182)

> I am tied to the stake, and I must stand the course.
> 　　(GLOUCESTER　3.7.57)

> The lamentable change is from the best;
> The worst returns to laughter.　　(EDGAR　4.1.5–6)

> World, world, O world!
> But that thy strange mutations make us hate thee,
> Life would not yield to age.　　(EDGAR　4.1.10–12)

> Full oft 'tis seen
> Our means secure us, and our mere defects
> Prove our commodities.　　(GLOUCESTER　4.1.19–21)

> The worst is not
> So long as we can say, "This is the worst."
> 　　(EDGAR　4.1.27–28)

As flies to wanton boys are we to the gods;
They kill us for their sport.   (GLOUCESTER   4.1.36–37)

If that the heavens do not their visible spirits
Send quickly down to tame these vile offenses,
It will come,
Humanity must perforce prey on itself,
Like monsters of the deep.   (ALBANY   4.2.47–51)

              This shows you are above,
You justicers, that these our nether crimes
So speedily can venge!   (ALBANY   4.2.79–81)

Ay, every inch a king.   (LEAR   4.6.107)

But to the girdle do the gods inherit;
Beneath is all the fiends'.   (LEAR   4.6.126–127)

There thou mightst behold the great image of authority: a
dog's obeyed in office.   (LEAR   4.6.157–159)

When we are born, we cry that we are come
To this great stage of fools.   (LEAR   4.6.182–183)

              I am bound
Upon a wheel of fire.   (LEAR   4.7.47–48)

I fear I am not in my perfect mind.   (LEAR   4.7.64)

              Men must endure
Their going hence, even as their coming hither;
Ripeness is all.   (EDGAR   5.2.9–11)

              and hear poor rogues
Talk of court news; and we'll talk with them too—
Who loses and who wins; who's in, who's out . . .
                        (LEAR   5.3.13–15)

The gods are just, and of our pleasant vices
Make instruments to plague us.   (EDGAR   5.3.173–174)

The wheel is come full circle.   (EDMUND 5.3.177)

Howl, howl, howl! O, you are men of stones! (LEAR 5.3.262)

KENT   Is this the promised end?
EDGAR   Or image of that horror?   (5.3.268–269)

                        Her voice was ever soft,
Gentle, and low, an excellent thing in woman.
                        (LEAR 5.3.277–278)

If Fortune brag of two she loved and hated,
One of them we behold.   (KENT 5.3.285–286)

The wonder is he hath endured so long.   (KENT 5.3.322)

Memorable Lines

Macbeth

FIRST WITCH
When shall we three meet again?
In thunder, lightning, or in rain?
SECOND WITCH
When the hurlyburly's done,
When the battle's lost and won. (1.1.1–4)

Fair is foul, and foul is fair.
Hover through the fog and filthy air. (WITCHES 1.1.11–12)

So foul and fair a day I have not seen. (MACBETH 1.3.38)

. . . oftentimes to win us to our harm
The instruments of darkness tell us truths,
Win us with honest trifles, to betray 's
In deepest consequence. (BANQUO 1.3.123–126)

Two truths are told,
As happy prologues to the swelling act
Of the imperial theme. (MACBETH 1.3.128–130)

This supernatural soliciting
Cannot be ill, cannot be good. (MACBETH 1.3.131–132)

Nothing in his life
Became him like the leaving it. (MALCOLM 1.4.7–8)

Yet do I fear thy nature;
It is too full o' the milk of human kindness
To catch the nearest way. (LADY MACBETH 1.5.16–18)

Thou wouldst be great,
Art not without ambition, but without
The illness should attend it. (LADY MACBETH 1.5.18–20)

The raven himself is hoarse
That croaks the fatal entrance of Duncan
Under my battlements. (LADY MACBETH 1.5.38–40)

Come, you spirits
That tend on mortal thoughts, unsex me here.
LADY MACBETH 1.5.40–41)

If it were done when 'tis done, then 'twere well
It were done quickly. (MACBETH 1.7.1–2)

. . . that but this blow
Might be the be-all and the end-all! (MACBETH 1.7.4–5)

Letting "I dare not" wait upon "I would,"
Like the poor cat i' th' adage? (LADY MACBETH 1.7.45–46)

We fail?
But screw your courage to the sticking place
And we'll not fail. (LADY MACBETH 1.7.60–62)

Bring forth men-children only! (MACBETH 1.7.73)

False face must hide what the false heart doth know.
(MACBETH 1.7.83)

Is this a dagger which I see before me,
The handle toward my hand? (MACBETH 2.1.34–35)

The bell invites me.
Hear it not, Duncan, for it is a knell
That summons thee to heaven or to hell.
(MACBETH 2.1.63–65)

Had he not resembled
My father as he slept, I had done 't.
(LADY MACBETH 2.2.12–13)

Methought I heard a voice cry "Sleep no more!
Macbeth does murder sleep," the innocent sleep,
Sleep that knits up the raveled sleave of care . . .

                                        (MACBETH   2.2.39–41)

Will all great Neptune's ocean wash this blood
Clean from my hand? No, this my hand will rather
The multitudinous seas incarnadine,
Making the green one red.   (MACBETH   2.2.64–67)

What's done is done.   (LADY MACBETH   3.2.14)

We have scorched the snake, not killed it.   (MACBETH   3.2.15)

Be innocent of the knowledge, dearest chuck,
Till thou applaud the deed.   (MACBETH   3.2.48–49)

                        Come, seeling night,
Scarf up the tender eye of pitiful day.   (MACBETH   3.2.49–50)

  I am cabined, cribbed, confined, bound in
To saucy doubts and fears.   (MACBETH   3.4.24–25)

It will have blood, they say; blood will have blood.
Stones have been known to move, and trees to speak.
                             (MACBETH   3.4.123–124)

Double, double, toil and trouble;
Fire burn, and cauldron bubble.   (WITCHES   4.1.10–11)

Eye of newt and toe of frog,
Wool of bat and tongue of dog . . .   (SECOND WITCH   4.1.14–15)

How now, you secret, black, and midnight hags?
                                (MACBETH   4.1.48)

Be bloody, bold, and resolute; laugh to scorn
The power of man, for none of woman born
Shall harm Macbeth.   (SECOND APPARITION   4.1.79–81)

Macbeth shall never vanquished be until
Great Birnam Wood to high Dunsinane Hill
Shall come against him.　　(THIRD APPARITION　4.1.92–94)

Saw you the Weird Sisters?　　　　(MACBETH　4.1.136)

Angels are bright still, though the brightest fell.
　　　　　　　　　　　　　　(MALCOLM　4.3.23)

What, all my pretty chickens and their dam
At one fell swoop?　　　　(MACDUFF　4.3.219–220)

Out, damned spot! Out, I say!　　(LADY MACBETH　5.1.34)

All the perfumes of Arabia will not sweeten this little hand.
　　　　　　　　　　　(LADY MACBETH　5.1.49–51)

Thou lily-livered boy.　　　　　　(MACBETH　5.3.15)

I have lived long enough. My way of life
Is fall'n into the sere, the yellow leaf.　(MACBETH　5.3.22–23)

Canst thou not minister to a mind diseased . . .
　　　　　　　　　　　　　　(MACBETH　5.3.42)

　　　　　　　　Therein the patient
Must minister to himself.　　　　(DOCTOR　5.3.47–48)

I have supped full with horrors.　　(MACBETH　5.5.13)

She should have died hereafter;
There would have been a time for such a word.
　　　　　　　　　　　　　　(MACBETH　5.5.17–18)

Tomorrow, and tomorrow, and tomorrow
Creeps in this petty pace from day to day
To the last syllable of recorded time,
And all our yesterdays have lighted fools
The way to dusty death. Out, out, brief candle!
　　　　　　　　　　　　　　(MACBETH　5.5.19–23)

Life's but a walking shadow, a poor player
That struts and frets his hour upon the stage
And then is heard no more. It is a tale
Told by an idiot, full of sound and fury,
Signifying nothing.   (MACBETH   5.5.24–28)

             Lay on, Macduff,
And damned be him that first cries, "Hold, enough!"
                  (MACBETH   5.8.33–34)

The time is free.   (MACDUFF   5.8.55)

Contributors

DAVID BEVINGTON, Phyllis Fay Horton Professor of Humanities at the University of Chicago, is editor of *The Complete Works of Shakespeare* (Scott, Foresman, 1980) and of *Medieval Drama* (Houghton Mifflin, 1975). His latest critical study is *Action Is Eloquence: Shakespeare's Language of Gesture* (Harvard University Press, 1984).

DAVID SCOTT KASTAN, Professor of English and Comparative Literature at Columbia University, is the author of *Shakespeare and the Shapes of Time* (University Press of New England, 1982).

JAMES HAMMERSMITH, Associate Professor of English at Auburn University, has published essays on various facets of Renaissance drama, including literary criticism, textual criticism, and printing history.

ROBERT KEAN TURNER, Professor of English at the University of Wisconsin–Milwaukee, is a general editor of the New Variorum Shakespeare (Modern Language Association of America) and a contributing editor to *The Dramatic Works in the Beaumont and Fletcher Canon* (Cambridge University Press, 1966–).

JAMES SHAPIRO, who coedited the bibliographies with David Scott Kastan, is Assistant Professor of English at Columbia University.

❖

JOSEPH PAPP, one of the most important forces in theater today, is the founder and producer of the New York Shakespeare Festival, America's largest and most prolific theatrical institution. Since 1954 Mr. Papp has produced or directed all but one of Shakespeare's plays—in Central Park, in schools, off and on Broadway, and at the Festival's permanent home, The Public Theater. He has also produced such award-winning plays and musical works as *Hair*, *A Chorus Line*, *Plenty*, and *The Mystery of Edwin Drood*, among many others.

THE BANTAM SHAKESPEARE COLLECTION

The Complete Works in 28 Volumes

Edited with Introductions by David Bevington

Forewords by Joseph Papp